Designing Sound

Designing Sound

Designing Sound

Andy Farnell

The MIT Press
Cambridge, Massachusetts
London, England

For information about special quantity discounts, please email special_sales@mitpress.mit.edu

This book was set in Century by Westchester Book Composition.

Printed and bound in the United States of America.

Library of Congress Cataloging-in-Publication Data

Farnell, Andy, 1969–.
Designing sound / Andy Farnell.
    p.   cm.
Includes bibliographical references and index.
ISBN 978-0-262-01441-0 (hardcover : alk. paper)
1. Computer sound processing. 2. Sound—Recording and reproducing—Digital techniques. 3. Sounds. 4. Motion pictures—Sound effects. 5. Animated films—Sound effects. 6. Video games—Sound effects. I. Title.
TK7881.4.F365   2010
006.5—dc22

2009050741

10 9 8

To Kate

To Kate

Contents

Acknowledgements   xxiii

1   Introduction   1

I Theory   5

2   Theory Introduction   7

3   Physical Sound   9

   3.1   Elementary Physics   9

        Energy   9

        Force   9

        Pressure   9

        Work   10

        Systems   10

        Power   10

        Energy Sources   10

        Matter and Mass   11

        Force, Distance, and Acceleration   11

        Displacement, Movement, and Freedom   12

        Excitation   12

   3.2   Materials   12

        Elasticity and Restoration   13

        Density   15

        Plasticity   16

        Structure and Strength   17

   3.3   Waves   17

        Wave Models   17

        Exchange of Forces   18

        Propagation   19

        Wave Types   20

        Amplitude   20

        Speed   21

        Group and Phase Velocity   22

        Wavelength   23

        Frequency and Period   23

        Simple Wave Math   23

Phase   24
Superposition and Phase Cancellation   24
3.4   Boundaries   25
Phase of Bending Waves at Solid Boundaries   26
Coupling   28
Reflection and Standing Waves   28
Modes   29
Visualising Sound Waves   30
Shape   30
Entropy and Heat   31
Loss and Damping   31
3.5   Analogues   32
Potential   32
Energy Inlet   33
Flow   33
Resistance   33
Tap or Outlet   34
Capacitance   34
Example Network Analogy   35
Example System Analysis   36
Acknowledgements   37
References   37
4   Oscillations   39
4.1   Oscillators   39
Period and Frequency   39
Frequency of a Spinning Object   39
Relaxation   41
Frequency of Relaxation Systems   42
Quantisation   43
4.2   Simple Harmonic Oscillators   43
Frequency of a Mass on Spring   44
Frequency of a Pendulum   46
Frequency of an LC Network   46
4.3   Complex Harmonic Oscillators   48
Oscillation of a String   48
Oscillation of a Bar or Rod   49
Oscillation of Cones, Membranes, Laminas   50
4.4   Driven Oscillations and Resonance   51
References   53
5   Acoustics   55
5.1   Acoustic Systems   55
Vibrations in Air   55
Radiation   56

Radiation Patterns   56

Spherical, Cylindrical, and Planar Waves   57

5.2   Intensity and Attenuation   58

Sound Pressure Level   58

Position and Correlation   58

Acoustic Sound Intensity   59

Geometric Attenuation   60

Transmission and Absorption   61

5.3   Other Propagation Effects   62

Reflection   62

Scattering   62

Dispersion   63

Refraction   63

Diffraction   64

Diffusion   65

Ground Effects   66

Oblique Boundary Loss   66

Wind Shear   67

Aberration   67

The Doppler Effect   67

Room Acoustics   67

Reverb Time   68

Outdoor Acoustics   70

5.4   Acoustic Oscillations   70

Turbulence   70

Reynolds Number   71

Sounds of Turbulence   71

Pipes   71

Radiation from Pipes and Horns   73

Helmholtz Oscillator   73

Textbooks   74

Papers   74

Online Resources   74

6   Psychoacoustics   77

6.1   Perceiving Sounds   77

Ears   77

Frequency Range of Human Hearing   78

Nonlinearity   78

Threshold of Hearing   78

Just Noticeable Difference   79

Localisation   79

Interaural Time Difference   79

Interaural Intensity Difference   80

Head Response Transfer Function   80

Distance   80

Source Identity   81
Perception of Loudness   81
Loudness Scales and Weighting   81
Duration and Loudness   82
Fatigue   83
Change of Loudness   83
Perception of Frequency   83
Pure Tone Discrimination   83
Critical Bands   83
Ranges   84
Resolution   85
Average of Close Components   85
Rapid Change of Amplitude   85
Phantom Fundamentals   86
Huggins Binaural Pitch   86
Bilsen Band Edge Pitch   86
Perception of Spectra   86
Perception of Harmonic and Inharmonic Spectra   87
Consonance, Harmony, and Roughness   87
Brightness, Dullness, and Spectral Centroid   88
Resonance, Flatness, and Formants   88
Perception of Temporal Structure   88
Granularity   89
Events and Flows   89
Envelopes   89
Attack   89
Transient and Rise Time   90
Slow Attacks   90
Decay   90
Sustain   90
Release   91
Effort and Movement   91
Precedence and Belonging   91
Gabor Limit for Duration   91
Hirsh Limit for Ordering   91
Streaming   92
Streaming by Pitch   92
Van Noorden Ambiguity   92
Spectral and Spacial Streams   92

6.2   Sound Cognition   93
Gestalt Effects   93
Discrimination   93
Scaling   94
Similarity   94
Matching   95

Classification   95
Identification   95
Recognition   95
Attention   96
Correspondence   96
Asynchronous Sound   96
Acousmatic Sound   97
The Audiovisual Contract   97
Absence   97
Concurrent Masking   98
Temporal Proximity Masking   98
6.3   Auditory Scene Analysis   99
Segregation   99
Schema Activation   100
Primitive Features   100
Harmonicity   100
Continuity   101
Momentum   101
Monotonicity   101
Temporal Correlation   102
Coherence   102
The Process of Scene Analysis   102
6.4   Auditory Memory   103
Short- and Long-term Memory   103
Auditory Pipeline   103
Verbal and Nonverbal Memory   103
Visual Augmentation   104
6.5   Listening Strategies   104
Listening Hierarchy   104
Reflexive   104
Connotative   105
Causal   105
Empathetic   105
Functional   105
Semantic   106
Critical   106
Reduced   106
Analytic Listening   106
Component Analysis   106
Signal Listening   107
Engaged   107
6.6   Physiological Responses to Sound   108
Stapedius Reflex   108
Startle Response   108
Orientation Response   108

Ecstatic Response   108
Stress Responses   109
Binaural Beat Entrainment   109
Psychotherapeutical Applications and Art   109
Cross-modal Perception   110

6.7   Sound, Language, and Knowledge   110
Imagining Sound   110
Talking about Sound   111
Noun Descriptions   111
Adjective and Adjunctive Descriptions   111
Gerund Verb Descriptions   111
Onomatopoeia and Alliteration   112
Reference Points   112
Procedural Knowledge   112
Declarative Domain Knowledge   112
Imperative Knowledge   113
Poetic Knowledge   113
Categorical Knowledge   113
Weak Cultural Domain Knowledge   113
Strong Cultural Domain Knowledge   113

Exercises   114
Exercise 1—Perception   114
Exercise 2—Language   114
Exercise 3—Knowledge and Communication   114

Acknowledgements   114

References   114
Books   114
Papers   115
Online Resources   117

7   Digital Signals   119

7.1   Signals   119
Transducers   119
Electronic, Continuous Signals   119
Sound Transducers   119
Information   119
Representing Signals   120
Digital Encoding   121
Digital-to-Analog Conversion   121
Analog-to-Digital Conversion   122
Digital Signal Processing   123
Floating Point Normalised Form   123
Smoothing Samples   124

7.2   Graphs   125
Spectra   125

Spectrograms 126

Waterfall Plots 127

7.3   Generating Digital Waveforms 128

Generating Samples 128

Buffering 128

The Sound of Zero (Silence) 129

The Sound of One (Constants) 129

Moving Signals 131

Sinusoidal Waves 132

Complex Harmonic Motion 134

Randomly Moving Signals 136

Suddenly Moving Signals 137

Slowly Moving Signals 139

Signal Programming Abstraction 141

A Csound Snippet 142

A CLM Snippet 142

Acknowledgements 143

References 143

Books 143

Papers 143

Online Resources 144

II   Tools   145

8   Tools Introduction 147

8.1   What You Will Need 147

8.2   Tools for Sound Design 147

8.3   Supporting Tools 148

9   Starting with Pure Data 149

9.1   Pure Data 149

Installing and Running Pure Data 150

Testing Pure Data 150

9.2   How Does Pure Data Work? 151

Objects 152

Connections 152

Data 152

Patches 152

A Deeper Look at Pd 153

Pure Data Software Architecture 153

Your First Patch 153

Creating a Canvas 155

New Object Placement 155

Edit Mode and Wiring 155

Initial Parameters   156
Modifying Objects   156
Number Input and Output   156
Toggling Edit Mode   156
More Edit Operations   157
Patch Files   157

9.3   Message Data and GUI Boxes   157
Selectors   158
Bang Message   158
Bang Box   158
Float Messages   158
Number Box   159
Toggle Box   159
Sliders and Other Numerical GUI Elements   159
General Messages   160
Message Box   160
Symbolic Messages   160
Symbol Box   161
Lists   161
Pointers   161
Tables, Arrays, and Graphs   161

9.4   Getting Help with Pure Data   162

Exercises   163
Exercise 1   163
Exercise 2   163
Exercise 3   163

References   163

10   Using Pure Data   165

10.1   Basic Objects and Principles of Operation   165
Hot and Cold Inlets   165
Bad Evaluation Order   165
Trigger Objects   166
Making Cold Inlets Hot   166
Float Objects   166
Int Objects   167
Symbol and List Objects   167
Merging Message Connections   167

10.2   Working with Time and Events   167
Metronome   167
A Counter Timebase   168
Time Objects   168
Select   169

10.3   Data Flow Control   169
Route   169

Moses   170
Spigot   170
Swap   170
Change   170
Send and Receive Objects   171
Broadcast Messages   171
Special Message Destinations   171
Message Sequences   171

10.4   List Objects and Operations   172
Packing and Unpacking Lists   172
Substitutions   173
Persistence   173
List Distribution   173
More Advanced List Operations   174

10.5   Input and Output   174
The Print Object   175
MIDI   175

10.6   Working with Numbers   177
Arithmetic Objects   177
Trigonometric Maths Objects   178
Random Numbers   178
Arithmetic Example   178
Comparative Objects   178
Boolean Logical Objects   178

10.7   Common Idioms   179
Constrained Counting   179
Accumulator   179
Rounding   180
Scaling   180
Looping with Until   180
Message Complement and Inverse   181
Random Selection   182
Weighted Random Selection   182
Delay Cascade   182
Last Float and Averages   182
Running Maximum (or Minimum)   183
Float Low Pass   183

11   Pure Data Audio   185

11.1   Audio Objects   185
Audio Connections   185
Blocks   185
Audio Object CPU Use   185

11.2   Audio Objects and Principles   186
Fanout and Merging   186

Time and Resolution   187
Audio Signal Block to Messages   187
Sending and Receiving Audio Signals   187
Audio Generators   187
Audio Line Objects   189
Audio Input and Output   189
Example: A Simple MIDI Monosynth   189
Audio Filter Objects   190
Audio Arithmetic Objects   191
Trigonometric and Math Objects   191
Audio Delay Objects   191

References   192

12   Abstraction   193
12.1   Subpatches   193
Copying Subpatches   194
Deep Subpatches   194
Abstractions   195
Scope and $0   196
12.2   Instantiation   196
12.3   Editing   197
12.4   Parameters   197
12.5   Defaults and States   198
12.6   Common Abstraction Techniques   199
Graph on Parent   199
Using List Inputs   200
Packing and Unpacking   200
Control Normalisation   201
Summation Chains   202
Routed Inputs   203

13   Shaping Sound   205
13.1   Amplitude-Dependent Signal Shaping   205
Simple Signal Arithmetic   205
Limits   207
Wave Shaping   207
Squaring and Roots   209
Curved Envelopes   210
13.2   Periodic Functions   211
Wrapping Ranges   211
Cosine Function   211
13.3   Other Functions   212
Polynomials   212
Expressions   213

13.4   Time-Dependent Signal Shaping   213
    Delay   214
    Phase Cancellation   214
    Filters   215
    User-Friendly Filters   215
    Integration   215
    Differentiation   217
References   217
14   Pure Data Essentials   219
14.1   Channel Strip   219
    Signal Switch   219
    Simple Level Control   219
    Using a Log Law Fader   220
    MIDI Fader   220
    Mute Button and Smooth Fades   221
    Panning   221
    Simple Linear Panner   221
    Square Root Panner   222
    Cosine Panner   222
    Crossfader   224
    Demultiplexer   224
14.2   Audio File Tools   225
    Monophonic Sampler   225
    File Recorder   226
    Loop Player   227
14.3   Events and Sequencing   227
    Timebase   227
    Select Sequencer   228
    Partitioning Time   229
    Dividing Time   229
    Event-Synchronised LFO   229
    List Sequencer   230
    Textfile Control   231
14.4   Effects   232
    Stereo Chorus/Flanger Effect   232
    Simple Reverberation   233
Exercises   235
    Exercise 1   235
    Exercise 2   235
    Exercise 3   235
    Exercise 4   235
Acknowledgements   235
References   235
    Online Resources   236

III Technique   237

15   Technique Introduction   239
  15.1   Techniques of Sound Design   239
    Layered Approach   239
    The Middle Layer   240
References   241
16   Strategic Production   243
  16.1   Working Methods   243
    Listen   243
    Stimulate   243
    Use Scale   243
    Vary Scope   243
    Keep Moving   244
    Balance Priorities   244
    Reuse and Share Successful Techniques   244
    Create a Comfortable Working Space   244
    Invite Input   245
  16.2   SE Approaches   245
    Structured Approach Summary   245
  16.3   Requirements Analysis Process   247
    Consensus of Vision   248
    Requirements Specification Document   249
    Writing Requirements Specifications   249
    Placeholders and Attachment   249
    Target Medium   250
  16.4   Research   250
    Papers, Books, TV Documentaries   250
    Schematics and Plans   251
    Analytical, Partial Recording   251
    Impulses and Test Excitations   252
    Physical Deconstruction   252
  16.5   Creating a Model   252
    Model Abstraction   253
  16.6   Analysis   254
    Waveform Analysis   254
    Spectral Analysis   254
    Physical Analysis   254
    Operational Analysis   254
    Model Parameterisation   254

16.7   Methods   255
       Piecewise   256
       Pure Additive   256
       Mixed Additive Composites   256
       Wavetables   256
       Subtractive   257
       Nonlinear   257
       Granular   257
       Physical   258

16.8   Implementation   258
       Encapsulation   259
       Internal Control   259
       Interface   259

16.9   Parameterisation   259
       Decoupling   259
       Orthogonality and Parameter Space   260
       Efficiency of Parameter Space   260
       Factoring/Collapsing   261

16.10 Practice and Psychology   261
       Design Cycle   261
       Objectification   262
       Expediency   262
       Flow   262
       Concentration, Familiarity, Simplicity   263
       Time and Vision   264

References   264
       Online Resources   265

17   Technique 1—Summation   267

17.1   Additive Synthesis   267

17.2   Discrete Summation Synthesis   270

17.3   Precomputation   273

References   274

18   Technique 2—Tables   277

18.1   Wavetable Synthesis   277

18.2   Practical Wavetables   278

18.3   Vector Synthesis   279

18.4   Wavescanning Synthesis   280

References   281

19   Technique 3—Nonlinear Functions   283

19.1   Waveshaping   283
       Table Transfer Functions   283

19.2   Chebyshev Polynomials   285

References   289

20   Technique 4—Modulation   291

   20.1   Amplitude Modulation   291

   20.2   Adding Sidebands   293

   20.3   Cascade AM, with Other Spectra   294

   20.4   Single Sideband Modulation   295

   20.5   Frequency Modulation   296

      Negative Frequencies   301

      Phase Modulation   303

References   303

21   Technique 5—Grains   305

   21.1   Granular Synthesis   305

      A Grain Generator   305

      Types of Granular Synthesis   307

      Sound Hybridisation   309

      A Granular Texture Source   310

   21.2   Time and Pitch Alteration   312

References   313

      Textbooks   313

      Papers   313

22   Game Audio   315

   22.1   Virtual Reality Fundamentals   315

      Game Objects   315

      Object Methods   315

      Object Views   315

      Object Behaviours   316

      The Players   316

      World Geometry   316

      Stages   317

      Platforms   317

      Game Logic   317

      Actors and Relevance   317

   22.2   Samples or Procedural Audio?   318

      Events versus Behaviours   318

      Limitations of Sample-Based Audio   318

   22.3   Traditional Game Audio Engine Functions   319

      Switching   319

      Sequence and Randomisation   319

      Blending   319

      Grouping and Buses   319

      Real-Time Controllers   319

Localisation   320
Ambiance   320
Attenuation and Damping   320
Replication and Alignment   320
Music Dialogue and Menus   320

22.4   Procedural Audio Advantages   321
Deferred Form   321
Default Forms   321
Variety   321
Variable Cost   322
Dynamic LOAD   322

22.5   Challenges for New Game Audio Systems   323
Dynamic Graph Configuration   323
Denormal and Drift Contingencies   323
Automatic Code Translation   324
Embedding a Pd Interpreter   324
Plugins   324
Cost Metrics   325
Hybrid Architectures   325
Hard Sounds   325

References   326
Books   326
Papers   326
Online Sources   326

IV   Practicals   **327**

23   Practicals Introduction   329
Practical Series—Artificial Sounds   331
24   Pedestrians   333
25   Phone Tones   337
26   DTMF Tones   343
27   Alarm Generator   347
28   Police   355
Practical Series—Idiophonics   365
29   Telephone Bell   367
30   Bouncing   383
31   Rolling   387
32   Creaking   395
33   Boing   401
Practical Series—Nature   407
34   Fire   409
35   Bubbles   419
36   Running Water   429

37   Pouring   437
38   Rain   441
39   Electricity   451
40   Thunder   459
41   Wind   471
Practical Series—Machines   483
42   Switches   485
43   Clocks   491
44   Motors   499
45   Cars   507
46   Fans   517
47   Jet Engine   523
48   Helicopter   529
Practical Series—Lifeforms   545
49   Footsteps   547
50   Insects   557
51   Birds   571
52   Mammals   579
Practical Series—Mayhem   591
53   Guns   593
54   Explosions   607
55   Rocket Launcher   617
Practical Series—Science-Fiction   627
56   Transporter   629
57   R2D2   635
58   Red Alert   641
      Cover Image Sources   647
      Index   649

Acknowledgements

This book is dedicated to my devoted and wonderful partner Kate who has always given me support and encouragement. And in loving memory of my father Benjamin Farnell, who passed away during its writing.

Thank you to friends and family who gave me the encouragement to finish this, Joan and John Hiscock, my kind and patient sister Vicky and her husband Jonathan Bond, for all their support. Also thank you to Lembit Rohumaa, a giant of generosity and enthusiasm who built Westbourne studio in the 1990s. Thank you to all those I've had the honour to work with in the studio and learn from their talents and thoughts about sound. To helpful members of various communities—this book would not exist without the tireless efforts of the open source software community. Thank you to all the proofreaders, expert advisors, and others who have contributed in innumerable ways. They include members of the pd-list and forum, members of music-dsp list and Yahoo sound design list: thank you for your patience, opinions, and honest criticisms. To all the Openlab guys and gals who have occasionally saved me from insanity by sharing a beer.

Sorry to anyone I missed. Thank you all.

Andrew Bucksbarg (telecommunications), Andrew Wilkie (musician and programmer), Andy Mellor (musician, programmer), Andy Tuke (programmer), Angela Travis (actor), Anthony Hughes (DJ), Augusta Annersley (psychology), Bart Malpas (musician), Carl Rohumaa (musician), Charles B. Maynes (sound designer), Charles Henry (signals math), Chris McCormick (game design), Christina Smith (musician), Chun Lee (Composer, programmer), Claude Heiland-Allen (digital artist, programmer), Coll Anderson (sound designer), Conor Patterson (digital artist), Cyrille Henry (interactive music), Daniel James (author and programmer), Darren Brown (musician), David Randall (Randy) Thom (sound designer), Derek Holzer (Pure Data), Domonic White (electronics, musician), Farella Dove (animator, VJ), Frank Barknecht (programmer, writer), Gavin Brockis (musician), Geoff Stokoe (physics), Grant Buckerfield (music producer, sound designer), Hans-Christoph Steiner (Pure Data), Ian (Bugs), Hathersall (filmmaker, programmer), Jim Cowdroy (musician), Jo Carter (teacher), Julie Wood (musician), Karen Collins (game audio), Kate Brown (psychotherapist, music), Kees van den Doel (procedural audio), Keith Brown (chemist), Leon Van Noorden (psychoacoustics), Marcus Voss (digital artist), Marius Schebella (Pure Data), Martin Peach (Pure Data), Mathieu Bouchard (math), Mike Driver (physics), Miller Puckette (computer music), Nick Dixon (musician, programmer), Norman Wilson (programmer), Patrice Colet (Pure Data), Patricia Allison (theatre), Paul Weir (composer), Paul (Wiggy) Neville (producer, musician), Paul Wyatt (musician), Peter Plessas (Pure Data), Peter Rounce (electronic engineer), Peter Rudkin (chemist), Philippe-Aubert Gauthier (acoustics), Rob Atwood (physics, programmer, artist), Rob Munroe (digital artist), Sarah Class (composer), Sarah Weatherall (film and radio), Shane Wells (electronics), Simon Clewer (programmer, physics), S (Jag) Jagannathan (digital artist, programmer), Steffen Juul (Pure Data), Steve Fricker (sound), Steven W. Smith (author, DSP), Steven Hodges (electronics, computing), Timothy Selby (electronics).

Packages used: Pure Data, Nyquist, Csound, Xfig, Inkscape, Gnu Octave, Gnuplot, LaTeX.

1
Introduction

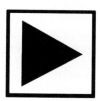

This is a textbook for anyone who wishes to understand and create sound effects starting from nothing. It's about sound as a process rather than sound as data, a subject sometimes called "procedural audio." The thesis of this book is that any sound can be generated from first principles, guided by analysis and synthesis. An idea evolving from this is that, in some ways, sounds so constructed are more realistic and useful than recordings because they capture behaviour. Although considerable work is required to create synthetic sounds with comparable realism to recordings the rewards are astonishing. Sounds which are impossible to record become accessible. Transformations are made available that cannot be achieved though any existing effects process. And fantastic sounds can be created by reasoned extrapolation. This considerably enhances the palette of the traditional sound designer beyond mixing and applying effects to existing material to include constructing and manipulating virtual sound objects. By doing so the designer obtains something with a remarkable property, something that has deferred form. Procedural sound is a living sound effect that can run as computer code and be changed in real time according to unpredictable events. The advantage of this for video games is enormous, though it has equally exciting applications for animations and other modern media.

About the Book

Aims

The aim is to explore basic principles of making ordinary, everyday sounds using a computer and easily available free software. We use the Pure Data (Pd) language to construct *sound objects*, which unlike recordings of sound can be used later in a flexible way. A practical, systematic approach to procedural audio is taught by example and supplemented with background knowledge to give a firm context. From here the technically inclined artist will be able to create his or her own sound objects for use in interactive applications and other projects. Although it is not intended to be a manual for Pure Data, a sufficient introduction to patching is provided to enable the reader to complete the exercises. References and external resources on sound and computer audio are provided. These include other important textbooks, websites, applications, scientific papers, and research supporting the material developed here.

Audience

Modern sound designers working in games, film, animation, and media where sound is part of an interactive process will all find this book useful. Designers using traditional methods but looking for a deeper understanding and finer degree of control in their work will likewise benefit. Music production, traditional recording, arrangement, mixdown, or working from sample libraries is not covered. It is assumed that the reader is already familiar these concepts and has the ability to use multitrack editors like Ardour and Pro Tools, plus the other necessary parts of a larger picture of sound design. It isn't aimed at complete beginners, but great effort is made to ease through the steep learning curve of digital signal processing (DSP) and synthesis at a gentle pace. Students of digital audio, sound production, music technology, film and game sound, and developers of audio software should all find something of interest here. It will appeal to those who know a little programming, but previous programming skills are not a requirement.

Using the Book

Requirements

This is neither a complete introduction to Pure Data, nor a compendium of sound synthesis theory. A sound designer requires a wide background knowledge, experience, imagination, and patience. A grasp of everyday physics is helpful in order to analyse and understand sonic processes. An ambitious goal of this text is to teach synthetic sound production using very little maths. Where possible I try to explain pieces of signal processing theory in only words and pictures. However, from time to time code or equations do appear to illustrate a point, particularly in the earlier theory chapters where formulas are given for reference.

Although crafting sound from numbers is an inherently mathematical process we are fortunate that tools exist which hide away messy details of signal programming to allow a more direct expression as visual code. To get the most from this book a serious student should embark upon supporting studies of digital audio and DSP theory. For a realistic baseline, familiarity with simple arithmetic, trigonometry, logic, and graphs is expected.

Previous experience patching with Pure Data or Max/MSP will give one a head start, but even without such experience the principles are easy to learn. Although Pure Data is the main vehicle for teaching this subject an attempt is made to discuss the principles in an application-agnostic way. Some of the content is readable and informative without the need for other resources, but to make the best use of it the reader should work alongside a computer set up as an audio workstation and complete the practical examples. The minimum system requirements for most examples are a 500MHz computer with 256MB of RAM, a sound card, loudspeakers or headphones, and a copy of the Pure Data program. A simple wave file editor, such as Audacity, capable of handling Microsoft .wav or Mac .aiff formats will be useful.

Structure

Many of the examples follow a pattern. First we discuss the nature and physics of a sound and talk about our goals and constraints. Next we explore the theory and gather food for developing synthesis models. After choosing a set of methods, each example is implemented, proceeding through several stages of refinement to produce a Pure Data program for the desired sound. To make good use of space and avoid repeating material I will sometimes present only the details of a program which change. As an ongoing subtext we will discuss, analyse, and refine the different synthesis techniques we use. So that you don't have to enter every Pure Data program by hand the examples are available online to download: <http://mitpress.mit.edu/designingsound>. There are audio examples to help you understand if Pure Data is not available.

Written Conventions

Pure Data is abbreviated as Pd, and since other similar DSP patcher tools exist you may like to take Pd as meaning "patch diagram" in the widest sense. For most commands, keyboard shortcuts are given as CTRL+s, RETURN and so forth. Note, for Mac users CTRL refers to the "command" key and where right click or left click are specified you should use the appropriate keyboard and click combination. Numbers are written as floating point decimals almost everywhere, especially where they refer to signals, as a constant reminder that all numbers are floats in Pd. In other contexts ordinary integers will be written as such. Graphs are provided to show signals. These are generally normalised −1.0 to +1.0, but absolute scales or values should not be taken too seriously unless the discussion focusses on them. Scales are often left out for the simplicity of showing just the signal. When we refer to a Pd object within text it will appear as a small container box, like metro. The contents of the box are the object name, in this case a metronome. The motto of Pd is "The diagram is the program." This ideal, upheld by its author Miller Puckette, makes Pd very interesting for publishing and teaching because one can implement the examples just by looking at the diagrams.

I
Theory

2
Theory Introduction

There ain't half been some
clever bastards.
—I. Dury

Three Pillars of Sound Design

We begin this journey with a blueprint. Computers are a wonderful vehicle that can take us to amazing places, but without theoretical underpinnings they are a car without a roadmap. They cannot show us a destination or a route, only a means of travelling. As sound designers we work within an enormous context, an incredibly rich landscape, encompassing physics, maths, psychology, and culture. The history of sound design goes back to before the Greeks and Romans[1] and brings with it such a body of terminology and theory that it's easy to get lost. Since we are concentrating on the general case of sound I will not dwell on musical instruments, song and musical scales, nor most of the five decades of analog electronic theory that precede digital representations. The following chapters are a rapid tour of what could easily fill three textbooks, if not an entire shelf. To provide a modern view that ties together these foundations I would like you to keep figure 2.1 in mind while reading. It shows sound design as a structure supported by three pillars, three bodies of knowledge, which are:

Physical

First we look at sound as a physical phenomenon, as vibrations within materials that involve an exchange of energy. These are the subjects of mechanics, material dynamics, oscillators and acoustics, covered in chapters 3, 4, and 5. Some equations will appear, but on the whole a qualitative approach is taken.

Mathematical

Mathematics plays an essential part for understanding how digital computers can make a facsimile of real-world dynamics. Chapter 7 will give an overview of digital audio signals. Although we venture into computer science in order to

---

1. The precursors of musical instruments are believed to be noise devices made by our primitive ancestors to scare away evil spirits.

see how to represent and transform such signals we will keep it light and avoid difficult analysis.

Psychological

And since sound is a sense, a human experience, psychoacoustics will be needed to help us understand how we perceive physical sounds, how we extract features and meaning from them, and how we categorise and memorise them. This is the topic of chapter 6. Our personal experiences are subjective and it is hard to objectively map internal encodings. However, the ideas presented here are known to hold true for most people and have solid experimental evidence from cognitive psychology.

Technique and Design

Bringing together these three supporting subjects, the physical, mathematical, and perceptual, we arrive at the final chapters in this part, which deal with technique. Here we will examine approaches to deconstructing sounds according to their physical basis and our experience of them. This reveals physical processes that tally with perceptual processes. Finally, we'll see how to turn these analytical models into new sounds with the desired behaviour, and see how to control them using signal-processing techniques.

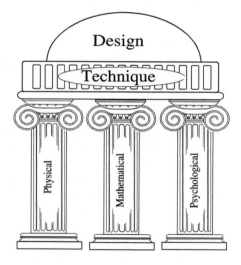

Figure 2.1
Theoretical underpinnings of sound design technique.

As you might expect, each of these topics overlaps with the others since they are part of a bigger picture. For example, the subject of physioacoustics connects psychoacoustics with the physics of sound. If you feel lost at any point during the next few chapters come back and look at figure 2.1 to take a wide view.

3
Physical Sound

Elementary Physics

Energy

Energy is a reference point in the universe. Perhaps it is the most fundamental of all things. We give it the symbol E. It is a constant that remains the same whatever else changes, and it can take many forms. Whenever something happens, from a rock rolling down a hill to a star exploding, some energy changes form. But the total amount of energy, the sum of all forms, remains the same. Its many forms include kinetic energy possessed by a moving object, thermal energy in a hot body, chemical potential energy in a battery, fuel, or food, or potential energy in a compressed spring or in a book just sitting on a shelf. We say an object can *contain* energy, or that energy is a *property of* an object. A hot firework and a falling rock both contain energy, in thermal or kinetic forms. The unit to measure energy is the Joule (J), but it cannot be determined directly, only by observing changes in energy.

Force

A *force* is the attempt of energy to move, which we write as F. Force is measured in Newtons, written N, so to describe a force of 10 Newtons we say $F = 10N$. In a reservoir the water exerts a huge force on the dam. But because the dam holds fast the water doesn't move and no energy changes. The water exerts a force on the dam, and the dam exerts a force on the water. This is Isaac Newton's third law, which says, whenever an object A exerts a force on another object B, then B will exert an equal force in the opposite direction on A. When the two forces are balanced, we say they are in *equilibrium*.

Pressure

When a force acts on a surface we say the surface experiences *pressure*, written p and measured in Pascals (Pa).[1] One Pa $= 1N/m^2$, so it is a force divided by an area and we can say

$$p = \frac{F}{A} \tag{3.1}$$

---
1. After French physicist and mathematician Blaise Pascal.

for a force F in Newtons and an area A in meters squared. At sea level on Earth there is always an ambient pressure of 101325Pa, called one standard atmosphere, so we usually measure any acoustic pressure relative to this quiescent background rather than dealing in absolute pressures. We don't take into account any direction the pressure acts in, so it is a scalar quantity, acting in all directions.

Work

Because energy can move we may harness and channel it to do *work*, which we give the symbol W. Work is a change of energy, also measured in Joules. So, another definition of energy is the ability to do work. It can cause things to get hotter, or move things, or emit light and radio waves. One way it can move is as sound, so sound can be thought of as changing energy. We use the symbol Δ to denote a change, and we can express work as a change of energy with the following formula.

$$W = \Delta E \tag{3.2}$$

Systems

In physics we talk about conservation of energy (as well as momentum and angular momentum). We always do so in the context of a closed system, isolated from the rest of the universe. But no such systems exist. In reality everything is connected, even in space where nothing can evade the reach of gravity and electromagnetic forces. Sound must be considered in this context, as part of an interconnected system. Here on Earth, objects rest on top of one another, or are surrounded by air or other fluids. These connections serve to transmit energy from one thing to another. Sounds can be explained as the flow of energy in a system, beginning with a source and ending at the furthest reaches of the system where sound energy eventually becomes heat. Somewhere within this system our ears, or a microphone, may observe the changing energy patterns.

Power

Power, measured in watts (W), is the rate at which work is done. One watt is the same as one Joule per second (1J/s), or how much energy changes state each second. When making a sound we are converting one kind of energy to another at a certain rate; in a trumpet or violin the force of air or the movement of a bow are converted to radiated sound energy. In an electronic amplifier with loudspeakers sound is produced from electrical energy. A perfect 100W amplifier and loudspeaker converts 100J of electrical energy to sound every second.

Energy Sources

So where does energy come from to make sound? Muscles in the chest of the trumpet player? The food that the violinist ate for breakfast? Most of the energy we experience on Earth comes from the Sun, and a tiny proportion comes from fission of matter within the planet (a hot liquid of heavy elements like iron, silicon, and uranium which undergoes a slow nuclear reaction at the planet's core). Every sound we hear is ultimately caused by these sources of energy doing work. When a branch falls from a tree it liberates gravitational potential energy stored from growth by photosynthesis. Growth that created the branch was slow, steady work against gravity. Now some of that energy becomes sound as the wood breaks and the branch crashes down. Energy is always trying to go from a high state to a low one, and this propensity to move makes it useful. It moves from wherever energy is high to wherever there is less energy, or more *degrees of freedom*, trying to spread itself as thinly as possible in the universe. This is called the *second law of thermodynamics*.

Matter and Mass

Some of the universe is made up of matter, a condensed form of energy. We are made of it, and so is the planet we live on. All matter has mass, measured in kilograms (kg), and has weight whilst in a gravitational field. The common understanding of matter is of indivisible atoms which have mass, within a space that has no mass. Another model sees it as a continuum of stuff where there are no sharp boundaries. Either is correct to a degree; matter is a spongy substance made of connected fields, and it can move about and contain energy. But single atoms are rare things. In some materials like metals and crystals atoms are packed together into a lattice. Instead of monatomic gases or liquids we usually find groups of atoms arranged into *molecules*. Where several different types of atom make up a molecule we call it a *compound*, such as crystaline salt which is made of sodium and chlorine atoms. The atomic or molecular model is great for understanding sound in a simple way, as a result of collisions between small points of mass. Think of a pool table or Newton's cradle toy and imagine sound as movement transferred from one ball to another.

Force, Distance, and Acceleration

Unless the forces acting on a mass are balanced, a change occurs. A mechanical force produces movement and does work, $W = F \times d$, for a distance d. We measure distance in meters, written as m, but two other concepts are very important: the rate of change of distance called *velocity* (or more commonly *speed*), and the rate of change of velocity, called *acceleration*. Velocity is given the symbol v and measured in meters per second, written m/s. Acceleration is measured in meters per second per second, written ms^{-2}, and we give it the symbol a.

   Newton's laws of motion are important because they ultimately explain how the air moves to make sound. The most important of these is the second law, stating that force equals mass times acceleration, $F = ma$. Shortly we will see how this gives rise to oscillations, a form of motion called *simple harmonic motion* which underpins many sounds. One Newton of force will accelerate 1kg at $1ms^{-2}$. Other kinds of forces are gravity (because it accelerates objects that have mass), magnetism, and electricity (because they too can accelerate objects and cause them to move). If you understand these basic concepts you have the physics foundations for everything else to do with sound.

Displacement, Movement, and Freedom

Tiny disturbances in the positions of molecules are responsible for sound. A *rest point* or *equilibrium position* is where a piece of matter is undisturbed by any vibrations. It's what we measure displacement relative to. The number of directions in which something can move determines its *degree of freedom*. Most real things have three degrees of translational movement (colloquially, up and down, left and right, forwards and backwards), and three degrees of rotational movement (pitch, roll, and yaw), but for many sound models we like to simplify things and imagine, for instance, that points on a string have only one degree of freedom. Displacement is a distance, so it's measured in meters, (m). However, more strictly it is a vector since the direction of displacement is important.

Excitation

An *excitation point* is the place where power is transmitted to an object. It can be frictional in the case of a scraping movement like a violin bow, or an impulse as during a collision. A material can be excited by turbulent airflow around it or by a sudden physical release that causes movement, such as with a plucked string. It can be excited by its own internal stresses when it breaks or deforms, like the creaking of heated steel beams. If it is made of a ferromagnetic metal something may be placed in a magnetic field where it will experience a force, as with some loudspeaker designs or an e-bow which can be used to play an electric guitar. A charged object in a strong electric field may be deflected if the field strength changes, which is the principle of electrostatic loudspeakers. But most kinds of excitation come through simple coupling, a direct force from another connected object that is vibrating. The thing bringing energy to the system is called the *excitor* and the thing that vibrates is *excited*. The excited thing can be a *resonator*, a concept we will develop shortly. In reality, because of Newton's third law both excitor and excited material usually contribute something to the sound, so the nature of both objects is important. The sound of a hammer hitting a nail is inseparable from the sound of a nail being hit with a hammer.[2]

┌─ SECTION 3.2 ───

Materials

We define materials to be any practical form of matter found in the real world. That could be glass, wood, paper, rocks, or scissors. It could also be steam, water, or ice, highlighting the first important property of materials which is *state*,[3] being solids, liquids, and gasses. These states reflect the way the matter is held together by forces. The forces holding all materials together are called *bonds*, of which there are several types, and some are stronger than others. In table 3.1 the five types of bonds and their strength are listed. As a rough guide, these break all matter into five classes, solid and crystalline chemical

---

2. Although with clever spectral techniques we can isolate the sounds of each part (see Cook 2002, p. 94).
3. We avoid using the physics term *phase* since that word has a special meaning in sound.

compounds with high melting points, metals, liquid and solid compounds with low melting points, organic compounds like oils and plastics, and large molecular compounds like cellulose and rubber. Each molecule is held in space by a

Table 3.1 Material bonds.

Type	Example	Youngs Modulus GPa
Covalent	Crystalline solids	200–1000
Metallic	Metals	60–200
Ionic	Soluble minerals	30–100
Hydrogen bond	Plastics	2–10
Van der Walls	Rubber, Wood	1–5

balance of electrostatic bonding forces that mutually attract and repel it from its neighbours. Newton's third law helps us understand why this affects sound. For every action there is an equal and opposite reaction. Written as $F_a = -F_b$, this means that because they are bonded together, if molecule a exerts a force on another one b, then b will provide an equal force in the opposite direction back to a to compensate. If one molecule gets too far from its neighbour it will be pulled back, and likewise it will be pushed away if two get too close. Thus sound travels through materials by causing a cascade of moving masses within this electrostatic bonding structure. The closer the molecular masses, and the more strongly bonded, the better and faster sound moves through something. It moves through steel very well, and quickly, at about 5000m/s, because iron atoms are packed close together and are well connected. Temperature affects the bonding, and sound obviously changes as state goes from solid, to liquid, and then to a gas. Ice sounds quite different from water. In carbon dioxide gas where the forces between distant molecules are relatively weak we find sound moves slowly at 259m/s. Of the 118 common elements, 63 are metals. That accounts for a wide range of physical properties, and more so if we allow alloys. Most metals are elastic, hard, dense, and acoustically very conductive.

Elasticity and Restoration

In addition to mass the other quality of matter that allows it to store mechanical energy, and makes sound vibrations possible, is *elasticity*. The chart in figure 3.1 elaborates on table 3.1 to show the elasticity for a range of materials. It goes by several names, sometimes called the *Young's modulus* (E) or *bulk modulus* (K) of a material, or *compressibility* when talking about gasses. We will look at these different definitions shortly. To begin with, all forces between molecules are balanced, in equilibrium. If a point of material is disturbed in space it changes its relationship to its neighbours. The material behaves as a temporary sponge to soak up mechanical energy. Increased and decreased forces of attraction and repulsion then act to pull the arrangement back into equilibrium. As the matter returns to its original configuration, with everything

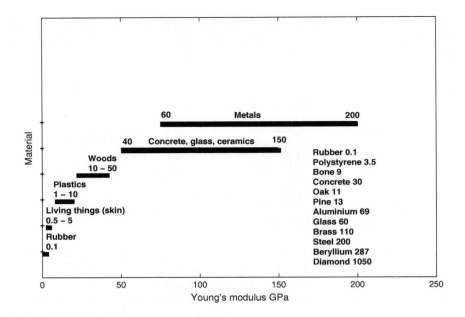

Figure 3.1
Elastic (Young's) modulus of some common materials $\times 10^9 \mathrm{N/m^2}$.

moving back to its rest point, all the energy held is released and the material is said to be *restored.*

More commonly we talk of the *stiffness* (k) of a material, which depends on E and the dimensions of the object. Stiffness is the distance (*strain*) a rod of material will move elastically for a given force (*stress*). For equal shapes, a stiff material like steel or diamond has a high value of E and only deforms a little bit for a large force, while a *flexible* material like rubber has a low value of E and easily stretches. To work out the stiffness of a string or rod we use

$$k = \frac{AE}{l} \tag{3.3}$$

where A is the cross-sectional area, and l is the total length. Stiffness is measured in Newtons per meter, so if a force is applied to a material and it moves by x meters then

$$k = \frac{F}{x} \tag{3.4}$$

Engineers combine these two equations to predict the movement and loads when designing machines or buildings, but we can use these formulas to find stiffness for calculating sound frequencies. Of course not all things happen to be strings or thin rods. For three-dimensional objects we may also want to know the bulk modulus K, which is how much a volume of material decreases for a certain pressure. To get the bulk modulus we need one more piece of information, the "squashiness" of the material. If you stretch a rubber band it gets thinner in the middle, or if you press down on a piece of modelling clay it grows fat as you squash it. This squashiness is called the *Poisson ratio* ν, and some values for common materials are given in figure 3.2. With the Poisson ratio ν and the

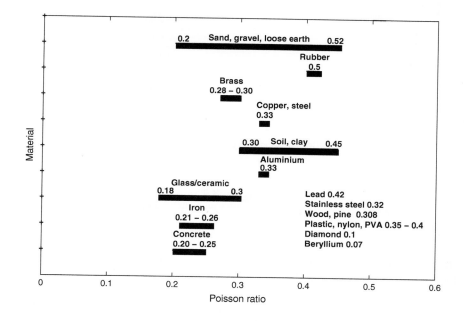

Figure 3.2
Poisson ratio (squash factor) of some common materials (no units).

Young's modulus E you can calculate the bulk modulus K as

$$K = \frac{E}{3(1 - 2\nu)} \tag{3.5}$$

This will come in handy in a moment when we calculate the speed of sound in a material.

Density

The density of a material is how closely its mass points are packed together. A large mass in a small volume has a high density, like diamond. The same mass spread out in a larger volume, like charcoal, has a low density, even though

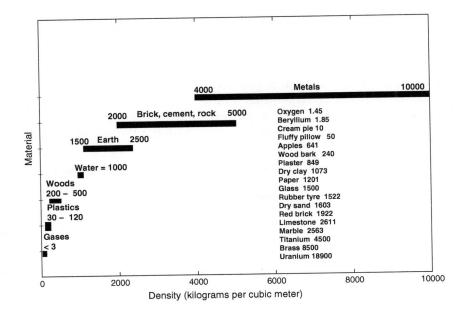

Figure 3.3
Density of some common materials $\times 1\text{kg/m}^3$.

these are the same element, carbon. Density ρ is mass m in kilograms divided by volume V in cubic meters, so

$$\rho = \frac{m}{V} \tag{3.6}$$

measured in kilograms per cubic meter (kg/m^3).

Plasticity

When a point stores energy elastically the energy is recoverable, and it is stored in a force. If a material moves in a plastic way, or *yields*, no energy is stored. The energy is transformed into heat. Plasticity is the opposite of elasticity. Plastic materials have points that don't return to their original positions, and after moving relative to each other they stay deformed. Such materials *absorb* sound and dampen vibrations. When you build a line of dominoes and push the end one over, it starts a chain reaction. Each domino falls onto its neighbour, which pushes the next neighbour, and so on. This movement of energy is a good approximation to an inelastic energy transfer. After the whole event has occurred, when everything is still again, a physical structure has been permanently moved or deformed. A material like this is said to be *plastic*. Many materials are thermoplastics which soften and become more plastic as they heat up. A candle taken from the freezer will sound like a wood or metal bar when dropped, compared to the dull thud of a warm softened candle. Other *thermosetting* materials harden and get more elastic with temperature.

Structure and Strength

Materials may have structure at many levels. We may see regular crystalline structure in metals and glass, or a chaotic and dispersed structure in graphite or clay. Complex structures exist, such as those found in wood where fibrous strands of cellulose are woven into vessels containing air or moisture. At the atomic and microstructural level metal is quite uniform in a way that wood is not. Glass or china ceramics fall between these two. Homogeneous structures, where each bit of the material is largely the same as all the other bits, tend to give purer tones than heterogeneous structures, where the material is composed of many different bits mixed up. Cellulose as corn starch in water, like dough or custard, is a lot less elastic than the same amount of cellulose arranged as wood. The difference here is material *strength*. Elasticity only works if the bonds aren't stretched too far, governed by two things. One is a constant factor for each material. The constant has no units, being a ratio, a nonfundamental unit made up of elasticity and plasticity in two modes, compression and tension. The other is temperature, which changes the strength. Since most things are thermoplastic they lose strength as they get hotter. A material that can crack, splinter, or deform changes its structure permanently. Like plasticity, if the material breaks any elastic energy is lost along with the potential for vibration. If a material is *hard*, like diamond or beryllium, the bonds may be so strong that sound is transmitted very fast; it is as if the whole structure moves together.

SECTION 3.3

Waves

We have talked about sound in an abstract way for some time now without ever alluding to its real nature. Now it's time to take a closer look at what sound really is. The things that carry energy from one place to another are called *waves* and they move by propagation through a *medium*. The medium, which is made to *vibrate*, is any intervening material between two points in space. Waves are imaginary things. Watch the surface of a pool as waves move on it; the water does not move along at the speed of the wave, it merely rises and falls. The local or instantaneous velocity of the medium is different from the speed of the wave. The wave is something else, less tangible; it is a pattern of change that spreads outwards.

Wave Models

If a wave is imaginary, how do we sense it? We can't directly see forces or accelerations; they exist to help us understand things. However, we can clearly see and measure displacement by the position of something, such as when water ripples over a pond. To help visualise waves we create imaginary *points* as a mathematical tool. Since atoms or molecules are too small for us to think about practically, a model of vibrating things needs fewer points, each representing more matter. They occupy no size but have a mass, and we arrange them into discrete spaces, planes or lines of points connected by bonds. By thinking about the movement of these imaginary points we can understand waves more easily.

Exchange of Forces

Let's return to our mathematical model of elastic material as a lattice of points and bonds in 3D space, like those coloured ball-and-spring models used for molecules in chemistry. It's an approximation of how matter behaves, in a sort of bouncy, wobbly way. All the forces causing vibration can be broken down into a sum of simpler forces. Some are pushing forces and some are pulling forces, acting the opposite way. Some are twisting forces with opposing ones that spin the other way. In a vibrating body they are all in a state of *dynamic equilibrium*. In this equilibrium energy moves backwards and forwards between two states, one of potential energy, or force, and one of kinetic energy, movement in space or velocity. The vibrations are a temporary dynamic equilibrium in which there is *equipartition* of energy. That means energy is held in a bistable state, alternately in one of two forms, a force or a movement. After excitation each point is trying to reach its equilibrium position, where it feels most at rest after being moved away from home by some disturbance. Before it finally settles back to its home position, when the sound stops, it moves around its rest point exchanging movement for force. These vibrations are what makes sound. The ones we hear come from the outside surface of the object, those in contact with the air. Shown in figure 3.4 is the movement of a displaced point as time progresses (down the diagram). Notice the force acting in the opposite direction to displacement.

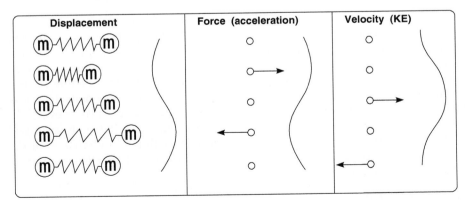

Figure 3.4
Transverse (solid bending) wave behaviour at another solid boundary.

Propagation

So, if we apply a force and displace a point so it moves relative to the points surrounding it, the others soon fall into line with the displaced point, either drawn into the space left behind the displacement or pushed forwards by the pressure ahead of it. In turn they exert a force on their neighbouring points, pushing or pulling them around in space. This effect propagates throughout the medium as a wavefront setting all the other points in its path into vibration. In an unbounded medium the wave propagates outward forever. In a finite vibrating solid, because of boundary conditions we will look at shortly, sound bounces around the material like ripples in a pool. The effect of this moving wavefront is a wave, and the time pattern of moving vibrations is called a *waveform*. Where the points of material are bunched up into a higher density it's called a *compression*, and conversely an area where they are more spread out than usual is a *rarefaction*. Sound waves in a gas are *longitudinal*, meaning the movement of material points is forwards and backwards in the same direction as the propagation. To visualise longitudinal propagation hold a long toy spring by one end and push it forwards and backwards. It simulates an elastic medium like

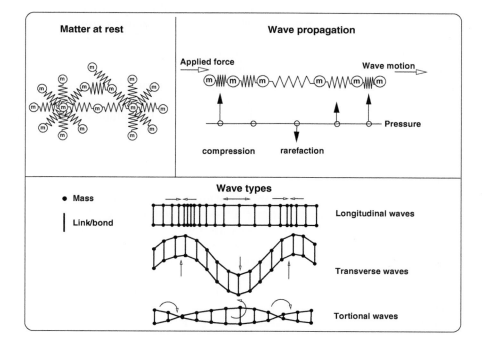

Figure 3.5
Propagation of waves.

a gas. Points that are compressed push outwards, trying to restore the springy medium to its original position. Because more compression waves are arriving behind the wavefront it tends to move forwards into the area of least resistance where the medium is at uniform density or where it has the greatest degree of freedom. This forwards movement of the wave is *propagation.*

At the peak of displacement the medium is not moving. Now the elasticity of the material comes into play. It flexes the points back towards their original position. The force carried by the wave is equal to the restoring force of the material. As the restoring force pulls them back the displaced points move so fast in the opposite direction they'll overshoot their original position. Where the restoring force is inversely proportional to the displacement then we get *simple harmonic motion,* as the displaced part swings back and forth around its rest point.

Wave Types

There are several kinds of waves determined by the directions of movement. As we just saw, longitudinal waves displace the medium in the same axis as the wave motion. There are also *transverse* waves that move in a direction perpendicular to the displacement of the medium. Transverse waves are like those seen on the surface of water.[4] Propagation of transverse waves is easy to see if you grab one end of a piece of string and shake it: the waves move from the point of displacement towards the end of the string at rest. Whereas sound waves travelling through the air move by longitudinal propagation, vibrating solids like a bell or plate may have either longitudinal or transverse waves happening. There is also a third, twisting kind of wave. To picture twisting or *torsion* waves imagine spinning a rope ladder. Whenever we talk of sound waves in air or other fluids, in an *acoustic* context, we mean longitudinal displacement waves. When talking about vibrations in solids we can either mean transverse waves or longitudinal waves.

Amplitude

Be careful of this term since there are many units used to quote amplitude and at least two often confusing variations. The amplitude of a wave is a *measured* quantity at some point. Usually we measure displacement in meters. But we can choose to measure any property, like presssure or velocity. In all cases it has both negative and positive magnitudes relative to the rest point. For sound waves a positive amount corresponds to a compression of the medium and a negative value to a rarefaction. Regular amplitude is measured between zero and the peak displacement. The difference between the most positive and most negative displacement of a wave is called the *range*, or peak to peak amplitude and is *twice the regular amplitude.*

---

4. Water waves are actually Rayleigh waves which move in small circles; the effect seen on the surface is the transverse component of these.

Speed

The speed of a wave is usually taken as constant within the life of a sound event in the same material. In the air, sound waves travel at about 340m/s, faster in a liquid, and even more so in a solid. So, as a simplification, all waves have a fixed speed in a uniform material, which depends only on the properties of the material and has the symbol c. Waves may change speed when moving between different materials or across temperature changes. In rare and extreme cases like explosions and supersonic booms, and to a small extent in all real (non-ideal) materials, this isn't perfectly true, but it is sufficiently accurate for most sound engineering. A deeper physical analysis shows that c also depends slightly on amplitude. We can calculate the speed of sound in a particular material from the elasticity and density. The formula works well for solids, slightly less so for rubber and liquids, and for gases we need to add an extra part to account for the fact that compressing a gas heats it. I won't give that formula here, only the general formula which is good for solids. To a good approximation:

$$c = \sqrt{K/\rho} \tag{3.7}$$

To show this works let's try it on some numbers. We will use steel since its properties are well documented and it's a common material found in sound design examples. We will also assume that we want the speed in a large volume of steel, rather than a thin rod or wire. For a thin solid we would directly use the stiffness, but for a volume first we need to find the bulk elastic modulus:

Young's modulus of steel $= 200 \times 10^9 \text{N/m}^2$

Density of steel $= 7900 \text{kg/m}^3$

Poisson ratio of steel $= 0.3$

Since

$$K = \frac{E}{3(1 - 2v)} \tag{3.8}$$

plugging in the numbers we get:

$$K = \frac{200 \times 10^9}{3 \times (1 - 0.6)}$$
$$= 1.67 \times 10^{11}$$

So, using the formula for the speed of sound:

$$c = \sqrt{\frac{K}{\rho}}$$
$$= \sqrt{\frac{1.67 \times 10^{11}}{7900}}$$
$$= 4597 \text{m/s}$$

Group and Phase Velocity

Earlier I described waves as an "imaginary" things, and we have seen that by propagation small particles can transfer power through a medium. This leads to an interesting and sometimes ambiguous use of the words *velocity* and *speed*. When thinking about the movement of points or particles we are sometimes interested in how fast a particle is moving at any instant. We call this the *particle velocity*. We will see soon that this determines the amount of viscous loss. In figure 3.6 the particle velocity is shown as the lighter dot which moves up and down.[5] One moment a particle velocity is large and in one direction, the next it is zero, and then it is negative and so on. Particle velocity is zero twice per cycle. If the amplitude increases you can see the distance travelled each cycle is greater, so the maximum particle velocity increases. So, the maximum particle velocity depends on frequency and amplitude.

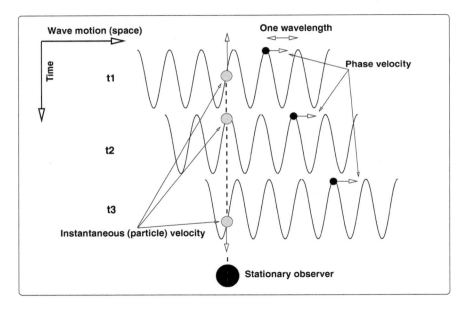

Figure 3.6
Velocity and wavelength of a moving wave.

Other times we are interested in the speed that the wave propagates through the medium, as calculated previously. To disambiguate it from the particle velocity we call it the *phase velocity*. It is the speed at which the waveform moves. In figure 3.6 a wave passes by a stationary observer at three times, (t1,

---

5. For clarity of the diagram I've shown it as a transverse wave, but in fact it has a longitudinal phase velocity in the same axis as the wave motion.

t2, t3). The phase velocity of propagation is shown by the darker dot which follows some feature (at the same phase) as it travels along. When talking about the "speed of sound" we are always talking about the phase (wave) velocity.

Another kind of wave velocity is called the *group velocity*, which is the speed at which energy travels. For most acoustic situations, the phase and the group velocity are equal. Group velocity is a constant that depends on the properties of the medium. Ripples on a pond show this effect. After a disturbance a group of waves will propagate outward, but within the group we see that the individual waves seem to move faster than the group, appearing at the rear of a cluster and moving forwards to disappear at the forward edge. Sometimes, when the group and phase velocity are not quite the same we see a wave distort as it propagates. In this case we say the medium is *dispersive*, because the propagation speed depends on frequency, so a wave containing several frequencies will change shape as the phase relation of its components alters (Graff 1991, p. 59). An example of this can be seen when water waves wash up on a beach. The phase velocity is trying to move ahead faster than the group velocity and so the wave curls over on itself.

Wavelength

Since waves take time to propagate some distance in space this introduces a delay between cycles of a wave measured at different locations in space. Indeed, this is how we are able to locate the source of a sound, because the waves from a vibrating object arrive at each ear at different times. Because waves propagate at a finite speed we sometimes talk about space and time in a comparable way, which leads us to the concept of *wavelength*. This is literally a measure of how long a wave is, in meters, and it's measured between the closest two points with the same displacement moving in the same direction. We give wavelength the symbol "lambda," written λ. One wavelength of a moving wave is also shown in figure 3.6.

Frequency and Period

The motion of some point, being displaced, returning through its rest point, overshooting, and then coming all the way back to its rest point once again, is one *cycle*, and the time taken to do this is the period (T) measured in seconds. A reciprocal view of the same thing, measured as the number of times this happens each second, is the *frequency* (f). Period and frequency are related as $f = 1/T$ and f has units of Hertz (Hz).

Simple Wave Math

As you have probably worked out, the concepts of speed, wavelength, and frequency are all connected by an equation. We can calculate the phase velocity (speed of sound) from frequency and wavelength with:

$$c = f\lambda \qquad (3.9)$$

To get the wavelength where we know speed and frequency we use:

$$\lambda = c/f \qquad (3.10)$$

And of course the final rearrangement gives us the frequency where we know c and λ as:

$$f = c/\lambda \tag{3.11}$$

The range of audible wavelengths in air is from 20mm for high frequencies up to 17m for the lowest. Real ranges of c vary from 100m/s in heavy gases to 12.8km/s in beryllium.

Phase

If you are driving on a roundabout, travelling in a circle, then halfway round you will be moving in the opposite direction, at 180°. To undo the change of direction the best thing to do is keep moving round until you have travelled through 360°. We can use perceptual frames of reference to understand the difference between an absolute relationship, like the distance from here to the post office, and a relative frame of reference, like "half-full." Phase can describe a thing's relation to itself (like upside-down or back-to-front). It describes an orientation with respect to an earlier orientation. All phases are circular or wrapped, so if you go far enough in one direction you get back to where you started. As a property of real waves, phase is best thought of as the relationship between a reference point, a snapshot of the wave that doesn't move, and a moving wave. Or, as a relationship between two identical copies of the same wave separated in time. When two waves match perfectly and both have positive peaks, negative peaks, and zeros that coincide, we say they are *in phase*. When the positive part of one wave coincides with the negative part of another identical one we say the two waves are *out of phase*, or the phase is *inverted*. Phase can be measured in degrees, and also in radians. Look again at figure 3.4 for a moment and notice that the acceleration is 90° out of phase with the velocity which follows from the formulas for velocity and acceleration in terms of force and mass.

Superposition and Phase Cancellation

Superposition is adding waves together. The amplitude of a new wave created by adding together two others at some moment in time, or point in space, is the sum of their individual amplitudes. Two waves of the same frequency which have the same phase match perfectly. They will reinforce each other when superposed, whereas two waves of opposite phase will cancel one another out. If two waves are travelling in opposite directions, as in figure 3.7, and meet at some point, they *interfere* with each other. Interference is something local to the point in space where they cross. For a moment they add to each other, and if the amplitudes A_a and A_b of two waves are each 1mm, then as their crests coincide there will be a peak of $A_a + A_b = 2$mm. After that they continue along their journey as if nothing had happened. Now, this might seem counter-intuitive, because what if the two waves were in opposite phase? Wouldn't they cancel out and destroy each other? Well, for a moment they do, but only at the exact point where they meet; after that the two waves carry on as normal. That's because waves carry energy which is a scalar quantity, so regardless of their direction or phase each contains a positive amount of energy. If they were

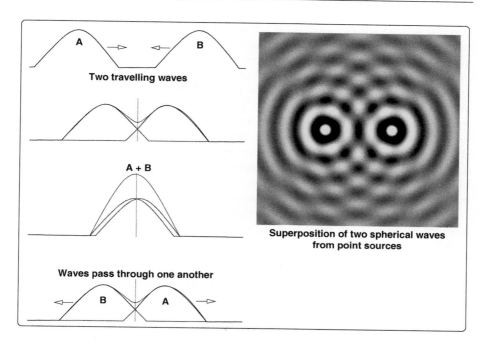

Figure 3.7
Superposition of moving waves.

able to annihilate each other then energy would be destroyed, which is impossible. So, superposition is a local phenomenon. You can see this in the right frame of figure 3.7, which shows the interference patterns created by two nearby sources vibrating at the same frequency. Each is sending out waves where the bright circles correspond to positive amplitudes (compressions) and the dark circles represent negative amplitudes (rarefactions). For any given frequency and speed of propagation there will be a pattern of stationary bright and dark spots where the waves locally reinforce or cancel each other. You can hear this if you set up a pair of loudspeakers to play a constant low sine wave at about 80Hz. Move your head from side to side and you will hear there are places where the sound seems louder than others. If you invert the phase of one channel there will be a point exactly halfway between the speakers where the sound goes to zero.

SECTION 3.4

Boundaries

A boundary is any change of material or material properties in the path of a wave. It could be the surface of a vibrating block of wood, in which case the medium is wood and the boundary material is air, or it could be the wall of a cave, in which case the medium is air and the boundary is rock. Three things can happen at a boundary depending on the difference between the medium and the boundary material. This difference can be summarised as the *boundary modulus*, a ratio of the elasticity and density of both materials. The modulus is one when the two materials are the same. In this case no reflection occurs. When the two mediums differ greatly, such as with water and air, a large proportion of the sound is reflected and very little is transmitted. For water and air this is about 99%; thus sounds above water do not really penetrate beneath the surface, and underwater sounds are very quiet in the air above. It is also found that the incidence angle can effect the intensity of the reflected wave. For both light and sound waves a very acute angle, *Brewster's angle*, may cause the reflection to suddenly vanish (see Elmore and Heald 1969, p. 159).

When considering changes happening at a boundary we need to be clear whether we talk of the wave particle's velocity, displacement, or pressure, and whether we are considering transverse bending waves in a solid or longitudinal acoustic pressure waves, since they have different behaviours.

Phase of Bending Waves at Solid Boundaries

For bending vibrations in a solid, if the boundary is a stiff and dense material then the wave is reflected back but its phase is inverted (figure 3.8). If the boundary is a dense but flexible material the wave is reflected back in phase. Newton's third law explains this. The point where the wave hits the boundary is subject to a force, but if it cannot move it exerts an equal but opposite force on the wave medium at that point. The displacement at the boundary is zero. This causes a new wave to emerge but travelling in the opposite direction and opposite phase. In a flexible solid material the boundary moves with the medium. It soaks up the force from the wave and stores it as potential energy,

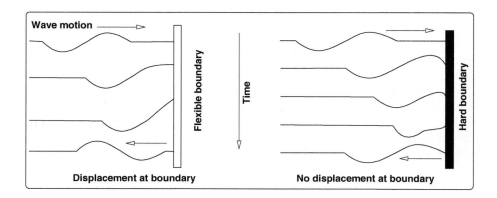

Figure 3.8
Transverse (solid bending) wave behaviour at another solid boundary.

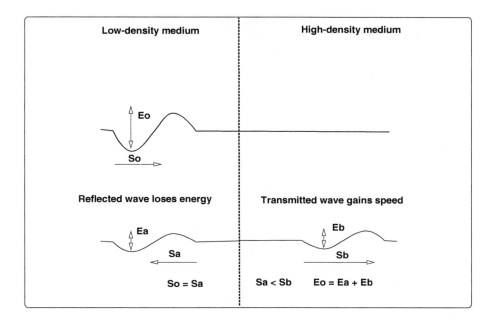

Figure 3.9
Change of wave speed across a boundary.

then emits it back into the medium as it restores. This new wave will be in the opposite direction but the same phase as the incident wave. The speed of a reflected wave in a solid will be the same as that of the incident wave, since it moves in the same medium. These effects are important when considering the coupling of materials such as drum skins or bar mountings, which we discuss below.

In either case, not all of the wave is reflected perfectly. In real materials some of it will propagate into the boundary material. In practice, of course, a mixture of all these things happens. Some energy is transmitted through the boundary and continues to propagate, some is reflected in phase, and some is reflected out of phase. Because of loss and transmission the amplitude of a reflected wave will always be less than the incident wave, but it will have the same wavelength and speed since it travels in the same medium. The transmitted wave, on the other hand, will have a different wavelength, since the density of the new medium and thus speed of propagation is different (figure 3.9). Finally, consider the direction of travel. If the incident wave is at 90° to the boundary (*normally incident* as in figure 3.10, right) then it will be reflected back in the same direction it arrived. But, as with light and a mirror, if the wave hits the boundary at an angle θ then it's reflected at the same angle θ on the other side of the normal line. And as light is refracted when moving from

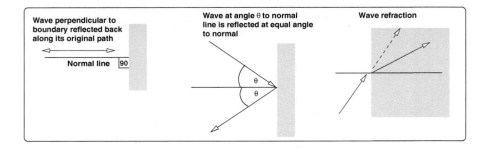

Figure 3.10
Wave behaviour at a boundary for reflected and refracted waves.

one medium to another, so is sound. The refracted wave in figure 3.10 follows Snell's law where the sine of the reflected and incident angles are in the same ratio as the speeds in each medium. Unlike light, low-frequency sound has large wavelengths. As long as the wavelength of a sound is small compared to the boundary size these rules hold true, but where the boundary is small or the wavelength is large the effects change. We hear this when sound is *occluded* by an obstacle and some of the frequencies pass around it while others are stopped. All these phenomena will become important later as we consider standing waves and modes, reverberation, and space acoustics.

Coupling

A sound may cross many boundaries from the source of energy and excitement to the point we hear it. Interfaces exist between materials with various properties, such as two kinds of wood in the bridge of a guitar. Some couplings are physically well connected, but others may be less obvious, long-distance, loose, or transient couplings. They form part of a chain in which each link causes the other to vibrate. As a later practical example, a design exercise involving lots of coupling is the sound of a vehicle. An engine alone is not the sound of a car. To properly simulate the whole car's sound we must also involve exhaust pipes, transmission noises, body resonances, and many other factors. To manage this complexity each part must be taken as a separate object in a connected whole. Loose couplings may be *discontinuous*, such as when two wine glasses are brought together. We can look at this in two ways, either as a nonlinear coupling or as a source of distinct new excitations (usually happening at the frequency of the driving source).

Reflection and Standing Waves

A reflected wave will encounter other wave-fronts travelling in the opposite direction and interfere with them. Whether the two waves reinforce each other or cancel each other out depends on their relative phases and frequencies. If a wave of the right frequency happens to bounce between two sides of an object so that its wavelength, or some multiple of it, is the same as the distance between reflections, a *standing wave* is created. A standing wave is best regarded as two waves travelling in opposite directions whose compressions and rarefactions reinforce each other. Standing waves depend on the geometry of a vibrating object. Certain lengths will encourage waves to appear at the certain frequencies, and *resonances* or *modes* emerge. Because most real objects aren't regular, many different frequencies combine in a complex dynamic process. The pattern of sound vibrations that emerge from an object is made of these resonances: waves bouncing around within the material.

Modes

Standing wave patterns tend towards the object's lowest-energy vibrational modes, those with the highest amplitude vibrations for the least energy input. It is a difficult dynamic process to describe without a good deal of math, so let's use analogy. Imagine the waves as if they were people in a town centre throughout a busy shopping day. Early in the morning when there are only a few people about, only the main high street has people on it. Later in the afternoon the town is swarming with people, visitors spread out onto the side streets to visit more obscure shops or to go to each other's homes. Some tourists get lost and take unlikely routes down side streets. This is similar to the modes, or paths that sound waves follow in the shape of an object. The more energy in the object, the more degrees of freedom will be explored. Some have a higher probability than others. The main high street is the easiest path. We call this the *primary mode*. It is the path down which sound energy moves easily to create the fundamental frequency of the object. The other smaller shopping streets form the secondary and tertiary paths. These correspond to other frequencies in the sound. The likelihood that an energy wave takes a secondary or higher path is related to how energetic the sound is. If it contains a lot of energy then waves spread out to use all the routes. Towards the evening visitors leave the town (some waves become heat and others are radiated as sound). The side streets empty and life returns mainly to the high street. This corresponds to the decay of energy in a sound through damping or radiation. Energy can move down from the tertiary and secondary modes back into the fundamental until finally it's the only strong harmonic left. The shape of standing waves can clearly be seen in some objects when we use sand particles or strobe lights to reveal them. Shown in figure 3.11 are some modes of a drum skin (as it makes an interesting demonstration), technically a circular membrane clamped at the circumference. The primary, denoted 0:0, is called the "umbrella" mode where the middle moves up and down. It corresponds to a half wavelength trapped within the limits of the circle. Other modes are given numbers to distinguish them, such as 1:2, the first circular mode plus the second diameter mode. All vibrating objects like bells, strings, or aircraft wings can be analysed in terms of modes. Modes depend on the material and the speed of sound in it, and the object's shape.

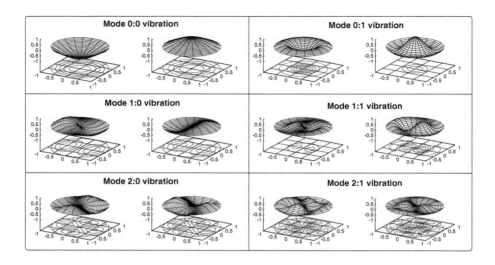

Figure 3.11
Some modes of a drum skin.

Visualising Sound Waves

If you hold a thin strip of paper or hair close to a loudspeaker vibrating at a low frequency it will show you the air molecules being displaced. Wheatstone devised a way to make sound waves visible in 1827 with his "kaleidophone," a metal rod with a small mirrored bead at the end. With this he could see sound waves as Lissajous patterns of light. He was following the work of Chladni who studied vibrations of plates by placing sand on them. One way of visualising longitudinal standing waves in a tube, an experiment performed by Kundt and often used in school physics lessons, is to put some fine sand in the tube so that it bunches up to reveal high and low pressure points. Buckminster Fuller and Hans Jenny found that wet dyes applied to surfaces could arrange themselves into patterns revealing the standing waves in solids like spheres and cubes. Using strobe lights we can take photographs or movies of vibrations as if they were in slow motion. Water droplets excited by a high-frequency sound field reveal their different spherical modes this way.

Shape

If we had a few drums or bells made from different materials and were able to listen to them all together we would quickly come to the conclusion that there is something about the sound, governed more by shape than material, that gives them all a similar character. Something that makes them drums and bells, and not, say, planks or bottles. In other words, we are able to hear shape, since it determines lengths, distances between boundaries, and modal paths inside and along the surface of a material. It affects the way frequencies build up and decay away, and which frequencies will be the strongest when the object vibrates.

Entropy and Heat

Sound can be seen as a stage in the life of energy as it does work and moves towards *entropy*. Entropy increases as energy spreads out and seeks more freedom. It hasn't been destroyed but it's been lost to us; it's become random or disordered and unable to do work. This is background heat. Heat can still do work if we have another body at a lower temperature, so hot objects may make sounds as they cool. Heat also flows like water or electricity from a high potential to lower one. In this great scheme the universe seems like a clock unwinding. When the universe reaches its maximum size all the energy that exists will be in this state of greatest entropy, at the lowest possible temperature, and everything will stop. Until then there is always something to be happy about, since there are plenty of pockets of energy at a high potential, and thus the possibility of energy flow, work, sound, and life.

Loss and Damping

So far we have thought about a perfect system where energy is always exchanged between kinetic and potential forms. In such a system an object set vibrating would continue to do so forever, and waves would propagate to eternity. The real universe is not like that, because of entropy. In figure 3.12 you see our familiar mass and spring pair representing a point of material and an elastic bond. But there is a new element attached to the mass. It represents a damper, or a mechanical resistance. The bar is supposed to be a piston that rubs against a rough material below so that friction occurs.

Both spring and damper connect the mass to a fixed reference point and the mass is set in motion with a brief force as before. Instead of oscillating back

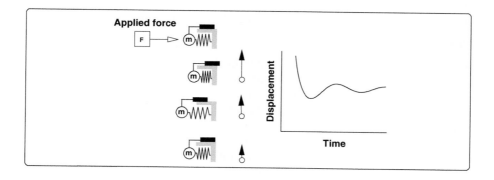

Figure 3.12
Loss in a mechanical system.

and forth forever the amplitude of each excursion decays away. The damper itself represents the lossy component of all real materials. As we have already examined, energy is never really lost; it becomes useless at doing work, and though we call it *loss* the sound energy actually becomes heat. If you play a musical instrument like trumpet or cello you probably already know that when any object makes a sound it gets a bit warmer. To quantify this we note that friction and loss are proportional to particle velocity: the faster the mass moves the more energy it loses.

SECTION 3.5

Analogues

You have heard of analog synthesisers and analog electronics, possibly even analog computers. But what does this word mean? From its Greek origins *ana-* meaning towards or upon, and *logos* meaning reasoning or logic, an *analogue* is a reasoned or systematic approach. In modern use it has come to mean a system of continuous measurement, but its important connotation is that of *analogy*, reasoning by appeal to some other similar system which shares features we want to describe. The roots of analog electronics come from the early days of cybernetics and computers between 1920 and 1950 when circuits were built as *analogies* of mechanical systems. It is possible to make electrical, mechanical, and acoustic analogs of vibrating systems. An analogous system will have equations of the same form but with different quantities. This is not limited to mechanics, acoustics, and electronics though, but applies also to chemical, electrostatic, social, and economic equations, which are of course not immediately relevant to the task at hand.

There are three physical systems we will consider now: mechanical, electrical, and acoustical. All are relevant to sound design, as you will see in later practical exercises, but the real reason for delving into these subjects in one swoop is to show the connection between all forces and behaviour. Beware that there are two versions of electro-acoustic-mechanical analogy in which the roles of variables exchange. The following system, called the *force-voltage* or *mobility* analog, is used in *network analysis* of which physical sound is one case.

Potential

All systems require potential for work to be done, energy in some state where it can flow. An example is water raised above sea level, used to generate electricity by damming a river. Gravitational potential energy (mgh) exists by dint of a mass m existing in a gravitational field (g) at some height (h) above the lowest potential. In fluid dynamics this is any state of pressure or elastic potential in a compressed gas. In electronics it's electrical potential held by a charge in a battery, a voltage measured as potential difference between two conductors in volts (V). In mechanics it is a stored force, such as a wound clock spring, or a source of power, such as a human working a machine.

Energy Inlet

Our network system should also include some kind of inlet through which potential flows. In a piano the string is excited by a hammer carrying kinetic energy. During impacts the energy inlet is briefly coupled to the rest of the system and then disconnects from it, while in frictional and turbulent excitations the inlet coupling is sustained.

Flow

Potential of water in a reservoir makes it move when released. Thus flow leads to a change in potential. Electrically this is current I, the flow of electrons through a wire. Mechanically it is velocity, and acoustically it is the volume current in cubic meters per second. When something is flowing it carries energy, which means it is reluctant to start or stop moving unless some energy is put into it or taken out. In mechanics mass is the quantity electrically analogous to inductance (L), and for sound we have a quantity (M) called the *inertance*. Inertance is the mass of moving medium divided by the cross-sectional area of the wavefront. Three network elements are shown in figure 3.13. The electrical component is a coil of wire which inducts current through it. The mechanical element is a mass which can carry energy by having a velocity, and the acoustic element is an open tube which carries a flow of acoustic energy when a wave moves within it.

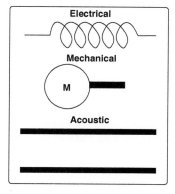

Figure 3.13
Inductance.

Resistance

Resisting flow turns some energy into heat and wastes it. An electrical resistance (R) measured in Ohms (Ω) gets hot when a current flows and reduces the current. Like the ticket barriers at the railway station during rush hour it simply wastes potential, gets everyone hot and angry, and causes a buildup of trapped potential behind it. In a mechanical system this is friction (B) given by a damper element. It produces a force against the movement proportional to the velocity it's trying to move at. In an acoustic system the resistance is due to viscosity; it is the dissipative property of the medium that turns flow into heat. Its measure is acoustic Ohms (R_a) and is the pressure of the sound wave at the wavefront divided by the volume velocity. The network element has a symbol which is a pipe containing some bars to represent a viscous or resistive obstacle.

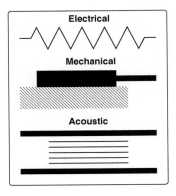

Figure 3.14
Resistance.

Tap or Outlet

The bridge of a guitar that couples the string to the sounding board, and the horn of a trumpet, are deliberate devices intended to take some of the vibrating energy away from the system and radiate it. These behave like resistances, because a loss occurs (energy is taken out of the system to somewhere else).

Capacitance

This is the propensity of an object to temporarily store some energy causing a localised potential. Unlike a battery or other potential source a capacitance is open, so it releases any accumulated energy as soon as it can. In electrical terms capacitance (C), measured in Farads (F), is the capacity to hold charge on two plates. The electrical network symbol reflects this. Mechanically, a capacitance is a spring, which we will examine shortly in some detail. It's an element that stores mechanical energy because of its elasticity. Mechanical capacitance is the inverse of the stiffness, $1/k$, and we call it the *compliance*, measured in meters per Newton. In acoustic terms a capacitance is a quality that opposes any change in the applied pressure. The larger the connected volume of a medium the greater its acoustical capacitance. The network symbol is drawn as a reservoir or container connected to the flow and is written C_a, also

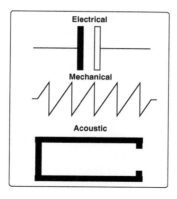

Figure 3.15
Capacitance.

in meters per Newton. It may be calculated from density ρ, propagation speed c, and volume V as $C_a = V/\rho c^2$.

Example Network Analogy

Bringing these elements together let's construct one example of an analog system. In figure 3.16 we see the electrical and mechanical elements of a hammered string. This can be thought of as a finite array of masses, springs, and dampers (or electrical capacitors, inductors, and resistors) excited by a burst of energy

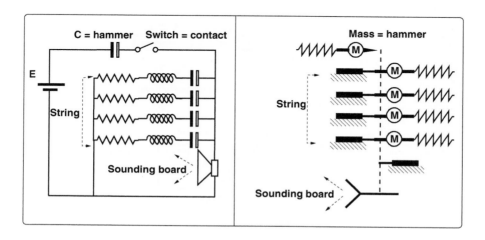

Figure 3.16
Analog systems (electrical, mechanical) of a hammered string.

carried by the hammer (either a mass or electrical capacitance) and radiated through an outlet which is the sounding board (shown as a mechanical surface or loudspeaker). What is interesting is that *any* sound-producing object, no matter how complex, can be reduced to a network system similar to this. A modern analysis is given by Jean-Marie Adrien in "Representations of Musical Signals" under the heading of "Modal Synthesis," and software systems to construct physical network models such as Cordis Anima and others have been developed where you can plug together masses, springs dampers, and energy sources. We will not be concerned with such a low-level "literal" approach so much as the general idea of interconnected systems which we can model in other ways, but it's worth keeping in mind that many systems can be modelled equivalently as an electrical circuit, a vibrating mechanical system, or an acoustic pressure system.

Example System Analysis

Most real objects are quite complex, having many subsystems that are connected together. We already mentioned the motor car as an example of something with many coupled subsystems. When considering *how* something makes a sound we often want to decompose it into parts and think about how each is coupled to the other. Flow of energy can be seen causally. An *entity-action* model like the ones shown in figure 3.17 can be a useful tool. Each part is connected by some kind of coupling that represents an energy transfer, shown as a diamond.

For each flow we can conduct a deeper physical analysis to explore the physics of the coupling, whether it's a continuous stick-slip friction, intermittent

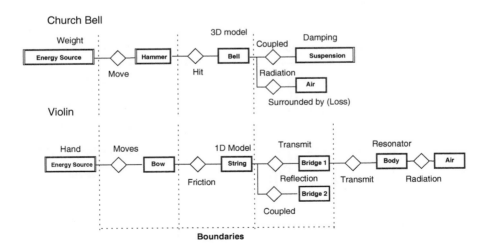

Figure 3.17
Entity-action deconstruction of a bell and violin.

contact, filter, capacitive reservoir, single impact, and so forth. Then we can split the design up into manageable parts, such as building the sounding board of a guitar separately from the strings. It also reveals input and output points which allow us to understand the control structure and any parameters that affect the behaviour.

Acknowledgements

Acknowledgement is given to Philippe-Aubert Gauthier, Charles Henry, and Cyrille Henry for suggestions and corrections.

References

Elmore, W. C., and Heald, M. A. (1969). *Physics of Waves.* Dover.
Graff, K. F. (1991). *Wave Motion in Elastic Solids.* Dover.
Morse, P. M. (1936, 1948). *Vibration and Sound.* McGraw-Hill.

4
Oscillations

SECTION 4.1

Oscillators

Having studied the energetic basis of sound it's time to see how these physical properties lead to systems that can oscillate and resonate. We should note that not all sounds are caused this way. Some short events like small electric sparks or a raindrop falling nearby may be seen as singular disturbances of the air, and the resulting sounds are determined more by acoustic propagations which we will study in the final part on physical sound. However, the vast majority of all sound makers, including all musical instruments, are oscillators, resonators, or a combination of both. In fact oscillators and resonators are very similar concepts, with the difference being where they appear in the chain of energy flow, either being primary sources of waves or systems driven (forced) by another source of wave vibrations.

Period and Frequency

Waves may be *periodic*, meaning they repeat in a pattern observed between two points in time or space, or *aperiodic*, meaning that their patterns are always changing. Periodic waves take a fixed amount of time to repeat each pattern, which we call the *period*, and they sound as though they have a definite pitch, whereas aperiodic waves usually sound complex or noisy as though they have no tone. The frequency of a periodic wave is the number of times it repeats a pattern every second. It is measured in Hertz (Hz) so that a 100Hz wave repeats 100 times a second. This is the reciprocal of its period. In other words the period is one divided by the frequency. So, the period of a 100Hz wave is 1/100th of a second, or 0.01 seconds.

Frequency of a Spinning Object

A perfectly smooth and perfectly circular spinning object is shown in figure 4.1. It makes no sound. If it is perfect, no matter how fast it spins it does not disturb the air. Of course no such objects exist in everyday life; most things have some eccentricity, like the egg shape next to it. When that spins it displaces some air and creates an area of high pressure one moment, followed by an area of low pressure in the same place. These disturbances propagate outwards as sound waves. The way the waves radiate is much simplified in the diagram. Perhaps you can visualise them spiralling out, much closer to how things happen in reality. Another simplification is that it's only spinning in one axis. Given two

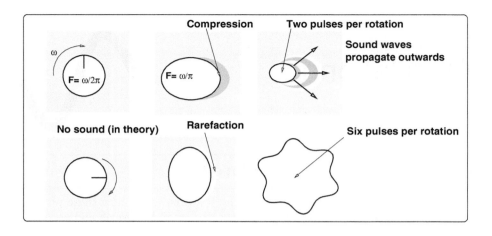

Figure 4.1
Frequency of a spinning object.

degrees of rotation you can probably see how this complicates things. Let's pre-
tend it's an egg, so it has symmetry in one axis but not the other. In this case
it doesn't matter that it spins round the symmetrical axis, because it displaces
no air by doing so. Next try to imagine it as a cube spinning in two axes so that
it moves corner over corner. We can split the motion into two frequencies, and
from some observation point the pattern of sound received will be the effect of
both rotations. This is where we should leave this subject until studying *modulation*, because what started out very simply, a perfect circle making no sound,
is about to become very complicated. Places where you'll find practical applications of this thinking are the sound of a fan or propeller, or bullet ricochets,
a sound determined by movement of an irregular object in three axes (called
spinning, *coning*, and *tumbling* motions). What we can say, as a general rule, is
the audible frequency of a spinning object is directly related to the frequency
it spins at. Notice the Greek "omega" symbol, ω, showing the spin rate. This
means *angular frequency*, the rate at which something spins round, measured
in radians. There are 2π radians (or 6.282) in one revolution. In other words,
using the terminology of degrees, we say $2\pi = 360°$. To convert from radians to
regular Hertz $f(\text{Hz}) = \omega/2 \times \pi$, or converting the other way round from Hertz
to radians, $\omega = 2\pi f$. Our egg-shaped object makes two compressions and rarefactions each time it rotates, so the sound we hear is at $f = 2\omega/2\pi = \omega/\pi$. The
regular object shown in the last frame has 6 raised points and produces a sound
at $6\omega/2\pi = 3\omega/\pi$ when spinning. Spinning discs with many teeth like this are
the basis of an old kind of predigital musical instrument called a tonewheel
organ. Another sound source that relies on this behaviour is the rotary siren.
This has a spinning disc with holes in it and a tube carrying air under pressure

that sits behind the disc. The sound is made by pulses of air escaping through
a hole as it passes over the tube; thus the frequency of a siren depends only on
the angular velocity of the disc and the number of holes. One interesting thing
about spinning objects is that they form a separate class from all other oscillators, since they are not resonators and don't depend on any other concepts
like force, capacitance, inertance, or resistance. These, as we shall see shortly,
are essential to all other types of oscillation, but spinning objects are *geometric
oscillators.*

Relaxation

If you ever had a bicycle that you wanted people to think was really a motorbike you probably had a "spokeydokey," a flexible card clipped to the bike
frame with a peg so that it pokes into the spokes of the wheel. The furthest
edge from the peg moves in the fashion shown at the bottom of figure 4.2,
a slowly rising and suddenly falling waveform sometimes called a *phasor.* As
a spoke pushes it sideways the card bends. The card edge moves linearly, at
the same constant speed of the spoke, until it is released. When this happens
it snaps back, because of the restoring force in the bendable card, and returns
to its original position. This cycle, where a force builds up and then releases,
is common in many natural things and their sounds; it is called a *relaxation
oscillator.* It is a periodic excitation of the medium, where energy builds up
and is then released.

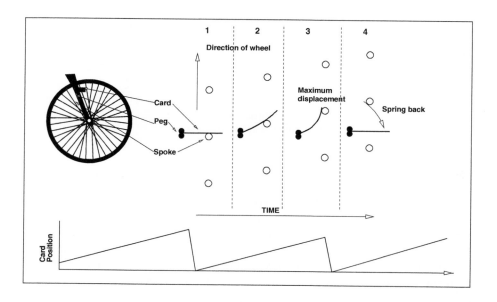

Figure 4.2
Spokeydokey.

Although a spokeydokey illustrates energy being stored and released it is not a real relaxation oscillator. It is another example of a spinning object, since the time at which the card returns is only determined by the angular velocity of the wheel. Some examples of proper relaxation oscillators are shown in figure 4.3: a balloon with its neck held under light constriction, and a flashing neon light. In both cases there is a source of energy. For the balloon, potential energy is stored as elasticity in rubber forcing the air towards an exit point. For the neon light, electrical energy is stored in a battery E, giving an electric potential. In each case there is a resistance constricting the flow of energy into a point that has capacitance C and a switch or release valve L that empties the capacitance when a threshold is reached. The width of the balloon neck is smaller than the area of air forced towards it, so it behaves as a resistance, and in the electrical circuit resistor R behaves in a similar fashion limiting current flow. The mouth of the balloon is held under tension so that enough force must accumulate to push the lips apart. When this happens a short burst of air is released which lowers the pressure in the neck temporarily. As air moves over the lips its velocity increases and so the pressure falls even more (Bernoulli principle), drawing the lips back together and sealing the balloon mouth. In

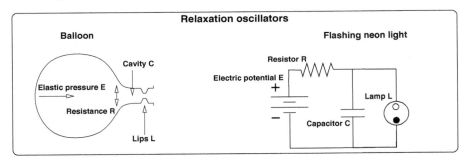

Figure 4.3
Example relaxation oscillators.

the case of the neon light electric charge flows through the resistor into the capacitor which fills up. As it does, the voltage (potential difference) across the neon tube increases. Once a certain potential is reached the gas becomes conductive (by ionisation) and a spark jumps across, releasing some energy as light. In both cases a momentary loss of energy changes the state of the system. The event that caused energy release ceases and a reservoir of potential begins to build up in the capacitance once again. This cycle of behaviour continues until the potential energy in the air or battery has all been used up.

Frequency of Relaxation Systems

The frequency of the balloon is rather too complex to explain here since it's an example of a relaxation oscillator *and* a Helmholtz resonator (which we will visit soon). The frequency of the electrical relaxation oscillator can be predicted quite easily, however. Neon gas becomes ionised and sparks at about 300V, and the voltage on the capacitor is determined by a well-known time constant. So long as the voltage available from the battery is greater than 300V the voltage across C will eventually reach the spark threshold. This is independent of the voltage and happens after T seconds where

$$T = \ln 2 RC \qquad (4.1)$$

Approximating the natural log of 2 and rewriting for frequency we get $F = 1/0.69RC$. Other examples of relaxation are found in the lips of a trumpet player and in our vocal cords when speaking or singing.

Quantisation

Closely related to simple relaxation is a situation where a relaxing system interfaces to a field or space in which an accelerating force acts (figure 4.4). A dripping tap, bubbles emerging from an underwater tube, and a ram jet engine are some examples. An equilibrium between opposing forces would normally keep the system stable, for example surface tension and weight, but a continuous flow of energy through some impedance causes the system to periodically release a packet of material or energy. Although it might not directly be the cause of sound waves, each of these packets can cause an excitement somewhere further along the system, like the splash-splash of a dripping tap.

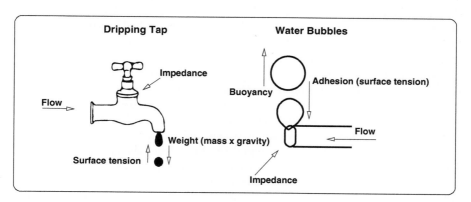

Figure 4.4
Quantisation of flow.

Simple Harmonic Oscillators

We have already mentioned simple harmonic motion while talking about how points of matter behave in a vibrating object, more properly described as the free vibrations of a lumped (discrete) system with a limited number of degrees of freedom and without exciting force. The main condition of simple harmonic motion occurs when the force acting on a body, and thus accelerating it, is proportional to and in the opposite direction from its displacement from the rest point. This is determined by a differential equation

$$A\frac{d^2x}{dt^2} = -Bx \tag{4.2}$$

where B is a constant of proportional restoration, x is the displacement, A is a variable that determines the period of movement (usually mass), and t is time. Solving the equation gives us a formula for the frequency of the system, and we shall briefly consider two common examples now, the undamped mass-spring and the pendulum.

Frequency of a Mass on Spring

A familiar school physics experiment is to calculate the frequency of a mass on a spring. In an idealised form it has only one degree of freedom: it can go up and down, but not side to side. Consider a spring and mass, here on Earth, at some time when it is just sitting there at rest. Gravity acts on the mass giving it weight, a force acting downwards. This force F is the mass m times the gravitational constant $g = 9.8$, so $F = m \times g$, and if the mass is 10kg then it creates a force (in Newtons N) of $10 \times 9.8 = 98$N. Another force is acting in the opposite direction, keeping the system in equilibrium. This is the support offered by the spring (and whatever the spring is attached to) in its rest position. Now, the spring has an elastic property, so if it is stretched or compressed some distance x by a force it will produce an opposing, restoring force proportional to that distance. The springiness is a constant k, measured in N/m. Hooke's law says that in a linear system, the restoring force is proportional to the displacement of the mass, and acts in a direction to restore equilibrium, so we write $F = -kx$. If the spring was initially unloaded and adding a mass m kg caused it to stretch by x m we know its springiness k to be $-mg/x$ since the force created by gravity mg must equal the force from the spring $-kx$ holding up the mass. Let's say our 10kg mass caused the spring to move 1cm, which makes $k = 98$N$/0.01$m$ = 9800$N/m. After working this out we can ignore gravity, because, maybe surprisingly, the frequency of a spring and mass doesn't depend on it. If you take the spring and mass out into space it will still oscillate at the same frequency. But what will that frequency be? Well, an oscillating mass must move, and a moving mass requires a force to either make it speed up or slow down. From Newton's second law, $F = m \times a$, where a is the acceleration in ms^{-2} and m is the mass. Assuming for a moment there are no losses, in keeping with conservation laws the forces must balance at all times. So at any time we have an equation $ma = -kx$. Remember that acceleration is the rate of change of velocity, and velocity is the rate of change of position. This leads us to a differential equation

$$m\frac{d^2x}{dt^2} = -kx \tag{4.3}$$

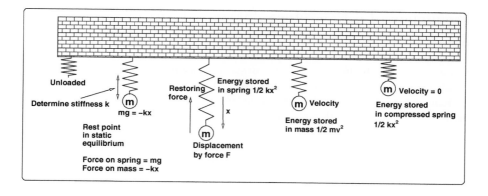

Figure 4.5
Spring-mass oscillation.

which is then written

$$\frac{d^2x}{dt^2} + \frac{kx}{m} = 0 \qquad (4.4)$$

There aren't many equations in this book—we try to avoid them and deal in "back of an envelope" engineering terms—but I have set this one clearly because it is possibly the most important and fundamental of them all. This describes the motion of a mass as a dynamic equilibrium of two forces. Energy is exchanged between two unstable states. When the mass passes through the equilibrium position no force will be acting on it, hence the stored, potential energy will also be zero. It will be at maximum velocity, so all the energy will be kinetic energy $E = mv^2/2$. At this same instant the acceleration will be momentarily zero since the mass is neither speeding up nor slowing down. At its maximum amplitude, at either extreme of movement, the velocity will be momentarily zero. At that time the acceleration, and the force of the spring, will be a maximum and so will the elastic potential energy $E = kx^2/2$. The simplified solution of this differential equation, which expresses x in terms of time t and maximum amplitude A, is

$$x = A\cos(\omega t) \qquad (4.5)$$

where

$$\omega = \sqrt{\frac{k}{m}} \qquad (4.6)$$

So the frequency of a mass on a spring depends only on mass and springiness (stiffness k). Let's plug the values for our 10kg mass and spring with $k = 9800$N/m into the equation to find its frequency.

$$\omega = \sqrt{\frac{9800}{10}} = 31.3\,\text{rad/s} \qquad (4.7)$$

And recalling that $\omega = 2\pi f$ we get $f = 31.3/6.282 = 4.72$ Hz.

Frequency of a Pendulum

A mass suspended from a string (having negligible mass itself) will swing at a constant rate depending only on the length of the string and gravity. The physics of pendula is one of the oldest understandings of oscillation, which Galileo used to explain harmonic ratios. The restoring force $mg\sin\theta$ is a component of the gravitational force mg acting in the direction of the equilibrium position. For small angles the assumption that this is proportional only to the angle (θ) works well enough. Because mass appears on both sides of the differential equation it is removed from the frequency calculation. So, assuming that $\sin\theta = \theta$ (small angle approximation), solving

$$\frac{d^2\theta}{dt^2} + \frac{g\theta}{l} = 0 \tag{4.8}$$

leads to

$$f = \frac{1}{2\pi\sqrt{\frac{l}{g}}} \tag{4.9}$$

Notice that the pendulum's frequency depends only on the length of the string and the strength of gravity. So two consequences are that its mass makes no difference, and a pendulum will not swing in space.

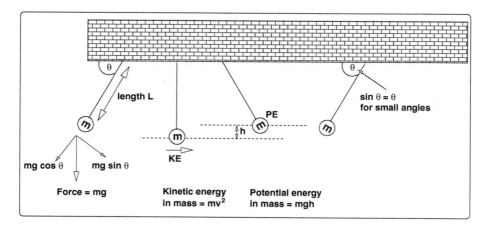

Figure 4.6
Pendulum oscillation.

Frequency of an LC Network

In a capacitor and a coil connected in parallel as shown in figure 4.7, electrical charge oscillates between them in a way analogous to the mass and spring. In

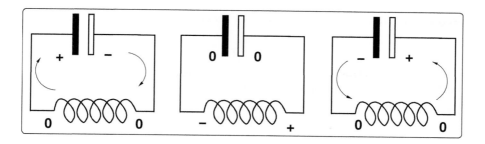

Figure 4.7
Electrical oscillator based on inductance and capacitance.

the circuit both elements are in parallel. In a closed network all voltages and currents must add up to zero (called Kirchhoff's law), so we get an unstable equilibrium just like with the force and kinetic energy in a mass and spring. Assume some potential is briefly applied to give a charge Q to the capacitor and then removed. In the initial condition the capacitor has a charge (+ and −), and the inductor has no current flowing through it. Electrons flow from the negative (−) side of the capacitor shown in the left part of figure 4.7 toward the positive plate until the capacitor's plates are discharged. When current I, which is the rate of change of charge dQ/dt, flows into or from a capacitor it changes the voltage on it (since $I = CdV/dt$), and when the current flowing through an inductor changes, dI/dt, the voltage across it changes, $V = LdI/dt$. In other words, the voltage across an inductor is proportional to the rate of change of current through it, and the current flowing onto a capacitor plates is proportional to the rate of change of voltage. Like the mass and spring, these act in *opposite directions*. A magnetic field builds up around the inductor generating a voltage equal and opposite to the electron flow from the capacitor. Once the capacitor is completely discharged through the inductor, no current flows and the magnetic field collapses. This change generates a new voltage (it gives back the energy it holds) to recharge the capacitor. This process repeats, causing an oscillation; the capacitor begins to discharge through the coil again, regenerating the magnetic field again, and so forth. The differential equation is

$$\frac{d^2 I(t)}{dt^2} = -\frac{1}{LC} I \qquad (4.10)$$

which can be solved to give current as a function of time $I = I_a \cos \omega t$ in which $\omega = 1/\sqrt{LC}$. Rewriting this for frequency gives us

$$f = \frac{1}{2\pi\sqrt{LC}} \qquad (4.11)$$

Interestingly the energy stored in an electrical capacitor is

$$E = \frac{1}{2}CV^2$$

and the energy stored in an electrical inductor is

$$E = \frac{1}{2}LI^2$$

so you can see how this analogy to a mechanical system ties up nicely.

SECTION 4.3

Complex Harmonic Oscillators

A single mass on a spring, a pendulum, and a simple electrical resonator all have a single frequency at which they will oscillate freely. These might be found as the primary source or *driving signal* in some situations, but much of the time we are concerned with more complex systems in real sound design. Strings, bars, plates, tubes, and membranes are all extents, in which there is a distribution of mass with more than one degree of freedom. When such systems oscillate they do so at many frequencies, depending on the modes we looked at in the last chapter. We don't have room to develop a mathematical analysis of each so I will just present the bare essentials, a formula for the fundamental frequency, a list of modes, and quick discussion of the spectrum.

Oscillation of a String

The natural frequency of a plucked string is

$$f = \frac{1}{2L}\sqrt{\frac{T}{m_u}} \tag{4.12}$$

where L is the length in meters, T is the tension in Newtons, and m_u is the mass per unit length in kilograms. A string can vibrate in all harmonic modes, that is to say we hear frequencies at f, $2f$, $3f$ ... In practice the strength of harmonics will depend on where the string is excited. If it is plucked or struck in the middle then only odd harmonics (1, 3, 5...) will be present, whereas exciting the string at 3/4 of its length brings out the even (2, 4, 6...) ones.

The question is often asked, how can a string simultaneously vibrate in more than one mode? Some modes of a vibrating string are shown in figure 4.8. These are the first four harmonics (fundamental plus three overtones). Each harmonic mode is a standing wave where the end points stay fixed, so with a node at each end they correspond to $\lambda/2$, λ, 2λ ... If some point on the string can only be in one place at once it seems impossible that all these modes can happen simultaneously. The principle of superposition makes sense of this. Of course the string remains as a single contour, but its shape is a complex mixture of all the harmonics added together.

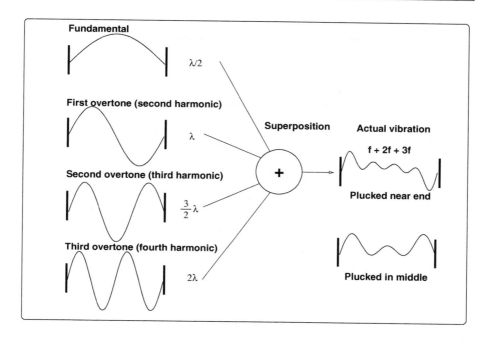

Figure 4.8
Vibrational modes of a string and a snapshot of the actual vibration pattern that results.

Oscillation of a Bar or Rod

Formulas for vibrating bars are given in Olson, Elmore and Heald (1969), and Benson (2006). For a deeper understanding you should refer to these textbooks. There are four cases to consider, a bar supported at one end, a bar supported at both ends, a bar resting on a central support, and a completely free bar. Let's deal with the more common ones, a free bar and a bar clamped at one end, as shown in figure 4.9. We assume the bar or rod is uniform in material and cross-sectional area. The first thing to calculate is an intermediate value called the *radius of gyration* (R). For a circular rod $R = a/2$ for a radius a. If the rod is hollow then

$$R = \frac{\sqrt{a^2 + b^2}}{2} \tag{4.13}$$

for an inner radius a and outer radius b. For a rectangular bar,

$$R = \frac{a}{\sqrt{12}} \tag{4.14}$$

With R we can easily get the fundamental as shown next. But to get the other harmonics is more difficult. They are not in a nice series like $f, 2f \ldots$ We need

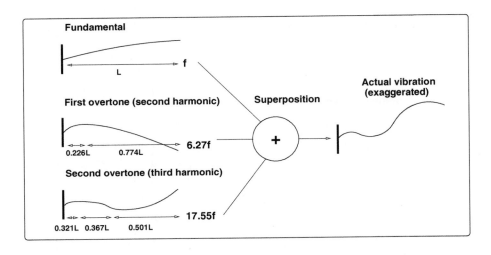

Figure 4.9
Vibrational modes of a bar clamped at one end.

to use a formula called the Euler–Bernoulli beam equation for a zero boundary condition. It's too complex to derive here, but it shows where the nodes appear (as shown in figure 4.9). Notice they bunch up towards the supported end causing a distortion that effectively warps the frequency spacing. For the fundamental, using Young's modulus E, the bar length l, and the material density ρ, for a bar supported at one end we get;

$$f = \frac{0.5596}{l^2}\sqrt{\frac{ER^2}{\rho}} \tag{4.15}$$

with harmonics in the series f, $6.267f$, $17.55f$, and $34.39f$. For a free bar we get a fundamental frequency

$$f = \frac{3.5594}{l^2}\sqrt{\frac{ER^2}{\rho}} \tag{4.16}$$

with a harmonic series f, $2.756f$, $5.404f$, and $8.933f$.

Oscillation of Cones, Membranes, Laminas

Many simple geometric objects have standard formulas for calculating their fundamental frequency and harmonic modes. Rather than give the all formulas here let's just touch on the general principles. You can find appropriate formulas in the textbooks listed in the reference section and from many other books on mechanical engineering. I will give formulas for other objects as we encounter them in the practical section. As a quick summary they fall into two classes, free vibrating objects and objects under tension. Objects such as strings or drum skins vibrate at a frequency related to their tension. This is intuitive from knowing that a drum skin can be tightened to give it a higher pitch. Free vibrating objects depend upon Young's modulus, the mass per area (or volume—given as density) and their dimensions (thickness, length, etc). Objects supported in one or more places tend to vibrate in fewer modes than their free equivalent, since the support points must be nodes (stationary points). Classes of objects commonly needed in sound design (and all known in engineering literature) are square and circular membranes under tension, free square and circular plates, equilateral triangular plates, and membranes, rods, bars and strings.

┌─ SECTION 4.4 ──
Driven Oscillations and Resonance
└──

We have used the term "natural frequency" in the preceding examples. And we have seen that a system made of many distributed masses, or one with several degrees of freedom, can vibrate at more than one frequency. In effect we have taken for granted that because the system is uniform each point will have the same natural frequency and all will move in sympathy. In reality most objects are *heterogeneous*, made up of many parts with different natural frequencies. So far we have considered what happens when a simple force is applied and then removed from a system. The point at which the force is removed is sometimes called the *initial condition*, and after that the system exhibits free vibration at its natural simple harmonic frequency until the energy is lost through damping and radiation.

Consider a different situation, which you can imagine as a complex system broken apart into a connected set of simpler points. None is really free, because it is coupled to the next point, and in this case we assume each point has a different natural frequency. Let's assume that one point (A) is vibrating strongly at its natural frequency. The adjacent point (B) undergoes *forced vibration*. Point A is the driving oscillator and B vibrates as a driven oscillator. It is a vibrating system under constant external excitation. Because the points are coupled, from Newton's laws we know that they can exchange forces. If we could momentarily separate them, then the position of point B, which it has been driven to by A, becomes its initial condition. Now, B can vibrate freely, but at a different frequency from A, so eventually they would be out of phase. Connecting them back together at this time would cause the forces to cancel and vibration would stop. Now, this is just a thought exercise to see how mutually coupled points behave. If the two points have different natural frequencies then the kinetic and potential energy changes will not be in phase, and we say that the second point offers an impedance to the first. Of course the relationship between A and B is mutual. The combined amplitude of A and B depends upon each other's natural frequencies. If both points have the *same* natural frequency the conflicting forces become zero. In other words the impedance offered by one point to the other becomes zero. This condition is called *resonance*.

In figure 4.10 you can see the *response* of two resonant systems. The x-axis in each graph is the frequency of the driving oscillator (in Hz) and the y-axis shows the amplitude of oscillation. The natural frequency (Ω) is the vertical middle line of the graph so the response is symmetrical for frequencies above and below it. Bandwidth is generally defined as the distance between two points -3dB down from (half of) the full scale amplitude.

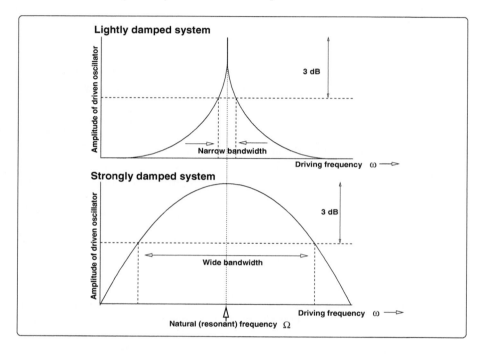

Figure 4.10
Resonance of a system with different damping.

So, we have changed the way we can look at an oscillator. Instead of a discrete point with a single frequency we can view it as an impedance to energy flow which depends on frequency. When the energy from the driving system (ω) exactly matches the natural frequency (Ω) then maximum flow occurs, and the amplitude of the driven system is also a maximum. For other frequencies the energy transfer doesn't just become zero, it diminishes as the difference between the driving frequency and the natural frequency becomes larger. We say the driven system behaves as a *filter*. If the driven system has very little damping (δ) then the impedance will be greater for a certain difference between the driving frequency and natural frequency, which we can write as $\omega - \Omega$. We say such a system has a *high resonance* and a *narrow bandwidth*. If the driven system is strongly damped then the amplitude will continue to be large even when the difference $\omega - \Omega$ is big. We say it has a *low resonance* and *wide bandwidth*. The general form of the equation for amplitude in terms of damping, natural, and driving frequency is

$$A(\omega) \propto \frac{\delta}{(\omega - \Omega)^2 + (\delta)^2}. \tag{4.17}$$

Because real objects have several degrees of freedom and are composed of heterogeneous points most vibrating objects have multiple resonant frequencies. A piece of wood will exhibit a whole range of resonances. We can treat a violin as a wooden resonator driven by another oscillator (a string). Recall the idea of *modes* and remember that the major spacing of these resonances will depend on the standing wave patterns due to the geometry of the object and the speed of sound in that material. However, the effects of material differences will mean that these are not neat, pure frequencies. The resonances will be bunched together in groups around the major modes, but there will be many of them accounting for slight variations of material properties. The precise sound of a violin depends on how the grain lies, the glue used, and what material is used for the bridge. To plot this *frequency response* we could measure the amplitude from the violin body while sweeping a pure sine frequency through a transducer coupled to the bridge. This fixed pattern of resonant high and low points can be modelled with a complex filter, called a *formant filter*, which we will meet later.

References

Benson, D. (2006). *Music: A Mathematical Offering*. Cambridge University Press.
Elmore, W. and Heald, M. (1969). *The Physics of Waves*. Dover.
Olson, Harry F. (1967). *Music, Physics, and Engineering*. Dover.

5
Acoustics

Acoustic Systems

Thus far we have considered the mechanical vibration of objects as sound waves move through them. Now we will progress to think about how sound radiated from objects behaves in the air up to the point it reaches our ears or a microphone, before we move to the study of psychoacoustics. Between the vibrations of solids and the movement of a microphone diaphragm or eardrum there is always an intervening medium. Almost exclusively this is air, a mixture of about 80 percent nitrogen and 20 percent oxygen, plus a collection of trace gases like argon and carbon dioxide.

Vibrations in Air

Unlike a vibrating solid, where we noted the existence of transverse and torsional waves, in acoustics we only consider longitudinal waves, and we are mainly concerned with the behaviour of a bulk volume. You may recall that the equations for a gas or liquid were complicated by the influence of the gas laws relating pressure, volume, and temperature. Because compressing a gas heats it, and air is a good thermal insulator so there's no time for the heat to flow away within the lifetime of a single wave cycle, the force (pressure) term of our differential equation is skewed. To correct for this we need to add a new factor called the *adiabatic index*, written γ. We won't look at the full wave equation for sound in air here, but there are some things we should remember that lead to a useful equation for the speed of sound in terms of pressure p and density ρ.

$$c = \sqrt{\gamma \frac{p}{\rho}} \tag{5.1}$$

The γ value doesn't change, but recalling that density is mass divided by volume and the initial (ambient) value of this is affected by temperature, we can get a new form of the equation

$$c = \sqrt{\frac{\gamma R T}{M}} \tag{5.2}$$

where R is the molar gas constant in joules per kilogram per mole, which is about 8.314J/kg/mol, T is the absolute temperature in Kelvin (K), and M is the molar mass (in kilograms per mole, which for dry air is 0.0289645kg/mol). This means the speed of sound in air is proportional to the square root of the air temperature. Variations in air temperature are common to many situations and we will see later how they cause sound to change direction through refraction.

Radiation

Radiation is the transfer of energy from a vibrating source to the surrounding medium. In order for us to hear a sound some energy must be lost from the source, so this continues our model of an energetic journey, flowing from the excitor to the observer. We assume that after radiating from a body the sound is effectively separated from the vibrating source. We sometimes take the direction of radiation to be an ideal line from a point, or the surface of a sphere. When the body is small compared to a large surrounding volume the waves are taken to emit in a straight line normal to the surface. This gives us the concept of sound "rays" and hence *ra(y)diation*.

Radiation Patterns

A point source or *monopole* can be imagined to throw out waves in a sphere. The best way to visualise this is to imagine a solid vibrating sphere moving in its 0 : 0 mode, called the *breathing* mode, where it expands and contracts. All points on the surface move outwards and inwards at the same time, so all sounds radiated normal to the sphere surface are in phase. No matter where an observer stands the sound intensity is uniform in all directions. See the left side of figure 5.1. Point sources vibrating in this way are a rare exception in reality,

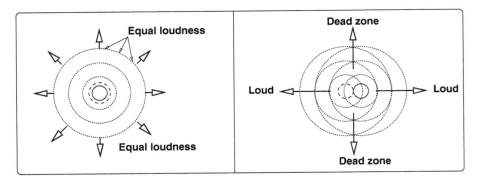

Figure 5.1
Left: A monopole in "breathing mode." Right: A dipole in "bending mode."

though a useful ideal model for digital representations. Real sources will have some length or thickness and, as we have seen earlier with vibrational modes, bits that are vibrating in different phases. The *dipole* effect is observed when recording a drum. When vibrating in its 0 : 0 or *umbrella mode*, a skin clearly has two phases, one on each side, that are opposite. A trick of "double miking" drums[1] is used by recording engineers so that they can be balanced in a mix much more effectively later by playing with the phases. Objects that vibrate this way, moving backwards and forwards, are generally said to be moving in *bending* modes, as shown on the right side of figure 5.1 where a circular cross section is moving between two positions. Perpendicular to the direction of movement is a line where no sound radiates, a *dead zone*. This can be seen in terms of interference, as we can approximate a dipole movement to two monopoles in opposite phases separated by a small distance. We have only thought about two modes, but we can extend this reasoning to imagine the complex radiation patterns observed by different shapes vibrating in *quadrupole*, *octupole*, and higher modes, and how the net effect at any observation point is the superposition of all these patterns.

Spherical, Cylindrical, and Planar Waves

Very close to the source we have the *near field* which, as a simplification, is smaller than the wavelength of a sound. Radiation here can be seen in a different way than for distances much greater than several wavelengths in the *far field*. Consider the round bar in figure 5.2. Each point along its length might be taken as a point source radiating in a sphere, but as we add more points so that the distance between them decreases, the superposition of all these sources becomes less lumpy, tending towards an expanding cylinder if we imagine looking along the axis of the bar. At still greater distances (shown on the right of figure 5.2 with an exaggerated distance) the curvature of the wave front gets less and less, and eventually the far field pattern tends towards a *plane wave*, meaning all parts of the wavefront move in parallel.

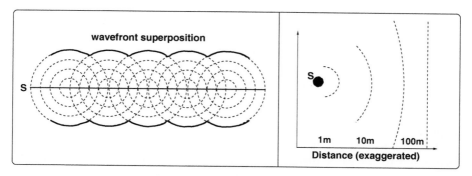

Figure 5.2
Left: Cylindrical radiation from a rod as the limit of separate point sources. Right: Change to planar waves as distance (exaggerated) becomes large.

---

1. Two identical microphones are used, one above the drum and one below, to catch both phases of the skin.

Intensity and Attenuation

Sound Pressure Level

Sound pressure p is a force per unit area, in N/m^2. The peak sound pressure of a wave is inversely proportional to the distance, so decreases as $1/r$ for a distance r from the source. Sound pressure is an absolute measurement and applies to a point in space where the measurement is made without taking the direction of the wave into account. Sound pressure level (SPL) is a ratio given in decibels. Since a decibel is a ratio we need a reference point to compare the absolute pressure per unit area to. We use $20\mu N/m^2$ as the smallest acoustically measurable value. To calculate SPL use

$$SPL = 20log_{10}\frac{p(N/m^2)}{2 \times 10^{-5}(N/m^2)} \tag{5.3}$$

There can be no acoustic waves with sound pressure levels greater than 194dB SPL because it would mean having rarefactions with less pressure than a complete vacuum, which is impossible. However, unipolar pulses of compression do exist with pressures greater than 194dB SPL, in explosions and lightning strikes.

Position and Correlation

As a practical approximation several sound sources may all emit the same waveform at exactly the same time. Either because they belong to the same object and are coupled by a material in which the speed of sound is extremely fast relative to the speed of sound in air, or perhaps because they are loudspeakers connected to the same circuit, we say each point emits in the same phase. Of course this is never strictly true as even electricity moves at a finite speed, but we will ignore this internal propagation for a moment. An observer at some distance comparable with the distances between the sources will hear a *coherent* sound. We say that the sources are *correlated*. The amplitude of any particular frequency will depend on the distance between two or more sources and thus on whether the superposition causes a reinforcement or cancellation of that frequency at that point.

A reinforcement will occur when the paths from the listener to each source correspond to the same distance modulo one wavelength. Conversely, a minimum amplitude will occur for a frequency or pair of distances that differ by some multiple of a half wavelength. In figure 5.3 (inset diagram) a particular frequency is in phase at point O but out of phase at point P. So long as the observer and sources remain fixed the spectrum stays fixed. If the listener or one of the sources moves then a sweeping notch filter effect may be heard as the change in distance causes different frequencies to reinforce or cancel at that position. The effect, shown in figure 5.3, is heard strongly when a source such as an aircraft moves across the sky and the sound arrives via two paths, one direct and another reflected from the ground.

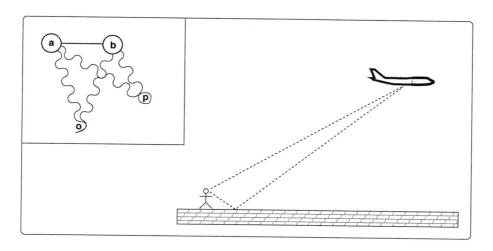

Figure 5.3
Left inset: Constructive and destructive superposition at two points relative to correlated sources. Right: Reflected waves are correlated (copies) and cause interference effects.

If the sounds are similar but each is produced by a separate mechanism, such as for a choir of singers or a swarm of bees, then there is no correlation between the sources. Waveforms from all the sources will already be constantly moving in and out of phase, or have slightly different frequencies, thus creating a thick swirling effect. Movement of either the listener or any of the sources will not produce a noticeable change in spectrum. We call such collections of sources *uncorrelated*. For large collections of sources this leads to significant differences in the observed *average* amplitude of complex spectra. Let's assume that the sources emit white noise so all frequencies are equally represented. For correlated sources the average received amplitude will be the sum of all individual amplitudes.

$$A_{cor} = A_a + A_b + A_c \ldots \tag{5.4}$$

But for uncorrelated sources like the choir or bee swarm the observed amplitude is the square root of the sum of the squares of individual amplitudes.

$$A_{uncor} = \sqrt{A_a^2 + A_b^2 + A_c^2 \ldots} \tag{5.5}$$

Acoustic Sound Intensity

Sound intensity I is the power per unit area. It takes into account the air velocity as well as pressure (by integrating their product in time), so is a vector that also accounts for the direction of energy flow. We measure this intensity in Watts per meter squared, written W/m^2, and it's proportional to the square of the sound pressure level, $I \propto p^2$. For harmonic plane waves a more useful formula in terms of density and phase velocity is

$$I = \pm \frac{p^2}{(2\rho c)} \tag{5.6}$$

Sound intensity level (SIL) is given in decibels rather than in absolute units of W/m^2. Since a decibel is a ratio we need a reference point to compare the absolute power per unit area to. We use 10^{-12}W/m^2 as a reference since it's about the quietest sound a human can hear. Sound intensity level is therefore given as

$$SIL = 10 log_{10} \frac{I(\mathrm{W/m^2})}{10^{-12}(\mathrm{W/m^2})} \tag{5.7}$$

Geometric Attenuation

For most applications we can be satisfied knowing the simplified models of radiation to work out formulas for geometric attenuation. In spherical and cylindrical models, as the sound propagates outwards the energy is spread thinner. The intensity of the sound, the ability of the energy to do work, decreases. As time and space grow, the energy is still passing through, but in ever more dilute form. Spherical and cylindrical radiation are shown in figure 5.4 where you can see how the area through which the wavefront moves varies with distance. For cylindrical propagation the height h of the slice remains constant so the area changes as $A = 2\pi r h$, or as the arc which is part of the circumference of a sector. Cylindrical radiation from a line source like a string or busy road loses power in proportion to the distance. This is sometimes stated as a 3dB (SIL) loss per doubling of distance. This comes from the formula for SIL and the fact that adding or subtracting the logarithms of numbers is the same as taking the logarithm of the same numbers multiplied or divided; thus if the intensity starts at $10 \log_{10}(2I)$ and ends up as $10 \log_{10}(I)$

$$10 \log_{10}(I) - 10 \log_{10}(2I) = 10 \log_{10}(1/2) = 3 \mathrm{dB}(loss) \tag{5.8}$$

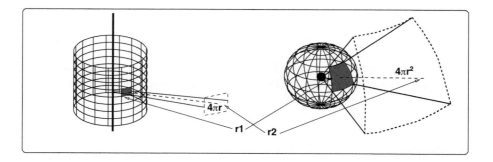

Figure 5.4
Geometry of the inverse square law.

For the spherical case the area increases as the surface of a sphere, ($A = 4\pi r^2$), so the power loss is proportional to the square of distance. At twice a given distance, the intensity (SIL) of a sound is one-quarter its original value, and at ten times the distance it is one-hundredth as much. This is sometimes stated as a 6dB loss per doubling of distance. At very large distances we can take the waves to be planar. They are no longer spreading, so they carry a constant energy per area regardless of distance. This is analogous to the assumption that sunlight is parallel: having travelled such a large distance its divergence is negligible. These losses are called *geometrical* because they have nothing to do with damping and friction; they depend only on distance.

Transmission and Absorption

Geometric loss of power/pressure and loss of energy by absorption are different things, and both must be considered when calculating the total attenuation of a sound at some distance. Attenuation occurring by absorption happens because of imperfect propagation that turns the sound energy to heat. Because of damping, as sound moves through a medium some is lost for every unit of distance travelled. In air or water *thermoviscous attenuation* happens because of the *viscosity* of the medium. Since the energy loss by a particle in a viscous fluid is proportional to its velocity, and the instantaneous velocity of particles is proportional to the sound frequency, then greater absorption losses occur for higher sound frequencies. This is known as Stokes law, which states that attenuation α is given by

$$\alpha = \frac{2\eta 2\pi f^2}{3\rho c^3} \qquad (5.9)$$

so it's proportional to the viscosity η and the square of the frequency f, and inversely proportional to the density of the medium ρ and the cube of the speed of sound in the medium c. Its units are Nepers per meter, but we can convert to decibels per meter by multiplying by 8.685889. Although the effect is small, it's significant over large distances where more high frequencies will be lost this way. It takes more than 12km for a 3dB loss to occur at 1kHz. Details may be found in ISO 9613-1/2, often used for environmental calculations.

In solids, absorption can also happen because of the *plasticity* of the medium and limitations on the *mean free path*. Wax, plastics, and the human body which contains fat all absorb sound by this method. Densely packed wool or sand absorbs energy since each part of it can move and dissipate energy without producing an elastic restoring force. Another factor contributing to loss is *molecular relaxation*. No materials are purely elastic or viscous; real mediums combine both properties leading to a *viscoelastic* model. Explanations of the real behaviour of materials, such as those by Maxwell, show that molecules experiencing a force (strain) give up a small amount of energy in a process of relaxation. Both kinds of loss depend on temperature, pressure (and hence amplitude of sound), the material properties of the medium, and the particle velocity (hence frequency of the sound). When air contains water vapour it introduces a greater loss than dry air. A typical loss is 0.02dB/m, which is very small and only heard over quite large distances outdoors. The frequency response shown by this type of loss is a band pass, attenuating low and high frequencies below 1kHz and above 5kHz depending on conditions.

Seen in a different way, absorption may be desirable. Sound insulating materials used to provide isolation between rooms require a high absorption. Given that the total energy output of something is equal to the input energy minus the absorption loss to heat, the remainder must be re-radiated from an absorbing object. This sound is *transmitted*. Because absorption is likely to be frequency selective an *occluding* object such as a wall will transmit a filtered version of the sound, usually with less high frequencies.

┌ SECTION 5.3 ───
| # Other Propagation Effects
└──

Reflection

Unlike the reflection of transverse waves in a solid, longitudinal acoustic waves, for which we are concerned with pressure, keep the same (pressure) phase on reflection. Their directional change is as for other waves, with the reflection angle being equal but opposite to the incidence angle with respect to the boundary normal. Like the modes of a vibrating solid we will hear similar effects caused by superposition of direct and reflected waves as shown in figure 5.5, and similar standing wave patterns will occur within a room or other acoustic space.

Scattering

If a plane wave, travelling in a single direction, hits a fairly small obstacle, then we may get *scattering*. This is slightly different from regular reflection when hitting a large solid wall. The object behaves as if it absorbs and re-radiates the sound; thus it changes the plane wave into a new spherical or cylindrical wave locally. The result is that more energy gets directed to the sides than in a normal reflection. There are two phenomena: *forwards scattering*, where new sound rays are spread into a cone ahead of the object; and *back scattering*, where the cone expands backwards towards the source. Scattering is a function of the object size and the frequency of the sound. The frequency of scattered sound is inversely proportional to the object size, and the intensity is proportional to the fourth power of the frequency. In a relatively sparse, free space, small objects like poles or trees tend to scatter high frequencies more; so if you fire a gunshot (which contains many frequencies) near the woods the reflected sound will seem higher in tone than a straight echo, while if you are inside the woods you will hear a lower tone as those frequencies are transmitted better through the trees.

Acoustic back scattering can occur in the air, such as when sound encounters turbulence like small vortices in the boundary between clouds and the atmosphere, or between different layers of the Earth's atmosphere; thus "sodar"[2] has

──────────────────────────────

2. Sound detection and ranging of clouds can show their external shape and internal composition rather like ultrasound scans of the body can, so it is a powerful weather-forecasting tool.

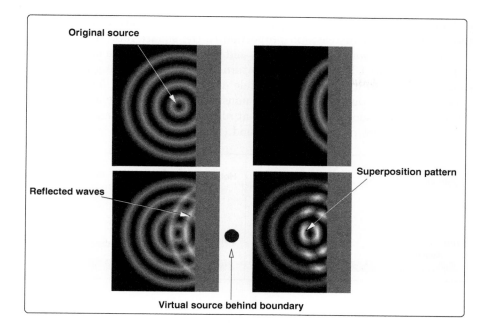

Figure 5.5
Acoustic wave behaviour at a solid boundary. Top left: Incident waves from source. Top right: Reflected waves only. Bottom: Loud spots caused by superposition (highlighted on right to emphasise pattern).

been used for weather forecasting. Because scattering would be hard to model as the result of many small objects it is best understood and modelled as the bulk property of some volume, based on the size and distribution of objects within.

Dispersion

Phase velocity is independent of frequency in pure, dry air which is a nondispersive medium. A dispersive medium deviates from the rules: it propagates waves at different speeds depending on their frequency. Carbon dioxide and water vapour both do this, and of course they are also found in air, but in most cases the effects are negligible. Over very large distances and with high frequencies (above 15kHz), the effects may be heard, as with thunder travelling over many kilometers. A strongly dispersed sound is like the effect known sometimes as a "spectral delay." It acts as a prism separating frequencies in time, producing an ill-defined "watery" effect.

Refraction

We have already seen that sound waves crossing a boundary between two mediums with different propagation properties may change speed. If a wave meets a change of medium obliquely then a change of direction may also occur. Since the speed of sound increases in proportion to the square root of temperature (moving faster in warm air than cold) and the air temperature decreases with altitude at about 6°C/km, a temperature gradient above the ground curves sound upwards so it is rapidly inaudible at ground level (fig. 5.6, left). Conversely, sound is sometimes heard at unusual distances where a temperature inversion occurs, such as above a lake at night, since sound carried upwards is then bent back down towards the ground (fig. 5.6, right).

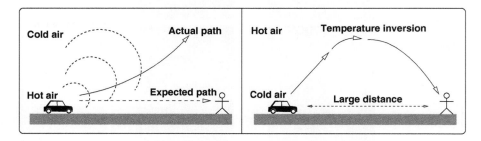

Figure 5.6
Sound refraction outdoors.

Diffraction

We have seen how many point sources approximate to a plane wave as we increase their number to the limit. Huygens' principle states the opposite, that we can continually re-appraise the propagation of a planar wave as if it were a collection of many point sources over the wavefront. If we sum the contributions of spherical waves from each point, then in the limit we return once again to a plane wave. Where a plane wave meets a partial occlusion like a high wall, or an exclusion such as a doorway, Huygens' principle states that the edge or hole can be approximated by a collection of point sources whose contribution forms a new wavefront (fig. 5.7, top left). This means that sound effectively bends around obstacles. In figure 5.7, top right, the listener receives two signals from the car, one transmitted through the wall by path C, and one refracted around the top of the wall via paths A and B. Without refraction the sound travelling path A would continue in a straight line and be inaudible.

Another effect of diffraction is to produce a position-dependent perception of frequency. We see in figure 5.7, bottom left, that different frequencies are refracted more or less. Low frequencies will bend around the wall more than high ones. If the wavefront of a harmonically complex sound is replaced by a number of point sources (figure 5.7, bottom right), for example because the sound hits a long line of fence posts, then an effect similar to the rainbow patterns observed when looking at an optical computer disk occurs. Distances between each new point source and an observer will vary. Where it matches

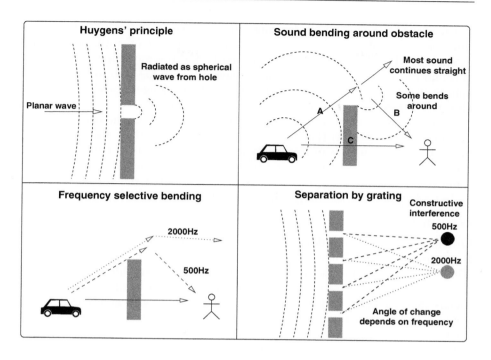

Figure 5.7
Sound diffraction effects.

some multiple of a particular wavelength, that frequency will interfere constructively (be in phase) with the sound of the same wavelength arriving from another point. We get a "hot spot" or loud area for that frequency. Different frequencies, and hence different wavelengths, will produce constructive interference at different listening points. This Fraunhofer diffraction causes sharp filtering of sound where the wavelength is comparable to the dimensions of a regular structure. It is noticeable with high frequencies reflected from corrugated walls, or with low frequencies, such as those from thunder, against a long row of houses.

Diffusion

Initially this concept may seem a lot like scattering, but it applies only to ordinary reflection from large, solid boundaries. A perfectly flat and reflective surface would obey the ideal reflection rules, with equal incidence and reflection angles for all frequencies. The opposite would be a perfectly *diffuse* surface which reflects incident sound of all frequencies in all directions. It is analogous to light in respect to a glossy (mirror-like) or matte (dull) finish. As you can picture, an irregular surface would have this property. However, the range of wavelengths for sounds in our hearing range is large, spanning from a few centimeters to several meters, so the tendency for a surface to offer diffuse reflection depends on the relative scale of its irregularity and the wavelength (frequency) of sound hitting it. A stone wall may behave diffusely for high frequencies but appear like a flat surface to low frequencies (with longer wavelengths). The ideal diffuser is somewhat like a coastline or rocky cliff face, having a random relief over a wide range of scales but also self-similarity in the distribution of its randomness. We call this a *Perlin noise surface*. In the presence of a diffuse reflector, a sound from any location will seem to emit from everywhere on the diffuse surface. In acoustic engineering, diffusion can be desirable to reduce room resonance and reduce discrete echo effects, but if the surface is diffuse and also highly reflective we get an unwelcome "woolly" or "muddy" effect.

Ground Effects

Ground effects occur by destructive or constructive interference of reflections from uneven ground. They happen most when the source is close to the ground. There is a correspondence between the attenuation or amplification, the relief of the terrain, and the wavelength of the sound. In other words, the mechanism means that the effect is dependent on the source frequency and height, and it appears to be strongest below 4m for most of the audio spectrum. The more uneven the terrain the stronger the frequency-dependent attenuation effects, with grass or rocky ground producing a greater effect than smooth hard ground. This suggests that the effect is increased by multiple reflections. Undulating ground with dips in the 10m to 100m range significantly attenuate low frequencies below 100Hz, small rocks and grassland produce a dip in the 200Hz to 1kHz range, while frequencies above 5kHz behave more like light rays and travel in a straight line unimpeded by ground effects (see Angelo Farina's models). Solid, even ground tends to produce a single reflection that adds to the direct wave, giving a 3dB amplification for most frequencies. We will see later that when the source is moving this can lead to a sweeping filter effect. As with diffraction, a surface with regular relief, such as a ploughed field, a line of houses, or a corrugated steel panel can produce a sharp notch or band filter effect, blocking or enhancing one small window of frequencies depending on the listener's location.

Oblique Boundary Loss

Oblique boundary loss is an effect that seems similar to ground attenuation but actually involves a different mechanism. High frequency sound travelling parallel to, or at a very sharp angle to, a surface can experience a loss due to a boundary layer. As explained in connection with turbulence there is a thin layer of any fluid close to a surface that is effectively stationary and resists sideways movement. This is stronger where the interface is to another fluid, so it affects sounds heard reflected from the surface of a still lake, the wet mossy walls of a cave, and to some extent vocal sounds produced in the trachea of a living creature.

Wind Shear

We often hear the expression "carried on the wind" to explain why sounds seem louder downwind than against it. Considering the relative velocities of a typical wind and that of sound, it should be obvious that the actual movement of the air has rather little effect on sound. The explanation is that because the wind blows faster above the ground than close to it (because of the boundary layer) the sound is curved downwards towards the listener by a velocity gradient, in an opposite fashion to the refraction effect described earlier. When combined with ground attenuation this can have the unexpected effect of making downwind sounds suddenly quieter as they are "blown into the ground" by refraction, or suddenly louder as sound that would be radiated upwards is curved down towards the listener.

Aberration

If a sound source is moving along a straight line at a tangent to a listener which passes through a point some distance d away, then sound waves will take some time to travel and be heard. If the source moves with velocity v and the sound waves with velocity c then the apparent sound source will be some distance behind the object D equal to the distance it has travelled during the time it took the sound to reach the listener.

$$D = \frac{vd}{c} \tag{5.10}$$

The Doppler Effect

A moving object causes the apparent frequencies of any sound it emits to be shifted up or down according to the component of its velocity relative to a stationary listener. The speed of sound c remains constant but movement towards the listener squashes the wavelength of the sound by $(1 - v/c)\lambda$, and for a source moving away the wave is stretched by $(1 + v/c)\lambda$. In terms of observed frequency change and source velocity this gives

$$f_{observed} = \frac{c}{c \pm V_{source}} \times f_{source} \tag{5.11}$$

where a plus indicates the source is moving toward the observer (higher observed frequency) and a minus means the source is moving away (lower observed frequency). In figure 5.8 you can see the speed of sound (c) remains the same, but the wavelength (λ) is squashed in the direction of travel when the source velocity (v) is non-zero.

Room Acoustics

Room acoustic theory combines an understanding of reflection, absorption, diffusion, scattering, boundary behaviour, and refraction and applies it to interior spaces. The task of the aesthetic acoustic engineer is close to that of an architect, to balance the desirable acoustic features of a space for its use. A concert hall should have a certain "liveness," but obviously not too much. A recording studio should have a flat and uncoloured response with very little natural

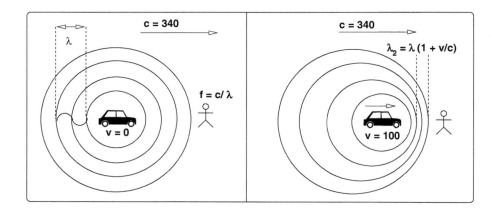

Figure 5.8
Doppler shift.

reverb. The engineer may need to take into account changes such as when an empty concert hall fills with people whose bodies absorb sound and raise the humidity and temperature of the air. In sound design, we are concerned with applying acoustic engineering knowledge in a similar way, but by selecting virtual material properties and dimensions of a room to obtain a given effect. A knowledge of room acoustics is obviously useful for realistic reverb design. A large part of room acoustics is therefore concerned with "wave tracing," following paths of reflection. As in vibrating solids, paths that bounce between two parallel faces generate standing waves, so we get the phenomenon of acoustic resonance. Below 20Hz (above 50ms) resonances become "flutter echos" or short "slapbacks" that ring as short but distinct echos bounce between parallel surfaces. As shown in figure 5.9, the path may encounter perfect reflections, transmissions, dead ends where it is absorbed, diffuse reflections, or resonances where it becomes trapped between close parallel surfaces. So the model gets rather complicated. For this reason we tend to use rules of thumb involving areas, bulk material properties, approximate frequency responses, and decay time rules.

Reverb Time

The time for a sound to decay away in a room is measured as the time for it to fall by 60dB from the intensity of the first reflection (written T_{60}). From an internal point of view, any loss due to absorption is characterized by an absorption coefficient (a), a fractional loss which is between 0.0 and 1.0 where 1.0 is a perfect absorber and 0.0 is a perfect reflector. The coefficient a is dependent on frequency and incidence angle. The usual coefficient given in tables is called the *random incidence coefficient*, which works well for diffuse surfaces. It is often specified for 1kHz, but for acoustic design you will want to look up the value

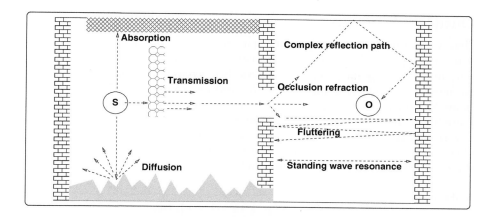

Figure 5.9
Some room acoustic processes.

in material tables to get values for a range of frequencies. As a rule of thumb the *Sabine formula* gives T_{60} as

$$T_{60} = \frac{kV}{Aa} \tag{5.12}$$

where A is the total area of the room in m^2, V is the volume of the room in m^3, k is the Sabine constant 0.161, and a is the absorption coefficient. A table of values for typical materials is given in table 5.1.

Table 5.1 Some absorption coefficients.

Material	125Hz	250Hz	500Hz	1kHz	2kHz	4kHz
Carpet	0.01	0.02	0.06	0.15	0.25	0.45
Concrete	0.01	0.02	0.04	0.06	0.08	0.1
Marble	0.01	0.01	0.01	0.01	0.02	0.02
Wood	0.15	0.11	0.1	0.07	0.06	0.07
Brick	0.03	0.03	0.03	0.04	0.05	0.07
Glass	0.18	0.06	0.04	0.03	0.02	0.02
Plaster	0.01	0.02	0.02	0.03	0.04	0.05
Fabric	0.04	0.05	0.11	0.18	0.3	0.35
Metal	0.19	0.69	0.99	0.88	0.52	0.27
People	0.25	0.35	0.42	0.46	0.5	0.5
Water	0.008	0.008	0.013	0.015	0.02	0.025

Outdoor Acoustics

Here we are interested in much of what applies to room acoustics, so there is some overlap, but diffraction, wind shear, ground effects, and dispersion really only apply to very large outdoor spaces. But we expect to find fewer parallel surfaces and small-scale resonances in rural environments than with human-made buildings. The acoustics of cities used for noise abatement and transport planning include both viewpoints. Generally speaking, outdoors we expect to find significant changes in temperature and ground incline. The paths of sound over water, over convex hills, into concave valleys, and through forests all produce remarkable alterations of amplitude and spectrum.

SECTION 5.4

Acoustic Oscillations

In the previous chapter we looked at oscillations in solid objects. Many of these principles also apply to a volume of gas; however, the role of excitor and resonator must be understood in different way. Many musical instruments, of the *wind instruments* family, exhibit excitation by relaxation or by turbulence, which we shall consider next.

Turbulence

Not all sounds are due to a balance of forces like simple harmonic motion. Noisy sounds involve forces that are not easy to predict. Quasi-periodic sources, like a flag flapping in the wind or the frictional sound of an object dragged on the ground, produce waves within a certain band, which can be statistically determined, but not at a regular pitch. An important phenomenon to understand for making water and wind sounds is turbulence.

Laminar Flow

For short distances and slow speeds, a fluid moves around things with an even flow, called the *laminar* mode. Each bit moves at a speed such that there are no big pressure differences between nearby volumes. Bernoulli determined that pressure decreases with speed, and that for a fluid to pass around an irregular object there must be some difference in speed. By geometry, the fluid must take more than one unequal path, and therefore there must be a difference in pressure somewhere. At low speeds this difference is spread evenly over a smooth pressure gradient that follows the contour of the object. Right next to the object's surface is a *boundary layer* where the drag caused by frictional forces greatly impedes the flow. Some distance away the flow is completely unaffected by the object. At all points between these extremes we find a steady gradient. In this case the flow makes no sound.

Chaos and Vortices

But when the fluid speed increases, a situation eventually arises where the difference in pressure between local flows is so strong that it starts to affect the procession of the main flow. In an incompressible fluid like water we can see that in order to go around an obstacle the fluid obtains some angular momentum; it begins to rotate in a clockwise or counterclockwise direction depending on which side of the object it passes. Since the velocities in the boundary layer decrease near the object and the fluid has some viscosity, there is angular shear between the molecules that tends to form rotating waves (*Tollmien–Schlichting waves*). These small vibrations grow into *vortices* and eventually giant movements called *eddies*. They continue to rotate after passing the obstacle, producing a *vortex chain*. As these interact they produce many small areas of varying velocity or pressure. In an elastic/compressible medium like air, temporary vacuums exert a force equal to or greater than the force of the fluid pushing along, and they pull some surrounding fluid in. Instead of laminar flow the air begins to move in and out, in a chaotic flow, or turbulence.

Reynolds Number

When exactly does the flow change from laminar to turbulent? The degree of turbulence is given by a *Reynolds number*, a ratio of inertial and viscous effects:

$$R = \frac{\rho V L}{\mu} \tag{5.13}$$

in which ρ is the density of the fluid, μ is its viscosity, L is the size of the impedance, and V is the velocity of flow. At a certain critical speed, a Reynolds number of about 2000, turbulence is introduced when the viscous forces (denominator) are not strong enough to support (or balance) the inertial forces (numerator). From this equation, larger objects, denser fluids, and faster flows tend towards turbulence.

Sounds of Turbulence

These chaotic patterns radiate out as longitudinal sound waves. It is rarely a harmonic or periodic movement; as it is so complex, it's not perceived as an orderly function of time. We hear a rushing-sound-like noise. However, beyond the critical point the Reynolds number correlates to the scale of vortices and chaotic pressure waves. As the fluid speed increases we get smaller scales and higher frequencies. Because of this statistical behaviour we get different sounds for different obstacle shapes and fluid speeds. Higher frequencies are heard for faster flows and smaller obstacles. The regularity of the obstacle also introduces some effects. Certain geometry, like perfectly round cables or poles, produces more focused, resonant signals like periodic whistling, while irregular geometry, like rocks and walls, produces the rushing-noise-like signals. A familiar scenario is where turbulence occurs within, or in close proximity to a resonant cavity such as a bottle or pipe. We will now look at this phenomenon of *acoustic resonance*.

Pipes

Turbulent flow causes compressions and rarefaction of air, but not necessarily in a periodic fashion. If objects are placed nearby that reflect waves generated by a turbulent flow, they may bounce back and coerce the vortices to adopt

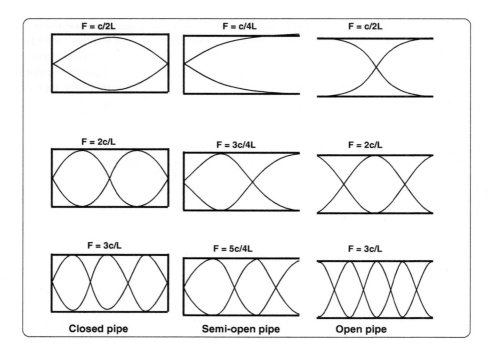

Figure 5.10
Resonances of pipes. Air velocity in closed, semi-open, and open pipes.

a periodic character.[3] If the cavity size and airflow are just right, a positive feedback cycle occurs, leading to a standing wave. In an open pipe there must be a particle velocity antinode, or pressure node, at the open end. If one end of the pipe is closed, then a velocity node (pressure antinode) must occur here, since at the boundary of a solid object no air will move. Using this idea we can predict the possible resonant modes for three kinds of situations: a pipe open at both ends, a pipe closed at both ends, and a pipe open at only one end.

Referring to figure 5.10 we see three types of pipe configuration and the standing waves that may appear. The fundamental frequency of a pipe closed at both ends occurs when there is a node at each end. The simplest wave that exactly fits into this arrangement is a half wavelength. Thus, for a pipe of length l:

$$f = \frac{c}{\lambda} = \frac{c}{2l} \tag{5.14}$$

Overtones can occur for any standing wave configuration that satisfies the correct placement of nodes at the ends, so these can happen at f, $2f$, $3f$, ... or

3. For turbulent excitations our rules about trying to nicely separate resonator and exciter break down—the two become merged into one complicated fluid dynamic process.

any integer harmonic. The case for a pipe which is open at both ends is similar, but with nodes replaced by antinodes. Again the fundamental is given by $c/2l$ and the harmonics are in an integer series. The case for a semi-open pipe is different. Here we must have a node at the closed end and an antinode at the open end. The smallest standing wave configuration that will fit is therefore a quarter wavelength, and so:

$$f = \frac{c}{\lambda} = \frac{c}{4l} \tag{5.15}$$

Furthermore, the only standing wave configurations that fit will be at f, $3f$, $5f$, $7f$, ... being the odd harmonic series.

Radiation from Pipes and Horns

In practice the frequency of a pipe isn't exactly as predicted by theory. Radiation from the end of the pipe appears as an impedance in a network model of the oscillator, and thus it changes the resonant frequency of the system. To get the accurate frequency for a pipe or horn we need to apply *end correction*. For a straight pipe we add $0.62R$ to get the effective length of a pipe with radius R. A tapered horn changes the acoustical impedance gradually, so providing a more efficient transfer of energy to the air. For a tapered horn, such as in a trumpet, we need to add $0.82R$ as an end correction.

Helmholtz Oscillator

A *Helmholtz oscillator* is a useful construction to understand. It occurs when an acoustic capacitance and inductance exist in series, such as for a bottle or a surfacing water bubble (seen later). A small aperture is connected to a volume such that the gas within it acts as a free mass, while the larger volume acts like a spring. A simplified illustration is shown in figure 5.11. If the gas in the neck is excited, say by one's blowing across the bottle mouth, then the gas will move up and down. By the Bernoulli principle there will be a reduction of air pressure over the opening and the gas in the neck will rise up. As it moves

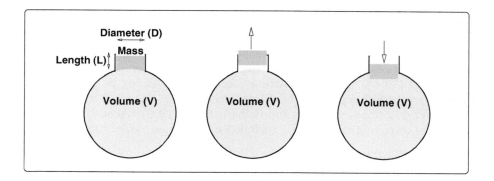

Figure 5.11
A Helmholtz resonator.

up, the pressure of main volume of gas in the vessel is lowered, so it pulls the
gas in the neck back down again. Since it has a small mass, given by the gas
density times the volume of the neck, it overshoots because of its inertance.
The gas in the vessel is then compressed, so it springs back, forcing the gas
in the neck up again. And the process repeats. The resonant frequency of a
Helmholtz oscillator is

$$f = \frac{cD}{4\pi} \sqrt{\frac{\pi}{VL}} \tag{5.16}$$

for a volume V, neck diameter D, neck length L, and speed of sound in air c.

Acknowledgements

Acknowledgement is given to Oleg Alexandrov for MATLAB code used to
make some illustrations in this chapter, and to Philippe-Aubert Gauthier, Peter
Plessas, Charles Henry, Cyrille Henry for suggestions and corrections.

References

Textbooks

Elmore, W., and Heald, M. (1969). *The Physics of Waves*. Dover.
Hartog, D. (1985). *Mechanical Vibrations*. Dover.
Morse P. M. (1936). *Vibration and Sound*. McGraw-Hill.
Morse, P. M., and Ingard, U. K. (1968). *Theoretical Acoustics*. Princeton University Press.
Kinsler, L. E., Frey, A. R., Coppens, A. B., and Sanders, J. V. (1999). *Fundamentals of Acoustics*. Wiley.

Papers

Foss, R. N (1978). "Ground plane wind shear interaction on acoustic transmission." Applied physics laboratory, Washington.
ISO 9613-1 (1993). "Acoustics, Attenuation of sound during propagation outdoors. Part 1—calculation of the absorption by the atmosphere."
ISO 9613-2 (1996). "Acoustics, Attenuation of sound during propagation outdoors. Part 2—General methods of calculation."
Wilson, D. K., Brasseur, J. G., and Gilbert, K. E. (1999) "Acoustic scattering and the spectrum of atmospheric turbulence." *J. Acoust. Soc. Am.* 105 (1).

Online Resources

"Hyperphysics" is a website of the Department of Physics and Astronomy at
Georgia University. It is a wonderful resource for relating physical concepts
and contains much useful information about sound and acoustics. <http://
hyperphysics.phy-astr.gsu.edu/hbase/hframe.html>

"Acoustics and Vibration Animations" is a collection of great simulations of moving, standing, and transmitted waves put together by Dan Russell, Professor of Applied Physics at Kettering University. <http://paws.kettering.edu/~drussell/demos.html>

A short essay entitled simply "Sound Waves" by Prof. J. B. Calvert provides a concise summary of many acoustic principles. <http://mysite.du.edu/~jcalvert/waves/soundwav.htm>

Tom Irvine runs a resource on acoustics with links and tutorials at his "vibration data" site. <http://vibrationdata.com>

Angelo Farina has published many excellent papers on environmental acoustics. <http://pcfarina.eng.unipr.it>

Ian Drumm wrote a "Guide to decibels and how to use them". Maintained at Salford University. <http://www.acoustics.salford.ac.uk/acoustics_info/decibels>

6
Psychoacoustics

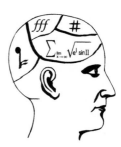

Perceiving Sounds

Psychoacoustics relates the measurable physical properties of waves, like amplitude and frequency, to the perception of sound and subjective phenomena, like loudness and pitch. It is the psychology part of sound. Although some of this chapter is technical, as much is human, emotive, and cultural. All these aspects must be combined in sound design to get the big picture. Understanding psychoacoustics and processes like streaming, categorisation, and masking make it easier for us to define the character of a sound in an efficient way. Sound cognition can be seen as layers, moving from hearing towards conscious understanding. Let's start at the lowest level in this scheme, which is physical, and properly speaking is a subset of psychoacoustics called *physioacoustics*.

Waves come from real physical vibrating objects like a bell or a loudspeaker, but they are not yet sounds. As a matter of definition, rather than a Zen puzzle, sounds are a perceptual experience, and without minds to experience them there are only vibrating waves. Waves cause your eardrum to vibrate and your brain to perceive a sensation. The sensation is not actually limited to the ears. We can feel low-frequency sounds between 1Hz and 20Hz in various parts of the body. Although we sometimes neglect to call these frequencies "sound" they are part of same physical phenomenon and experience. Occasionally we may see visual manifestations of sound. Shaking windows or sand on drum skins can reveal sound to our eyes. At high intensities, such as in explosions, sound can knock down or shatter objects.

Ears

It is customary to show a diagram of the ear at this point. Let us break with tradition since you probably remember from biology classes how the ears work. There is the outer part, the familiar shape of an ear, the *pinna, meatus*, and *lobes*. In humans the pinna acts partly as an amplifier and partly as a filter used for locating sounds. The meatus, while primarily serving to connect and separate the outer and inner ear, also serves as a resonant cavity, around 2kHz, which is useful for amplifying speech. Exactly what the ear lobes do isn't understood, but they seem to behave usefully as dampers on the pinna at certain frequencies and may have a role in our sense of balance. The eardrum or *tympanic membrane* acts as the main transducer to convert air pressure waves into vibrations in the middle ear. Then there are the inner workings (ossicles) of *malleus, incus, stapes*, which transmit sound to the *cochlea*. The ossicles match the impedance of the eardrum to the fluid contained in the cochlea and provide further amplification through leverage. The cochlea is a tapering cavity. Because it tapers, different frequencies cause resonances at different locations. Inside it is covered with a carpet of small hairs, known as the *basilar membrane*, which turn vibrations into nerve signals. Additionally there is a set of outer hairs on which the smaller inner hairs rest. They move up and down to tune the cochlea and have a role in attention and selection of sounds.

Frequency Range of Human Hearing

For sounds above about 20Hz ears produce a sensation of hearing, all the way up to between 10kHz and 20kHz, depending on age. It is important to know the human hearing range because it limits the range of frequencies we need to analyse or process synthetically. The majority of natural sounds like speech and music have frequencies in the middle of this range, between 300Hz and 3kHz. But harmonics from real sounds extend right through the range and beyond. Natural sounds are not band limited. Even apparently dull sounds like bubbling mud or collisions between wooden bricks have weak components going right through the hearing range.

Nonlinearity

The basilar membrane is not actually a linear system. Distortion introduced by the ear itself leads to the nonlinearity of loudness perception. It is actually a complex cybernetic system with feedback that makes it deliberately nonlinear, as we will see later when considering attention. Outer hair cells serve to enhance or dampen specific frequencies in response to input. One reason for having nonlinear hearing controlled by outer cells is that we can average the input energy for better dynamic resolution, so if a second tone is added to an existing one at a different frequency the first tone apparently diminishes in volume, which is called *two tone suppression*. The nonlinear frequency response of the overall system causes *cubic difference tones*, a form of harmonic distortion.

Threshold of Hearing

What is the quietest sound we can hear? As we will see shortly, the quietest perceivable sound depends on its frequency. Indeed, the effects of amplitude, frequency, and spectrum are not independent, but combine to produce a complex picture of perception. As a reference point we pick 1kHz as the frequency to define $1 \times 10^{-12}\text{W/m}^2$ as the quietest perceivable sound. It is a remarkably small amount of energy. In fact, we can actually hear heat as white noise. The human ear is such a sensitive, adaptive transducer that in certain conditions the Brownian motion of air molecules against the eardrum is audible. After prolonged periods of exposure to absolute silence (a disconcerting situation you can experience only on a lifeless volcanic island or in a specially constructed room) people report hearing a faint hissing sound. This isn't a neurological artifact, it's random thermal noise. Interestingly, the smallest visible intensity is thought to be one single photon of light, so we are basically tuned by evolution to perceive down to the limit of our physical world.

Just Noticeable Difference

To perceive something we must *notice* it. Whatever aspect of sound we want to measure the "just noticeable difference" (*JND*) is the smallest change that produces a perceptual effect. This measure is used in psychoacoustic experiments, and is always relative to another value. So, we may ask, what is the smallest frequency deviation from a 100Hz tone that we can notice? JND is most often seen in connection with amplitude changes.

Localisation

As two eyes allow us to perceive depth of field through stereoscopic vision, so a pair of ears allows us to locate sound sources according to the differences between the received signals. Stated simply, four factors are attended to. Two angles (normally given in degrees) specify the source direction, with the azimuth angle placing the source on a circle around us and the elevation angle as a measure of where the sound lies above or below. Furthermore, the distance of the object and its size are perceived as part of this stage. Small objects appear to emit from a point source whilst large objects emit from a volumetric extent. A general rule is that higher frequency sounds with sharp attacks are localised better than low ones with soft attacks. We localise sounds best at their start times, in the first few milliseconds of the attack transient. Sustained sounds are harder to locate. Another rule is that we are better at localising sound in a free space, outdoors, than in a small room where there are lots of reflections. And one last general rule is that we perceive location better if we are able to move our heads and get several takes on the sound. Tilting the head to get better elevation perception, or turning to face the sound are important actions in accurate localisation. Two phenomena are known to play a role: *interaural time difference* and *interaural intensity difference*. Interaural means "between the two ears," so the first is a measure of the relative amplitudes arriving at each ear (e.g., the action of *panning* in a stereo system). The second depends on what we already know about propagation, that sound takes a finite time to travel a distance in space. Both are combined in a model known as the *head transfer function*.

Interaural Time Difference

The interaural time difference (ITD) is the time difference between the arrival of the same sound at each ear. Simply, if the sound arrives at the right ear before the left it's very likely the source is located in the right field. ITD is most effective at frequencies below 700Hz because of the wavelengths involved. The brain appears to be doing a cross correlation of the sources, so when more than a whole wavelength will fit into the interaural distance, about 15 to 25cm, then ambiguity arises. This happens above 1.5kHz where ITD stops working. If the radius of the head is r and θ is the angle from the middle (the direction of the nose), then if c is the speed of sound

$$ITD = r\frac{(\theta + \sin(\theta))}{c} \tag{6.1}$$

When we already have the ITD and want to know the angle, a simplified rearrangement of the formula gives

$$\sin^{-1}\theta = \frac{c \times ITD}{2r} \tag{6.2}$$

Interaural Intensity Difference

Simply, if the sound is louder in the right ear than the left it's very likely the source is located in the right field. With only two ears we are not able to determine the exact sound source location using interaural intensity difference (IID). Sources emanating from points on a curve with the same azimuth yield the same interaural intensity difference. So this information constrains the possible locations but is only one part of the whole picture. The absolute intensity difference is actually rather small, so the occlusion offered by the head, the *acoustic shadow* it casts, plays an important part, particularly for higher frequencies. Localisation requires using both pieces of information and making a best guess from the available data. IID becomes effective above 700Hz but really works properly above 1.5kHz, for complementary reasons to the ITD range. When IID cues contradict ITD ones, the ITD information wins if the frequencies are mainly above 1.5kHz.

Head Response Transfer Function

Because both IID and ITD produce ambiguity, without further information our brains make use of extra information to perceive elevation and avoid front-back confusion. The nose plays a vital role in this. Having an obstruction on one side of the head means the sound paths around it are not symmetrical, so we are able to distinguish front and rear sources. The pinna of each ear acts as an amplifier that favours signals in the direction we are looking, and since sounds from behind must pass around it this adds to the front-rear discrimination. The nose and cheekbones act to sweep sounds from the front towards the ears, and being soft and fleshy they absorb some sounds in a way that helps us tell they come from the front. Additionally the damping effects of hair and the position of neck and shoulders contribute to our sense of sonic orientation. Since these phenomena apparently rely on diffraction and absorption effects they are sensitive to frequency. Higher frequencies don't travel around the head as well as low frequencies, so they are heard less on the opposite side. Sounds around 2kHz are more likely to be directionally confused.

Distance

We aren't very good at gauging distance unless we know something about the source. Familiar things like voices or the sound of a car can be judged fairly well since we have an internal measure of how loud we expect it to be. For strange sounds heard in the open it's harder to tell whether it's a quiet sound close to us, or a loud sound at a distance. What we do is make some assumptions about sound from its spectrum. Since higher frequencies are attenuated more with distance, if the sound fits the profile of something that should have a high-frequency component, and that part is missing or quiet, then we perceive it as farther away. Another psychoacoustic process is to use the environment to judge the distance. If we are adjusted to a certain environment, like a room, then we use the ratio of direct to reflected sound as a guide.

Source Identity

Given a choice of correlated sources we assign the nearest plausible source to be the loudest. If you have two radios in the same room tuned to the same station then the sound will seem to come from the closest one, even if that is quieter than the other. This effect can be used in virtual modelling as a way to factor out redundant correlated sources and subsume the source into one closest emitter. The same psychoacoustic process is at work when we construct a stereo field from two loudspeakers. If you sit between equidistant sources you do not hear two separate left and right sounds but one that seems to come from the middle.

Perception of Loudness

The intensity of a sound is an objective measure of energy received by the ear. It is proportional to amplitude, either in terms of absolute sound pressure level or sound intensity level in power per unit area. The *loudness* of a sound is a subjective value which depends on frequency and other factors. Our perception of loudness isn't the same as sound pressure level or sound intensity level, which can be confusing.[1] Loudness is measured in *sones*, another relative ratio, which has a relation to *phons*, described below. One sone is defined as the loudness of a 1kHz sine wave at 40dB SPL. An increase of 10dB SPL is perceived to be twice as loud in sones, 20dB SPL as four times louder, and 40dB SPL as sixteen times louder.

Loudness Scales and Weighting

Some frequencies seem louder to our ears than others. Sounds in the mid-range seem louder than low-frequency and high-frequency sounds of the same pressure level, which is unsurprising given an evolutionary influence towards selecting speech as the most important range. Several "equal loudness" curves have been developed in the past, including the Fletcher-Munson and Robinson-Dadson curves. The most recent DIN/ISO 225 curve combines the best features of earlier ones and eliminates some errors. Of course there is no such thing as an absolutely objective equal loudness curve, just a best approximation to one that works well for most people. The DIN/ISO 226 curve specifies the *phon* such that 1 phon is equal to 1dB SPL at 1kHz. It is not a unit but a contour or set of data points for subjectively measured loudness for pure tones of certain frequencies. In figure 6.1 you can see the curve for 80 phon-dB(ISO226). Notice

---

1. At the interface of audio engineering and psychoacoustics the proliferation of scales and units is confusing even to seasoned professionals and academics.

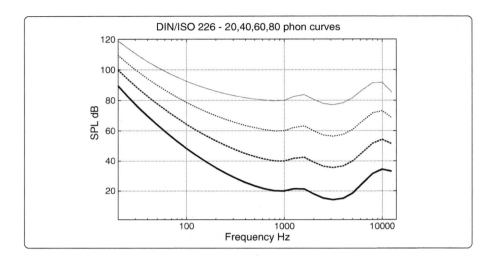

Figure 6.1
Equal loudness curves for 20 phon, 40 phon, 60 phon, and 80 phon.

that at 1kHz it is exactly 80dB SPL, but varies either side of this. Other curves between 20dB (ISO226) and 80dB (ISO226) show a slight change in shape. They become slightly flatter for louder signals.

Sound level meters employ "weighting filters" to compensate for frequency dependency and produce a reading more appropriate to what we actually hear. As with all standards the choice is considerable, and there are A, B, C, ... types. Two which have endured are the A weighting scale used in environmental noise measurement, and the ITU-R 468 scale given by the BBC. This scale is used in broadcasting and mastering since it works better for music and speech containing a noisy component. It also employs *psophometric weighting*, which accounts for our perception of transient events which may have a large peak energy but are subjectively quieter, while A weighting uses a regular RMS averaging. When sound loudness measurements are given they may be qualified by a parenthesised unit which specifies the weighting scale, so you may see 100dB(A) or 100dB(ITU) given.

Duration and Loudness

As just mentioned, a short sound may seem quieter because it does not stimulate the ear for very long, even if its peak intensity is large. Perception of loudness for short sounds increases with their duration, so that the power is integrated over time to increase the total energy carried. This effect, called *temporal integration*, can be used in sound design to make gunshots or short impacts have more apparent volume by stretching them a few milliseconds. It is effective for durations of up to about 200ms.

Fatigue

Steady sounds made of pure tones begin to sound quieter after we have been exposed to them for a while. This depends on their absolute intensity (Bekesey) and whether they are interrupted, but after about a minute a steady tone will seem subjectively quieter by half. Whether this occurs in the cochlea or is a function of attention remains to be clarified, because even a brief interruption can restore the initial loudness, and "interesting" sounds that modulate at low frequencies fatigue us less and thus remain subjectively loud.

Change of Loudness

The smallest perceptible change of intensity is a function of frequency for pure tones, and is also a function of actual loudness. The least sensitivity to loudness changes occurs in the lower-frequency range for sounds of a few hundred Hertz. As frequency increases above 1kHz, the ability to discriminate amplitude change gets much better and follows a curve similar to equal loudness, giving the best discrimination in the vocal range and then falling off again above about 4kHz. Also, we can hear changes in loudness better when the sound is louder, but not too loud, which is why you should mix at the appropriate volume. The best loudness discrimination is within the range just above a normal conversation, around 60dB SPL to 70dB SPL. Another way of interpreting the same data is to ask the question, what is the minimum level a tone needs to be in order to be heard as a separate sound in the presence of an existing tone of the same frequency? This gives us the JND for *intensity masking*.

Perception of Frequency

Just as *intensity* and *loudness* are absolute and perceptual terms, the psychological counterpart for *frequency* is *pitch*. There are several models of pitch perception, but for general sound synthesis it's not as important as for musical uses. Musical pitch is not as simple as it seems, which makes music interesting. For general sound purposes we tend to be concerned with a less sophisticated model of pitch where absolute frequencies play a stronger role.

Pure Tone Discrimination

Our *resolving power* is the ability to hear two simultaneous tones of different but close frequencies as separate. If they are too close then they fuse into a single note. It's different when they are played alternately. The *differential threshold* between changes of a frequency in time is smaller than for simultaneous ones. This introduces the concept of masking, which we will consider shortly.

Critical Bands

The critical band model comes about by viewing the cochlea as a spectrum analyser[2] with a finite resolution between bands. The cochlea has thousands of tiny hairs. Each is activated by a small range of frequencies in the area

---

2. It's not entirely true that the cochlea is a "spectrum analyser" since a more modern view of the spiking neuron process shows pitch is encoded as time-separated nerve impulses as well as physically localised stimuli.

that the cochlea is tuned. We call this *location information* since it pertains to places along the basilar membrane where stimulation occurs; it shouldn't be confused with localisation, which is about the position of a source outside the head. These are grouped into about 24 critical bands of 1/3 octave each, much like a graphic equaliser. An alternative scale for perceived frequency which is different from musical pitch is called the *Bark scale* (Heinrich Barkhausen). To get the Bark frequency in terms of Hertz you can use:

$$Bark = 13 \tan^{-1} 0.00076f + 3.5 \tan^{-1}(f/7500)^2 \qquad (6.3)$$

This produces a number between 1 and 24, so giving 24 critical bands over the average human hearing range of 20Hz to 15kHz.

Ranges

Many frequency ranges (also containing all the critical bands) are expressed in more common language in various branches of sound and music. The oldest and simplest division, shown at the top of figure 6.2, is into *bass*, *mid-range*, and *treble* bands, such as found on a basic tone control. Sound producers have long used a more elaborate system of names that stops short of identifying each critical hearing band and lumps together areas of the audio spectrum in a way that's useful for talking about vocals and instruments. The *sub* is rarely occupied by real instruments and really refers to a central channel or *subwoofer* loudspeaker used to add depth to thunder and other loud effects in cinematic or dance club PA systems. The bass and *upper bass* ranges deal with kick drums, bass guitar fundamental, and the lower octaves of piano and guitar, while the mid-range is split into further areas that relate to vocal, string, and brass sweet spots. Higher ranges include *presence* for adding clarity to vocals and instruments, *top* for cymbals and noisy sounds, and *air* which includes all the highest overtones up to the limit of the system. Some researchers (e.g., Leipp 1977) have quantified these for analytical use into so-called *sensible bands*. The lower scale in figure 6.2 shows the divisions of a 32-band graphic equaliser.

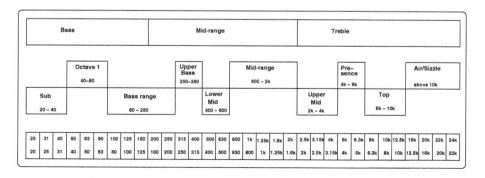

Figure 6.2
Common descriptions for ranges within the sound spectrum.

Resolution

Because the cochlea is formed from a finite number of hair cells there is a limit
to the resolution of frequencies. However, there is not a one-to-one correspondence between hair cells and possible frequencies we can hear, which would only
allow about 18,000 discrete frequencies. Instead we combine two kinds of information: timing information where the neurons fire on each cycle of a waveform,
and location information where a group of several neurons in a critical band
resonate because of where they are in the cochlea. The neurons can only fire up
to a certain speed (estimated by some to be up to 1kHz). Although an individual neuron may only fire at a certain rate, the output of several neurons may be
combined later on, giving a better resolution. This process is not linear by any
means. At the low end we have no problem hearing the difference between 100Hz
and 105Hz, a difference of only 5Hz. These frequencies are easily distinguishable. But at the top end the same difference between 16000Hz and 16005Hz is
not distinguishable. So we say these frequencies are *unresolvable*. When hearing
these two high frequencies together, we perceive a beating tone of 5Hz, which
is easily encoded by the neuron timing, so we know there is more than one
frequency in this range. It isn't clear, though, whether these might be 16000Hz
and 16005Hz, or 16000Hz and 15995Hz, since both pairings will give a 5Hz
beating pattern; thus there is ambiguity in perception. By the time we get up
to 20kHz, available to a healthy youngster, the critical bandwidth is so large
that 20kHz and 21kHz stimulate the same area, but the beat difference is too
fast to encode with timing. At this point all frequencies are unresolvable, even
though they may create a sensation. So, hearing employs several channels of
information. When the timing information from multiple neurons is combined
with the location information plus our ability to use beating between critical
bands to disambiguate frequencies, the resolution of the ear is quite remarkable.

Average of Close Components

Many real waves contain more than one close frequency, but are still periodic.
Their perceived frequency is not necessarily the period of the entire wave pattern. The peaks and zeros will be encoded by neural timing, and the individual
frequencies will stimulate critical band locations. The perception of pitch for
those falling within a critical band is formed from both these indicators and
so appears to be somewhere between the two. For example, a mixture of 20Hz
and 30Hz is periodic at 10Hz, but is heard as a sound at about 25Hz.

Rapid Change of Amplitude

Amplitude changes can have a small effect on pitch. An exponential change of
amplitude for a sinusoidal wave modifies the apparent pitch (Hartmann 1977,
2004). This is best regarded as a perceptual feature and is not really the same
as sidebands resulting from modulation, which introduce measurable frequencies, although there is clearly some underlying connection here. As an example,
the fast dynamics of a gunshot or thunder clap can make it seem higher in
frequency than it really is during the attack phase.

Phantom Fundamentals

Some sounds are heard to have a pitch below any frequency actually present (Seebeck 1841; Schouten 1940). Certain spectra *suggest* a fundamental frequency that doesn't exist in reality. This is true of the oboe and some other woodwind sounds. The phenomenon can be used to "make space" at the lower end of the audio spectrum and is exploited by some sub-bass effect processors that distort a signal to introduce a phantom frequency below the real fundamental. The general rule (Goldstein 1973), although hard to put rigorously, is that if a series of harmonics is arranged such that it seems a fundamental *should* have been present, then it will be heard. This is why a male voice can clearly be heard on a telephone even though the signal is strongly high-pass filtered above the fundamental range.

Huggins Binaural Pitch

Pitch may be apparent even where there is no physical periodic component. White noise presented to both ears but shifted by a small period T in one ear can result in the perception of a tone at $1/T$ in the middle (Cramer and Huggins 1958). The phenomenon is connected to IID processing and a function of the brain that attempts to minimise the signal to noise ratio of sounds by correlating input from each ear (Bilsen 1977). This is connected to the deep colour of stereo phasing and flanging effects, and is useful in sound design when considering such things as a passing jet plane which seems to emit a falling and rising tone even though the resonance cannot be accounted for by acoustic properties alone.

Bilsen Band Edge Pitch

A very steep ("brick wall") filter applied to broadband noise can create the perception of a pitch at the cutoff frequency, even if the filter is maximally flat. This is important in sound design, especially when creating subtle natural effects such as rainfall where colour should be avoided and specific noise distributions are vital to the effect.

Perception of Spectra

Once again we introduce a new term, *timbre*, for the subjective, perceptual quality of a measurable quantity which is the spectrum. Of course a spectrum is not a scalar quantity with one dimension, but a matrix of values. Accordingly, we cannot rank timbres in a simple order; rather they form a space (Wessel 1976; Grey 1975; Wessel and Grey 1978) in which certain sounds are close to each other and others are far away. Bear in mind that timbre refers to a static spectrum, with a fundamental frequency and a series of overtones. This is just a snapshot in the frequency domain and does not capture the evolution of the sound. When we talk about timbre we are talking about the instantaneous perceptual sensation produced by a steady spectrum.

Perception of Harmonic and Inharmonic Spectra

In earlier chapters we have learned that vibrating bodies can produce a spectrum that is harmonic, where every frequency has some simple integer relationship to the fundamental, or inharmonic, where the frequencies are related in a more complex way with nonintegral intervals. Harmonic spectra are perceived as "pure" or *consonant* timbres, while inharmonic ones may be called "rough" or *dissonant*. Interestingly, a pure timbre does not require that the harmonics line up perfectly with absolute integer values; rather it requires that they form a steady (monotonic) progression. So, for example, the series 100Hz, 199Hz, 396.01Hz, and 788.06Hz sounds perfectly pure. Each overtone is almost an octave, 1.99 times the previous one. Because a note consisting of nonintegral harmonics isn't dissonant it seems reasonable that absolute scales are not hardwired into the brain, but learned. On the other hand, 100Hz, 200Hz, 400Hz, and 411Hz sounds rough and inharmonic even though the first three terms are perfect octaves. The thing about the first example is that it sounds perfectly pure until we try to play it in a scale, where it sounds wrong, while the latter seems intrinsically "rough" but is uniform and consistent when played in a harmonic scale.

Consonance, Harmony, and Roughness

The above phenomenon displays the principle of *local consonance*, the relationship of a spectrum to shifted copies of itself. It is why certain instruments sound better in certain scales. It also explains the complex relationship between timbre and harmony that gives rise to the fascinating arts of orchestration and arrangement in composition. While we are straying into musical territory it's also worth noting that harmony rules such as chordal consonance and dissonance fall out of this principle too. If the overtones of a note line up with those of other notes in a scale then the timbre is harmonic in that scale. Helmholtz explained consonance and dissonance in terms of beating. Close frequencies that give rise to slow phase shifting produce an annoying sensation in the ear where the beat frequency is above a few Hertz. Harmonics that line up precisely do not result in beating. More recent studies (Plomp and Levelt 1965) seem to indicate that it is ambiguous stimulation of hair cells in the cochleas critical bands that causes the unpleasant roughness, and a plot can be made of the perceived dissonance between two sine waves. This dissonance curve shows that the most roughness occurs with a separation of about a semitone (the eleventh interval), or a quarter of a critical band width, $0.25 * 1$Bark. Above this dissonance falls (consonance increases) as the separation increases towards the octave, but does not magically change at "special" intervals like the fifth. Again, this reinforces that Western musical concepts are not perceptually innate as some texts have claimed. As sound designers working on nonmusical work we can still use this wisdom. Roughness as an unpleasant effect may be better understood as the *doom tone*. It is an interference rhythm composed of cycles in the 4Hz to 8Hz range resulting from dangerous high-energy phenomenon like stampeding animals and high speed wind. When it modulates higher frequency components, the resulting critical band ambiguity leads to an unsettling effect.

Brightness, Dullness, and Spectral Centroid

A subjective scale used much in music is the *brightness* or *dullness* of a sound. Bright sounds simply have more high overtones than dull ones. But having a few loud high frequencies is not sufficient to make a sound bright. The best measure of whether a sound is dull or bright involves finding its spectral "centre of gravity" or *spectral centroid*. This is a weighted mean, so we find it by adding up the strengths of frequencies in each critical band (times the band number) and dividing by the total of all the bands. For N critical bands around frequency f_n each containing energy x_n

$$Centre\ of\ spectrum = \frac{\sum_{n=0}^{N-1} f_n \times x_n}{\sum_{n=0}^{N-1} x_n} \qquad (6.4)$$

There must also be sufficient continuity in the spectrum to produce a bright timbre. A predominantly low-frequency spectrum with an isolated high component will be heard as a dull sound with a separate "artifact" on top of it. Brightness is used as a scaling dimension in many timbre space studies (Wessel 1973; Grey 1975; Moorer, Grey, and Snell 1977–78) and characterises frictional and nonlinear processes (bowed string and horns). The *attack* portion (see below) of a sound is very important in the perception of brightness (Helmholtz, Wessel 1973; Grey 1975, Schaeffer 1977). If a sound begins with a bright transient the rest of the sound is weighted as brighter. A dull timbre has a low spectral centroid, or no unresolvable harmonics in the speech range. Such sounds appear damped or muted.

Resonance, Flatness, and Formants

Resonant timbres have a *sharp*, narrow spectrum with most of the frequencies clumped around a one or more fixed points. Alternatively, a timbre is described as *flat* or *wide* where the spectrum is evenly distributed. Noisy sources like a cymbal give wide, flat timbres, while a wooden flute gives a sharp, resonant timbre. Many acoustic instruments like guitar and violin have several fixed resonances. A single note cannot reveal these, since it would be impossible to tell which come from the exciter (string) and which are part of the resonator (body), but if two or more different notes are played the common resonance becomes apparent. In perceptual terms we refer to this fixed resonant feature as a *formant*. Sounds that have a combination of sharp resonance and formants in the 300Hz to 1kHz range sound voice-like.

Perception of Temporal Structure

The following items deal with the way we divide sounds up in time. Broadly, we can use three *scales* in which to place sounds. The first division is between microstructure and macrostrcuture. Microstructure is everything below one second. It is the trill of a flute, the syllables of a word, or the individual crackles in a fire. Macrostructure is everything longer, from the sentences that make up a dialogue to the thematic development throughout a symphony. In this scale we consider tens of seconds, minutes, and hours. The microstructure needs further dividing into short, very short and "nano-scale" sounds. Important perceptual boundaries occur within this range, which we will consider next.

Granularity

This term really applies to the microstructure of sound. Sounds less than about 20ms are heard differently from those that are longer. Gabor (1946) and Stockhausen both contribute to this concept, and granular synthesis is one of the practical methods that come out of it. At the lower limit the idea of events fuses with the perception of pitch. As a very tight drum roll speeds up, it ceases to be a sequence of discrete beats at about 18Hz and becomes a pitch. Granularity also applies in the 50ms to 150ms range across the Miller/Van Noorden threshold, and again over the one second barrier. This effectively partitions sonic microstructure into three broad areas of granularity where slightly different rules apply.

Events and Flows

When we are taught maths at school, we first learn integers. Multiples of one make sense to the young mind, as do *events* like "three o'clock" and "tea time". Later we learn that these are fictions, that everything is always in motion; and so we introduce another fiction more soothing to the adult mind, which is the idea of *real numbers* and continuous flows. As mental tools both are equally valid, and it is merely a matter of utility whether we choose to deal with events or streams. It is fairly safe to say that what happens on the macrostructural level constitute events: a particular bar in a piece of music, a particular scene in a film. And it is fairly safe to say that what happens on the microstructural level, the samples and waveforms that make up a sound, are continuous flows.

Envelopes

A nice way of dividing events and flows into meaningful frames is to consider the change of energy occurring within a system. Is it growing? Is it diminishing? Is it steady? Four words are commonly used in sound design to describe the *envelope* of a sound: *attack*, *decay*, *sustain*, and *release*. These words can apply to any variable quality such as amplitude, frequency, or timbre. Control envelopes used in synthesis are often abbreviated *ADSR* to reflect these stages.

Attack

The period at the start of a sound where it moves from zero to maximum energy is called the *attack*. For percussive sounds this is very quick. Attack times of less than 10ms are generally heard as a click, though most real sounds do not have an instantaneous attack, even if it is very fast, because some energy is absorbed into the body before being radiated as sound. The smaller the object, the faster this initial energetic absorption will be. A sound that could be considered to have a near zero attack might be a small glass marble dropped onto a tiled floor. It is useful to further break the attack into two more stages, the *transient* and the *rise*.

Transient and Rise Time

A *transient* corresponds to the excitation stage. It is often considerably louder than the rest of the sound and is always short. Typical transients are between 5ms and 50ms long. It may contain sound from both the excited object and the excitor, for example a drum stick or bell hammer. The *rise* occurs while vibrational energy is still building up in the system. As a rule it is often shorter than one period of the primary mode, or the length of the object divided by the speed of sound in the material. Often it reaches its maximum before the transient has finished; thus the two seem inseparable. A good example where this is not the case is a gong. When hitting a gong the transient of the beater on metal precedes a short period where the initial excitation wave spreads through the body. The beater impact creates short-lived high frequencies locally, but the spread of the displacement is a fairly low-frequency event after which the major vibrational modes emerge and the gong bursts into life.

Slow Attacks

The attack may also be very long. In a gently bowed string the amplitude continues to increase until the restoring force from the string and the force applied to the bow reach a maximal dynamic equilibrium limited by friction, which may take several seconds. A sound that might be considered to have only attack is an object sliding off an inclined surface into the air. In this case it continues to accelerate with frictional excitation making a louder and louder sound until it falls off the edge of the surface. Another example is a simple fireworks rocket. Ignoring that it usually fades into the distance, the sound output rises in intensity until it burns out or explodes, since an increasing surface area of fuel burns.

Decay

Decay applies to systems where energy continues to be supplied after the transient stage. Such sounds are usually frictional or turbulent, such as dragging a sack over the ground, or blowing a trumpet. Decay happens after the initial energy input to the system overshoots the sustainable level. After this the system reaches some kind of steady dynamic equilibrium called the *sustain*.

Sustain

During this period energy input to the system equals energy output (minus internal loss to heat), so the portion of energy that makes up the sound remains steady. A good example is a bowed string. Schaeffer (1977) refers to this as *energetic maintenance* in his sonic taxonomy. The sustain stage usually produces a steady sound output, but this is not always true. Again the bowed string provides a good example, because periodically the bow must change direction, so while the overall level of energy transfer is quite even there are points where it waxes and wanes. An interesting counterexample is a marble rolling down a long uniform slope. Strictly the system is in a *release* stage, since stored energy is being given up at a constant rate. However, the sound energy produced is constant and seems sustained. Water flowing over a waterfall is a sustained process. The upstream river provides a constant source of energy, the downstream river provides a sink into which the water disappears, and the waterfall itself is merely an inefficiency in the flow that turns some energy from the moving water into sound and heat.

Release

This occurs once we stop putting energy into the system, but it still contains some stored energy and continues making sound for a while. For moving objects this value corresponds to momentum, or to storage capacity for fluids. Release always tends to zero; it is the final stage of a sound.

Effort and Movement

Possibly valuable, though less rigorous or quantifiable interpretations of sound dynamics, come from Pierre Schaeffer (1977), Michel Chion (1994), and Rudolf Laban (1988). Schaeffer's 1966 Solfège is extended by Chion to develop species, dimension, gauge, stretch, weight, relief, impact, articulation, sustenance, shape, maintenance, facture, and impulsion as dynamic descriptors. Laban's work on dance incorporates the mass and movement of the human form to describe the feelings of gestures that may apply to sound. Starting with the ideas of effort, space, time, weight, and flow, a set of axiomatic gesture classes are formed, such press, glide, wring, float, dab, slash, flick, and thrust.

Precedence and Belonging

In breaking up a sound into its structural elements, the *Haas effect* or *precedence effect* determines where we perceive the separation of source and environment to lie. Reflections received after about 30ms are assigned to the environment and heard as separate echoes. Those happening within 30ms of a sound are fused into it and ascribed to the same object. Thus, although the body of a classical guitar is an acoustic resonator that produces multiple echoes within its cavity, these all blend into the same apparent source. They seem to belong to the guitar, and not to the room. A hand clap in a large hall will create discrete echoes. The echoes seem to belong to the room, not the hands.

Gabor Limit for Duration

The Gabor limit marks the minimum duration for which a sound can be said to have a pitch. Anything shorter than about 10ms to 20ms doesn't contain enough wavecycles to stimulate a sensation of pitch and is heard as a click. The apparent frequency (or perhaps this is a good place to use the ambiguous word *tone*) of the click depends only on its duration. Shorter clicks sound higher/sharper while longer clicks sound lower/duller.

Hirsh Limit for Ordering

Short sounds were presented to listeners with random offset timings by scientists (Hirsh and Sherrick 1961). Sometimes A would precede B by a short interval, and sometimes it would be the other way about. Occasionally, just by chance, the two sounds would start simultaneously. It was found that when the separation was about 20ms or less the two sounds could not be ordered above chance.

Streaming

Closely connected to perceived ordering of sounds is *streaming*, which is where we group components of a sound together in the belief that they belong to same thing. Some telephone rings and birdcalls are composed of short, high and low tones in quick sequence, but you hear them as a single trill instead of being composed of separate steady tones. When a number of similar sounds occur in quick succession, we say they achieve *fusion* and become one sound. Individual raindrops make a "pit-pat" sound when the fall is light, but in a torrential downpour the sound becomes a single wall of noise. The opposite is true when the density of an apparently coherent sound falls below a certain threshold and begins to break up into individually identifiable parts. We call this the *fission* point, or the *temporal coherence boundary*. With a small difference in spectrum and frequency, listeners perceive an integrated stream with a contour they can follow. As the spectrum or frequencies diverge they begin to hear two separate streams, one high and one low. At this point attention can focus on either stream separately, but not on the whole pattern.

Streaming by Pitch

Experiments done with alternating high- and low-pitched tones (Miller and Heise 1950) show that fission and fusion occur in the area of 50ms to 150ms depending on the frequency separation of the tones (measured in semitones). For larger frequency separations, the tones do not fuse until the alternation rate is higher. The precise rates required for fission and fusion depend on the individual listener. The phenomena seen with streaming pure tones indicate that pitch and temporal identification compete with each other.

Van Noorden Ambiguity

An ambiguity discovered by Van Noorden (1975) is an area between fission and fusion states (from 100ms up to 1500ms) where the listener can choose to hear the sound in one of two ways (influenced by suggestion or initial conditions), rather like those Gestalt optical illusions of a cube that switches perspective. Van Noorden conducted an experiment where he changed the frequency and alternation period until an integrated trill became two streams of separate sounds, then moved one or the other variable back until the streams integrated once again. He found that *hysteresis* happened: the fission and fusion boundaries were not the same and depended on which side you approached from and the attentional setting.

Spectral and Spacial Streams

As well as depending on frequency and timing, our tendency to group sounds is also influenced by their spectrum. The notion of a discrete *timbre space* (Wessel 1979) is useful. Up to a certain limit there are many sounds we would classify as a flute, and if we hear a melody played by an instrument that changes its spectrum within these limits we assume it is from the same source. Beyond the limit, moving in the direction of an oboe, there comes a point where we hear another instrument playing the notes with an altered spectrum and we assume two musicians are playing together. Two sounds with very different harmonic structures create a clear boundary that separates them, even if they share some common overtones. Localisation also plays a part, so we tend to ascribe sounds to a common source if they appear to originate from the same location.

SECTION 6.2

Sound Cognition

Much of how we organise sound at a higher level is still a mystery. Some of it may be entirely personal and subjective, but large parts of the general structure are well understood. We have different faculties (Fodor 1983) which are responsible for specialised tasks, like separate brain areas for music, language and scene analysis. Characteristics or dysfunctions like *amusia*[3] (Sacks 2007) confirm the role of localised (neurological) faculties.

Gestalt Effects

Richard Warren performed tests on listeners in which phonemes in spoken sentences were completely replaced (not merely masked) by short extraneous noises, like objects bumping or a cough. Later the listeners recalled the words perfectly, as if they had been complete, and could not even identify places where replacements had occurred. This experiment highlights that perception (generally, not just with auditory senses) is a holistic process that recognises overall patterns. The "phi phenomenon," according to Gestalt psychologists, is our ever-present tendency to organise disparate, granular events into a coherent and sensible whole. Bear in mind that during this process the brain plays tricks on us, so what we "perceive" isn't always what we "hear," which is not always what is *actually there* (as a measurable pressure wave).

Discrimination

Our ability to perceive information in a sound determines whether that information is relevant to us. If some feature or quality is present in one sound but absent or changed in another and we cannot tell them apart we may assume that the information is irrelevant to the perceptual process. An example is the phase relationship between waves in a sustained periodic sound, which can be completely changed without any effect on the listener. There are minimum changes in frequency and amplitude that are perceived, and our ability to discriminate timing markers as individual events is limited. Discrimination only requires that we feel a sense of difference between two sounds, not that we need to say anything concrete about them. For example, experiments show that we can tell two similar rapid tone sequences apart with absolute certainty, but

---

3. *Amusia*: complete "blindness" to musical forms in someone who has no problem with ordinary sound processing.

the actual differences are ineffable. We only perceive some mysterious quality difference without being able to explain it (Broadbent and Ladefoged 1959).

Scaling

If we can discriminate a quality then it may have some scale or dimensions against which to measure it. Scaling is the act of applying something quantitative to distinguish sounds. The hardness of a bell hammer and the distance of the observer from the bell are two physical parameters that lead to obvious scalings. They reliably map something measurable in the physical domain to something humans can say about the sound, something in the perceptual domain. Not all physical parameters affect a sound. An obvious case is the mass of a pendulum, which doesn't even figure in behaviour, or the independence of volume in liquid sounds (splashing in a river sounds the same as splashing in the ocean; it's depth that has an effect). Some physical parameters affect a sound in more than one way. Temperature has a multitude of influences on the microstructural sound of a fire burning. In sound design we wish to reduce the set of parameters to the minimum needed to perceptually capture the sound.

Similarity

The similarity of two sounds from the same object tells us something about that object. Imagine a recording of a tin can being hit softly then successively harder with a beater. If we split up the recording and play back the hits randomly we would still be able to rank them back to the correct order by listening to them carefully. The change in amplitude from quiet to loud and the shift in spectra as more energy is imparted form a recognisable ordering. You could do the same for a bottle and rank all the hits in order when it is hit differently with the same beater. You would instantly know that any two sounds pulled from the two different recordings were of different objects, because of their frequency patterns. You could compare examples of each hit with the same energy from the same beater to reveal a third new parameter, the beater. To know the parametric dimensions of a sound we can use tests of similarity to discover them. As sound designers we do this all the time: we move a fader and compare the before and after versions according to some space or multidimensional grid of features. If a group of people is presented all possible pairs of examples from a set of sounds and asked to rate similarity, the salient features of the sound are revealed statistically. This is called *multidimensional scaling*. Algorithms such as the Kohonen self-organising map can be used to cluster sounds and provide a *similarity space*. Both are approaches to analysing the *timbre space* of the sound object to try and discover parameters. We can use this concept the other way around too. If we already know the timbre space of an instrument or sound-producing object, because we make it from a model, then we can predict the similarity of various settings from what we know about discrimination of sound features. In creative terms this offers a powerful device. Juxtaposition of similar sounds can provide a strong associative link, such as the falling raindrops blended with machine-gun-fire in the war film *Saving private Ryan*.

Matching

A match is a definite association of a sound to a class or set of things. It doesn't have to be conscious or verbalised with a name; it's enough that we feel a sense of familiarity and know what that sound is. Walking in the rainforest our ancestor instantly knows the difference between raindrops on the leaves and the sound of a twig snapping. Survival requirements create fast responses or instincts towards the attack characteristics of a sound, allowing an approaching predator to be quickly matched against an apparently very similar alternative sound, just another raindrop falling on a leaf.

Classification

Classification is similar to matching, only we must verbalise some class or set we think the sound belongs to. Sets can be arbitrary and overlapping. We can have bouncy sounds, rough or smooth ones, or happy, annoying, grainy, or fluffy ones. Two sounds can fall into the same set when they share one or more important features.

Identification

At some level, comparisons are made to sounds stored in long-term memory. Identification is more than a match, and it is more precise than a classification of features; it is a concrete statement of what we think a sound is, what it signifies, and what the thing is that makes it. Examples are "A motorbike," and "A stone dropped into water." Some parts of an identification may be superfluous, such as the stone as opposed to an orange. We mean "*something* dropped into water" but use the stone as a template from a familiar match. Some parts of the identification may be wrong, which indicates a degree of *confusion*. It may be a petrol lawnmower, not a motorbike. Lacking biker skills I may have identified a Harley Davidson when in fact I heard a Moto Guzzi. Identifications and confusions are very important to sound designers on the level where visuals are to be matched to sound, on Foley stages, "wild sound" recording sessions, and sound editing rooms. The skilful sound designer picks similarities and creates deceptive matches and identifications such as using a cabbage for a flesh-stabbing sound, or an electric razor and plastic cup for a light-saber sound. Identification is strongly influenced by the accompanying visuals and the context that is set by them.

Recognition

Recognition is the strongest of all. While identification can happen for sounds we have never heard before, recognition involves some correlation with a unique internal model. A passing vehicle may belong to a stranger and is thus *a* motorbike, as opposed to the one with a customised exhaust and strange rattle in the fuel tank mounting that I recognise as *Tom's 1980 air-cooled V-twin Moto Guzzi*. What is really interesting is that this familiarity is not limited to specific sound instances. Certain sounds in modern life are "samples" and are recognised as specific unchanging instances of sounds we have heard before. Examples may be brand sounds like the "Intel Logo" or a "Nokia ringtone," or familiar recordings like the Wilhelm scream. Each time we hear them the same pattern of bits produces more or less the exact same waveform. However, humans can recognise sounds by their intrinsic mechanism. The sound of a familiar voice speaking words we have never heard before is one example. Tom's Moto Guzzi is making patterns of vibrations it has never made before, yet it's recognisable as that definite article from its general behaviour.

Attention

Attention is what we pay to important or pleasing signals. We focus on sonic objects just as we focus on things we see. Even though signals arrive from many sources all jumbled into the same wave we can pick out the individual transmitters like radio stations. The so-called *cocktail party effect* is an example of attention. So, attention is some tuning of perception. Many experiments have been done that conclude that attention is something that happens at quite a low level in the brain/nervous system. Much as we can focus on objects with our eyes, in hearing we are able to tune the ear to filter out things we are not expecting, or don't want to hear. For humans this happens at the neural level, probably because we don't have "ear lids"; but some animals can direct their ears to attend to different sources.

Correspondence

Attention is sharply focused by visual *correspondence*, involving innate processing to compensate for movement and distance perception. In a cinematic context the deliberate or implied bindings of explicit visual events to sounds is *diegesis* (from the Greek meaning "a story told"). Naturally we try to bind things we see to things we hear. When a pot falls off the table and breaks, each piece of china has its own frequency that matches its size. With a proper correspondence between the sounds and images of pieces landing we feel the scene makes sense. Although the scene is composed of many events in quick succession and many concurrent processes, we are able to give several things our attention at once. How many is unsurprisingly about 5 or 6, or Miller's number. In a collection of sources, like a passing stampede of galloping horses, only one may be in the visual frame at any time. That is the one that has focus and the object to which we try and bind attention. It is *synchronised* sound. In the background we see many other horses moving by. Should we synchronise sounds to every single hoof to get a realistic effect? No; in fact we only need to synchronise the few in focus, and add a general filler effect to account for the rest. Randy Thom suggests that in cinematic sound an adequate efficiency can go as far as using only one single or maybe a pair of front sounds against a background texture. In the audiovisual realm we often group things as one, two, and lots.

Asynchronous Sound

In contrast to ordinary correspondence and synchrony in an audiovisual context *asynchronous* sound augments a visual event with a nonliteral interpretation, not neccesarily meaning there is no time relationship between event and sound, but rather that they are not literally synchronised to on-screen visual events. Examples might be the replacement of a gunshot with a firework as the movie fades to a celebratory scene after the villain is dead, or a scream with a siren and flashing lights to indicate that the police arrive, without having to explicitly show that part of the narrative.

Acousmatic Sound

Deriving from Pythagoras, and meaning "heard without being seen," the idea of *acousmatic* sound takes it one step further than asynchronous sources. Schaeffer (1977) developed the acousmatic concept as that of sound divorced from any known mechanism or source, sound to be taken on face value purely for its sonic features, so it connects to Chion's (1994) reduced listening mode. Cinematically all such sounds are necessarily asynchronous. There are different theoretical interpretations of how such sound is able to communicate on a different level to *diegetic* and synchronous sources. Context and anticipation play a big part. The sound may be quite mysterious, unknown and used for its connotative properties. On the other hand, through priming or established convention it may communicate any abstract quality, a mental state (happiness, confusion, anger) or a characterisation ("bad guy" sound). In this respect, acousmatic sources overlap with the musical score in a soundtrack. In a different way, to distinguish from simple asynchrony, the deliberate absence of a visual element may allow acousmatic sound to take over in a more powerful way, such as in Michael Moore's *Fahrenheit 9/11* where documenting known events in the absence of a familiar spectacle produced a more chilling and horrible reinterpretation by forcing focus onto the energy of impact sounds and screams.

The Audiovisual Contract

Seeing and hearing at the same time produces a different, holistic effect, than either sense alone. Taking this simplification of correspondence further, Bregman's (1990) findings on constructive narrative are rephrased by Chion (1994) as a deliberate suspension of separation. The audio-spectator "agrees to forget that sound is coming from loudspeakers and picture from the screen." This fusion of senses, called multi-modal integration, is central to sound design because it allows us great flexibility with both sonic and visual objects so long as a plausible synchronisation and object-sound mechanism exists. This can be stretched so far as to work perfectly well when one of the elements is merely a metaphor, thus opening immense possibilities to creative sound design.

Absence

In the case notes of famous psychiatrist Oliver Sacks there's a story about a man who lived close to a railway line. He complained of waking every night with a jump at exactly the same time, as if hearing a loud sound. Microphones placed in the bedroom recorded no sounds and psychoanalysis yielded no explanation. Eventually, further investigation revealed that for twenty years a late freight train had passed the house at exactly the same time each night while he slept, but had recently stopped. The patient, subconsciously familiar and attuned to the passing train, was responding to the train *not* passing the house. Look at a line of fence posts or the teeth in a person's smile where one is missing. The absent thing stands out. This reversal of ground and form is common in psychology; we notice difference, even when that difference is absence. With sound, a missing pulse in a regular stream or a missing harmonic in an otherwise regular series can stand out. We actually hear the thing that's not there. The *Duifhuis effect* happens when you slow down a periodic waveform with a missing harmonic to a low frequency. The missing harmonic is heard explicitly (and often mistaken for aliasing). This effect can be explained in terms of Fourier construction and physioacoustic stimulation of the basilar membrane (Hartmann and Lin 1977). I will not attempt to explain it here, but it's worth remembering that some features or annoying artifacts in a sound cannot be traced by looking for what is there so much as what *should be* there.

Concurrent Masking

Unrelated sounds in close temporal or spectral proximity can interfere with one another. Sometimes one of them completely swamps the other so that it's no longer audible. *Concurrent masking* (or *simultaneous masking*) is when one sound happens right on top of another. Obviously, by superposition, the two sounds blend to become one, but our perception of the individual sounds is affected. In a rock drum kit the snare, hi-hat, and kick drum occupy very different spectral bands, so each instrument is clearly audible in rhythms with two or more sounds occurring on the same beat. If the two sounds are relatively similar, and one is significantly louder than the other, the quiet one will not be heard. That is to say, a mix of two sounds where one is masked by the other is indistinguishable from the masking sound alone. This is explained in terms of *critical band masking*, which says that each critical band is only capable of transcoding information from one sound at once. If two sounds contain overtones that share a critical band, they fuse. If one sound contains only parts that occupy a subset of the critical bands from another sound, the latter is dominant and will completely subsume the first sound (*in-band masking*). This is an important part of psychoacoustic data reduction used in the MP3 algorithm. Sounds in one critical band can be masked by sounds in neighboring critical bands too (*interband masking*). If a narrow band sound is flanked by another sound correlated in two neighbouring bands, above and below, then it is masked. The other sound is said to spread, and the *spreading function* depends on frequency and amplitude. Higher frequencies are more easily masked by spread than lower ones because each band occupies a wider frequency range in Hertz than those at the lower end of the spectrum.

Temporal Proximity Masking

As we have already seen, sounds separated by short time intervals have an effect on each other. Forwards (post) and backwards (pre) masking occur for two sounds in quick time succession. A quiet sound immediately following or preceding a loud sound can be masked even though it is clearly in a space of its own. It is as if our brain is distracted by the dominant sound and forgets about the lesser one. These aren't quite the same going forwards and backwards in time. Forwards masking happens around 100ms to 200ms afterwards, while backwards masking only works for 30ms to 100ms before.

┌─ SECTION 6.3 ──
│   **Auditory Scene Analysis**
└──

How do we make sense of complex sound scenes? An example given by one of the pioneers of *auditory scene analysis*, Albert Bregman (1990), is to imagine hearing the sound of dinner plates sliding over each other and then falling to the ground with some rolling around and some breaking. Afterwards you can answer specific questions such as "How many plates were there?" "How far did they fall?" "Did all the plates break?" "How big were the plates?" and so on. Applications of auditory scene analysis might be fire alarms where we can augment heat and smoke detectors with microphones that can detect for the sound of fire, baby alarms that can discriminate distress from contented gurglings, or intruder alarms that recognise human footsteps. This kind of work is a branch of artificial intelligence (AI) sometimes called *machine listening*, with interesting work being conducted at MIT Media Lab and Queen Mary College London. The fire and baby alarms were project suggestions for my DSP students. As sound designers we find auditory scene analysis valuable from a constructionist point of view. Knowledge about how the human brain deconstructs sound can be used in reverse to engineer sounds with the intended effects.

Segregation

Complex pressure waveforms arriving at the ears may have no obvious time domain boundaries that indicate individual events or causes. To break a complex sound apart we employ several strategies simultaneously. The first of these is *segregation*, itself composed of several substrategies that attempt to identify individual objects or events within a composite stream of information. Several simultaneous sources, such as a car engine, speaking voices, and background music, will all have frequency components that overlap in time. The frequencies themselves are not constant, but move in *trajectories* or *gestures*. A trajectory is a motion in a high-dimensional space but can be thought of in a simpler way as a path in lower dimensions, say, as a squiggly line in 3D.

Although a trajectory may intersect with other trajectories from other sounds, it is usually obvious from looking at the direction of the lines before and after crossing which one is which. In computer vision we first perform edge detection to find the boundaries of objects. However, some objects will be behind others, so to overcome this loss of information resulting from partial occlusion the computer must "connect the dots" and make inferences about lines that are implicit in the pattern. In auditory scene analysis we call this guessing or interpolation of lost features *closure*. Of course we naturally do this as humans, and similarly our auditory faculties are able piece together the "missing" frequencies in a composite sound. The physical counterpart to occlusion of sound waves, where an object lies in the propagation path, is not what we mean here. In psychoacoustics the sonic analogy to visual occlusion is masking, where frequencies are not so much missing as overlapping. Although the waves from all sounds arrive at the ear, some may be effectively hidden by others.

Schema Activation

A schema is a pattern or template stored by the brain that incoming stimulus is compared to. A cognitive psychology approach says that certain trajectories activate prelearned schemas. Fortunately this doesn't work like searching a file system, it happens through parallel processing that matches certain features in a treelike way, so matching or recognition happens almost immediately. Conscious attention allows us to guide or filter the possible schemas and search according to expectations, but attention plays a part even when we don't consciously attend. Each stage of a trajectory enhances or diminishes possible choices from a lexicon of schemas. In other words, sounds behave in an expected way, even when they are unfamiliar.

Primitive Features

So, what are the rules that underlie this process? Mainly they are simple rules of physics. In other words, we have an innate understanding of everyday physics deeply ingrained into our perception of sound. In a musical context Beck (2000) describes this as "acoustic viability." This is important to us as sound designers because we can suppose that if we pay proper attention to physics during construction then sounds will "make sense." Bregman (1990) calls this the *primitive auditory scene analysis level*. Some, such as Shepard (1957), follow an "aquired" hypothesis that regularity from the physical world is quickly learned by all animals during formative development. Having been exposed to examples every waking and sleeping moment of our lives it is perfectly reasonable that such patterns are deeply ingrained into our low-level perception. Others tend to favour a "strong" version analogous to Chomsky's (1957) innate grammar hypothesis, that we are born with a certain propensity to recognise primitive features, such as the octave. This may follow from the structure of the cochlea, the behaviour of spiking neurons, or the predefined structure of the auditory neural pathways; for example in Broca's area (Musso 2003).

Harmonicity

One primitive feature is the regularity of harmonic structure. From our previous exploration of sound physics we know that simple harmonic oscillations and resonances often lead to a series of frequencies related by a mathematical rule. In the simplest cases of a vibrating string or pipe these are multiples of a single harmonic interval. When we hear a flute we do not suppose that each harmonic comes from a separate instrument, but that the whole series results from the same source. This even works for inharmonic overtone patterns such as those from square laminas or nonlinear systems. It is as if our brains implicitly understand the mathematical rules of the production mechanism so long as they are relatively natural.

Continuity

If natural sounds sources are limited by the rules of physics then we expect the signals from them to behave in a constrained way. One such constraint is *continuity*, which implies some kind of low pass filter or slew rate limitation on how fast some dimension of a sound trajectory may change. When it changes faster than the allowed "speed limit" we tend to perceive this as a new sound, since it would be impossible for the old sound to change in this way. An example (by Warren 1972, 1982) reveals *homophonic continuity* when a steady sound is briefly increased in amplitude. Instead of hearing one object that quickly moves closer and then recedes we tend to hear a new sound suddenly appear in the foreground while the existing sound continues in the background at its previous level. If the change is reasonably slow then it appears to be one source that grows louder and then quieter.

Bregman found this applied strongly to localisation. If a sound equally present in both ears was gradually increased in one ear, then the expected perception of movement occurred. However, if the sound increased too rapidly (less than 100ms) then listeners discarded this as an impossible event, since the source would have to move too rapidly, and instead heard a second source emerge in the direction of the louder sound while the original continued unaltered in the established position. The perception of this speed limit depends on the perceived size of the source. Smaller, lighter objects such as a buzzing fly can be presumed to change their behaviour rapidly, while larger heavier objects seem to violate the perceptual speed limit for slower changes. This is reflected in the wide range of continuity thresholds found for different sounds (Warren 1972; Bregman 1990; Darwin 2005), ranging from 40ms to 600ms.

Momentum

We use the term *momentum* here to distinguish it from continuity and monotonicity. Although they are related concepts, broadly a *principle of good continuity*, they are not quite the same thing. Warren found that a continuous pure tone interrupted by bursts of noise was heard as an unbroken stream with bursts of noise added on top. Since the noise contains some of the frequency of the pure tone it seems to be briefly masked by the noise rather than replaced by it. Naturally, it is a more likely occurrence than the tone abruptly stopping, being replaced by noise, and then resuming. It is as if the sound carries a weight or momentum, making short interruptions seem less plausible.

Monotonicity

Continuity of change can also apply to a sequence of obviously separate events from the same source. Monotonicity is the tendency for an established pattern to continue in the same direction of evolution. The interval between the bounces of a ball always decreases. If the interval is small we might assume the ball is very bouncy, but it never *increases* unless some new event occurs to add energy, such as someone pushing down on the ball. Most natural phenomena are characterised by a decaying energy function and we easily hear any new injection of energy into the system as a new event. Sounds that unexpectedly break with an established pattern of change tend to be heard as new events or new sources (Bregman and Dannenbring 1973).

Temporal Correlation

Bregman (1990) summarises temporal correlation as *"Unrelated sounds seldom start or stop at exactly the same time."* Imagine starting some complex machine with gears and wheels. It is a composite source made up of many clicks and whirring noises, yet we lump them together as the same object. If the speed or mechanical intensity of the machine increases we tend to perceive this as a continuation of the original behaviour so long as the frequencies and patterns of the new behaviour match more or less with those of the old. If some component of a composite sound is isolated and played so that it starts before the rest then it is heard as a separate source throughout the duration of the sound that starts later, even though it is actually a component of that sound. Bregman calls this the *old plus new* strategy.

Coherence

In the words of Bregman (1990), "Many changes that take place in an acoustic event will affect all the components of the resulting sound in the same way at the same time." I would revise this to read in a *related* way, because it is impossible to blindly postulate the underlying parameters of a sound well enough to say *same*. Sometimes explained as the *principle of common fate*, another way of explaining this is in terms of common underlying cause. The changes occurring to many parameters in a vibrating body are often linked back through a causal chain to a single source. For example, the sound of footsteps on gravel contains many tiny bursts of frequency, each caused by a small stone moving against another, but the common parameter is the pressure of the foot on the ground. All the tiny components move together (around a statistical mean), not just in amplitude but also in frequency.

The Process of Scene Analysis

Let's try and pull some of these threads together. We do not have room to go into detail about this complex topic, but as a summary auditory scene analysis is a process of streaming, grouping, correlation, and matching schemas. The overall process is not a linear one and is not easily explained by any one sub-process. Rather, it is a result of them contributing in parallel to a bigger picture. Since schemas seem to compete with each other, familiar tricks known from other branches of psychology, such as priming, are useful in influencing the perception of a sound where two similar schemas compete. This is useful to understand for sound design, since a lot of what we do is "trickery" based on providing expectations for the listener.

┌─ SECTION 6.4 ──
│   # Auditory Memory
└───

An old-fashioned view of memory suggests a library of sounds located in a specific area of the brain. More modern views emerging from research tell us that there is no such "place" where memories reside. Rather, memory is an emergent property of the whole auditory system, as neural biases and schemas are slowly annealed by new experiences. In other words, it is the act of listening that modifies the apparatus we have for that task, creating new expectations and patterns.

Short- and Long-term Memory

Like other memory faculties, there seem to be short- and long-term changes, so auditory memory can be understood on at least two levels corresponding to immediate memory: an *echoic store* that quickly fades, and long-term or *episodic memory* that can last a lifetime. The echoic memory serves as a short buffer of a few seconds. Sounds here have not been encoded to any higher level. The echoic store seems separate from another faculty of short-term auditory memory for encoded sounds, which is quite like persistence of vision. It is a temporary stimulation of schemas that "resonate" for a while but then fade out, leaving no long-term change. Long-term memory involves a permanent neurological change, often requiring intense or repeated experience, and some measure of time to crystallise. What we do know is that speech and music each seem to involve separate faculties where episodic memory is formed.

Auditory Pipeline

An experiment conducted by Crowder (1969) works much like the musical puzzle toy "Simon." By appending more and more items to a sound sequence and measuring the recall of previous items, he found several interesting trends. The suffixed item is always recalled with great clarity if no further sounds arrive. This is more than *positional bias* in that new items actively erase those preceding them closely in time. Items further back in the pipeline seem to fare better. This suggests that a certain *encoding period* is required for sounds to take hold in auditory short-term memory. Another experiment (Massaro 1970) confirms this by showing how the intertone interval affects sequence recall. Fast melodies with intervals less than 100ms produce very poor memories. Recall improves with intervals up to about 350ms where it levels off.

Verbal and Nonverbal Memory

Because we have a highly developed faculty for processing speech, it follows that if a sound can be recognised and specifically tagged with a name then we can take advantage of verbal memories. Clearly a well-trained musician with perfect pitch can remember a melody sequence better if able to translate it into *categorical* symbolic form like E, G, B, D, F. This is not the same process used where we remember the tone sensation of hearing those notes. This *precategorical* memory is what interests us the most for sound design, partly because it affects perception of subsequent sound events within short time scales. Categorical memory is important in work, such as recalling pieces of music, or finding sound effects in a library. Precategorical memory concerns the ineffable, feelings associated with sound, priming and expectations that are important to understand when constructing film soundtracks.

Visual Augmentation

Because, as we have seen above, perception is a Gestalt process, we integrate other sensory cues into the process of forming memories. Many legal cases dealing with eyewitness testimony have exposed the unreliability of this Gestalt synthesis. Questions such as "Who shot first?" or "Which car hit the pedestrian?" can be hard to answer where sound and vision conspire to create ambiguous memories. The stronger schema tends to override the lesser ones, even modifying real memories to create a new memory (of what we think we saw or heard) to reduce *cognitive dissonance*. Experiments on sound memory generally remove all visual stimulus with a blindfold or reduced lighting to avoid this. In connection with *correspondence*, discussed above, this is important to us as sound designers. Deliberately *framed* events with visual focus exert a far stronger influence on our recall of a scene than acousmatic (out-of-frame) events.

SECTION 6.5

Listening Strategies

In this section we move away from the low-level perception and memory of sound to think about activities that happen in the higher brain. This overlaps with *attention*, but at a more conscious level, where intent and feelings which can be given verbal descriptions play a role.

Listening Hierarchy

Some researchers have proposed different ways we listen to sounds and have placed them into categories that indicate some type or level of unconscious or conscious thought while listening. The following paragraphs deal with listening modes, Schaeffer (1977) and Chion's (1994) categorical listening modes summarised by Tuuri, Mustonen, and Pirhonen (2007), and incorporate some of David Huron's (2002) musical listening observations as well as my own interpretations. From a sound designer's point of view we are interested in the utility of these for constructive and analytical tasks. They are not exclusive; most activities for designing sound occupy more than one category.

Reflexive

Reflexive responses are base, instinctive responses that we don't have much control over except in engaged listening (e.g., the way two jazz musicians respond "automatically to one another"). The startle response, defence reflex, and orientation response are common gut reactions to sounds, discussed in more detail later under the heading of *physiological responses*. But this category also includes low-level experiences of sound, which can evoke primitive feelings. Certain fast attack characteristics and suggestions of high energy transfer can cause immediate sensations of fear and vigilance. Many of these are probably evolved faculties from surviving in hostile environments with predators. Some, possibly hardwired for all animals, include universally relevant features for all living things, danger (high energy transfer, disorder, and predators), food (familiar sounds of prey associated with eating), mates (responses to calls of the opposite sex), and safety (sounds of the parent, group, etc.).

Connotative

Connotative response involves activation of our lower-level schemas that attend to features of a sound during the preconscious and preverbal identification, matching, and recognition stages. These responses are partial matches to learned features which may not have names or be directly understood by the listener. The resonance of a growl tells us the physics of a beast's anatomy and helps us identify a threatening or harmlessly small animal hidden in the forest. Those spectral features are part of an evolved connotative faculty we have for identifying size from the sound of animals. These are abstract preidentification features that tell us something about a sound source without us needing to know exactly what it is. In a city there are many more unusual and unexpected sounds like foreign conversations and new beeps and alarms which we recognise connotatively without knowing more.

Causal

During causal processing we deconstruct a sound into identifiable objects and a sequence of energy paths that explain the sound as a causal set of actions or flows. A recording of dinner plates sliding then bouncing and smashing constructs a vivid sound scene in which we can hear the individual events and link them together into an understandable whole. Much of Bregman's (1990) scene analysis deals with features that indicate causality such as shared timeframes, spectra, and microstructural detail.

Empathetic

Empathetic processing connects sounds to schemas about some other entity's state of mind or being. It is the extent to which we personify sounds and attach ourselves to them. The sounds of a crying baby, a loved one's voice, or an angry shouting mob give us feelings about the identity and intention of the source and guide our expectations.

Functional

A boat whistle, car horn, or ringtone are functional, as is somebody shouting the word "Stop!" They denote a specific purpose and are strongly identified with an object that informs, warns, marks, or orients us or the source by sound.

A bat squeak and sonar ping are functional, using echolocation to navigate, but unless you are a bat, biologist, or submariner the functional dimension may not be apparent. Birdcall is largely functional, as is the sound of a rattlesnake. The functionality depends on the intent of the signified, and if you are party to the semantic content of the sound its significance may be vital to your survival. Hunting dogs and lions use short clicks or yips to inform one another of where they are and optimise the chances of the pack making a successful kill.

Semantic

Semantic listening is a recognition activity where sounds are matched to immediately relevant meanings. A telephone ringing is a signifier that someone wants to talk to us. If we are expecting a call it may have extended semantics for us. Obviously language is a special case of this where words have meanings within a complex system of sequence, grammar, context, and so forth.

Critical

Critical listening judges the contextual appropriateness or correctness of a sound. A telephone ringing at 4:00 AM, a swear word, or an out-of-tune piano might provoke critical activity in most people. As sound designers we become bothered by complex questions about alignment, phase, clicks, and timbres that most people could not interpret or care about, so the task of sound design involves a lot of critical listening. In practical application, an expert who is applying soundtracks to pictures knows that Scooby-Doo bongos are appropriate for a cartoon comedy when the bad guys give chase, but not in a gritty reality drama.

Reduced

At times the listener consciously switches off all other perceptual channels to focus only on the sound in its abstract form. *Reduced listening* (Schaeffer 1977) is an important skill in sound design and is probably something that only humans do when enjoying music. It is different from engaged listening because we are only passively involved with the source.

Analytic Listening

When we combine all other modes in a *conscious* attempt to deconstruct sound and reveal deeper meaning, we engage in *analytical listening*. Trying to discern where someone was born from their accent or a doctor listening to a heartbeat are examples of this mode. My grandfather was an expert engineer who would walk around a car listening to the engine for a long while before making pronouncements about tapits, tuning, or piston rings. Even before lifting the bonnet to see the engine his diagnosis was seldom wrong.

Component Analysis

A particular type of analytical listening is peculiar to sound designers. Computers and brains alike may try to reduce a complex sound into the smallest set of features that adequately describes it. This data reduction is exploited in audio codecs, for example using the Karhunen–Loève transform, which is an automatic statistical linear method for grouping the energy from a sound into as few parameters as possible. Principal *component anaysis* is of interest here because as sound designers we are often doing a similar thing. As a listening mode we attempt to construct a *parametric model* that captures the sound with the least number of variables, while making them as meaningful as possible for the range of behaviours we want. We are trying to expose the underlying structure or mechanism through sound, separating out causal groupings. Later when we look at synthetic fire we will see that something like 5 or 10 parameters can capture the phenomenon quite well and thus give us the possibility of synthesising a wide range of burning effects just by combining these variables in different ways.

Signal Listening

Signal listening or *anticipatory* listening occurs when we expect some important sound. Truax (2000) used the expression "listening-in-readiness" for awaiting some expected sound event. It could be the alarm clock, when you wake up at 7:59 to hear it ringing at 8:00. It could be the sound of an animal you thought you heard crawling in the corner. This involves some remarkable neural and physiological activity. What happens during signal listening is the ear and auditory system tune to the expected sound—so much so that we may mistakenly hear other sounds as the target signal. It is known that the ear can actually *emit* sound (tinnitus is one case), but the reason for this is the less well-known process in which the cochlea hairs are not entirely passive but are part of a cybernetic system that uses feedback to tune to anticipated signals. It's possible that the heightened vigilance of paranoia leading to "hearing voices" is partly explained by this; the voices seem real because their source is very low down in the audio cognition stack, so that a passing car becomes a whispering voice when the voice is anticipated.

Engaged

Engaged listening is a supercritical state of experience that involves some degree of *interactivity*, being complete understanding and *involvement* with the sound we are hearing and its causal process. The sound may drive physical responses, while the responses also drive the sound. This tight coupling happens in such activities as singing, tap dancing, or playing a musical instrument. There is a feedback loop where, within expectations, we know and understand the sound scene which responds to our actions, or us to it. This is the experience a musician in a band enjoys and one we aspire to as sound designers. We are listening to the sound in the moment we are involved in changing it. Curiously, for the sound designer this supercritical mode of listening happens because we build the model of the sound ourselves and are judging the results to make immediate changes. Sadly, even with powerful computers, interfacing difficulties make the turnaround time for changing a model too long for a sound designer to get "in the zone" the way a musician can, but the rewarding feelings are similar.

┌─ SECTION 6.6 ───┐
│   **Physiological Responses to Sound**   │
└───┘

Sound can have an immediate and unconscious effect on human beings. This may be connected to the fact that even with the neurological ability to focus and filter sound without "ear lids" it is still an involuntary activity, especially when one is caught unaware by an unexpected noise.

Stapedius Reflex

Very loud sounds can cause the ear to shut down temporarily to protect itself, in a reaction known as the *stapedius reflex*. Muscles contract to dampen the ossicles and impede transmission to the cochlea. Hearing quickly returns to normal. It also occurs partially during speaking or singing, so that we hear our own voices more quietly than we otherwise would.

Startle Response

For survival humans evolved to recognise the difference between a snapping twig, a lightning bolt, and a raindrop on a nearby leaf within the first milliseconds of perception. Long before much time has passed, where front brain processing occurs to recognise or categorise sounds we can respond to features in the attack part of a sound. Certain patterns that suggest high energy or a sudden release of force cause an immediate *startle response*. A person may involuntarily move his head backwards as if dodging an unseen threat, move his hand and legs defensively, or blink. Heart rate increases and the person's attention is focused so he becomes more attentive to subsequent sound events.

Orientation Response

A loud or sharp sound off-axis may provoke an immediate instinct to turn your head towards the source in an *orientation response*. As we have already considered, this is partly due to the need to move the head to enhance localisation, but it is also driven by the desire to see the sound source and make further identification.

Ecstatic Response

Huron (2002) lists *ecstatic listening* as a response, particularly to music, that creates a sensation of shivers, called *frisson* in physiological terms. It may also be a response to the sound of a loved one's voice or a particular sound with strong emotional meaning. The experience may last several seconds. It involves waves of goose bumps, shivering and tickling sensations in the back, arms, shoulders, and neck and may also give rise to blushing and lacrimation or full-blown spontaneous crying. Most people describe this as a *good* feeling, an ecstatic moment. For most the experience is entirely involuntary. Since it was discovered that opiate suppressants inhibit this response it is clear that it involves release of peptides by the hypothalamus. In other words, sound can be a drug.

Stress Responses

Effects of *stress, responses* include raised blood pressure, sweating, disorientation, and confusion. As sound designers we should concentrate on the useful application of stress responses. Deliberate acivation of startle and stapedius responses, doom tone, and high energy suggestions all raise adrenalin levels. In a secure and limited context the effect is exciting and a powerful augmentation to action films and games. In the worst case it is quite literally assult, in the legal sense of the use of physical force (which is what sound is) and invasive behaviour. Theatre sound systems are restricted to a safe level (between 80 and 105 dB SPL) for health reasons, but even with this potential sound pressure many stress responses can be invoked. Noise abatement and environmental health is a complex and far-reaching topic, and the effects of prolonged stress responses to noise are known to include cardiovascular disease, depression, increased aggression, and many other ailments (see Field 1993; Treasure 2007). Sound has been used as torture since ancient Chinese times up until the present day in the United States. However, we should remain aware that these responses and their consequences are not absolutes and that consent and personal choice play a part. In nightclubs, raves, and festivals all over the world you will find people who happily expose themselves to sound patterns above 100dB for pleasure, while the same sound, if unwanted, would be extremely stressful.

Binaural Beat Entrainment

It is known that pure nonmusical tones can also have an effect on mood when listened to for long periods. Binaural difference conditioning involves presenting two tones, one to each ear, so that the beat frequency between them stimulates corresponding neural activity in the brain. Exact understanding of this still escapes us and much pseudo-science accompanies the phenomenon. However, the basis for binaural entrainment seems reasonable since interhemispherical communication via the corpus callosum requires a long signal pathway influencing many other faculties. It certainly has interesting applications in sleep, learning, and awareness research. The long listening times required and exclusivity of ear channeling limit the potential use for sound design.

Psychotherapeutic Applications and Art

I will say very little on the topic of psychotherapeutic applications of sound (which is a shame because there are entire shelves of fascinating material to discuss). There is literature ranging from credible, scientifically sound studies to absolute bunk. We cannot ignore the deep emotional impact of sound and its potential effect on the well-being of the human mind and body, nor the fact that this clearly overlaps with artistic goals. As for its value, there is no doubt from the work done by Beth-Abraham, Nordoff-Robbins, Warwick University, and other institutions that sound and music offer extremely powerful therapeutic strategies. For sound designers involved in artistic projects I think this is actually a ripe area to draw from, since the goal is not just to augment a visual experience but to use sound in its own right to affect emotional change. Interesting writing on subjects from trauma recovery to the impact of environmental sound on learning, productivity, aggression, and attachment would make useful background studies for any sound designer. Notable authors include Lozanov (1978), Nordoff and Robbins (1971), Sacks (2007), Treasure (2007), Tomaino (2003), and Bonny (2002).

Cross-modal Perception

Recent discoveries are challenging the established idea of well-separated faculties (in the sense of Fodor 1983). Researchers (Wang and Barone 2008) have noticed that the visual cortex may be involved in sound processing, particularly in multi-sensory input. Moving objects in the peripheral visual field corresponding to sounds may affect enhanced auditory perception; and likewise, accompanying sounds may enhance or produce visual sensations. This is not the same as the often debilitating phenomenon of synesthesia, but may be related. In other experiments (Jousmaki and Hari 2006) connections between sound and touch have been established such that feeling can be influenced by sounds played at the same time. In other work (Schurmann et al. 2004) it has been shown that vibrations received through the hands or feet can influence the perception of loudness. These discoveries have interesting implications for film sound designers and game developers using force feedback devices.

SECTION 6.7

Sound, Language, and Knowledge

> Captain Jack stood on the deck of the Black Crow, a slight summer breeze wafted bubbles of drunken laughter from the saloon of the Eyepatch and Stump, and echos of shrieking seagulls haunted the cobbles of the old dockside . . . Yaaar!

Imagining Sound

Imagine yourself in a pirate film set in days of yore. On the quayside, watching Captain Jack's ship roll in to the harbour, you can hear the mumble and chatter of voices, the breeze in the rigging of ships, dogs barking in the streets. These are the same sounds our ancestors have been hearing for thousands of years; they have a firm basis in the physics and biology of our lives. When we use "sound words" to evoke a scene we deal with a powerful emotional device. Hearing is one of earliest developmental senses, as we listen even in the womb, and like smells (the olfactory senses), they invoke activity in deep and primal part of our brains that pictures do not. Our capacity for imagining sound is profound. If you concentrate you can almost *"hear"* sounds in your head, not only concrete memorised sounds but hypothetical ones and the abstract qualities of sounds as separate cognitive devices. For example, when reading we have an internal voice. Play with modifying that internal voice as you continue reading now. Try with an angry or happy voice. I like to read the newspapers in Homer Simpson's most sarcastic voice, because what they say is *always so true.*

Talking about Sound

Concentrate now on some everyday sounds like passing cars or animals. Or try some absurd, abstract sounds like paint drying. Obviously I have no idea what you're thinking, because our internal schemas and archetypes are quite unique. The problem then is how to move from an imagined sound to its realisation. Let's consider the means for expressing these imagined sounds. What words come to mind? How would you tell someone else what you're hearing in your head?

Noun Descriptions

Nouns are the enemy in sound design. When we say "airplane sound" it may invoke one of many different strong schemas that are all categorically "airplanes" but as different as apples and badgers. The Red Baron's Fokker triplane sounds nothing like a fighter jet. When we work from unqualified simple nouns, linguistic ambiguity makes them insufficient. In fact, sometimes the object actually has no sonic meaning in the description at all. The sound of "a dripping tap" has plenty to do with the bath material, depth of water, room reverberation, and so on, but rather little to do with taps. The same word means different things to different people. When I say "police siren" you might immediately hear a slow wail or a fast trumpeting sound, whatever best fits your strongest personal schema of that sound. In New York the sirens sound different from those in Berlin or Amsterdam, but we recognise each quite easily.

Adjective and Adjunctive Descriptions

Good sound words are adjectives. This is where richness is found in the English language to denote a quality of an otherwise ambiguous noun. A "hollow bell" suggests odd harmonics, since "hollow" sounds like oboes and empty tubes have that quality. Adjectives and adjuncts are more useful than nouns in sound description but less powerful than verbs. A good use of the adjectives "softness" and "hardness" for sound would convey the state of a material quite literally, while "plastic" and "springy" can be fairly reliably used to convey an expected degree of damping.

Gerund Verb Descriptions

Instead of having separate words for each sound in the world we have words that describe what they do more than what they are. When employing verbs for sound we often do so creatively, with like participles and gerund forms. So we have a pretty big vocabulary of hissing, whistling, groaning, creaking, scraping, farting, crackling, crunching ways to talk about sound. These verbs are a form of imperative and poetic knowledge, describing the thing that makes the sound in terms of what it does. This makes sense, because sound is a branch of dynamics: it is all about what happens when changes occur.

Onomatopoeia and Alliteration

Direct vocalisation of sounds is essential in the studio to communicate, and sound designers do it all the time. It is quite acceptable to use vocalised place-holders in a draft soundtrack by dubbing over the visuals. In fact this can create a very expressive guide. This is where your teachers were wrong, because reading comics is the only way to appreciate the vocabulary of "Twunk . . . boyoyoyoying!" Onomatopoeia and alliteration are used to convey the "flump" of a mattress and the "chitter-chatter" of an engine. Alliteration carries insistence, sequence, and timing. A "higgledypiggledy" sound suggests much about its structural design. Given the ineffability of sound there is nothing childish about such use, although some serious designers take a while to embrace the studio culture where it is acceptable to use such speech.

Reference Points

Traditional sound designers build up a vocabulary of reference sounds. Scooby-Doo bongos, the Wilhelm scream, light sabers, and so on are cultural and professional reference points used to label archetypal devices. These higher-level creative markers are not really part of synthetic sound design, but understanding them will greatly inform design choices.

Procedural Knowledge

Imagine that aliens came to watch cartoons with you and they want to know why Mr Bouncy makes a boinging noise when he jumps along the ground. You explain with great patience that it's not actually the sound Mr Bouncy makes, but a ruler being twanged on a desk. After explaining that a ruler is a 30cm piece of thin, stiff wood and a desk is a solid and heavy piece of furniture and that after pushing it down with your finger and suddenly releasing it you have to move the ruler while allowing it to vibrate, the aliens will be enlightened. They will have all the knowledge they need to make Mr Bouncy's sound, given desks, rulers, and fingers. We almost completely described the sound by describing the physical properties of the thing that made it, and the process by which it occurred. Its connotations and other signifiers are irrelevant.

Declarative Domain Knowledge

Part of the above involves *domain* knowledge about what things are, for example what a ruler is. Some of it, like desks and rulers, is common experience, but sound designers need to develop a good worldly knowledge of sonic objects. A composer presumably knows all the instruments of an orchestra and can refer to a cello instead of "the scrapey low-sounding thing." Sometimes this can be extremely detailed and specialised, such as knowing makes and models of steam whistles and Klaxon horns, or the precise architecture of a computer sound chip along with a particular hardware method it uses to create sounds.

Imperative Knowledge

These are observations about things that happen to make a sound. The way the ruler must be placed on the desk with some part of it fixed, and the displacement with a finger to excite motion, are *imperative statements*.

Poetic Knowledge

Poetic knowledge is about the intersections or extensions of categorical, procedural, and domain knowledge that are conveyed through metaphor and simile. It is about what something is "like." "Buzzing like bees" or "popping like a cork" are phrases binding domain reference points to abstract sound ideas that share something with them. Poetic knowledge defines the target by giving us something against which to compare it.

Categorical Knowledge

When disambiguating sounds we use more specific domain knowledge, usually related to the finer physical behaviour or origin of an object. We ask, for instance, is it a four-litre petrol engine, or a two-stroke motorbike engine? Is it a European long-tailed wibble-warbler or an African long-tailed wibble-warbler? Some of these details map directly onto sonic features, such as the tone of an engine or the chirps of a birdcall.

Weak Cultural Domain Knowledge

There are qualities that cannot be measured or universally agreed upon, but are nevertheless shared within groups. Some are weak and change with time or context. The definition of "dramatic" or "epic" is not very reliable. Certain terms enjoy periods of vogue within sectors of industry, and as such they are weak. Being asked for musical scores to be "cinematic" three times a day gets very annoying. Very weak terms like "black" should also be avoided in the studio, not because of racial connotations in this case, but because they are ambiguous to the point of being useless. "Black" can also mean depressive, or dark in tone; or it can mean strong and starkly defined. Weak cultural domain knowledge is occasionally useful as a buffer to communicate between groups who don't speak each other's language, like management and producers from different sectors of industry. The danger with vogue words is not only their ambiguity so much as a tendency for those who don't want to seem outsiders to adopt and blindly abuse them.

Strong Cultural Domain Knowledge

These are mildly quantifiable (ordinal or cardinal) context-dependent terms. They are well understood and useful for communication but still vague. What exactly is "allegro" or "purity"? Terms that come from classical music theory have very well-defined properties. Those translated from Italian map onto specific tempos and rhythms, so "tuneful and happy" isn't as ambiguous as you might think. The "consonance" of two notes or a chord in context can be defined well, but we should never forget that these terms are dependent on

Western culture and that a different tuning system or audience can change the interpretation.

Exercises

Exercise 1—Perception

It is very instructive to experience many of the psychology experiments referenced in this chapter. Hear for yourself the effects of masking, sequence fusion and fission, Gabor grains and Sheppard tones. See if you can locate psychoacoustic applets and data on the net, and compare your own experiences to those of a typical listener.

Exercise 2—Language

Take the role of the script writer and continue with the pirate story of "Old Blind Jack's Treasure." Try to make life easy for the sound designer; be playful with words and think of rich language to describe the things going on in the sound scene like "crackling logs," "groaning timbers," and "twittering wenches." Use analogy, metaphor, and onomatopoeia, to paint the sound scene in words.

Exercise 3—Knowledge and Communication

Without touching a synthesiser or microphone try to provide a formal specification of a sound. Give as many details as you can, procedural and technical, then swap specifications with a partner before trying to implement each other's sounds.

Acknowledgements

Thanks to Leon Van Noorden and Danijel Milosevic for help with this chapter and to Jeff Tackett for his MATLAB ISO266 function.

References

Books

Bonny, H. (2002). *Music and Conciousness: The Evolution of Guided Imagery and Music*. Barcelona.

Boulanger, R. C., et al. (2000). *The Csound Book*. MIT Press.

Bregman, A. S. (1990). *Auditory Scene Analysis: The Perceptual Organization of Sound*. MIT Press.

Chion, M. (1994). *Audio-Vision: Sound on Screen*. Columbia University Press.

Chomsky, N. (1957). *Syntactic Structures*. Mouton.

Fodor, J. A. (1983). *The Modularity of Mind*. MIT Press.

Hartmann, W. M. (2004). *Signals, Sound, and Sensation*. Springer/AIP Press.

Helmholtz, H. von (1863/2005). *On the Sensations of Tone as a Physiological Basis for the Theory of Music*. Kessinger.

Laban, R. v. (1988). *The Mastery of Movement*. Northcote House.

Lozanov, G. (1978). *Outlines of Suggestopedia*. Gordon & Breach.

McAdams, S., and Bigand, E. (1993). *Thinking in Sound: The Cognitive Psychology of Human Audition*. Oxford University Press.

Moore, B. C. J. (2003). *An Introduction to the Psychology of Hearing*. Academic Press.

Nordoff, P., and Robbins, C. (1971). *Music Therapy in Special Education*. John Day.

Sacks, O. (2007). *Musicophilia: Tales of Music and the Brain*. Vintage.

Schaeffer, P. (1977/2002). *Trait des objets musicaux*. Seuil.

Talbot Smith, M. (ed.) (1999). *Audio Engineer's Reference Book*. 2nd ed. Focal Press.

Treasure, J. (2007). *Sound Business*. Management Books.

Truax, B. (2000). *Acoustic Communication*. Praeger.

Warren, R. M. (1982). *Auditory Perception: A New Synthesis*. Pergamon Press.

Papers

Almonte, F., Jirsa, V. K., Large, E. W., and Tuller, B. (2005). "Integration and segregation in auditory streaming." *Physica D* 212: 137–159.

Beck, S. D. (2000). "Designing acoustically viable instruments in Csound." In R. C. Boulanger et al., *The Csound Book* (p. 157). MIT Press.

Bilsen, F. A. (1977). "Pitch of noise signals: Evidence for a central spectrum." *J. Acoust. Soc. Am.* 61: 150–161.

Birchfield, S. T., and Gangishetty, R. "Acoustic localisation by interaural level difference." IEEE Int. Conf. on Acoustics, Speech, and Signal Processing (ICASSP).

Bregman, A. S., and Dannenbring, G. (1973). "The effect of continuity on auditory stream segregation." *Percep. Psychophys.* 13: 308–312.

Broadbent, D. E., and Ladefoged, P. (1959). "Auditory perception of temporal order." *J. Acoust. Soc. Am.* 31: 1539.

Cosi, P., De Poli, G., and Lauzzana, G. (1994). "Auditory modelling and self-organizing neural networks for timbre classification." *J. New Music Res.* 23: 71–98.

Cramer, E. M., and Huggins, W. H. (1958). "Creation of pitch through binaural internaction." *J. Acoust. Soc. Am.* 61 413–417.

Crowder, R. G., and Morton, J. (1969). "Precategorical acoustic storage." *Percep. Psychophys.* 5: 365–373.

Darwin, C. J. (2005). "Simultaneous grouping and auditory continuity." *Percep. Psychophys.* 67(8): 1384–1390.

Field, J. M. (1993). "Effect of personal and situational variables upon noise annoyance in residential areas." *J. Acoust. Soc. Am.* 93: 2753–2763.

Fletcher, H., and Munson, W. A. (1933). "Loudness, its definition, measurement, and calculation." *J. Acoust. Soc. Am.* 5: 82–108.

Gabor, D. (1946). "Theory of communication." *J. IEE (London)* 93(26): 429–457.

Geddes, W. K. E. (1968). "The assessment of noise in audio frequncy circuits." Research report 1968/8-EL17, British Broadcasting Corporation, Engineering Division.

Grey, J. M. (1975). "Exploration of musical timbre." Stanford Univ. Dept. of Music Tech. Rep. STAN-M-2.

Hartmann, W. M. (1977). "The effect of amplitude envelope on the pitch of sine wave tones." *J. Acoust. Soc. Am.* 63: 1105–1113.

Huron, D. (2002). "Listening styles and listening strategies." Society for Music Theory 2002 Conference. Columbus, Ohio.

Huvenne, M., and Defrance, S. (2007). "On audiovisual composition: Research towards new terminology."

Jian-Yu, Lin, and Hartmann, W. M. (1997). "On the Duifhuis pitch effect." *J. Acoust. Soc. Am.* 101(2).

Jousmäki, V., and Hari, R. (1998). "Parchment-skin illusion: Sound-biased touch." *Curr. Biol.* 8(6).

Kendall, R., and Carterette, E. (1996). "Difference thresholds for timbre related to spectral centroid." In *Proc. 4th Int. Conf. on Music Perception and Cognition* (pp. 91–95). Montreal: ICMPC.

Leipp, E. (1977). "L'integrateur de densite spectrale, IDS et ses applications." *Bulletin du Groupe d'Acoustique Musicale* 94, laboratoire d'Acoustique Musicale.

Massaro, D. W. (1970). "Retroactive interference in short-term recognition memory for pitch." *J. Exper. Psychol.* 83: 32–39.

McCabe, S. L., and Denham, M. J. (1997). "A model of auditory streaming." *J. Acoust. Soc. Am.* 101: 1611–1621.

Miller, B. A., and Heise, G. A. (1950). "The trill threshold." *J. Acoust. Soc. Am.* 22: 637–638.

Moorer, J. A., Grey, J. M., and Snell, J. A. I. (1977–1978). "Lexicon of analyzed tones (parts I/II/III: [Violin tone] [clarinet and oboe tones] [the trumpet])." *Comp. Music J.* 1(2–3): 39–45, 12–29, 23–31.

Musso, M., Moro, A., Glauche, V., Ritjntjes, M., Reichenbach, J., Büched, C., and Weiller, C. (2003). "Broca's area and language instinct." *Nat. Neurosci.* 6: 774–781.

Plomp, R., and Levelt, W. J. M. (1965). "Tonal consonance and critical bandwidth." *J. Acoust. Soc. Am.* 38: 548–560.

Robinson, D. W., and Dadson, R. S. (1956). "A re-determination of the equal-loudness relations for pure tones." *Brit. J. Appl. Phys.* 7: 166–181.

Schürmann, M., Caetano, G., Hlushchuk, Y., Jousmäki, V., and Hari, R. (2006). "Touch activates human auditory corext." *NeuroImage* 30(4): 1325–1331.

Schürmann, M., Caetano, G., Jousmäki, V., and Hari, R. (2004). "Hands help hearing: Facilitatory audiotactile interaction at low sound-intensity levels." *J. Acoust. Soc. Am.* 115: 830–832.

Seebeck, A. (1841). "Beobachtungen über einige Bedingungen der Entstehung von Tonen." *Annal. Physik Chemie* 53: 417–436.

Sethares, W. A. (1993). "Local consonance and the relationship between timbre and scale." *J. Acoust. Soc. Am.* 94: 1218–1228.

Shepard, R. N. (1957). "Stimulus and response generalization." *Psychomet.* 22:325–345.

Shouten, J. F. (1940). "The residue: A new concept in subjective sound analysis." *Proc. of Koninklijke Nederlandse Akademie van Wetenschappen* 43: 356–365.

Tomaino, C. (2003). "Rationale for the inclusion of music therapy in PS Section T of the minimum data set 3.0 (Nursing home resident assessment and care screening)." Supp. to information from the American Music Theory Association, December.

Tuuri, K., Mustonen, M.-S., and Pirhonen, A. (2007). "Same sound different meanings: A novel scheme for modes of listening." 2nd Audio Mostly Conference on Interaction with Sound. Ilmenau, Germany.

van Noorden, L. P. A. S. (1975). "Temporal coherence in the perception of tone sequences." Technische Hogeschool Eindhovern, the Netherlands.

Wang, Y., and Barone, P. (2008). "Visuo-auditory interactions in the primary visual cortex of the behaving monkey: Electrophysiological evidence." *BMC Neurosci.* 9.

Warren, R. M., Obusek, C. J., and Ackroff, J. M. (1972). "Auditory induction: Perceptual synthesis of absent sounds." *Science* 176: 1149–1151.

Wessel, D. L. (1973). "Psychoacoustics and music: A report from Michigan State University." *PAGE: Bull. of the Comp. Arts Soc.* 30.

Wessel, D. L. (1976). "Perceptually based controls for additive synthesis." In *Int. Comp. Mus. Conf. (ICMC).* MIT Press.

Wessel, D. L. (1979). "Timbre space as a musical control structure." *Comp. Music J.* 2(3).

Wessel, D. L., and Grey, J. M. (1978). "Conceptual structures for the representation of musical material." IRCAM Technical Report No. 14.

Online Resources

<http://www.stockhausen.org>

David Worrall Notes on psychophysics from Australian Centre for the Arts and Technology, Australian National University: <http://www.avatar.com.au/courses/PPofM>

7
Digital Signals

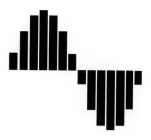

Signals

Transducers

A transducer is a machine[1] designed to convert changes in one kind of energy to changes in another kind. A video camera *encodes* changes in light into electrical *signals*. A microphone *encodes* changes in air pressure into electrical signals. Most transducers have an opposite that behaves the other way about, to *decode* signals back into the original energy form. A projector turns electrical video signals into light patterns and a loudspeaker turns electrical variations into sound.

Electronic, Continuous Signals

Just as sound is the human experience of waves, a *signal* is a machine representation of waves. A signal is a changing value, usually electrical, that represents something like amplitude, slope, or frequency. Natural signals, like the voltage on a capacitor, or the position of the sun in the sky, change so immeasurably smoothly that we say they vary *continuously*. Between every tiny division we could possibly measure more detail, more change within change. Mathematically speaking, we require *real* numbers to describe these signals.

Sound Transducers

There are many ways to transduce the vibrations that make sound. Electrostatic transducers use crystals or thin insulators which can be made to move or change shape when a high-voltage electric field is applied. Likewise, when moved they produce changes in an electrical field. Electromagnetic transducers use magnets and coils of wire to convert movement into electricity or vice versa. Resistive transducers rely on changes in material properties when a force is applied, such as carbon which changes its electrical conductivity with pressure.

Information

If a phenomenon like a sound or image can be converted into something else, and later that thing can be used to recreate the original phenomenon, what

---

1. A "machine" is defined as something that converts one *form* of energy to another. Notice carefully the words used—a "transducer" converts *changes* in energy.

is the intermediate thing? According to Shannon and Weaver (Shannon 1948; Weaver and Shannon 1963) it is *information*. Information can exist in the here and now, as *real-time signals* or as a pattern stored somewhere as a recording which can be replayed to produce the original real-time signal. There are always two parts to information. One is public, explicit, and sent over a *channel*. We call it *data*. The other is a private, implicit part that must be shared by both encoder and decoder in order to make sense of the data. This part describes the *format* of the data; in information-speak, it attaches *semantics* to *syntax*. In other words, without understanding what the data means we cannot decode it. The data *represents* a real signal. It is not an actual signal, just as the words printed on this page are not the actual thoughts in my mind as I write. As you read these words the format that we both share (an understanding of English) allows you to decode them into thoughts in your head which, hopefully, approximate my own ideas.

Representing Signals

The most common and useful representation of sound vibrations is a displacement graph. It shows the physical distance some point has moved away from a its rest point, at some time. If we make it correspond directly to the position of a loudspeaker cone, by turning it into an electrical current and passing it through a coil in a magnetic field, the displacement data can be used to reconstruct the sound. Hopefully it will be the same sound as would be heard if you had your ear close to that point where the microphone recorded it. This will happen when it is replayed at the same rate as it was recorded. You can see a displacement graph in figure 7.1. Time moves from left to right along the x-axis numbered from 0 to 10. Let's assume these numbers represent

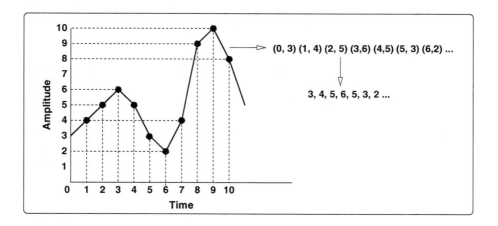

Figure 7.1
Displacement graph representing part of a sound.

milliseconds. Amplitude, or displacement, represented by an electrical signal is marked on the y-axis going from 0 to 10. Let's assume this represents volts.

Unlike real signals, digital sound signals are *sampled*. A stream of numbers called *samples* is captured or played back at a certain rate, called the *sampling rate*. Sampling gives us discontinuous or discrete signals where each step is a value that represents an amplitude at a single point in time. Obviously this means we throw away some information since there are some places on the graph, between the sample points, which are not encoded. However, with enough discrete sample points it's possible to accurately encode a sound signal. How many is enough? Sampling theory says that we need at least twice the number of sample points per second as the highest frequency in a signal. So to cover the human hearing range of 0Hz to 20,000Hz we need 40,000 sample points every second. Shown next to the graph is a list of time value pairs: (0,3)(1,4)(2,5), and so on. Because the time axis increments by one on each step we can ignore time and make it implicit, so we can just store the sequence as (3, 4, 5 ...). So digital sound is just a sequence of numbers. Each number represents a possible position for the diaphragm in your loudspeakers or headphones. The highest and lowest number that can be represented sets the *dynamic range* of our sound. A speaker can only move so far before it breaks, so sound cards and amplifiers are designed to limit movement to a maximum value called the *full-scale deflection*.

Digital Encoding

The range of numbers representing the signal amplitude determines the *dynamic range* that can be encoded. Storing data as binary means that if n bits are used to store each amplitude value, $(2^n) - 1$ possible values can be represented. Too few bits cause *quantisation distortion*, which makes the sound grainy and lacking in detail. With 16 bits we have 65,535 possible values, and with 32 bits we get 4,294,967,295 values. Today many digital audio systems operate with 64 bits. To get the dynamic range of a digital encoding system in decibels we can assume that if one bit represents the threshold of hearing, then the formula

$$\text{range} = 20\log_{10}(2^n - 1) \approx 6.0206n \text{ dB} \tag{7.1}$$

gives a dynamic range of 98dB for 16 bits, 192dB for 32 bits, and interestingly for 64 bits we get 385dB, far more than the possible dynamic range of natural sounds. So two variables determine the quality of a digital signal: the sampling rate which sets the highest frequency we can capture, and the bit depth which determines the quantisation resolution. A typical high-quality digital audio system uses a sampling rate of 48kHz or 96kHz with a bit depth of 32 bits.

Digital-to-Analog Conversion

In a moment we will look at how analog signals are converted to digital numbers, but before doing so it makes sense to explore the opposite process. Recall that binary numbers consist of only ones and zeros, like the four-bit number 1001. Moving right to left, each digit represents an increasing power of two,

1, 2, 4, 8 ..., so 1001 represents one 8, no 4 or 2, and one 1, which make a total of 9. So, to convert a binary number to its ordinary numerical value we add each 1 or 0 weighted by its position value. The circuit shown in figure 7.2 does this using resistors. If two resistors R1 and R2 are placed between a voltage V and zero volts they will divide the voltage in a ratio. If R1 connects to the voltage source and R2 to zero volts then the voltage between them will be $V \times R2/(R1+R2)$. The resistors at the right in figure 7.2 form what is called an R2R ladder, which divides the voltage into $1/2V$, $1/4V$, $1/8V$, ..., halving it each time. The transistors T0, T1, T2 act as switches, controlled by a bit value, to connect these voltage sources to the same wire where they are summed. So, assume the supply voltage is 16V; then the 3-bit pattern 101 will produce a total voltage of

$$(1 \times 16/2) + (0 \times 16/4) + (1 \times 16/8) = 8 + 0 + 2 = 10\text{V} \qquad (7.2)$$

In this case the *least significant bit* represents 2V, and the binary number 101, which represents a denary value of 5, produces 10V. In practice a digital-to-analog converter (DAC) will have between 16 and 24 bits, and the resistors will be extremely accurate laser trimmed, thermally compensated devices built into an integrated circuit.

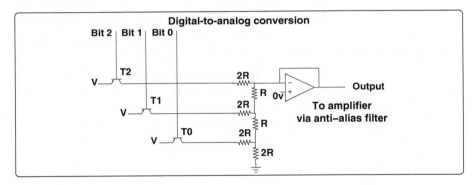

Figure 7.2
Digital-to-analog conversion using a resistor ladder.

Analog-to-Digital Conversion

Now we can look at analog-to-digital conversion, because one easy way to understand this uses a DAC. In figure 7.3 there is a DAC connected to a binary counter. The clock that drives the counter runs much faster than the sampling rate. On every clock cycle the counter either increments or decrements depending on which input is selected. These inputs are fed from a comparator, a circuit that compares the present input voltage with the output of the DAC. If the input voltage is lower than the DAC output the counter decreases, and

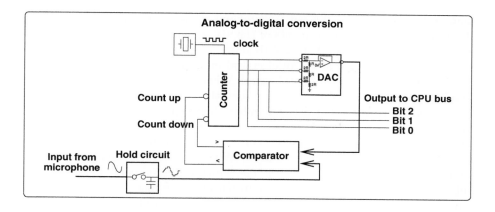

Figure 7.3
Analog-to-digital conversion by approximation.

it increases if the input voltage is higher. Thus the counter converges on the binary representation of the instantaneous input voltage. When the counter doesn't change anymore, the binary number at its output is sent to the CPU as the result. To briefly hold the input voltage steady a *sample hold* stage is applied while convergence takes place.

Digital Signal Processing

Continuous, analog signals from a microphone are encoded with an analog-to-digital converter (ADC) and turned back into an analog signal so we can hear them by a digital-to-analog converter (DAC). Due to technology limitations most of these are 24-bit. Which raises the question, why use a 32- or 64-bit representation if the input and output are less accurate? Surely the processing only need be as good as the weakest link in the chain? The answer is that processing digital signals leads to errors, such as *truncation* or *rounding* errors. Using 64 bits allows them to be added (mixed) or divided (attenuated) with better accuracy.

Floating Point Normalised Form

In fact for most digital signal processing (DSP) operations we don't actually represent samples as integers 0 to 4294967295. Instead *floating point* (decimal point) numbers in the range −1.0 to +1.0 are used. A normalised signal is one which occupies the greatest possible dynamic range, so that the highest part of the wave and the lowest part fit perfectly within the dynamic range. A normalised signal gives the best resolution, because it makes best use of the available accuracy, thus reducing errors due to quantisation. In Pure Data, signals have an absolute dynamic range of 2.0, between −1.0 and +1.0. The representation of a signal from microphone to floating point digital data is shown in figure 7.4. Displacements of the air are converted to a voltage by the microphone, in this case 0V to 2V (it doesn't really matter exactly what this range is, but 2V is typical for an electrical microphone signal), and then by a 24-bit ADC into a sampled digital signal. When moving from a lower bit depth to a higher one the usual method is to pad the less significant bits with zeros. On the right you can see a list of numbers between −1.0 and +1.0 typical of the way digital sound data is stored. A value of 1.0 represents the loudspeaker cone pushed outwards as far as it will go, and −1.0 for where the cone has moved inwards to its furthest position. When no signal is being sent to the loudspeaker, the cone rests in the middle, which will happen for a value of zero. Software and hardware limits signals to within the full-scale deflection of the sound system to ensure nothing breaks, so if we accidentally send a value of 2.0 it is limited to 1.0 and no harm is caused.

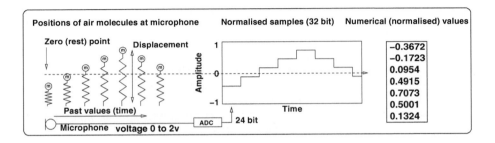

Figure 7.4
Sampling using normalised floating point numbers.

Smoothing Samples

A frequently asked question is "What about the gaps between samples?" How does a changing sequence of numbers become a continuous signal again to make sound? The DAC is part of a sound card which does two other things for us. One is to hold sample levels shown in figure 7.5(A) at the last value so that we obtain a waveform that looks like a rising and falling staircase shown in figure 7.5(B). The time between each step will be 1/`sample rate`. A low pass filter with a cutoff of half the sampling frequency is then applied, which smooths out the steps. You have probably seen filters do this in graphics applications by using Bezier or spline functions. The result is a smoothly varying sound waveform like that shown in figure 7.5(C). We will not go into any discussion of sampling theory here, but note that `sampling frequency/2` is a special number called the *Nyquist point* and is the maximum frequency of any sound that can be encoded for a given sampling rate.

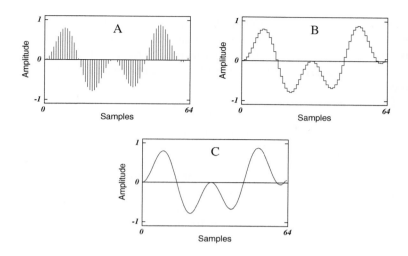

Figure 7.5
Digital audio signals as sampled numbers. A: Raw samples. B: Step function. C: Smooth filtered output.

SECTION 7.2

Graphs

As we know, a sound waveform is a pattern of pressure changes in time, and can be drawn as a two-dimensional picture or graph with time as one axis and amplitude as the other. When we plot amplitude against time this way it's called a *time domain* view of the wave. We will meet some other representations of signals in this book which are helpful to see what is happening in a sound.

Spectra

A sound wave can contain more than one frequency. The spectrum of a composite wave is a two-dimensional representation of the frequencies it contains and their relative amounts at some point in time. When we plot amplitude against frequency we call this the *frequency domain* view of a wave. A spectrum plot is the measured values of each frequency occurring within some time window, so it is a short-term snapshot of the frequencies at some point in the sound. There are two kinds of spectrum plot. Most times we only use the type that shows the *"real"* part of a spectrum, one that does not contain phase information.[2]

---

2. A spectrum that contains real and imaginary parts captures the phase of each frequency too. From these two pieces of information it is possible to reconstruct the waveform exactly. The original waveform cannot be accurately reconstructed from only the real spectrum, so it represents a kind of data loss.

Many time domain waveforms may have the same real spectrum so there are more unique time domain waveforms than real spectra. A short segment of a bass guitar waveform is shown on the left in figure 7.6. It is about 0.01s long. Notice that it swings negative and positive of the zero (rest point) and is encoded in a normalised range or −1.0 to +1.0. Next to it is a spectrum snapshot. There is no time axis in the spectrum; it only represents the frequencies that exist in the window to the left. The y-axis shows the relative amplitudes of several frequencies from 0 (none present) to 1.0 (which is scaled to fit the strongest frequency). Along the x-axis are frequencies from 0Hz (DC) to 4kHz. You can see two important things from this graph. First, the amplitude at 0Hz is not zero, which means there is a small DC offset to the waveform within the sampled area (which is normal—since we picked an arbitrary segment to analyse), and second, the frequencies seem to be spaced regularly—which is something else we might expect to see from a periodic waveform.

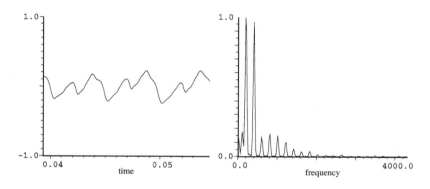

Figure 7.6
A time domain graph of a section of bass waveform and its spectrum.

Spectrograms

A spectrum plot isn't enough to capture all of a sound; for that we have spectrograms. In real sounds the spectrum changes in time too. The shifting frequencies over time create movement within the sound. A spectrogram is a series of spectrum plots laid out in time as a surface or as light or dark areas on a 2D map. Time moves along the x-axis and the other denotes frequency. The intensity of any frequency at some time is given by the brightness or darkness of a pixel at the appropriate coordinates. In figure 7.7 there is a longer (0.06s) section of the same bass waveform. Its spectrogram is shown on the right. In this case *darker* areas indicate a stronger frequency. There are some things we can see from this graph. First, not all the frequencies remain strong throughout the sound; some decay away. Second, there is a pitch change. Notice that the frequencies slope

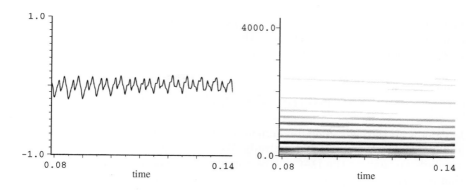

Figure 7.7
A longer piece of bass waveform and a spectrogram of the same period.

down slightly towards the end. Lastly, there is a grey area at the bottom of the
plot indicating some noisy low-frequency components.

Waterfall Plots

Probably the best way to visualise an entire sound is using a waterfall plot. You
should practice looking at these and getting a feel for how to read them. It is
essentially the same as the spectrogram but plots the wave as a 3D surface. In
figure 7.8 the left frame shows a time domain plot of a complete bass note that
lasts about 0.3s. On the right is a waterfall plot. Because it has been rotated
so we can see it better, the frequency and amplitude axes are meaningless. The
scales only makes sense when the plot is viewed from the side or above. In the

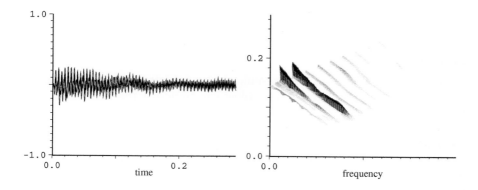

Figure 7.8
The entire bass note and its waterfall spectrogram.

view shown, from slightly above and to one side, we see that the strengths of frequencies vary with the height of the surface. This is a nice way to see the relative evolution of the components.

SECTION 7.3

Generating Digital Waveforms

Let's now go through some fundamental concepts. We want to understand how audio signals are constructed digitally. We will think for a moment about how numbers are sent to the DAC in the sound card. Then we will look at a collection of "primary" signals which introduce some interesting concepts. Each has at least one special property.

Generating Samples

Let us assume we have a function, a little piece of computer code that can send a number to the DAC. We call it **out()**. Whatever number (called the function argument) goes in the brackets gets sent, so **out(0.5)** sends 0.5 to the soundcard. Consider this very simple pseudocode program:

```
while(1){
    out(0.0);
}
```

Having 1 as the condition for a while loop means it will perform the instructions within its braces forever. There is only one instruction: to send a single sample with the value 0.0 to the sound card DAC. If we ran this program we would quickly see a problem. The sound card would be overwhelmed with data and cause the program to crash with a "buffer overflow" or similar report. The problem is that the DAC requires data to be given at a constant rate, perhaps 44,100 or 48,000 samples per second. One thing we could do is insert a useless instruction after the output function to waste some time. That's a bad idea for many reasons. First, it will tie up the computer doing nothing useful most of the time. Second, when we need to do some computations to make sound they will also take some time, so we would have to constantly adjust the waiting time.

Buffering

To avoid this timing mess we use buffers. You will often see controls for your sound card or audio programs that allow you to adjust the buffer settings. A buffer is like a queue of things called *blocks* that the supplying program puts at one end and the consuming program or device takes off the other. To reduce the number of times this has to happen it's better that each block contains more than one sample, so each program can operate on a bunch of samples at a time. A typical choice of block size is 64 samples. So long as the buffer is reasonably full both programs can go about their business in their own time. If the buffer gets too empty then the sound card can tell the sound-generating program to make more blocks. If the buffer gets too full then the sound card can ask it to slow down. So long as the buffer has something in it the DAC will have something to do. To ask the generating program for another block the sound card *calls a function*. This *call back* function fills up a block with new data and passes it back, where it gets appended to the end of the buffer.

```
void  fillblock ()
{
int  sample  =  63;
float  block [64];
   while ( sample −−){
     block [ sample ]  =  0.0;
     }
}
```

In the pseudo code[3] snippet above our call back function is called `fillblock()`, which stuffs an array of 64 floating point numbers with zeros. The current sample is decremented on each pass through the loop and the loop exits when `sample` is zero. The only thing that can go wrong is if the generating program is so busy it cannot supply new blocks in time. Then we get stutters, clicks, and dropouts as the DAC starves and stops outputting any audio.

The Sound of Zero (Silence)

So, to make sound we send streams of numbers wrapped up in blocks. A stream of blocks containing all zeros like above will make no sound. This is how we make silence. Why bother to point this out? Well, many assume that when the sound card is silent it is receiving no data, but that is not true. Once a sound-generating program connects to the DAC it sends a constant stream of data, even if the values of it are zero. Within the programs we make this will also be true: even when there is apparently nothing happening, blocks are still flowing.

The Sound of One (Constants)

Let's assume a sound synthesis program is idle and spewing out zero-filled blocks. To begin with, at time 0.0, the loudspeaker will be in its central position, receiving no voltage, and all will be silent. The moment we issue an instruction to send a value of 1.0 to the output we hear a loud click. Consider this program, which fills up blocks forever. It has a variable `time` to keep track of the total number of samples output. Once the time passes a threshold it stops filling the blocks with zero and starts filling them with 1.0 instead. The output is shown in the graph in figure 7.9.

```
float  block [64];
int  sample;
int  time  =  0;
```

---

3. This "C-like" pseudo language assumes conditional evaluation with post decrement and array numbering from zero.

```
while(1){
    fillblock();
}

void fillblock()
{
sample = 63;
  while(sample--) {
        if (time < 14700) {
            block[sample] = 0.0;
        }
        else {
            block[sample] = 1.0;
        }
        time++;
    }
}
```

The loudspeaker cone moves from its rest position quickly outwards to its maximum. This happens at about 0.3 seconds in the graph shown in figure 7.9. It will stay there without moving for all time. Due to space limitations in the book we cut out most of the "all time" part, and the graph shows 1 second of output. After hearing the first click there is silence. We don't keep hearing the number 1.0 as a sound. Even though the system of software, sound card, and amplifier keep telling the loudspeaker cone to stay pushed outwards we hear nothing. In truth, the speaker cone does not stay pushed out all this time, which would be very harmful. The sound card and amplifier take care of blocking any constant "DC" (direct current) signals. So, let's ask the question, what is the sound of one? The answer is "no sound at all." A constant-valued signal makes no sound. Sound is about changes. The only sound we have heard so far is a brief click, known as a *step impulse*, when the output suddenly changed from 0.0 to 1.0. Measuring change is to talk about *frequency*, and here we shall

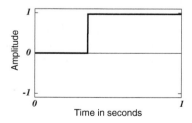

Figure 7.9
A constant signal.

note that a DC signal has a frequency of zero: it sounds like nothing, no matter what its continuous value is. The silence generated by a constant value of 1.0 is indistinguishable from the silence made by a constant value of 0.0.

Moving Signals

Let's look now at a signal that keeps on moving. If sound is change then let's keep our signal changing and hear the result. If we start with the number zero and repeatedly add a small value to it, say 0.001 on each loop of the program, it will grow in size. Now we will have a signal that moves upwards, but keeps on growing. It will quickly reach 1.0, then exceed the full-scale deflection of the system, which we don't want. We want to keep it moving within the range of 0.0 to 1.0, so we add a new instruction to reset the sample value back to 0.0 every time it exceeds a threshold. Our pseudocode becomes:

```
float block[64];
float phase = 0;
int sample;
    while(1){
        fillblock();
    }


void fillblock()
{
sample = 63;
    while(sample--) {
        block[sample] = phase;
        phase = phase + 0.01;
            if (phase > 0.99) {
                phase = 0.0;
            }
    }
}
```

```
O━┳ Keypoint
Sound is a branch of dynamics: it's all about changes.
```

Running this program you should hear a buzz at a constant frequency. Because it moves in a pattern our ears can interpret it as a sound. The pattern repeats over and over, so it is a *periodic signal*. On each cycle the same thing happens. The signal, as shown in figure 7.10, starts off at 0.0, rises until it passes 0.99, and then returns to zero. The amount added on each step, the slope of the signal, determines how long the cycle will last. In other words, it controls the frequency. The name we give this waveform is a *phasor*.

A phasor is sometimes called a *sawtooth wave* for obvious reasons, but strictly it is not. It has one unusual property: that it is asymmetrical and

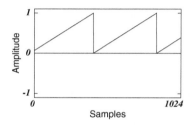

Figure 7.10
A phasor signal.

does not go below 0.0. Because it moves between 0.0 and 1.0 its average value is not zero. It is easy to turn a phasor into a true sawtooth wave, which we will do later, but it's worth noting the purpose of this object is far more fundamental than making buzzing sounds, precisely because of this range. Often we use a phasor as a timebase or input to other objects to produce more complex waveforms. Many sounds you construct will start with this essential operation. A phasor embodies the idea of a rotation in time when we allow the interval between 0.0 and 1.0 to represent an angle over the range of 360°. Mathematically, it is a function of time (t)

$$f(\omega t) = t - \lfloor t \rfloor \tag{7.3}$$

where $\lfloor t \rfloor$ is the floor function giving the largest integer less than or equal to t. So, as t grows $f(\omega t)$ repeats and is never greater than 1.0.

Remember that for periodic functions we are only really interested in what happens over one cycle, because all the others are copies of the same thing. A phasor gives us a signal representing time that is bounded. It describes one period and then we reset it to zero and reuse the same range. Without it we would run into computational problems using an ever-increasing raw time value t because our floating point representation would eventually be insufficient.

Sinusoidal Waves

We have seen simple harmonic motion where each point is being pulled back to its equilibrium position by a force proportional to its displacement, and we have recognised that this is fundamental to sound production. The next snippet of pseudo code creates a signal of the periodic function of time

$$f(t) = \cos(\omega t) \tag{7.4}$$

Here the ω represents 2π radians (360°), to fully cover the domain of the cos() function—in other words, one full cycle.

```
float  PI = 3.14159265358;
float  TWOPI = 2.0 * PI;
float  DELTA = 0.001;
void  fillblock()
{
sample = 63;
   while(sample--) {
        block[sample] = cos(TWOPI * phase);
        phase = phase + DELTA;
           if (phase > 0.99999) {
               phase = 0.0;
           }
      }
}
```

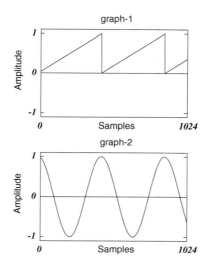

Figure 7.11
Cosine from phasor.

As seen in figure 7.12 it is identical to the graph seen by projecting the motion of a point on a rotating wheel by viewing it from the side and plotting this against time. This geometrical equivalence gives us a way to compute the waveform. The displacement in one axis of a point rotating in a plane can be obtained by taking the cosine of the angle through which it has changed. Because **sine** and **cosine** are periodic functions we may use a phasor to index one full cycle. The phasor, shown above the cosinusoidal waveform in figure 7.11, resets at the point the function wraps. Notice that we use radians instead of degrees in most computer code, so a multiplier of $2 \times \pi$ is used. Notice also that

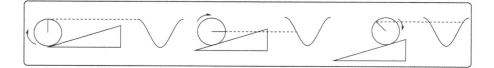

Figure 7.12
Relationship between phasor and angle.

we always try to minimise redundant computations inside the inner loop, so the variable TWOPI is calculated only once outside the function. To help visualise this function, imagine a cylinder or wheel moving over a surface that represents the slope of the phasor as shown in figure 7.12. The length of the diagonal slope will be exactly the circumference of the wheel, $2\pi \times r$ for a radius r. Each time one phasor cycle happens it advances the wheel by one rotation. We are simulating something that turns a linear motion into a spinning motion. Notice that one cycle swings both positive and negative of the waveform centre line. Half of the range of the phasor is the producing the positive part, and half is producing the negative part. For a cosine wave the wheel starts with pointing to 12 o'clock, and for a sine wave the wheel begins pointing at 9 o'clock. The difference between cosine and sine is the phase on which they start.

> **O━ Keypoint**
> The phasor is a fundamental source from which we can derive all other periodic waveforms.

Complex Harmonic Motion

Adding together some simple waves gives us more complex waves, a process called *mixing*. Each wave rides on top of the other so that the height of the total wave is the sum of them both. This is the process of superposition which we have already met and see naturally with water waves. For two separate frequencies we will use two phasors. Later we will see how several harmonically related sinusoids can be derived from a single phasor.

```
float  phase1 = 0;
float  phase2 = 0;
float  PI = 3.14159265358;
float  TWOPI = 2.0 * PI;
float  DELTA1 = 0.001;
float  DELTA2 = 0.024;
void  fillblock()
```

```
{
sample = 63;
float sum;
  while(sample--) {
      sum = (cos(TWOPI * phase1)+cos(TWOPI * phase2));
      block[sample] = 0.5 * sum;
      phase1 = phase1 + DELTA1;
      phase2 = phase2 + DELTA2;
        if (phase1 >= 1.0) {
           phase1 = 0.0;
        }
        if (phase2 >= 1.0) {
           phase2 = 0.0;
        }
   }
 }
}
```

The maximum possible value for the combined amplitude is the sum of the amplitudes of the two waves being mixed. Because each is in the range −1.0 to 1.0 (a peak-to-peak range of 2.0), then the minimum and maximum will be −2.0 and 2.0 (a total peak-to-peak range of 4.0). So, when we mix signals we follow the addition part with a scaling part to put the signal back into the correct range, which we have done here by dividing by two. The waveform and spectrum of a mixture two sinusoidal waves, one at a frequency of 900Hz and

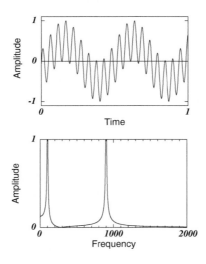

Figure 7.13
900Hz + 100Hz.

the other at 100Hz, are shown in figure 7.13. Notice it is a repeating waveform, but unlike the single cosine wave or phasor this waveform doesn't repeat at nice intervals where it coincides with zero quite so often; it repeats every 25 cycles, which is the lowest common factor of 900 and 100.

O🔑 Keypoint

All sounds except the cosine/sine wave are made up of several frequencies, which form a spectrum.

Randomly Moving Signals

Let's consider another fundamental signal, one that has a random number for every sample, called *noise*. It makes the fizzing, whooshing sound of TV static or air escaping under high pressure. If the numbers are completely random we call it *white noise*. The range of random values is between -1.0 and 1.0, so white noise is symmetrical. Noise tries to fill up every part of the graph, which means white noise actually shows up mostly black in the waveform graph. And, theoretically, it contains every frequency, so it shows up as a dark area in a spectrum snapshot. These are shown in figure 7.14. Some (rather inefficient) pseudo code for generating 32-bit symmetrical white noise is given next. We generate random numbers in the range 0 to 2, then subtract 1 to make them symmetrically normalised. More commonly, a method based on a recurring formula and known as *linear congruential pseudo-random generation* is directly implemented. It is much faster than "high-quality" random number generators and therefore fine for sound. For a good discussion of noise see Smith 2003; ffitch 2000.

```
srand ();
void fillblock ()
{
int random_number;
float normalised_rand;
sample = 63;
   while(sample−−) {
        random_number = rand() % 4294967295;
        normalised_rand = (random_number/2147483648) − 1.0;
        block[sample] = normalised_rand;
   }
}
```

On each step the sample value is a random number, independent of any before it. Because of this, noise is nonperiodic by definition. In fact, computers cannot generate truly random numbers, so *pseudo-random noise* is used. This is a very long and complex repeating sequence with values that are so hard to predict they seem random. So, a necessary first step in the above code is for the **srand()** function to "seed" the generator used by another function **rand()**,

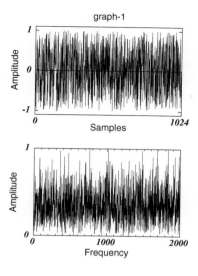

graph-1

Figure 7.14
White noise.

thus giving it a more unpredictable output. Why is white noise white? One way of looking at it is to think about the frequencies that are in the mix. Perfect white noise has an equal mixture of all the frequencies in the human hearing range. This corresponds well to the effect of combining all the colours in the human visual range as light to get white light. In theory, noise has the property that it contains all those frequencies equally at all times. This is impossible in reality; different blends of frequencies fade in and out. At any moment a spectrum snapshot will show different patterns, but on average all frequencies are equally represented in any short time. Thinking of the graph as a photograph, the longer we "leave the film exposed for," by using a longer average, the more we see the graph fill up until it is a steady line high on the scale, showing that on average all the frequencies appear equally.

O━┱ Keypoint

Noise contains a great many frequencies, theoretically all frequencies.

Suddenly Moving Signals

Another fundamental signal to look at is the *impulse*. We don't call it an "impulse wave," because technically it's not a wave. Like noise it is not periodic, but unlike noise, which is a continuous signal, an impulse exists for just a moment in time. If we set only one sample in the stream to 1.0 while all the rest are zero we get a very short and rather quiet click. It sounds a bit like the step impulse we first heard as a signal change between 0.0 and 1.0, but this kind of impulse is a single sample of 1.0 that returns immediately to 0.0. The time domain graph and spectrum snapshot are shown in figure 7.15. The code sets a single bit to 1.0 (in this case in the middle of the graph to make it easier to see) and all previous and subsequent bits to zero. This is sometimes called the *Kronecker delta function.*

```
float block[64];
int sample;
int time = 0;
    while(1){
        fillblock ();
    }

void fillblock ()
{
sample = 63;
    while(sample--) {
        if (time == 512) {
            block[sample] = 1.0;
        }
        else {
            block[sample] = 0.0;
        }
        time++;
    }
}
```

Impulses behave a bit like noise by trying to fill up the entire spectrum with frequencies. Again, they are a mathematical abstraction, and real impulses do not behave exactly as their theoretical models. They are revealing tools, or analytical things for the most part, but they are very useful in sonic construction. But here's a riddle. How can all the frequencies happen at once in time? That's impossible. Frequency is about changes in time, and if time diminishes to zero then surely there can be *no* frequencies? Well, this isn't a book about wave mechanics, so let's not go too deeply into uncertainty principles, but you may have realised that the more we know about the precise position of a signal in space-time the less we know about its frequency, and vice versa. In reality the frequencies *appear* to be there because of the sharpness of an impulse.

In the spectrum graph you can see the frequencies the impulse occupies. Actually this is partly an artefact of the measuring process, the Fourier algorithm, but that's good because it shows us that the theory of impulses as packets of "all frequencies" is consistent with itself and other parts of DSP theory. The dark band is the average level of the graph; if we could measure the average of all the frequencies in a set of perfect impulses it would be a straight line in this dark area, showing an equal representation for all frequencies. But the best way

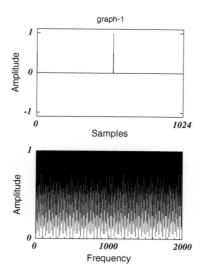

Figure 7.15
An impulse spike.

to show that an impulse is made of all frequencies is to work in reverse. If we add all frequencies then surely we can make an impulse. Let's begin summing individual sine waves with the same phase, as shown in figure 7.16. With only two we see that the time domain amplitude peaks where they reinforce each other. Each time we divide the total amplitude by the number of contributions to the sum, so that the signal will fit into our graph. With 4 and then 8 waves notice how the peak becomes increasingly narrower and the other surrounding waves become smaller. Eventually, with thousands of waves added together in phase, we end up with zero everywhere except in one place, where we get a single impulse spike.

O━┱ Keypoint
Very fast, short sounds are called *impulses* and contain all frequencies in an instant.

Slowly Moving Signals

At the other end of the time scale from impulses are signals that change very slowly but are not constants. Instead of taking milliseconds to change they take seconds or even minutes to conduct their movement. Often these are used to control the loudness or spectra of other signals. They move too slowly to be

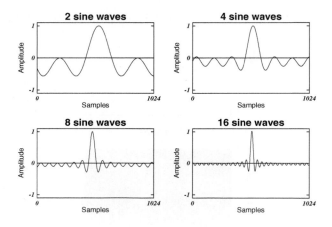

Figure 7.16
Impulse as a sum of all frequencies.

heard as sounds themselves and are referred to as *envelope* or *line* signals in many situations. The pseudo code listing shows a very simple attack and decay line that rises to 1.0 and then falls to 0.0 over a certain number of samples.

```
float  block[64];
float  env = 0;
int  time = 0;
float  attacktime = 256;
float  decaytime = 768;
float  attackslope = 1.0/attacktime;
float  decayslope = 1.0/decaytime;
int  sample;
while(1)  fillblock();

void  fillblock()
{
sample = 63;
  while(sample--) {
      block[sample] = env;
        if (time < attacktime) {
            env = env + attackslope;
        }
        else if (time < attacktime + decaytime) {
            env = env - decayslope;
        }
  }
}
```

We can use a signal as an envelope to modify the volume of another sound. To do this we multiply the line output by the signal we want to modify. We say that one signal *modulates* the other. The line signal is modulating a 100Hz sine wave in the waveform plot of figure 7.17. It produces a symmetrical signal because the sine signal contains positive and negative values but the envelope is only positive. A positive number times a negative one gives a negative one, so an envelope signal in the range 0.0 to 1.0 works fine as a volume control.

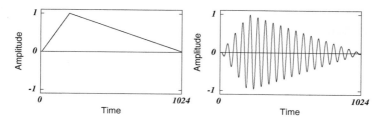

Figure 7.17
Envelope control signals.

Signal Programming Abstraction

So, how do we multiply a line generator by a wave generator in code? Suppose we had already defined a sine wave generator as a function taking a frequency argument, and a line generator taking attack and decay times. How would each function know the global time? It would be tedious to pass it to every function.

```
while(sample--) {
    block[sample] = line(10,100,time)*sinewave(440,time);
}
```

What we really want is a much better language than C for sound design. Low-level languages are great for efficiently designing basic functions, or objects, sometimes called *unit generators*. By doing so we obtain a layer of abstraction, hiding away the messy details like sample rates, time, buffers, and memory allocation. Since the 1960s many computer languages have been developed specifically for sound (Geiger 2005; Roads 1996). Most have been designed for musical applications, giving them features which are superfluous but not necessarily in conflict with our needs as sound designers. Two contrasting, historically important classes are the imperative MUSIC-N type languages originating with Max Mathews, from which Csound (Vercoe) descends, and the functional Lisp based family like Common Lisp Music (Schottstaedt) and Nyquist (Dannenberg). The two code snippets below (from Geiger 2005) illustrate these.

A Csound Snippet

```
instr 1
asig oscil       10000, 440, 1
out asig
endin
Score:
f1     0    256  10   1;    a sine wave function table
i1     0    1000 0
```

A CLM Snippet

```
(definstrument simp ()
    (let* ((j 0))
      (run (loop for i from 0 below 44100 do
            (outa i (sin(* j 2.0 pi (/ frequency *srate*)))))
(incf j)))))
(with-sound () (simp))
```

Both examples above play a 440Hz sine tone. Notice how Csound is like an assembly language with intermediate variables and fixed unit generator opcodes like oscil. It is also split into instrument definitions (called an *orchestra*) and timing definitions (called a *score*). Lisp, on the other hand, is a functional language where there aren't really any variables. Everything is a function, or a function of a function. Both are very powerful in their own ways. Csound makes abstractions that can be used in time; CLM can use the powerful *lambda abstraction* to make reusable code templates, so that very complex operations can be succinctly expressed at a high level. Unfortunately, both are difficult to learn and use for different reasons. More modern languages like Chuck and Supercollider offer improvements, but development time is still long when using them because complex syntax must be learned. The language I have chosen for this book is Pure Data (Puckette). A Pure Data program that does the same thing as the above examples is shown in figure 7.18. Nothing else really comes

Figure 7.18
A Pd program to make a 440Hz sine signal.

close to the power of dataflow expressed visually. There is no syntax other than boxes that represent unit generators and connections. The level of abstraction is perfect. It hides away everything you don't need to worry about, allowing you to concentrate on sound algorithm design. The following chapters are an introduction to this language before we get down to the practical business of designing sound.

Acknowledgements

Acknowledgement is given to Charles Henry, Miller Puckette, and Philippe-Aubert Gauthier for suggestions and corrections.

References

Books

Chamberlin, H. (1985). *Musical Applications of Microprocessors.* Hayden.
Dodge, C., and Jerse, T. A. (1985). *Computer Music: Synthesis, Composition, and Performance.* Schirmer.
Greenebaum, K., and Barzel, R. (2004). *Audio Anecdotes: Tools, Tips, and Techniques for Digital Audio.* A. K. Peters.
Kahrs, M., and Brandenburg, K. (eds.) (1998). *Applications of Digital Signal Processing to Audio and Acoustics.* Kluwer.
Moore, F. R. (1990). *Elements of Computer Music.* Prentice Hall.
Pohlmann, Ken C. (1995). *Principles of Digital Audio,* (3rd ed.) Mcgraw-Hill. (Essential reading.)
Puckette, M. (2007). *The Theory and Technique of Electronic Music.* World Scientific.
Roads, C. (1996). *The Computer Music Tutorial.* MIT Press.
Roads, C., DePoli, G., and Piccialli, A. (1991). *Representations of Musical Signals.* MIT Press.
Roads, C., and Strawn, J. (1987). *Foundations of Computer Music.* MIT Press.
Smith, S. W. (2003). *The Scientist and Engineer's Guide to Digital Signal Processing.* California Technical Pub.
Weaver, W. and Shannon, C. (1963). *The Mathematical Theory of Communication.* University of Illinois Press.

Papers

ffitch, J. (2000). "A look at random numbers, noise, and chaos with Csound." In *The Csound Book: Perspectives in Software Synthesis, Sound Design, Signal Processing,and Programming,* ed. R. Boulanger. MIT Press.
Geiger, G. (2005). "Abstraction in computer music software systems." Universitat Pompeu Fabra.
Shannon, C. (1948). "A mathematical theory of communication." *Bell Sys. Tech. J.* 27: 379–423, 623–656.

Online Resources

Music-DSP is the name of a mailing list run from Columbia University. There is also a music-dsp website with many examples of code for oscillators, filters, and other DSP operations. <http://music.columbia.edu/mailman/listinfo/music-dsp>

DSP-Related is another well-known website with lots of information and a forum. <http://www.dsprelated.com/>

Julius O. Smith maintains one of the best pedagogical guides to filters on the Internet at Stanford University CCRMA. <http://ccrma.standford.edu/~jos/>

II

Tools

8
Tools Introduction

If the only tool you have is a
hammer everything looks like
a nail.
—Anonymous

SECTION 8.1
What You Will Need

- A computer with at least a 500MHz processor.
- Sound card, loudspeakers or headphones, and a microphone.
- Notepad and pencil.
- A sturdy pair of walking boots.
- A flask of weak lemon drink.
- Patient neighbours/family.

SECTION 8.2
Tools for Sound Design

In his book *How to Be Creative* Hugh Macleod gives away one of the best
secrets about being a successful producer, that there is no correlation between
creativity and ownership of equipment: as an artist gets more proficient the
number of tools goes down. The following chapters provide a basic introduction to one of the most powerful audio programming environments ever devised.
You can often tell an extremely powerful tool by its Spartan appearance. It does
not need to advertise itself. There are no flashing graphics or whizzbangs, just
a command prompt or a blank canvas. What this is saying is "I am ready to do
your bidding, Master." Many get stuck here, because they never thought about
what they want to do, expecting the tools to lead them rather than the other
way about.

The initial appearance of Pd can be intimidating, so to get beyond "Now
what?" it's time to embark on a short crash course in dataflow patching so
you can complete the practical elements of the book. The first chapter explains
how dataflow patchers work and provides you with an overview of the most
common Pd objects. You can examine all the examples, which are available

to download from the Internet. Do not hesitate to hack and experiment with these. When you are comfortable with the main concepts read the chapter on abstraction. Start building your own patches and abstractions as soon as possible. The last chapter in this part provides some essential components to begin making sound, including sample tools, effects, and ideas to construct your own mixer and sequencer.

SECTION 8.3

Supporting Tools

The above list in section 8.1 is only half in jest. The walking boots will come in handy, as will a good microphone and small digital recorder with some spare batteries. The computer cannot provide the answer and means to every sound design problem, so getting hold of material to work with is an essential part of the process. Sound libraries are useful, but there's no substitute for seeing and studying the things you are going to deconstruct and design. In later chapters I will discuss the techniques of analytical recording, somewhat different from studio or regular field recording where you intend to use the results as the final product. A good monitoring space is vital too. This is not a book on studio design, but it's worth saying that each link in the chain counts. Possibly the weakest link is loudspeakers and listening space. Work at a reasonable level, not too loud or quiet. Use nearfield monitors so your ears are able to resolve detail.

Additionally, an audio editor will be useful. Any of the major packages are good, Sound Forge, Cool Edit, Pro Tools, etc. I like one called Snd, which is used to prepare the spectrographs and wave printouts in this book, but it is not an easy tool to use. Audacity is a good all round editor that runs on many platforms, reads and writes many file types, and is free. The last tool worth mentioning is patience and persistence. Sometimes you can't crack a sound in one session. Walk away, come back later—preferably armed with some more knowledge, reading, or time spent listening to target examples—and sneak up on it when it's not expecting you. Breakthroughs often happen when you aren't expecting them, or when you adapt a process for something else you were working on that suddenly seems appropriate.

9
Starting with
Pure Data

Pure Data

Pure Data is a visual signal programming language which makes it easy to construct programs to operate on signals. We are going to use it extensively in this textbook as a tool for sound design. The program is in active development and improving all the time. It is a free alternative to Max/MSP that many see as an improvement.

The primary application of Pure Data is processing sound, which is what it was designed for. However, it has grown into a general-purpose signal-processing environment with many other uses. Collections of video-processing externals exist called Gem, PDP, and Gridflow, which can be used to create 3D scenes and manipulate 2D images. It has a great collection of interfacing objects, so you can easily attach joysticks, sensors, and motors to prototype robotics or make interactive media installations. It is also a wonderful teaching tool for audio signal processing. Its economy of visual expression is a blessing: it doesn't look too fancy, which makes looking at complex programs much easier on the eye. There is a very powerful idea behind "The diagram is the program." Each patch contains its complete state visually so you can reproduce any example just from the diagram. That makes it a visual description of sound.

The question is often asked, "Is Pure Data a programming language?" The answer is yes; in fact, it is a Turing complete language capable of doing anything that can be expressed algorithmically, but there are tasks such as building text applications or websites that Pure Data is ill suited to. It is a specialised programming language that does the job it was designed for very well, namely processing signals. It is like many other GUI frameworks or DSP environments which operate inside a "canned loop"[1] and are not truly open programming languages. There is a limited concept of iteration, programmatic branching, and conditional behaviour. At heart dataflow programming is very simple. If you understand object oriented programming, think of the objects as having methods which are called by data, and can only return data. Behind the scenes Pure Data is quite sophisticated. To make signal programming simple it hides

---

1. A *canned loop* is used to refer to languages in which the real low-level programmatic flow is handled by an interpreter that the user is unaware of.

away behaviour like deallocation of deleted objects and manages the execution
graph of a multirate DSP object interpreter and scheduler.

Installing and Running Pure Data

Grab the latest version for your computer platform by searching the Internet
for it. There are versions available for Mac, Windows and Linux systems. On
Debian-based Linux systems you can easily install it by typing:

```
$ apt-get install puredata
```

Ubuntu and RedHat users will find the appropriate installer in their package
management systems, and MacOSX or Windows users will find an installer
program online. Try to use the most up-to-date version with libraries. The
pd-extended build includes extra libraries so you don't need to install them
separately. When you run it you should see a console window that looks something like figure 9.1.

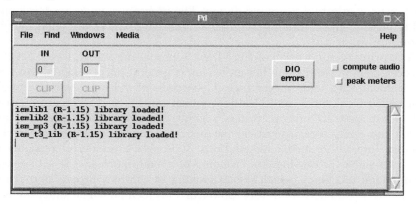

Figure 9.1
Pure Data console.

Testing Pure Data

The first thing to do is turn on the audio and test it. Start by entering the
Media menu on the top bar and select Audio ON (or either check the compute
audio box in the console window, or press CTRL+/ on the keyboard.) From the
Media→Test-Audio-and-MIDI menu, turn on the test signal (fig. 9.2). You
should hear a clear tone through your speakers, quiet when set to −40.0dB and
much louder when set to −20.0dB. When you are satisfied that Pure Data is
making sound, close the test window and continue reading. If you don't hear
a sound you may need to choose the correct audio settings for your machine.
The audio settings summary will look like that shown in figure 9.3. Choices
available might be Jack, ASIO, OSS, ALSA, or the name of a specific device
you have installed as a sound card. Most times the default settings will work. If

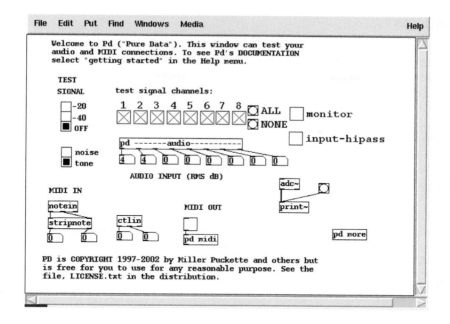

Figure 9.2
Test signal.

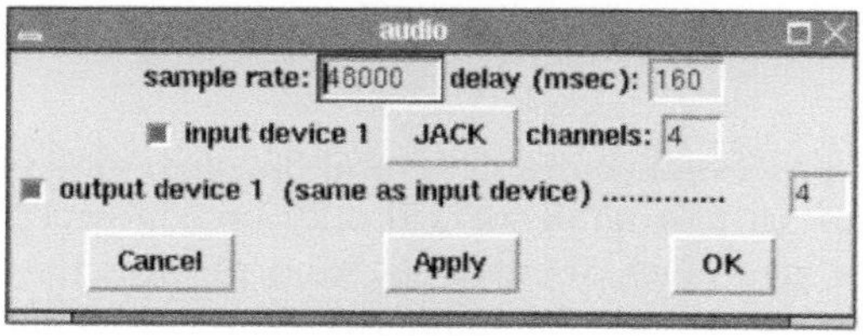

Figure 9.3
Audio settings pane.

you are using Jack (recommended), then check that Jack audio is running with `qjackctl` on Linux or `jack-pilot` on MacOSX. Sample rate is automatically taken from the sound card.

┌─ SECTION 9.2 ─────────────────────────────────
How Does Pure Data Work?

Pure Data uses a kind of programming called *dataflow*, because the data flows along connections and through objects which process it. The output of one process feeds into the input of another, and there may be many steps in the flow.

Objects

Here is a box ⬚. A musical box, wound up and ready to play. We call these boxes *objects*. Stuff goes in, stuff comes out. For it to pass into or out of them, objects must have *inlets* or *outlets*. Inlets are at the top of an object box, outlets are at the bottom. Here is an object that has two inlets and one outlet: ⬚. They are shown by small "tabs" on the edge of the object box. Objects contain processes or procedures which change the things appearing at their inlets and then send the results to one or more outlets. Each object performs some simple function and has a name appearing in its box that identifies what it does. There are two kinds of object, *intrinsics* which are part of the core Pd program, and *externals* which are separate files containing add-ons to the core functions. Collections of externals are called *libraries* and can be added to extend the functionality of Pd. Most of the time you will neither know nor care whether an object is intrinsic or external. In this book and elsewhere the words *process*, *function*, and *unit* are all occasionally used to refer to the object boxes in Pd.

Connections

The connections between objects are sometimes called *cords* or *wires*. They are drawn in a straight line between the outlet of one object and the inlet of another. It is okay for them to cross, but you should try to avoid this since it makes the patch diagram harder to read. At present there are two degrees of thickness for cords. Thin ones carry message data and fatter ones carry audio signals. *Max/MSP* and probably future versions of Pd will offer different colours to indicate the data types carried by wires.

Data

The "stuff" being processed comes in several flavours: video frames, sound signals, and messages. In this book we will only be concerned with sounds and messages. Objects give clues about what kind of data they process by their name. For example, an object that adds together two sound signals looks like ⬚. The + means that this is an addition object, and the $\sim$ (tilde character) means that its object operates on signals. Objects without the tilde are used to process messages, which we shall concentrate on before studying audio signal processing.

Patches

A collection of objects wired together is a *program* or *patch*. For historical reasons *program* and *patch*[2] are used to mean the same thing in sound synthesis. Patches are an older way of describing a synthesiser built from modular units connected together with patch cords. Because inlets and outlets are at the top and bottom of objects, the data flow is generally down the patch. Some objects

---

2. A different meaning of patch from the one programmers use to describe changes made to a program to remove bugs.

have more than one inlet or more than one outlet, so signals and messages can be a function of many others and may in turn generate multiple new data streams. To construct a program we place processing objects onto an empty area called a *canvas*, then connect them together with wires representing pathways for data to flow along. At each step of a Pure Data program any new input data is fed into objects, triggering them to compute a result. This result is fed into the next connected object and so on until the entire chain of objects, starting with the first and ending with the last, have all been computed. The program then proceeds to the next step, which is to do the same thing all over again, forever. Each object maintains a state which persists throughout the execution of the program but may change at each step. Message-processing objects sit idle until they receive some data rather than constantly processing an empty stream, so we say Pure Data is an *event-driven system*. Audio-processing objects are always running, unless you explicitly tell them to switch off.

A Deeper Look at Pd

Before moving on to make some patches consider a quick aside about how Pd actually interprets its patches and how it works in a wider context. A patch, or dataflow graph, is navigated by the interpreter to decide when to compute certain operations. This *traversal* is *right to left* and *depth first*, which is a computer science way of saying it looks ahead and tries to go as deep as it can before moving on to anything higher, and moves from right to left at any branches. This is another way of saying it wants to know what depends on what before deciding to calculate anything. Although we think of data flowing down the graph, the nodes in figure 9.4 are numbered to show how Pd really thinks about things. Most of the time this isn't very important unless you have to debug a subtle error.

Pure Data Software Architecture

Pure Data actually consists of more than one program. The main part called **pd** performs all the real work and is the interpreter, scheduler, and audio engine. A separate program is usually launched whenever you start the main engine, which is called the **pd-gui**. This is the part you will interact with when building Pure Data programs. It creates files to be read by **pd** and automatically passes them to the engine. There is a third program called the **pd-watchdog**, which runs as a completely separate process. The job of the watchdog is to keep an eye on the execution of programs by the engine and to try to gracefully halt the program if it runs into serious trouble or exceeds available CPU resources. The context of the **pd** program is shown in figure 9.5 in terms of other files and devices.

Your First Patch

Let's now begin to create a Pd patch as an introductory exercise. We will create some objects and wire them together as a way to explore the interface.

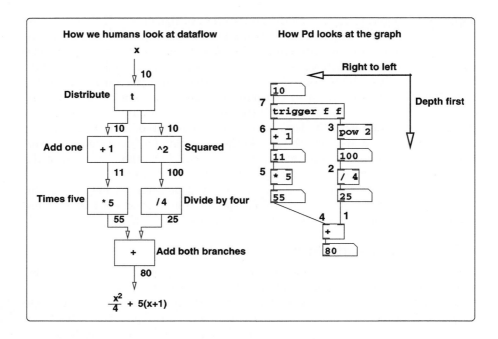

Figure 9.4
Dataflow computation.

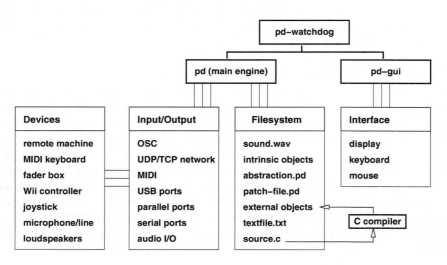

Figure 9.5
Pure Data software architecture.

Creating a Canvas

A *canvas* is the name for the sheet or window on which you place objects. You can resize a canvas to make it as big as you like. When it is smaller than the patch it contains, horizontal and vertical scrollbars will allow you to change the area displayed. When you save a canvas, its size and position on the desktop are stored. From the console menu select File→New or type CTRL+n at the keyboard. A new blank canvas will appear on your desktop.

New Object Placement

To place an object on the canvas, select Put→Object from the menu or use CTRL+1 on the keyboard. An active, dotted box will appear. Move it somewhere on the canvas using the mouse and click to fix it in place. You can now type the name of the new object, so type the multiplication character * into the box. When you have finished typing, click anywhere on the blank canvas to complete the operation. When Pure Data recognises the object name you give, it immediately changes the object box boundary to a solid line and adds a number of inlets and outlets. You should see a ⊡ on the canvas now.

Figure 9.6
Objects on a canvas.

Pure Data searches the paths it knows for objects, which includes the current working directory. If it doesn't recognise an object because it can't find a definition anywhere, the boundary of the object box remains dotted. Try creating another object and typing some nonsense into it; the boundary will stay dotted and no inlets or outlets will be assigned. To delete the object, place the mouse cursor close to it, click and hold in order to draw a selection box around it, then hit delete on the keyboard. Create another object beneath the last one with an addition symbol so that your canvas looks like figure 9.6.

Edit Mode and Wiring

When you create a new object from the menu, Pd automatically enters edit mode, so if you just completed the instructions above you should currently be in edit mode. In this mode you can make connections between objects or delete objects and connections.

Figure 9.7
Wiring objects.

Hovering over an outlet will change the mouse cursor to a new "wiring tool." If you click and hold the mouse when the tool is active you will be able to drag a connection away from the object. Hovering over a compatible inlet while in this state will allow you to release the mouse and make a new connection. Connect together the two objects you made so that your canvas looks like figure 9.7. If you want to delete a connection, it's easy; click on the connection to select it and then hit the delete key. When in edit mode you can move any object to another place by clicking over it and dragging with the mouse. Any connections already made to the object will follow along. You can pick up and move more than one object if you draw a selection box around them first.

Initial Parameters

Most objects can take some initial parameters or *arguments*, but these aren't always required. Objects can be created without these if you are going to pass data via the inlets as the patch is running. The ⊡ object can be written as ⊡ 3 to create an object which always adds 3 to its input. Uninitialised values generally resort to zero, so the default behaviour of ⊡ would be to add 0 to its input, which is the same as doing nothing. Contrast this with the default behaviour of ⊡, which always gives zero.

Modifying Objects

You can also change the contents of any object box to alter the name and function, or to add parameters.

Figure 9.8
Changing objects.

In figure 9.8 the objects have been changed to give them initial parameters. The multiply object is given a parameter of 5, which means it multiplies its input by 5 no matter what comes in. If the input is 4 then the output will be 20. To change the contents of an object click on the middle of the box where the name is and type the new text. Alternatively, click once, and then again at the end of the text to append new stuff, such as adding 5 and 3 to the objects shown in figure 9.8.

Number Input and Output

Figure 9.9
Number boxes.

One of the easiest ways to create and view numerical data is to use *number boxes*. These can act as input devices to generate numbers, or as displays to show you the data on a wire. Create one by choosing Put→Number from the canvas menu, or use CTRL+3, and place it above the ⊡ object. Wire it to the left inlet. Place another below the ⊡ object and wire the object outlet to the top of the number box as shown in figure 9.9.

Toggling Edit Mode

Pressing CTRL+e on the keyboard will also enter edit mode. This key combination toggles modes, so hitting CTRL+e again exits edit mode. Exit edit mode now by hitting CTRL+e or selecting Edit→Edit mode from the canvas menu. The mouse cursor will change and you will no longer be able to move or modify object boxes. However, in this mode you can operate the patch components such as buttons and sliders normally. Place the mouse in the top number box, click and hold, and move it upwards. This input number value will change, and it will send messages to the objects below it. You will see the second number box change too as the patch computes the equation $y = 5x + 3$. To reenter edit mode hit CTRL+E again or place a new object.

More Edit Operations

Other familiar editing operations are available while in edit mode. You can cut or copy objects to a buffer or paste them back into the canvas, or to another canvas opened with the same instance of Pd. Take care with pasting objects in the buffer because they will appear directly on top of the last object copied. To select a group of objects you can drag a box around them with the mouse. Holding SHIFT while selecting allows multiple separate objects to be added to the buffer.

- CTRL+a Select all objects on canvas.
- CTRL+d Duplicate the selection.
- CTRL+c Copy the selection.
- CTRL+v Paste the selection.
- CTRL+x Cut the selection.
- SHIFT   Select multiple objects.

Duplicating a group of objects will also duplicate any connections between them. You may modify an object once created and wired up without having it disconnect so long as the new one is compatible the existing inlets and outlets, for example replacing ⬚ with ⬚. Clicking on the object text will allow you to retype the name and, if valid, the old object is deleted and its replacement remains connected as before.

Patch Files

Pd files are regular text files in which patches are stored. Their names always end with a **.pd** file extension. Each consists of a *netlist*, which is a collection of object definitions and connections between them. The file format is terse and difficult to understand, which is why we use the GUI for editing. Often there is a one-to-one correspondence between a patch, a single canvas, and a file, but you can work using multiple files if you like because all canvases opened by the same instance of Pd can communicate via global variables or through send and receive objects. Patch files shouldn't really be modified in a text editor unless you are an expert Pure Data user, though a plaintext format is useful because you can do things like search for and replace all occurrences of an object. To save the current canvas into a file select File→Save from the menu or use the keyboard shortcut CTRL+s. If you have not saved the file previously a dialogue panel will open to let you choose a location and file name. This would be a good time to create a folder for your Pd patches somewhere convenient. Loading a patch, as you would expect, is achieved with File→Open or CTRL+o.

┌ SECTION 9.3 ───
Message Data and GUI Boxes

We will briefly tour the basic data types that Pd uses along with GUI objects that can display or generate that data for us. The message data itself should not be confused with the objects that can be used to display or input it, so we distinguish messages from boxes. A *message* is an event, or a piece of data that gets sent between two objects. It is invisible as it travels down the wires, unless we print it or view it in some other way like with the number boxes above. A message can be very short, only one number or character, or very long, perhaps holding an entire musical score or synthesiser parameter set. Messages can be floating point numbers, lists, symbols, or pointers which are references to other types like datastructures. Messages happen in *logical time*, which means that they aren't synchronised to any real timebase. Pd processes them as fast as it can, so when you change the input number box, the output number box changes instantly. Let's look at some other message types we'll encounter while building patches to create sound. All GUI objects can be placed on a canvas using the `Put` menu or using keyboard shortcuts `CTRL+1` through `CTRL+8`, and all have *properties* which you can access by right-clicking them while in edit mode and selecting the `properties` pop-up menu item. Properties include things like colour, ranges, labels, and size and are set per instance.

Selectors

With the exception of a bang message, all other message types carry an invisible *selector*, which is a symbol at the head of the message. This describes the "type" of the remaining message, whether it represents a symbol, number, pointer, or list. Object boxes and GUI components are only able to handle appropriate messages. When a message arrives at an inlet the object looks at the selector and searches to see if it knows of an appropriate *method* to deal with it. An error results when an incompatible data type arrives at an inlet, so for example, if you supply a symbol type message to a `delay` object it will complain:

```
error: delay: no method for 'symbol'
```

Bang Message

This is the most fundamental and smallest message. It just means "compute something." Bangs cause most objects to output their current value or advance to their next state. Other messages have an implicit bang so they don't need to be followed with a bang to make them work. A bang has no value; it is just a bang.

Bang Box

A bang box looks like this ⬚ and sends and receives a bang message. It briefly changes colour, like this ◼, whenever it is clicked or upon receipt of a bang message to show you one has been sent or received. These may be used as buttons to initiate actions or as indicators to show events.

Float Messages

"Floats" is another name for numbers. As well as regular (integer) numbers like 1, 2, 3 and negative numbers like −10 we need numbers with decimal points like

−198753.2 or 10.576 to accurately represent numerical data. These are called *floating point numbers*, because of the way computers represent the decimal point position. If you understand some computer science then it's worth noting that there are no integers in Pd; everything is a float, even if it appears to be an integer, so 1 is really 1.0000000. Current versions of Pd use a 32-bit float representation, so they are between −8388608 and 8388608.

Number Box

For float numbers we have already met the number box, which is a dual-purpose GUI element. Its function is to either display a number or allow you to input one. A bevelled top right corner like this ⬚ denotes that this object is a number box. Numbers received on the inlet are displayed and passed directly to the outlet. To input a number click and hold the mouse over the value field and move the mouse up or down. You can also type in numbers. Click on a number box, type the number and hit RETURN. Number boxes are a compact replacement for faders. By default it will display up to five digits including a sign if negative, −9999 to 99999, but you can change this by editing its properties. Holding SHIFT while moving the mouse allows a finer degree of control. It is also possible to set an upper and lower limit from the properties dialogue.

Toggle Box

Another object that works with floats is a toggle box. Like a checkbox on any standard GUI or web form, this has only two states, on or off. When clicked a cross appears in the box like this ⊠ and it sends out a number 1; clicking again causes it to send out a number 0 and removes the cross so that it looks like this ☐. It also has an inlet which sets the value, so it can be used to display a binary state. Sending a bang to the inlet of a toggle box does not cause the current value to be output; instead it flips the toggle to the opposite state and outputs this value. Editing properties also allows you to send numbers other than 1 for the active state.

Sliders and Other Numerical GUI Elements

GUI elements for horizontal and vertical sliders can be used as input and display elements. Their default range is 0 to 127, nice for MIDI controllers, but like all other GUI objects this can be changed in their properties window. Unlike those found in some other GUI systems, Pd sliders do not have a step value. Shown in figure 9.10 are some GUI objects at their standard sizes. They can be ornamented with labels or created in any colour. Resizing the slider to make it bigger will increase the step resolution. A radio box provides a set of mutually exclusive buttons which output a number starting at zero. Again, they work equally well as indicators or input elements. A better way to visually display an audio level is to use a VU meter. This is set up to indicate decibels, so it has a rather strange scale from −99.0 to +12.0. Audio signals that range from −1.0 to +1.0 must first be scaled using the appropriate object. The VU is one of the few GUI elements that acts only as a display.

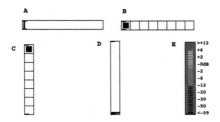

Figure 9.10
GUI Objects A: Horizontal slider. B: Horizontal radio box. C: Vertical radio box. D: Vertical
slider. E: VU meter.

General Messages

Floats and bangs are types of message, but messages can be more general.
Other message types can be created by prepending a *selector* that gives them
special meanings. For example, to construct lists we can prepend a *list* selector
to a set of other types.

Message Box

These are visual containers for user-definable messages. They can be used to
input or store a message. The right edge of a message box is curved inwards
like this ⌐, and it always has only one inlet and one outlet. They behave as
GUI elements, so when you click a message box it sends its contents to the
outlet. This action can also be triggered if the message box receives a bang
message on its inlet. Message boxes do some clever thinking for us. If we store
something like 5.0 it knows that is a float and outputs a float type, but if we
create a message with text then it will send out a list of symbols; so it is type aware,
which saves us having to say things like "float 1.0" as we would in C programs.
It can also abbreviate floating point numbers like 1.0 to 1, which saves time
when inputting integer values, but it knows that they are really floats.

Symbolic Messages

A *symbol* generally is a word or some text. A symbol can represent anything;
it is the most basic textual message in Pure Data. Technically a symbol in Pd
can contain any printable or nonprintable character. But most of the time you
will only encounter symbols made out of letters, numbers, and some interpunc-
tuation characters like a dash, dot, or underscore. The Pd editor does some
automatic conversions: words that can also be interpreted as a number (like
3.141 or $1e + 20$) are converted to a float internally (but $+20$ still is a symbol!). Whitespace is used by the editor to separate symbols from each other,
so you cannot type a symbol including a space character into a message box.
To generate symbols with backslash-escaped whitespace or other special characters inside, use the makefilename symbol maker object. The openpanel file dialogue
object preserves and escapes spaces and other special characters in filenames,

too. Valid symbols are *badger*, *sound_2*, or *all_your_base*, but not *hello there* (which is two symbols) or *20* (which will be interpreted as a float, 20.0).

Symbol Box

For displaying or inputting text you may use a ⟨symbol⟩ box. Click on the display field and type any text that is a valid symbol and then hit ENTER/RETURN. This will send a symbol message to the outlet of the box. Likewise, if a symbol message is received at the inlet it will be displayed as text. Sending a bang message to a symbol box makes it output any symbol it already contains.

Lists

A list is an ordered collection of any things, floats, symbols, or pointers that are treated as one. Lists of floats might be used for building melody sequences or setting the time values for an envelope generator. Lists of symbols can be used to represent text data from a file or keyboard input. Most of the time we will be interested in lists of numbers. A list like {*2 127 3.14159 12*} has four elements; the first element is 2.0 and the last is 12.0. Internally, Pure Data recognises a list because it has a *list selector* at the start, so it treats all following parts of the message as ordered list elements. When a list is sent as a message all its elements are sent at once. A list selector is attached to the beginning of the message to determine its type. The selector is the word "list," which has a special meaning to Pd. Lists may be of mixed types like {*5 6 pick up sticks*}, which has two floats and three symbols. When a list message contains only one item which is a float it is automatically changed (cast) back to a float. Lists can be created in several ways, by using a message box, or by using ⟨pack⟩, which we will meet later, to pack data elements into a list.

Pointers

As in other programming languages, a *pointer* is the address of some other piece of data. We can use them to build more complex data structures, such as a pointer to a list of pointers to lists of floats and symbols. Special objects exist for creating and dereferencing pointers, but since they are an advanced topic we will not explore them further in this book.

Tables, Arrays, and Graphs

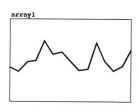

Figure 9.11
An array.

A *table* is sometimes used interchangeably with an *array* to mean a two-dimensional data structure. An array is one of the few invisible objects. Once declared it just exists in memory. To see it, a separate *graph* like that shown in figure 9.11 allows us to view its contents.

Graphs have the wonderful property that they are also GUI elements. You can draw data directly into a graph using the mouse and it will modify the array it is attached to. You can see a graph of **array1** in figure 9.11 that has been drawn by hand. Similarly, if the data in an array changes and it's attached to a visible graph then the graph will show the data as it updates. This is perfect for drawing detailed envelopes or making an oscilloscope display of rapidly changing signals.

To create a new array select Put→Array from the menu and complete the dialogue box to set up its name, size, and display characteristics. On the canvas a graph will appear showing an array with all its values initialised to zero. The Y-axis range is −1.0 to +1.0 by default, so the data line will be in the centre. If the save contents box is checked then the array data will be saved along with the patch file. Be aware that long sound files stored in arrays will make large patch files when saved this way. Three draw styles are available: points, polygon, and Bezier, to show the data with varying degrees of smoothing. It is possible to use the same graph to display more than one array, which is very useful when you wish to see the relationship between two or more sets of data. To get this behaviour use the in last graph option when creating an array.

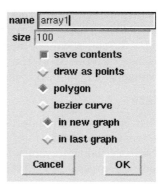

Figure 9.12
Create array.

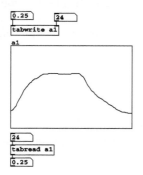

Figure 9.13
Accessing an array.

Data is written into or read from a table by an index number which refers to a position within it. The index is a whole number. To read and write arrays, several kinds of accessor object are available. The `tabread` and `tabwrite` objects allow you to communicate with arrays using messages. Later we will meet `tabread4~` and `tabwrite~` objects that can read and write audio signals. The array **a1** shown in figure 9.13 is written by the `tabwrite` object above it, which specifies the target array name as a parameter. The right inlet sets the index and the left one sets the value. Below it a `tabread` object takes the index on its inlet and returns the current value.

SECTION 9.4

Getting Help with Pure Data

At <**http://puredata.hurleur.com/**> there is an active, friendly forum, and the mailing list can be subscribed to at **pd-list@iem.at**.

Exercises

Exercise 1

On Linux, type `pd --help` at the console to see the available startup options. On Windows or MacOSX read the help documentation that comes with your downloaded distribution.

Exercise 2

Use the `Help` menu, select `browse help`, and read through some built-in documentation pages. Be familiar with the `control examples` and `audio examples` sections.

Exercise 3

Visit the online `pdwiki` at <http://puredata.org> to look at the enormous range of objects available in `pd-extended`.

References

Arduino I/O boards: http://www.arduino.cc/.

Puckette, M. (1996). "Pure Data." *Proceedings, International Computer Music Conference.* San Francisco: International Computer Music Association, pp. 269–272.

Puckette, M. (1996). "Pure Data: Another integrated computer music environment." *Proceedings, Second Intercollege Computer Music Concerts*, Tachikawa, Japan, pp. 37–41.

Puckette, M. (1997). "Pure Data: Recent progress." *Proceedings, Third Intercollege Computer Music Festival.* Tokyo, Japan, pp. 1–4.

Puckette, M. (2007). *The Theory and Technique of Electronic Music.* World Scientific Press.

Winkler, T. (1998). *Composing Interactive Music: Techniques and Ideas Using Max.* MIT Press.

Zimmer, F. (editor) (2006). *Bang—A Pure Data Book.* Wolke-Verlag.

References

10
Using Pure Data

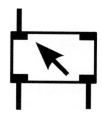

Basic Objects and Principles of Operation

Now that we are familiar with the basics of Pd, let's look at some essential objects and rules for connecting them together. There are about 20 message objects you should try to learn by heart because almost everything else is built from them.

Hot and Cold Inlets

Most objects operating on messages have a "hot" inlet and (optionally) one or more "cold" inlets. Messages received at the hot inlet, usually the leftmost one, will cause computation to happen and output to be generated. Messages on a cold inlet will update the internal value of an object but not cause it to output the result yet. This seems strange at first, like a bug. The reason for it is so that we can order evaluation. This means waiting for subparts of a program to finish in the right order before proceeding to the next step. From maths you know that brackets describe the order of a calculation. The result of $4 \times 10 - 3$ is not the same as $4 \times (10 - 3)$, we need to calculate the parenthesised parts first. A Pd program works the same way: you need to wait for the results from certain parts before moving on.

Figure 10.1
Hot and cold inlets.

In figure 10.1 a new number box is added to right inlet of ⊡. This new value represents a constant multiplier k so we can compute $y = kx + 3$. It overrides the 5 given as an initial parameter when changed. In figure 10.1 it's set to 3 so we have $y = 3x + 3$. Experiment setting it to another value and then changing the left number box. Notice that changes to the right number box don't immediately affect the output, because it connects to the cold inlet of ⊡, but changes to the left number box cause the output to change, because it is connected to the hot inlet of ⊡.

Bad Evaluation Order

A problem arises when messages fan out from a single outlet into other operations. Look at the two patches in figure 10.2. Can you tell the difference? It is impossible to tell just by looking that one is a working patch and the other contains a nasty error. Each is an attempt to double the value of a number by connecting it to both sides of a ⊡. When connections are made this way the

Figure 10.2
Bad ordering.

behaviour is undefined, but usually happens in the order the connections were made. The first one works because the right (cold) inlet was connected before the left (hot) one. In the second patch the arriving number is added to the *last* number received because the hot inlet is addressed first. Try making these patches by connecting the inlets to ⬚ in a different order. If you accidentally create errors this way they are hard to debug.

Trigger Objects

A trigger is an object that splits a message up into parts and sends them over several outlets in order. It solves the evaluation order problem by making the order explicit.

Figure 10.3
Ordering with trigger.

The order of output is right to left, so a `trigger bang float` object outputs a float on the right outlet first, then a bang on the left one. This can be abbreviated as `t b f`. Proper use of triggers ensures correct operation of units further down the connection graph. The arguments to a trigger may be **s** for symbol, **f** for float, **b** for bang, **p** for pointers, and **a** for any. The "any" type will pass lists and pointers too. The patch in figure 10.3 always works correctly, whatever order you connect to the ⬚ inlets. The float from the right outlet of `t f f` is always sent to the cold inlet of ⬚ first, and the left one to the hot inlet afterwards.

Making Cold Inlets Hot

Figure 10.4
Warming an inlet.

An immediate use for our new knowledge of triggers is to make an arithmetic operator like ⬚ respond to either of its inlets immediately. Make the patch shown in figure 10.4 and try changing the number boxes. When the left one is changed it sends a float number message to the left (hot) inlet which updates the output as usual. But now, when you change the right number box it is split by `t b f` into two messages, a float which is sent to the cold (right) inlet of ⬚, and a bang, which is sent to the hot inlet immediately afterwards. When it receives a bang on its hot inlet, ⬚ computes the sum of the two numbers last seen on its inlets, which gives the right result.

Float Objects

The object ⬚ is very common. A shorthand for `float`, which you can also use if you like to make things clearer, it holds the value of a single floating point number. You might like to think of it as a variable, a temporary place to store a number. There are two inlets on ⬚; the rightmost one will set the value of the object, and the leftmost one will both set the value and/or output it depending on what message it receives. If it receives a bang message it will just output whatever value is currently stored, but if the message is a float it will override the currently stored value with a new float and immediately output that. This gives us a way to both set and query the object contents.

Int Objects

Although we have noted that integers don't really exist in Pd, not in a way that a programmer would understand, whole numbers certainly do. `int` stores a float as if it were an integer in that it provides a rounding (truncation) function of any extra decimal places. Thus 1.6789 becomes 1.0000, equal to 1, when passed to `int`.

Symbol and List Objects

As for numbers, there are likewise object boxes to store lists and symbols in a temporary location. Both work just like their numerical counterparts. A list can be given to the right inlet of `list` and recalled by banging the left inlet. Similarly `symbol` can store a single symbol until it is needed.

Merging Message Connections

When several message connections are all connected to the same inlet that's fine. The object will process each of them as they arrive, though it's up to you to ensure that they arrive in the right order to do what you expect. Be aware of race hazards when the sequence is important.

Figure 10.5
Messages to same inlet.

Messages arriving from different sources at the same hot inlet have no effect on each another; they remain separate and are simply interleaved in the order they arrive, each producing output. But be mindful that where several connections are made to a cold inlet only the last one to arrive will be relevant. Each of the number boxes in figure 10.5 connects to the same cold inlet of the float box `f` and a bang button to the hot inlet. Whenever the bang button is pressed the output will be whatever is currently stored in `f`, which will be the last number box changed. Which number box was updated last in figure 10.5? It was the middle one with a value of 11.

SECTION 10.2

Working with Time and Events

With our simple knowledge of objects we can now begin making patches that work on functions of time, the basis of all sound and music.

Metronome

Figure 10.6
Metronome.

Perhaps the most important primitive operation is to get a beat or timebase. To get a regular series of bang events `metro` provides a clock. Tempo is given as a period in milliseconds rather than beats per minute (as is usual with most music programs).

The left inlet toggles the metronome on and off when it receives a 1 or 0, while the right one allows you to set the period. Periods that are fractions of a millisecond are allowed. The `metro` emits a bang as soon as it is switched on and the following bang occurs after the time period. In figure 10.6 the time period is 1000ms (equal to 1 second). The bang button here is used as an indicator. As soon as you click the message box to send 1 to `metro` it begins sending out bangs which make the bang button flash once per second, until you send a 0 message to turn it off.

A Counter Timebase

We could use the metronome to trigger a sound repeatedly, like a steady drum beat, but on their own a series of bang events aren't much use. Although they are separated in time we cannot keep track of time this way because bang messages contain no information.

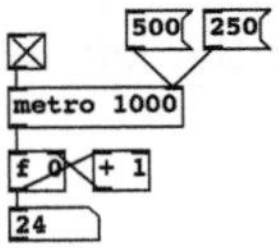

Figure 10.7
Counter.

In figure 10.7 we see the metronome again. This time the messages to start and stop it have been conveniently replaced by a toggle switch. I have also added two new messages which can change the period and thus make the metronome faster or slower. The interesting part is just below the metronome. A float box receives bang messages on its hot inlet. Its initial value is 0, so upon receiving the first bang message it outputs a float number 0 which the number box then displays. Were it not for the `+ 1` object the patch would continue outputting 0 once per beat forever. However, look closely at the wiring of these two objects: `f` and `+ 1` are connected to form an *incrementor* or *counter*. Each time `f` recieves a bang it ouputs the number currently stored to `+ 1` which adds 1 to it. This is fed back into the cold inlet of `f` which updates its value, now 1. The next time a bang arrives, 1 is output, which goes round again through `+ 1` and becomes 2. This repeats as long as bang messages arrive: each time the output increases by 1. If you start the metronome in figure 10.7 you will see the number box slowly counting up, once per second. Clicking the message boxes to change the period will make it count up faster with a 500ms delay between beats (twice per second), or still faster at 4 times per second (250ms period).

Time Objects

Three related objects help us manipulate time in the message domain. `timer` accurately measures the interval between receiving two bang messages, the first on its left inlet and the second on its right inlet. It is shown on the left in figure 10.8.

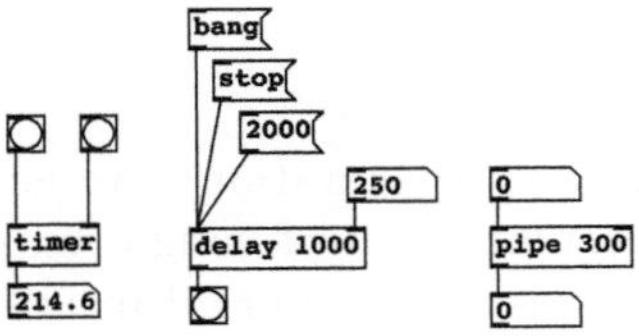

Clicking the first bang button will reset and start `timer` and then hitting the second one will output the time elapsed (in ms). Notice that `timer` is unusual; it's one of the few objects where the right inlet behaves as the hot control. `delay` shown in the middle of figure 10.8 will output a single bang message a certain time period after receiving a bang on its left inlet. This interval is set

Figure 10.8
Time objects.

by its first argument or right inlet, or by the value of a float arriving at its left inlet, so there are three ways of setting the time delay. If a new bang arrives, any pending one is cancelled and a new delay is initiated. If a `stop` message arrives, then `delay` is reset and all pending events are cancelled. Sometimes we want to delay a stream of number messages by a fixed amount, which is where `pipe` comes in. This allocates a memory buffer that moves messages from its inlet to its outlet, taking a time set by its first argument or second inlet. If you change the top number box of the right patch in figure 10.8 you will see the lower number box follow it, but lagging behind by 300ms.

Select

This object outputs a bang on one of its outlets matching something in its argument list. For example, `select 2 4 6` will output a bang on its second outlet if it receives a number 4, or on its third outlet when a number 6 arrives. Messages that do not match any argument are passed through to the rightmost outlet.

Figure 10.9
Simple sequencer.

This makes it rather easy to begin making simple sequences. The patch in figure 10.9 cycles around four steps, blinking each bang button in turn. It is a metronome running with a 300ms period and a counter. On the first step the counter holds 0, and when this is output to `select` it sends a bang to its first outlet which matches 0. As the counter increments, successive outlets of `select` produce a bang, until the fourth one is reached. When this happens a message containing 0 is triggered which feeds into the cold inlet of `f` resetting the counter to 0.

SECTION 10.3

Data Flow Control

In this section are a few common objects used to control the flow of data around patches. As you have just seen, `select` can send bang messages along a choice of connections, so it gives us a kind of selective flow.

Route

Figure 10.10
Routing values.

Route behaves in a similar fashion to select, only it operates on lists. If the first element of a list matches an argument, the remainder of the list is passed to the corresponding outlet.

So, `route badger mushroom snake` will send 20.0 to its third outlet when it receives the message {*snake 20*}. Nonmatching lists are passed unchanged to the rightmost outlet. Arguments can be numbers or symbols, but we tend to use symbols because a combination of `route` with lists is a great way to give parameters names so we don't forget what they are for.

We have a few named values in figure 10.10 for synthesiser controls. Each message box contains a two-element list, a name-value pair. When `route` encounters one that matches one of its arguments it sends it to the correct number box.

Moses

This is a "stream splitter" which sends numbers below a threshold to its left outlet, and numbers greater than or equal to the threshold to the right outlet. The threshold is set by the first argument or a value appearing on the right inlet. `moses 20` splits any incoming numbers at 20.0.

Spigot

This is a switch that can control any stream of messages including lists and symbols. A zero on the right inlet of `spigot` stops any messages on the left inlet passing to the outlet. Any non-zero number turns the spigot on.

Swap

Figure 10.11
Swapping values.

It might look like a very trivial thing to do, and you may ask—why not just cross two wires? In fact `swap` is a really useful object. It just exchanges the two values on its inlets and passes them to its outlets, but it can take an argument, so it always exchanges a number with a constant. It's useful when this constant is 1 as shown later for calculating complement $1 - x$ and inverse $1/x$ of a number, or where it is 100 for calculating values as a percent.

Change

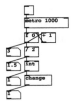

Figure 10.12
Pass values that change.

This is useful if we have a stream of numbers, perhaps from a physical controller like a joystick that is polled at regular intervals, but we only want to know values when they change. It is frequently seen preceded by `int` to denoise a jittery signal or when dividing timebases. In figure 10.12 we see a counter that has been stopped after reaching 3. The components below it are designed to divide the timebase in half. That is to say, for a sequence $\{1, 2, 3, 4, 5, 6 \ldots\}$ we will get $\{1, 2, 3 \ldots\}$. There should be half as many numbers in the output during the same time interval. In other words, the output changes half as often as the input. Since the counter has just passed 3 the output of `/` is 1.5 and `int` truncates this to 1. But this is the second time we have seen 1 appear, since the same number was sent when the input was 2. Without using `change` we would get $\{1, 1, 2, 2, 3, 3 \ldots\}$ as output.

Send and Receive Objects

Figure 10.13
Sends.

These are very useful when patches get too visually dense, or when you are working with patches spread across many canvases. **send** and **receive** objects, abbreviated as **s** and **r**, work as named pairs. Anything that goes into the send unit is transmitted by an invisible wire and appears immediately on the receiver, so whatever goes into **send bob** reappears at **receive bob**.

Matching sends and receives have global names by default and can exist in different canvases loaded at the same time. So if the **receive** objects in figure 10.14 are in a different patch they will still pick up the send values from figure 10.13. The relationship is one to many, so only one send can have a particular name but can be picked up by multiple **receive** objects with the same name. In the latest versions of Pd the destination is dynamic and can be changed by a message on the right inlet.

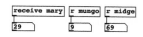

Figure 10.14
Receives.

Broadcast Messages

As we have just seen, there is an "invisible" environment through which messages may travel as well as through wires. A message box containing a message that begins with a semicolon is *broadcast*, and Pd will route it to any destination that matches the first symbol. This way, activating the message box `; foo 20(` is the same as sending a float message with a value of 20 to the object `s foo`.

Special Message Destinations

This method can be used to address arrays with special commands, to talk to GUI elements that have a defined *receive symbol* or as an alternative way to talk to **receive** objects. If you want to change the size of arrays dynamically they recognise a special *resize* message. There is also a special destination (which always exists) called `pd` which is the audio engine. It can act on broadcast messages like `; pd dsp 1(` to turn on the audio computation from a patch. Some examples are shown in figure 10.15.

Message Sequences

Several messages can be stored in the same message box as a sequence if separated by commas, so `2, 3, 4, 5(` is a message box that will send four values one after another when clicked or banged. This happens instantly (in *logical time*). This is often confusing to beginners when comparing sequences to lists. When you send the contents of a message box containing a sequence all the elements are sent in one go, but as separate messages in a stream. Lists, on the other hand, which are not separated by commas, also send all the elements at the

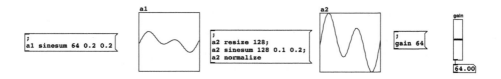

Figure 10.15
Special message broadcasts.

same time, but as a single list message. Lists and sequences can be mixed, so a message box might contain a sequence of lists.

List Objects and Operations

Lists can be quite an advanced topic and we could devote an entire chapter to this subject. Pd has all the capabilities of a full programming language like LISP, using only list operations, but like that language all the more complex functions are defined in terms of just a few intrinsic operations and abstractions. The *list-abs* collection by Frank Barknecht and others is available in *pd-extended*. It contains scores of advanced operations like sorting, reversing, inserting, searching, and performing conditional operations on every element of a list. Here we will look at a handful of very simple objects and leave it as an exercise to the reader to research the more advanced capabilities of lists for building sequencers and data analysis tools.

Packing and Unpacking Lists

The usual way to create and disassemble lists is to use `pack` and `unpack`. Arguments are given to each which are type identifiers, so `pack f f f f` is an object that will wrap up four floats given on its inlets into a single list. They should be presented in right-to-left order so that the hot inlet is filled last. You can also give float values directly as arguments of a `pack` object where you want them to be fixed; so `pack 1 f f 4` is legal, the first and last list elements will be 1 and 4 unless overridden by the inlets, and the two middle ones will be variable.

Start by changing the right number in figure 10.16, then the one to its left, then click on the symbol boxes and type a short string before hitting RETURN. When you enter the last symbol connected to the hot inlet of `pack`, you will see the data received by figure 10.17 appear in the display boxes after it is unpacked.

The `unpack s s f f` will expect two symbols and two floats and send them to its four outlets. Items are packed and unpacked in the sequence given in the list, but in right-

Figure 10.16
List packing.

to-left order. That means the floats from `unpack s s f f` will appear first, starting

with the rightmost one, then the two symbols ending on
the leftmost one. Of course this happens so quickly you
cannot see the ordering, but it makes sense to happen
this way so that if you are unpacking data, changing it,
and repacking into a list, everything occurs in the right
order. Note that the types of data in the list must match
the arguments of each object. Unless you use the **a** (any)
type, Pd will complain if you try to pack or unpack a
mismatched type.

Figure 10.17
List unpacking.

Substitutions

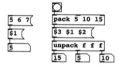

Figure 10.18
Dollar substitution.

A message box can also act as a template. When an
item in a message box is written $1, it behaves as an
empty slot that assumes the value of the first element of
a given list. Each of the dollar arguments $1, $2, and so on
are replaced by the corresponding item in the input list.
The message box then sends the new message with any
slots filled in. List elements can be substituted in multiple positions as seen in figure 10.18. The list {5 10 15}
becomes {15 5 10} when put through the substitution
$3 $1 $2.

Persistence

You will often want to set up a patch so it's in a certain state when loaded.
It's possible to tell most GUI objects to output the last value they had when
the patch was saved. You can do this by setting the **init** checkbox in the
properties panel. But what if the data you want to keep comes from another
source, like an external MIDI fader board? A useful object is loadbang which
generates a bang message as soon as the patch loads.

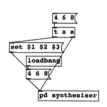

Figure 10.19
Persistence using messages.

You can use this in combination with a message
box to initialise some values. The contents of message
boxes are saved and loaded with the patch. When you
need to stop working on a project but have it load the
last state next time around then list data can be saved
in the patch with a message box by using the special
set prefix. If a message box receives a list prefixed by
set it will be filled with the list, but will not immediately ouput it. The arrangement in figure 10.19 is
used to keep a 3 element list for **pd synthesiser** in
a message box that will be saved with the patch, then
generate it to initialise the synthesiser again when the patch is reloaded.

List Distribution

An object with 2 or more message inlets will distribute a list of parameters to
all inlets using only the first inlet.

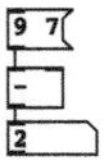

The number of elements in the list must match the number of inlets and their types must be compatible. In figure 10.20 a message box contains a list of two numbers, 9 and 7. When a pair of values like this are sent to $\boxed{-}$ with its right inlet unconnected they are spread over the two inlets, in the order they appear, thus $9 - 7 = 2$.

Figure 10.20
Distribution.

More Advanced List Operations

To concatenate two lists together we use $\boxed{\texttt{list append}}$. It takes two lists and creates a new one, with the second list attached to the end of the first. If given an argument it will append this to every list it receives. It may be worth knowing that $\boxed{\texttt{list}}$ is an alias for $\boxed{\texttt{list append}}$. You can choose to type in either in order to make it clearer what you are doing. Very similar is $\boxed{\texttt{list prepend}}$ which does almost the same thing, but returns a new list with the argument or list at the second inlet concatenated to the beginning. For disassembling lists we can use $\boxed{\texttt{list split}}$. This takes a list on its left inlet and a number on the right inlet (or as an argument) which indicates the position to split the list. It produces two new lists: one containing elements below the split point appears on the left outlet, and the remainder of the list appears on the right. If the supplied list is shorter than the split number then the entire list is passed unchanged to the right outlet. The $\boxed{\texttt{list trim}}$ object strips off any selector at the start, leaving the raw elements.

┌─ SECTION 10.5 ──┐

Input and Output

└──┘

There are plenty of objects in Pd for reading keyboards, mice, system timers, serial ports, and USBs. There's not enough room in this book to do much more than summarise them, so please refer to the Pd online documentation for your platform. Many of these are available only as external objects, but several are built into the Pd core. Some depend on the platform used; for example, $\boxed{\texttt{comport}}$ and $\boxed{\texttt{key}}$ are only available on Linux and MacOS. One of the most useful externals available is $\boxed{\texttt{hid}}$, which is the "human interface device." With this you can connect joysticks, game controllers, dance mats, steering wheels, graphics tablets, and all kinds of fun things. File IO is available using $\boxed{\texttt{textfile}}$ and $\boxed{\texttt{qlist}}$ objects, objects are available to make database transactions to MySQL, and of course audio file IO is simple using a range of objects like $\boxed{\texttt{writesf~}}$ and $\boxed{\texttt{readsf~}}$. MIDI files can be imported and written with similar objects. Network access is available through $\boxed{\texttt{netsend}}$ and $\boxed{\texttt{netreceive}}$, which offer UDP or TCP services. Open Sound Control is available using the external OSC library by Martin Peach or $\boxed{\texttt{dumpOSC}}$ and $\boxed{\texttt{sendOSC}}$ objects. You can even generate or open compressed audio streams using $\boxed{\texttt{mp3cast~}}$ (by Yves Degoyon) and similar externals, and you can run code from other languages like python and lua. A popular hardware peripheral for use in combination with Pd is the Arduino board, which gives a number of buffered analog and digital lines, serial and parallel, for robotics and control applications. Nearly all of this is quite beyond the scope of this book. The way you set up your DAW and build your sound design studio is an individual matter, but Pd should not disappoint you when it comes to I/O connectivity. We will now look at a few common input and output channels.

The Print Object

Where would we be without a `print` object? Not much use for making sound, but vital for debugging patches. Message domain data is dumped to the console so you can see what is going on. You can give it a nonnumerical argument which will prefix any output and make it easier to find in a long printout.

MIDI

When working with musical keyboards there are objects to help integrate these devices so you can build patches with traditional synthesiser and sampler behaviours. For sound design, this is great for attaching MIDI fader boards to control parameters, and of course musical interface devices like breath controllers and MIDI guitars can be used. Hook up any MIDI source to Pd by activating a MIDI device from the `Media->MIDI` menu (you can check that this is working from `Media->Test Audio and MIDI`).

Notes in

You can create single events to trigger from individual keys, or have layers and velocity fades by adding extra logic.

The `notein` object produces note number, velocity, and channel values on its left, middle, and right outlets. You may assign an object to listen to only one channel by giving it an argument from 1 to 15. Remember that note-off messages are equivalent to a note-on with zero velocity in many MIDI implementations, and Pd follows this method. You therefore need to add extra logic before connecting an oscillator or sample player to `notein` so that zero-valued MIDI notes are not played.

Figure 10.21
MIDI note in.

Notes out

Another object `noteout` sends MIDI to external devices. The first, second, and third inlets set note number, velocity, and channel respectively. The channel is 1 by default. Make sure you have something connected that can play back MIDI and set the patch shown in figure 10.22 running with its toggle switch. Every 200ms it produces a C on a random octave with a random velocity value between 0 and 127. Without further ado these could be sent to `noteout`, but it would cause each MIDI note to "hang," since we never send a note-off message. To properly construct MIDI notes you need `makenote` which takes a note number and velocity, and a duration (in milliseconds) as its third argument. After the duration has expired it automatically adds a note-off. If more than one physical MIDI port is enabled then `noteout` sends channels 1 to 16 to port 1 and channels 17 to 32 to port 2, etc.

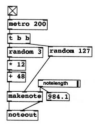

Figure 10.22
MIDI note generation.

Continuous controllers

Two MIDI input/output objects are provided to receive and send continuous controllers, `ctlin` and `ctlout`. Their three connections provide, or let you set, the controller value, controller number, and MIDI channel. They can be instantiated with arguments, so `ctlin 10 1` picks up controller 10 (pan position) on MIDI channel 1.

MIDI to frequency

Two numerical conversion utilities are provided to convert between MIDI note numbers and Hz. To get from MIDI to Hz use `mtof`. To convert a frequency in Hz to a MIDI note number use `ftom`.

Other MIDI objects

For pitchbend, program changes, system exclusive, aftertouch, and other MIDI functions you may use any of the objects summarised in figure 10.23. System exclusive messages may be sent by hand crafting raw MIDI bytes and outputting via the `midiout` object. Most follow the inlet and outlet template of `notein` and `noteout` having a channel as the last argument, except for `midiin` and `sysexin` which receive omni (all channels) data.

MIDI in object		MIDI out object	
Object	Function	Object	Function
`notein`	Get note data	`noteout`	Send note data.
`bendin`	Get pitchbend data −63 to +64	`bendout`	Send pitchbend data −64 to +64.
`pgmin`	Get program changes.	`pgmout`	Send program changes.
`ctlin`	Get continuous controller messages.	`ctlout`	Send continuous controller messages.
`touchin`	Get channel aftertouch data.	`touchout`	Send channel aftertouch data.
`polytouchin`	Polyphonic touch data in	`polytouchout`	Polyphonic touch output
`midiin`	Get unformatted raw MIDI	`midiout`	Send raw MIDI to device.
`sysexin`	Get system exclusive data	No output counterpart	Use `midiout` object

Figure 10.23
List of MIDI objects.

Working with Numbers

Arithmetic Objects

Objects that operate on ordinary numbers to provide basic maths functions are summarised in figure 10.24. All have hot left and cold right inlets and all take

Object	Function
`+ `	Add two floating point numbers
`- `	Subtract number on right inlet from number on left inlet
`/ `	Divide lefthand number by number on right inlet
`* `	Multiply two floating point numbers
`div`	Integer divide, how many times the number on the right inlet divides exactly into the number on the left inlet
`mod`	Modulo, the smallest remainder of dividing the left number into any integer multiple of the right number

Figure 10.24
Table of message arithmetic operators.

Object	Function
`cos`	The cosine of a number given in radians. Domain: $-\pi/2$ to $+\pi/2$. Range: -1.0 to $+1.0$.
`sin`	The sine of a number in radians, domain $-\pi/2$ to $+\pi/2$, range -1.0 to $+1.0$
`tan`	Tangent of number given in radians. Range: 0.0 to ∞ at $\pm\pi/2$
`atan`	Arctangent of any number in domain $\pm\infty$ Range: $\pm\pi/2$
`atan2`	Arctangent of the quotient of two numbers in Cartesian plane. Domain: any floats representing X, Y pair. Range: angle in radians $\pm\pi$
`exp`	Exponential function e^x for any number. Range 0.0 to ∞
`log`	Natural log (base e) of any number. Domain: 0.0 to ∞. Range: $\pm\infty$ ($-\infty$ is -1000.0)
`abs`	Absolute value of any number. Domain $\pm\infty$. Range 0.0 to ∞
`sqrt`	The square root of any positive number. Domain 0.0 to ∞
`pow`	Exponentiate the left inlet to the power of the right inlet. Domain: positive left values only.

Figure 10.25
Table of message trigonometric and higher math operators.

one argument that initialises the value otherwise received on the right inlet. Note the difference between arithmetic division with [/] and the [div] object. The modulo operator gives the remainder of dividing the left number by the right.

Trigonometric Maths Objects

A summary of higher maths functions is given in figure 10.25.

Random Numbers

A useful ability is to make random numbers. The [random] object gives integers over the range given by its argument including zero, so [random 10] gives 10 possible values from 0 to 9.

Arithmetic Example

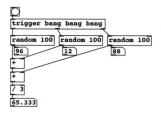

An example is given in figure 10.26 to show correct ordering in a patch to calculate the mean of three random numbers. We don't have to make every inlet hot, just ensure that everything arrives in the correct sequence by triggering the [random] objects properly. The first [random] (on the right) supplies the cold inlet of the lower [+], the middle one to the cold inlet of the upper [+]. When the final (left) [random] is generated it passes to the hot inlet of the first [+], which computes the sum and passes it to the second [+] hot inlet. Finally we divide by 3 to get the mean value.

Figure 10.26
Mean of three random floats.

Comparative Objects

In figure 10.27 you can see a summary of comparative objects. Output is either 1 or 0 depending on whether the comparison is true or false. All have hot left inlets and cold right inlets and can take an argument to initialise the righthand value.

Boolean Logical Objects

There are a whole bunch of logical objects in Pd including bitwise operations that work exactly like C code. Most of them aren't of much interest to us in this book, but we will mention the two important ones, [||] and [&&]. The output of [||], logical OR, is true if either of its inputs are true. The output of [&&], logical AND, is true only when both its inputs are true. In Pd any non-zero number is "true," so the logical inverter or "not" function is unnecessary because there are many ways of achieving this using other objects. For example, you can make a logical inverter by using [==] with 1 as its argument.

Object	Function
>	True if the number at the left inlet is greater than the right inlet.
<	True if the number at the left inlet is less than the right inlet.
>=	True if the number at the left inlet is greater than or equal to the right inlet.
<=	True if the number at the left inlet is less than or equal to the right inlet.
==	True if the number at the left inlet is equal to the right inlet.
!=	True if the number at the left inlet is not equal to the right inlet.

Figure 10.27
List of comparative operators.

SECTION 10.7

Common Idioms

There are design patterns that crop up frequently in all types of programming. Later we will look at abstraction and how to encapsulate code into new objects so you don't find yourself writing the same thing again and again. Here I will introduce a few very common patterns.

Constrained Counting

We have already seen how to make a counter by repeatedly incrementing the value stored in a float box. To turn an increasing or decreasing counter into a cycle for repeated sequences there is an easier way than resetting the counter when it matches an upper limit: we wrap the numbers using mod. By inserting mod into the feedback path before the increment we can ensure the counter stays bounded. Further mod units can be added to the number stream to generate polyrhythmic sequences. You will frequently see variations on the idiom shown in figure 10.28. This is the way we produce multirate timebases for musical sequencers, rolling objects, or machine sounds that have complex repetitive patterns.

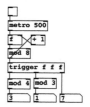

Figure 10.28
Constrained counter.

Accumulator

A similar construct to a counter is the accumulator or integrator. This reverses the positions of f and + to create an integrator that stores the sum of all previous number messages sent to it. Such an arrangement is useful for turning

Figure 10.29
Accumulator.

"up and down" messages from an input controller into a position. Whether to use a counter or accumulator is a subtle choice. Although you can change the increment step of the counter by placing a new value on the right inlet of ⊞ it will not take effect until the previous value in 𝖿 has been used. An accumulator, on the other hand, can be made to jump different intervals immediately by the value sent to it. Note this important difference: an accumulator takes floats as an input while a counter takes bang messages.

Rounding

Figure 10.30
Rounding.

An integer function, **int**, also abbreviated **i**, gives the whole part of a floating point number. This is a *truncation*, which just throws away any decimal digits. For positive numbers it gives the *floor* function, written $\lfloor x \rfloor$, which is the integer *less than or equal to* the input value. But take note of what happens for *negative* values, applying **int** to -3.4 will give -3.0, an integer *greater than or equal to* the input. Truncation is shown on the left in figure 10.30. To get a regular rounding for positive numbers, to pick the *closest* integer, use the method shown on the right in figure 10.30. This will return 1 for an input of 0.5 or more and 0 for an input of 0.49999999 or less.

Scaling

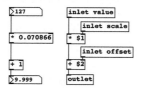

Figure 10.31
Scaling.

This is such a common idiom you will see it almost everywhere. Given some input values such as 0 to 127, we may wish to map them to another set of values, such as 1 to 10. This is the same as changing the slope and zero intersect of a line following $y = mx + c$. To work out the values you first obtain the bottom value or *offset*, in this case $+1$. Then a *multiplier* value is needed to scale for the upper value, which given an input of 127 would satisfy $10 = 1 + 127x$, so moving the offset we get $9 = 127x$, and dividing by 127 we get $x = 9/127$ or $x = 0.070866$. You can make a subpatch or an abstraction for this as shown in figure 13.1, but since only two objects are used it's more sensible to do scaling and offset as you need it.

Looping with Until

Unfortunately, because it must be designed this way, **until** has the potential to cause a complete system lockup. Be very careful to understand what you are doing with this. A bang message on the left inlet of **until** will set it producing bang messages as fast as the system can handle! These do not stop *until* a bang message is received on the right inlet. Its purpose is to behave as a fast loop construct performing message domain computation quickly. This way you can fill an entire wavetable or calculate a complex formula in the time it takes to

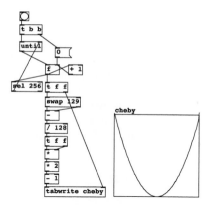

Figure 10.32
Using until.

process a single audio block. Always make sure the right inlet is connected to a valid terminating condition. In figure 10.32 you can see an example that computes the second Chebyshev polynomial according to $y = 2x^2 - 1$ for the range -1.0 to $+1.0$ and fills a 256-step table with the result. As soon as the bang button is pressed a counter is reset to zero, and then `until` begins sending out bangs. These cause the counter to rapidly increment until `select` matches 256, whereupon a bang is sent to the right inlet of `until`, stopping the process. All this will happen in a fraction of a millisecond. Meanwhile we use the counter output to calculate a Chebyshev curve and put it into the table.

Figure 10.33
For 256.

A safer way to use `until` is shown in figure 10.33. If you know in advance that you want to perform a fixed number of operations, then use it like a **for loop**. In this case you pass a non-zero float to the left inlet. There is no terminating condition; it stops when the specified number of bangs has been sent—256 bangs in the example shown.

Message Complement and Inverse

Figure 10.34
Message reciprocal and inverse.

Here is how we obtain the number that is $1 - x$ for any x. The *complement* of x is useful when you want to balance two numbers so they add up to a constant value, such as in panning. The `swap` object exchanges its inlet values, or any left inlet value with its first argument. Therefore, what happens with the lefthand example of figure 10.34 is the ☐ calculates $1 - x$, which for an input of 0.25 gives 0.75. Similarly, the inverse of a float message $1/x$ can be calculated by replacing the ☐ with a ☐.

Random Selection

To choose one of several events at random, a combination of `random` and `select` will generate a bang message on the select outlet corresponding to one of its arguments. With an initial argument of 4 `random` produces a *range* of 4 random integer numbers starting at 0, so we use `select 0 1 2 3` to select amongst them. Each has an equal probability, so every outlet will be triggered 25% of the time on average.

Figure 10.35
Random select.

Weighted Random Selection

Figure 10.36
Weighted random select.

A simple way to get a bunch of events with a certain probability distribution is to generate uniformly distributed numbers and stream them with `moses`. For example, `moses 10` sends integers greater than 9.0 to its right outlet. A cascade of `moses` objects will distribute them in a ratio over the combined outlets when the sum of all ratios equals the range of random numbers. The outlets of `moses 10` distribute the numbers in the ratio 1 : 9. When the right outlet is further split by `moses 50` as in figure 10.36, numbers in the range 0.0 to 100.0 are split in the ratio 10 : 40 : 50, and since the distribution of input numbers is uniform they are sent to one of three outlets with 10%, 40%, and 50% probability.

Delay Cascade

Sometimes we want a quick succession of bangs in a certain fixed timing pattern. An easy way to do this is to cascade `delay` objects. Each `delay 100` in figure 10.37 adds a delay of 100 milliseconds. Notice the abbreviated form of the object name is used.

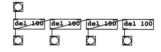

Figure 10.37
Delay cascade.

Last Float and Averages

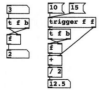

Figure 10.38
Last value and averaging.

If you have a stream of float values and want to keep the previous value to compare to the current one then the idiom shown on the left in figure 10.38 will do the job. Notice how a trigger is employed to first bang the *last* value stored in the float box and then update it with the current value via the right inlet. This can be turned into a simple "low pass" or averaging filter for float messages as shown on the right in figure 10.38. If you add the previous value to the current one and divide by two you obtain the average. In the example shown the values were 10 followed by 15, resulting in $(10 + 15)/2 = 12.5$.

Running Maximum (or Minimum)

Giving a very small argument and connecting whatever passes through it back to its right inlet gives us a way to keep track of the largest value. In figure 10.39 the greatest past value in the stream has been 35. Giving a very large argument to `min` provides the opposite behaviour for tracking a lowest value. If you need to reset the maximum or minimum tracker just send a very large or small float value to the cold inlet to start again.

Figure 10.39
Biggest so far.

Float Low Pass

Using only `*` and `+` as shown in figure 10.40 we can low pass filter a stream of float values. This is useful to smooth data from an external controller where values are occasionally anomalous. It follows the filter equation $y_n = Ax_n + Bx_{n-1}$. The strength of the filter is set by the ratio $A : B$. Both A and B should be between 0.0 and 1.0 and add up to 1.0. Note that this method will not converge on the exact input value, so you might like to follow it with `int` if you need numbers rounded to integer values.

Figure 10.40
Low pass for floats.

11
Pure Data Audio

Audio Objects

We have looked at Pd in enough detail now to move on to the next level. You have a basic grasp of dataflow programming and know how to make patches that process numbers and symbols. But why has no mention been made of audio yet? Surely it is the main purpose of our study? The reason for this is that audio signal processing is a little more complex in Pd than the numbers and symbols we have so far considered, so I wanted to leave this until now.

Audio Connections

I have already mentioned that there are two kinds of objects and data for messages and signals. Corresponding to these there are two kinds of connections, audio connections and message connections. There is no need to do anything special to make the right kind of connection. When you connect two objects together, Pd will work out what type of outlet you are attempting to connect to what kind of inlet and create the appropriate connection. If you try to connect an audio signal to a message inlet, then Pd will not let you, or it will complain if there is an allowable but ambiguous connection. Audio objects always have a name ending with a tilde (~) and the connections between them look fatter than ordinary message connections.

Blocks

The signal data travelling down audio cords is made of *samples*, single floating point values in a sequence that forms an audio signal. Samples are grouped together in *blocks*.

A block, sometimes called a *vector*, typically has 64 samples inside it, but you can change this in certain circumstances. Objects operating on signal blocks behave like ordinary message objects; they can add, subtract, delay, or store blocks of data, but they do so by processing one whole block at a time. In figure 11.1 streams of blocks are fed to the two inlets. Blocks appearing at the outlet have values which are the sum of the corresponding values in the two input blocks. Because they process signals made of blocks, audio objects do a lot more work than objects that process messages.

Audio Object CPU Use

All the message objects we looked at in the last chapters only use CPU when event-driven dataflow occurs, so most of the time they sit idle and consume no resources. Many of the boxes we put on our sound design canvases will be audio objects, so it's worth noting that they use up some CPU power just being

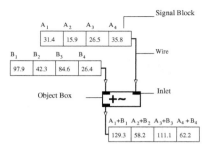

Figure 11.1
Object processing data.

idle. Whenever `compute audio` is switched on they are processing a constant stream of signal blocks, even if the blocks contain only zeros. Unlike messages, which are processed in logical time, signals are processed synchronously with the sound card sample rate. This *real-time* constraint means glitches will occur unless every signal object in the patch can be computed before the next block is sent out. Pd will not simply give up when this happens; it will struggle along trying to maintain real-time processing, so you need to listen carefully. As you hit the CPU limit of the computer you may hear crackles or pops. The DIO indicator on the Pd console shows when *over-run* errors have occurred. Click this to reset it. It is also worth knowing how audio computation relates to message computation. Message operations are executed at the beginning of each pass of audio block processing, so a patch where audio depends on message operations which don't complete in time will also fail to produce correct output.

┌─ SECTION 11.2 ───
│
│ # Audio Objects and Principles
│
└──

There are a few ways that audio objects differ from message objects, so let's look at those rules now before starting to create sounds.

Fanout and Merging

Figure 11.2
Signal fanout is okay.

You can connect the same signal outlet to as many other audio signal inlets as you like; blocks are sent in an order which corresponds to the creation of the connections, much like message connections. But unlike messages, most of the time this will have no effect whatsoever, so you can treat audio signals that fan out as if they were perfect simultaneous copies. Very seldom you may meet rare and interesting problems, especially with delays and feedback, that can be fixed by reordering audio signals (see chapter 7 of Puckette 2007 regarding time shifts and block delays).

When several signal connections all come into the same signal inlet that's also fine. In this case they are implicitly summed, so you may need to scale your signal to reduce its range again at the output of the object. You can connect as many signals to the same inlet as you like, but sometimes it makes a patch easier to understand if you explicitly sum them with a `+~` unit.

Figure 11.3
Merging signals is okay.

Time and Resolution

Time is measured in seconds, milliseconds (one thousandth of a second, written 1ms) or samples. Most Pd times are in ms. Where time is measured in samples, this depends on the sampling rate of the program or the sound card of the computer system on which it runs. The current sample rate is returned by the `samplerate~` object. Typically a sample is 1/44100th of a second and is the smallest unit of time that can be measured as a signal. But the time resolution also depends on the object doing the computation. For example, `metro` and `vline~` are able to deal in fractions of a millisecond, even less than one sample. Timing irregularities can occur where some objects are only accurate to one block boundary and some are not.

Audio Signal Block to Messages

To see the contents of a signal block we can take a snapshot or an average. The `env~` object provides the RMS value of one block of audio data scaled 0 to 100 in dB, while `snapshot~` gives the instantaneous value of the last sample in the previous block. To view an entire block for debugging, `print~` can be used. It accepts an audio signal and a bang message on the same inlet and prints the current audio block contents when banged.

Sending and Receiving Audio Signals

Audio equivalents of `send` and `receive` are written `send~` and `receive~`, with shortened forms `s~` and `r~`. Unlike message sends, only one audio send can exist with a given name. If you want to create a signal bus with many-to-one connectivity, use `throw~` and `catch~` instead. Within subpatches and abstractions we use the signal objects `inlet~` and `outlet~` to create inlets and outlets.

Audio Generators

Only a few objects are signal sources. The most important and simple one is the `phasor~`. This outputs an asymmetrical periodic ramp wave and is used at the heart of many other digital oscillators we are going to make. Its left inlet specifies the frequency in Hz, and its right inlet sets the phase, between 0.0 and 1.0. The first and only argument is for frequency, so a typical instance of a phasor looks like `phasor~ 110`. For sinusoidal waveforms we can use `osc~`. Again, frequency and phase are set by the left and right inlets, or frequency is set by the creation parameter. A sinusoidal oscillator at concert A pitch is defined by `osc~ 440`. White noise is another commonly used source in sound design. The

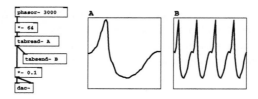

Figure 11.4
Table oscillator.

noise generator in Pd is simply `noise~` and has no creation arguments. Its output is in the range −1.0 to 1.0. Looped waveforms stored in an array can be used to implement *wavetable* synthesis using the `tabosc4~` object. This is a 4-point interpolating table ocillator and requires an array that is a power of 2, plus 3 (e.g. 0 to 258) in order to work properly. It can be instantiated like `phasor~` or `osc~` with a frequency argument. A table oscillator running at 3kHz is shown in figure 11.4. It takes the waveform stored in array A and loops around this at the frequency given by its argument or left inlet value. To make sound samplers we

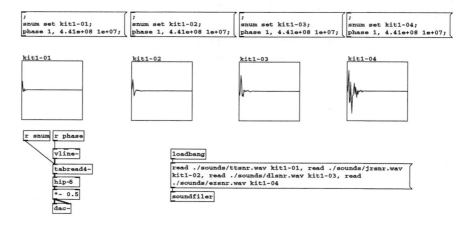

Figure 11.5
Sample replay from arrays.

need to read and write audio data from an array. The index to `tabread~` and its interpolating friend `tabread4~` is a sample number, so you need to supply a signal with the correct slope and magnitude to get the proper playback rate. You can use the special `set` message to reassign `tabread4~` to read from another array. The message boxes in figure 11.5 allow a single object to play back from more than one sample table. First the target array is given via a message to **snum**, and then a message is sent to **phase** which sets `vline~` moving up at 44,100 samples per second. The arrays are initially loaded, using a multipart message, from a **sounds** folder in the current patch directory.

Audio Line Objects

For signal rate control data the `line~` object is useful. It is generally programmed with a sequence of lists. Each list consists of a pair of numbers: the first is a level to move to and the second is the time in milliseconds to take getting there. The range is usually between 1.0 and 0.0 when used as an audio control signal, but it can be any value such as when using `line~` to index a table. A more versatile line object is called `vline~`, which we will meet in much more detail later. Amongst its advantages are very accurate sub-millisecond timing and the ability to read multisegment lists in one go and to delay stages of movement. Both these objects are essential for constructing envelope generators and other control signals.

Audio Input and Output

Audio IO is achieved with the `adc~` and `dac~` objects. By default these offer two inlets or outlets for stereo operation, but you can request as many additional sound channels as your sound system will handle by giving them numerical arguments.

Example: A Simple MIDI Monosynth

Using the objects we've just discussed let's create a little MIDI keyboard-controlled music synthesiser as shown in figure 11.6. Numbers appearing at the left outlet of `notein` control the frequency of an oscillator. MIDI numbers are converted to a Hertz frequency by `mtof`. The MIDI standard, or rather general adherence to it, is a bit woolly by allowing note-off to also be a note-on with a velocity of zero. Pd follows this definition, so when a key is released it produces a note with a zero velocity. For this simple example we remove it with `stripnote`, which only passes note-on messages when their velocity is greater than zero. The velocity value, ranging between 1 and 127, is scaled to between 0 and 1 in order to provide a rudimentary amplitude control.

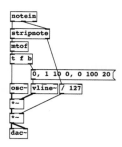

Figure 11.6
MIDI note control.

So, here's a great place to elaborate on the anatomy of the message used to control `vline~` as shown in figure 11.7. The syntax makes perfect sense, but sometimes it's hard to visualise without practice. The general form has three numbers per list. It says: *"go to some value,"* given by the first number, then *"take a certain time to get there,"* which is the second number in each list. The last number in the list is a time to wait before executing the command, so it adds an extra *"wait for a time before doing it."* What makes `vline~` cool is you

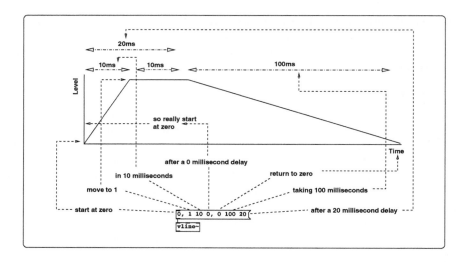

Figure 11.7
Anatomy of vline message.

can send a sequence of list messages in any order, and so long as they make temporal sense `vline~` will execute them all. This means you can make very complex control envelopes. Any missing arguments in a list are dropped in right-to-left order, so a valid exception is seen in the first element of figure 11.7 where a single 0 means *"jump immediately to zero"* (don't bother to wait or take any time getting there).

Audio Filter Objects

Six or seven filters are used in this book. We will not look at them in much detail until we need to because there is a lot to say about their usage in each case. Simple one-pole and one-zero real filters are given by `rpole~` and `rzero~`. Complex one-pole and one-zero filters are `cpole~` and `czero~`. A static biquad filter `biquad~` also comes with a selection of helper objects to calculate coefficients for common configurations, and `lop~`, `hip~`, and `bp~ 1` provide the standard low, high, and band pass responses. These are easy to use and allow message rate control of their cutoff frequencies and, in the case of bandpass, resonance. The first and only argument of the low and high pass filters is frequency, so typical instances may look like `lop~ 500` and `hip~ 500`. Bandpass takes a second parameter for resonance like this `bp~ 100 3`. Fast signal rate control of cutoff is possible using the versatile `vcf~` "voltage controlled filter." Its first argument is cutoff frequency and its second argument is resonance, so you might use it like `vcf~ 100 2`. With high resonances this provides a sharp filter that can give narrow bands. An even more colourful filter for use in music synthesiser designs is available as an external called `moog~`, which provides a classic design that can self-oscillate.

Audio Arithmetic Objects

Audio signal objects for simple arithmetic are summarised in figure 11.8.

Object	Function
`+~`	Add two signals (either input will also accept a message)
`-~`	Subtract righthand signal from lefthand signal
`/~`	Divide lefthand signal by right signal
`*~`	Signal multiplication
`wrap~`	Signal wrap, constrain any signal between 0.0 and 1.0

Figure 11.8
List of arithmetic operators.

Trigonometric and Math Objects

A summary of higher maths functions is given in figure 11.9. Some signal units are abstractions defined in terms of more elementary intrinsic objects, and those marked * are only available through external libraries in some Pd versions.

Object	Function
`cos~`	Signal version of cosine function. Domain: -1.0 to $+1.0$. Note the input domain is "rotation normalised."
`sin~`	Not intrinsic but defined in terms of signal cosine by subtracting 0.25 from the input.
`atan~` *	Signal version of arctangent with normalised range.
`log~`	Signal version of natural log.
`abs~` *	Signal version of abs.
`sqrt~`	A square root for signals.
`q8_sqrt~`	A fast square root with less accuracy.
`pow~`	Signal version of power function.

Figure 11.9
List of trig and higher math operators.

Audio Delay Objects

Delaying an audio signal requires us to create a memory buffer using `delwrite~`. Two arguments must be supplied at creation time: a unique name for the memory buffer and a maximum size in milliseconds. For example, `delwrite~ mydelay 500` creates a named delay buffer "mydelay" of size 500ms. This object can now be used to write audio data to the delay buffer through its left inlet. Getting delayed signals back from a buffer needs `delread~`. The only argument needed is the name of a buffer to read from, so `delread~ mydelay` will listen to the contents of `mydelay`. The delay time is set by a second argument, or by the left inlet. It can range from zero to the maximum buffer size. Setting a delay time larger than the buffer results in a delay of the maximum size. It is not possible to alter the maximum size of a `delwrite~` buffer once created. But it is possible to change the delay time of `delread~` for chorus and other effects. This often results in clicks and pops[1] so we have a `vd~` variable-delay object. Instead of moving the read point, `vd~` changes the rate at which it reads the buffer, so we get tape echo and Doppler-shift-type effects. Using `vd~` is as easy as before: create an object that reads from a named buffer like `vd~ mydelay`. The left inlet (or argument following the name) sets the delay time.

References

Puckette, M.(2007). *The Theory and Technique of Electronic Music.* World Scientific.

---

1. Hearing clicks when moving a delay read point is normal, not a bug. There is no reason to assume that waveforms will align nicely once we jump to a new location in the buffer. An advanced solution crossfades between more than one buffer.

12
Abstraction

┌ SECTION 12.1

Subpatches

Any patch canvas can contain *subpatches* which have their own canvas but reside within the same file as the main patch, called the *parent*. They have inlets and outlets, which you define, so they behave very much like regular objects. When you save a canvas all subpatches that belong to it are automatically saved. A subpatch is just a neat way to hide code, it does not automatically offer the benefit of local scope.[1]

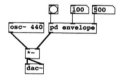

Any object that you create with a name beginning with pd will be a subpatch. If we create a subpatch called `pd envelope` as seen in figure 12.1 a new canvas will appear, and we can make `inlet` and `outlet` objects inside it as shown in figure 12.2. These appear as connections on the outside of the subpatch box in the same order they appear left to right inside the subpatch. I've given extra (optional) name parameters to the subpatch inlets and outlets. These are unnecessary, but when you have a subpatch with several inlets or outlets it's good to give them names to keep track of things and remind yourself of their function.

Figure 12.1
Using an envelope
subpatch.

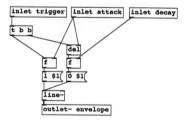

Figure 12.2
Inside the envelope subpatch.

To use `pd envelope` we supply a bang on the first inlet to trigger it, and two values for attack and decay. In figure 12.1 it modulates the output of an oscillator

---

1. As an advanced topic subpatches can be used as target name for dynamic patching commands or to hold data structures.

running at 440Hz before the signal is sent to `dac~`. The envelope has a trigger inlet for a message to bang two floats stored from the remaining inlets, one for the attack time in milliseconds and one for the decay time in milliseconds. The attack time also sets the period of a delay so that the decay portion of the envelope is not triggered until the attack part has finished. These values are substituted into the time parameter of a 2-element list for `line~`.

Copying Subpatches

So long as we haven't used any objects requiring unique names any subpatch can be copied. Select `pd envelope` and hit **CTRL+D** to duplicate it. Having made one envelope generator it's a few simple steps to turn it into a MIDI mono synthesiser (shown in figure 12.3) based on an earlier example by replacing the `osc~` with a `phasor~` and adding a filter controlled by the second envelope in the range 0 to 2000Hz. Try duplicating the envelope again to add a pitch sweep to the synthesiser.

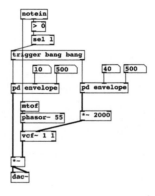

Figure 12.3
Simple mono MIDI synth made using two copies of the same envelope subpatch.

Deep Subpatches

Consider an object giving us the vector magnitude of two numbers. This is the same as the hypotenuse c of a right triangle with opposite and adjacent sides a and b and has the formula $c = \sqrt{a^2 + b^2}$. There is no intrinsic object to compute this, so let's make our own subpatch to do the job as an exercise.

Figure 12.4
Vector magnitude.

We begin by creating a new object box and typing `pd magnitude` into it. A new blank canvas will immediately open for us to define the internals. Inside this new canvas, create two new object boxes at the top by typing the word `inlet` into each. Create one more object box at the bottom as an `outlet`. Two input numbers a and b will come in through these inlets and the result c will go to the outlet.

When turning a formula into a dataflow patch it sometimes helps to think in reverse, from the bottom up
towards the top. In words, c is the square root of the
sum of two other terms, the square of a and the square
of b. Begin by creating a $sqrt$ object and connecting it to
the outlet. Now create and connect a $+$ object to the
inlet of the $sqrt$. All we need to complete the example is
an object that gives us the square of a number. We will
define our own as a way to show that subpatches can contain other subpatches. And in fact this can go as deep as
you like. It is one of the *principles of abstraction* that we

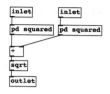

Figure 12.5
Subpatch calculates
$\sqrt{a^2 + b^2}$.

can define new objects, build bigger objects from those, and still bigger objects
in turn. Make a new object `pd squared`, and when the canvas opens add the
parts shown in figure 12.6.

Figure 12.6
Subpatch to compute x^2.

To square a number you multiply it by itself.
Remember why we use a trigger to split the input before
sending it to each inlet of the multiply. We must respect
evaluation order, so the trigger here distributes both
copies of its input from right to left; the "cold" right
inlet of $*$ is filled first, then the "hot" left inlet. Close
this canvas and connect up your new $pd\ squared$ subpatch.
Notice it now has an inlet and outlet on its box. Since
we need two of them, duplicate it by selecting then hitting CTRL+D on the keyboard. Your complete subpatch
to calculate magnitude should look like figure 12.5. Close this canvas to return
to the original topmost level and see $pd\ magnitude$ now defined with two inlets
and one outlet. Connect some number boxes to these as in figure 12.4 and test
it out.

Abstractions

An abstraction is something that distances an idea from an object; it captures
the essence and generalises it. It makes it useful in other contexts. Superficially an abstraction is a subpatch that exists in a separate file, but there is
more to it. Subpatches add modularity and make patches easier to understand,
which is one good reason to use them. However, although a subpatch seems
like a separate object it is still part of a larger thing. *Abstractions* are reusable
components written in plain Pd, but with two important properties. They can
be loaded many times by many patches, and although the same code defines
all instances each instance can have a separate internal namespace. They can
also take creation arguments, so you can create multiple instances each with a
different behaviour by typing different creation arguments in the object box.
Basically, they behave like regular programming functions that can be called
by many other parts of the program in different ways.

Scope and $0

Some objects like arrays and send objects must have a unique identifier, otherwise the interpreter cannot be sure which one we are referring to. In programming we have the idea of *scope*, which is like a frame of reference. If I am talking to Simon in the same room as Kate I don't need to use Kate's surname every time I speak. Simon assumes, from context, that the Kate I am referring to is the most immediate one. We say that Kate has *local scope*. If we create an array within a patch and call it `array1`, then that's fine so long as only one copy of it exists.

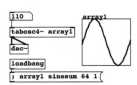

Consider the table oscillator patch in figure 12.7, which uses an array to hold a sine wave. There are three significant parts, a `tabosc4~` running at 110Hz, a table to hold one cycle of the waveform, and an initialisation message to fill the table with a waveform. What if we want to make a multi-oscillator synthesiser using this method, but with a square wave in one table and a triangle wave in another? We could make a subpatch of this arrangement and copy it, or just copy everything shown here within the main canvas. But if we do that without changing the array name, Pd will say:

Figure 12.7
Table oscillator patch.

```
warning: array1: multiply defined
warning: array1: multiply defined
```

The warning message is given twice because while checking the first array it notices another one with the same name, then later, while checking the duplicate array, it notices the first one has the same name. This is a serious warning, and if we ignore it erratic, ill-defined behaviour will result. We could rename each array we create as `array1`, `array2`, `array3`, etc, but that becomes tedious. What we can to do is make the table oscillator an abstraction and give the array a special name that will give it local scope. To do this, select everything with CTRL+E, CTRL+A, and make a new file from the file menu (or you can use CTRL+N as a shortcut to make a new canvas). Paste the objects into the new canvas with CTRL+V and save it as `my-tabosc.pd` in a directory called `tableoscillator`. The name of the directory isn't important, but it is important that we know where this abstraction lives so that other patches that will use it can find it. Now create another new blank file and save it as `wavetablesynth` in the *same* directory as the abstraction. This is a patch that will use the abstraction. By default a patch can find any abstraction that lives in the same directory as itself.

┌─ SECTION 12.2 ───┐

Instantiation

Create a new object in the empty patch and type `my-tabosc` in the object box. Now you have an instance of the abstraction. Open it just as you would edit a normal subpatch and make the changes as shown in figure 12.8.

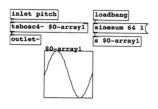

Figure 12.8
Table oscillator abstraction.

First we have replaced the number box with an inlet so that pitch data can come from outside the abstraction. Instead of a `dac~` the audio signal appears on an outlet we've provided. The most important change is the name of the array. Changing it to `$0-array1` gives it a special property. Adding the `$0-` prefix makes it local to the abstraction because at run time, `$0-` is replaced by a unique per-instance number. Of course we have renamed the array referenced by `tabosc4~` too. Notice another slight change in the table initialisation code: the message to create a sine wave is sent explicitly through a `send` because `$0-` inside a message box is treated in a different way.

┌─ SECTION 12.3 ───

Editing

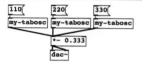

Figure 12.9
Three harmonics using the table oscillator abstraction.

Now that we have an abstracted table oscillator let's instantiate a few copies. In figure 12.9 there are three copies. Notice that no error messages appear at the console, as far as Pd is concerned each table is now unique. There is something important to note here, though. If you open one of the abstraction instances and begin to edit it the changes you make will immediately take effect as with a subpatch, but they will only affect that instance. Not until you save an edited abstraction do the changes take place in *all* instances of the abstraction. Unlike subpatches, abstractions will not automatically be saved along with their parent patch and must be saved explicitly. Always be extra careful when editing abstractions to consider what the effects will be on all patches that use them. As you begin to build a library of reusable abstractions you may sometimes make a change for the benefit of one project that breaks another. How do you get around this problem? The answer is to develop a disciplined use of namespaces, prefixing each abstraction with something unique until you are sure you have a finished, general version that can used in all patches and will not change any more. It is also good practice to write help files for your abstractions. A file in the same directory as an abstraction, with the same name but ending -help.pd, will be displayed when using the object help facility.

┌─ SECTION 12.4 ───

Parameters

Making local data and variables is only one of the benefits of abstraction. A far more powerful property is that an abstraction passes any parameters given as creation arguments through local variables $1, $2, $3.... In traditional programming terms this behaviour is more like a function than a code block. Each instance of an abstraction can be created with completely different initial

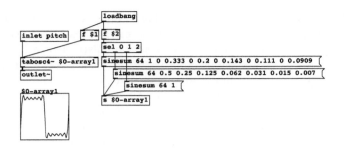

Figure 12.10
Table oscillator abstraction with initialised frequency and shape.

arguments. Let's see this in action by modifying our table oscillator to take arguments for initial frequency and waveform.

In figure 12.10 we see several interesting changes. First, there are two `float` boxes that have **$n** parameters. You can use as many of these as you like and each of them will contain the nth creation parameter. They are all banged when the abstraction is loaded by the `loadbang`. The first sets the initial pitch of the oscillator, though of course this can still be overridden by later messages at the pitch inlet. The second activates one of three messages via `select` which contain harmonic series of square, sawtooth, and sine waves respectively.

┌─ SECTION 12.5 ───

Defaults and States

A quick word about default parameters. Try creating some instances of the abstraction in figure 12.10 (shown as `my-tabsosc2` in figure 12.11).[2] Give one a first parameter of 100Hz but no second parameter. What happens is useful: the missing parameter is taken to be zero. That's because `float` defaults to zero for an undefined argument. That's fine most of the time, because you can arrange for a zero to produce the behaviour you want. But what happens if you create the object with no parameters at all? The frequency is set to 0Hz of course, which is probably useful behaviour, but let's say we wanted to have the oscillator start at 440Hz when the pitch is unspecified. You can do this with `sel 0` so that zero value floats trigger a message with the desired default. Be careful choosing default behaviours for abstractions, as they are one of the most common causes of problems later when the defaults that seemed good in one case are wrong in another. Another important point pertains to initial parameters of GUI components, which will be clearer in just a moment when we consider abstractions with built-in interfaces. Any object that persistently maintains state (keeps its value between saves and loads) will be the same for *all* instances of the abstraction loaded. It can only have one set of values

─────────────────────────────────

2. The graphs with connections to them shown here, and elsewhere in the book, are abstractions that contain everything necessary to display a small time or spectrum graph from signals received at an inlet. This is done to save space by not showing this in every diagram.

(those saved in the abstraction file). In other words, it is the abstraction *class* that holds state, not the object instances. This is annoying when you have several instances of the same abstraction in a patch and want them to individually maintain persistent state. To do this you need a state-saving wrapper like `memento` or `sssad`, but that is a bit beyond the scope of this textbook.

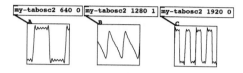

Figure 12.11
Three different waveforms and frequencies from the same table oscillator abstraction.

┌─ SECTION 12.6 ──────────────────────────────

Common Abstraction Techniques

Here are a few tricks regularly used with abstractions and subpatches. With these you can create neat and tidy patches and manage large projects made of reusable general components.

Graph on Parent

It's easy to build nice-looking interfaces in Pd using GUI components like sliders and buttons. As a rule it is best to collect all interface components for an application together in one place and send the values to where they are needed deeper within subpatches. At some point it's necessary to expose the interface to the user, so that when an object is created it appears with a selection of GUI components laid out in a neat way.

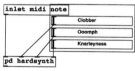

Figure 12.12
Graph on parent synth.

"Graph on Parent" (or GOP) is a property of the canvas which lets you see inside from outside the object box. Normal objects like oscillators are not visible, but GUI components, including graphs, are. GOP abstractions can be nested, so that controls exposed in one abstraction are visible in a higher abstraction if it is also set to be GOP. In figure 12.12 we see a subpatch which is a MIDI synthesiser with three controls. We have added three sliders and connected them to the synth. Now we want to make this abstraction, called GOP-hardsynth, into a GOP abstraction that reveals the controls. Click anywhere on a blank part of the canvas, choose **properties**, and activate the GOP toggle button. A frame will appear in the middle of the canvas. In the canvas properties box, set the size to *width* = 140 and *height* = 80, which will nicely frame three standard-size sliders with a little border. Move the sliders into the frame, save the abstraction and exit.

Figure 12.13
Appearance of a GOP
abstraction.

Here is what the abstraction looks like when you create an instance (fig. 12.13). Notice that the name of the abstraction appears at the top, which is why we left a little top margin to give this space. Although the inlet box partly enters the frame in figure 12.12 it cannot be seen in the abstraction instance because only GUI elements are displayed. Coloured *canvases*[3] also appear in GOP abstractions, so if you want decorations they can be used to make things prettier. Any canvases appear above the name in the drawing order so if you want to hide the name make a canvas that fills up the whole GOP window. The abstraction name can be turned off altogether from the **properties** menu by activating **hide object name and arguments**.

Using List Inputs

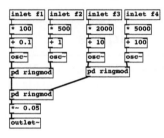

Figure 12.14
Preconditioning normalised
inlets.

The patch in figure 12.14 is a fairly arbitrary example (a 4 source cross ring modulator). It's the kind of thing you might develop while working on a sound or composition. This is the way you might construct a patch during initial experiments, with a separate inlet for each parameter you want to modify. There are four inlets in this case, one for each different frequency that goes into the modulator stages. The first trick to take note of is the control preconditioners all lined up nicely at the top. These set the range and offset of each parameter so we can use uniform controls as explained below.

Packing and Unpacking

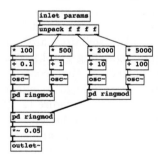

Figure 12.15
Using a list input.

What we've done here in figure 12.15 is simply replace the inlets with a single inlet that carries a list. The list is then unpacked into its individual members which are distributed to each internal parameter. Remember that lists are unpacked right to left, so if there was any computational order that needed taking care of you should start from the rightmost value and move left. This modification to the patch means we can use the flexible arrangement shown in figure 12.16 called a "programmer." It's just a collection of normalised sliders connected to a `pack` object so that a new list is transmitted each time a fader is moved. In order to do this it is necessary to insert `trigger bang float`

---

3. Here the word "canvas" is just used to mean a decorative background, different from the regular meaning of patch window.

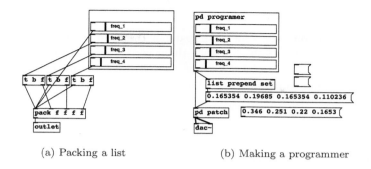

(a) Packing a list   (b) Making a programmer

Figure 12.16
Packing and using parameter lists.

objects between each slider as shown in figure 12.16 (left). These go on all
but the far left inlet. Doing so ensures that the float value is loaded into `pack`
before all the values are sent again. By prepending the keyword `set` to a list,
a message box that receives it will store those values. Now we have a way of
creating patch presets, because the message box always contains a snapshot
of the current fader values. You can see in figure 12.16 (right) some empty
messages ready to be filled and one that's been copied, ready to use later as a
preset.

Control Normalisation

Most patches require different parameter sets with some control ranges between
0.0 and 1.0, maybe some between 0.0 and 20000, maybe some bipolar ones
−100.0 to +100.0 and so on. But all the sliders in the interface of figure 12.17
have ranges from 0.0 to 1.0. We say the control surface is *normalised*.

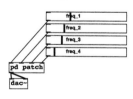

If you build an interface where the input parameters have mixed ranges it can get confusing. It means
you generally need a customised set of sliders for
each patch. A better alternative is to normalise the
controls, making each input range 0.0 to 1.0 and
then adapting the control ranges as required inside
the patch. Pre-conditioning means adapting the input
parameters to best fit the synthesis parameters. Normalisation is just one of the tasks carried out at this
stage. Occasionally you will see a `log` or `sqrt` used to
adjust the parameter curves. Preconditioning opera-
tions belong together as close to where the control signals are to be used as
possible. They nearly always follow the same pattern: multiplier, then offset,
then curve adjustment.

Figure 12.17
All faders are normalised
0.0 to 1.0.

Summation Chains

Sometimes when you have a lot of subpatches that will be summed to produce an output it's nicer to be able to stack them vertically instead of having many connections going to one place. Giving each an inlet (as in figure 12.18) and placing a ⊞ object as part of the subpatch makes for easier to read patches.

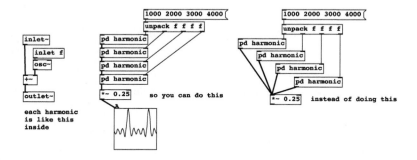

Figure 12.18
Stacking subpatches that sum with an inlet.

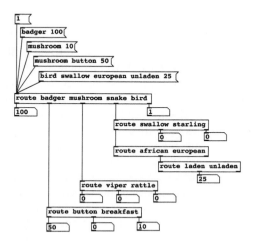

Figure 12.19
Route can channel named parameters to a destination.

Routed Inputs

A powerful way to assign parameters to destinations while making them human-readable is to use `route`. Look at figure 12.19 to see how you can construct arbitrary paths like URLs to break subpatches into individually addressable areas.

13
Shaping Sound

The signal generators we've seen so far are the phasor, cosinusoidal oscillator, and noise source. While these alone seem limited they may be combined using shaping operations to produce a great many new signals. We are going to make transformations on waveforms, pushing them a little this way or that, moulding them into new things. This subject is dealt with in two sections: amplitude-dependent shaping where the output depends only on current input values, and time-dependent signal shaping where the output is a function of current and past signal values.

SECTION 13.1
Amplitude-Dependent Signal Shaping

Simple Signal Arithmetic

Arithmetic is at the foundation of signal processing. Examine many patches and you will find, on average, the most common object is the humble multiply, followed closely by addition. Just as all mathematics builds on a few simple arithmetic axioms, complex DSP operations can be reduced to adds and multiplies. Though it's rarely of practical use, it's worth noting that multiplication can be seen as repeated addition, so to multiply a signal by two we can connect it to both inlets of `+~` and it will be added to itself. The opposite of addition is subtraction. If you are subtracting a constant value from a signal it's okay to use `+~`, but express the subtracted amount as a negative number, as with `+~ -0.5`, though of course there is a `-~` unit too. Addition and multiplication are commutative (symmetrical) operators, so it doesn't matter which way round you connect two signals to a unit. On the other hand, subtraction and division have ordered arguments: the right value is subtracted from, or is the divisor of, the left one. It is common to divide by a constant, so `*~` is generally used with an argument that's the reciprocal of the required divisor. For example, instead of dividing by two, multiply by half. There are two reasons for this. First, divides were traditionally more expensive so many programmers are entrenched in the habit of avoiding divides where a multiply will do. Second, an accidental divide by zero traditionally causes problems, even crashing the program. Neither of these things are actually true of Pd running on a modern processor, but because of such legacies you'll find many algorithms written accordingly. Reserve divides for when you need to divide by a variable signal, and multiply by decimal fractions everywhere else unless you need rational numbers with good accuracy.

This habit highlights the importance of the function and makes your patches easier to understand. Arithmetic operations are used to scale, shift, and invert signals, as the following examples illustrate.

A signal is scaled simply by multiplying it by a fixed amount, which changes the difference between the lowest and highest values and thus the peak to peak amplitude. This is seen in figure 13.1 where the signal from the oscillator is halved in amplitude.

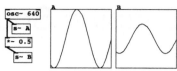

Figure 13.1
Scaling a signal.

Shifting involves moving a signal up or down in level by a constant. This affects the absolute amplitude in one direction only, so it is possible to distort a signal by pushing it outside the limits of the system, but it does not affect its peak to peak amplitude or apparent loudness since we cannot hear a constant (DC) offset. Shifting is normally used to place signals into the correct range for a subsequent operation, or, if the result of an operation yields a signal that isn't centered properly to correct it, shifting swings it about zero again. In figure 13.2 the cosine signal is shifted upwards by adding 0.5.

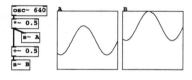

Figure 13.2
Shifting a signal.

In figure 13.3 a signal is inverted, reflecting it around the zero line, by multiplying by −1.0. It still crosses zero at the same places, but its direction and magnitude is the opposite everywhere. Inverting a signal changes its phase by π, 180° or 0.5 in rotation normalised form, but that has no effect on how it sounds since we cannot hear absolute phase.

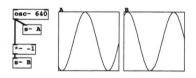

Figure 13.3
Inverting a signal.

The complement of a signal a in the range 0.0 to 1.0 is defined as $1 - a$. As the phasor in figure 13.4 moves upwards the complement moves downwards, mirroring its movement. This is different from the inverse; it has the same direction as the inverse but retains the sign and is only defined for the positive range between 0.0 and 1.0. It is used frequently to obtain a control signal for amplitude or filter cutoff

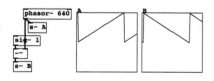

Figure 13.4
Signal complement.

that moves in the opposite direction to another control signal.

For a signal a in the range 0.0 to x the reciprocal is defined as $1/a$. When a is very large then $1/a$ is close to zero, and when a is close to zero then $1/a$ is very large. Usually, since we are dealing with normalised signals, the largest input is $a = 1.0$, so because $1/1.0 = 1.0$ the reciprocal is also 1.0. The graph of $1/a$ for a between 0.0 and 1.0 is a curve, so a typical use of the reciprocal is shown in figure 13.5. A curve is produced according to $1/(1 + a)$. Since the maximum amplitude of the divisor is 2.0 the minimum of the output signal is 0.5.

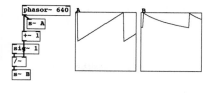

Figure 13.5
Signal reciprocal.

Limits

Sometimes we want to constrain a signal within a certain range. The `min~` unit outputs the minimum of its two inlets or arguments. Thus `min~ 1` is the minimum of one and whatever signal is on the left inlet; in other words, it clamps the signal to a maximum value of one if it exceeds it. Conversely, `max~ 0` returns the maximum of zero and its signal, which means that signals going below zero are clamped there forming a lower bound. You can see the effect of this on a cosine signal in figure 13.6.

Think about this carefully; the terminology seems to be reversed but it is correct. You use `max~` to create a minimum possible value and `min~` to create a maximum possible value. There is a slightly less confusing alternative `clip~` for situations where you don't want to adjust the limit using another signal. The left inlet of `clip~` is a signal and the remaining two inlets or arguments are the values of upper and lower limits; so, for example, `clip~ -0.5 0.5` will limit any signal to a range of one centered about zero.

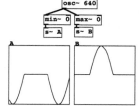

Figure 13.6
Min and max of a signal.

Wave Shaping

Using these principles we can start with one waveform and apply operations to create others like square, triangle, pulse, or any other shape. The choice of starting waveform is usually a phasor, since anything can be derived from it. Sometimes it's best to minimise the number of operations, so a cosine wave is the best starting point.

One method of making a square wave is shown in figure 13.7. An ordinary cosine oscillator is multiplied by a large number and then clipped. If you picture a graph of a greatly magnified cosine waveform, its slope will have become extremely steep, crossing through the area between -1.0 and 1.0 almost vertically. Once clipped to a normalised range what remains is a square wave, limited to between 1.0 and -1.0 and crossing suddenly halfway through. This method produces a waveform that isn't band-limited, so when used in synthesis you should keep it to a fairly low-frequency range to avoid aliasing.

A triangle wave moves up in a linear fashion just like a phasor, but when it reaches the peak it changes direction and returns to its lowest value at the

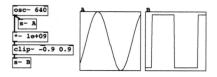

Figure 13.7
Square wave.

same rate instead of jumping instantly back to zero. It is a little more complicated to understand than the square wave. We can make a signal travel more or less in a given time interval by multiplying it by a constant amount. If a signal is multiplied by 2.0 it will travel twice as far in the same time as it did before, so multiplication affects the slope of signals. Also, as we have just seen, multiplying a signal by -1.0 inverts it. That's another way of saying it reverses the slope, so the waveform now moves in the opposite direction. One way of making a triangle wave employs these two principles.

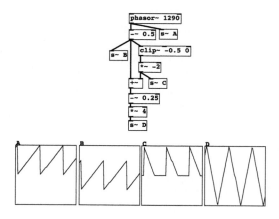

Figure 13.8
Triangle.

Starting with a phasor (graph A) at the top of figure 13.8, and shifting it down by 0.5 (graph B), the first half of it, from 0.0 to 0.5, is doing what we want. If we take half and isolate it with clip~ we can then multiply by -1.0 to change the slope, and by 2.0 to double the amplitude, which is the same as multiplying by -2.0. During the first half of the source phasor, between 0.5 and 1.0, the right branch produces a falling waveform (graph C). When we add

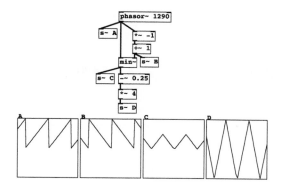

Figure 13.9
Another way to make a triangle wave.

that back to the other half, which is shifted down by 0.5 the sum is a triangle wave once normalised (graph D).

An alternative formula for a triangle wave, which may be slightly easier to understand, uses min~ and is shown in figure 13.9. Starting with a phasor again, (graph A) and adding one to the inverse produces a negative moving phasor with the same sign but opposite phase (graph B). Taking the minima of these two signals gives us a triangle wave, positive with amplitude 0.5 (graph C). This is recentered and normalised (graph D).

Squaring and Roots

One common function of a signal a is a^2, another way of writing $a \times a$. A multiplier is the easiest way to perform squaring. If you connect a signal to both inlets of a multiplier it is multiplied by itself. The effect of squaring a signal is twofold. Its amplitude is scaled as a function of its own amplitude. Amplitude values that are already high are increased more, while values closer to zero are increased less. Another result is that the output signal is only positive. Since a minus times a minus gives a plus, there are no squares that are negative. The reverse of this procedure is to determine a value r which if multiplied by itself gives the input a. We say r is the square root of a. Because finding square roots is a common DSP operation that requires a number of steps, there's a built-in sqrt~ object in Pd. Without creating complex (imaginary) numbers there are no square roots to negative numbers, so the output of sqrt~ is zero for these values. The effect of making the straight phasor line between 0.0 and 1.0 into a curve is clear in figure 13.10, graph A; likewise the curve bends the other way for the square root in graph B. Remembering that a minus times a minus gives a plus you can see that whatever the sign of a signal appearing at both inlets of the multiplier, a positive signal is output in graph C. Making either sign of the cosine wave positive like this doubles the frequency. In graph D an absence of negative square roots produces a broken sequence of positive pulses, and the

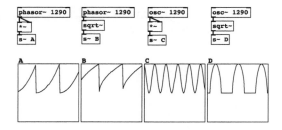

Figure 13.10
Square roots.

effect of the square root operation is to change the cosine curve to a parabolic (circular) curve (notice it is more rounded).

Curved Envelopes

We frequently wish to create a curve from a rising or falling control signal in the range 0.0 to 1.0. Taking the square, third, fourth, or higher powers produces increasingly steep curves, the class of *parabolic* curves. The quartic envelope is frequently used as a cheap approximation to natural decay curves. Similarly, taking successive square roots of a normalised signal will bend the curve the other way.[1] In figure 13.11 three identical line segments are generated each of

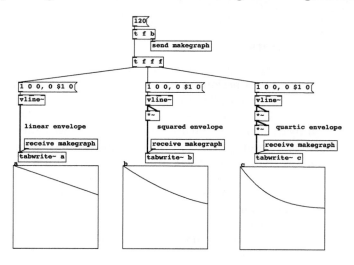

Figure 13.11
Linear, squared, and quartic decays.

---

1. See McCartney 1997 for other identities useful in making efficient natural envelopes.

length 120ms. At the same time all `tabwrite~` objects are triggered, so the graphs are synchronised. All curves take the same amount of time to reach zero, but as more squaring operations are added, raising the input to higher powers, the faster the curve decays during its initial stage.

┌─ SECTION 13.2 ──┐

Periodic Functions

└──┘

A periodic function is bounded in range for an infinite domain. In other words, no matter how big the input value, it comes back to the place it started from and repeats that range in a loop.

Wrapping Ranges

The `wrap~` object provides just such a behaviour. It is like a signal version of `mod`. If the input a to `wrap~` exceeds 1.0 then it returns $a - 1.0$. And if the input exceeds 2.0 it gives us $a - 2.0$. Wrap is the "fractional" part of a number in relation to a division, in this case the unit 1, $a - \lfloor a \rfloor$. Let's say we have a normalised phasor which is cycling up once per second. If we pass it through `wrap~` it will be unaffected. A normalised phasor never exceeds 1.0 and so passes through unchanged. But if we double the amplitude of the phasor by multiplying by 2.0 and then wrap it, something else happens, as seen in figure 13.12.

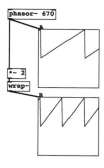

Figure 13.12
Wrapping.

Imagine the graph of a in a range of 0.0 to 2.0 is drawn on tracing paper, and then the paper is cut into two strips of height 1.0 which are placed on top of one another. Each time the phasor passes 1.0 it is wrapped back to the bottom. Consequently the frequency doubles but its peak amplitude stays at 1.0. This way we can create periodic functions from a steadily growing input, so a line that rises at a constant rate can be turned into a phasor with `wrap~`. Even more useful, we can obtain an exact number of phasor cycles in a certain time period by making the line rise at a particular rate. The `vline~` in figure 13.13 moves from 0.0 to 1.0 in 10ms. Multiplying by 3 means it moves from 0.0 to 3.0 in 10ms, and wrapping it produces three phasor cycles in a period of $10/3 = 3.333$ms, giving a frequency of $1/3.333 \times 1000 = 300$Hz.

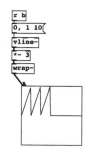

Figure 13.13
Wrapping a line.

Cosine Function

The reason for saying that the phasor is the most primitive waveform is that even a cosinusoidal oscillator can be derived from it. Notice in figure 13.14 that although the phasor is always positive in the range 0.0 to 1.0 (unipolar), the `cos~`

operation produces a *bipolar* waveform in the
range −1.0 to 1.0. One complete period of the
cosine corresponds to 2π, 360°, or in rotation
normalised form, 1.0. When the phasor is at 0.0
the cosine is 1.0. When the phasor is at 0.25
the cosine crosses zero moving downwards. It
reaches the bottom of its cycle when the phasor is 0.5. So there are two zero crossing points,
one when the phasor is 0.25 and another when
it is 0.75. When the phasor is 1.0 the cosine
has completed a full cycle and returned to its
original position.

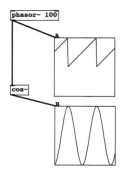

Figure 13.14
Cosine of a phasor.

SECTION 13.3

Other Functions

From time to time we will use other functions like exponentiation, raising to a
variable power, or doing the opposite by taking the log of a value. In each case
we will examine the use in context. A very useful technique is that arbitrary
curve shapes can be formed from *polynomials*.

Polynomials

A polynomial is expressed as a sum of different power terms. The graph of $2x^2$ gives
a gently increasing slope and the graph of
$18x^3 + 23x^2 - 5x$ shows a simple hump weighted
towards the rear which could be useful for
certain kinds of sound control envelope. There
are some rules for making them. The number of
times the curve can change direction is determined by which powers are summed. Each of
these is called a *term*. A polynomial with some
factor of the a^2 term can turn around once, so
we say it has one *turning point*. Adding an a^3
term gives us two turning points, and so on.
The multiplier of each term is called the *coefficient* and sets the amount that term effects
the shape. Polynomials are tricky to work with

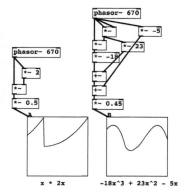

x * 2x   −18x^3 + 23x^2 − 5x

Figure 13.15
Polynomials.

because it's not easy to find the coefficients to get a desired curve. The usual
method is to start with a polynomial with a known shape and carefully tweak
the coefficients to get the new shape you want. We will encounter some later,

like cubic polynomials, that can be used to make natural-sounding envelope curves.

Expressions

Expressions are objects with which you can write a single line of arbitrary processing code in a programmatic way. Each of many possible signal inlets x, y, z correspond to variables $\$v(x, y, z)$ in the expression, and the result is returned at the outlet. This example shows how we generate a mix of two sine waves, one 5 times the frequency of the other. The available functions are very like those found in C and follow the maths syntax of most programming languages. Although expressions are very versatile they should only be used as a last resort, when you cannot build from more primitive objects. They are less efficient than inbuilt objects and more difficult to read. The expression shown in figure 13.16 implements $A sin(2\pi\omega) + B sin(10\pi\omega)$ for a periodic phasor ω and two mix coefficients where $B = 1 - A$. The equivalent patch made from primitives is shown at the bottom of figure 13.16.

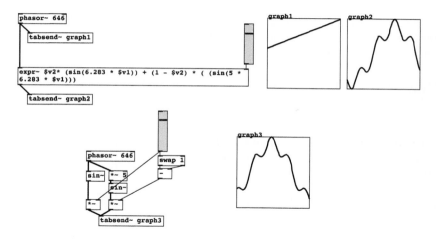

Figure 13.16

Using an expression to create an audio signal function.

SECTION 13.4

Time-Dependent Signal Shaping

So far we have considered ways to change the amplitude of a signal as a function of one or more other variables. These are all instantaneous changes which depend only on the current value of the input sample. If we want a signal to change its behaviour based on its previous features then we need to use time shaping.

Delay

To shift a signal in time we use a delay. Delays
are at the heart of many important procedures
like reverb, filters, and chorusing. Unlike most
other Pd operations, delays are used as two separate objects. The first is a write unit that works
like `send~` but sends the signal to an invisible area
of memory. The second object is for reading from
the same memory area after a certain time. So
you always use `delwrite~` and `delread~` as pairs. The
first argument to `delwrite~` is a unique name for
the delay and the second is the maximum memory (as time in milliseconds) to allocate. On its
own a delay just produces a perfect copy of an
input signal a fixed number of milliseconds later.
Here we see a 0.5ms pulse created by taking the
square of a fast line from one to zero. The second
graph shows the same waveform as the first but
it happens 10ms later.

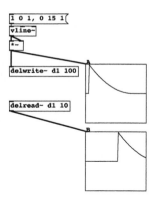

Figure 13.17
Delay.

Phase Cancellation

Assuming that two adjacent cycles of a periodic
waveform are largely the same, then if we delay
that periodic signal by time equal to half its period
we have changed its phase by 180°. In the patch
shown here the two signals are out of phase. Mixing the original signal back with a copy that is
antiphase annihilates both signals, leaving nothing. In figure 13.18 a sinusoidal signal at 312Hz
is sent to a delay **d1**. Since the input frequency
is 312Hz its period is 3.2051ms, and half that
is 1.60256ms. The delayed signal will be out of
phase by half of the input signal period. What
would happen if the delay were set so that the
two signals were perfectly in phase? In that case
instead of being zero the output would be a waveform with twice the input amplitude. For delay
times between these two cases the output amplitude varies between 0.0 and 2.0. We can say for a
given frequency component the output amplitude
depends on the delay time. However, let's assume
the delay is fixed and put it another way—for a

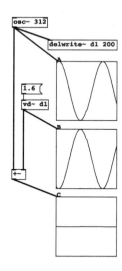

Figure 13.18
Antiphase.

given delay time the output amplitude depends on the input frequency. What
we have created is a simple filter.

Filters

When delay time and period coincide we call the loud part (twice the input amplitude) created by reinforcement a *pole*, and when the delay time equals half the period we call the quiet part where the waves cancel out a *zero*. Very basic but flexible filters are provided in Pd called `rpole~` and `rzero~`. They are tricky to set up unless you learn a little more about DSP filter theory, because the frequencies of the poles or zeros are determined by a normalised number that represents the range of 0Hz to $SR/2$Hz, where SR is the sampling rate of the patch. Simple filters can be understood by an equation governing how the output samples are computed as a function of the current or past samples. There are two kinds: those whose output depends only on past values of the *input*, which are called *finite impulse response* filters (FIR), and those whose output depends on past input values and on past *output* values. In other words, this kind has a feedback loop around the delay elements. Because the effect of a signal value could theoretically circulate forever we call this kind recursive or *infinite impulse response* filters (IIR).

User-Friendly Filters

Filters may have many poles and zeros, but instead of calculating these from delay times, sampling rates, and wave periods, we prefer to use filters designed with preset behaviours. The behaviour of a filter is determined by a built-in calculator that works out the coefficients to set poles, zeros, and feedback levels for one or more internal delays. Instead of poles and zeros we use a different terminology and talk about bands which are passed or stopped. A band has a center frequency, specified in Hz, the middle of the range where it has the most effect, and also a bandwidth which is the range of frequencies it operates over. Narrow bands affect fewer frequencies than wider bands. In many filter designs you can change the bandwidth and the frequency independently. Four commonly encountered filters are the low pass, high pass, band pass, and band cut or notch filter, shown in figure 13.19. The graphs show the spectrum of white noise after it's been passed through each of the filters. The noise would normally fill up the graph evenly, so you can see how each of the filters cuts away at a different part of the spectrum. The high pass allows more signals above its centre frequency through than ones below. It is the opposite of the low pass, which prefers low frequencies. The notch filter carves out a swathe of frequencies in the middle of the spectrum, which is the opposite of the band pass, which allows a group of frequencies in the middle through but rejects those on either side.

Integration

Another way of looking at the behaviour of filters is to consider their effect on the slope or phase of moving signals. One of the ways that recursive (IIR) filters can be used is like an accumulator. If the feedback is very high the current input is added to all previous ones. Integration is used to compute the area under a

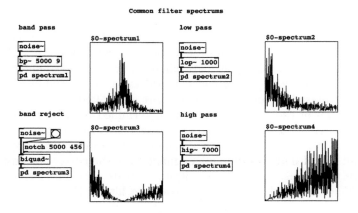

Figure 13.19
Common user-friendly filter shapes.

curve, so it can be useful for us to work out the total energy contained in a signal. It can also be used to shape waveforms; see Roberts 2009.

Integrating a square wave gives us a triangle wave. If a constant signal value is given to an integrator its output will move up or down at a constant rate. In fact this is the basis of a phasor, so a filter can be seen as the most fundamental signal generator as well as a way to shape signals. Thus we have come full circle and can see the words of the great master, "It's all the same thing." A square wave is produced by the method shown in figure 13.7, first amplifying a cosinusoidal wave by a large value and then clipping it. As the square wave alternates between +1.0 and −1.0 the integrator output first slopes up at a constant rate, and then slopes down at a constant rate. A scaling factor is added to place the resulting triangle wave within the bounds of the graph. Experiment with integrating a cosinusoidal wave. What happens? The integral of $\cos(x)$ is $\sin(x)$, or in other words we have shifted $\cos(x)$ by 90°. If the same operation is applied again, to a sine wave, we get back to a cosine wave out of phase with the first one, a shift of 180°. In other words, the integral of $\sin(x)$ is $-\cos(x)$. This can be more properly written as a definite integral

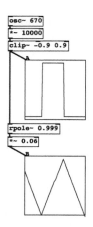

Figure 13.20
Integration.

$$\int \cos(x)\,dx = \sin(x) \tag{13.1}$$

or as

$$\int \sin(x)\,dx = -\cos(x) \tag{13.2}$$

Differentiation

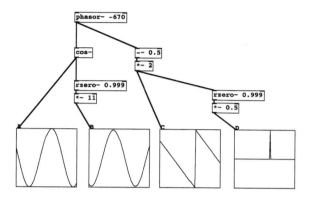

Figure 13.21
Differentiation.

The opposite of integrating a signal is differentiation. This gives us the instantaneous slope of a signal, or in other words the gradient of a line tangential to the signal. What do you suppose will be the effect of differentiating a cosine wave? The scaling factors in figure 13.21 are given for the benefit of the graphs. Perhaps you can see from the first graph that

$$\frac{d}{dx}\cos(x) = -\sin(x) \tag{13.3}$$

and

$$\frac{d}{dx}\sin(x) = \cos(x) \tag{13.4}$$

More useful, perhaps, is the result of differentiating a sawtooth wave. While the sawtooth moves slowly its gradient is a small constant, but at the moment it suddenly returns the gradient is very high. So, differentiating a sawtooth is a way for us to obtain a brief impulse spike.

References

McCartney, J. (1997). "Synthesis without Lookup Tables." *Comp. Music J.* 21(3).
Roberts, R. (2009). "A child's garden of waveforms." Unpublished ms.

14
Pure Data Essentials

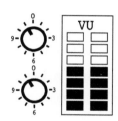

This chapter will present some commonly used configurations for mixing, reading and writing files, communication, and sequencing. You may want to build up a library of abstractions for things you do again and again, or to find existing ones from the pd-extended distribution. All the same, it helps to understand how these are built from primitive objects, since you may wish to customise them to your own needs.

SECTION 14.1

Channel Strip

For most work you will use Pd with multiple audio outlets and an external mixing desk. But you might find you want to develop software which implements its own mixing. All mixing desks consist of a few basic elements like gain controls, buses, panners, and mute or channel select buttons. Here we introduce some basic concepts that can be plugged together to make complex mixers.

Signal Switch

All we have to do to control the level of a signal is multiply it by a number between 0.0 and 1.0. The simplest form of this is a signal switch where we connect a toggle to one side of a ⊡ and an audio signal to the other (figure 14.1). The toggle outputs either 1 or 0, so the signal is either on or off. You will use this frequently to temporarily block a signal. Because the toggle changes value abruptly it usually produces a click, so don't use this simple signal switch when recording audio; for

Figure 14.1
Signal switch.

that you must apply some smoothing, as in the mute button below.

Simple Level Control

To create a level fader, start with a vertical slider and set its **properties** to a lower value of 0.0 and upper value of 1.0. In figure 14.2 the slider is connected to one inlet of ⊡ and the signal to the other, just like the signal switch above except the slider gives a continuous change between 0.0 and 1.0. A number box displays the current fader value, 0.5 for a halfway position here. A sine oscillator at 40Hz provides a test signal. It is okay to mix messages and audio signals on opposite sides of ⊡ like this, but because the

Figure 14.2
Direct level control.

slider generates messages any updates will only happen on each block, normally every 64 samples. Move it up and down quickly and listen to the result. Fading is not perfectly smooth. You will hear a clicking sound when you move the slider. This *zipper noise* is caused by the level suddenly jumping to a new value on a block boundary.

Using a Log Law Fader

The behaviour of slider objects can be changed. If you set its properties to log instead of linear, smaller values are spread out over a wider range and larger values are squashed into the upper part of the movement. This gives you a finer degree of control over level and is how most real mixing desks work. The smallest value the slider will output is 0.01. With its top value as 1.0 it will also output 1.0 when fully moved. Between these values it follows a logarithmic curve. When set to halfway it outputs a value of about 0.1, and at three quarters of full movement its

Figure 14.3
Log level control.

output is a little over 0.3. It doesn't reach an output of 0.5 until nearly nine-tenths of its full movement (shown in figure 14.3). This means half the output range is squashed into the final 10 percent of the movement range, so be careful when you have this log law fader connected to a loud amplifier. Often log law faders are limited to constrain their range, which can be done with a `clip` unit.

MIDI Fader

You won't always want to control a mix from Pd GUI sliders; sometimes you might wish to use a MIDI fader board or other external control surface. These generally provide a linear control signal in the range 0 to 127 in integer steps, which is also the default range of GUI sliders. To convert a MIDI controller message into the range 0.0 to 1.0, it is divided by 127 (the same as multiplying by 0.0078745), as shown in figure 14.4. The normalised output can be further scaled to a log curve, or multiplied by 100 to obtain a decibel scale and converted via the `dbtorms` object.

Figure 14.4
Scaling a level.

To connect the fader to an external MIDI device you need to add a `ctlin` object. The first outlet gives the current fader value, the second indicates the continuous controller number and the third provides the current MIDI channel. Volume messages are sent on controller number 7. We combine the outlets using `==` and `spigot` so that only volume control messages on a particular channel are passed to the fader. The patch shown in figure 14.5 has an audio inlet and outlet. It has an inlet to set the MIDI channel. It can be subpatched or abstracted to form one of several components in a complete MIDI controlled fader board.

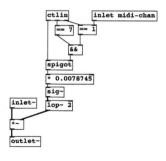

Figure 14.5
MIDI level.

Mute Button and Smooth Fades

After carefully adjusting a level you may want to temporarily silence a channel without moving the slider. A *mute button* solves this problem. The fader value is stored at the cold inlet of a `*` while the left inlet receives a Boolean value from a toggle switch. The usual sense of a mute button is that the channel is silent when the mute is active, so first the toggle output is inverted. Some solutions to zipper noise use `line` or `line~` objects to interpolate the slider values. Using `line` is efficient but somewhat unsatisfactory, since we are still interfacing a message to a signal and will hear clicks on each block boundary even though the jumps are smaller. Better is to use `line~`, but this can introduce corners into the control signal if the slider moves several times during a fade. A good way to obtain a smooth fade is to convert messages to a signal with `sig~` and then low pass filter it with `lop~`. A cutoff value of 1Hz will make a fade that smoothly adjusts over 1 second.

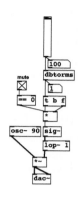

Figure 14.6
Mute switch.

Panning

"Pan" is short for *panorama*, meaning a view in all directions. The purpose of a pan control is to place a *mono* or *point* source within a listening panorama. It should be distinguished from *balance*, which positions a sound already containing stereo information. The field of an audio panorama is called the *image*, and with plain old stereo we are limited to a theoretical *image width* of 180°. In practice a narrower width of 90° or 60° is used. Some software applications specify the pan position in degrees, but this is fairly meaningless unless you know precisely how the loudspeakers are arranged or whether the listener is using headphones. Mixing a stereo image for anything other than movie theatres is always a compromise to account for the unknown final listening arrangement. In movie sound, however, the specifications of theatre PA systems are reliable enough to accurately predict the listener's experience.

Simple Linear Panner

In the simplest case a pan control provides for two speakers, left and right. It requires that an increase on one side has a corresponding decrease on the other. In the centre position the sound is distributed equally to both loudspeakers. The pan patch in figure 14.7 shows a signal inlet and control message inlet at the top and two signal outlets at the bottom, one for the left channel and one for the right. Each outlet is preceded by a multiplier to set the level for that channel, so the patch is essentially two level controls in one. As with our

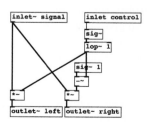

Figure 14.7
Simple panner.

level control, zipper noise is removed by converting control messages to a signal and then smoothing them with a filter. The resulting control signal, which is in the range 0.0 to 1.0, is fed to the left channel multiplier, while its complement (obtained by subtracting it from 1.0) governs the right side. With a control signal of 0.5 both sides are multiplied by 0.5. If the control signal moves to 0.75 then the opposing side will be 0.25. When the control signal reaches 1.0 the complement will be 0.0, so one side of the stereo image will be completely silent.

Square Root Panner

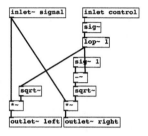

Figure 14.8
Root law panner.

The problem with simple linear panning is that when a signal of amplitude 1.0 is divided in half and sent to two loudspeakers, so each receives an amplitude of 0.5, the result is quieter than sending an amplitude of 1.0 to only one speaker. This doesn't seem intuitive to begin with, but remember loudness is a consequence of sound power level, which is the square of amplitude.

Let's say our amplitude of 1.0 represents a current of 10A. In one loudspeaker we get a power of $10^2 = 100$W. Now we send it equally amongst two speakers, each receiving a current of 5A. The power from each speaker is therefore $5^2 = 25$W, and the sum of them both is only 50W. The real loudness has halved! To remedy this we can modify the curve used to multiply each channel, giving it a new *taper*. Taking the square root of the control signal for one channel and the square root of the complement of the control signal for the other gives panning that follows an *equal power law*. This has a 3dB amplitude increase in the centre position.

Cosine Panner

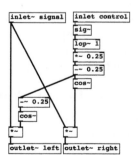

Figure 14.9
Cos-sin law panner.

Though the square root law panner gives a correct amplitude reduction for centre position, it has a problem of its own. The curve of $\sqrt{A}$ is perpendicular to the x-axis as it approaches it, so when we adjust the panning close to one side the image suddenly disappears completely from the other. An alternative taper follows the *sine-cosine law*. This also gives a smaller amplitude reduction in the centre position, but it approaches the edges of the image smoothly, at 45 degrees. The cosine panner is not only better in this regard but slightly cheaper in CPU cycles since it's easier to compute a cosine than a square root. It also mimics the placement of the source on a circle around the listener and is nice for classical music, as an orchestra is generally arranged in a semicircle; however, some engineers and producers prefer the root law panner because it has a nicer response around the centre position and signals are rarely panned hard left or right. (The right and left outlets in fig. 14.9 are reversed.)

Figure 14.10 shows the taper of each panning law. You can see that the linear method is 3dB lower than the others in the centre position and that the root and cosine laws have different approaches at the edge of the image.

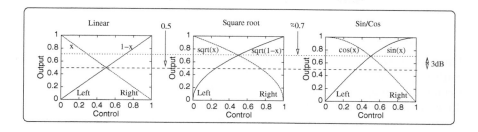

Figure 14.10
Linear, root, and sin/cos panning laws.

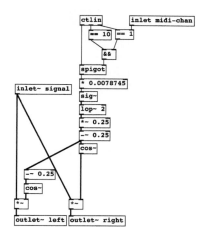

Figure 14.11
MIDI panner.

Combining the cosine panner patch with a `ctlin` we now have a MIDI-controlled pan unit to add to the MIDI-controlled fader. Pan information is sent on controller number 10, with 64 representing the centre position. Once again an inlet is provided to select the MIDI channel the patch responds to. You may like to expand this idea into a complete MIDI fader board by adding a mute, bus outlet, and auxiliary send/return loop. It might be a good solution to combine the level control, panning, mute, and routing into a single abstraction that takes the desired MIDI channel and output bus as creation arguments. Remember to use dollar notation to create local variables if you intend to override MIDI control with duplicate controls from GUI objects.

Crossfader

The opposite of a pan control, a reverse panner if you like, is a crossfader. When you want to smoothly transfer between two sound sources by mixing them to a common signal path, the patch shown in figure 14.12 can be used. There are three signal inlets; two of them are signals to be mixed, and one is a control signal to set the ratio (of course a message domain version would work equally well with appropriate antizipper smoothing). It can be used in the final stage of a reverb effects unit to set the wet/dry proportion, or in a DJ console to crossfade between two tunes. Just like the simple panner, the control signal is split into two parts, a direct version and the complement, with each modulating an input signal. The output is the sum of both multipliers.

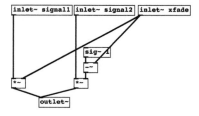

Figure 14.12
Crossfader.

Demultiplexer

A demultiplexer or signal source selector is a multiway switch that can choose between a number of signal sources. Figure 14.13 is useful in synthesiser construction where you want to select from a few different waveforms. In this design the choice is exclusive, so only one input channel can be sent to the output at any time. A number at the control inlet causes `select` to choose one of four possible messages to send to `unpack`. The first turns off all channels, the second switches on only channel one, and so forth. The Boolean values appearing in the `unpack` output are converted to signals and then low passed at 80Hz to give a fast but click-free transition.

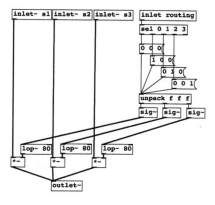

Figure 14.13
Demultiplex.

Audio File Tools

Monophonic Sampler

A useful object to have around is a simple sampler that can grab a few seconds of audio input and play it back. Audio arrives at the first inlet and is scaled by a gain stage before being fed to `tabwrite~`. It's nice to have a gain control so that you don't have to mess with the level of the signal you are recording elsewhere. In figure 14.14 a table of 88200 samples is created called `$0-a1`, so we have a couple of seconds recording time. Obviously this can be changed in the code or a control created to use the `resize` method. When it receives a bang, `tabwrite~` starts recording from the beginning of the table. To play back the recording we issue a bang to `tabplay~`, which connects directly to the outlet. The use of dollar arguments means this patch can be abstracted and multiple instances created; it's not unusual to want a bunch of samplers when working on a sound.

Using the sampler is very easy. Create an instance and connect it to a signal source via the first inlet. In figure 14.15 the left audio input is taken from `adc~`. A slider with a range 0.0 to 1.0

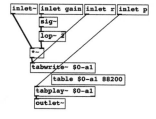

Figure 14.14
Simple sampler.

Figure 14.15
Using a sampler.

connects to the gain inlet, and two bang buttons are used to start recording or playback. Sound files of up to 3min can be stored happily in memory. Beyond this limit you need to use other objects for 32-bit machines, because the sound quality will suffer due to pointer inaccuracies. If you have files longer than 3 minutes then you may want to think about using disk-based storage and playback.

File Recorder

When creating sounds for use in other applications, like multitracks or samplers, you could choose to record the output of Pd directly from the dac~ using your favourite wave file editor or software like Time Machine. This could mean editing long recordings later, so sometimes you want to just write fixed-length files directly from Pd.

In figure 14.16 we see a file writer in use, which I will show you how to make in a moment. It catches audio, perhaps from other patches, on a bus called `audio`. It was created with two arguments: the length of each file to record (in this case 1s) and the name of an existing folder beneath the current working directory in which to put them. Each time you hit the **start** button a new file is written to disk, and then the **done** indicator tells you when it's finished. A numerical suffix is appended to each

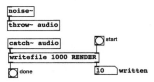

Figure 14.16
Using a file writer.

file, which you can see on the second outlet, in order to keep track of how many files you've created. The internals of the file writer are shown in figure 14.17.

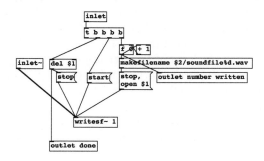

Figure 14.17
Making a file writer.

Audio comes into the first inlet and to the writesf~ object which has an argument of 1, so it writes a single-channel (mono) file. There are three commands that writesf~ needs: the name of a file to open for writing, a start command, and a stop command. Each bang on the second inlet increments a counter, and the value of this is appended to the current file name using makefilename, which can substitute numerical values into a string like the C **printf** statement does. This string is then substituted after the **open** keyword in the following message. As soon as this is done a **start** message is sent to `writesf-` and a bang to the `delay`, which waits for a period given by the first argument before stopping `writesf-`.

Loop Player

A looping sample player is useful in many situations, to create a texture from looped background samples or to provide a beat from a drum loop, especially if you need a continuous sound to test some process with. In figure 14.18 we see a patch that should be created as an abstraction so that many can be instantiated if required. Its operation is unsophisticated, just playing a loop of a sound file forever. When the abstraction receives a bang, `openpanel` is activated and provides a nice file dialogue for you to choose a sound file. You should pick a Microsoft .wav or Mac .aiff type; either stereo or mono will do, but this player patch will only give mono output. The name and path of this file is passed through the trigger "any" outlet and packed as the first part of a list along with a

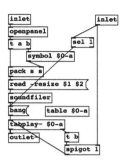

Figure 14.18
Sample loop player.

second part which is a symbol **$0-a**. The second symbol is the name of our storage table, the place in memory where the contents of the sound file will be put once read. It has the prefix **$0-** to give it local scope, so we can have many sample loop players in a patch. Now the elements of the list will be substituted in $1 and $2 of the message **read -resize $1 $2**, which forms a complete command to `soundfiler` telling it to read in a sound file and put it in an array, resizing the array as required. Once this operation is complete, `soundfiler` returns the number of bytes read, which in this case we ignore and simply trigger a new bang message to start `tabplay-`. Notice the argument is the name of the array living in the table just above it. `tabplay-` will now play once through the file at its original sample rate, so there is no need to tune it. When it has finished, the right outlet emits a bang. We take this bang, buffering it through another trigger and apply it back to the `tabplay-` inlet, which means it plays the sound forever in a loop. A zero arriving at the second inlet allows you to stop the loop playing.

SECTION 14.3

Events and Sequencing

Now let's look at a few concepts used for creating time, sequences, and event triggers.

Timebase

At the heart of many audio scenes or musical constructions is a timebase to drive events. We've already seen how to construct a simple timebase from a metronome and counter. A more useful timebase is given in figure 14.19 that

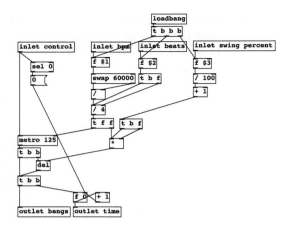

Figure 14.19
A more useful musical timebase abstraction with BPM and swing.

allows you to specify the tempo as beats per minute (BPM) and to add a "swing"[1] to the beat. Notice first that start and stop control via the first inlet also resets the counter when the timebase is stopped. Bangs from `metro` are duplicated with a `delay` object so we can position every other beat relative to the main rhythm. To convert beats per minute to a period in milliseconds it is divided by 60000 and multiplied by the number of beats per bar. The last parameter provides swing as a percentage, which is added to the delay prior to incrementing the counter.

Select Sequencer

The simplest way to obtain regular patterns for repetitive sounds is by using `mod` to wrap the incoming time to a small range, say 8 beats, and then use `select` to trigger events within this range. You do not have to fill out all the select values. So, for example, to produce a single trigger at $time = 1024$ you can connect one `select` matching this number. A good practice is to broadcast a global time message so that other patches can pick up a common reference. In figure 14.20 the output from the timebase abstraction goes to a `send`. To create a sequencer where you can manually set the time at

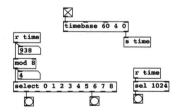

Figure 14.20
Select based triggering.

---

1. Swing is where every other beat is moved slightly in time, giving a different feel to the rhythm.

which an event is triggered, use a combination of ⊟ and ⸤select⸥ with a number box attached to the cold inlet of ⊟ and the current time going to the left inlet.

Partitioning Time

For long musical compositions, interactive installations, or generating event structures for a long
game or animation, you may want to offset timing sequences by a large number but keep the relative timings within a section. This is how bars
and measures work in a traditional sequencer. In
figure 14.21 ⸤moses⸥ is used to split the global time
into smaller frames of reference. A chain of ⸤moses⸥
objects splits off numbers that fall within a range.
You can see that the last value present on the left
outlet of the first split was 127. Numbers of 128 or
more are passing through the right outlet and into
the second ⸤moses⸥, which partitions values between
128 and 255. We subtract the base value of 128
from this stream to reposition it, as if it were a
sequence starting at zero. This can be further pro-

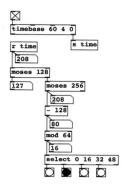

Figure 14.21
Bar offset by partitioning time.

cessed, such as wrapping it into the range 0 to 64 to create 2 bars of 64 beats
in the range 128 to 256. In figure 14.21 you see the timebase at 208, which is
in the second bar of the partitioned timeframe.

Dividing Time

With time expressed as a number you can perform arithmetic on it to obtain different rates. Be aware that
although the value of numerical time changes with a different scale it still updates at the rate set by the timebase.
Since for musical purposes you want to express time in
whole beats and bars, a problem is presented. Dividing
time by two and rounding it to an integer means two messages will now be sent with the same value. To get around
this problem, ⸤change⸥ is used so that redundant messages
are eliminated. Using ⸤int⸥ means values are rounded to
the time floor, so if rhythms constructed this way seem
one beat out of alignment you can try using a "closest
integer" rounding explained earlier. Sometimes rounding
time is not what you want, as shown in the next example.

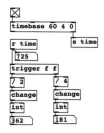

Figure 14.22
Dividing time into
different rates.

Event-Synchronised LFO

An application and pitfall of timebase division is shown in figure 14.23 where
low-frequency control signals are derived from the timebase. Notice how the
sine wave is not interpolated, so you get two or four consecutive equal values
when using a divided timebase. This makes the LFO jumpy, so to avoid it we

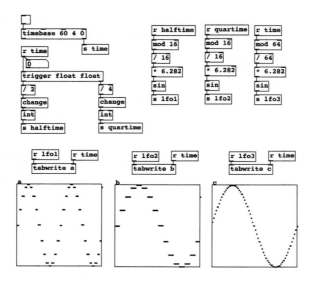

Figure 14.23
Synchronous message LFOs.

scale the raw time values before the trig operation using a higher and .
This illustrates why you should often use a timebase that is a large multiple
(say 64 times) of the real event rate you want. You might use this to create
interesting polyrhythms or elaborate slow-moving control signals for wind, rain,
or spinning objects.

List Sequencer

An alternative to an absolute timebase is using lists and delays to make a relative time sequencer. Events are stored in a list, which we define to have a
particular meaning to a sequencer that will interpret it. In this case the list is
read in pairs, an event type and a time offset from the last event. So, a list
like {*1 0 2 200 1 400*} describes three events and two event types. Event 1
occurs at *time* = 0, and then at *time* = 200 event 2 occurs, followed by event
1 again at *time* = 200 + 400 = 600. Times are in milliseconds, and event types
usually correspond to an object name or a MIDI note number. The patch in
figure 14.24 is hard to follow, so I will describe it in detail. The sequence list
arrives at the first inlet of `list split 2` where it is chopped at the second element. The first two elements pass to the `unpack` where they are separated and
processed, while the remainder of the list passes out of the second outlet of
`list split 2` and into the right inlet of `list append`. Returning to `unpack`, our first half
of the current pair, which identifies a float event type, is sent to the cold inlet
of a `float` where it waits, while the second part, which represents a time delay,

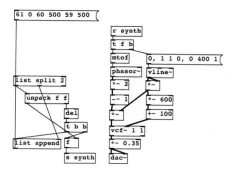

Figure 14.24
An asynchronous list sequencer.

is passed to `delay`. After a delay corresponding to this second value, `delay` emits a bang message which flushes out the value stored in `float` for output. Finally, `list append` is banged so the remainder of the list is passed back to `list split 2` and the whole process repeats, chomping 2 elements off each time until the list is empty. On the right in figure 14.24 is a simple monophonic music synthesiser used to test the sequencer. It converts MIDI note numbers to Hertz with `mtof` and provides a filtered sawtooth wave with a 400ms curved decay envelope. To scale the sequence delay times, and thus change the tempo without rewriting the entire list, you can make each time offset be a scaling factor for the delay which is then multiplied by some other fraction. List sequencers of this type behave asynchronously, so they don't need a timebase.

Textfile Control

Eventually, lists stored in message boxes become unwieldy for large data sets and it's time to move to secondary storage with textfiles. The `textfile` object provides an easy way to write and read plain text files. These can have any format you like, but a general method is to use a comma or line break delimited structure to store events or program data. It is somewhat beyond this textbook to describe the many ways you can use this object, so I will present only one example of how to implement a text-file-based MIDI sequencer. A combination of `textfile` and `route` can provide complex score control for music or games. If you need even larger data sets with rapid access, an SQL object is available in `pd-extended` which can interface to a database.

Starting at the top left corner of figure 14.25 you can see a monophonic synthesiser used to test the patch. Replace this with a MIDI note out function if you like. The remainder of the patch consists of two sections, one to store and write the sequence and one to read and play it back. Recording commences when the **start-record** button is pressed. This causes a **clear** message to be

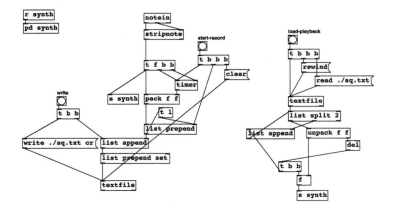

Figure 14.25
A MIDI sequencer that uses textfiles to store data.

sent to `textfile`, the list accumulator is cleared and the `timer` object reset. When a note is received by `notein` and then reduced to just its note-on value by `stripnote`, it passes to the trigger unit below which dispatches two bangs to `timer`. The result of this is for `timer` to output the time since the last bang it received, then restart from zero. This time value, along with the current MIDI note number, is packed by `pack` into a pair and appended to the list accumulator. When you are done playing, hit the `write` button to flush the list into `textfile` and write it to a file called `sq.txt` in the current working directory. Moving to the load and replay side of things, banging the `load-replay` button reads in the textfile and issues a `rewind` message, setting `textfile` to the start of the sequence. It then receives a bang which squirts the whole list into a list sequencer like the one we just looked at.

SECTION 14.4

Effects

For the last part of this chapter I am going to introduce simple effects. Chorus and reverb are used to add depth and space to a sound. They are particularly useful in music making, but also have utility in game sound effects to thicken up weaker sources. Always use them sparingly and be aware that it is probably better to make use of effects available in your external mixer, as plugins, or as part of the game audio engine.

Stereo Chorus/Flanger Effect

The effect of chorus is to produce a multitude of sources by doubling up many copies of the same sound. To do this we use several delays and position them

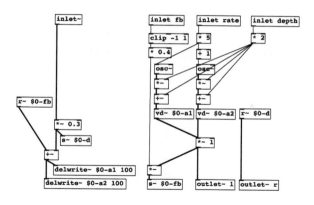

Figure 14.26
A chorus-type effect.

slightly apart. The aim is to deliberately cause beating and swirling as the copies move in and out of phase with one another. In figure 14.26 an input signal at the first inlet is split three ways. An attenuated copy is fed directly to the right stereo outlet while two other copies are fed to separate delay lines. In the centre you see two variable delay taps, $\boxed{\text{vd}\texttt{\char126}}$, which are summed.

A small part, scaled by the feedback value on the second inlet, is sent back to be mixed in with the input signal, while another copy is sent to the left stereo outlet. So there is a dry copy of the signal on one side of the stereo image and two time-shifted copies on the other. By slowly varying the delay times with a couple of signal rate LFOs a swirling chorus effect is achieved. The low-frequency oscillators are always 1Hz apart and vary between 1Hz and 5Hz. It is necessary to limit the feedback control to be sure the effect cannot become unstable. Notice that feedback can be applied in positive or negative phase to create a notching effect (phaser/flanger)

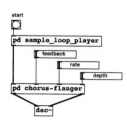

Figure 14.27
Testing the chorus.

and a reinforcing effect (chorus). Testing out the effect is best with a sample loop player. Try loading a few drum loops or music loop clips.

Simple Reverberation

A reverb simulates dense reflections as a sound bounces around inside some space. There are several ways of achieving this effect, such as convolving a sound with the impulse response of a room or using all-pass filters to do a similar thing. In figure 14.28 you can see a design for a recirculating reverb type that uses only delay lines. There are four delays that mutually feed back into one another, so once a signal is introduced into the patch it will circulate through a

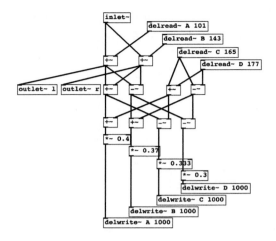

Figure 14.28
A recirculating Schroeder reverb effect.

complex path. So that reinforcement doesn't make the signal level keep growing, some feedback paths are negative. The recirculating design is known as a *Schroeder reverb* (this example by Claude Heiland-Allen) and mimics four walls of a room. As you can see the number of feedback paths gets hard to patch if we move to 6 walls (with floor and ceiling) or to more complex room shapes. Reverb design is a fine art. Choosing the exact feedback and delay values is not easy. If they are wrong then a feedback path may exist for certain frequencies, producing an unstable effect. This can be hard to detect in practice and complex to predict in theory. An apparently well-designed reverb can mysteriously explode after many seconds or even minutes, so a common design safety measure is to attenuate the feedback paths as the reverb decays away. What defines the reverb time is the point at which the reverb has fallen to −60dB of the first reflection intensity. A good design should not be too coloured, which means feedback paths must not be too short, leading to a pitched effect. The minimum delay time should be at least a quarter of the reverberation time, and the lengths of delays should be prime, or collectively coprime.[2] The density of the reverb is important too. Too little and you will hear individual echos; too much and the effect will become muddy and noisy. Schroeder suggests 1000 echoes per second for a reasonable reverb effect. If you look in the **extra** directory that comes with Pd there are three nice reverb abstractions, `rev1~`, `rev2~`, and `rev3~`, by Miller Puckette.

---

2. Integers comprising a set with no common factors are said to be collectively coprime.

Exercises

Exercise 1

Create any one of the following effects.

- Guitar tremolo effect
- Multistage phaser
- Multitap tempo-sync delay
- A high quality vocal reverb

Exercise 2

Create a sequencer that provides any two of the following.

- Hierarchical structure
- Microtonal tuning scales
- Polyrhythmic capabilities
- A way to load and save your compositions

Exercise 3

Design and implement a mixing desk with at least three of the following.

- MIDI or OSC parameter automation
- Switchable fader and pan laws
- Surround sound panning (e.g. 5.1, quadraphonic)
- Effect send and return bus
- Accurate signal level monitoring
- Group buses and mute groups
- Scene store and recall

Exercise 4

Essay: Research data structures in Pd. How can graphical representations help composition? What are the limitations of graphics in Pd? Generally, what are the challenges for expressing music and sound signals visually?

Acknowledgements

I would like to thank Frank Barknecht, Steffen Juul, Marius Schebella, Joan Hiscock, Philippe-Aubert Gauthier, Charles Henry, Cyrille Henry, and Thomas Grill for their valuable help in preparing this chapter.

References

Case, A. (2007). *Sound FX: Unlocking the Creative Potential of Recording Studio Effects*. Focal.

Gardner, W. G. (1998). "Reverberation algorithms." In M. Kahrs and K. Brandenburg (eds.), *Applications of Digital Signal Processing to Audio and Acoustics*, pp. 85–131. Kluwer.

Izhaki, R. (2007). *Mixing Audio: Concepts, Practices, and Tools*. Focal.

Penttinen, H., and Tikander, M. (2001). Spank the reverb. In *Reverb Algorithms: Course Report for Audio Signal Processing S-89.128*.

Schroeder, M. R. (1962). "Natural sounding artificial reverberation." *J. Audio Eng. Soc.* 10, no. 3: 219–224.

Zoelzer, U. (2008). *Digital Audio Signal Processing*. Wiley.

Online Resources

<http://puredata.info> is the site of the main Pure Data portal.

<http://crca.ucsd.edu> is the current home of official Pure Data documentation by Miller Puckette.

Beau Sievers, "The Amateur Gentleman's Introduction to Music Synthesis": an introductory online resource geared toward synth building in Pure Data. <http://beausievers.com/synth/synthbasics>

<http://www.musicdsp.org> is the home of the music DSP list archive, with categorised source code and comments.

<http://www.dafx.de> is the home of the DAFx (Digital Audio Effects) project, containing many resources.

III

Technique

15
Technique Introduction

The ideal engineer is a composite.
He is not a scientist, he is not a
mathematician, he is not a
sociologist or a writer; but he
may use the knowledge and
techniques of any or all of these
disciplines in solving engineering
problems.
—N. Dougherty

SECTION 15.1
Techniques of Sound Design

This is the third part of the book, before we move on to the practicals. Up to this point we have looked at a theoretical basis for sound, including elementary physics, acoustics, psychoacoustics, and the idea of digital signals. Additionally, I have introduced Pure Data, a wonderful tool for developing procedural audio. Before we can begin practicing it's necessary to know how to apply this knowledge to the task of designing sounds, so we need to zoom out once again and take a larger view.

Layered Approach

All of these subjects can be seen as the bottom layer shown in figure 15.1. A general principle is that good design is done top down, then implemented bottom up. By this we mean that the most important guiding factors are the abstract, artistic aims that form the top layer. To get somewhere, we need to know where we are going and why. This is the part of sound design driven by artistic considerations. Books on cinematic and theatrical design by authors such as D. Sonnenschein, T. Gibbs, W. Whittington, J. Cancellaro, and G. Childs are full of interesting wisdom that will help you understand this top layer. Here we have only a little room to sketch out the basic principles. Given a clear set of aesthetic and behavioural goals we can move towards a *model*. Then we start building the sound from the most basic principles, from the bottom back towards the top.

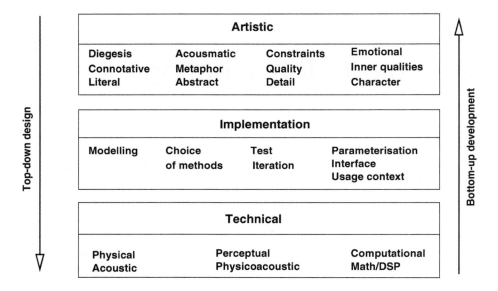

Figure 15.1
Overview of technique.

The top layer defines the purpose of the sound, constraints, and indicators, like how the sound will be heard. Will it be a literal (diegetic) accompaniment to an on-screen narrative, or will it be a suggestive background? On what device will it be played, a small handheld mobile device, or a high-quality theatre surround sound system? What is it trying to communicate, in terms of emotion, power relationships, inner psychological worlds, or abstract feelings? How will it relate to other sounds, dialogue lines, actors' movements, and so forth?

The Middle Layer

The middle layer is how we get from a model to a satisfactory finished product. Implementation is the act of turning a model, which is something that exists in the designer's mind, into something real and audible. Next we need a *grimwa*, a book of spells and tricks that will come in handy for our practical work to make real sounds from models. These are stock techniques that allow us to attack a design in a structured way. Once the physical and spectral parts of a sound are understood, well-known approaches to shaping waveforms and spectra can be used to get the results we want. Within the design process we refer to these as the *methods*. Some are explained in the following chapters, structured into additive, table-based, modulation, shaping, and granular methods. This is by no means a complete list of synthesis methods, but it covers the essential principles on which other more esoteric ones are based.

We also need a framework within which to practice, so I have included an explanation of a formal process that treats sound design as a software engineering task as well as a short chapter to give a context for sounds designed for real-time execution in virtual reality and video games.

References

Beauchamp, R. (2005). *Designing Sound for Animation.* Focal.

Childs, G. W. (2006). *Creating Music and Sound for Games.* CTI.

Chion, M. (1994). *Audio-Vision: Sound on Screen.* Columbia University Press.

Collins, K. (2008). *Game Sound: An Introduction to the History, Theory, and Practice of Video Game Music and Sound Design.* MIT Press.

Gibbs, T. (2007). *The Fundamentals of Sonic Art and Sound Design.* AVA.

Kaye, D., and LeBrecht J. (2000). *Sound and Music for the Theatre: The Art and Technique of Design.* Focal.

Marks, A. (2008). *The Complete Guide to Game Audio: For Composers, Musicians, Sound Designers, Game Developers,* 2nd ed. Focal.

Sider, L. (ed.) (2003). *Soundscape: School of Sound Lectures 1998–2001.* Wallflower.

Sonnenschein, D. (2001). *Sound Design: The Expressive Power of Music, Voice, and Sound Effects in Cinema.* Wiese.

Viers, R. (2008). *The Sound Effects Bible: How to Create and Record Hollywood Style Sound Effects.* Wiese.

Weis, B. (1985). *Film Sound: Theory and Practice.* Columbia University Press.

Wishart, T. (1994). *Audible Design: A Plain and Easy Introduction to Sound Composition.* Waterstones.

Wishart, T., and Emmerson, S. (1996). *On Sonic Art.* Routledge.

Whittington, W. (2007). *Sound Design and Science Fiction.* University of Texas Press.

Wyatt, H., and Amyes, T. (2004). *Audio Post Production for Television and Film: An Introduction to Technology and Techniques.* Focal.

Yewdall, D. L. (2007). *The Practical Art of Motion Picture Sound.* Focal.

16
Strategic Production

Working Methods

How do you move from an idea about a sound to hearing it? Can we formalise intuitive, creative leaps in order to produce consistent results? What are the recurring design patterns that can be used in a coherent methodology?

Listen

Good sound design is more analysis than synthesis. Most of it is component analytical, reduced, critical, and semantic listening. Keep an ear open for similar sounds or ones with similar mechanisms. Make connections between patterns like a water splash and breaking glass, or a squeaking wheel and an animal sound.

Stimulate

Sometimes it's necessary to get the brain working by exercise, to warm it up and start connections happening. Some designers say they like to randomly listen to sounds for a while. All artists engage in aleatoric or improvisational stimulation; frottage (Max Ernst), word association, and random collage are all techniques discussed in the wonderful book *The Creative Process* (Ghiselin 1952), which contains short essays by brilliant minds from every discipline like Henri Poincaré, W. B. Yeats, A. E. Housman, D. H. Lawrence, Samuel Taylor Coleridge, Max Ernst, John Dryden, Albert Einstein, and dozens of others. Develop your own mental workout to defeat the block that you often face with a new project or when you start work cold.

Use Scale

Make use of similar features that exist on shorter or longer timescales, or that are shifted in frequency. For example, a model for a heavy sack dragged over dirt can become the light brush of a duster when speeded up, a snapping matchstick can be a breaking tree branch, and a small wooden brick can become a heavy box when slowed down. This will give you material for analysis or composition without difficult recording methods needed for very delicate or unwieldy sounds.

Vary Scope

Work like a painter, occasionally stepping back to see the whole picture (semantic listening) and sometimes zooming in on very fine features invisible to the ordinary listener (component analytical listening). Stepping back is important because sound can be seductive and hypnotic. It is easy to get stuck in a certain perspective and lose sight of the whole.

Keep Moving

The ability to let the work flow requires occasionally letting go of technical considerations and engaging in reduced listening, which allows an intuitive impression to form. This requires taking rests to avoid fatigue. A few minutes taking a walk or making a cup of tea can work wonders.

Balance Priorities

There are three (reasonably orthogonal) axes or dimensions that must be juggled while working. It is said in all fields of design, pick any two from good, fast, and cheap. The question is, will it do? You cannot afford to be too much of a perfectionist, or too slapdash. Here are the equivalents in technical sound design.

1. Computational efficiency
2. Development speed
3. Aesthetic quality

For procedural video game sound I would say that currently 1 and 3 are most important, in that order. Fast and elegant code is desirable for many reasons, but it also buys you space to trade against 3, because if you can do something cheaply you can afford to use more of it. Aesthetic quality for a large class of sounds improves with the ability to add varied concurrent instances. Off-line design for film and animation makes 1 less important and 3 much more so.

Reuse and Share Successful Techniques

Build up a library of techniques and reusable components. Improve upon them stepwise. It shouldn't need to be said, but never be afraid to share techniques; don't believe the fallacy that "your gain is my loss." No professionals are one-trick wonders. Sharing can vastly improve your own methods. Sometimes you find you only really understand something as you attempt to verbalise it, and that cements it in your repertoire.

Create a Comfortable Working Space

Metaphorically, you need a tidy, well-organised desk. Most digital art forms require concentration and freedom from distractions. A new, unfamiliar system is initially very much slower to work with than a familiar one. When switching software packages or development environments you should find you adjust to previous productivity levels within one or two months of regular use. If you move from studio to studio, take a familiar file system and toolset with you as a laptop, or create an online workspace.

Invite Input

Most of the time you know when something is right, and you are the best judge of it. Yet, sound can throw up surprisingly subjective reactions and misinterpretations. Seek other opinions when you get the chance. That in itself is a difficult task. It's something you need to do casually. Most people are pleasant and keen to offer encouragement rather than objective criticism; they are often reluctant to venture a strong opinion even when they feel it deeply. The other side of this is to maintain confidence and vision, even ignoring advice when you know in your heart that something is right.

SECTION 16.2

SE Approaches

I've tried and failed to give rigorous accounts of the sound design process before. They always end up as personal, anecdotal accounts. It is a process that's hard to put into words. What follows is my best shot at putting it within a framework based loosely on Sommerville's (2004) approach from classic software engineering. It's a laborious process, one that with time you will learn to perform unconsciously, but the one thing to recommend it is that if you follow it you will always get adequate results. A software engineering approach to design is interesting, because in a way what we are producing is software assets. Once all programs were produced in an ad hoc fashion. Of course it is true that good work, done by creative people, involves intuitive leaps. A structured and reasoned approach to code or sound design is an ideal, and a sadly mythical one. But let us indulge in it for a while. We will visit each part in detail in later sections, but it helps to collect these points together first as a short list and then as quick explanations. Here are the steps.

1. Lifecycle
2. Requirements analysis
3. Research and acquisition
4. Model building
5. Method analysis
6. Implementation
7. Integration
8. Test and iteration
9. Maintenance

Structured Approach Summary

Lifecycle

All designs have a lifecycle, starting as a need and ending with a satisfactory solution that has a finite lifetime. Stages may overlap, as in the so-called *waterfall model*, but generally each must be completed before the next can be begun.

Requirements analysis

The lifecycle starts with a specification of requirements. A script, edited film, or game plan sets out what will be needed. You must study and clarify this before moving ahead.

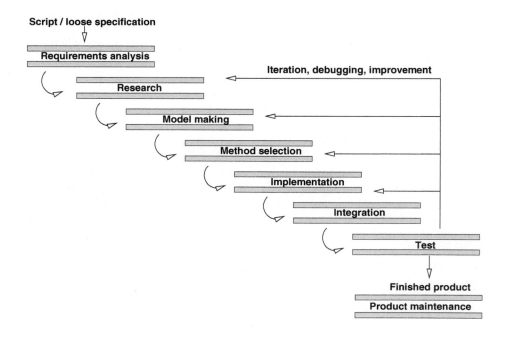

Figure 16.1
Stages in developing sound objects.

Research

No requirements specification goes very deep. The next step is to break it down into chunks and conduct research to gain detailed, specific information about each part. This may involve collecting documents or analysing data.

Model building

This is equivalent to drawing up a map and waypoints or to sketching a flowchart of the whole problem. You do not need to know specific implementation details yet. The model is a definition of an object or set of objects that reflects all the behaviours set out in the requirements analysis and lists well-formed outcomes for each.

Method analysis

This is the stage of creating a sound algorithm. It maps the model onto the implementation and usually consists of a collection of stock methods. In software engineering, these are design patterns. In procedural sound design, they are DSP blocks in a process chain like "single sideband modulator" or "dynamic formant filter." We don't specify the implementation yet, so a model is portable between different DSP systems or programming languages. Sometimes we express a model as a block diagram.

Implementation

Actually building the sound object by plugging together unit generators, predesigned filters, and control logic is the implementation. It results in runnable code taking a set of input data and producing audio as output.

Integration

Next we place our media into the finished product. This process can assume many forms. It could involve creating instances of sound objects in a DAW environment, recording them to multitrack, triggering from EDLs, MIDI data, Lau, or Python scripts in a game mockup, or embedding code into other runtime objects. It may even be handled by a completely different team, but even if you are not directly involved you should at least understand the challenges of this step.

Test and iteration

Here we measure the performance of the implementation against expectations. Very seldom does the synthetic sound designer move straight from a conceptual model to a satisfactory solution in one step. Patches must usually be tweaked and improved. As you gain more knowledge and experience in synthesis, development time will get shorter. Because you will rarely make the correct implementation the first time, this stage actually consists of any or all of the previous stages done again. In the worst case it may mean going back as far the research or requirements stage. In the best case it may mean a few tweaks to the implementation details.

Maintenance

Once the product is released you may be required to revisit it. A film or music album may be remixed. A game may need add-on packs, or patches, or a sequel that uses old material. An installation may be expanded or redesigned in light of public feedback. This is where well-commented code and modular design strategies will reward you.

SECTION 16.3

Requirements Analysis Process

The first thing is to know what you want. This may change as new information comes to light, but the better the initial specifications the less work will be

wasted along the way. Requirements specification is a process where you work
to clarify as much as possible with the rest of the production team, and the end
result is a requirements specification document. It has many parts, including
entity descriptions, process specifications, milestones, metrics, stage times, test
plans, and so forth. They all work together to give the best possible description of the goal, what we agree is a satisfactory result, and how to achieve it.
The process often begins when you are handed an initial inventory, taken from
scripts or brainstorming sessions. It could be as simple as a list of objects or
props, though more likely it will include behaviours, uses in specific situations,
and a list of scenes or stages where the objects are used. Fleshing this out
means asking questions, looking at models and characters, reading scripts, or
watching cuts of a movie while imagining the soundscapes involved. Be aware
that if parallel production methods are being used instead of a stage-by-stage
approach, the entire crew will also be involved in a dynamic process.

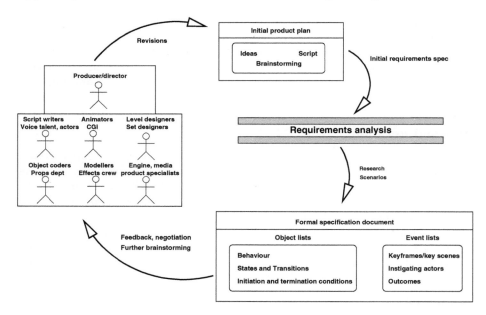

Figure 16.2
The process of developing a sound requirements specification.

Consensus of Vision

At this stage there will be a lot of revisions, negotiations, and discussions, so
don't get attached to any particular ideas too early. What you are hoping to get
into the requirements specification document is a list of all objects and their
uses, key scenes, and aesthetic guidance about characterisations. For example,

when a jet plane passes overhead in a scene description, you want to know: What is its speed? Is it in frame? What altitude? What kind of jet is it, a passenger jet or a fighter jet? How long does it take to pass? For a game, you need to know much more about possible behaviours. Can the player fly it, requiring in-cockpit sounds? If it gets shot down, is there an engine failure sound? What are the different positions it can be observed from? Only in the distance, or close up on the runway? And the list goes on ... in fact there may be hundreds of items to deal with for each object, and there may be hundreds of objects. Meanwhile, all the other team members will be working on their own scenes and objects, trying to reach a coherent consensus. Anticipate variations and extensions, and try to fill any gaps as you go.

Requirements Specification Document

Requirements analysis means both the process we have just described, and a document which is the output of this consultation, often called the *spec*, or *production plan*. Historically the spec is a weighty paper document, but in a modern production it is entirely electronic, taking the form of a database used to generate code templates and placeholder files. Other document *views* can be generated from this, such as edit decision lists or location recording instructions. The database is an interactive asset management system, so that chunks of work can be "ticked off" as they are done to provide the project manager with a rapid overview.

Writing Requirements Specifications

Scene descriptors are useful. A scene is a list of all the entities in scope and actions that can happen. This may be open ended (player-driven) or scripted. They can be exhaustively enumerated in a matrix, sometimes called an *entity-action model*. Any scripts which define a narrative, whether fixed or programmatic, are very valuable. Inevitably some sound actions are missed out of scripts, but a good sound designer can infer sonic events and interactions from a coherent script. Use reference points and archetypes, examples of similar sounds, specific library titles, or written descriptions of sounds to define them.

Placeholders and Attachment

For the product to take shape, asset slots are temporarily filled with sounds. In a music track this might be a looped beat from a library that a real drummer will play later; or a piece of music that fits the mood of a scene may be used in a film. The danger with placeholders is that people become attached to them and they can influence production in negative ways. Worst of all, unless rigorous data management is used in big projects, a placeholder can slip through into the final product and cause terrible legal problems over copyright. Always thoroughly tag any nonoriginal material that goes in as a placeholder. A good trick for placeholders is to deliberately make them awful. This acts as a constant reminder and motivation to flesh out the production with at least prototypes of original material. Another problem with attachment is that you're robbing yourself because of effort invested. We've all fallen foul of this fallacy, I'm sure.

After working on a problem for ages and the results are still bad, one is reluctant to make any of the bold, spontaneous moves that could solve it. Sometimes the only answer is to throw it away and start again; in the end it will save time to do so.

Target Medium

A good requirements specification explains the target medium properly, enabling you to take advantage of existing capabilities like 5.1 surround sound and EAX localisation. Limitations of mobile devices with small speakers or headphones with limited frequency and dynamic range are highlighted. This really pertains to the integration stage, but a prior knowledge of the final target capabilities means you can make decisions about what material to use. The best strategy is to work in the highest quality until the last moment before making data compressed or reducing the sample rate of your code. It is common for products to cross media formats these days. Games become films, or radio shows become television features or audio books. Working on cross-format material means keeping options open. Always keep the original high-quality cuts in backup; that way you won't have to repeat the whole process again. The target can extend to knowledge about the audience, and the situation in which sound will be heard (in an airport lounge, at home, or in the car).

SECTION 16.4

Research

During the research stage you want to collect as much information as possible about the sounds you will design, for suitability, accuracy, and authenticity. Although primarily technical you might want to work with market researchers to better understand the audience, or with other team members to properly understand characters and inventory. Action and adventure projects tend to focus on the realism and power of weapons and vehicles. Documentary and educational projects obviously require thorough investigation. Using some tiger sounds in a wildlife documentary about lions, because they sound okay, is a big no-no! You can be sure someone out there happens to be an expert on big cats. If, on the other hand, it's for a children's animation, then you'll probably get away with it. The end product of the research stage is all the material necessary to either properly record the sound, source it from a library, or construct a synthetic model.

Papers, Books, TV Documentaries

How does a Natterjack toad make a sound? What is the rate of wing beating for a housefly? What is the elastic modulus of polycarbonate? These kinds of questions will trouble you at some time or other when designing sound. Use the library, the Internet, scientific journals, textbooks, or documentaries to find out.

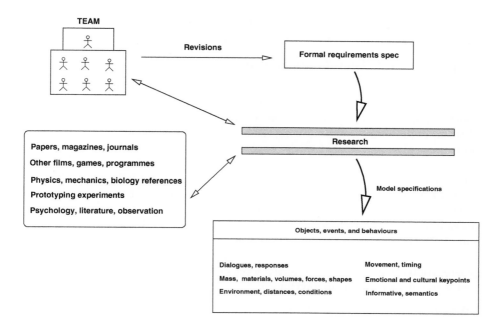

Figure 16.3
Research stages: preparing to make the model.

Schematics and Plans

It is helpful if you can get the diagrams of something you are modelling, maybe from a maintenance manual, or the plans of a building for which you want to model the acoustic space. For a jet engine I was able to calculate the possible resonances of the combustion chamber after being given detailed drawings. If you have access to the objects but no plans then simply measuring distances can help.

Analytical, Partial Recording

During normal recording the main concern is to capture a finished product. Microphones are positioned to obtain the best all-round aspects of the target sound. In analytical recording we want to capture the components of the sound and any useful sonic information that helps us understand the process. This can require a lot more planning. When recording an engine, for example, you may want to focus on the exhaust, the engine mounting, cooling fans, and other components that will be mixed together later to obtain all-round perspective and distance combinations. If you can isolate some components, all the better. For example, when at a railway yard you may be able to get the sound of wheels on the track without an engine. Record as many features of the object as you can, like buttons, levers, doors, etc.

Impulses and Test Excitations

The jet engine example demonstrates another useful technique. Most already have a spark gap built in as the ignition source. A spark can produce a very short impulse which reveals the sonic character of a space by way of reverb; it gives us an impulse response. Firing the ignition spark when no other sounds are happening gives a snapshot of the engine cavity.[1] Of course this is an unusual case; most things don't happen to have an almost perfect impulse source built into them, so you must take your own along. A small gas lighter or "clacker" used for some sound-controlled toys is useful. This is great for capturing the interior of vehicles or similar spaces. Other times you simply want to tap the outside of a rigid body to get an impression of its material makeup and impact sound. With either the impulse source or the object you use for tapping out excitations, it's important to use the *same* thing consistently. A drumstick with plastic coated tip is ideal since it has a reasonable weight, is easily replaceable, and won't dent or damage anything.

Physical Deconstruction

Sometimes there's no other solution but physically dismantling something to get at the innards and record them. If you can isolate an excitation source from the resonance of the housing, this is extremely revealing. For instance, the alarm clock example demonstrates that a large part of the sound comes from the body, which amplifies the clockwork mechanism. The internal works produce a much quieter and detailed sound that is obscured by the body. Taking the clock apart and placing a contact microphone on the ticking internal assembly provides only the cog sounds, very different from the assembled clock. Tapping the body provides a response for a space into which the mechanism can be placed later. Convolution methods mean you can then hybridise sources and excitors, such as using the large wooden body of a grandfather clock with the ticking of small watch to make a third imaginary object, a "grandfather watch."

┌─ SECTION 16.5 ───
Creating a Model
└──

Our model is one part of an intermediate stage between the real object and its procedural counterpart. The model only exists in the mind of the designer, although pencil and paper sketches may help you formulate it. It is a simplification of the properties and behaviours of the object. For example, a car model says that it has an internal combustion engine of four cylinders connected to

---

1. Be very careful using a spark impulse source in any situation where there may be flammable gases. Remember many such gases are heavier than air and may collect in the bottom of a space.

an exhaust pipe and a transmission shaft connected to four wheels with rubber tyres, a clutch, a brake, a body, a windscreen, and so on. It also specifies a set of behaviours like switching the engine on, revving the engine speed, engaging a gear, moving forward, braking, and maybe skidding on the road to make a squeal. It provides a relationship between subsystems that might be considered object models in their own right, like doors that can open and slam.

Model Abstraction

A model contains declarative knowledge about what something is and the way it behaves in reality. In itself it doesn't tell us how to synthesise a sound unless we build a complete one-to-one physical model of everything. It's possible to solve sound synthesis this way, using only declarative knowledge to make a model, but it takes an enormous amount of computing power to do so. Also, it isn't as useful as it might seem, because we end up needing far too much control data. As hinted in earlier chapters, the process of model building involves component and system analysis to break the object apart. It also requires simplification, data reduction, to factor out boring details and leave the essential bones. What we are left with is the smallest set of parametric controls, or object methods, that capture the behaviour of that sound object for its intended use.

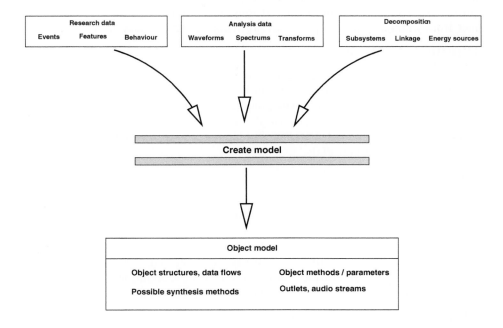

Figure 16.4
Modelling stage: building an object model.

┌─ SECTION 16.6 ───┐

Analysis

└──┘

Building a model may require some analysis. This is where we study examples of real sounds, perhaps those collected during analytical recording. It can be as simple as an informal *by ear* analysis, making note of timings and so on. Usually though, you will want to apply different software tools to the job. We have already looked at the representations of sound signals, so let's recap how they can help us analytically.

Waveform Analysis

Looking at the sound in a basic waveform editor can reveal a lot to an experienced designer. Is there a large DC component associated with an overpressure? What is the ratio of the attack transient to the body of the sound? Are there noticeable periodic features, for example phasing, that might indicate two sources or a reflection?

Spectral Analysis

We know that sounds are made of many individual frequencies in a constantly changing spectrum. By looking at the spectra of real sounds we can try to make new ones like them. Waterfall plots and spectrum snapshots help us to map out the evolution of frequencies in time. It may be possible to group features *by eye* just from watching spectra evolve or studying the trajectories in a sonogram.

Physical Analysis

With an understanding of what forces and movements occur in a real or hypothetical material model we can attempt to simulate the waves that would be produced. This may involve developing mathematical equations from simplified model components, for example plates, beams, spheres, or stretched skins. These equations let us calculate the fundamental frequency or overtones from the size, shape, and materials.

Operational Analysis

An operator combines two things to make something else. Operational analysis is breaking the sound into a set of transforms that unite the physical, spectral, and wave signature models. This can be seen as breaking the model up into a chain of excitors, resonators, and feedback paths. Special tools exist to help with this step, although not all are freely available. For example, the Praat suite works from the operational assumption that the sound is a voice and can give the formant filter coefficients needed to model a vocal sound.

Model Parameterisation

Shortly we will look at the interesting process of parameterisation, or how to choose the smallest set of controls. With correct parameterisation we create not only single sounds, but entire classes of sounds that vary along useful behavioural lines. We can construct "explosion" objects which have variable degrees of power, detonation speed, containment materials, and so on, waterfalls that are specified in volume of water per second, fluid viscosity, and height, or cows whose nostril size and lung capacity are tweakable. This solves current sound design problems and future ones. Most interestingly it allows dynamic parameterisation of real-time synthesised sounds, which is particularly useful for games and animations based on physics data.

SECTION 16.7

Methods

By analogy, you are an artist who has been commissioned to produce a tribute to the King. You have done all the research and have an extremely detailed model in your mind: the gait and posture, the smile, little blemishes, everything right down to the guitar strings on his Gibson Super 400. But you haven't yet decided whether it will be a sculpture or a painting. And in either case, will it be bronze or marble, oils or watercolour? Methods are the middle layer in a sandwich between models and implementations. A method is a technique that maps a model onto an implementation. No one method gives us all sounds. They overlap and have different uses. This is the heart of procedural sound design practice, understanding "synthesis algorithms" and how they make certain sounds, and it is the greatest part of what this book is trying to teach.

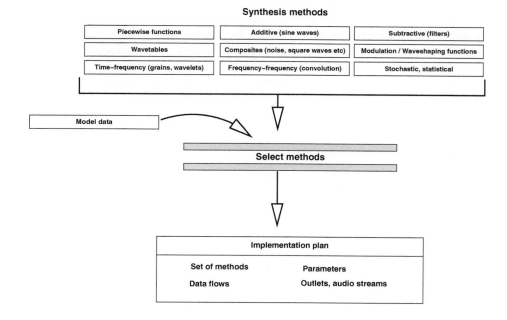

Figure 16.5
Choosing appropriate methods.

Each method is some kind of shortcut or approximation that can be used to realise part of a sound. Artistically, sound design is not as rigid as painting or sculpture. We get to use brass, clay, oil paints, chicken wire, and *papier mache* all in the same creation. The only rule is that efficient methods are needed for real-time applications, so we focus on fast methods. A short summary of some well-known methods follows.

Piecewise

Sometimes we don't know an elegant and subtle way to get a result, so we use a brute force methodology that ignores any niceties like resources or time efficiency. With piecewise approximation we look at the waveform or spectrum of a sound, then create functions, piece by piece, that produce the same data. It's a method that shows a lack of understanding about the deeper nature of the problem and just "seems to work." But direct or piecewise time domain approximation of waveforms is fine-grain, tricky work. Piecewise spectral construction is similar—somewhat more abstract, but no easier. They are really clumsy and naive methods limited to short sounds, but occasionally they are useful when we simply have no other model that works. When you do the police siren exercise you will see an example of a piecewise method. We will only look at the time domain waveform and work out some functions to give that shape without any care for a deeper understanding.

Pure Additive

This is a constructionist design approach. Our atomic unit of construction is a *single frequency*. We use superposition to add together many oscillators. By definition, each oscillator is a sine or cosine wave with one frequency and phase. Each can have a start and end time separate from the others, and its own envelope control to vary the loudness, so not every frequency is present all the time. A disadvantage of the additive approach is the work required to create many separate oscillators and envelope controls. Its strong application is struck, rigid bodies that have a degree of spectral flux within well-defined constraints.

Mixed Additive Composites

Instead of adding together sine waves we start with more complex nonelementary waveforms like sawtooth, triangle, square, pulse, and noise. This approach is common to early analog music synthesisers like the Moog, Korg, and Roland machines. A great range of musically useful sounds can be made by mixing only three or four elementary waveforms, but the technique can be extended to the general case of synthesis by enriching the palette and using a finer control system than found with music synthesisers. Its advantages are simplicity and cost efficiency, but only a limited range of sounds can be produced this way.

Wavetables

A similar approach is *wavetable* synthesis. Instead of starting with a few primitive wavecycles we use a large palette of complex waves drawn from real recordings and crossfade or layer them together. This approach is at the heart of many

1990s music synthesisers like the PPG, Roland JV1080, and Korg wavestation. It shares something with the brute force piecewise approach, in that we can only create sounds by splicing together existing chunks, again giving a limited range of sounds. It is also very memory hungry as it needs to store the wavetables, so it loses many of the advantages of true procedural sound.

Subtractive

The metaphor with *subtractive synthesis* is one of sculpture. You start with a block of marble and "remove everything that isn't *David*." The block of marble is white noise. We use filters to take away the bits we don't want, leaving a broad sketch of what's desired. Perhaps it's better called *selective synthesis*, which is an extension of this metaphor with a scalable block of marble. You can create extra bits where you need them by boosting some frequencies, or stretching the block. To sculpt in this way, resonant filters that can boost as well as cut certain frequencies are needed. Of course this is all relative in the dimensions of a sound signal, because boosting one frequency is the same as reducing all the others. It's important to keep this metaphor in mind, because subtractive synthesis, like sculpture, is a *revealing* process. If the original block of marble does not contain *David* (because it is too small or contains holes like Swiss cheese), then we can't reveal him. This happens for all real white noise sources which contain only a finite number of frequencies at any instant.

Nonlinear

Modeling clay is a good metaphor for nonlinear methods. The start point is a single frequency or group of frequencies which we distort and shape. Distorting a wave adds or removes frequencies. Though it falls between additive and subtractive techniques as an approach, it's conceptually harder to understand than either. Two common ways of doing this are *modulation* and *waveshaping*, which can be shown to be equivalent. It's somewhat analogous to scalable vector graphics programs that build pictures from a set of basis functions or primitives like circles, squares, and lines, and a stack of transformations that distort them in space. The strength of the nonlinear approach is sounds with a lot of spectral flux, such as musical brass and string instruments, and complex struck bodies like bells and other metal objects.

Granular

Whereas an additive approach is construction in the frequency domain, and piecewise approximation is construction in the time domain, granular synthesis is construction in the *time-frequency domain*. We composit thousands of tiny *grains* of sound, each of which is very short and contains a little burst of frequencies. The distribution of the grains and their frequency creates a new sound. They may be sparsely distributed or very dense where some may overlap. The strength of the granular approach is textures such as water, fire, wind, rain, crowds of people, flocks or swarms, anything that is composed of many sources acting together. Its disadvantages are computational cost and lack of precision.

Physical

A physical approach attempts to model the propagation, resonance, and damping of sound energy within a system using delays or finite element models. We take materials and couplings to be filters and follow the flow of energy through the system from its source to the listener. The advantage of the approach is that it is easy to understand at the highest level because there's a direct correspondence between software processes and physical components. The disadvantages of purely physical models are computational cost, potential instability, and memory use for delay buffers.

SECTION 16.8

Implementation

Methods have *implementations*, which are the lowest and computationally simplest ways of looking at sound. Implementations are the nuts and bolts, the times and divides, cosine functions, the basic arithmetic and trigonometric elements of signal processing. They are performed by combining objects, some of which are "atomic," into more complex structures. You will build functions or abstractions that implement the more basic DSP methods and combine them into larger systems. In dataflow this is done through connections, and in other languages by forming statements and functional flows.

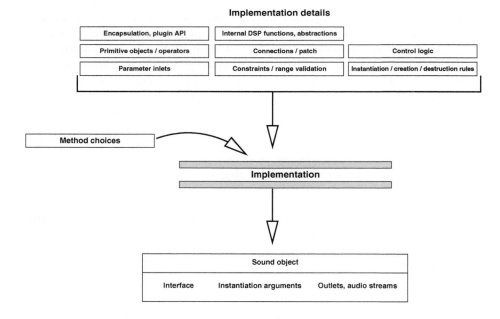

Figure 16.6
Implementing the sound object.

Encapsulation

As a sound object designer you will eventually want to export plugins and code components for game sound or other multimedia platforms. Keeping the implementation open and separate is a useful strategy for keeping portable code. If you can, begin experimenting with hearing implementations from different languages. Try using Supercollider, Csound, Chuck, or other frameworks to implement the exercises in this book, to reinforce the idea that your methods and models can work equally well independent of implementation details like the programming language or development environment. Dan Stowell (2009) has translated some of the practicals in this book to Supercollider code.

Internal Control

Where automatic instantiation and garbage collection isn't provided, some work is needed to make sure that objects can be created and destroyed properly. Attention should be paid to default arguments, range checking of creation and run-time parameters, and cost minimisation by shutting down DSP flows that are not in use. In Pure Data you can use the `switch~` object for this purpose.

Interface

Do you want a set of sliders to be virtual or from a MIDI fader box? Are you going to control the object using Lua script or with OSC protocol? Will it be a stand-alone application for an exhibit or art installation? The top-level view of a sound object is everything we offer to the world to program it. For embedded objects, it is a set of public-class methods. It should be a clean set of properly scaled parameters, the fewest needed to give the widest range of meaningful control. Whether you intend to run the sound object from a game engine or a MIDI violin, constructing an interface layer should be seen as part of the work for building a sound object.

SECTION 16.9

Parameterisation

Parameterisation is a special topic that applies to making good designs. Again, it borrows a little from traditional software engineering, but also from practical experience of designing many synthesisers and sounds. It is not a separate step, but a philosophy that should be kept in mind throughout every design. You cannot add good parameterisation as an afterthought.

Decoupling

An important concept is the decoupling of control structures from synthesis structures. If we imagine a piano as a synthesiser, then the pianist and her score sheet are the control structure. The same piano can perform any number of musical pieces by replacing the pianist or the score. In the same way, many sounds we want to design depend as much on the data fed in as on the signal-processing program making the actual waveforms. Often it's hard to see where that line between synthesis (implementation) and performance (control) should lie. Sometimes, having built a synthesiser, we must remove parts of its structure up to the controlling application or performer when it becomes apparent that they don't belong so tightly coupled to the DSP. Other times we find that the interface is too complex, or there are redundant controls that can be merged back into the DSP. But usually, if we look hard at the problem and think a little beforehand, there will be an obvious line at which to make the break and define a clean interface. This also applies intradesign, between objects used to build the implementation. Each should have a clear, well-defined role and not become enmeshed in the business of its neighbours. In software engineering we call this proper *cohesion*.

Orthogonality and Parameter Space

Let's think for a moment about the concept of independent and codependent parameters. Sometimes we are lucky or clever enough to find that we have built something where every knob and control has a unique and well-defined purpose. Other times we are faced with a set of controls that all seem to change one another in some way. A good example is the difference between flying a plane and a helicopter. The latter is a far more difficult beast to master because of the way its controls interact. Two parameters are *orthogonal* if they can be represented as separate dimensions perpendicular to one another in some space. For example, in 3D we have a frame of reference giving us three directions, up-down, left-right, and forwards-backwards, which we usually denote with something like x, y, and z. It's possible to have a vector in this space, say a diagonal across the x, y axes. Think of a joystick which controls two parameters in a plane. Moving along the diagonal affects both parameters. If we replaced the diagonal movement with a single slider then we would have codependency, since we cannot change parameter x without now changing parameter y. There are two useful things we often want to do. The first is to separate codependent parameters so that we can modify them in isolation, and the other is to collapse parameters into a single one to reduce the number of controls. Often, we build a synthesiser that presents us with a large number of parameters, too many to sensibly control. We find that many of them are redundant. If you think of these parameters as defining a space, just like three-dimensional x, y, z space but with more dimensions, then we say that *useful* parameter space is smaller than the total parameter space.

Efficiency of Parameter Space

Later, when we study additive synthesis of bell sounds, and then bird sounds using modulation techniques, we will see two opposite examples. The first requires a large number of parameters to produce only a few rather similar sounds. The latter has only a few parameters, but it produces a vast number of very different sounds. A model and implementation are good when they offer an efficient parameter space; we say the design *captures* the sound well.

Factoring/Collapsing

An aviation analogy for a moment, you may have heard: "There are old pilots and bold pilots, but no old, bold pilots." The parameter space of age and courage has a mutually exclusive area; the product of age and courage is a constant. Reducing a large parameter space to a smaller set of more useful controls is rather like this. It involves removing the parameter combinations that don't make any sense. Let's say we have a model for some imaginary process like a rigid body impact. For this, we have three parameters, attack time, decay time, and the frequency of a filter. But we notice that all the sounds we are interested in combine these parameters as a subset (subspace) of all the possible ones. When the attack time is sharp, the decay time is long and the filter frequency is higher. It seems there are never sharp attacks with low-filter frequencies and short decays. If we can find three functions that map a single parameter on to the other three, let's call it *impact energy*, then we can collapse the space and reduce the complexity of the interface. We end up with one parameter that captures all the behaviour we want.

┌─ SECTION 16.10 ───┐
│ # Practice and Psychology   │
└──┘

The above process depicts an ideal. It is the perfect chain of work that assumes that everything follows in a neat sequence and we get everything right the first time so it's only necessary to go through the steps once. In reality, design requires several passes, and not all the steps will happen in a nice order. Analysis always comes before synthesis. Each time we approach a new sound we will ask questions to deconstruct the sound into its essential physical production mechanisms. Armed with these, we attempt to fit them to known synthesis tricks or methods that can efficiently emulate physical behaviours while offering useful controls. Finally, we will build a level of behavioural abstraction on top of this to give control. In real life each step will be imperfect and require us to revise the analysis, model, methods, and implementation over and over again. This can be seen as a cycle, with the designer sitting in the middle trying to balance all the parts in a circle of work. A more modern software engineering practice that describes this process is called "agile development," where fast iteration over smaller chunks of the design and frequent updates to the design document are made. The motto "fail early, fail often" discourages too much design without testing.

Design Cycle

Returning to the painting analogy, how does a painter go about creating a new work? In *still life studies* a bowl of fruit sits on the table for the artist to faithfully copy. Or a human model might strike a few poses to inspire. Other times the painter only has imagination, but might still fetch objects to the studio to study, or walk around town observing people to absorb their dress and manner. You can probably already see many connections between this and sound design, but let's state the analogy clearly. A sound artist has a canvas, like a painter. Instead of brush strokes it consists of objects, data tables, and lines of computer code. To look at the canvas one auditions the current implementation. Let's assume the result is not good enough. It is unfinished. We then make a comparison of the workpiece to the target, whether it be something in the imagination or a concrete example. We try to define the differences between what we have and what we want. This is called the *design task*. Then we adjust what we have, performing further research and analysis as necessary to create a set of changes which, when applied to the implementation, bring it closer to the target. This iteration repeats many times until the result is close enough to what we want. We may need to revise the model. Or maybe we need to select different methods—or merely change the data controlling the implementation.

Objectification

Throughout the task cycle the sound qua object never exists in a petrified form. Aside from the fact that we can listen to examples or reference points, we are constantly engaged in a balancing act between an internal object, a mental representation of the target sound and its behaviour (which the rec spec tries to formalise), and the work we have done so far. The work canvas is an *external object* (in a psychodynamic sense), a cold and unreachable implementation of the designer's ideal. Each time we audition it we affect the internal (idealised) object. The internal object is ripe with connotations, memories of similar prototypes, feelings, and so forth, but as it converges with the implementation a deadening (finalisation/petrification) occurs. This is the same for all artists. A painter cannot avoid looking at the painting nor a sculptor from touching the clay, but sound is more delicate, so this psychodynamic interpretation is most important in sound because of its fleeting transience. Unless we are careful the external object will overwhelm the internal one; it will "sell itself to us" and erase the original vision.

Expediency

So, as a cognitive-ergonomic consideration, speed is very important during production. Because it is difficult to keep a desired sound in your imagination without the listening process interfering with the target during audition, working on a running sound object is essential. But systems that require the design to be compiled before audition are almost useless, since they take too long. Even a 5-second gap between action and response can be devastating to the design task. This is why we choose to use real-time dataflow systems for object design and why languages like C++ are almost impossible to use creatively. Compiled languages are great for creating the basic building blocks, since they offer the ability to write robust, reusable, and efficient code, but you should not confuse the tasks of tool building with actual creative sound object building.

Flow

This leads us to the concept of flow (as outlined by Csikszentmihalyi 1916), an optimal state of mind in which to enter and work within the design cycle. In

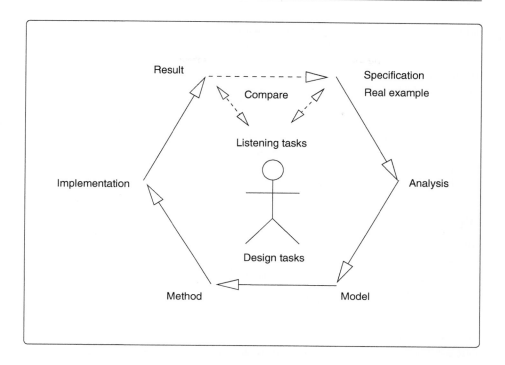

Figure 16.7
Iterative design process.

a nutshell it can be summarised as "work hard, play hard, at the same time—because work is play." Programming, and particularly procedural sound design, is both challenging and rewarding. With experience, the feeling of imagining a sound, developing a model, and hearing it converge on the intended goal is exhilarating. For this to occur one must maintain skills and challenges equally within an optimal time and motivation window. If you are not challenged by choosing to push the limits of a design you will suffer boredom. If you overreach beyond your skills or tiredness limit the task becomes negatively stressful. Many almost revel in the notion of high pressure and "crunch time performance." They like to boast about how 90 percent of the work was completed in the last 10 percent of the timetable. Let's be frank here: this is poor planning cast in a redeeming light. Hard work and happiness are not mutually exclusive. Confusions of effort with progress (see Brooks 1975) and time with money are the enemy here.

Concentration, Familiarity, Simplicity

A good design cycle relies on a mixture of expediency, clarity of execution, and conscious control over feelings and memories in order to hold the ideal in mind while crafting the workpiece. It is a task that demands a lot of focus.

I have seen many designers and producers get "wowed" by technology and so overwhelmed with possibility that their creative impulse is "stolen" from them. Without losing the passion for the art it is necessary to develop a somewhat urbane, even cavalier detachment from the tools. A racing driver does not marvel at the design of the car during the race. That is not to say he is completely disinterested; rather that focus on the task makes the tool "transparent." Many producers say they do better work in familiar surroundings with a trusty beaten-up old mixing desk than in the "glamour" and pressure of a £5000/ day studio with the latest Pro Tools software and a 128-channel SSL desk. Redundant technological possibilities are a distraction that upset focus. A racing car does not have a stereo on the dashboard.

Time and Vision

We experience sound in a different way than we experience images. Viewing a procedural sound canvas is more like looking at a sculpture. It must be seen from many points of view for one to fully take in the whole. This requires exploring the behavioural parameter space of the sound by trying several different sets of input data. The best thing for this is probably a MIDI (or better OSC) fader board and MIDI keyboard to trigger events rapidly. For a painter the canvas exists at all points in time; time and brushstrokes may change it, but it always exists in time. You can look at a painting and see its entirety with a single glance. Sound on the other hand is a function *of* time. You are only ever listening to a tiny bit of the whole at some instant. Understanding how this is different from the visual art can really help us work with sound. It takes one minute to audition a sound that is 60 seconds long, no more, no less; there aren't really any shortcuts. Tools exist that can fast-forward sound without upsetting the pitch; they are great for editing raw material, but because sound is an experience that relies on timing, this isn't as much use as it seems. So, a fundamental "problem" is that because sound is a function of time it must be heard in real time to be understood. If we engage in a process that requires us to listen through the whole piece each time we make an adjustment we will use a lot of time; therefore it's necessary to plan sounds at a higher level so that we can zoom in and work on features of them which are *outside time*. It is the abstraction provided by the model that makes this possible.

References

These are eclectic, but all contain something of great value for the sound designer.

Bely, A. (1922). *Glossolalia: Poem about Sound*. Translation 2000, Thomas R. Beyer.

Brooks, F. P. (1975). *The Mythical Man-Month: Essays on Software Engineering*. Addison-Wesley. (2nd ed., 1995.)

Cameron, J. (1997). *The Artist's Way*. Pan.

Csikszentmihalyi, M. (1996). *Creativity: Flow and the Psychology of Discovery and Invention*. Harper Perennial.

Ghiselin, B (ed.) (1952). *The Creative Process*. Regents of University of California.

Hofstadter, D. R. (1979). *Gödel, Escher, Bach: An Eternal Golden Braid*. Basic Books.

Sommerville, I. (2004). *Software Engineering*, 7th ed. Addison Wesley.

Tarkovsky, Andrey A. (1988). *Sculpting in Time: Reflections on the Cinema*. University of Texas Press.

Online Resources

Sven Carlsson's site: <http://filmsound.org>.

Dan Stowell, "Designing Sound in Supercollider" Wiki book entry: <http://en.wikibooks.org/wiki/Designing_Sound_in_SuperCollider>.

17
Technique 1
Summation

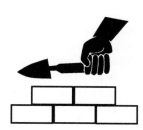

Additive Synthesis

With this technique we work in the frequency domain and build sounds piece by piece. Here we revisit as a synthesis method what we have known informally all along, that almost any arbitrary function of time can be expressed in terms of simpler functions,[1] and through the work of Bernoulli, D'Alembert, Euler, Fourier, and Gauss we arrive at some special cases for harmonic periodic sounds which are the sum of sinusoidals. In Fourier's harmonic theory any periodic waveform, which only need be defined over the interval $0–2\pi$, is the sum of a trigonometric series

$$f(\theta) = \frac{1}{2}a_0 + \sum_{k=0}^{\infty} a_k \cos(k\theta) + b_k \sin(k\theta) \qquad (17.1)$$

in which θ is $2\pi\omega t + \phi$, where ϕ is the initial phase of a sinusoid. The coefficients of this expression are sinusoidal and cosinusoidal components in a simple integer series; where the sound is harmonic they are all multiples of the lowest, fundamental frequency. This describes a static, steady state spectrum (and as a mathematical feature, one that is assumed to be infinite in duration). Calculating one period is enough, since all the others are the same. But if we reevaluate the equation with a different set of coefficients every few milliseconds we can get dynamic, evolving sounds with attacks and endings. This is called *discrete time Fourier synthesis*, and we can use a *discrete time Fourier transform* (DTFT) to analyse an existing sound into a set of coefficients and then use those to resynthesise the sound. If we replay analysis data to an array of oscillators we recover the original sound, but it leaves little room for actual design unless we can manipulate and transform the intermediate parameters.

It's one of the oldest digital methods. Max Mathews and Jean Claude Risset did much of the groundwork for additive synthesis in the 1950s and 1960s. Since the number of harmonics in most real sounds is very large, to do practical additive synthesis we must employ *data reduction*, to boil the sound down to its most important features. We look for envelopes that can be used with more

---

1. In fact not every function works, because of convergence problems.

than one partial, reducing the synthesis to groups of sinusoids that behave in a similar way. We can also threshold oscillator functions, switching them on or off dynamically so as not to waste CPU resources on inconsequential components (Lagrange and Marchand 2001). Finally, as we will see shortly, we can break sounds down into principle components that have efficient representations for their class, for instance making the harmonic parts from a closed form expression and using only a few extra oscillators to fill in the inharmonics.

A practical consideration is how to represent additive parameters. How do we store them so they are useful and flexible to play with? We could place each component from a Fourier analysis into its own array, but that would require quite a lot of space. You can imagine that the analysis data from a harmonic sound has been sampled to give us the four envelopes seen in figure 17.1. They are shown in a format appropriate for `vline~`, but it is often better to store them in *breakpoint* format, which consists of time-value pairs corresponding to each corner where the line changes direction. Each "track" corresponds to the amplitude of one oscillator.

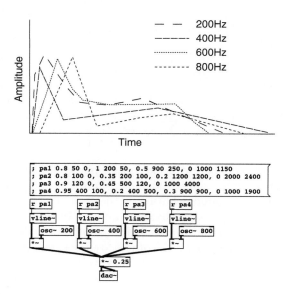

Figure 17.1
Breakpoint envelopes in additive synthesis.

Generally the partial envelopes extracted from a real sound by Fourier or other types of analysis will be complicated, so data reduction must be applied to turn them into simple envelopes. This process uses a mixture of curve fitting, minima and maxima identification and downsampling (see Moré 1977). Those in figure 17.1 look very much like a spectral waterfall plot viewed from the side so we can see their time relationship optimally. For many sounds we find that just a few envelopes describe a number of *groups* with similar structures. Instead of storing all the envelopes we can store the group basis curves and derive all the other envelopes by means of interpolation or applying shaping functions.

Several variations on the general idea of additive synthesis are worth discussing. First, on the importance of phase, recall that we can often discard this information and still hear a good result, but if we want to reconstruct an exact time-domain waveform the phase of each component is needed. Because the analysis-synthesis process can be expressed by equations using complex numbers, the amplitude part is sometimes called the *real part* and the *imaginary part* represents the phase. Some sounds, particularly those with transients, require us to keep phases properly aligned, while others are much more forgiving of absolute component alignment. This gives us two approaches to additive synthesis, one in which we have a bank of free running oscillators and we only supply the *real*, amplitude part, and another where we use a synchronous oscillator bank or modify the phases with the *imaginary* (phase) part of the data. figure 17.2 demonstrates a bell sound and a struck wire sound. One uses free running independent oscillators while the other requires that all oscillators have a common phase. Apart from this difference the patches are almost identical. Try replacing the `partial` abstractions with `spartial` in the bell sound to hear the difference.

O━ Keypoint
The phase of partials can be important in additive synthesis.

Second, since most real sounds are partly inharmonic, and it's only possible to synthesise harmonic waveforms with a pure Fourier method, we rarely use a fixed-frequency oscillator bank. We can generalise the additive method to partials that are not harmonic. As well as having the amplitudes change we also supply data to change the frequency of each partial. Some partials will not sound all the time. It's generally true that a sound is much more busy at the start, so we need a lot of partials there. As the sound evolves fewer partials are needed in most cases. In the end this leads to a lot of data and the need for careful management of it. Figure 17.3 shows a data structure used in Pd to hold the changing frequencies of partials of a bell sound. You can see that the fundamental wobbles around throughout the sound and that there is a bending of all frequencies at the start due to nonlinearity in the attack.

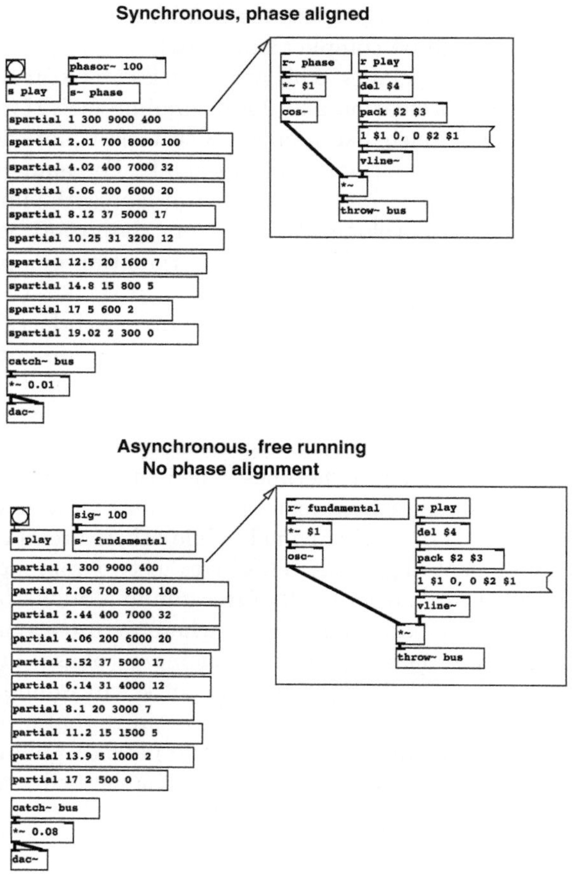

Synchronous, phase aligned

Asynchronous, free running
No phase alignment

Figure 17.2
Different approaches to phase in practical additive design.

SECTION 17.2

Discrete Summation Synthesis

A wonderful mathematical identity can be used to get a useful shortcut. The sum of a geometric series can be written in a simpler way as a fraction of powers.

$$\sum_{k=0}^{n-1} z^k = \frac{1 - z^n}{1 - z}$$

Likewise, for periodic functions a sum of trigonometric functions having a uniform relationship can be expressed as a much simpler formula requiring only

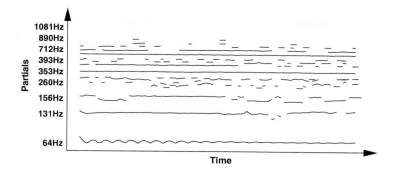

Figure 17.3

Partial tracing: See Pure Data help example 4.15-sinusoidal-tracker.

a sine and cosine term and a division. This is called the *closed form* expression of an infinite sum, or a *discrete summation formula* (DSF), and it saves an enormous amount of CPU provided we want a spectrum that can be described in this regular way. It was developed into a synthesis method in the early 1970s (Moorer 1976). Moorer (1976) gives the textbook by Jolley (1961) as a reference, and the general form of the equation in which θ and β are two periodic functions

$$\sum_{k=0}^{N} a^k \sin(\theta + \beta) =$$

$$\frac{\sin\theta - a\sin(\theta - \beta) - a^{N+1}[\sin(\theta + (N+1)\beta) - a\sin(\theta + N\beta)]}{1 + a^2 - 2a\cos\beta}$$

which he then develops into simplified special cases for synthesising several different classes of spectra. In its most flexible form we can specify the number of harmonics too, which makes it band-limited. But here we'll look at a simplified form that is easier to understand. The technique requires only two oscillators to produce inharmonic spectra. In use it's a bit like modulation techniques where we have an index that affects the brightness by extending the harmonic series, and a modulator frequency that sets the spacing. For harmonic spectra we will see it's possible to use only one phasor, in which case the spacing is an integer that we obtain by wrapping. The equation given in Moorer's paper

$$\sum_{k=0}^{N} a^k \sin(\theta + k\beta) = \frac{\sin\theta - a\sin(\theta - \beta)}{1 + a^2 - 2a\cos\beta} \qquad (17.2)$$

leads us to the Pure Data implementation of figure 17.4 in which we have a control for the fundamental frequency, one for the harmonic spacing (distance), and one for the harmonic decay (index). With *index* < 1.0 the harmonics tend towards zero. It's possible to make spectra that grow, or double-sided spectra like those we get from AM and FM. However, because this simplification approximates an infinite sum; without modifying the patch we will get aliasing if the index is set greater than 1.0.

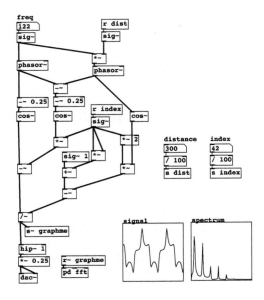

Figure 17.4
Discrete summation form of additive synthesis.

One of the problems with the approach is that the amplitude grows as the spectrum gets brighter, so a normalising function is needed to keep the waveform within sensible bounds. Moorer suggests several variations of scaling by $1/\sqrt{1 - a^{index}}$, but this isn't so good for symmetrical spectra or those containing folded components that reinforce or negate existing ones, so experimenting may be necessary.

A commonly used method for generating band limited pulses is given by Dodge and Jerse (1985). If n is the number of harmonics, a is the amplitude, and θ is a phasor:

$$\frac{a}{n}\sum_{k=1}^{n}\cos(k\theta) = \frac{a}{2n}\left\{\frac{\sin([2n+1]\theta/2)}{\sin(\theta/2)} - 1\right\}$$

Note that in the implementation of figure 17.5 I use the shorthand form $\boxed{\text{sin-}}$, which is an abstraction, to make the translation between the equation and the patch easier to understand.

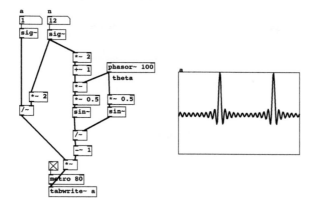

Figure 17.5
Closed form for band limited pulse.

Precomputation

Pure Data, Csound, Supercollider, and almost every other DSP sound design environment provide a way to generate waveforms additively so that they can be stored in a table. This has the advantage of offering a band-limited spectrum so that for transpositions up to the point where the highest harmonic equals the Nyquist frequency (*samplerate*/2) there will be no aliasing. The disadvantage is that precomputing waveforms requires memory and a little CPU time before the patch can run. For low frequencies the waveforms sound somewhat empty and cold. Of course we can always add more harmonics, but we must be mindful that the advantage of band limitation trades off against the richness of the waveform for low frequencies. It's possible to make a compromise if we use more memory to make a band-limited oscillator that switches tables to ones using fewer harmonics as the frequency increases. Playing back a stored table requires the `tabosc4~` object. In Pure Data the table must be a power of two plus three for interpolation to work. This brings us to the method of wavetable synthesis, which we will explore more fully in a moment. For now let's see how to precompute some classic waveforms as the sum of sinusoids. We use a `sinesum` command in a message box giving the table name, size, and a list of harmonic amplitudes which are labelled h_1 to h_9 in figure 17.6. For a sinewave we need only one harmonic with an amplitude of 1.0 in the first position. A square wave is obtained by setting all the odd harmonics to $1/n$ for h_n. To get a triangle wave set odd $h_n = 1/n^2$ with alternate positive and negative signs. And for a sawtooth set $h_n = 1/n$. In figure 17.7 we see a message containing the construction commands, which are of course written as decimals. Some loss of accuracy occurs when writing irrationals to two or three places, but you can give more

Waveform	h1	h2	h3	h4	h5	h6	h7	h8	h9
Sine	1	0	0	0	0	0	0	0	0
Square	1	0	1/3	0	1/5	0	1/7	0	1/9
Triangle	1	0	-1/9	0	1/25	0	-1/49	0	1/81
Sawtooth	1	1/2	1/3	1/4	1/5	1/6	1/7	1/8	1/9

Figure 17.6
Harmonics of classic waveforms.

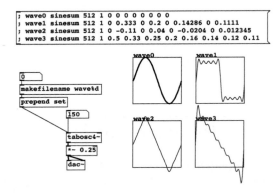

Figure 17.7
Precomputed waveforms using additive synthesis.

accuracy if you like. Notice also that the triangle and sawtooth converge on a peak amplitude greater than 1.0.

References

Dodge, C., and Jerse, T. A. (1985). *Computer Music: Synthesis, Composition, and Performance*. Schirmer Books.

Horner, A., and Beauchamp, J. (1996). "Piecewise-Linear Approximation of Additive Synthesis Envelopes, A Comparison of Various Methods." *Computer Music Journal*, 20, no. 2.

Jolley, L. B. W (1961). *Summation of Series*. Dover.

Lagrange, M., and Marchand, S. (2001). "Real-time additive synthesis of sound by taking advantage of psychoacoustics." *Proc. COST G-6 Conference on Digital Audio Effects (DAFX-01)*, Limerick, Ireland. DAFX.

Moorer, J. A. (1976). "The Synthesis of Complex Audio Spectra by Means of Discrete Summation Formulas." *J. Aud. Eng. Soc.* 24, no. 9: 717–727.

Moré, J. J. (1977). "The Levenberg-Marquardt algorithm: Implementation and theory." In *Lecture Notes in Mathematics*, edited by G. A. Watson. Springer-Verlag.

Stilson, T., and Smith, J. O. (1996). "Alias-free digital synthesis of classic analog waveforms" In *Proc. 1996 Int. Computer Music Conf.*

18
Technique 2
Tables

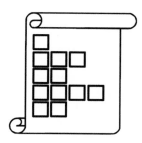

Wavetable Synthesis

Wavetable synthesis employs lookup tables which contain stored functions. We have already seen how to shape a periodic function of time with another function, which we call *waveshaping*; for instance, we saw a trivial case when producing a cosine wave by connecting a `phasor~` to a `cos~` object. Waveshaping will be explored in more detail in the next section. The built-in `cos~` object could be replaced with a lookup table that does the same thing; only, because the function is stored in a table rather than computed, we would then prefer to say it's a *wavetable lookup*. It has probably occurred to you that we can change the function to obtain any other waveforms, and we have already seen how to do this by filling a table with the sum of sinusoids. This should highlight the connection between additive synthesis and wavetables; a wavetable is a periodic function, starting and ending on zero, so it must be expressible as a sum of sines. Study figure 18.1 for a moment and hopefully you will see another connection.

Waveshaping and wavetable synthesis are somewhat connected, at least in a degenerate case. In the former we have a sinusoidal or more complex periodic waveform that is passed through a nonlinear function, often a lookup table, to modify its spectrum. The first column of figure 18.1 shows this when the function is linear. Our wavetable is a line running through zero between −1.0 and 1.0, and the index to the table is a sinusoidal wave. In this case, where we view the process as waveshaping we can use a nonlinear function and change the amplitude or shape of the input waveform but keep the function fixed. Notice how the index is placed centrally around the middle of a 128-point table by subtracting 64, because the input wave is bipolar.

In the case of wavetable synthesis we use a phasor as an index to a periodic function. We keep the indexing waveform fixed but dynamically modify the shaping function. This is shown in the second column of figure 18.1. The table is filled with a cycle of a cosine wave and we index it with a phasor. Notice how the index covers the table domain using the full 128 points because the input wave is unipolar and positive.

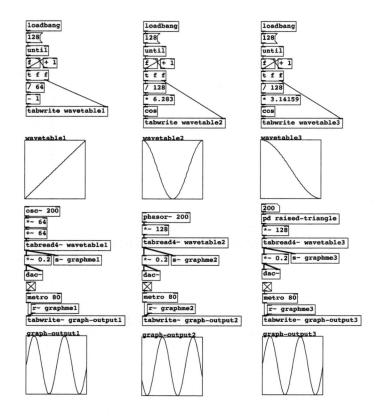

Figure 18.1
A useful identity: waveshaping and wavetable synthesis have a trivial equivalence.

The last column shows how we can use smaller tables for symmetrical functions by only storing half of it. Instead of a phasor we use a raised triangle wave to scan around the middle ($y = 0$) of the stored function. This provides an interesting advantage that the function endpoints do not have to match up. So we can use nonperiodic functions such as polynomials that have interesting turning points where we want.

┌─ SECTION 18.2 ───

Practical Wavetables

Figure 18.2 demonstrates some techniques for employing wavetables. Remember that `tabread4~` is an interpolating reader, so your tables should really have an extra three points if you want to avoid small glitches. We see two ways of changing the sound. The first is to issue a command to change the table contents, either by computing a new function and filling the table, or using one of

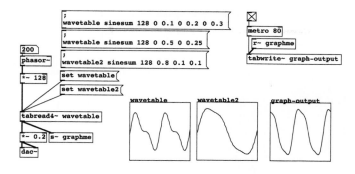

Figure 18.2
Using wavetables in Pure Data.

the built in wave constructors like `sinesum`. Another way is to `set` <tabread4~> to reference a different table by giving it a message with the new table name as an argument.

This is okay for obtaining a fixed spectrum, but how do we make dynamic sounds? One way of doing this is wavetable switching by changing the index offset into a lookup table that stores several periodic functions. These could be single cycles of any evolving waveform. In effect this a perversion of timestretching because we can move forwards or backwards through an evolving sound at any rate without causing clicks, but we can't make jumps between arbitrary cycles.

This highlights the difficulty for wavetable synthesis, which is working out a way to change the table contents without causing a click, in other words to keep the phase changing smoothly. One method is to write behind the phasor index, but this causes problems rather like those of file locking if a table is shared between oscillators. A good solution is to crossfade between two or more tables so that you update one that isn't currently being read. This brings us nicely to the subject of wavescanning and vector synthesis techniques.

SECTION 18.3

Vector Synthesis

Vector synthesis is really a control strategy, but it is commonly used with a wavetable synthesis layer, so this is a good place to explore it. A useful object in Pure Data is the table lookup oscillator <tabosc4~>, which essentially does what we have seen above in a neat package.

Vector synthesis can be considered a form of additive synthesis that blends more complex spectra. It belongs in the family of so-called S+S (sample plus synthesis) methods where oscillators that replay prestored wavetables are combined with a fade matrix, envelope generators, and filters. This strategy is

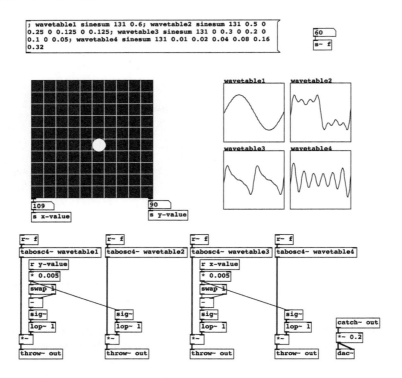

Figure 18.3
A 2D synth using an external GUI object.

typical of many digital music synthesisers from the 1990s such as the Sequential Circuits Prophet VS vector synthesizer.

In figure 18.3 we see four wavetables filled with preconstructed waveforms and mixed according to the position of a marker on a 2D plane. This patch requires the `grid` external by Yves Degoyon which is available in extended versions of Pure Data. I find it a useful tool for sound design, especially in combination with a controller surface like the Korg KaossPad, a joystick, or a multi-axis MIDI controller wheel via the `ctlin` object. Each position on the grid produces a unique blend of waveforms, and if movements can be recorded and then played back it forms a complex envelope generator.

SECTION 18.4

Wavescanning Synthesis

Wavescanning is a hybrid method that falls somewhere between waveshaping, granular synthesis, and wavetable synthesis by taking any sound file as a source and using a triangle or sine to index it. We pay no attention to any period/phase

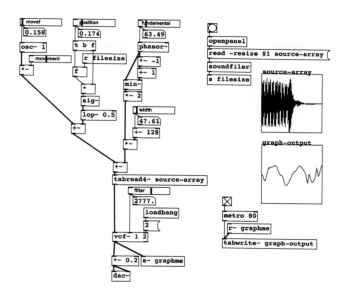

Figure 18.4
A wavescanner with useful musical controls.

boundaries within the sample; we simply use it as raw material. The cool part happens when we scan slowly through the file by adding an offset to the average index position. Figure 18.4 shows a patch that can produce some very interesting dynamic spectra like the PPG or Synclavier devices.

First we produce a triangle wave from a phasor. Multiplying it by a scale factor allows us to change the width of the scan, to squash or stretch the excursion of the index. Adding a slow moving LFO gives the sound a thicker and more unpredictable quality if we want. A filter after the table lookup can help reduce high harmonics that are formed as sidebands when the scan width is very narrow.

References

Bristow-Johnson, R. *Wavetable Synthesis 101: A Fundamental Perspective.* Wave Mechanics, Inc.

Horner, A., Beauchamp, J., and Haken, L. (1993). "Methods for Multiple Wavetable Synthesis of Musical Instrument Tones." *J. Audio Eng. Soc.* 41, no. 5: 336–356.

19
Technique 3
Nonlinear Functions

Waveshaping

Here we use a function called a *transfer function* to map a bipolar normalised input signal onto another one for the purposes of changing its spectrum. The process is *nonlinear*, meaning the rules of superposition are not obeyed and we get more harmonics out than we put in. Of course we could use a linear transfer function, $f(x) = x$, which would give us exactly the same output as the input. Let's start with this degenerate case of waveshaping to demonstrate the idea and show one of the simplest implementations using a lookup table.

Table Transfer Functions

The domain of the input signal in figure 19.1 is -1.0 to $+1.0$ and the output has the same range. The left-hand function is simply $y = x$, so the output follows whatever input is supplied. The output is drawn perpendicular to the input so you can see how this simple function maps every input onto a corresponding output. The net result of this waveshaper is the same as a perfect wire: it does nothing.

On the right in figure 19.1 we see a nonlinear transfer. This is the hyperbolic tangent function $y = \tanh(x)$. Obviously the output, which is $\tanh(\sin(x))$, has a different time domain waveform than the input, but it also has a different spectrum. In figure 19.2 you can see how to do this in practice. There is a cosinusoidal oscillator which is scaled to index a table of 258 values centred on zero. A line segment makes a short envelope which modulates the oscillator amplitude before and after the shaping function. To do the shaping function we use a `tabread4~` which reads from the array `xfer`. Two procedures on the right of the patch can fill the array with either a line or a curve.

O━ Keypoint
Waveshaping is a nonlinear method that distorts a signal.

The idea is that we fill the table with a function which provides the spectrum we want when driven with a signal we already have. In figure 19.3 we see the effect of using the identity function $y = x$, a straight diagonal line.

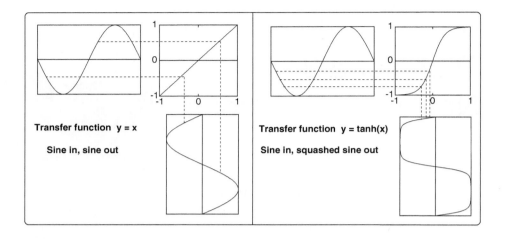

Figure 19.1
Waveshaping with identity and tanh transfer functions.

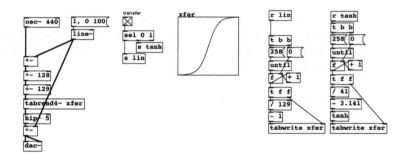

Figure 19.2
A table-based waveshaper noise.

But there is more to it. Look at the slope of $\tanh(x)$ near the middle, for small values around zero. It is almost a straight line. As the amplitude of the input signal tends towards zero the function is more linear. This means the spectrum of the output (as well as its amplitude) depends on the amplitude of the input. That's great for synthesis of natural sounds, because louder sounds usually contain more harmonics. In figure 19.4 the same input produces a distorted and harmonically richer sound when its amplitude is high, but decays back towards a sinusoidal wave as the amplitude decreases.

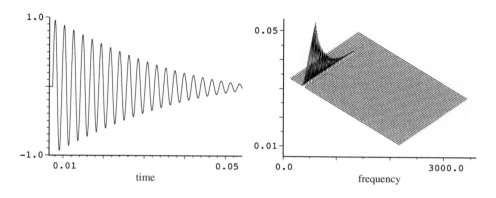

Figure 19.3
A linear transfer function has no effect.

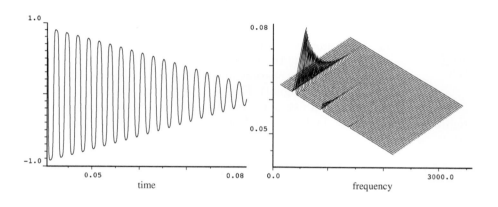

Figure 19.4
A tanh transfer function makes more harmonics when the input is louder.

┌─ SECTION 19.2 ─────────────────────────────────

Chebyshev Polynomials

Remember polynomials were mentioned in the section on shaping. Let's take a closer look at these now. A particular class of polynomial functions, discovered by nineteenth-century Russian mathematician Pafnuty Lvovich Chebyshev, have some interesting properties. The functions listed in figure 19.5 are known as Chebyshev polynomials of the first kind and given the symbol T_n, with the subscript denoting the nth polynomial in the series. You may notice a relationship between Pascal's triangle and the terms.

$$T_0(x) = 1$$
$$T_1(x) = x$$
$$T_2(x) = 2x^2 - 1$$
$$T_3(x) = 4x^3 - 3x$$
$$T_4(x) = 8x^4 - 8x^2 + 1$$
$$T_5(x) = 16x^5 - 20x^3 + 5x$$
$$T_6(x) = 32x^6 - 48x^4 + 18x^2 - 1$$
$$T_7(x) = 64x^7 - 112x^5 + 56x^3 - 7x$$
$$T_8(x) = 128x^8 - 256x^6 + 160x^4 - 32x^2 + 1$$
$$T_9(x) = 256x^9 - 576x^7 + 432x^5 - 120x^3 + 9x$$

Figure 19.5
The first ten Chebyshev polynomials.

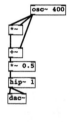

Figure 19.6
Doubling.

For sound design they offer a great shortcut in the synthesis method of waveshaping. If a pure sinusoidal wave with frequency f is applied, the result is a harmonically shifted version at nf for T_n. The amplitude of the new harmonic can be made to depend on the input amplitude too. Let's ignore T_0 and T_1 since one has a range that's a constant and the other is the identity (which gives the input signal). But we can look at the first useful one, T_2, which is a frequency doubler. For practical purposes we can ignore the multiplier and offset and reduce the analysis to that of x^2.

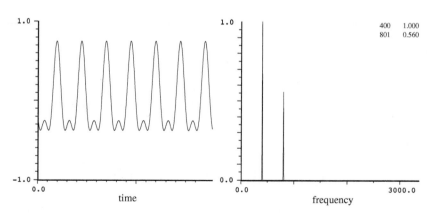

Figure 19.7
The second Chebyshev polynomial T_2 creates a $2f$ component from f.

We already looked at the properties of squaring a signal in the context of envelope curves. When a sine wave is squared the result is a new sine wave at twice the frequency raised above zero. A way of looking at this is that since x^2 is the same as $x \times x$ then we are multiplying, or modulating, a signal with itself. In the frequency domain this gives us a sum and difference. The sum will be $x + x = 2x$, making twice the original frequency. The difference, $x - x = 0$, gives a frequency of zero, or a DC offset. Another clue is to remember that the squares of negative numbers are positive, so for a bipolar input we will only get a unipolar output, and so the output must always be above zero. The patch of figure 19.6 shows a squared sine added to an unmodified copy. A `hip~` object removes the DC offset, so the signal sits around zero as seen in the time domain graph of figure 19.7. In the right-hand graph we see a spectrum snapshot showing the new harmonic at twice the input frequency.

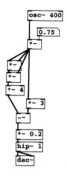

We can extend this principle to get the second, third, and higher harmonics. For the first few Chebyshev polynomials it's not too difficult to implement them directly using basic arithmetic objects. Figure 19.8 shows a patch for T_3 using a few multiply operations. Chebyshev polynomials are alternately odd and even functions. Only the functions that are odd contain the original frequency; those that are even produce the first harmonic instead. This one is odd because it implements $4x^3 + 3x$. In this example we can blend between the fundamental and second harmonic by varying the amplitude, so there is no need to explicitly mix in a copy of the driving sinusoid if we need it. To demonstrate the rapid growth of complexity, one more example for T_4 is given in figure 19.9.

Figure 19.8
A third harmonic.

🔑 Keypoint

Chebyshev polynomials can be used to add specific harmonics.

It's an even function since $T_4(x) = 8x^4 - 8x^2 + 1$ contains only even coefficients (plus a constant we can ignore). Notice that every other coefficient term is subtracted or added to the previous. This causes some harmonics to be created out of phase and cancel with others. Because of this the output amplitude is always within a normalised range. In fact Chebyshev polynomials are special, carefully constructed cases of more general rules that let us predict a spectrum from any polynomial function. By combining polynomials we can theoretically produce any spectra at a much lower cost than using oscillators additively. Furthermore, they can then be factored and simplified to produce a single polynomial (perhaps with a great many terms) that will produce the spectrum we

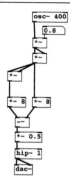

Figure 19.9
Chebyshev T_4.

want from a single oscillator. Figure 19.10 shows the spectrum and time domain waveform of a sine shaped by T_3.

Although we can reuse the output of x^2 to get x^4, x^8, this would be a good place to start using the more flexible $\boxed{\texttt{POW~}}$ object. For functions higher than about T_5 or T_6 another method is needed, so it's time to use expressions or a table lookup implementation. Tables should be created at load time. Figure 19.11 shows how a table is made by computing each entry using $\boxed{\texttt{until}}$, a counter, and an expression. The driving oscillator is scaled to index the array as before.

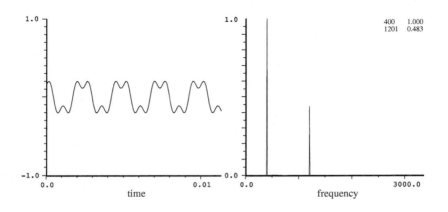

Figure 19.10
The second Chebyshev polynomial T_3 creates a $3f$ component from f.

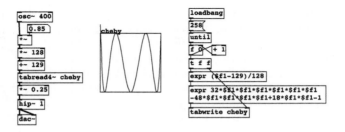

Figure 19.11
Higher-order polynomials are better implemented using tables.

References

Arfib, D. (1979). "Digital synthesis of of complex spectra by means of multiplication of non-linear distorted sine-waves." *J. AES* 27, no. 10.

Beauchamp, J. (1979). "Brass tone synthesis by spectrum evolution matching with non-linear functions." *CMJ* 3, no. 2.

Le Brun, M. (1979). "Digital waveshaping synthesis." *J. AES* 27, no. 4: 250–266.

20
Technique 4
Modulation

Amplitude Modulation

Remember that modulation means changing something in accordance with something else. In this case we are changing the amplitude of one signal with another. To do amplitude modulation (AM), we multiply the two signals, call them A and B, to get a third signal C. That can be written simply in the time domain as

$$C = A \times B \qquad (20.1)$$

We looked at modulation with slowly moving signals earlier while studying control envelopes. A familiar effect, often used with guitar, is *tremolo*, in which the audio signal is amplitude modulated with a slowly moving periodic wave of about 4Hz. In this section we consider what happens when modulating one audio signal with another. Let's begin by assuming that both are simple sinusoidal signals in the lower audible range of a few hundred Hertz.

Traditionally one of the input signals is called the *carrier* (at frequency f_c), the thing that is being modulated, and we call the other one the *modulator* (at frequency f_m), the thing that is doing the modulating. For the trivial case of amplitude modulation it doesn't matter which is which, because multiplication is commutative (symmetrical): $A \times B = B \times A$. Let's look at a patch to do this in figure 20.1, and the result in figure 20.2.

Figure 20.1
$A \times B$.

The patch is simple. We take two signals from cosinusoidal oscillators and combine them with a ⚹ object. What will the resulting amplitude be if both signals are normalised? If signal A is in the range -1.0 to 1.0 and so is B, then the lowest the amplitude can be is $-1.0 \times 1.0 = -1.0$ and the highest it can be is 1.0×1.0 or -1.0×-1.0, both of which give 1.0, so we get a normalised signal back out. But what frequencies will we get? Figure 20.2 shows the answer, and maybe it isn't what you expect, since neither of the original frequencies is present. We see $f_c + f_m$ and $f_c - f_m$.

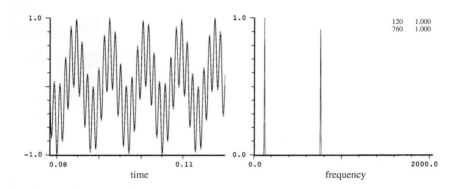

Figure 20.2
Multiplying two audio signals. The spectrum of the new signal is different from either of the inputs.

We multiplied two signals at 320Hz and 440Hz, and we got two frequencies, one at 760Hz and one at 120Hz. Multiplying two pure frequencies gives two new ones which are their sum and difference. We call these *sidebands* of the original frequencies. In this case the *upper sideband* or sum is 320Hz + 440Hz = 760Hz, and the *lower sideband* or difference is 440Hz − 320Hz = 120Hz. This can be seen mathematically from a trigonometric identity called the *cosine product to sum rule* which explains simple modulation.

$$\cos(a)\cos(b) = \frac{1}{2}\cos(a + b) + \frac{1}{2}\cos(a - b) \qquad (20.2)$$

The amplitude of each input signal was 1.0, but since the output amplitude is 1.0 and there are two frequencies present, each must contribute an amplitude of 0.5. This can also be seen to follow from the cosine product equation. Note that the spectrograph in figure 20.2 shows the amplitudes as 1.0 because it performs normalisation during analysis to display the relative amplitudes; in actual fact these two frequencies are half the amplitude of the modulator input. So, what are the practical applications of simple modulation? As described above, neither of the original frequencies is present in the output, so it's a way of shifting a spectrum.

When using slowly moving envelope signals to modulate a signal we take its spectrum to be fixed and assume the amplitudes of all the frequencies rise and fall together. Most of the time that's true, but as is apparent from the previous equations, changing the amplitude of a signal rapidly changes its spectrum.

This seems a bit weird to begin with. But where have we seen this before? It is implied by Gabor and Fourier ...

O⇁ Keypoint
As we make shorter and sharper changes to a signal it gains higher frequencies.

┌ SECTION 20.2 ─────────────────────────────────────

Adding Sidebands

Above, we started with two oscillators producing two frequencies, and we ended up with two new frequencies. It seems a long way round to get rather little advantage. If we had wanted 760Hz and 120Hz, why not just set the oscillators to those frequencies? But of course we still have the two original sine signals to play with. We could add those in and end up with four frequencies in total. So, one of the main uses of AM in synthesis is to construct new and more complex spectra by adding sidebands.

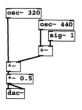

Figure 20.3
Ring modulator.

Figure 51.4 shows a patch called a *ring modulator* which is a common idiom in synthesisers and effects. This time it matters which we call the carrier and modulator. The carrier is the 320Hz signal connecting to the left of ⌈*⁻⌉, and the modulator is the 440Hz one connecting to the right side. Notice that we add a constant DC offset to the modulator. This means that some amount of the carrier signal will appear in the output unaltered, but the modulator frequency will not appear directly. Instead we will get two sidebands of *carrier* + 440Hz and *carrier* − 440Hz added to the original carrier.

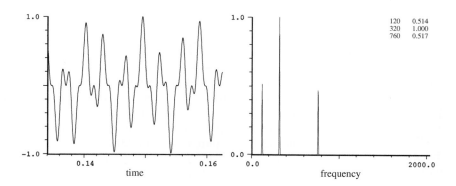

Figure 20.4
Ring modulator, showing the carrier plus two sidebands produced by modulation.

In the spectrograph of figure 20.4 you can see the relative amplitudes of the carrier and sidebands, with the sidebands having half the amplitude. No signal is present at 440Hz.

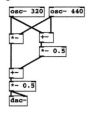

If we want to get as many components in the spectrum as possible, the patch of figure 20.5 can be used. There are four possible frequencies: the carrier, the modulator, and two sidebands. The spectrum is shown on the right of figure 20.6 in which all bands have equal amplitude. Because the amplitude sum of the carrier and modulator will be twice that of the modulated signal we use half of it so that all the harmonics are of equal amplitude. So far we haven't said anything about the phases of sidebands, but you might notice that the time domain waveform is raised by 0.5 because of the way the signals combine.

Figure 20.5
All band modulator.

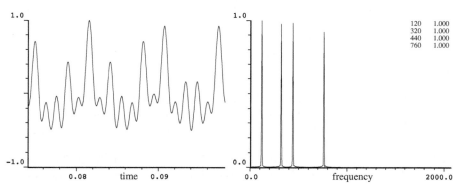

Figure 20.6
All band amplitude modulation giving sum, difference, and both originals.

SECTION 20.3

Cascade AM, with Other Spectra

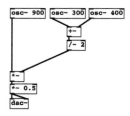

Figure 20.7
AM with two harmonics.

This process can be repeated two or more times to add more harmonics. If a signal containing more than one frequency, let's call them f_a and f_b, is modulated with a new signal of frequency f_m, as shown by the patch in figure 20.7, then we get sidebands at $f_a + f_m, f_a - f_m, f_b + f_m, f_b - f_m$, which can be seen in figure 20.8. Starting with one signal containing 300Hz and 400Hz, and modulating with 900Hz we obtain 900Hz + 400Hz = 1300Hz, 900Hz − 400Hz = 500Hz, 900Hz + 300Hz = 1200Hz, and 900Hz − 300Hz = 600Hz. We can chain ring modulators or all sideband modulators to multiply harmonics and get ever denser spectra. Starting with two oscillators we can get 4 harmonics, then add another oscillator to get 8, and so on.

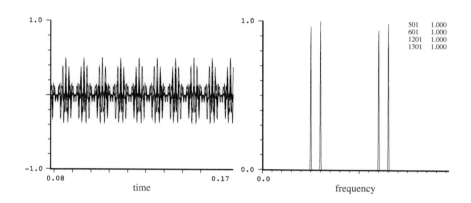

Figure 20.8
Modulating a signal containing more than one harmonic.

SECTION 20.4

Single Sideband Modulation

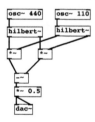

Figure 20.9
Single sideband
modulation.

One of the problems with simple AM-like ring modulation is that we often get more harmonics than are required, and often they appear in places we don't want. Sometimes it would be nice if we could obtain only one extra sideband. It would be useful to make a frequency shifter, a patch that would move all the harmonics in a signal up or down by a fixed interval like that shown in figure 20.9.

The *Hilbert transform*, sometimes called the *singular integral*, is an operation that shifts the phase of a signal by 90° or $\frac{\pi}{2}$, and we can write it as $H(f)(t)$ for a function of time, f. So, $H(\sin(t)) = -\cos(t)$. In Pure Data we have an abstraction `hilbert~` that provides two outputs separated in phase by $\frac{\pi}{2}$, called a *quadrature shift*. What it enables us to do is cancel out one of the sidebands when doing modulation. In figure 20.9 we are performing a normal multiplication to get two shifted version of the carrier, an upper and lower sideband, but we also perform this on a quadrature version of the signal. Because of phase shifting the lower sideband in the left branch of the patch will be 180° or π out of phase with the one from the right branch. When we combine the two by subtraction the lower sideband vanishes, leaving only the upper one. The result is seen in figure 20.10, showing that we end up with a pure 550Hz sinusoidal wave after modulating 440Hz and 110Hz signals. Frequency shifting of this kind can be used to create harmony and chorus effects.

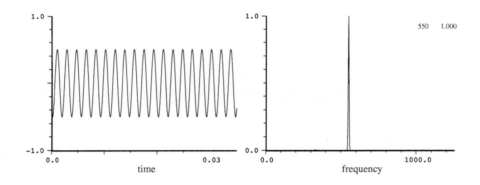

Figure 20.10
Using a Hilbert transform to obtain a single sideband.

Frequency Modulation

Frequency modulation is another way of synthesising complex spectra. When we modulate the frequency of a signal very slowly it's called *vibrato*. As the modulating frequency increases into the audio range it causes new sidebands to appear, a bit like AM. In some ways it is more flexible than AM, in some ways less so. Let's look at a few configurations and spectra to see how it differs and learn where it might be useful for sound design.

Figure 20.11 shows the simplest form of the FM idea. This time we are not multiplying a signal by the modulator, but changing the frequency of another oscillator. The output of the top oscillator connects to the frequency inlet of the bottom one, so the top oscillator is modulating the frequency of the bottom one. As it stands this is a useless patch, but it shows the essential principle.

Figure 20.11
FM.

A more realistic demonstration of FM is shown in figure 20.12. The modulator and carrier are output to left and right channels so we can see their relationship in figure 20.13. This time we provide an offset which sets the *carrier frequency* to 100Hz, and add another signal on top of this. The signal we add is the modulator scaled by a new number which we call the *frequency deviation*. In this case the deviation is 30, so the carrier will wobble around between 70Hz and 130Hz. I've added a number to control the modulator frequency too,

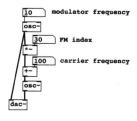

Figure 20.12
Real FM patch.

so we have three parameters to play with in a basic FM patch: the *carrier frequency* (f_c), the *modulation frequency* (f_m), and the *deviation*, which is sometimes called the *FM amount*. The *FM index* is often given as a small number, which is the ratio of the *frequency deviation* (Δf) to the modulation frequency, so $i = \Delta f / f_m$, but it is sometimes given in percent. Strictly it should not be measured in Hertz, but in some of our discussion we will talk about the index as a *frequency deviation*, which isn't really correct, since the unit amplitude of the modulator is 1Hz. Notice in figure 20.13 that the modulator is always positive. The carrier gets squashed and stretched in frequency. Where the modulator is at a maximum or minimum the carrier frequency is a maximum or minimum.

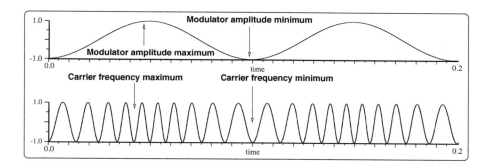

Figure 20.13
FM with a carrier of 100Hz, modulator of 10Hz, and an index of 30Hz.

If you listen to the patch above you will hear an effect more like a fast vibrato. As the modulator frequency increases the wobbling starts to fuse into the carrier frequency, creating a richer timbre. Increasing the index will make the sound brighter. So what is happening to the spectrum?

In figure 20.14 we see the first patch that demonstrates the sidebands introduced by FM. The modulator is 200Hz and the carrier is 600Hz, but the index is zero. On the right in figure 20.14 the only harmonic is the sinusoidal carrier, and the spectrum has a single component at 600Hz.

O━ Keypoint
If the FM index is zero we only get the carrier.

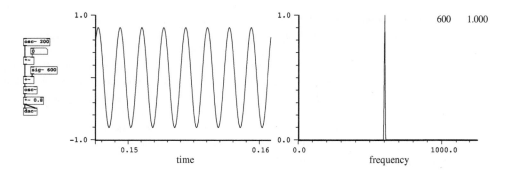

Figure 20.14
FM with a carrier of 600Hz, modulator of 200Hz, and an index of 0Hz.

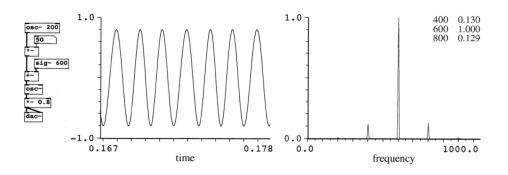

Figure 20.15
FM with a carrier of 600Hz, modulator of 200Hz, and an index of 50Hz.

Now we start to increase the index, adding a 50Hz excursion to either side of the carrier. You can see in figure 20.15 that two sidebands have emerged at 400Hz and 800Hz. At the moment this looks rather like AM with sidebands at $f_c + f_m$ and $f_c - f_m$.

O—🔑 Keypoint
In FM, the sidebands spread out on either side of the carrier at integer multiples of the modulator frequency.

What happens as we increase the index further? In figure 20.16 we have a modulation amount of 200Hz, and you can see four sidebands. As well as the previous two at 400Hz and 800Hz, we now have two more at 200Hz and 1000Hz

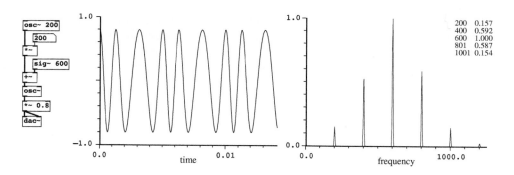

Figure 20.16
FM with a carrier of 600Hz, modulator of 200Hz, and an index of 200Hz.

(ignoring the small FFT error in the plot). Notice the distance between these sidebands.

We can express this result by noting the sidebands are at $f_c + f_m$, $f_c - f_m$, $f_c + 2f_m$, and $f_c - 2f_m$. Is this a general rule that can be extrapolated? Yes, in fact, the formula for FM gives the sidebands as being at integer ratios of the modulator above and below the carrier. As for amplitude modulation, we can see how this arises if we look at some slightly scary-looking equations. Starting with something we already know, a sinusoidal or cosinusoidal wave is a periodic function of time given by

$$f(t) = \cos(\omega t) \tag{20.3}$$

or by

$$f(t) = \sin(\omega t) \tag{20.4}$$

in which ω is the angular frequency and t is time. The value of t is the phasor or increment in our oscillator, and in Pure Data we can basically ignore ω or its expansion to $2\pi f$ because of rotation normalised ranges. We can express the FM process as another similar equation for a new function of time where an extra value is added to the phasor.

$$f(t) = \cos(\omega_c t + f(\omega_m t)) \tag{20.5}$$

The new thing is another function of time. In other words, a new oscillator with angular frequency ω_m. So, let's make that explicit by filling out the new time variant function to get

$$f(t) = \cos(\omega_c t + i\sin(\omega_m t)) \tag{20.6}$$

The value i is the FM index since it scales how much the $\sin(\omega t)$ part affects the outer cosine term. If it is used as a rate of change of increment, then we call the process FM; if it is a change that is merely added to the phase (which is done by rearranging the formula) then we call it PM, meaning *phase modulation*. The two are essentially equivalent, but I will show an example of PM later for completeness. Now, to see what spectrum this gives, a few tricks using trigonometric identities are applied. We use the sum to product (opposite of the previously seen product to sum) rule

$$\cos(a + b) = \cos(a)\cos(b) - \sin(a)\sin(b) \tag{20.7}$$

with

$$\cos(a)\cos(b) = \frac{1}{2}(\cos(a - b) + \cos(a + b)) \tag{20.8}$$

and

$$\sin(a)\sin(b) = \frac{1}{2}(\cos(a - b) - \cos(a + b)) \tag{20.9}$$

and by substitution and expansion obtain the full FM formula

$$\begin{aligned}
&\cos(\omega_c t + i\sin\omega_m t) \\
=\ & J_0(i)\cos(\omega_c t) && (20.10) \\
-\ & J_1(i)(\cos((\omega_c - \omega_m)t) - \cos((\omega_c + \omega_m)t)) && (20.11) \\
+\ & J_2(i)(\cos((\omega_c - 2\omega_m)t) + \cos((\omega_c + 2\omega_m)t)) && (20.12) \\
-\ & J_3(i)(\cos((\omega_c - 3\omega_m)t) - \cos((\omega_c + 3\omega_m)t)) && (20.13) \\
+\ & \dots && (20.14)
\end{aligned}$$

So, you can see where the series of components $f_c \pm nf_m$ comes from, and also note that components are alternately in different phases. But what are the functions $J_0 \dots J_n$ all about? They are called *Bessel functions* of the first kind. Their appearance is a bit too complicated to explain in this context, but each is a continuous function defined for an integer that looks a bit like a damped oscillation (see fig. 20.17) and each has a different phase relationship from its neighbours. In practice they scale the sideband amplitude according to the modulation index, so as we increase the index the sidebands wobble up and down in a fairly complex way.

O—ᴛ Keypoint
The amplitude of the *n*th FM sideband is determined by the *n*+1th Bessel function of the modulation index.

For small index values, FM provides a regular double sided, symmetrical spectrum much like AM, but instead of only producing the sum and difference it yields a series of new partials that decay away on either side of the carrier. When we say they *decay away*, what does this mean? Well, in fact there are really more partials than we can see. Those at $f_c \pm 3f_m$ are also present, but are too small to be detected. As the index increases they will start to appear much stronger, along with others at $f_c \pm 4f_m$, $f_c \pm 5f_m$, $f_c \pm 6f_m$, and so on.

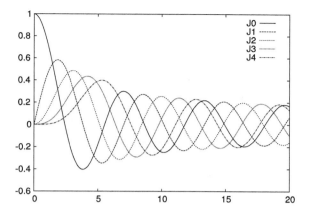

Figure 20.17
The first five Bessel functions of the first kind.

The ones that are loud enough to be considered part of the spectrum, say above −40dB, can be described as the *bandwidth* of the spectrum. As an estimate of the bandwidth you can use Carson's rule, which says the sidebands will extend outwards to twice the sum of the frequency deviation and the modulation frequency, $B = 2(\Delta f + f_m)$.

Another thing to take note of is the amplitude of the time domain waveform. It remains at a steady level. If we had composed this same spectrum additively there would be bumps in the amplitude due to the relative phases of the components, but with FM we get a uniformly "loud" signal that always retains the amplitude of the carrier signal. This is useful to remember for when FM is used in a hybrid method, such as in combination with waveshaping or granular synthesis.

Looking at figure 20.18, we are ready to take a deeper look at FM in order to explain what is happening to the spectrum. It no longer appears to be symmetrical around the carrier, and the regular double-sided decay of the sidebands seems to have changed. For an index greater than 1.0 (when $\Delta f \geq f_m$) we see a new behaviour.

Negative Frequencies

Let's break it down again and look at a simplified FM patch in which the modulation can produce negative frequencies.

What do we mean by a negative frequency? To answer that let's plug some numbers into the patch, setting the first modulating oscillator to 10Hz and making the sweep carrier be 100Hz. In figure 20.19 I have sent the modulator to one output channel and the modulated carrier to the other. Take a look at figure 20.20 where these are shown together. When the amplitude of the 10Hz modulator is 1.0, the frequency of the carrier is 100Hz. This is true at the

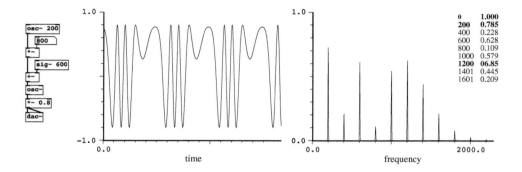

0	1.000
200	0.785
400	0.228
600	0.628
800	0.109
1000	0.579
1200	06.85
1401	0.445
1601	0.209

Figure 20.18
FM with a carrier of 600Hz, modulator of 200Hz, and an index of 800Hz.

point where the top waveform hits a maximum, which corresponds to the middle cycle of the first group of three in the bottom trace. When the modulator amplitude is somewhere about halfway the carrier is oscillating at about 50Hz.

Figure 20.19
Basic FM patch.

It's not easy to pick any point on the lower waveform and say that the oscillator has a precise frequency there, because the modulator is continuously changing its frequency. The result is that carrier becomes distorted, squashed, and then stretched in frequency. You can see what happens as the modulator reaches zero, the carrier reaches a frequency of 0Hz and comes to a halt. But look what happens as the modulator swings negative towards −1.0. The carrier changes direction. It still reaches a frequency of 100Hz when the modulator amplitude hits −1.0, but its phase has flipped.

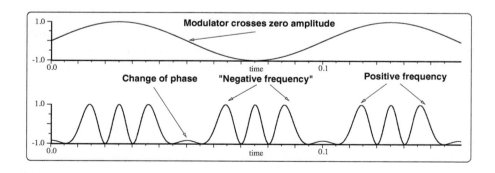

Figure 20.20
Negative frequencies cause a change of phase.

Negative frequencies are folded back into the spectrum with their phase inverted. Much like aliasing caused by frequencies that *fold-over* above the Nyquist point we say ones that get reflected at the bottom *fold-under*. If they combine with real, positive phase components, they cancel out, so we start to get holes in the spectrum.

Phase Modulation

If you compare figure 20.21 to figure 20.12 the similarities should be obvious. But ponder the subtle difference for a moment and think about the FM formula.

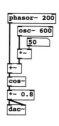

Instead of supplying a steady signal via `sig~` to a `osc~` oscillator that already contains a phase increment we have a separate `phasor~` which indexes a `cos~` function. This does exactly the same thing as the combined oscillator. But instead of changing the carrier frequency we are adding a new time variant signal to the phase. Since a change in the rate of change of phase is the same as a change in frequency, we are doing the same thing as FM. However, we have the advantage that the phase accumulator is available separately. This means we can derive other time variant functions from it which will maintain the same overall phase coherence. The upshot is to greatly simplify the design of complex FM patches in which we have more than one modulator signal combined.

Figure 20.21
Phase modulation.

  Keypoint
"Negative frequencies" produce harmonics inverted in phase.

References

Carson, J. R. (1922) "Notes on the theory of modulation." *Proc. IRE* 10, no. 1: 57–64.

Chowning, J. M. (1973) "The synthesis of complex audio spectra by means of frequency modulation." *J. Audio Eng. Soc.* 21: 526–534.

Chowning, J., and Bristow, D. (1986). *FM Theory and Applications by Musicians for Musicians.* Yamaha Music Foundation, Tokyo.

Truax, B. (1977). "Organizational techniques for C:M ratios in frequency modulation." *CMJ* 1–4: 39–45.

21
Technique 5
Grains

Granular Synthesis

Granular synthesis derives from Gabor's theory of acoustic quanta (Gabor 1944). It is painting in sound with a pointillistic style. It is always seen as a computationally expensive method, and something requiring a lot of control data. It has been explored by composers and synthesists (Truax 1988; Xenakis 1971; Roads 1978; Stockhausen) to produce sounds not possible by any other methods. With this method we create a steady state spectrum by combining many short bursts of sound called *grains*. Usually the grains overlap, so the process requires concurrency/polyphony. There are several variations on the basic method, some which have nonoverlapping grains, some which use shorter or longer grains, some employing random distributions of timing and grain size, and some that are more uniform. We will examine a few of the more common approaches now.

A Grain Generator

A grain is simply a waveform modulated by a short envelope. In theory any envelope shape can be used, but it should be time symmetrical. For efficiency, a triangular, trapezoid, or raised cosine window is often the choice but the best is the Gaussian or bell-shaped curve. Figure 21.1 illustrates the main principle of granular synthesis. On the top row you can see a bell curve envelope and the wave packet formed when a continuous sinusoidal waveform is modulated with it.

O⟋ Keypoint
Granular synthesis uses short packets of sound layered or sequenced to make more complex sounds.

   The bottom row shows how three copies of the envelope overlap in time. In a real-time implementation we could actually use two alternating envelopes; at the point where the second envelope reaches a maximum the first is zero, so it can be reused if the source waveform or lookup table can be exchanged

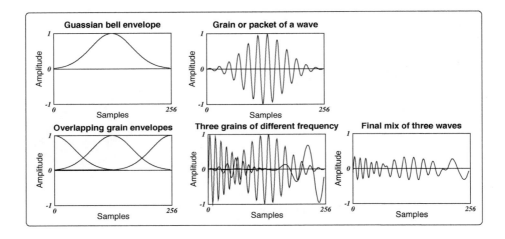

Figure 21.1
Granular synthesis of multiple sources using overlapping grains.

instantly. The second graph on the bottom row shows superimposed plots of three grains at different frequencies, and the final figure shows how they look when mixed into a continuous smooth waveform.

Figure 21.2 further illustrates why we need to do this instead of simply mixing or adjoining short sections of waveforms, and the diagram also provides an experimental framework in Pure Data that you can modify and play with to make offline renders of different grain mixtures. Two waveforms are created with different frequencies in the second row of figure 21.2, and the last graph shows what happens if we mix these. At the midpoints of both tables, where the transition occurs, there is no reason why an arbitrary waveform should have any particular value. If the values are very different when we mix the waves a bump or discontinuity occurs which will result in a click. The bottom row has two tables in which we have enveloped grains. They start and end on zero, and the shape of the Gaussian curve approaches zero asymptotically to the time axis, so we always get a smooth blend. We can move the start and end points of the curve backwards or forwards to get more or less overlap and the transition will remain smooth.

Figure 21.3 gives the three subpatches required to implement figure 21.2. The first shows how a signal expression is used to obtain the Gaussian curve from an exponential function. The second shows how we can take any segment of waveform, multiply it by the curve, and store it in a temporary new wavetable as a grain. In practice we might use a source of sampled audio in the wavetable and give an offset to choose different start points from the source material. Blending the grains is an interesting issue, and in the third part of figure 21.3 you can see a non-real-time solution that fills another array with a crossfade between two grains. For creating very dense granular sounds it's often best to

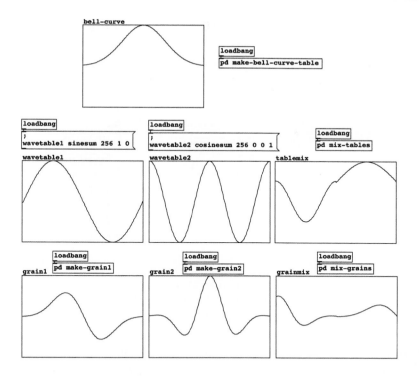

Figure 21.2
A Gaussian bell curve envelope used to form grains that can be mixed without clicking.

prerender textures, which is why I have demonstrated this offline approach. In Pure Data we can do something like the Csound `grain` opcode and make a grain *compositor* that overlays thousands of grains into the same array by repeatedly passing over and mixing, much like a sound-on-sound technique. The problem with this approach is that noise accumulates from digital errors, so in a moment we will look at how to combine grains in parallel and in real time.

Types of Granular Synthesis

There are many ways that grains can be combined. We can choose different durations and amplitudes for each grain envelope. We can choose different time distributions and overlaps. And we can also choose what waveform to put in each grain. Together, these possible parameters lead to several techniques that each have strengths for making different kinds of sounds.

Synchronous granular synthesis and PSOLA

Two familiar effects are *time-stretching* and *pitch-shifting*, which can be seen as two sides of a common process called pitch synchronous overlap and *add*

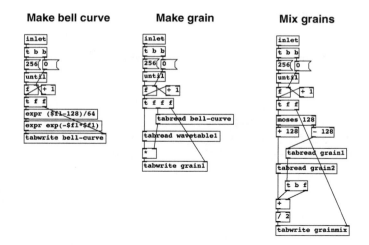

Figure 21.3
Operations on tables for granular synthesis.

(PSOLA). A sound can be divided into short segments that overlap and then each is played back in sequence so that the original sound is obtained. To time stretch a sound we add extra copies of the grains by changing the length and overlap duration so that the total length is greater or less than the original. In this case all the grains are taken from the same source (as seen in the first part of figure 21.4) and played back at the same original pitch, but the position they are chosen from slowly increments through the source file. For pitch shifting the playback rate of each grain waveform is altered and the grain envelope parameters are then chosen to obtain the original sound sample length. Both methods can add undesirable artifacts, a pitched quality at the frequency of the grain stream. Choosing the best frequency, duration, and overlap depends on the source material and most commercial time-stretch and pitch-shift plugins use an algorithm that analyses the sound first to choose the best parameters. The effect can be lessened by adding jitter, some random fluctuation to the grain sequence, which brings us to the subject of asynchronous granular synthesis.

Asynchronous granular synthesis

The second part of figure 21.4 illustrates a technique more commonly used to create sustained versions of dynamic sounds by randomly selecting grains from around a certain point in the source waveform and then mixing them randomly in time. Often the location in the source file is chosen from a Gaussian distribution, or maybe completely at random. Another technique is to use *random walks* around some point in the file or the *zigzag* method where the time direction reverses occasionally. This works well for turning strings, voices, and noisy sounds into rich textures. Although the grains themselves may be completely

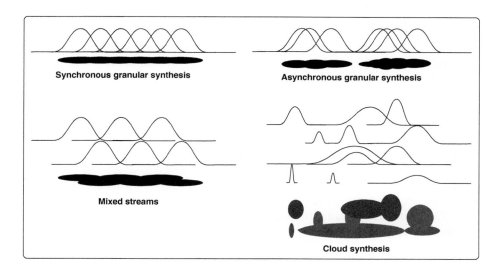

Figure 21.4
Types of granular synthesis.

aperiodic, the resulting texture retains the pitch of the original source material. Notice below the envelope graph I have drawn an artistic depiction of the resulting texture. In this case its amplitude will warble up and down since the superposition of grains whose contents are in phase will produce peaks while those places where the grain density is low or the packet contents are out of phase will cause quiet spots. Asynchronous granular synthesis is often improved by the use of some light reverb to spread out the unpredictable amplitude contours.

Sound Hybridisation

Granular techniques offer a useful kind of cross synthesis if we combine grains from two or more source waveforms. This can be done statistically, or it can be more carefully controlled by sequencing. A "round robin" or shuffling algorithm can give rise to sounds that take on the quality of two or more others when they are combined at the granular scale. The third diagram in figure 21.4 depicts two interleaved streams of grains from different sources. Taking this concept to the limit we can design entirely new sounds from fragments of existing ones in a way that mixing and splicing by hand would make impossible. The last part of figure 21.4 shows what is sometimes called *cloud* synthesis, because we take bits from many streams and combine them with different grain density, duration, overlap, randomness, or spacial position.

A Granular Texture Source

Let's explore further with a quick practical. We will make a tool that can be used to create continuous layers of sound from a short sample. It works well for voice, string, brass, and other pitched sources. Starting with figure 21.5 we see an abstraction that provides the main function, a flexible grain generator we shall call `grainvoice`. It relies on two arrays, which will be globally visible in the parent patch: one to store the source waveform, called `source-array`, and another to hold the grain envelope curve, called `grain-env`. The latter is fixed at 2,048 points, but the former may be resized to fit any sound sample we supply. The core component is a `vline~` object, which receives a message to create a line going from 0.0 to 1.0 over a certain time interval. This time interval is the grain duration, which is substituted into the second element of the second list. The line segment simultaneously addresses both tables, and their results are multiplied.

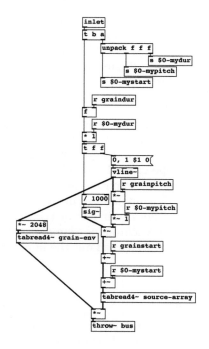

Figure 21.5
A real-time grain generator.

Parameters `grainpitch`, `graindur`, and `grainstart` control the sound. These are given in two forms. First, global versions set the pitch, duration, and start point for all the grain generators in the entire patch. These are modified by local versions (prefixed $0-my) which set the parameters unique to a voice instance. To obtain the envelope index we multiply by the table size of 2,048. To get the table index we need to multiply by the sample rate. In this example the sample rate is 44,100, so you should load a compatible sound file or make the patch adaptive using `samplerate~`. Each grain voice uses `throw~` to send its output to a summation point in the main patch.

Four instances of the grain voice are used in figure 21.6. The main patch consists of five groups of objects, so let's deal with each group in turn. At the top left is a file loader comprising `openpanel`, and a message to tell `soundfiler` to load the given file reference into array **source-array** (resizing as necessary). Beneath is a subpatch to fill the grain envelope table. Keen eyes may notice the Gaussian bell function has been replaced by a raised cosine window, sometimes

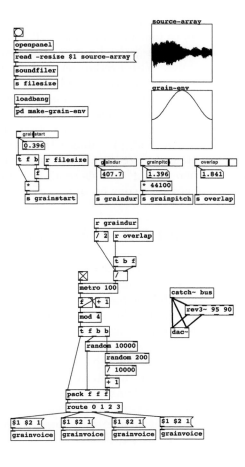

Figure 21.6
A sustained texture pad using four overlapping grain generators.

called a *Hanning window*, which is computed as $0.5 + \cos(x)/2$ between $-\pi$ and π. To the right of these subpatches are graphs of the two tables.

In the middle of the patch is a set of controls. Notice that `soundfiler` returns the size of the file loaded, in samples, which is broadcast to `filesize`. The first control uses this to scale the `grainstart` parameter so that 0.0 is always the start of the file and 1.0 is always the end. Grain duration is simply given in milliseconds, with a slider range between 10ms and 2000ms. The grain pitch is centered on 1.0, which plays back at the usual 44.1kHz. Moving this slider left or right of the middle slows or speeds up the sample replay. Finally there is an `overlap` parameter, which we shall examine in a moment. It ranges between 1.0 and 2.0.

The main part of the patch is at the bottom. It is a round-robin sequencer based on a `metro` driving a counter which prepends a number between 0 and 3 to a list via `pack`. These two-element lists containing a couple of random numbers are then distributed by `route` to four possible voices. The metronome period is calculated in accordance with the grain duration, but here is where we also involve the `overlap` parameter. With overlap set to 2 the clock period is 1/4 of the grain duration so the first grain will finish in time to be retriggered. For smaller values there will be less grain overlap. This changes the density of the texture. You may like to play with the random values that are substituted into the local grain voice parameters. These give a start offset of up to $10,000$ samples and a pitch variance of 2 percent, providing a thick chorusing effect. More focussed textures can be obtained by reducing the pitch and timing variation of the grains, whereas more chaotic, "fat" sounds result from bigger variations. To sweeten the patch I have included a copy of Miller's `rev3~` reverb at the output.

SECTION 21.2

Time and Pitch Alteration

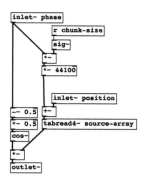

Figure 21.7
Another grain generator.

Here is a two-phase PSOLA effect adapted from a Pure Data help example. With it you can change the pitch or playback rate of a sound sample stored in a table. The core component is the grain generator seen in figure 21.7 of which there are two. A `position` signal value slowly sweeps through the file, but added on top of this is a more rapidly moving phasor that arrives on the `phase` inlet. This is scaled by `chunk-size`. Each cycle of the phasor produces a raised cosine window that modulates the chunk of sample data read from the source table. So, this grain generator uses a computed function instead of a lookup table for its envelope. Notice also that it's fixed to work at a 44.1kHz sampling rate. Below in figure 21.8 you can see two copies which are summed. Each is driven by two signals, a position value obtained from the `vline~` line generator on the

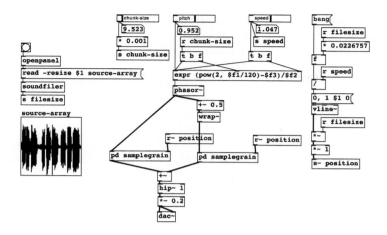

Figure 21.8
Time stretch and pitch shift using overlapping grains on opposite phases.

right-hand side, and a phasor for the grains. One of the phasors is made 180°
out of phase with the other.

On top of the patch is an expression that computes the grain length from
the playback speed, pitch, and chunk size controls. To use the patch, first load
a sample, which will return its file size to the line generator for use in computing the line length. Then set up the speed and pitch controls. Pitch is in cents
around a middle zero position, while speed is a factor with one (normal speed)
in the centre.

References

Textbooks

Roads, C. (1996). *The Computer Music Tutorial*. MIT Press.
Tolonen, T., Valimaki, V. and Karjalainen, M. (1998). *Evaluation of Modern
Sound Synthesis Methods*. Technical report 48, Laboratory of Acoustics and
Audio Signal Processing, Dept. Electrical Engineering, Helsinki University of
Technology.
Roads, C. (2004). *Microsound*. MIT Press.
Xenakis, I. (1971). *Formalized Music: Thought and Mathematics in Composi-
tion*. Indiana University Press. (2nd ed., Pendragon, 2001.)

Papers

Cavaliere, S., and Aldo Piccialli, A. (1997). "Granular synthesis of musical signals." In *Musical Signal Processing* (ed. Curtis Roads et al.). Routledge.
De Poli, G., and Piccialli, A. (1991). "Pitch-synchronous granular synthesis."

In *Representations of Musical Signals*, 187–219, ed. Giovanni de Poli, Aldo Piccialli, and Curtis Roads, MIT Press.

Gabor, D. (1947) "Acoustical quanta and the theory of hearing." *Nature* 159, no. 4044: 591–594.

Jones, D., and Parks, T. (1988). "Generation and combinations of grains for music synthesis." *Comp. Music J.* 12, no. 2: 27–33.

Keller, D., and Truax, B. "Ecologically-based granular synthesis." <http://ccrma.stanford.edu/~dkeller/.pdf/KellerTruax98.pdf>.

Miranda, E. (1995). "Granular synthesis of sounds by means of a cellular automaton." *Leonardo* 28, no. 4: 297–300.

Roads, C. (1978). "Automated granular synthesis of sound." *Computer Music Journal* 2, no. 2: 61–62.

Truax, B. (1988). "Real-time granular synthesis with a digital signal processor." *Comp. Music J.* 12, no. 2: 14–26.

22
Game Audio

Virtual Reality Fundamentals

Game Objects

Because games are written within an object oriented framework it is fair to say that everything in a game is an object. By this we mean that the game world is composed of discrete entities, things that have a name, an appearance, a set of behaviours, and so forth. Objects may be composed of other objects either by attachment or containment. They may have visible attributes such as location, orientation, and colour, and hidden attributes like age, buoyancy, and hardness. Together these provide all those properties we might normally ascribe to everyday things when talking about the real world.

Object Methods

So, our set of objects forms a model of a world. It can have trees, cars, buildings, animals, and people. Each may be created or destroyed, moved around, or otherwise interacted with. Interactions take place through a system of *methods*. Each object has a set of methods to provide its outward behaviour, whether it can roll, break, float or sink, catch fire, be used as a vehicle, and so on. Methods may also modify hidden attributes, such as damaging or repairing an object. Objects may act on each other by performing an *action*. When a user performs an action he or she interacts with an object and a method is invoked. Often it sets in motion calculations which then modify the visual appearance and hidden properties. For the visual domain, this activates computations in the graphics engine, so objects may be seen to spin around, shatter, or bounce.

Object Views

Computer graphics have dominated games for almost two decades. Huge improvements have been made in creating photorealistic renditions of objects. I will say little about this here other than to explain the general idea as far as necessary to talk about sound. Each object with a physical appearance has a *mesh*, a simplified three-dimensional structure that describes its outer boundary. This can be interpolated to give apparent smoothness or deformed to change the object during collisions or animated movement. The mesh only describes the shape of the object; to give it visual substance it must be covered in *textures*. These provide the exterior colours and patterns such as brickwork patterns for a wall or the scales of a dinosaur skin. To create a view of the world and the objects it contains two further pieces are needed. The first is a *viewpoint* or *camera* which acts as the eyes of the observer. The second is a source of *lighting* to illuminate the objects, cast shadows, and create an illusion of depth. These components are brought together in a *rendering engine* that takes the positions of the objects and the camera, their movement, orientation, lighting, and textures, and creates a 2D moving image that we call a *view*.

Object Behaviours

All the above leads to a wonderful visual experience that characterises the modern 3D graphical video game. But on its own, a visual experience of a virtual world does not make a game. Apart from what we see it's necessary to give abstract behaviours and properties to objects. These may include health, age, ownership, cost, etc. The rules of the game stipulate allowable behaviours and allowable actions by players. For example, a player character may have a given strength that limits the number of objects he can pick up and carry as personal inventory.

The Players

Perhaps the most fundamental object is the *player object*, which is an example of a *character*. It represents both a viewpoint, a state, and an input/output subsystem. It is the presence, within an artificial world, of the *real* human player whose actions it represents. Characters are "living," animated objects that may be controlled by human players or by AI. A common perspective is *first person*, where the view is cast through the eyes of the player object. The camera is set at head height, at the front of the player's character mesh, and can move from side to side or up and down as the human player controls the head movement of his or her player object. This is the most popular configuration and leads to an *immersive* experience of being within the player character as a "spirit" or a homunculus that possesses the player object. Another perspective is *third person* where the human player observes a view outside of the character he or she controls. This may be fixed above and behind, or may allow free movement around the world in which the character exists. The somewhat schizophrenic *second-person* perspective puts the player in the body of another character observing the first (controlled) character object. This is rarely seen except in cut scenes and asides. For multiplayer games there will be more than one human-controlled player object within a world, each with its own unique viewpoint.

World Geometry

A special object is the actual *world* itself. The sky, the ground, rivers and pools, the walls of buildings. Of course this is not a single object, but a collection of others. Together they define the landscape, what exists, and where. When we talk about world geometry, for the most part we mean inanimate things. We mean this within the context of a special and important behaviour called *collision*. In this sense the physical boundaries of object meshes provide a set of constraints about what may move where; so, for instance, solid things may not move through one another. Combined with calculations from the *physics engine* this provides observable behaviours. Soft things may be penetrated by hard things, elastic things will bounce when they collide, holes may be dug in the ground or walls knocked down; but even where the geometry is deformable it remains part of the class of world objects.

Stages

Virtual worlds can be enormous. It is now possible to represent entire planets complete with cities in a video game. But, as in real life, at any moment we are aware of only a limited context. Most of the time we inhabit a room, or a street from which only a few buildings are visible, and even at the top of a hill or flying in a plane the horizon limits our view. To fit enough objects into memory the world is compartmentalised into *stages* or *levels*. When it becomes possible for information to travel between two adjoining stages, both must be loaded; otherwise, by clever processes of occlusion, clipping, culling, and space partitioning, only the parts of the world we can interact with "exist."

Platforms

Though most of the world geometry is fixed, there are some things that can move around, and by attachment they can carry other objects around too. Lifts, escalators, and vehicles are typical urban human-made platforms. These permit a degree of control. Noncontrollable natural platform examples might be fluids such as rivers or wind flows that can sweep things along. Sometimes we subsume platforms into a more general class called *movers*, which may include anything that can translate (in x, y, z dimensions) or rotate about an axis (such as a swinging door). Platforms must incorporate the physical concepts of mass, momentum, friction, and so forth.

Game Logic

Not all objects have an appearance or manifest function. Some are invisible objects whose function is hidden to the player, like path waypoints, triggers, score keepers, and so on. They form a kind of invisible program that exists within the space of the virtual world. For example, a door may have a lock that requires a key to open. Only when the player possesses the correct key object and uses it (by applying an appropriate action) will the door open.

Actors and Relevance

Actors are anything that's *relevant* to the game logic. They may be animate characters, player objects, weapons, vehicle platforms, or whatever. What distinguishes them from inanimate world geometry or incidental objects is their relevance, which defines the *focus* of the game. Actors may have a special property of *instigation* which they inherit from other actors in order to model causality. If object A collides with object B which then collides with object C, we say A is the instigator and the sequence ABC is the *causal chain*. Further ways of discriminating relevant from irrelevant information might use distance, occlusion by intervening objects, or time. Relevance affects the way objects are drawn by the graphics engine. Distant objects are not rendered in as much detail as close ones. As we will see shortly, this *level of detail* (written *LOD*) is also important to sound.

SECTION 22.2

Samples or Procedural Audio?

Armed with a superficial understanding of what is happening in game code, we can prepare to think about the sonic properties of objects. Before doing so let's talk briefly about the traditional way that game audio has been done over the last two decades. Firstly, we must note that sound has not always been done with samples, or what I call the *data model* of game audio. In fact, game audio started using procedural technology. Early game consoles and personal computers had synthesiser chips that produced sound effects and music in real time, but once sample technology matured it quickly took over because of its perceived realism. Thus synthesised sound was relegated to the scrapheap.

Events vs. Behaviours

To take a long view of the last two decades and understand why procedural sound is set to make a huge comeback, we need to understand the limitations of sampled sound and the ambiguity in the word "realistic." Sampled sound is nothing more than a recording. The limitation that immediately presents itself is that sampled sound is fixed in time. No matter what clever tricks of blending, layering, filtering, and truncation we apply, the fact remains that samples are a one-off process. A recording captures the digital signal of a single instance of a sound, but not its behaviour. What this has meant for game audio over the last two decades is that the entire approach has been *event based*. Traditional game audio binds each action to an event which triggers a sound sample. Some real-time modification can be applied, such as distance damping, or combining alternative samples in a random or granular way to get more variation. But none of these techniques is able to map the underlying physical behaviour of an object to its sound. Contrast this with the visual domain where graphics are all about continuous behaviour, controlled by streams of parameters based on physics. By analogy to traditional game sound technology, an event-based graphical game would only be a series of static photographs, much like the popular Myst game of the 1980s.

Limitations of Sample-Based Audio

Current game audio engine technology is largely geared to handling this events-plus-samples approach. Accordingly the sample replay and post-processing DSP is severely dissociated from the underlying physics engine and the graphical rendering engine. Many functions and approaches are directed towards disguising this schism between faculties. In software engineering terms, game audio is badly coupled and incohesive. Examples of problems are aligning loops with movements, thus limiting either a visual or audio action to have a predetermined length, or the endless quest for new methods to alleviate the repetitive quality of samples drawn from a limited data set by using random factors.

Traditional Game Audio Engine Functions

Below is a quick summary of traditional game audio engine functions. Many of these are relevant to a procedural approach, albeit in a slightly different way than for samples.

Switching

When an object comes into play, either because it comes within range of the player or acquires relevance, it must be activated. This may involve a pre-fetch phase where a soundbank is loaded from secondary storage. Although modern game sound systems have hundreds or even thousands of channels it is still necessary to manage voice playback in a sensible way. Like the polyphony assignment for traditional samplers, a game audio system prioritises sounds. Those that fall below an amplitude threshold where they are masked by others are dropped and the object instance containing the table replay code is destroyed. Activation may be by triggers or events within the world.

Sequence and Randomisation

Composite or concatenated sounds may be constructed by ordering or randomly selecting segments. Examples are footsteps or weapons sounds that comprise many small clicks or discrete partials in combination.

Blending

Crossfading and mixing of sample data is used much like it is in a normal sampler. Velocity crossfades for impact intensity are no different from a multi-sampled piano. For example, we may have five or six versions of a door slam, each recorded with increasing force. At run time one sample would be selected according to the speed the door closes.

Grouping and Buses

Most game audio systems incorporate a mixer much like a traditional large-frame multibus desk with groups, auxiliary sends, inserts, and buses. The difference between a digital desk used for music and one used in game audio is more to do with how it is used. In traditional music the configuration of the desk stays largely the same throughout the mix of a piece of media, but in a game the entire structure can be quickly and radically changed in a dynamic way. Reconfiguring the routing of the entire mix system at the millisecond or sample accurate level without clicking or dropouts is the strength of game audio mixers.

Real-Time Controllers

Continuous real-time parameterisation from arbitrary qualities can be applied to a sound source. Object speed, distance, age, rotation, or even temperature are possible. Presently these are usually routed to filter cutoff or pitch controls, since the range of dynamic real-time control for nonsynthetic sounds is poor.

Localisation

Simple panning or interaural phase shift according to head transfer response is applied to the sound in order to place it perceptually for the player actor. Relative actor speed, orientation, and the propagation medium (air, fog, water, etc.) all contribute to how the sound is received. This is closely connected to "ambiance" below. Specialised DSP routines are built in to many game consoles and game-oriented sound cards. One of these, which provides an easy-to-use API, is called EAX.

Ambiance

This is an extension of localisation which creates much more realistic sound by contextualising it. Reverb, delay, Doppler shift, and filtering are applied to place point sources or extents within the environment. Echos can be taken from the proximity of nearby large objects or world geometry so that sound sources obtain natural ambiance as the player moves from outdoors, through a forest, into a cave, and then into a corridor or room. Fast real-time convolution or wave-tracing can be used to interpolate between environments as the player moves around.

Attenuation and Damping

This is directly linked to distance but may also apply filters to affect fogging (absorption), or material damping caused by intervening objects that occlude sound. Localisation, ambiance, and attenuation are all aspects of the same process, placing dry discrete sources or volumetric extents into a natural-sounding mix.

Replication and Alignment

If we ignore Einstein for a moment and assume the existence of a synchronous global timeframe, then networked clients in a multiplayer game would all march like an army in lockstep. In reality clients do not do this; they are more like a loose crowd following along asynchronously because of network latency. The server maintains an authoritative "worldview" which is broadcast to all clients. This data may include new objects and their sounds as well as time-tagged packets that indicate the relative rather than absolute timing between events. It is necessary to reschedule some sound events pushing them forwards (if possible) or backwards a few milliseconds to make them correspond to visual elements. Without this, network packet ordering and jitter would scramble the sequence and timing of events and make the sound and vision disjoint. Variable delays are used to align sounds to correct positions or states by interpolation on the client.

Music Dialogue and Menus

These are often given special treatment and have their own groups or subsystems. Dialogue is often available in several languages and can contain sentences of differing length or even have an entirely different semantic structure. Where music is dynamic or interactive this is currently achieved by mixing multitrack sections according to a composition matrix of "stems" that reflects emotive game states. Short musical effects or "stings" can be overlaid for punctuation, and atmospheres can be slowly blended together to affect shifting moods. Menu sounds require a separate code environment because they exist outside the game and may continue to be used even when all world objects or the level itself has been destroyed.

SECTION 22.4
Procedural Audio Advantages

Deferred Form

The sample-based data model requires that most of the work is done in advance, prior to execution on the platform. Many decisions are made in advance and cast in stone. Procedural audio, on the other hand, is highly dynamic and flexible; it defers many decisions until run time. Data-driven audio uses prior assignment of polyphony limits or priorities for masking, but dynamic procedural audio can make more flexible choices at run time so long as we satisfy the problem of predicting execution cost. This means that critical aesthetic choices can be made later in the process, such as having the sound mixers work with a desk "in-world" during the final phase of production, much like a film is mixed. They can focus on important scenes and remix the music and effects for maximum impact. With run-time dynamic mixing, it is possible to "set focus" on an object that the player is looking at or a significant actor that requires highlighting in context.

Default Forms

Perhaps the most interesting advantage, from an overall game development view, is the idea of automatically generating sounds. Because the growth of sound assets is combinatorial, the increasing size of virtual worlds means it's becoming hard to generate enough assets for a game. A procedural audio engine that derives from the physics engine and model attributes like material, shape, velocity, etc., can provide sounds automatically. This doesn't remove the sound designer, but it provides a "background," a basic set of default behaviours for all objects. The sound designer can then derive special cases where sound quality is important, picking key scenes or events to elaborate on. This means that no sound is accidentally missed because an asset was not bound to an event.

Variety

Further advantages of procedural audio are versatility, uniqueness, dynamic level of detail, and localised intelligence. Let's consider the first of these for a moment. As we mentioned above, a recorded sound always plays precisely the same way, whereas procedural sound may be interactive with continuous real-time parameters being applied. This advantage is understood for generative music which can change its motifs, structure, and balance to reflect emotional dimensions. But it works equally well for sound effects. The sound of flying bullets or airplane propellers can adapt to velocity in ways that are impossible with current resampling or pitch-shifting techniques. Synthesised crowds can burst into applause or shouting; complex weather systems where the wind speed affects the sound of rainfall; rain that sounds different when falling on roofs or into water; realistic footsteps that automatically adapt to player speed, ground texture, and incline—the dynamic possibilities are practically endless. We will consider dynamic level of detail shortly because this is closely tied up with computational cost models, but it is also related to dynamic mixing, which allows us to force focus in a sound mix according to game variables.

Variable Cost

Playing back sample data has a fixed cost. It doesn't matter what the sound is; it always requires the same amount of computing power to do it. Procedural sound has a variable cost: the more complex the sound is the more work it requires. What is not immediately apparent is that the dynamic cost of procedural audio is a great advantage in the limiting condition. With only a few sounds, sampled methods vastly outperform procedural audio in terms of cost and realism. However, as the number of sounds grows past a few dozen, the fixed cost of samples starts to work against it. Some procedural sounds are hard to produce, for example an engine sound, while some are extremely easy and cheap to produce, for example wind or fire sounds. Because of this we reach a point in a typical sound scene where the curves cross and procedural sound starts to outperform sample data. What makes this even more attractive is the concept of dynamic level of audio detail (LOAD).

In mixing a sound scene we may fade out distant or irrelevant sounds, usually by distance or fogging effects that work with a simple radius, or by zoning that attenuates sounds behind walls. Until a sampled sound drops below the hearing or masking threshold it consumes the same resources regardless of how much it is attenuated. With dynamic LOAD techniques a synthetic source can gracefully blend in and out of a sound scene producing a variable cost. We can employ psychoacoustic, perceptual methods to constructing only the parts of the sound that are most relevant (Fouad et al. 1997), or cull unneeded frequencies in a spectral model (Raghuvanshi and Lin 2006). What this means is that for a complex sound scene the cost of peripheral sounds is reduced beyond that of sampled sources. The magic cutoff point where procedural sound begins to outperform sampled sources is a density of a few hundred sources.

Dynamic LOAD

Instead of simply applying filters to attenuate recorded sources we are able to cleverly tailor a procedural synthetic sound to use less resources as it fades into the distance. Think of a helicopter sound. When in the distance the only sound audible is the "chop chop" of the rotor blades. But as it approaches we hear the tail rotor and engine. Similarly the sound of running water is a detailed pattern of sine waves when close, but as it fades into the distance the detail can be replaced by cheaply executable noise approximations. Psychoacoustic models of perception and Gabor's granular theory of sound suggest this is the correct way to do level of detail. Making sounds with less focus consume less resources is merely a bonus from a computational point of view. This can lead to perceptually sparser, cleaner mixes, without the "grey goo" phenomena that comes from the superposition of an overwhelming number of channels of sampled audio. LOAD utilises many similar principles to those used in audio compression like MPEG layer 3. Different behavioural models for swarms, volumetric extents, composites, and causally linked sequences may take advantage of critical band and temporal masking. Because we get to compute them at run time we can take account of live dynamics or other constraints like framing, focus, player task, relevance, etc.

SECTION 22.5

Challenges for New Game Audio Systems

As technology is still in development it's important to realise that no audio engine currently offers all the necessary pieces of the jigsaw needed for perfect procedural audio. Pure Data and Max currently offer the best DSP development environment, but even where their run-time schedulers can be embedded into game code they suffer limitations that must be solved to obtain a highly robust and flexible real-time game audio engine. There are competing philosophies that must be weighed up as we converge on the ideal system. Parallelism, threading, object inheritance, and granularity are some of the issues on the table at the time of writing this. For an excellent overview of audio computation systems see Günter Geiger's thesis (Geiger 2006). I will briefly mention a few of the more interesting issues next.

Dynamic Graph Configuration

Ideally we want to be able to construct DSP graphs on the fly, to add, delete, and modify objects without causing clicks or dropouts. If it is necessary to remove one object and replace it with another before one signal block has computed that there is a potential for overrun. One approach is to hot swap objects via an intermediate crossfade. A new object X is inserted in parallel with object A, which we wish to replace. X is a wrapper that contains B, the replacement object, but can deactivate and deallocate the wrapping code leaving only B. Once inserted a signal crossfade occurs over several blocks as the threading/ timing allows, and then the wrapper is pulled off B. A problem arises as the DSP graph becomes large. To insert or delete a node it is necessary to traverse and sort the entire graph. Several data structures are interesting candidates for building DSP schedulers, including adjacency matrices of pointers, various tree structures, and linked graphs. Pure Data and Max both use the linked structure approach, because it is flexible both at run time and at design time, but it suffers unpredictable traversal times that mean dynamic reconfiguration is a problem.

Denormal and Drift Contingencies

In native code a problem arises with an accumulating phasor or long exponential decay envelope where floating point numbers eventually degenerate into *denormal form.* On many processors this leads to an immense performance hit or a complete lockup of the program. Objects we have looked at so far in this book are, on the whole, well written and perform for hours or days without reaching a pathological state. But it is not always possible to code DSP with both an efficient and safety critical approach, so some thought needs to be given to long-term behaviour. Bearing in mind that some oscillators drift in phase and accuracy, some effort should be given to avoiding designs that are sensitive to this and to testing properly to make sure long-running ambient keypoint actors don't degenerate. Many players will leave a game running for days, and VR software installations for world simulators must be expected to run with up-times of months or optimistically years. The most obvious approach is to reset objects on a periodic basis. But unless this method is built into the object, the only choice is to delete and reinstantiate running code. In a large DSP graph this can be a headache if it means the whole graph must be rebuilt, and it could cause unexpected clicks or dropouts. A scheme that works well is to give all objects a finite but large lifetime after which they will fade out and self-destruct. In almost all reasonable scenarios a player does not expect to hear a running sound for days on end. If a list of objects that *should* or *could* be active in a given space is kept then these objects can be reactivated when there is player activity in the vicinity of them.

Automatic Code Translation

As we have seen, Pd/Max is a powerful design platform, but how can we obtain code that runs independently of a specific engine? The form of a dataflow algorithm is certainly attractive. It's easy to understand and portable, being a netlist in a regular text file. Turning a sound object design into something for a specific platform requires rewriting it, usually as C++, a time-consuming business. An attractive tool is FAUST, which provides an intermediate form of symbolic DSP algebra compatible with dataflow concepts and can automatically generate optimised C++. The missing step is to translate directly from dataflow into C++ classes to provide polymorphic object inheritance.

Embedding a Pd Interpreter

This is the most attractive solution to my mind. Electronic Arts decided to put together a programming team (Jolly, Danks, Saint Girons, Ajjanegadde, James) to embed Pure Data directly into the game audio engine for a game called Spore. This allowed composers (Eno and others) to write procedural scores for the game. Research and development at Sony may include Pd in future game console designs.

Plugins

An approach taken by the Audiokinetic Wwise engine is for a VST plugin framework. It's well established and practically an industry standard for hosting synthesis code. FAUST can automatically generate plugins for a number of architectures including LADSPA and VST, which can then be hosted within a proprietary game audio engine. Pd as a plugin within a game audio engine framework is also an attractive route.

Cost Metrics

Variable cost was mentioned as an advantage but is a double edged sword; it's also a disadvantage. Like variable interest rates, whether it's a friend or foe depends on your investments. Because the cost of producing a synthetic sound can be hard to predict prior to execution, we don't know how to allocate resources. This problem is common to other dynamic content production methods, and it requires that we can either guess the cost of an operation in advance and carefully schedule resources, limit the cost at run time, or produce methods which gracefully degrade as they run out of resources rather than suddenly breaking. Assigning maximum costs to objects is not difficult. We add up the cycles for the worst case. Audio DSP code seldom has unpredictable branches; in fact it has few branches at all, so pipelined systems tend to behave extremely well. However, with dynamic level of detail we can't easily predict the cost reductions, because they depend on run-time dynamics. If ten players all suddenly decide to smash the windows in a building and an explosion of particles is spawned, the audio engine must cap the resources.

Hybrid Architectures

A compromise is to restructure programs to include a precomputation stage for intermediate forms that will remain fixed throughout the lifetime of object instances. This short wait would replace what are currently load times with data model media. Some objects already do this of course, such as table oscillators, but sound object designers should give thought to this general principle. There are many cases where a small amount of precomputation can provide massive run-time speedups within the inner code loops. Taking this approach further, we arrive at the concept of hybrid procedural/data modelling. During low load periods, offline processing occurs to fill data tables with anticipated media. This can occur when objects come within effective radius or during a stage load. Of course some of the behavioural advantages are lost, but a fair compromise is to mix precomputed media with real-time streams to get the best of aesthetic quality, cost, and behavioural flexibility.

Hard Sounds

There are some places that procedural or hybrid behavioural audio shouldn't be expected to offer much advantage—at least not within the next ten years. Voice actors are an obvious point. Monsters and creatures are a borderline case. Although we will look at some principles for making living creatures they represent a challenge. Realistic models are likely to remain expensive and we are better served by samples in most cases. However, the possibilities for dynamics with living things makes this an attractive area for research. Music is also an interesting case. Much research has been done on dynamic game music. Some believe it yields soulless and two-dimensional results. Although many algorithmic composition techniques exist and musical rules can be formalised in code, it is impossible to replace the human creativity a real composer brings to interpreting and augmenting a scene. The role of real-time computation, as for many sound effects, is probably to produce "second-tier" musical backgrounds while real composers produce the main features.

References

Books

Boer, J. (2002). *Game Audio Programming.* Charles River Media.
Brandon, A. (2004). *Audio for Games: Planning, Process, and Production.* New Riders.
Collins, K. (2008). *Game Sound: An Introduction to the History, Theory, and Practice of Video Game Music and Sound Design.* MIT Press.
Marks, A. (2001). *Game Audio: For Composers, Musicians, Sound Designers, and Developers.* CMP.
Wilde, M. (2004). *Audio Programming for Interactive Games.* Focal Press.

Papers

Fouad, H., Hahn, J. K., and Ballas, J. (1997). "Perceptually based scheduling algorithms for real-time synthesis of complex sonic environments." George Washington University and Naval Research Laboratory, Washington, D.C.
Geiger, G. (2006). "Abstraction in computer music software systems." University Pompeu Fabra, Barcelona, E.S.
Raghuvanshi, N., and Lin, M. C. (2006). "Interactive sound synthesis for large-scale environments." Dept. of Computer Science, University of North Carolina at Chapel Hill.

Online Sources

Collins, K. "Game sound." <http://www.gamessound.com>
Kilborn, M. <http://www.markkilborn.com/resources.php>
Young, K. <http://www.gamesound.org>

IV

Practicals

23
Practicals Introduction

The path is made by walking.
—African proverb

Practical Synthetic Sound Design

Once you have worked through the next thirty or so exercises you should be ready to tackle most sound design problems from first principles. No set of exercises can hope to exhaustively prepare a designer for every eventuality, so I've picked some common examples that are typical of their general class upon which you can build with further research and experience. Mostly, each exercise increases in difficulty, and later ones will tend to assume you have completed those before. They are split into the following categories.

Artificial

This is the class of sounds that have no real-world counterpart. They can usually be described by a formal specification. Such sounds include telephone dial tones, alarms, and indicators.

Natural Forces

These sounds result from energetic dynamics in nature like wind, rain, thunder, and fire.

Idiophonics

This category includes rigid body collisions or nonlinear interactions between moving parts that do not change size or mass. Such sounds are produced by friction, scraping, rolling, impact, crushing, and fragmentation.

Machines

Machines extend the idiophonic class into complex human-made devices with several moving parts. This class includes motors, fans and propellers, engines, and vehicles.

Life

The most complex sound sources are animate beings. Their material makeup and control systems provide a great challenge to model. Examples are birds, insects, and mammal sounds.

Project Mayhem

Here we investigate the class of high-energy and high-speed sounds where everyday acoustic theory breaks down. This includes supersonic objects such as bullets, shockwaves, and explosions.

Sci Fi

The final section challenges the designer's creativity and exercises ideas of metaphor, simile, and implication to conjure up fantastic sound effects for unreal objects.

Practical Series
Artificial Sounds

Embrace simplicity.
—Lao-Tzu

Artificial Sounds

The chapters in this series are about sounds with no real-world counterpart. By this we mean things like telephone beeps, alarms, or electronic button activates. They are simple sounds. What makes them interesting is that they can be generated according to a specification. This illustrates the point that, if given a thorough specification, we can proceed quickly to implementation without the more difficult analysis stage. Sometimes the specification is published as a standards document. Other times, a model and method are easy to obtain from simple analysis, as shown in the first exercise. It's a great place to start because each can be synthesised using simple techniques.

The Practicals

Five practical exercises of increasing difficulty follow.

- Pedestrian crossing, a simple beeping sound. Introduces basic analysis and synthesis.
- Phone tones, making more complex signalling tones from specification. Bring observer points and energetic analysis into the picture.
- DTMF tones, working from precise specification. Think about code reuse and simple interface building.
- Alarms: investigate alert and indicator sounds. This introduces the idea of functional specification and the meaning of sounds (semantics).
- Police: a more detailed electroacoustic example with some more analysis and synthesis. Explore the idea of data reduction through different synthesis methods.

24
Practical 1
Pedestrians

Aims

In this practical we will construct a simple beeping tone as used for UK pedestrian crossings and introduce some basic analytical procedures. We will discuss the design and purpose of the beeping and discover there are reasons why it sounds the way it does.

Analysis

This practical was inspired by a discussion on the Yahoo sound design list when a filmmaker wanted a particular type of British road crossing signal. Being an artificial, publicly recognised sound, it is given by a government standards document. However, getting an audio example was simple enough since I live near to a main road. The recording, captured about 3m away from the source, is

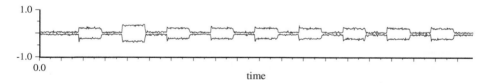

Figure 24.1
Recording of a pedestrian crossing signal near a busy road.

shown in figure 24.1. Notice the background noise level from car engines and general street sounds. There are three points of interest: the timing of the beeps, their frequency, and the waveform of the signal. Let's begin by measuring the timing. The x-axis scale of figure 24.2 is in seconds, so one beep lasts for 100ms. The off time is also 100ms. We call the ratio of on time to off time the *duty cycle* of the signal. In this case it is 1:1, sometimes given as a percentage for the on part, thus 50 percent.

Next we wish to find out something about the waveform. Experienced ears can guess a frequency below 5kHz with good accuracy. I guessed about 2kHz, but let's see what the spectrum analysis thinks. It is immediately clear from

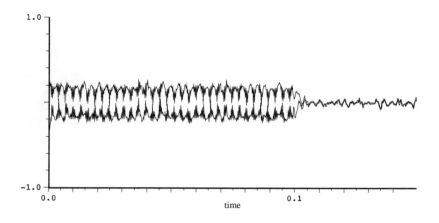

Figure 24.2
Measuring the timing pattern of the beeps.

the plot in figure 24.3 that there's one strong frequency. The list of numbers on the right side is called the *peaks list* and it shows some weak frequencies at the low end of the spectrum, probably originating from traffic sounds. The main peak is given as 2.5kHz. We can also tell from the spectrum that the beep does not have any other significant harmonics.[1]

Model

Our model can be succinctly summarised thus: The pedestrian crossing signal is a 2.5kHz sinusoidal wave broken at 100ms with a 50 percent duty cycle.

Method

We will use a 2.5kHz sine wave oscillator and multiply it by a control signal that alternates between 0 and 1 every 100ms.

DSP Implementation

There are several ways to implement the described model even once we decide to use a simple oscillator and control gate. For this exercise I will introduce one simple solution, using a counter.

---

1. Zooming in on the spectrum plot reveals weak components at 5kHz and 7.5kHz, which shows it has a little distortion, but we shall ignore this here.

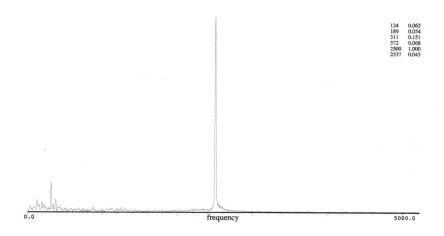

124	0.062
189	0.054
311	0.151
372	0.068
2500	1.000
2537	0.045

Figure 24.3
Spectrum plot of one beep from a pedestrian crossing sound.

Counter-Controlled Beeping

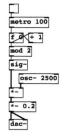

Figure 24.4
Crossing beeps.

The patch shown in figure 24.4 works as follows. A toggle switch activates a metronome with a fixed period of 100ms. Ten times per second, a bang message passes into the hot inlet of a float box which is wired as a counter with an increment of 1. The counter advances upwards without limit. Taking modulo 2 of the counter output gives an alternation between 0 and 1, since $2\,mod\,2 = 0$, $3\,mod\,2 = 1$, $4\,mod\,2 = 0$, etc. From this we derive an audio signal via `sig~` as a modulator. The output of a sine oscillator set to a frequency of 2500Hz is multiplied by the 1 or 0 signal. A fixed scaling of 0.2 is applied to make the output a little quieter. It is sent to both channels of the DAC. Ensure that `compute audio` is switched on. Start the metronome by activating the toggle and you should hear a regular beeping sound.

Results

Source   . . . .   <http://mitpress.mit.edu/designingsound/pedestrian.html>

Conclusions

By analysing recordings we can extract useful data. A simple indicator sound can be made by modulating a constant tone on and off.

Limitations

One problem is that turning off the metro doesn't always stop the tone. If the state of the counter is 1 at the moment it is switched off it remains that way, with the tone constantly sounding. The result is also somewhat inaccurate. The real crossing sound has some harmonic distortion caused by the transducer, a sudden attack transient caused by the abrupt tone switching, and resonance from its housing.

Practical Design Considerations

The tone switching causes a click at the start of each tone burst. In this case it is desirable. To see why, consider some other features of the sound. Why choose 2.5kHz? There are two sides to the road and at least two beepers to aid sight-impaired pedestrians (or fully sighted people in bright sunlight). At a staggered crossing where there are several beepers we need to know which one is active for safety reasons. The choice of 2.5kHz is deliberate. It is high enough in frequency to be easily located but not too high to be inaudible to elderly pedestrians. Recall that a sharp attack makes a sound easier to locate. In practice the transducer is housed to make the sound as local to the crossing and easy to locate using IID cues as possible. So the choice of frequency and modulation method is not accidental.

Deviations from Specification

The recorded tone did not exactly match the specifications document, which defines a range of tolerences rather than precise values. The duty cycle and modulation frequency matched properly, but the tone frequency is given as (as low as) 1kHz but measured closer to 2.5kHz.

Exercises

Exercise 1

Record and analyse another simple indicator sound. You could try a microwave oven timer or a simple electronic doorbell. Specify a model for the sound and synthesise it as well as you can.

Exercise 2

Listen to the sounds next time you cross a big city road. What do you notice about the tone, directionality, and timing of the crossing signals? How do you think these help road safety?

References

UK Highways Agency (2005). *TR2509: Performance specification for audible equipment for use at pedestrian crossings*.

25
Practical 2
Phone Tones

Aims

In this practical we explore working from specification. Sometimes you get handed everything you need and the important task is to implement it as faithfully as possible. Imagine you have received a script for the following scene:

> spy 1: *Picks up telephone* (**sfx: Dialing tone from handset**)
> spy 1: *Dials number* (**sfx: Ringing tone from handset**)
> spy 2: "Hello, this is the Badger."
> spy 1: "This is Fox. The dog has the bone, the seagull flies tonight."
> spy 2: "Good, Fox. Now the Americans will pay for their deception...hold on..."
> (**sfx: click—telephone line goes dead**)

Create the sound effects for telephone tones heard through the handset when making the call.

Analysis

These are the sounds heard on the receiver, through the handset. The first two correspond to different signalling states within the phone system that occur before both parties are ready to talk and the system switches to a voice link. The dial tone is a constant, low-frequency purring sound that indicates the system is ready to make a call. Normally it is followed by dialling the number, done either with DTMF tones[1] or with pulse dialling. If a number is recognised by the exchange, the ringing tone occurs. It is a higher-pitched broken tone that occurs between dialling a number and the other person picking up.

Model

The signals are electronic in nature. They are specified by a standards document that gives the ideal model so there is no work to do here but implement what we are given. The tone specifications are explained in the CCITT standard for telephony as follows:

---

1. DTMF tones are examined in a later practical.

Tone name	Frequencies	Modulation	Purpose
Dial tone	440Hz + 350Hz	Continuous	Indicate ready to receive
Ringing tone	480Hz + 440Hz	On 2s, off 4s	Indicate remote ring

Figure 25.1
Table of signalling tones.

Observation Point

This makes a nice example to explore the observer concept. How does what the listener hears differ from the ideal model? There are three possible scenarios not explained by the above script. We could be listening through the ears of Fox, talking to his contact. We would hear the sounds through the handset, loud and close. Alternatively, the audio scene may be from the viewpoint of a third person in the room with Fox. We would hear Fox speaking with room acoustics, but the voice of Badger and the dialling tones as thin, distant, and filtered. Finally, we might "zoom out" to reveal Special Agent Smith listening in on a telephone tap. From his viewpoint the signals come directly from the line, and both voices and tones are treated accordingly. For this example let's assume we are listening from the perspective of Fox, the first spy.

Method

We construct both the tones by addition of sine waves. There are only two frequencies in each so the job is easy. `osc~` objects will be used for this. To make the ringing tone broken we modulate it with a low-frequency control signal in the message domain. Next we construct a crude model of a telephone line and handset that adds distortion and bandwidth limiting using `clip~` and `bp~ 1`, then listen to the dialling and ringing sounds through it.

DSP Implementation

Figure 25.2
CCITT dialing tone.

First create a sinewave oscillator `osc~` object. Set its first and only creation parameter for frequency to 350Hz. Now copy this object using CTRL-D, and place the copy close to the first oscillator. Change its frequency to 440Hz. Connect both of them to one `+~`, each to a different side. This explicitly adds the signals. Remember that signals are *implicitly* summed, so this patch could be done without the `+~` object, but it is a nice way to make clear what is happening. To scale this to a reasonable listening level we multiply by 0.125. Finally, connect to both sides of the

DAC, and you should hear the dial tone (fig. 25.2). In land-based telephone systems, tones are produced at the exchange not the handset itself (as for mobile devices), since the tones are part of the signalling protocol. The observation point is therefore at the end of some channel or connection, classically an electrical connection that is very long and therefore far from ideal. Also the signal will be observed through the handset transducer, a small loudspeaker with a limited frequency range. What will this combination of telephone line and handset do to the signal? Full analysis of the line, which is a complicated affair involving the inductance, capacitance, and resistance of the wire, is unnecessary since we are making an approximation. It's enough to know that the effect of passing through the line is some distortion, a loss of some frequencies, and accentuation of some other frequencies. The line and handset behave like a cascade of band-pass filters.

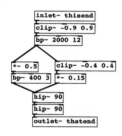

One inlet and one outlet are connected by a chain of units to crudely approximate a phone line and handset. The subpatch in figure 25.3 appears as `pd tline` in subsequent examples. First some distortion is introduced using `clip~`. This widens the spectrum, introducing odd harmonics and causing some loss at the two original frequencies. Next we mimic the band-limiting effect of the wire with a resonant filter centered on 2kHz. Both our original frequencies are within the range of the filter response, but what we are interested in is the effect this line filter will have on the extra harmonics from the distortion. Next the general effect of a small louspeaker is added.

Figure 25.3
Approximation of
transmisson medium.

The sounds we are interested in are around 400Hz, so let's place the centre of our filter there and remove all low frequencies. There will also be some distortion from the loudspeaker, which we add in parallel.

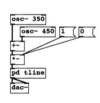

Now we can use the telephone line with the dial-tone patch. Look at figure 25.4 and you will see I've multiplied the dial-tone signal by a message rate 1 or 0 to switch it on or off. Try this with the `*~` *following* the line as an experiment. Do you notice the subtle difference to the change in tone during switching? When switched at the other side of the line from the listener, a sudden disconnect drives a high-frequency impulse over the channel. The telephone line makes its own sound as it behaves like a resonator. Patches for the ringing tone and busy tone are shown in figure 25.5. They are very similar frequency pairs to the dialling tone but with different modulation timings. Build them to hear the effect and check the timings and frequencies against the CCITT documentation.

Figure 25.4
Dialing tone over
a line.

Old-Style Pulse Dialer

Before DTMF technology telephone systems used pulse dialling. Instead of sending a tone to the exchange the phone sent a series of pulses. The character

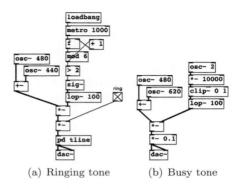

(a) Ringing tone   (b) Busy tone

Figure 25.5
More signalling tones.

of this sound is determined by answering the question, where does the energy come from? For a modern cell phone, energy comes from the handset. In the case of old pulse dialling phones it comes from the exchange, which sends a current down the phone line. It comes back on the other side of the line carrying voice signals, making a circuit. The sound of a remotely switched current is what we call the *impulse response* of the circuit. When we look at excitation methods of physical bodies later we will see that an impulse equates to hitting something.

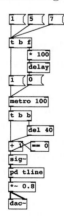

Figure 25.6
Pulse dial.

An old rotary dialler makes and breaks the line connection to the exchange. The short pulses are DC, so have no frequency except at their start and end points, which are step impulses. On each connection, current flows down the line from the exchange and back again. The characteristic sound of an analog pulse-dial telephone therefore depends almost entirely on the line and handset, on the character of miles of copper wire and a small plastic box. In figure 25.6 a message causes 1 to be sent to a metronome, switching it on. The metronome has a period of 100ms. At the same time a delay is scheduled to emit a bang, 100ms times the incoming number message later, which turns the metronome off. So a message of 7 switches the metronome on for 700ms, and there will be 7 bangs. Each bang from `metro` is duplicated by a trigger and delayed by `delay` to produce a 40ms pulse. This approximates the duty cycle of a typical pulse dialler. The `+ == 0` is a toggle idiom, with an initial state of zero. It behaves like a counter that can only count 0 or 1, so it's a condensed version of the counter and *mod* 2 operation we used before.

Results

Source   . . . .   <http://mitpress.mit.edu/designingsound/
phonetones.html>

Conclusions

Sounds can be *defined* as well as existing because of a physical process. They
can be given by precise specifications. Telephone dial and ring tones are completely synthetic, human-made things. Yet we should take into account all real,
physical processes that may affect the sound, like the electrical effect of the
telephone line and the acoustic properties of the handset. The observer point
and intevening processes are relative to the source of energy in a model. Here
we can approximate the physical effects by a chain of distortions and filters.

Exercises

Exercise 1

Combine all the sound effects from this exersise to make a complete "audio
scene" with pickup, dial tone, dialling, and ringing tone (or busy signal).

Exercise 2

Work on refining the remote disconnect click as heard by a nearby listener.
Listen to the sound design from some Hitchcock movies for that classic phone
disconnect sound.

Exercise 3

What causes crackles on a phone line? How would you add these to the line
model as an effect?

Exercise 4

Create the sounds of a 2600 Baud modem dialling in, establishing a carrier,
and transferring data.

References

"Technical Features of Push-Button Telephone Sets." (1988) In *CCITT Volume
VI: General Recommendations on Telephone Switching and Signalling.* International Telecommunication Union. (AKA the "blue book.")

26
Practical 3
DTMF Tones

1	2	3
4	5	6
7	8	9
*	0	#

Aims

Construct a telephone dialler using "Dual Tone Multi Frequency" modulation. The dialler has a keypad containing 16 buttons for the numbers 0 to 9, four letters A, B, C, and D, and two special symbols, hash and star. On each keypress the dialler will send a 200ms beep corresponding to the CCITT/DTMF standard tone for that keypress.

Analysis

Begin by researching the CCITT standard to see how audio is used in the dialling or address signalling part of a phone call. The tones are pairings from a choice of 8 frequencies that are picked for their noninteraction on a noisy audio bandwidth line.[1] The specification sets out some limits like the duration of the DTMF tone, which must be 50ms or more. The minimum interval between digits is 45ms and the maximum is 3 seconds.

	1209Hz	1336Hz	1477Hz	1633Hz
697Hz	1	2	3	A
770Hz	4	5	6	B
852Hz	7	8	9	C
941Hz	*	0	#	D

Figure 26.1
Table of DTMF tones.

Model

Once again, there is no physical model; all signals are elecronic in nature. They are specified by a standards document that gives the ideal model, so again there is no model to think about: we just copy the specifications as faithfully as possible.

---

1. Unless a channel that mixes two signals is linear we get intermodulation distortion, new products at integer combinations of the input frequencies. DTMF tones are chosen so that even on a badly distorted line these artifacts won't be confused with recognised frequencies.

Method

First construct a subpatch that produces a pair of tones. Create a lookup using message boxes to map keypresses onto a set of tone pairs. Then add a keypad to activate the oscillators from entries in the lookup and operate a control gate to switch them on and off.

DSP Implementation

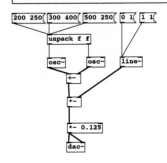

The message boxes along the top of figure 26.2 represent some test frequencies and two control messages. The first are lists of number pairs, the frequencies of two tones given in Hertz which are unpacked and sent to two separate sinewave oscillators. The sum of the oscillator signals is multiplied by a control signal from a line generator. The two messages on the right are $\{destination,\ time\}$ pairs that change the state of the line generator very fast, in $1.0ms$, to a value of 1.0 or back again to 0.0. Play around with switching the signal on and off and selecting different frequency pairs. If we can control this patch to select the right fre-

Figure 26.2
Dual tone dial signal.

quencies and make it switch the tone on then off when a key is pressed, the job is almost done. Everything needed to make the dialler work is shown in figure 26.3. Each button in the keypad has its *send-symbol* set to one of the receive destinations labelled $0-n. In the lookup section below, a corresponding receive object picks up bang messages and passes a list of tone pairs to the destination **dialme**. Messages received at **dialme** are unpacked and fed to the two oscillators. First we trigger a message to set the line generator on. After a delay of $200ms$ a message is sent to return the line generator to 0.0. A final high pass removes any unwanted low-frequency components.

Results

Source   ....   <http://mitpress.mit.edu/designingsound/
                             dtmf.html>

Pressing any of the buttons produces a short beep corresponding to one of the standard DTMF dialling tones.

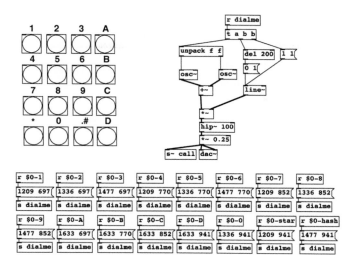

Figure 26.3
Keypad and table.

Conclusions

Lists stored in message boxes can be used to make a lookup table for driving several oscillators. This way we can reuse the same two oscillators for all DTMF tones. A keypad interface can be made by setting the **send symbol** property of each bang button to a message destination.

Exercises

Exercise 1

Try using the **key** object (if available on your system) to get presses from your computer keyboard to trigger DTMF tones.

Exercise 2

Why exactly are these particular frequencies chosen? Research a little about transmission theory (line propagation) and the distortion of signals and imagine these tones have travelled a bad line with noise added. How might you improve this design to make it more reliable?

Exercise 3 (Advanced)

How would you design a decoder to turn the audio signal back into numbers?

References

"Technical Features of Push-Button Telephone Sets." (1988). In *CCITT Volume VI: General Recommendations on Telephone Switching and Signalling*. International Telecommunication Union.

27
Practical 4
Alarm Generator

Aims

Construct an alarm tone that can be used for alerts or warnings on doors, telephones, or moving equipment. Its purpose is to convey information with different meanings and degrees of urgency. It should be able to produce a range of alarm sounds each with clearly separate identities, yet be simple enough to use only a few objects.

Analysis

A point of this exercise is to understand sound design from soft specifications. Sometimes we can't study an existing sound, because there isn't one. Nor do we have a concrete specification to work from. What we'll do is develop a flexible tone generator that can be used to explore ideas from the psychoacoustics chapter, then use it to make some sounds with particular characters. We know that some sound sequences are more arresting. A regular series is more pleasing than an irregular one. Modulation period can indicate urgency. Melodic sequences with consonant relationships are more pleasing than dissonant ones. Some sound spectra are more annoying or attention grabbing, while others produce a sense of happiness and well-being. Think of the soft "bong" sound used in passenger aircraft. One bong—fasten seatbelts. Two bongs—cross-check for takeoff. Three bongs—we're all going to die. But whatever the meaning it has a mellow, friendly presence.

Model

Again we are constructing an electronic sound, so there is no physical model. We are free to design any sound we like so long as it fulfils the stated aims. The model is therefore based entirely on the aims and analysis, a set of goals, and psychoacoustic principles. We will construct a patch capable of sequencing simple tones in the 0 to $2kHz$ range. It will be able to produce short melodies with a variable spectrum for different characters.

Method

Oscillators will provide the signal sources. Each tone will have its own oscillator. Switching between them will be done using modulation, multiplying each sources by a control signal.

DSP Implementation

LFO-Controlled Alarm

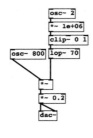

Figure 27.1
Alarm 2.

Here is a different way of doing what we did for the pedestrian crossing beeps. A low-frequency square wave oscillator (LFO) in the signal domain is used to modulate a sine tone.

Two sinewave oscillators are used in patch figure 27.1. One is a $800Hz$ source, which is modulated by a control signal arriving on the right side of the multiply. The LFO consists of four objects. First we take a sine wave at $2Hz$ (a period of 0.5 seconds) and multiply it by a large number. Then we clip it into the range 0.0 to 1.0 again. The result is a square wave that moves quickly between 0.0 and 1.0 at the same frequency as the sine oscillator. To remove the sharp edges a low-pass filter with a slope of 0.014 seconds is used (the filter cuts above $70Hz$), which gives a softer switching of the amplitude and avoids sudden clicks.

Two-Tone Alarm

If we have two states to our control signal then surely it's easy to replace the silence by another tone. This is done by taking the complement of a signal. Since our control signal (a) lies in the range 0.0 to 1.0 its complement is one minus the original signal (written $1 - a$). We can use a combination of [sig~] and [-~]

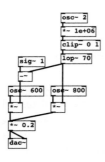

Figure 27.2
Alarm 3.

to do this. When the output of the LFO is 1.0 then the opposite signal is 0.0, and vice versa.

In this patch (fig. 27.2) we use the same LFO with a period of 0.5 seconds and a low-pass filter to give a soft transition. This time two sine oscillators provide signals at $800Hz$ and $600Hz$. Each is connected through a multiplier. One of them is modulated directly by the square wave, and the other by the complement of the LFO signal. Both are summed and scaled by 0.2. When the output of the LFO is 1.0 then the $800Hz$ signal is multiplied by 1.0 and passes to the output, but the $600Hz$ signal is multiplied by $(1 - 1 = 0)$ and isn't heard. In the opposite state the $800Hz$ sine signal is multiplied by 0.0 and $600Hz$ by $(1 - 0 = 1)$, so we hear that instead.

Three-Tone Alarm

This principle can be extended to any number of sources. Two tones are limited to an alternating ABAB effect, though we also know how to create silence, by multiplying by zero. In theory, then, we can create sequences of three elements, like A-BBB-, (where - is a silence) to produce one short A and one long B tone separated by equal silences. To suggest rising or falling patterns we must introduce a third pitch C, so that the relationship $A > B > C$ or $A < B < C$ can exist for them. In figure 27.3 we see a couple of ways of doing this. The

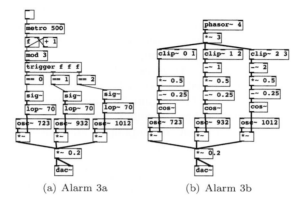

(a) Alarm 3a   (b) Alarm 3b

Figure 27.3
Two ways of making the 3 tone alarm.

first example extends our earlier message domain approach. Instead of counting modulo 2 the numbers are divided into cycles of 3, counting 0, 1, 2, 0, 1, 2.... Three ⊟ objects each produce an exclusive one when matched, or zero when not matched. This is used to switch on one of three sine oscillators. The second method (fig. 27.3b) works in the signal domain. By stretching the phasor signal in amplitude by a factor of three, then dividing it into three segments using clip~ objects, we get three little phasors for the price of one. Subtracting the split point returns each phasor's starting amplitude to zero. Each begins in time where the previous one ends. When doing this we say we *split the phase* into three. Each can be used as a separate control signal to modulate an oscillator amplitude. The result would be a sequence of tones fading in, but by scaling, shifting, and taking the cosine of each phase we get smooth "humps" (half sine cycles), so each tone flows nicely into the next without clicks.

Multitone Alarm

Listen to the alarm of figure 27.3 and experiment with changing some values. You should be able to get a range of trills and rising or falling sequences. Next we will develop this patch into an even more flexible and programmable generator.

Let's start by modifying the oscillators. So far we have used sinusoidal waves with a single frequency, but we really want a palette of different spectra to choose from. Three parts of a multialarm generator are shown in figure 27.4. Concentrating on the leftmost subpatch we see an application of waveshaping.

New Spectra from Old

Refer to figure 27.4a and recall that we can express a (co)sinusoidal wave function as $x = \cos(\omega t)$, where ω is the angular frequency and t is the time. This is the familiar single-frequency wave used in the previous exercise. Applying another cosine function to the wave, we have $x = \cos(\cos(\omega t))$, which results in a richer sound, with harmonics in the series 2ω, 4ω, 6ω, 8ω.... Recall also that shifting cos by $90°$ gives us sin, which we can do by adding a small offset of 0.25. This new waveshaping function, $x = \sin(\cos(\omega t))$, gives another harmonic series, ω, 3ω, 5ω, 7ω.... An offset value at 0.125, exactly between 0.0 and 0.25 gives a mixture of odd and even harmonics. So, what we have is a way to vary the spectrum (timbre) of our oscillator between a hollow, square wavelike sound and a bright stringlike sound. Note that a change from all odd to all even harmonics is equivalent to jumping up an octave. A subpatch made of this arrangement is named pd cosc.

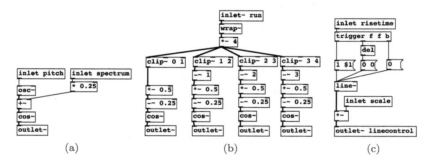

(a)   (b)   (c)

Figure 27.4
Components of multialarm.

A Four-Phase Wrapping Oscillator

The middle subpatch (fig. 27.4b) is a development of figure 27.3b, but now we have four phases. Instead of scanning continuously with a phasor we've replaced it with a wrap-, which is fed from the subpatch inlet. If we apply a rising line signal to the inlet our four-phase splitter it will scan up (left to right). If the applied line is decreasing it will scan down (right to left). The rate of scanning will depend on the slope of the line. Once again we turn our four little subphasors into half sine cycles to give a smooth modulator that doesn't make clicks. A subpatch containing this arrangement, with one inlet and four outlets, is named pd 4phase-osc.

A One-Shot Line Generator

The last part we need is a line generator, shown in figure 27.4c. It will drive the four-phase oscillator which will provide a sequence of short modulation pulses, which will in turn modulate four different pd cosc oscillators with variable spectra. It works as follows. A float arriving at the inlet sets the run time, the time for the line̲~ to rise to 1.0. The line̲~ is always reset to zero by the first message, then rises to 1.0 in the time substituted in the second position of the leftmost message. Meanwhile a delay is activated. It will emit a bang to trigger the middle message and reset line̲~ again after the run time. Finally, there is a scale factor applied to the result which arrives through a second subpatch inlet. If this is set to 1.0 the line will scan as normal. If it is set to 2.0 the four-phase oscillator will scan twice around, sending out 8 pulses in the pattern 1, 2, 3, 4, 1, 2, 3, 4. Other values can give us longer or shorter subsequences. A subpatch containing this arrangement, with two inlets and one outlet, is named pd timebase.

Integrating the Parts

Putting it all together gets us to the patch shown in figure 27.5. Number boxes supply the run time and scale factor to the timebase. Four sliders set the frequencies of each oscillator and a fifth sets the spectrum of all oscillators.[1] A hip̲~ is applied as a DC trap filter so that frequencies of 0Hz work as silence.

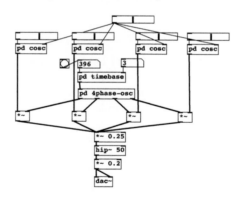

Figure 27.5
Multiringer with controls.

Programming It

Before leaving this practical let us develop something new and introduce some concepts of encapsulation and programming. Then we can talk about particular

---

1. You might like to experiment with giving each oscillator its own spectrum control, but for simplicity I have made them common.

sounds as numbers. See the changes made in figure 27.6. The sliders and number boxes have been replaced with a `unpack` fed from an inlet. The whole patch is now wrapped by one more layer of subpatching and addressed by a single parameter list. I have also rearranged the layout to make it a bit easier to read.

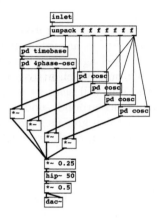

Figure 27.6
Programmable subpatch.

So, how do we program it? Parameter lists are made using the patch shown to the left of figure 27.7, which was explained in the tools chapters. This programmer fills a message box with the values from the sliders, which you can then click to hear the sound. Some example messages are given on the right of the patch.

Results

◀   Source   . . . .   <http://mitpress.mit.edu/designingsound/alarms.html>

Let's describe each sound to highlight the versatility of this patch. You should build or download the patches, or listen to the audio examples while reading the descriptions.

Happy blips—380 2 349 0 0 0 1

Two short, mellow blips. These indicate a good operation, positive action.

Affirmative—238 1 317 0 0 476 0

Two longer blips rising slightly in pitch. Definitely a positive indicator.

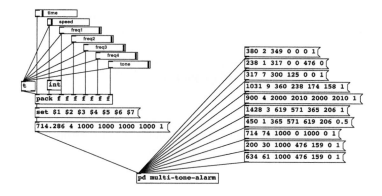

Figure 27.7
Programming multiringer.

Activate—317 7 300 125 0 0 1

Fast sequence of mid-range blips. Indicates some process or action starting.

Invaders—1031 9 360 238 174 158 1

Classic "Space Invaders" type tone sequence. A lively and arresting alert but without negative connotations.

Information—900 4 2000 2010 2000 2010 1

Fast high-frequency pips. Character-by-character readout at the bottom of the screen when identifying CIA secret HQ.

Message alert—1428 3 619 571 365 206 1

Three descending sequences with pleasing interval. Possibly a good ring tone for arriving messages.

Finished—450 1 365 571 619 206 0.5

Four-tone sequence with a feeling of finality; a power-off sound.

Error code—714 74 1000 0 1000 0 1

Atonal buzzing sound. An error has occurred.

Wrong buzzer—200 30 1000 476 159 0 1, 634 61 1000 476 159 0 1

BZZZZzzzzzt! You are wrong. So very wrong!

Conclusions

A versatile range of alarms and indicators can be achieved by sequencing short segments of various frequencies and spectra. A compact cyclic tone sequencer can be realised in the signal domain by splitting the phase of a slower signal.

Spectral variation can be easily and cheaply obtained by wave shaping. Complex patches can be encapsulated to offer a single entry point and programming method.

Exercises

Exercise 1

An annoying feature of the design is that when you adjust the sequence *length* parameter the sequence *rate* changes. Redesign the patch to decouple these two parameters.

28

Practical 5
Police

Aims

We will create the sound of an American-style police siren. In doing so we will delve deeper into analysis and deconstruction with regard to energy flow. There will be some discussion of synthesis methods and how waveforms relate to spectra. We will partly work from waveform specification, but this time our analysis will include circuit schematics combined with other domain knowledge about the construction of an electronic siren. This is also our first serious venture into electroacoustics where the transducer and environment will be more significant.

Analysis

Let's begin with spectral analysis of an example recording. An interesting feature to note in figure 28.1 is the bump in the time-domain graph. It is significant because we know (from inspection of the spectrogram) that the sound is a frequency sweep, up and down, so a sudden bump is a fair indicator of a resonance. It is immediately apparent from the spectrogram that the signal is not sinusoidal. There are several harmonics moving in parallel, seen as copies stacked on top of the lowest component. A closer look at the spectrogram also reveals a copy shifted in time (most prominently in one of the mid-range harmonics). This suggests an echo, so it tells us something about the environmental makeup of the sound. Though the plot is slightly blurred it's possible to estimate the frequency sweep from the fundamental frequency (lowest trace). It's the one between 0Hz and 1000Hz.

Model

Let's begin by considering the energy model. Remember that energy flows from a source towards entropy, and along the way part of it exists as sound waves. A summary of the energetic model in figure 28.2 shows movement from an electrical source towards the listener.

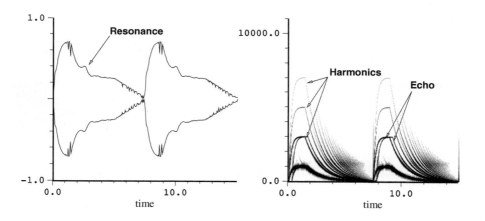

Figure 28.1
Police siren: Spectrogram.

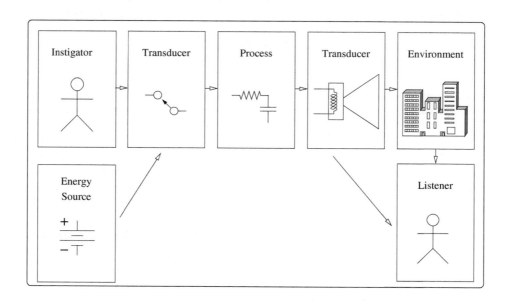

Figure 28.2
Police siren: Model.

Energy Source

Electrical potential energy is stored in a battery. In practice this is a lead-acid automotive battery supplemented by the engine alternator when it is running. It supplies around 5A to the siren at 12V, giving 60W of power. An electronic siren is reasonably efficient, converting about 50 percent or 30W of electrical power to sound.

Instigator

A switch on the car dashboard is operated by the driver. It connects the battery to the siren so that current flows. The rate of the siren sweep and its frequency are independent of the voltage supplied and the vehicle speed. There is often just one control, on or off, but sometimes there is a control to set the siren sweep rate.

Oscillation Process

An electronic circuit at the heart of the siren has two oscillators based on RC networks. The first is a low-frequency oscillator creating a slow-frequency sweep. Typical sweep frequencies are between 0.1Hz and 3Hz. It modulates the frequency of a second oscillator, which operates between about 100Hz and 1kHz. This signal is amplified by a power transistor before being applied to the coil of a horn transducer. A transistor oscillator found in many electronic sirens is shown in figure 28.3. It is called an *astable multivibrator*, or sometimes an

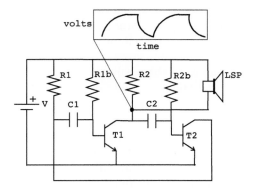

Figure 28.3
Transistor astable oscillator.

astable flip-flop, meaning it has no stable state. There are two transistors, **T1** and **T2**, each of which changes the state of the other; thus the circuit flip-flops between two states. A transistor switches on once the voltage on a capacitor rises above a certain threshold. When switched on, the transistor allows a current to flow through a resistor onto another capacitor that will eventually cause the second transistor to switch on. When this happens the second

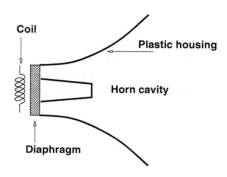

Figure 28.4
Siren transducer and horn.

transistor drains current from the first capacitor and causes the first transistor to switch off.

So, the circuit alternates between two states, one in which transistor **T1** is switched on and **T2** off, and another where transistor **T2** is on while **T1** is off. The voltage, which corresponds to the output waveform, is shown at a point in the circuit where **C2** connects to **R2**. It follows the recognisable charge and discharge cycle of a capacitor. This diagram shows only one oscillator. A complete siren circuit uses two of these oscillators, one for the low-frequency sweep and one to produce the audio waveform. Given the values of each electronic component we could work from the circuit schematic to determine the exact oscillation frequency, but that's unnecessary since we can tell it well enough by listening. Notice the same wave shape seen in the spectrogram frequency plot. This is the LFO rising and falling.

Horn

In order to produce an acoustic wave from an electrical signal a device similar to that in figure 28.4 uses a coil to create a magnetic field which moves a ferromagnetic diaphragm. The diaphragm is mounted so that it has a limited movement and can flex inwards and outwards. In many ways it's similar to a loudspeaker, but is optimised for power output rather than sound quality. Unlike a high-quality loudspeaker, the movement of the diaphragm is not linear with respect to the applied force, so some distortion is introduced.

The main function of the horn is to act as an acoustic amplifier, but it also adds some directionality to the sound. If it is taken to be approximately conical it behaves like an open tube, favouring odd and even harmonics equally. But the horn does not behave as a perfect acoustic amplifier. Far from it. Its material has a resonance and its geometric construction is quite like that of a bell. In some regards we should also treat it as a fairly well-damped plastic bell driven by the signal it is trying to amplify. Of course this introduces further distortion and colouring to the sound.

Environment

In isolation the siren would produce a loud but uncharacteristic sound. Much of the quality identifying a police siren comes from environmental factors. The siren is part of a larger object, the vehicle. It is mounted by bolts to a roof assembly that can transmit some sound to the vehicle itself, a little of which will resonate and be amplified by the metal roof acting as a sounding board. If the vehicle were moving we would expect to hear some Doppler shift, but we won't model that in this practical. Finally, the vehicle-mounted siren cannot be taken in isolation. Some sound will come to the listener directly, so long as there is an open line of sight between vehicle and observer, and some will be reflected from buildings. In figure 28.5 two buildings flank the vehicle with a

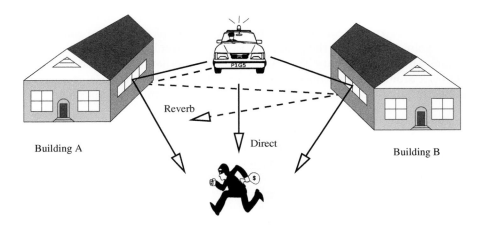

Figure 28.5
Echoes from objects in environment.

listener in the middle. At least four possible signals should be considered: the direct sound that passes only through the air to the observer, an echo from building A, an echo from building B at a different time, and *reverberant* sounds that bounce between both buildings several times before reaching the listener.

Method

We will create an oscillator that directly copies the waveform of a transistor astable. This is the technique of piecewise time-domain approximation, by copying the target waveform. The horn and environmental features will be achieved using `clip~` and a `bp~` filter to first distort then filter the waveform towards something like the response of a plastic horn. Finally, environment effects are added using `delwrite~` and `delread~` objects to give some echoes.

DSP Implementation

Log Waveform Oscillator

A phasor~ is scaled by 2.0 and split into two streams. One branch is truncated to stay below 1.0, then subtracted from 1.0 to give us its complement. The other is truncated to stay above 1.0 and a fixed value of 1.0 subtracted from it to shift it back down into the range 0.0 to 1.0. This gives us two halves of the original waveform as separate signals, one for the rising part and one for the falling part. Since we want the falling half-cycle to be an upside-down version of the rising one we take the complement again. Next we raise a constant 2.71828, the natural number e, to the power of each signal. This gives us the wave shape of a charging capacitor. Both curves are in the same direction, but we want one of them to be the mirror image of the other. So we take the signal complement once again, this time on the rising half-cycle. The resulting signals are shown in graphs a1 and a2 of figure 28.6. Adding these together, scaling and then shifting back around zero produces a waveform like that of the transistor oscillator, shown in graph a3 of figure 28.6, which has a logarithmic rise and fall.

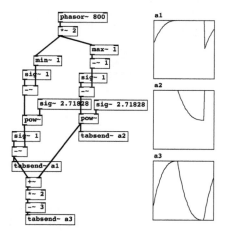

Figure 28.6
Oscillator to mimic capacitor charge/discharge.

Distortion and Filter

The distortion of the diaphragm is quite severe. For all but small movements it behaves in a nonlinear way. In practice the diaphragm is heavily overdriven,

Figure 28.7
Plastic horn.

which squares off the waveform. Several parallel band-pass filters would more accurately model resonances created by the horn and vehicle body, but for this exercise a single filter centred around 1.5kHz is sufficient. Distortion from the diaphragm appears before filtering by the horn, which means that harmonics introduced by the distortion are filtered. This increases odd harmonics in a region around 1.5kHz.

Environment Echo

This abstraction has one inlet and one outlet, so it is not an attempt to make a stereo echo that accounts for position. The inlet connects to three `throw~` objects, b1, b2, and b3, corresponding to buildings in the vicinity of the siren. A direct version of the input is sent straight to the output and scaled. Three `delwrite~` objects implement fixed delays which are summed at a common node and recirculated to all the delays again. A scaling value of 0.1 is sufficient to produce a reverberation effect without allowing too much feedback to cause excessive colouring or instability. Part of this signal is tapped off and sent to the output as our echo/reverb effect.

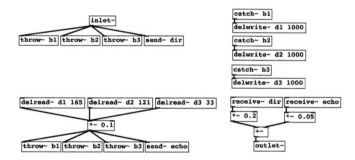

Figure 28.8
Environmental echoes from buildings.

Putting It Together

All components of the siren effect, two oscillators, horn simulation, and environment echo, are connected together as shown in figure 28.9. Two message boxes set the sweep frequency of the LFO to either 0.1Hz or 3Hz. To connect the two oscillators it is necessary to scale and offset the LFO signal so it sweeps over a range of 800Hz starting above 300Hz. The second oscillator is another instance of the first oscillator abstraction. Output from the second oscillator feeds into the horn simulation and then to the environment before being sent to the audio output. It will start as soon as the patch is loaded, so you may like to add a switch to turn the effect on and off.

Figure 28.9
All parts.

Comparing the output to a recording of a real police siren you should hear it's a fairly good approximation. A smoother, less brash effect can be obtained by experimenting with the horn distortion and filter. The values used in this exercise are quite strong in order to accentuate the effect, so experiment with different clipping values. Because the filter is quite resonant the amplitude peaks at a certain point in the sweep. This corresponds to the bump in the analysis signal. You may be able to hear this in a good recording of a police siren. This effect tends to be accentuated with distance in a city. Sometimes, when the source is very distant, you cannot hear the lower parts of the sweep near 300Hz at all, they are absorbed by the environment and you only hear occasional bumps from the high part of each sweep popping out above the ambient traffic noise. A less resonant filter will give a more even sweep, as heard much closer.

Critique of Method

We will look later at better methods of synthesising sound. If there is a "theory" about how to teach synthesis, it says: start with additive synthesis because it's the easiest to understand. The method we've used here is to approximate the time-domain waveform piece by piece. So why have I introduced this "brute force" time-domain approach now? Because it shows up the weaknesses of what might otherwise seem a practical and straightforward way to make sounds. Let's review the charge sheet:

- It's hard work. It needs many wave functions for anything but the simplest periodic musical instrument. We were lucky this time, in that we could work from a schematic giving the behaviour of a capacitor charging and discharging. But without an underlying behaviour to study it is sometimes very hard to find functions that approximate a waveform of unknown origin.

- It's confusing. There are no meaningful parameters for the oscillator model that affect timbre. We say the model is "brittle" because it works for only one particular arrangement of wave functions. But if we try and change any values it collapses and we get meaningless noise out. Imagine we had 8 segments to make a more complicated periodic wave. Changing one in the middle would either require us to recalculate all the others or cause a discontinuity.

- It can be expensive. For a simple periodic waveform with only two segments it's fairly effective, but the cost grows rapidly as more function segments are chained together.

- We don't learn much. In a way we are cheating. All we have done is copy the time domain wave of the sound and expressed it as functions without really understanding anything about what we are copying. It can be

said that not much *data reduction* has been achieved, because we haven't
reduced the behaviour to a smaller set of parameters.[1] Let's try and do
that next to give an example.

Spectral Approximation in the Time Domain

Although it was a sensible starting point, taking the electronic model too literally caused unnecessary complexity. What if we could replace all the logarithmic
curve business with something much simpler? Remember from psychoacoustic
theory that our ears hear spectrums, not waveforms. So, can we find another
waveform with the same spectrum that is easier to generate? In figure 28.10

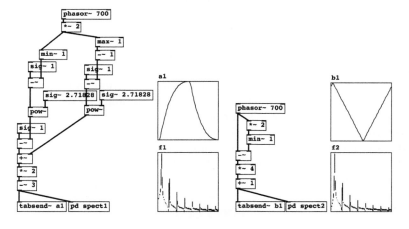

Figure 28.10
Triangle waveform and spectral equivalence to logarithmic waveform.

an interesting shortcut is revealed. Our oscillator that mimics the RC circuit
is shown on the left with its waveform shown in graph a1 and its spectrum
appearing in graph f1. Alongside it is a triangle wave oscillator with waveform
and spectrum shown in graphs b1 and f2. Look at the two spectra. They are the
same (or very close indeed). But the triangle wave is far simpler to construct:
we just split a phasor, flip one side, and add together the two slopes.

O━ Keypoint
Many time domain waveforms share the same spectrum. A spectrum contains
less information than a waveform.

---

1. As well as in synthesis the idea of data reduction is central to audio data compression
such as MPEG3. This is a kind of analysis and resynthesis optimised for data reduction by
spotting duplicates that can be reused and irrelevant information that can be discarded.

As an exercise try replacing the second oscillator with a triangle wave. Notice that even though they have the same spectra the distortion stage affects each differently. Notice also that we cannot replace the first oscillator with a triangle wave without changing the character of the pitch sweep. These results should help you understand the differences between using a signal for its time domain (waveform) properties and using it for its frequency domain (spectral) properties.

Results

Source   ....   <http://mitpress.mit.edu/designingsound/police.html>

Conclusions

We've considered an energetic model of sound production and traced the flow of energy as a signal through the entire process. In doing so we have explored pitch, spectrum, and loudness and thought about how the electronic, physical, and environmental aspects of a signal affect the sound produced. We've discovered a practical application of the link between spectra and waveforms and seen why piecewise approximation of a signal can be naive. With that in mind we have introduced the idea of data reduction as a form of optimisation.

Exercises

Exercise 1

Experiment with improving the environment model, adding more buildings, damping, and other acoustic effects.

Exercise 2

Use a variable delay to add Doppler to the sound and create the effect of a passing siren.

Practical Series
Idiophonics

Everything in the world has a
spirit which is released by its
sound.
—Oskar Fischinger

Simple Material Interactions

Idio means to stand alone and separate, so idiophonics is about simple interactions between discrete, ordinary, everyday objects. It includes collisions, crushing, rubbing, scraping, and bouncing. The objects are generally materially homogeneous, geometrically regular, and maintain their shape and size throughout the sounding process. So we could consider knocking on a door or dropping a tin can to be idiophonic processes. The term develops the orchestral category for musical instruments, idiophones, which consists of simple percussion instruments like snare drums, shakers, castanets, and tubular bells. All the same, these can be elaborate as designed for musical use. Strictly, a piano is a percussion instrument, yet it clearly does *not* belong this category. Although the materials and event descriptions are simple this doesn't mean the underlying physical processes are any less complex than other sounds. Crushing and some forms of frictional excitation are complicated subjects. Shattering, as with breaking a window, is not included in this category because of the complex dynamics and change of shape.

Collisions and Other Excitations

The category of idiophonics is important in game sound. The majority of casual sounds are rigid body collisions for simple material objects. Most inventory items are given a "dropped" sound; footsteps are a collision and crushing process (although their complexity means we will study them separately later on). Movers like doors, train carriages, and boxes are collisions or frictions between solid structures made of wood or metal. Rolling will be seen as repeated small collisions, while the noise of stick-slip friction is a kind of small-scale tangential collision if we wish to look at it that way. Acoustic resonance and the effect of blowing are not considered here, mainly because in the absence of wind it's a human-generated event restricted to musical instruments. However, that said, steam and air movement in pipes, locomotives, and other vehicles is a topic of later chapters under the heading "machines."

Forces

With the majority of idiophonic events being collisions, we will be thinking of kinetic energy as the source. It may have been given to a body by falling, or by being pushed by some other actor. We don't need to think about the primary instigator (and the preceding energy system), only to know the mass and velocity of an object at the time we want to create its sound. This is an area where gravity comes into play. It influences the sound of dragged or pushed objects, the swinging of chains and ropes, and the decaying motion of a bouncing object. We also wish to understand friction and fluid viscosity as damping forces. In real-time physics engines they are used to limit the movement of objects, but they play an equal role in sound objects to determine decay times and spectral evolution when things interact.

The Practicals

It would be nice to have room in this textbook to consider a whole range of processes, especially fragmentation which is a fascinating subject, but we will limit ourselves to the following studies which cover a useful range of concepts.

- A telephone bell, as an extended study of a struck object.
- Bouncing ball, as a decaying series of impacts.
- Creaking door sound, as a study of friction.
- Rolling tin can, as regular and irregular movement of an object.
- Twanging ruler, as a study of plucking, nonlinearity, and discontinuity.

References

Vicario, G.B., Rocchesso, D., Fernström, M., and Tekniska Hoegskolan, K. (2001). "The sounding object." <http://www.soundobject.org>. Project jointly by University of Udine Dipartimento di Scienze Filosofiche e Storico-Sociali, University of Verona Dipartimento di Informatica, University of Limerick, Speech, Music, and Hearing centre KTH-Stockholm.

29
Practical 6
Telephone Bell

Aims

In this practical we are going to create the sound of an old style telephone bell from the era of 1930–1960. As usual we will follow the design pattern that should by now be familiar. First we will analyse the sound and the nature of the production mechanism, thinking about the components, structures, and behaviours. Then we will propose a model, using knowledge about the form and physical principles of the sound. Next we will use the model, to determine one or more synthesis methods, and finally we will choose DSP tricks to approximate the signals we hope to hear.

Analysis

Bell

There are many types of bell, but the sound we want to create is actually two small bells with an electrically operated hammer that rattles between them.

Electromagnetic Buzzer

An alarm bell for an old-style telephone or fire alarm is an electromechanical device that produces a continuous ringing. A hammer (or striker) repeatedly hits two bells in alternation. The energy comes from a battery which causes a current to flow through one of two electromagnets. In figure 29.1 the current flows through the metal (electrically conductive) fulcrum and (ferromagnetic) rocker, which serve two purposes, being both a pivot on which the hammer can swing and part of the electric circuit. The device is arranged so that current initially flows through one electromagnet, either EA or EB. When electromagnet EA is active it pulls the rocker towards it until contact is made, which routes the current to EB. Likewise, EB pulls the magnetic rocker back until electrical contact is made through EA again. This operation should seem familiar: it is an electromechanical astable device, similar to the transistor circuit we examined for the police siren. Energy from the battery is converted into kinetic energy in the reciprocating hammer via a magnetic field.

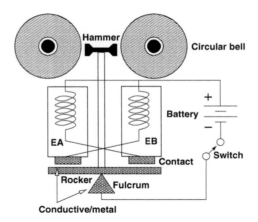

Figure 29.1
Electromechanical bell.

Model

Size

Bells come in a wide range of shapes and sizes. Big Ben, a cousin of the Liberty Bell cast by Whitechapel Foundry in 1858, is 2.7m wide and about 2m high. It is so large its 13 tons of metal took three furnaces to melt and 20 days to cool to a solid. And at the other end of the scale, some musical instrument bells, such as on a tambourine, mini barbell chimes, or a bell-rattle like a cabassa, are as small as a few millimeters across. The telephone bell we are going to simulate is approximately 6cm in diameter.

Shape

The general shape of a bell is a curved skin, a bit like a half cycle of a sine wave rotated around in space, although tubes and semisphere shapes are common too. Our telephone bell has an almost semispherical shape. Whatever their shape all bells have a common feature, at least one elliptical path. Bells usually have a high degree of rotational symmetry, a circular aspect, although some have an egg-shaped cross section and, as an atypical case, a cowbell is almost square.

Material

They are most often made of metal, perhaps brass, bronze, or another alloy chosen for its springiness. Brass has a propagation speed of about 5000m/s. From this we can estimate the frequency of the prominent component using a little geometry and arithmetic. For a 6cm diameter the circumference is 0.18m, so a wavefront moves around it in 0.011 seconds. This means it would form a perfect standing wave, with the bell expanding and compressing along its diameter at about 900Hz. As we will see shortly, this isn't necessarily the lowest frequency. The fundamental will probably be an octave below at 450Hz.

Damping

The bell is mounted on a rubber grommet, which offers a fair degree of damping. Let's estimate how much of a damping factor the bell has for a small supporting area in contact with it. The bulk modulus of brass compared to that of rubber is $1 \times 10^5 \text{N/m}^2$ against $160 \times 10^9 \text{N/m}^2$. That is a huge difference, four orders of magnitude, so rubber acts as a very strong damper. The energy returned will be about 1/1000 of that hitting the boundary. But only a small area of the bell surface touches the grommet, let's say 0.1 percent, so we can cross three zeros from that and estimate a damping factor of about $\frac{1}{10}$th. By itself the damping factor is no use. We need to know how long the bell would ring if it were perfectly suspended and the only losses were to the air (radiation) and entropy. To know this we need to know how much energy it's hit with, and how much loss of energy per second occurs. Experimentally and theoretically this comes out at about 30 seconds, but we'll skip examining that stage in detail so we can summarise and move on. It's important to work from ballpark figures and experimental data in sound design; we don't need to know very precise values so much as crude ratios and heuristics to guide us to the right area, then we attach fine-grain controls to zoom in on the exact parameters for the sound we want. Let's add one more estimate to our model: the bell rings for about 3 seconds.

What Happens?

A bell is brought to life when something impacts with it, like a hammer, stick, or another bell. The size and energy of the beater tend to be in proportion to the bell so that it rings as loudly as possible without damage, and as a rough guide it is frequently made of a very similar material to the bell itself. These facts already tell us a something about bell sounds. Let's consider separately three properties: shape, material makeup—both chemical and structural—and the excitation, or what hits it. Then let's consider what happens and how those properties play a role in the sound that emerges by causing energy to be focused into certain modes or regular vibrations as it propagates within the bell. Imagine the striker hitting a bell. This is shown in the centre of figure 29.2 where we see the bell from the side and from the bottom in several modes of vibration. During the very short time they are connected, energy from the hammer deforms the bell. For a moment the shape of the bell is no longer semispherical/round but becomes a slightly oval shape. Energy propagates throughout the whole body of the bell, exciting it into many modes of oscillation that fall into particular patterns typical of a circular object.

The fundamental mode is determined by the diameter of the bell lip. In this mode the whole bell distorts back and forth between two oval shapes where the irregular axis is at $90°$ to the previous one. Some of this energy quickly moves into other circular modes, a third harmonic appearing at 60°, a fourth at 45°, and so on. These primary modes are all harmonic, corresponding to some integer division of the bell circumference into sectors. Look at the first mode in figure 29.2, which is unusual and is connected to the remaining inharmonic modes. The whole bell lip expands and contracts, so the top of the bell must contract downwards and upwards. This leads to a division which makes a cross section with the bell axis, usually appearing about one-third of the way up, and there's another one that happens higher up.

Now we can divide the bell surface into areas and imagine them moving inwards and outwards in complex patterns. These are denoted by the mode numbers like (3,2) which means the bell is vibrating in a 120° circular mode while flexing at two points along its axis, or (5,1) which means it is vibrating at 72° and flexing at one point. Historically, bell designers have given special names to these modes, and their relationship to the overtone produced is well known. Names such as the "tierce," "quint," "nominal," and "prime" are used to denote them. An interesting one is the first (0,1) mode where the entire bell expands and conracts around its centre. This "breathing mode" is an octave below the first natural frequency; sometimes it's called the "hum." While these modes give us ideas about which frequencies are likely from all (general) bells, exactly which modes are loud or quiet for a given bell depends on how it is struck and its exact shape and material structure.

High-frequency energy from the initial hit decays away the fastest because there are no corresponding resonant modes; so the bell sound starts out bright, with lots of frequencies, and these quickly shift into a handful of primary and secondary modes. As time goes by all the energy becomes heat, the bell stops vibrating at audible frequencies and amplitudes, and the sound dies away. The telephone bell we are considering deviates a little from this theory. It is more like a distorted semisphere with slightly elongated parallel sides, so it has some of the behaviour of a sphere and some of the behaviour of a tube. Both these shapes have their own rules for vibrational modes, so practically speaking it's hard to use theory alone to predict the overtones.

Spectral Analysis

What we could do is take a few real bells, hopefully similar to the target telephone bell, and see what spectrum they give. One trick I learned from a jazz drummer is that as with guitar strings you can selectively damp a cymbal or bell by touching it in the right place. This lets you make recordings that separate out some of the overtones and make the analysis clearer. Let's take a look at a spectrogram of a bell (actually a 10cm thin-walled brass bowl very similar to the bells found in phones) and use these frequencies to help with the model.

The spectrums are thresholded, simplified so that only the strongest frequencies come through. I have taken three snapshots, at the start, middle, and end of the sound, so the evolution of frequencies can be seen. Neither these diagrams nor the 3D plot given in figure 29.6 adequately show the moment-by-moment growth and decay of the spectrum. It's something you really need to do for yourself with a good analysis package. As you step through a sound file

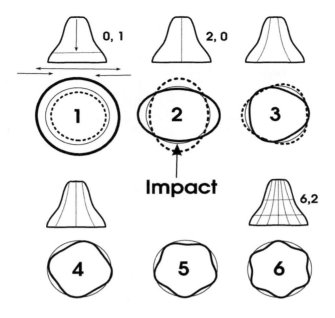

Figure 29.2
Modes of a bell.

you will see the individual components move, and the way they move can give clues about what is happening at a physical level.

Looking at figure 29.3 we see the initial burst of many frequencies. Like a football game, you can see plenty from the initial positions, but can't really predict much about what will happen next. Anything could happen during the game. The strongest partial is at 3.016kHz with two other strong ones at 1.219kHz and 5.316kHz. There's also a spike of high frequency, which is probably the hit from the metal beater at 11.6kHz. Notice the grouping around the bottom, between 400Hz and 1kHz. There are two strong peaks in this cluster at 484Hz and 948Hz.

With two points of reference a lot more is revealed. The initial burst near 11kHz has completely gone, so we can assume this was the striker hitting the bell. Much of the energy has now shifted into 483Hz, which seems a likely candidate for the fundamental, and a second mid-range peak has emerged near 1.229kHz at 1.439kHz. Notice that the harmonics move around slightly. The current 1.229kHz is almost certainly the "same" modal resonance as 1.219kHz (a small difference of 10Hz).

The question to ask now is, can we see any harmonic patterns or groupings? Well, $483 \times 2 = 966$, not far from 959Hz, so perhaps this peak is related to the fundamental this way, and $483 \times 3 = 1449$, which might indicate a third

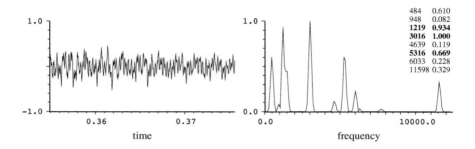

484	0.610
948	0.082
1219	**0.934**
3016	**1.000**
4639	0.119
5316	**0.669**
6033	0.228
11598	0.329

Figure 29.3
Attack portion of spectrum.

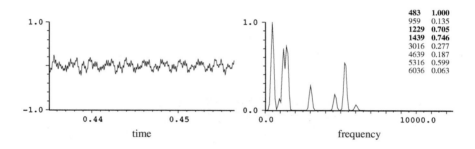

483	**1.000**
959	0.135
1229	**0.705**
1439	**0.746**
3016	0.277
4639	0.187
5316	0.599
6036	0.063

Figure 29.4
Mid-portion of spectrum.

harmonic. The rest don't seem to have integer relationships to the candidate fundamental. This could mean two things, both questions of interpretation or frame of reference. Either we picked the wrong fundamental or the others are all inharmonic partials. The only candidate left for a fundamental is 1229Hz; it seem unlikely that the first two will die out, and 1229Hz isn't harmonically related to anything else on offer.

Moving to the last snapshot in figure 29.6 we see the final state of decay. Everything has moved down to the first three partials that are all harmonically related, with a little bit left at 4.639kHz. You can see this whole process play out in the 3D plot of figure 29.6. The graph is rotated in order to better see the evolution in all three axes, so time moves from bottom left to top right and frequencies closer to us are higher.

What we want to do is express these frequencies as ratios of the identified fundamental. Clearly two of them are very easy, being in 1:2 and 1:3 ratio with the fundamental. Dividing by 483 the others are about 1:6, 1:9.5, 1:11, 1:12.5,

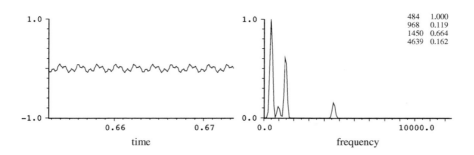

Figure 29.5
Tail portion of spectrum.

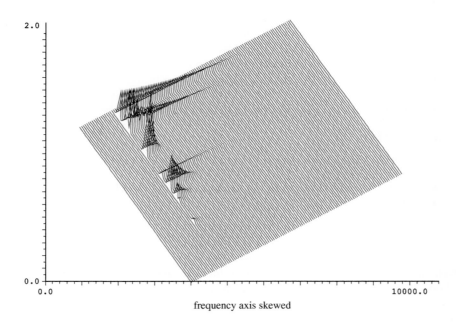

Figure 29.6
3D time/freq plot of bell sound.

and 1:24. We see that there are three groups of decay, 1:24, 1:12, and 1:6 decay away fastest, followed by 1:11 and 1:9, while 1:1, 1:2, and 1:3 have the greatest longevity. The 3D plot also reveals a burst of energy around the 1:3 ratio in the attack. This is the cluster of peaks we saw in the first snapshot around 1kHz. It tends to indicate an instability or situation where a bunch of resonances nearly divide to a common mode, but not quite. Following a spectrogram in real time you will often see bands dancing around a certain point, sometimes exhanging energy between two or more peaks in a regular pattern before finally settling on one dominant mode. In this case it is around the range 1:2.5 to 1:3.5 (which is more obvious from listening than looking at the graphs).

Summary of Model

So, the shape, material and structure, and excitation determine how waves propagate around the object and how its resonances create certain modes of vibration. In this system, energy movements are heard as sound, or die away through dissipation. Objects of regular shape and material makeup focus sound into more definite frequencies than irregular and inconsistent ones. Let's take stock of some things we know:

- The shape, size, and material of a bell remain fixed.
- The excitation is very short compared to the length of the sound.
- A bell is usually made from a dense, elastic, and regular material.
- There are a number of pure sinusoidal components in a bell sound.
- Their relationship is initially complex, but simplifies with time.
- They each evolve in different ways through the duration of a bell note.
- Eventually all die to nothing. Energy is radiated as sound or lost to entropy.
- Overall, the spectrum of a bell is quite sparse.

Specification

And let's recap on specific parameters that define our target sound.

- The fundamental frequency of the bell is about 450Hz to 500Hz.
- It dies away in about 3 seconds, give or take a fudge factor.

Method

Remember what we are focusing on: a specific kind of bell, an old-style telephone bell, made of brass, a couple of inches across, struck repeatedly with a small hammer connected to a buzzer. That gives us at least three components to consider: the hammer, the bell, and the buzzer. Additionally, we need to be thinking about any housing or case that the bell operates in, sources of energy, and objects that act as sinks of acoustic energy or radiators. So, turning to the method, how can declarative knowledge, stuff about what a bell is and how it makes a sound, be moved to imperative or procedural knowledge, stuff about how to implement the bell and select tools from our DSP box of tricks? Now is the time to consider why we might choose one synthesis method over another, and so we need a little computational wisdom to help know which approach might be the most efficient. For real-time implementation in games we also care which is easiest to code, most flexible at run time, and which presents the most useful interface to application components above. Then we can fill out the specific parameters, exactly what frequencies will be produced. Let's now think of some tricks we can employ from the knowledge we have.

The Bell(s)

The method we are going to choose for the bell is an additive approach. The main reason for that is point 8 of our model, that the sound contains a fairly sparse arrangement of pure tones. So we will add many sinusoidal waves together, one for each frequency. However, the frequencies are not static; they are a blend which evolves over time with some changing at a different rate from others. So we may need more than one control envelope.

Efficiency

Only a few oscillators are needed. Since the sparseness of the bell spectrum is what makes additive a good choice we only need a handful of oscillators to get a fair emulation. The few high-energy, high-frequency harmonics from the hammer impact could be approximated by a little burst of noise. After that short (30ms) time the vibrational modes have settled into maybe 10 or 12 important harmonics. In this example we'll use 5 bunches of 3 harmonics, a total of 15 partials plus the striker sound.

Flexibility

Ratios are better than absolute values. Remember that the shape of the bell doesn't change (apart from the distortions which are part of the sound), so tuning a bell is more about its scale. Rather than specifying fixed frequencies for each harmonic it's better to start with only the fundamental and express all the other harmonics as ratios. This way, by changing the fundamental you can tune the bell and all the other harmonics will follow suit correctly. When adding a second bell later you'll see why this was a good move, and how easy it is to change one parameter for the fundamental rather than rewriting them all.

Make Use of the Physics

The harmonics form groups. Although each harmonic has an individual evolution, some harmonics seem to behave in a related way. Studies of bell sounds show that the partials grow and decay in groups, and groups of groups, as they interact. For example, the circular modes are quite distinct from the bending modes. Couldn't we lump some of these frequencies together in order to simplify the control of them? Controlling groups of harmonics that tend to decay together with the same envelope is a way for us to cheat and use a little less processor power than controlling the level of every harmonic individually. Won't grouping harmonics by modes cause a reduction in quality? Certainly, but the trick is to decide where the cutoff between detail and cost lies, and in this case we can make significant shortcuts.

Bell Hammer

For the hammer we could choose a noise-based method. It's hard to model every frequency excited by the hammer striking the bell, and would be pointless overkill. The transient is so short and complex it approximates to a burst of noise. In an earlier published design I used only a noise generator and short envelope to get this. Here, an additional group of 4 high frequencies is used to more closely follow the analysis with a noise component added.

Casing

What about the housing for the telephone bell? That's something that depends on the design of the phone. More modern ones come in smaller plastic housings, while old style ones were made of a denser and harder material called Bakelite. Since we have a certain era in mind (circa 1950), we'll use that knowledge to specify a heavy Bakelite box. The sound would certainly encounter some reflections in this box, and because of its hardness it would transmit and radiate the sound well. A good method for creating a small acoustic space is to use delays. Two short delays, one corresponding to the width of the box and the other to its length are sufficient. Of course, you are thinking, the box also has height. That is true, but like the simplification made with the partials of the bell we can make things less complicated by simplifying the acoustic space.

The Buzzer

Rocking backwards and forwards on its fulcrum the hammer strikes two bells alternately. An estimate of the frequency this happens at is 10Hz. So what does this control system add to the sound? First, it produces a little sound of its own, although this is quiet relative to the bell intensity. It is coupled to the housing so any rattling made by the buzzer will be amplified. Second, consider the timing: such an electromechanical system will have a little variation in the time it takes to move from side to side, so it is not perfectly periodic. We could also add a little randomness to this movement to give the effect more realistic character.

DSP Implementation

The foregoing discussion has been lengthy, but now we have everything needed to begin building. The following sections will detail each component before we finally assemble them into the required sound object.

Bell Oscillator

Here's our oscillator (figure 29.7). It hardly seems worth making an abstraction of, does it? Just two parts excluding the inlet and outlets, a `osc~` to make the waveform, and a `*~` to control the amplitude. But we'll be using a few of these, so making an abstraction, however trivial, will save on some patching later. A pitch value in Hertz will come through the first inlet, and an amplitude value from 0.0 to 1.0 through the second inlet.

Figure 29.7
The oscillator.

Envelope Generator

Figure 29.8
Envelope generator.

The heart of this component is the versatile line generator vline~ which takes a message and produces a slowly moving signal. The message in this case says go to 1.0 in 0.0 milliseconds after a 0.0 millisecond delay, then go to 0.0 in $1 milliseconds after a zero delay. The value $1 gets substituted into the message from whatever arrives at the decay inlet, a floating point number between about 10 and 500. So, if we send this abstraction a number 250.51, its output will immediately jump to 1.0 and then take 250.51ms to return to zero. However, it will not return to zero in a linear fashion. The extra *~ gives the square of the line segment, so it curves rapidly and then more gently towards zero.

One Partial

A partial, as shown in figure 29.9, is a combination of the envelope and oscillator. Now we have something more useful to produce a sound. If we pass it a list of three elements, representing frequency, amplitude, and decay time, a short sound consisting of a single decaying cosinusoidal wave will be output.

Figure 29.9
A partial.

The values are all passed in through a single inlet as a list, and then unpacked to go to their respective destinations. The list will correspond to frequency, amplitude, decay. The oscillator is modulated by the envelope output. We won't use this component as it is, because it only provides one partial and we want to control groups of partials with the same envelope, so next let us modify this a bit and combine several oscillators into a group.

Group

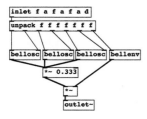

Figure 29.10
Group of three oscillators.

We extend the above patch by adding two more oscillators, which need some more outlets from the unpack. As shown in figure 29.10, at the top is an inlet that carries a list of seven elements, three pairs of frequencies and amplitudes, and a decay time for the group envelope. Since the maximum amplitude of all three oscillators might be 3.0, the sum is scaled by one-third. It doesn't matter if you do the scaling before of after the envelope multiplication. Now we are ready to test this component and hear the most basic bell sound.

Testing the Group

Hearing the group oscillator is as simple as connecting a message and dac~ as shown in figure 29.11,
with an extra attenuator so it isn't too loud. The
decay time is a short 800ms and for the frequencies
and amplitudes I picked some numbers at random.
They give a fairly inharmonic metal sound. What
we will do next is take several groups and combine
them.

Figure 29.11
Test a group.

Adding a Striker

The sound of the little hammer hitting the bell creates a
brief transient containing lots of frequencies. They're not
just the extra overtones in the bell that die away almost
instantly, but also the sound of the hammer vibrating, and
the lever on which it is mounted. This is approximated by
a short burst of noise to produce a click. Only 10ms is
needed, and a quartic decay makes sure the click dies away
rapidly. Because of the high frequencies in the noise only
a small level is needed to create the right effect, hence the
0.1 multiplier. Shown in figure 29.12 is a subpatch that will
be combined into the final patch shortly. It receives a bang
message via **r striker** and outputs its signal via a throw~
to a local destination **$0-striker**.

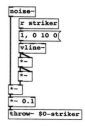

Figure 29.12
Bell striker.

Building the Bell

At last, all the threads can be drawn together into a finished implementation. In
figure 29.13 you can see how this is achieved, providing a bell whose amplitude,
fundamental (pitch), and overall decay (duration) can be set independently of
the harmonic structure. Each of five pack objects collects the values obtained
by multiplying out the frequency and amplitude ratios taken from the analysis.
The analysis I performed was made by looking at more spectrograms than there
is room to present here, so there are some extra partials carefully placed into
groups that we haven't fully discussed. You can either copy this example, or
you may like to experiment with analysing your own bell recording and filling
out some different values. This patch will be tidied away into a subpatch for
the next step where we build the buzzer and housing.

Making a Box

The resonator in figure 29.14 sends its input signal into two delays that feed
back into each other. Between them is a fixed filter that mimics the material
properties of the box and a clip~ that serves to limit the signal and introduce a
little distortion to create a brighter sound. An old telephone has a box about
20cm to 30cm (12 inches) square. From the speed of sound being 340m/s we get

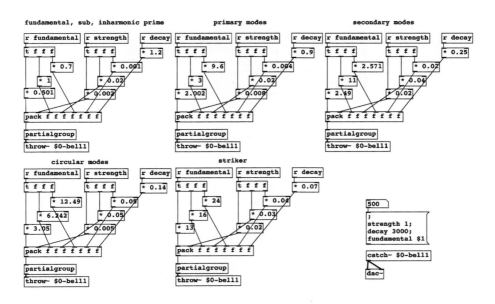

Figure 29.13
All the groups of the bell in ratio.

a resonance of 0.3/340ms or about 1.1kHz. Two delays are used with the length being slightly longer than the width. Tapping some Bakelite shows resonances somewhere between a hard wood and plastic, and for a plate about 5mm thick resonances were seen at 1kHz, 500Hz, and 300Hz. Choosing the exact values for the patch in figure 29.14 requires a bit of tweaking by hand. You want to find two values for the acoustic resonance and set the width, length, and feedback to give a good effect, while at the same time you must pick filter values that give a nice hollow radiated tone. Picking feedback values close to 0.7 gives good results; then tune the filters to get the quality of a plastic box without accidentally sending the acoustic resonator into unstable feedback.

A Buzzer with Two Bells

Finally we combine all the elements as shown in figure 29.15. Two copies of the bell are needed, and they must be modified slightly so you can send them individual frequency and triggering messages. Using a counter with **mod** and **select** gives alternating bang messages. Since the bells will not be identical, a slight difference of frequency makes the effect much more realistic. I found values of 650Hz and 653Hz worked okay for this model. The last stage sums both bells and the striker noise, and feeds some of this through the casing patch.

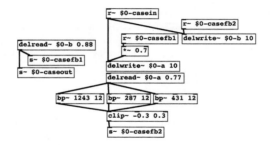

Figure 29.14
Casing.

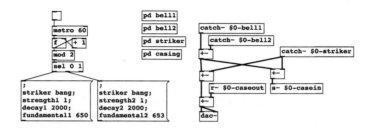

Figure 29.15
Telephone bell effect: all components together.

Results

Source . . . . <http://mitpress.mit.edu/designingsound/
telephonebell.html>

Conclusions

A traditional telephone bell is an electromechanical vibrator with a hammer that strikes two small bells. We have thought about the flow of energy from electricity into sound vibrations and the material and geometric factors that lead a rigid body to vibrate in certain modes. We have looked at analysis using snapshot spectrograms and resynthesis by additive methods. Efficiency through approximation and reuse of components are understood, and we have experimented with making small acoustic "waveguides" to simulate an enclosure.

Exercises

Exercise 1

Research some famous church bells such as the Coventry Cathedral bells resynthesised by B. Hibbert (after analysis work of A. A. Hughes). Make an additive synthesiser that reconstructs these from the published overtone and amplitude data.

Exercise 2

Research tubular bells, cowbells, Tibeten singing bowls, or some other struck bell-like source. Attempt to resynthesise it based on *your own* spectral analysis study. You should submit your spectral analysis graphs with features marked. Include a discussion of the vibrational and acoustic modes. You may find good material on the physics forum or in the *Journal of Vibration and Acoustics*.

References

Adrien, J. M. (1991). "The missing link: Modal synthesis." In *Representations of Music Signals*, ed. G. De Poli, A. Piccialli, and C. Roads. MIT Press.

Benson, D. J. (207). "A mathematicians guide to the orchestra 3.21—The Bell." In *Music: A Mathematical Offering*, chapter 3, pp. 138–142.

Cook, P. R. (2002). "Two and three dimensions." In *Real Sound Synthesis for Interactive Applications*, chapter 12. Peters.

Florens J. L., and Cadoz, C. (1991). "The physical model." In *Representations of Music Signals*, ed. G. De Poli, A. Piccialli, and C. Roads. MIT Press.

Olsen, H. F. (1952). "Resonators and radiators." In *Music, Physics, and Engineering*, chapter 4, pp. 59–107. Dover.

Risset, J. C., and Mathews, M. V. (1969). "Analysis of musical-instrument tones." *Physics Today* 22, no. 2: 23–30.

30
Practical 7
Bouncing

Aims

In this exercise we will look at bouncing. We will consider the sound of a ball falling under gravity onto a hard surface, although generally the principles may also apply to the case where two elastic objects such as wine glasses are brought together with a constant force.

Analysis

Work must be done if you lift a ball to some height above a surface, and this is stored as gravitational potential energy. When the ball is released it accelerates downwards under a constant gravitational force gaining kinetic energy. By Newton's Second Law acceleration causes the velocity to increase, and since kinetic energy is a function of mass and velocity, it also increases. When it hits a surface the ball is deformed in an elastic collision, releasing some energy as sound. The remaining energy is briefly stored as elastic potential. On striking the surface the ball has an upward force acting on it which deforms its shape. As the restoring force acts to return the ball to its original shape an equal and opposite force acts upwards on the ball (Newton's Third Law), causing it to bounce into the air again.

While rising, the ball is still subject to the force of gravity. An acceleration occurs in the same direction as before, but this time it is in the opposite direction to the velocity so the ball decelerates until it comes to a stop in midair. The entire process repeats again from this point. Since a sound is made there must be some loss from the system, so the ball will not reach its original height. As the process repeats there will be less energy in the ball, so each bounce will be successively smaller and the time between bounces will decrease.

Unlike rigid bodies considered elsewhere, the deformation of the ball is quite considerable. Its shape and density are not fixed during the collision, as sound is produced. This causes some nonlinear effects that change the pitch and tone of the impact sound depending on the amount of energy exchanged. The first bounce, from the greatest height, deforms the ball the most and alters its pitch much more than subsequent bounces. As the ball comes to rest, making smaller bounces with less deformation, the pitch and timbre envelope tend towards more constant values. The amount of loss, and thus the intensity of sound, is roughly proportional to the impact velocity, so as the bounces become

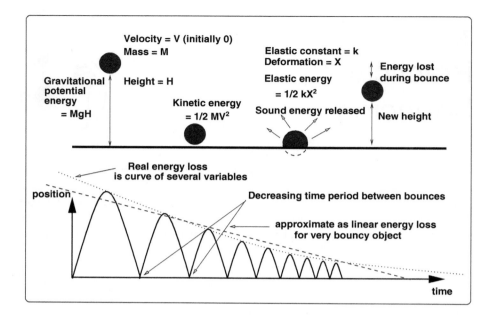

Figure 30.1
Energy exchange in a bouncing object.

smaller the sound also becomes quieter. The impact sound will vary enormously depending on size, density, material content, and distribution of the ball. A glass marble, solid rubber ball and hollow football each have quite different characters. The vibrational modes of a sphere are determined by Bessel functions so we could make a quite detailed model if we wanted. However, here we are more concerned with the decaying energy model that characterises a bouncing object, so we will substitute a simple approximation for the impact sound. What is important is how the sound changes with the impact velocity, since this is the psychoacoustic information that makes us hear a bouncing ball.

Model

Instead of directly modelling the kinetic energy, gravity, and bouncing, a shortcut can be made which only considers the sonically relevant parameters. We have a system that produces a decaying pattern of events in which the event frequency increases while the spectrum, duration, and total amplitude of each event diminishes. We will have just one parameter, which corresponds to the height of the ball. This will determine the time to fall and thus the final velocity. The decrease in bounce period is roughly linear, so we can use a metronome to make bounce events that increase in frequency.

Method

Two parts will be considered separately, one for generating the impact sound and one for generating the bounce event pattern. We will use FM synthesis to give control of a spectrum that varies between a sine wave and a denser bunch of harmonics. A decay envelope will be applied to control the amplitude and FM amount for each impact. This will be repeatedly triggered by a metronome. At the same time we will apply a linear envelope to the metronome period and to the envelope decay time, amplitude, and modulation frequency. Together this will produce the effect of bounces decreasing in energy.

Implementation

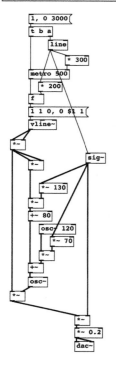

The initial message works with `line` to make a linear envelope taking 3 seconds to reach zero. We split a bang message off to start the metronome and pass the remaining list to `line`. Initially the bounce event period will be 300ms, the main output amplitude via `sig~` will be 1.0, and the decay time stored in `float` will be 200ms. As the line decreases towards zero the period at the right inlet of `metro` will decrease towards zero and so will the output amplitude and decay time. Each time `vline~` is triggered it moves to 1.0 in 1.0ms and then from 1.0 to 0.0 over the decay time passed from `float` and substituted in $1. The amplitude curve of each bounce is a square law decay (on the left-hand side), while the carrier frequency of an FM stage is swept by a 4th power decaying curve. Frequency sweeps between 210Hz and 80Hz occurring on each bounce are added to the main oscillator running at a fixed frequency of 120Hz to give a low "thud." The part above 80Hz represents the nonlinear deformation that happens in the attack part of the impact, while most of the body of the sound is at a frequency close to 80Hz. Scaling the modulation by 70Hz according to the bounce height gives a richer spectrum for more energetic bounces and an almost pure sine wave of 80Hz at zero height. This implementation is imperfect since the decay time of the bounce pattern is independent of the initial metronome period, so that for small initial height value it won't work correctly. This could be fixed by employing an event pattern generator based on delays.

Figure 30.2
Bouncing ball.

Results

Source   . . . .   <http://mitpress.mit.edu/designingsound/
                                  bouncing.html>

Conclusions

A bouncing object is characterised by its physical behaviour where over time energy is lost from the system as sound and heat. The bounces get closer together and less energetic. The rate of energy loss can be approximated as linear. The energy in each impact is given by the height from which the object falls on each bounce. Mapping timbre, amplitude, and decay time to the bounce energy provides the correct effect.

Exercises

Exercise 1

If a perfectly elastic sphere hit a perfectly hard, elastic plane, could it bounce forever? If so, what sound would it make? Improve the model to account for air resistance or for an imperfect surface that has a soft absorbent property. (Hint: drag is proportional to velocity.)

Exercise 2

Replace the DSP synthesis with another model for a struck idiophonic object like a glass or metal. Study spectrograms to see how changing impact energy alters the spectrum, especially during the attack.

31
Practical 8
Rolling

Aims

Produce the sound of a rolling object like an empty drink can blowing along uneven ground in the wind.

Analysis

A rolling object with mass obtains rotational kinetic energy, either because gravity acts on it or because something (like a boot when we kick it) applies an impulsive force to it. Friction holds the bottom surface of the object to the ground so the rest of the body moves around this pivot. A perfectly smooth cylinder or sphere on an ideal frictionless plane would not roll unless given an initial rotational moment; it would just slide. So the act of rolling, and the sound produced, depends on the irregularity of the object surface and the ground it moves on.

Model

Consider the regular triangular object on the left in figure 31.1. It is rigid and moves without slipping. When at rest on its base it produces an even force and pressure on the ground, and the ground supports it with an opposite and equal force. To roll it clockwise so that it moves up onto the bottom right corner, work must be done to move center of mass upwards. Because it balances on a corner a smaller surface area supports the same weight, so the pressure increases. There will be 3 steps of 120° in each rotation during which the patterns shown in the graphs below will repeat. Each time the potential energy rises with the center of mass until it reaches its highest point, and kinetic energy (in the x-axis direction) decreases to zero, then increases in an opposite (negative) direction. After 60° of rotation we no longer need to supply energy; instead the unstable object falls under gravity. At a time where the original apex (now the bottom right corner) impacts the ground there is a vector of velocity that causes a sudden spike of force as the object gives up any energy that went into the movement. During the collision, energy is lost to heat and sound as it excites the body of the object and the surface. As we add sides to the object, each additional side

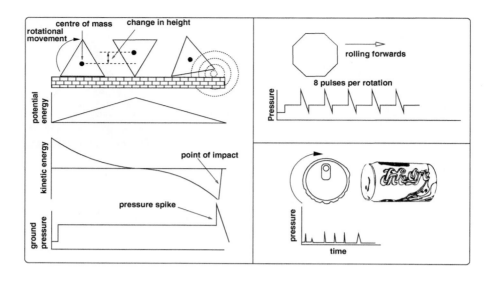

Figure 31.1
A rolling drink can.

means the energy needed to raise the center of mass and the impulse of energy given up on each step of rotation tends towards zero. A regular octagon (shown in the top right panel in fig. 31.1) emits eight smaller impulses during a rotation. Extending this to the limit, the object eventually approximates the circular section of the drink can shown bottom right. Of course no real object has perfect geometry, and a drink can still contains small dents and bumps. As this object rolls it creates a pattern of impulses that repeats over for each rotation. Let's take a look at this from another perspective: if the object were perfectly circular and the ground were uneven then we could imagine a converse effect. This is how Rath (2003) develops a rolling model in which the uneven surface is significant in comparison to the size of the rolling object. In figure 31.2 we see a cylinder or ball moving over a bumpy surface. To overcome each peak it must rotate around the maxima, producing a signature that follows the contours of the surface.

Model

Our model will consist of four parts: a model of momentum and impulsive force, a repeating source of impulses that correspond to the contour around the circumference of the rolling object, a model for uneven ground texture, and a struck model for the actual sound made by a drink can hit on the side. So, the collision pattern consists of the repeating rolling sound made by the spinning

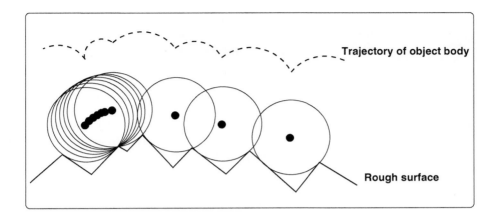

Figure 31.2
Rath's model of a perfect object rolling on an uneven surface.

object and a bumping signature from uneven ground, which is responsible for low-frequency components as the object translates up and down. Strictly this only works for a cylinder that has one degree of rotational freedom. A sphere could roll in a fashion that gives rise to a nonrepeating impulse pattern, although as a necessary condition for the object being spherical there would be a high degree of similarity and gradual change to this pattern.

Method

Simple bandpass filters will serve us for the drink can. Repeated rolling patterns will be obtained by phase synchronous wrapping of a phasor signal common to several functions. A good approximation to ground bumping is obtained from shaped noise.

Implementation

Again, our main purpose here is exploring the pressure signature of a rolling object rather than accurately modelling the can, so a crude model will suffice. We would normally attack this by looking at the modes of bending and acoustic resonance, namely ring modes (around the circumference), longitudinal vibration modes (squashing and stretching of the can along its cylindrical axis), vibrational bending modes (side-to-side deformation of the can), and acoustical resonance (in this case a tube partially closed at one and fully closed at the

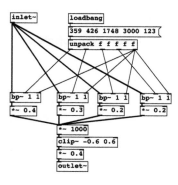

Figure 31.3
A simple approximation to a
drink can.

other). We might also note that a drink can has
very thin walls (slender cylinder behaviour) but
rigid end pieces (effectively solid compared to
the skin). However, we are only interested in the
strongest modes of excitation from impacts on
the side, so let's just take a look at a spectrum
of a real drink can.

You can clearly see a pair of frequencies at
359Hz and 426Hz, and a couple of higher ones
at 1748Hz and 3150Hz (only the strongest three
are listed in the peaks). There seems to be a bit
of spreading around both areas, because the thin
can walls behave in a rather nonlinear way, and
maybe a couple of other areas of energy around
$1,500$Hz.

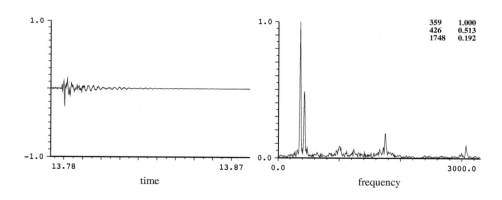

Figure 31.4
Hitting an aluminium drink can on the side.

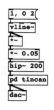

Figure 31.5
Testing out the
tin can.

An approximation made from four noise bands is shown in
figure 31.3. It's a straightforward resonator with a message and
unpack mechanism to initialise the filters at load time. Adding
a `clip~` introduces some distortion to widen up the noise bands
harmonically. Here in figure 31.5 is a little test patch that takes
the square of a short line segment, high pass filters it, and uses
that as an impulse to the resonator so we can hit the drink can
and hear it. Next we will create the rolling pressure signature
and connect it to this drink can model. By carefully setting the
levels, any small impulses will produce relatively pure tones,
but stronger ones overdrive the `clip~` and give richer harmonics,
which produces a brighter sound.

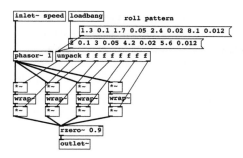

Figure 31.6
A repeating roll pattern.

Rolling speed is determined by a signal on the first inlet, which sets a phasor frequency. Four copies of this go to four multipliers, which scale the amplitude and thus the slope. When wrapped, each scaled phasor will have its transition in a different place, according to the multiplier value. For example, a multiplier of 3 will produce 3 transitions of the wrapped phasor for every period of the original. Each of these signals is then scaled in amplitude before being summed at `rzero~`, which behaves as a differentiator. A short impulse appears at the point of each phasor transition, so by configuring the pre- and postwrap multipliers we obtain a repeating pattern of impulses. This subpatch becomes pd `regular-roll` in the final example.

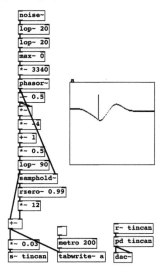

Figure 31.7
Ground bumping.

Irregular bumping due to ground texture is produced by the patch shown in figure 31.7. It is designed to create an undulating waveform with impulse spikes appearing at the minima of parabolic excursions. Starting at the top we have a noise source strongly low pass filtered and then constrained to a positive range. A multiplier boosts this weak signal to create a frequency control for a phasor centred around a few hundred Hertz. The following 5 objects form a pulse shaper, producing a circular curve which is then low pass filtered to remove some of the sharp edges where the curve abruptly changes direction. The aim here is to create a low-frequency bumping signal to drive the drink can model. In parallel with this, a `samphold~` turns the slowly moving wave into a step waveform with edges that coincide with phasor transitions. Differentiating this gives impulses at the bottom of each dip, where the rolling cylinder would impact with the next rising slope. This subpatch becomes pd irregular-ground in the final example. Before using these subpatches in the main patch, the test objects shown in figure 31.7 may be removed and the send object replaced with a signal outlet.

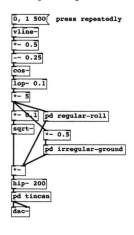

Our final arrangement is shown in figure 31.8 and consists of both irregular and regular rolling generators coupled to the can model. Amplitude control with a root law seems to work well since even very low roll speeds are quite loud, and while faster rolling does increase the energy of impacts the sound intensity is not that much louder in practice (the nonlinearity of the can seems to cause saturation). Amplitude and roll speed are given by a pulse generator and low pass filter that act to integrate "pushes" given to the can. In other words, this models momentum, mass, and loss. Pressing the message box will produce a 500ms half cosine and give a little push to the can which sets it rolling, but it will quickly stop as the level in the low pass filter decays. Pressing the message several times quickly will set the can rolling faster and for longer. This is a good scheme to use in game control logic where a decoupled sound control layer is to be driven by relatively infrequent periodic events.

Figure 31.8
Complete rolling can patch.

Results

Source   . . . .   <http://mitpress.mit.edu/designingsound/rolling.html>

Conclusions

A rolling object produces a pattern of excitations that are partly due to the irregularity of the object partly due to the irregularity of the ground. A model of mass and frictional loss can easily be made using just a low pass filter. We can crudely model a drink can using two or three narrow band filters used additively and a waveshaping function to get brighter sounds for harder impact.

Exercises

Exercise 1

Replace the drink can with another material model like a rock or glass bottle.

Exercise 2

Combine the rolling model with a bouncing control scheme and simulate a complex motion in which the object may pitch, tumble and roll onto its ends. Produce a more sophisticated object model that excites different overtones depending on the impact position.

References

Rath, M. "An expressive real-time sound model of rolling." (2003). *Proc. 6th Int. Conference on Digital Audio Effects (DAFx-03)*. London.

Van den Doel, K., Kry, P. G., and Pai, D. K. (2001). "FoleyAutomatic: Physically-based Sound Effects for Interactive Simulation and Animation." *Computer Graphics (ACM SIGGRAPH 01 Conference Proceedings)*, pp. 537–544. SIGGRAPH.

32

Practical 9
Creaking

Aims

Investigate the physics of friction and its application to creaking doors and squeaky floor boards.

Analysis

Friction is a fundamental bit of physics that applies to everything from architecture to holding your pants up. It affects sound in many ways, in the rusty hinges of a door, in a window cleaner's sponge, in mechanical brakes and joints, and in the squeaky transmission shafts of vehicle engines. The general physical process includes many sonic descriptions as well as creaking, such as squeaking, squealing, grinding, or rubbing sounds.

Stick-Slip Motion

To avoid relativism we should define two objects, one to be an immovable reference or *base* and the other to be the *mover* which travels over the surface of the base. The mover M pushes against the base with a force normal to its surface. This might be due to the mover having weight (Mg), such as when pushing a heavy box along the ground, or it might be an applied force, such as when cleaning a window with a sponge. Additionally, there is another tangential force F_w trying to push the mover over the base. This is because of some work we are tying to do, like opening a door. Because the surfaces are not perfectly smooth on a microscopic scale, some protrusions of one surface will rest in the dips of the other. A diagram (fig. 32.1) showing this may help understand how the surfaces become locked together. Sticking describes a point in time where the velocity of the mover is zero or very small. Force F_w still acts on the mover, but it is balanced by a *static friction* force F_s that stops the mover. Slight movement, called *shear*, can happen at this time. It is due to the flexibility of bonds between their surfaces, but from our point of view is negligible. *Slip* describes a period of time during which the mover slides over the surface. The tangential force becomes greater than the static frictional force and the mover is set free. When this happens *kinetic friction* applies, and acts to slow down the mover. Notice I've mentioned two kinds of friction, static and dynamic (or

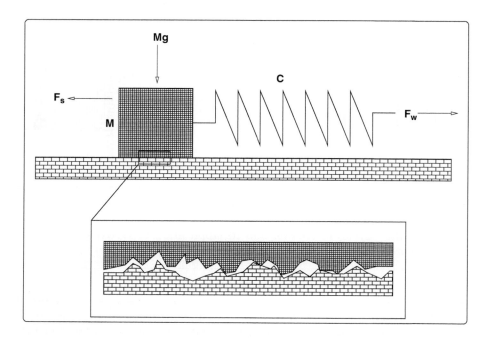

Figure 32.1
Frictional forces and surface interface at a microscopic level.

kinetic) types. It's because these two kinds of friction exist that we get a periodic behaviour, like a relaxation oscillation, but a little more complex than the simple on/off threshold behaviours we have considered before. In figure 32.1 a spring connects the source supplying force F_w to the mover M. It gives a mechanical capacitance C by virtue of its tension. Once the mover overcomes static friction it accelerates quickly forwards, much faster than F_w is pulling the spring along, so reducing the tension in the spring. Kinetic friction, which is much less than static friction, acts on the mover until it slows to a halt, at which point it becomes stuck again until enough force has built up in the spring.

The sonic effect of this motion is summarised by figure 32.2. Displacement of the mover D_m occurs in steps compared to the constant displacement of the leading object doing the work, D_w. The longer the time interval between steps, the greater force has accumulated and the higher the peak velocity. Impulses are generated when the mover quickly lurches forwards, and in practice these tend to come in short clusters with a large movement followed by several smaller ones. The complexity of frictional stick-slip movement arises because the coefficient of kinetic friction depends on velocity, but not in a simple way. At slow speeds it increases with velocity, up to a maximum; then beyond that it begins

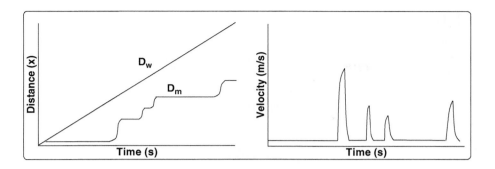

Figure 32.2
Velocity and displacement of a mover sticking and slipping.

to decrease with increasing velocity. The movement also creates heat, which affects the surface properties. This effect on rubber is known by racing drivers and is why cars drive a warm up lap to soften the tyres and increase their friction. Because the surface is random on a microscopic scale we cannot predict the exact instant of slip (otherwise earthquake prediction would not be so hard), but on a statistical level the macro-behaviour can be so predictable as to sound perfectly periodic. Periodicity is increased where the stick-slip interface belongs to a mass coupled to a resonant system like the spring. The resonant system will trend to produce regular peaks in the force and cause slip to happen in sympathy with its resonant frequency, as happens in a bowed string.

Model

A squeaky door hinge is a two-part coupling where friction causes a series of stick-slip impulses, and the door, which may be of many materials or sizes, acts as an amplifier for these pulses. On its own the stick-slip model only shows us the velocity of the mover. It doesn't tell us how this might sound other than the frequency of stick-slip movements is proportional to the applied force. Any sounds produced are going to depend on excitations of both parts, mover, and base. In a squeaky door the base is one part of the hinge. The hinge is a small metal plate coupled to a much larger wooden or metal sounding board. The mover is the other half of the hinge that rotates over the lower part with the weight of the door acting as the normal force. In a creaking floorboard the mover and base may be two wooden boards pressed against one another, where the mover is the board that's trodden on and the base is an adjacent board that it rubs against. Each burst of movement may itself consist of noisy excitations, but in creaking objects they are generally short and can be treated as single impulses. If we apply an impulsive pattern appropriate for stick-slip friction to a material model of the base and mover, we should get a reasonable approximation of creaking sounds.

Method

We will use a slow moving line to mimic mass/momentum and apply this to
an event generator. Each event will create an impulse that feeds a resonator
appropriate for a large, thick rectangular body.

DSP Implementation

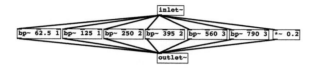

Figure 32.3
Formants for a wooden door.

Start with the door itself. Stick-slip pulses will be
passed through a static formant designed for a square
wooden door effect (fig. 32.3). The lowest frequency
is 62.5Hz, although this is a subharmonic given for a
little extra weight, the proper harmonic series starts
on 125Hz. These frequencies are chosen for an unsupported rectangular membrane and follow the ratios
1:1.58:2.24:2.92:2:2.55:3.16. Also, some (0.2) direct signal is passed through in parallel with the formant filters.

A patch written mainly in the message domain is
shown in figure 32.4. It turns an applied force (in the
range 0.0 to 1.0) at its inlet to a sequence of audio pulses
at its outlet. First of all, some smoothing is applied
to the control input with a `line` giving a 100ms lag.
This effectively gives the mover some mass and momentum so it doesn't respond too lightly to volatile control
changes. A trigger splits off a left branch which turns the
metronome on once the control passes a threshold of 0.3.
This mimics the initial force needed to overcome static
friction and set the mover going, and thus we don't get
an unfeasibly low-frequency slipping. In the right branch
the metronome period is calculated. The control scale is
inverted so it has the correct direction and is multiplied
by 60, then added to a minimum offset of 3ms. This
connects to the cold inlet of `metro` because the period is
updated by the addition of a random number on each
metronome cycle. Random numbers are proportional to

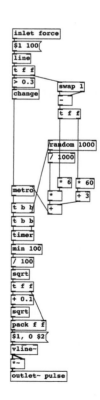

Figure 32.4
Stick-slip friction model.

the period, so when the movement is slow and the period between creaks is large so is the random number. So the random range diminishes in keeping with the creaking frequency. The sequence of bangs so produced activates a `timer` whose output increases with the time between each bang. This is how we model the buildup of force so that the amplitude of each slip is proportional to the time since the last one. Since `timer` runs in real rather than logical time, a limit of 100ms is placed on this value to prevent an unreasonably loud sound happening should the patch stall for any reason. The value is normalised and then a square root function applied (twice for the amplitude and once for the decay time). We do this to scale the slip amplitudes and create a good volume curve. After packing into a list, the amplitude and decay time of a line segment are set. A more natural square law decay is applied to this audio signal before output.

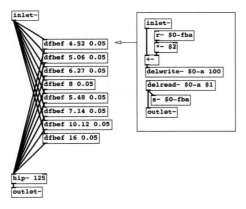

Figure 32.5
Square panel resonator for wooden door and the delay element abstraction used to make it.

Next we apply a delay-based resonator. Again the series is chosen for a rectangular membrane with a fundamental mode of 125Hz, although these must be expressed as periods. A small abstraction is shown in figure 32.5 along with a rectangular wooden panel resonator using several of these.

Combining these components is straightforward. Stick-slip impulses are imbued with a wooden ringing by the formant bank and then given to a resonator that gives the sound some life. The brightness and tone can easily be changed by playing with the direct signal passed by the formant subpatch, or by narrowing the filters. For different sized doors, small floorboards, or different materials you should recalculate the resonator and formant characteristics. You may like to do some research on the stick-slip character of other materials too. Some adjustment of the impulsive/noise excitation will be needed to

Figure 32.6
Creaking door.

get metal grinding or other kinds of material scraping. Lots of variation can be obtained by shaping the stick-slip pulses in different ways, but some more complex interactions like squealing leather or sponges will need more than one stick-slip source, since the sound is a combination of many stick-slip events happening together.

Results

Source   ....   <http://mitpress.mit.edu/designingsound/ creaking.html>

Conclusions

A creaking door can be modelled as a stick-slip friction model imparting impulses to a solid radiator which acts as a fixed formant filter and acoustic amplifier.

Exercises

Exercise 1

Improve the squeaky hinge by having several stick-slip sources acting in parallel (more than one hinge). Try adding another excitation source such as a door handle or lock to the same resonator to get an integrated effect.

Exercise 2

Analyse some other friction models such as a heavy box being pushed over the ground or a squeaking sponge on a wet window pane.

References

Cook, P. (2002). "Exciting and controlling sound modes." In *Real Sound Synthesis for Interactive Applications*, chapter 14, pp. 175–177. A. K. Peters.

33
Practical 10
Boing

Aims

To make the familiar comedy sound (as for Mr Bounce or Zebedee), which is a twanged rule or bar held at the edge of a solid surface.

Analysis

Remember that not all sounds need to be literal. Some sounds are representative or suggestive, but that does not mean they aren't rooted in real physics or aren't clearly definable. This makes an interesting study because although the meaning of the sound is abstract, the production mechanism is concrete.

Making a Twang

A wooden rule is held over the edge of a table so that about half of it hangs over the edge. As you press firmly down on the supported end with one finger the other end is displaced so that the whole length bends. Suddenly releasing the unsupported end causes it to swing back quickly and then oscillate. For the best sound effect precisely enough pressure should be applied to the supported end to allow overshoot. In other words the supporting finger acts as a pivot that lets the bar lift above the table and collide with it on the way down. The result is a complex sound that we can analyse as two separate oscillating modes.

Nonlinear Oscillation

Bending the bar to give sufficient initial force causes a clear nonlinearity (bending) in the pitch. An initial frequency of 5Hz to 20Hz above the final frequency is typical. In addition the finger pressure or position of the bar may be modulated to produce a vibrato effect.

Discontinuity

Depending on the pressure applied, several different modes are at work. As it moves into the highest position and disconnects with the table we can view the system as a mixture of two possible modes: as a freely vibrating bar damped at one end or as a clamped bar. Both of these modes are present and exhibit different vibrational patterns; the result is a mixture of the two. Upon hitting the table a new excitation occurs. On the downward cycle we can view the

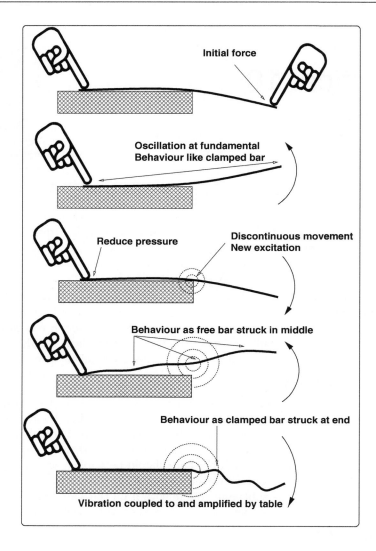

Figure 33.1
A vibrating rod with nonlinear contact.

system as a clamped bar of approximately half the original length being struck at its supporting end. This is a periodic impulse that excites higher frequencies than the fundamental. In fact the system is quite complex. If we choose to view it as two separate vibrational processes we have one set of modes modulating another. It isn't clear exactly where it will strike the table since there are nodes at other positions than the initial centre of curvature giving the fundamental. Further, each time the bar is excited again by collision in its clamped half-length position, new vibration patterns will be imparted to it.

Modes of the Free and Clamped Bar

From Olson (1967) and Benson (2007) we see the general formula for a vibrating bar is

$$F_n = M \frac{2\pi}{l^2} \sqrt{\frac{EK^2}{\rho}} \tag{33.1}$$

where E is Young's modulus, K is the radius of gyration, ρ is the material density, l is the length of the bar, and for the fundamental F and subsequent overtone multiples F_n

$$M = \begin{cases} 0.5596_n & \text{if bar is clamped} \\ 1.1333_n & \text{if bar is free} \end{cases}$$

Fortunately we only have to estimate the fundamental for a 30cm wooden bar, which comes out at about 300Hz; the remaining series of inharmonic frequencies can be obtained by plugging values in to the equation to get the first, second, and third overtones. These, as a multiple of the fundamental are:

Modes of vibrating bar

Mode	Clamped bar	Free bar
Fundamental	f	f
First overtone	6.276f	2.756f
Second overtone	17.55f	5.404f
Third overtone	34.39f	8.933f

Model

First we will create a struck free bar model based on noise and narrow band pass filters with resonances chosen for a wooden-sounding effect. Then we create a second oscillator with the spectrum of a clamped bar and modulate it with a pitch envelope to give a nonlinear frequency decay. Modulating the first source with the second and mixing the two together gives us a fair approximation of the twanged wooden bar. This stops short of modelling the discontinuity properly, but provides an adequate effect to demonstrate the usefulness of our analysis.

Method

The struck bar is implemented as several narrow band pass filters in parallel. The clamped modes are obtained by additive synthesis, and phase locked to a single source that also has its phase reset on each triggering (so the vibration

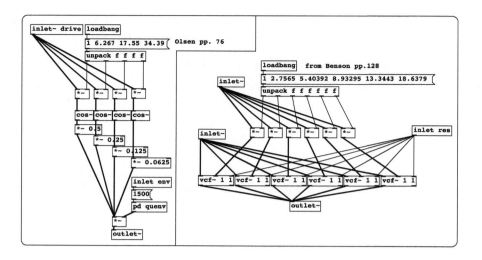

Figure 33.2
Subpatches for the clamped and free vibrational modes.

always starts from the same place). Some vibrato is added to the fundamental, which helps suggest nonlinearity and gives a more pleasing comical effect when exaggerated.

DSP Implementation

Four sinusoidal components are derived from a common phase in the frequency ratios unpacked from the initial message in the first part of figure 33.2. Their amplitudes are scaled in a decaying geometric progression 0.5, 0.25, 0.125, etc. Before output the sum is modulated by a quartic envelope with a fixed decay of 1500ms.

In the second part of figure 33.2 six band pass filters that have modulated centre frequencies are positioned for the inharmonic series 1, 2.7565, 5.40392, 8.93295, 13.3443, and 18.6379. This will be driven by a low pass filtered noise source so the amplitudes of each band decay away with increasing frequency. Assemble the two subpatches as shown in figure 33.3. A 16th power envelope modulates the fundamental phasor by 6Hz. This high-order envelope gives a very sudden change of frequency in the attack with a much longer movement over a small range for the remainder of the sound. It isn't shown for conciseness, because you can make it yourself either by using `pow~` or by cascading multiplies to do repeated squaring. To give the phasor a falling waveform, a multiplier of −1 is included. Excitation for the free mode bar is obtained by taking the

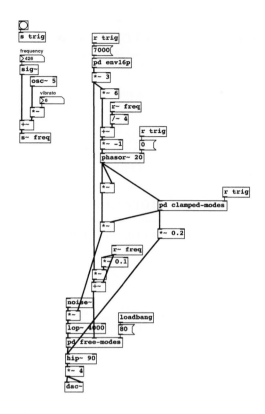

Figure 33.3
Twanging effect with modes for free and clamped bars in modulation.

square of the fundamental phasor to modulate the clamped waveform and a noise source. On each trigger the phase is reset to zero.

Results

Source   . . . .   <http://mitpress.mit.edu/designingsound/boing.html>

Conclusions

A discontinuous effect can cause periodic impacts which are themselves short excitations of the vibrating object. Different modes of vibration can be modelled separately and combined.

Exercises

Exercise 1

Modify the model to include a discontinuity where the bar alternates between length l and $l/2$ on each cycle.

Exercise 2

Investigate the properties of either a coiled stiff spring or lamellophone such as the marranzano ("jaw harp"[1]). Model either using any appropriate method.

References

Benson, D. J, (2007). *Music: A Mathematical Offering*. Cambridge University Press.
Olson, H. F. (1967). *Music, Physics, and Engineering*, 2nd ed. Dover.

---

1. Or "Jew's harp," which has no connection with Judaism, and is thus considered a derogatory name. It is actually an early Chinese instrument.

Practical Series
Nature

Nature hates calculators.
—Ralph Waldo Emerson

Natural Elements

Earth, water, air, and fire. Corresponding to four states solid, liquid, gas, and plasma, these are the elemental forms recognised by all cultures throughout history. Although attributed by North Western culture to the Greeks Empedocles and Aristotle they have symbolic counterparts in the alchemic, religious, and magical traditions of almost all cultures, including documented counterparts amongst Hindu, Chinese, Arabic, African, and Native American peoples.

Of course, we need to take these loosely in a modern interpretation, such as fitting electricity (including lightning) into the fire/plasma category. And since "Earth" is not a dynamic element, we have already covered it under the heading of idiophonics, that is, rigid body collisions. Two concepts will interest us much more in the following practicals, turbulence and statistical distributions.

The Practicals

- Fire, in the familiar form of a bonfire. We consider the process of combustion and the physical forces present that cause sound, a perfect example for component analysis.
- Bubbles, an example that leads us to examine both gases and liquids simultaneously, so we can treat it as a general look at the properties of fluids.
- Flowing water: constructing a model of flowing liquids to see how fluid friction, turbulence, depth and speed of flow all contribute to the sound.
- Poured liquids. Continuing from the previous practical, a model of liquids in a vessel is developed.
- Rain: the ideas of pressure signatures, volumetric extents, and statistical distributions are introduced.

- Electricity: an archetypal sparking sound is constructed based on ideas of irregular flow and cascade events (ionisation and flashover). The chirp impulse is introduced as a useful tool for modelling loud sounds.
- Thunder: we consider a compromise between spectral and physical models for this difficult case of an extremely energetic event. Some environmental acoustics and the N-Wave models of Few, Ribner, and Roy are discussed.
- Wind: the central role of turbulence in natural sounds is investigated. We also consider the role of causality, thresholding functions, and space for constructing real-time procedural audio scenes.

34
Practical 11
Fire

In this practical we will study a common and useful natural sound effect, fire. We will analyse the physical and acoustic properties of fire and combine several contributory signals to create a composite effect.

Analysis

What Is Fire?

Fire is a complex phenomenon. It is an example of a composite sound effect, having many contributory parts, and it is an example of a volumetric extent, coming from more than one location. Fire is an oxidisation reaction that has gone out of control. It starts when fuel gets hot and starts to oxidise. This generates heat in an exothermic reaction. The hotter something gets the better it oxidises and the more it oxidises the hotter it gets, ever more rapidly in a runaway process. This positive feedback causes a reaction that is self-sustaining and will increase in size and rate so long as fuel and oxygen are supplied. The following things usually happen.

Liquefaction and Boiling

As they heat, some solids melt and then boil. In wood, resins and oils are forced to the surface under pressure. In other materials, wax or plastics may melt and flow from the initial fuel. Some of these change to a vapour state, causing bubbles.

Outgassing

Recall Boyle's law, one of the many gas laws from kinetic theory, which says the product of pressure P and volume V is a constant for a fixed temperature T (written $PV = kT$). So if temperature increases, either the volume increases or pressure builds up. In the first case gas must escape from the fuel and comes out making a hissing sound. Where the escape path is impeded by trapped liquids we may hear periodic buildup and relaxations of pressure which sound strongly pitched.

Explosion

Where there is an immovable constriction and gases cannot escape to the surface because they build up in a sealed cavity, pressure will increase until it causes an explosion. The gas does not ignite or burn inside the fuel; it simply forces the solid fuel apart.

Stress

Explosive pressure isn't the only cause of disintegrating solid state materials. Thermal expansion of solid materials causes them to creak and groan.

Disintegration

Eventually the stress may build up until the fuel starts to disintegrate, making loud cracking sounds. This can cause large-scale structural shifts as pieces of fuel fall away or collapse on top of one another. If constrained they may fracture suddenly, as glass does when heated.

Flames

Gases released are often flammable themselves; they are a fuel too. With a high enough temperature flammable gas released by the reaction ignites into flames. Flames do not burn throughout their entire volume but on a *combustion front*, a skin covering the outside of the flame where it mixes with oxygen. Even where oxygen is premixed in a forced flame we can see the same effect in a clean Bunsen burner, with combustion happening on an exterior front.

Convection

In the free atmosphere, hot gaseous byproducts of the reaction, perhaps water vapour and carbon dioxide, expand. The density of hot gas is lower than the surrounding air and so, because it is lighter, it rises, leading to a low pressure around the flame. This is called *convection*. The temporary low pressure sucks surrounding air and fresh oxygen into the fray.

Flame Acoustics

The tendency of the combustion front to propagate is determined by the cross-sectional area and the pressure of the gaseous state fuel (Razus et al. 2003). Flames tend to pass into areas if they are a larger adjacent free volume at lower pressure. Lower pressure above the flame draws it upwards. The flame itself acts as a resonant cavity, a tube of low-pressure gas that oscillates chaotically from side to side as cool air rushes in to replace convected air. You can see this happening in a candle flame that flickers even when there is no wind. Expanding and rising gas changes the shape of the flame, elongating it into a thinner, taller volume. But to talk about a gas being lighter or heavier we must consider weight, which is a product of mass and gravity. A flame in zero gravity forms a perfect sphere. In Earth gravity, however, the cooling gas is heavier, so it falls back down causing instabilities around the flame and making it oscillate.

The energy exchange model in this case can be thought of as kinetic energy of a light, hot, rising gas and potential energy of a heavy, cold gas. The inflow of air around the base of the flame leads to vortices, turbulent patterns that shift the flame sideways or in spiral formations. All of these movements lead to low-frequency sounds. They are usually manifest as roaring, fluttering sounds in the $3 - 80$Hz range. Popping or gaseous state explosions happen where the flammable gas and air mixture is suddenly at an ideal pressure and temperature. This happens when the heat production from burning happens exactly in phase with an increase in pressure as a flame collapses. Placing a candle in a tube of the correct diameter to create a flame resonance causes a regular popping sound. The reverse principle is used in rocket engine design to minimise stress on the combustion chamber by modulating the fuel flow.

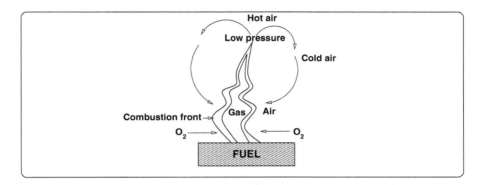

Figure 34.1
Flame gas dynamics.

Smouldering

Smouldering is combustion without flames where the oxidation reaction happens over the fuel surface. A fine, low-level sound that lies between hissing and crackling can be heard in some rare cases such as yellow or white hot glowing charcoal. Here the source can be considered intense Brownian motion amplified by the acoustic properties of the surface.

Radiation

Fire can spread without direct contact. Nearby objects absorb electromagnetic radiation of infrared wavelengths and heat up. The black body interpretation of radiation and absorption means darker materials will tend to absorb more energy than shiny objects like metals, which reflect the radiation away. Nearby objects with a low flash point, like paper and wood, will begin to produce vapour and may burst into flame. We should therefore consider the larger environment. Near to a fire we may hear creaks and groans from stresses in structures that are rapidly heating up or cooling down, but aren't burning.

Model

All these processes in our model lead to a diverse bunch of sounds. Listed below are ten common sonic features of fire and their causes. I've ranked the list in order of importance to the sound of fire. We are going to pick only the most significant three components and combine them to create a realistic fire sound, but for truly great fire effects you might like to work your way down the remaining items on the list as a future exercise.

- lapping—combustion of gases in the air, on the combustion front (flames)
- crackling—small scale explosions caused by stresses in the fuel
- hissing—regular outgassing, release of trapped vapour
- bubbling—boiling of liquids
- creaking—internal stress of fuel expansion or nearby structures
- fizzing—aerial conflagration of small particles
- whining—periodic relaxations during outgassing
- roaring—low-frequency turbulent cycles of flames
- popping—gaseous phase explosion where heat and pressure are in phase
- clattering—settling of fuel under gravity

Method

In terms of acoustic intensity, lapping, crackling, and hissing form the dominant part of the sound of fire. We will compose each separately using subtractive synthesis based on filtered white noise, then combine these additively into the correct texture. Each sonic component will be created in its own subpatch. Several instances of each component are then blended together according to a single control for the *intensity* of the fire.

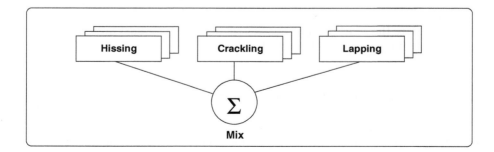

Figure 34.2
Fire components.

DSP Implementation

Hissing

Figure 34.3
Hissing1.

With only a white noise generator we already have a fair starting point for a hissing sound. But it's a constant noise. Hissing in a fire comes and goes, usually in short bursts with silence in between. What we need to do is modulate the hissing with a random low-frequency signal, but where do we get one of those? An easy way is to use another noise generator through a low pass filter. Remember that white noise contains every frequency, so it must contain some low ones as well as high ones. The low pass filter selects the ones we want. Build and listen to the patch in figure 34.3. What is wrong with this sound?

Changing the Hissing Dynamics

What's lacking in this first attempt is correct loudness and distribution. It's still an almost constant noise, occasionally getting louder or quieter. The hissing from a real fire seems much more volatile and violent. Hisses come though in loud bursts, appearing much more suddenly and much more loudly than the gentle modulation above. We need to modify the dynamics of the low-frequency modulator and we do this by taking the square of the modulating signal. Taking the square of a normalised signal makes values close to 1.0 pass through unaltered but makes lower values much quieter. It expands the dynamic range of the modulator signal. Because the average level is now lower we must amplify the result to get back to a sensible level. Listen to the patch of figure 34.4 and compare it with the previous patch. What differences do you hear? There should be bits where the hissing almost completely disappears leaving silence, with occasional loud bursts of noise.

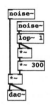

Figure 34.4
Hissing2.

O— Keypoint
Raising a normalised signal to a fixed power expands its dynamics. Conversely, taking the root of a normalised signal compresses its dynamics.

That's almost what we want, but the sound is still a little too regular. Let us continue applying the squaring technique to increase dynamic range. We increase the expansion to the 4th power by squaring again. This time the signal almost vanishes, so we need to boost it again, by ten times. This value needs to be carefully selected. A 4th power is a large expansion and we can easily end up with a signal that is far too quiet one moment and much too loud the

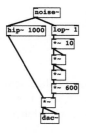

next. The trick is to balance the makeup gain block with the preamplification. I started with 2.0 and 2,000 then adjusted both values until it sounded right. You will frequently need to use this technique of adjusting the input and output ranges of a function. Sometimes the best values must be found by trial and error. The best way is to attach some sliders to the multiplication blocks and then play with them until it works. Once you have the correct values you may hard-code them back in as fixed values and remove any variables like sliders.

Figure 34.5
Hissing3.

O━ Keypoint

Instead of calculating scaling values sometimes you must find the sweet spot of a function by hand. Use sliders to fine tune the domain and range before fixing these values in code.

Changing the Hissing Tone

Listen carefully to your work at this point and compare it to some examples of recorded fire. There are a few too many low frequencies in the hissing sound that make it sound a bit "wide." Adding a `hip~` filter fixes this. Roughly, the sound of escaping gas is related to the volume moving relative to the aperture size. Gas escaping from a burning solid forces its way through tiny cracks and channels just a few millimeters wide creating a high pitched sound.

Optimisations

Remember that we intend to run our procedural sounds in real time. One of our goals in designing practical procedural sound effects is to use the minimum processing power required to achieve the desired effect. Often we need to work through our code, making small improvements on the first attempt. Notice the optimisation which incrementally improves our hissing sound generator. We have reused the same noise source to derive both the low-frequency modulator and the high-frequency signal source. This is okay to do here, but for a number of reasons we will discuss shortly it isn't always acceptable to reuse signal generators in this way.

Crackling

Fire crackles are short, sharp explosions, often in wood, coal, or other solids where a piece of material disintegrates under pressure. Because our effect is for a hypothetical, generalised fire, we don't know the exact size and material of the fragments.

We will construct a crackle generator that can approximate
a range of tones that might be found in burning coal, wood, and
cardboard. Again we start with a noise source. To get a short
snap begin by modulating it with a tight envelope of 20ms.
The envelope is produced using a line segment generator which
jumps immediately to 1.0, then quickly decays back to zero.
Again we obtain a square law decay, closer to a natural envelope found in real sounds.

Figure 34.6
Crackling1.

Crackle Density and Control

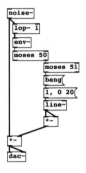

Figure 34.7
Crackling2.

As it stands we must manually fire the envelope generator
in figure 34.6 by pressing the bang message. That's no good.
We need it to automatically produce intermittent crackles
at random times. In figure 34.7 we obtain a random trigger. Again a `lop~` provides a slowly moving random source.
Instead of using it directly as a modulator we convert it to a
control signal, using the `env~` unit which gives the RMS value
of the input signal as a control rate float between 0.0 and
100, representing the decibel amplitude. A pair of stream
splitters using `moses` create a window right in the middle of
this range. Each time the input signal crosses into this range
it passes through and triggers the line envelope. Remember that the values here are floats, not integers, so a `select`
object would be inappropriate. Changing the low pass filter
frequency alters the signal volatility and hence the number
of times per second it crosses its midpoint. This gives us a
simple way to control crackle density.

Crackle Tone

Right now, every crackle sounds the same. We would like
a bit of variety in the sounds. To get some colour and
variation we can do two things. First we can make the
decay time of each crackle a little different. Recall the
Gabor period and that short sounds have a somewhat
different property than longer ones. By varying their
duration we create clicks that seem to change in tone.
We substitute a random number into the decay time
of the envelope. Since we started with a fixed decay of
20ms let's make it a random range up to 30ms. Furthermore, we can explicitly make the tone of each crackle
unique using a resonant filter. That's achieved by adding
a random number to the frequency input of our filter.
Of course we need to choose an appropriate range of
random numbers here too. Those between 100 and 1000
give good frequencies for burning wood, but in the patch
of figure 34.8 we allow crackles over most of the audio

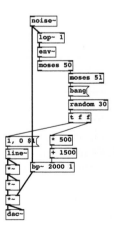

Figure 34.8
Crackling3.

spectrum, between 1.5kHz and 16.5kHz. Now we have crackles that vary in tone and duration. This combination gives a realistic result.

Flames

Figure 34.9
Lapping1.

So far so good. But our fire is still missing one essential element: the roaring, lapping sound made by burning gas. The sound of flames burning is a low "woofing" noise. To focus the frequencies into the right range a `lop~` unit is used. On its own a single `lop~` unit is too mild; we still have a lot of mid and high frequencies getting through. Also the tone of a real flame has a resonance to it.

Resonance comes about because the pressure created by the burning gas effectively creates a tube of air in which the sound resonates. So how do we achieve this? By using a resonant band pass filter we get a little closer to the sound we want. A couple of small problems remain. There's a bit too much low frequency in the sound. Components below 20Hz are inaudible but they still have an effect on the digital sound signal.

Figure 34.10
Lapping2.

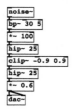

Figure 34.11
Lapping3.

Frequencies close to zero waste the available dynamic range. We remove them here using a `hip~` unit at 25Hz. Also the flame generator and the hiss generator suffer from being a bit too lively in dynamics. Sometimes they go over level when played loudly, but when we attenuate them they are too quiet. We can fix this problem by using a `clip~` unit to cap the level. This limiting, even though it introduces distortion, is acceptable here because the signal goes over level infrequently and the distortions introduced actually improve the sound somewhat. For rare cases where the modulation drifts too high and causes the `clip~` to briefly lock at a constant DC signal, an extra `hip~` fixes things.

Putting It All Together

To create the composite effect, the parts are now mixed. We create a single unit consisting of three separate parts. Before wrapping up this exercise let's make an optimisation. Each of the units that generate lapping, crackling, and hissing are based on a noise generator, so can't we just factor it out and use the same generator for all of them? This is an interesting question, one we have already considered when building the hiss generator. The answer is "It depends." For some applications this would be a bad idea; it would reduce the degree of variation in the sound because all the units would react in unison to a common signal. But for fire the

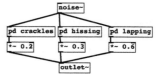

Figure 34.12
Fire generator.

answer is surprisingly **yes**. It's not only an optimisation, it's an improvement and a great idea. Why? Because the noises we hear have a common causal linkage. Fire tends to rise up and wane in such a way that crackles, hiss, and lapping all move together, so making the noise source a common unit improves the overall sound in a subtle way by adding some coherency.

O— Keypoint
DSP optimisation by reuse depends on causal correlation. Some sounds are features of the same underlying process and signals can be combined, while others are independent and must be kept separate.

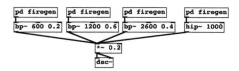

Figure 34.13
Fire-all.

Finally, we want a big roaring fire, not the small sound our single fire generator gives. Let's arrange a bunch of them, each with slightly different settings, into the mix to create a big fire sound. A collection of four fire generators that gives an impressive sound is shown in figure 34.13. Should we factor out the noise generator one more time? This time the answer is no: we want some degree of chaos and incoherency in the mix, so let's allow each fire generator to have its own random basis.

Results

◀ Source . . . . <http://mitpress.mit.edu/designingsound/
fire.html>

Conclusions

Physics-based component analysis can be a powerful tool. Reducing a sound to separate phenomena and synthesising each separately provides a great deal of control. For extents like fire and water a subtractive approach starting from white noise is appropriate. Optimisations can be made by factoring out generators or resonators if all components share a causal link that includes them.

Exercises

Exercise 1

To simulate an absolutely top whack fire we would build unit generators for each of the model components. But simply having them all running together would be naive. There is a proper causal linkage between events in a fire. To get the fire to build up properly we would start with a little smouldering, then crackling and lapping, building up to grand ensemble of boiling and fizzing when the fire is most active. Certain occurrences like hissing and bubbling may go together in groups. A wood fire is often said to "spit" as oils inside the wood evaporate, which is immediately followed by an upsurge in the amount of flames as flammable fuels vapourise. Have a go at creating some of the other texture generators. Perhaps you can create a common control to set the intensity of your fire with distinct levels of combustion in which different generators become more active.

Exercise 2

A spectrogram analysis of fire would be too confusing to print in this textbook and of limited use, so I have avoided it and relied on the physical analysis. See if you can obtain a high-resolution spectrogram of a real fire recording and try to match features we have discussed to components heard in the recording. Print out the spectrograph on a large sheet or use a graphics package to notate the spectrogram to show where you think crackles, hisses, pops, or other features appear.

Exercise 3

Try to reverse the process in exercise 1 and produce the sound of a fire being extinguished with water. Listen to some recordings of this first. Explain why you might hear a big increase in shrieking and whining components. What is happening to the water?

References

Razus, D., Oancea, D., Chirila, F., Ionescu, N. I. (2003). "Transmission of an explosion between linked vessels." *Fire Safety Journal* 38, no. 2 (March 2003): 147–163.

35

Practical 12
Bubbles

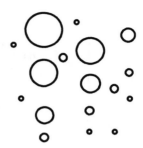

Produce the sound of liquid bubbling, taking into account physical factors such as fluid density, viscosity, depth, rate of bubble formation, and the nature of the gas source.

Analysis

The bubbles we are interested in here are fluids within other fluids, specifically gas bubbles in a liquid. A bubble is little piece of something that is where it doesn't belong. It doesn't belong there because it's in conflict with its environment and doesn't mix with it. Were this not the case bubbles would either float happily about underwater or the air would redissolve back into the water. On all sides are water molecules pressing inwards trying to crush the bubble. It therefore assumes the minimum surface area possible, which is a sphere. We take water to be an incompressible fluid and the air to be elastic. In this view the air in the bubble is a spring and the surrounding water is a mass. Consider a complementary phenomenon, a balloon filled with water. If you've made balloon water bombs you understand how they wobble like a jelly. Underwater a bubble wobbles like a jelly too, albeit under a slightly different balance of forces. In figure 35.1 we see the familiar time and spectrogram analysis of a sample sound. It's the sound of bubbles surfacing in a bath tub. The plot was made with a small window for good time resolution, so it looks a bit blurred. Study it briefly now. We will return to this later and it will make much more sense.

Quantisation of Regular Gas Flow

It's quite clear that bubbles are discrete events. Bubbles from some source of gas under pressure appear in a quantised form by a process of relaxation, much like a dripping tap. Recall from our earlier studies of oscillations that a dripping tap and underwater bubbles are complementary phenomena, a case of *quantisation*, where the energy stream is split into packets or quanta (droplets or bubbles here). A dripping tap or bubbling gas under constant pressure releases each drop or bubble at regular intervals. One force must overcome another force that resists movement. For a drip the surface tension of the water holds it back.

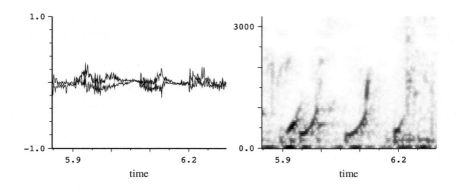

Figure 35.1
Bubble analysis.

Once the drip becomes big and heavy enough it detaches from the reservoir of water building in the tap and falls under gravity. For bubbles, the driving force is the pressure of the gas and the opposing force is surface tension, working to adhere the bubble to the larger body of gas. Pressure around the bubble trying to force it into a sphere will eventually overcome the surface tension and the bubble *pinches off*. However, it's rarely the case that water bubbles form under constant pressure; instead they tend to come in bursts which decay in frequency followed by a period of few bubbles, and then another burst. The reason for this involves some complex dynamics; let us just say that once some bubbles have started moving other bubbles find it easier to break through for a short while. We will revisit this concept again when we look at electricity, a phenomenon that shares some behaviour with fluids.

Speed of Bubble Motion

An alternative way of thinking about the bubble is as a place where there isn't any water: it's not the bubble moving up so much as the water falling down. Wherever the water is, it always falls with a constant force of gravity, and so the bubble rises with the same force, which we call the *upthrust*. The force exerted on a submerged body by buoyancy equals the weight of displaced fluid, which is Archimedes' Principle. Ignoring fluid friction for a moment, a constant force causes a constant acceleration (g), which is the gravitational constant, approximately 9.8. So bubbles emerging from the bottom of a pond will get further apart as they rise towards the surface.

Terminal Velocity

Additionally, a bubble rising through water experiences forces of fluid friction and turbulence. These create an opposing force proportional to velocity, so just as a body falling in the air reaches a terminal (maximum) velocity, so it is for a bubble when the frictional forces due to its upward velocity match the upthrust. A rising air bubble in water reaches a velocity of approximately

$$\frac{2}{3}\sqrt{gR} \qquad (35.1)$$

for a bubble of radius R. Everything apart from the radius is a constant. What this means to the sound is that whatever the bubble size it quickly reaches its final velocity. Now suppose a bunch of bubbles, some big, some small, were created deep in the water. The bigger ones will arrive at the surface first, followed by the smaller ones.

Size of Bubbles

In water, the volume of air halves for every 10m of depth, corresponding to a pressure increase of 1 atmosphere. The pressure increases linearly with depth, so the volume of a rising bubble increases as it moves towards the surface. This is not visible in a bath or glass of water. It's an effect that only happens in very deep water, say at least 10m deep. Bubble size can also change depending on how long the bubble remains in a liquid that contains dissolved gases. Where bubbles are formed by cavitation of dissolved gases, they tend to grow in size as they absorb more gas, something that happens in fizzy drinks. For practical purposes you can assume that a bubble keeps the same size throughout its life.

Excitation

There are three ways a bubble can be excited to make a noise. When the bubble comes from an underwater source of gas, the shock of separation from the larger body imparts an impulse to the bubble. Picture the bubble just the moment before it pinches off by watching the bubbles in a fish tank aeration pipe: it is elongated, but when the bubble pinches it snaps backwards and oscillates. A similar process happens when raindrops or stones hit water: a column of air protrudes momentarily into the water, but as the fluid collapses behind it the same pinching occurs. Another kind of impulse is imparted to a bubble during *cavitation*. This is when a bubble simply pops into existence during a pressure or temperature change in a liquid. The mode of this oscillation is slightly different from pinched bubbles since it involves a uniform explosive formation. Finally, there is the "singing bubble," which obtains its acoustic energy through frictional excitation when rising; these bubbles tend to rise in a spiral or zigzag because of their oscillating exteriors.

Underwater Bubbles

The bubble is strongly damped, so pinched and cavitated bubbles make only a short sound, less than a tenth of a second. Singing bubbles emit a sine wave mixed with a noisy component due to turbulence. Both of these are very quiet sounds that come from bubbles while they are submerged. When the bubble is much larger, deviations in shape will cause modulation of pitch. Big, non-spherical bubbles sometimes sound a bit wobbly, whereas smaller ones sound tightly pitched. Very large bubbles oscillate across two or more axes according to Laplacian equations and exhibit sounds rather like slowly modulated FM. Finally, the perception of pitch depends on the observer. Sounds from underwater don't travel into the air unless the fluid is contained in some kind of tank with thin walls. What we hear in air, where the speed of sound is slower than the liquid in which the event originated, has a different pitch.

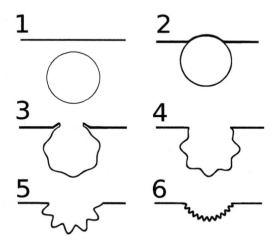

Figure 35.2
Surfacing bubble.

Frequency

The actual pitch of a bubble depends on a few things. The larger the bubble the lower the sound. But that is a very simple view. The pitch also depends on the ratio of the gas elasticity to the surrounding liquid elasticity, the restoring force, which in turn depends on pressure, which in turn depends on height in the water. The full equations for a bubble's pitch as a function of height, temperature, pressure, fluid density, and size are too complex to derive here, even in words, but for the curious the Minnaert Formula

$$f = \frac{1}{2\pi R} \times \sqrt{\frac{3\gamma P}{\rho}} \tag{35.2}$$

relates pressure P, water density ρ, ratio of gas specific heat γ, and radius R to frequency. Notice the familiar structure of the equations right-hand side, a solution to another second-order differential system. Experiments give us a value of 3kHz for a 1mm bubble.

Surfacing Bubble Sounds

What we are actually creating in this patch is the sound of a surfacing bubble, depicted in figure 35.2. This is what most people think of as "bubble sounds," not the hissing, ringing, or clicks of singing and cavitating bubbles. Excitation comes from the bubble surface being torn apart as the liquid skin maintained by surface tension breaks, forming a Helmholtz resonator.

Because it's a sphere, as it emerges the cavity diminishes, and because the same energy is squashed into an ever smaller space the frequency increases. The result is an exponentially rising sinusoidal wave in the 1kHz to 4kHz range. An idealised graph of this curve (e^x) is shown in figure 35.3 for comparison to figure 35.1. Refer back to the spectrogram analysis now and you should be able to identify the exponential rise of the two middle examples. As time moves forward the curve gets rapidly steeper.

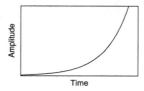

Figure 35.3
Exponential rise.

Model

An underwater source produces bubbles of varying size which rise to the surface where they pop and ring. This produces sine waves because the oscillation is strongly damped, with exponentially rising frequency because of the changing geometry. The sounds are of a fairly constant duration because the bubble velocities are relatively uniform; thus the time taken to emerge depends only on diameter. The larger (lower-frequency) ones emerge first followed by the smaller ones; thus the sound pattern tends to rise in frequency.

Method

The patch is split into two sections so we can decouple the production of underwater bubbles from their sound at the surface. A pseudo-random stream of events is derived from a sequence of small prime numbers. This drives a sound generator based on an exponential envelope and sinusoidal wave generator.

DSP Implementation

Bubbling Pattern

The timing part consists of a metronome and counter combined with a modulo operator to provide a circular counter. The abstraction in figure 35.4 has two inlets. The first is to start the metronome. The time between each increment of the counter is initially 15ms, which gives a regular timebase, and another inlet is provided to set the period. The cycle range is set by the first abstraction argument, which is substituted in the first argument of [mod]. We instantiate this object with a value of 200 so it counts between 0 and 199. What we actually want, though, is not a regular series of events. To simulate relaxation of flow a regular random source is inappropriate, which is why we haven't used an approach like that for the fire crackling generator. Something slightly different is called for here. We use a select block to output a bang when an integer between 0 and 199 matches one of its arguments. Do you recognise the numbers in the select block of figure 35.5? They are small primes in diverging ascendancy. Humans are very good at picking out patterns; we tend to notice any periodicity in a sequence if we listen to it long enough, but the primes create an illusion of a nonperiodic source because they have no common factors.

Figure 35.4
Cycle.

Furthermore, having every event produce a bubble would still be too much, so a way of culling a few events is required. Removing one in every two events is sufficient for a realistic bubbling pattern; however, we don't just want to remove each alternate event, we want to cull them randomly. By doing this the stream of events will sometimes contain longer gaps and sometimes shorter ones while still retaining the overall feel of a steady average rate. A number between 0 and 100 is generated for each event and fed to a stream splitter with a midpoint of 50. Because the random numbers are evenly distributed, on average half the events will make it through. Any number that passes through the splitter invokes a bang message. An extra inlet is given to the abstraction to adjust the probability (density) of bubbles.

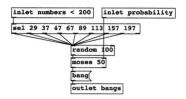

Figure 35.5
Bubble pattern.

Sound Generation

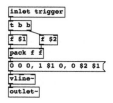

Figure 35.6
Attack decay
envelope.

The bubble sound patch will use two envelope generators, one for the pitch and another for the amplitude. First we'll make the amplitude envelope, which is a linear attack-decay line. In figure 35.6 two floats are obtained from the abstraction arguments, one for the attack time and one for the decay time, both in ms. A bang appearing at the inlet causes both of these to be packed and then substituted in a list for the vline~. It starts at 0.0, then moves to 1.0 over the attack time, and then back to 0.0 over the decay time after a delay equal to the attack time. The result is a triangular envelope peaking at 1.0 and taking a total time of *attack* + *decay*. This abstraction is named adenv.

An exponential curve generator is shown in figure 35.7. The behaviour of this abstraction, which mimics the geometry of an emerging bubble is at the heart of our sound. A float value for the duration (initially 10 so we don't accidentally produce a loud click) is provided by the first abstraction argument. Upon receiving a bang this number is substituted into a list for `vline~` as the time to rise between 0.0 to 1.0. Unlike the linear envelope, we do not use the output of `vline~` directly. First it is shaped by the function e^x, made from a constant `sig~` and a `pow~` object. This abstraction is named expcurve.

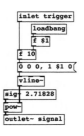

Figure 35.7
Expcurve.

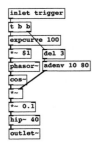

Both envelope generators are combined with an oscillator in figure 35.8. You can see the exponential curve for pitch is created with a period of 100ms, while the linear attack decay envelope has a fast attack (10ms) and slightly slower decay (80ms). So that the amplitude peaks at precisely the right point in the pitch sweep, a delay is added before it triggers. To have bubbles at different pitches we scale the pitch envelope by the first abstraction argument; typically this will be between 1kHz and 3kHz. The final output is scaled by 0.1 to get a sensible volume and a high-pass filter removes any very low frequencies.

Figure 35.8
Bubblesound1.

Putting It Together

This part is easy: all we have to do is connect the event generator to the bubble sound generator to get some results. If several instances of the bubble sound with slightly different frequencies are connected via a random selector we get a more interesting effect. We haven't dealt with the issue of bubble size yet, so we assume fairly consistent bubble sizes with similar frequencies. If you tweak the parameters in the above example you will notice that attack and pitch are linked; moving the attack also alters the apparent pitch of the bubble. This codependency is a feature of the simple model we've used, where moving the attack changes the point at which the amplitude peaks during the pitch rise.

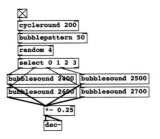

Figure 35.9
Several bubbles.

Polyphony

Listening to the patch above you will quickly notice a problem. By randomly selecting which bubble will sound from uniformly distributed numbers there's nothing to stop the same bubble generator being picked twice. If this happens

before it has finished playing then retriggering the envelopes causes the sound
to be abruptly truncated. Another limitation is that we only have four bubble pitches entered as fixed abstraction parameters. It would be nice to have a
source of bubbles that are not only random in time without the possibility of
being cut short, but random in pitch too.

Bubble Factory

The next patch rewrites the bubble sound and pattern generator to give control over the density and average pitch. It uses *round-robin* allocation. This
allocates in repeating order, 1, 2, 3, 4, 1, 2, 3, 4.... With this method we can
be sure that no bubble will cut short the previous one so long as its duration
is less than the time to cycle round all generators. Two more improvements
can be made. When the bubble pitch is high (for smaller bubbles) the duration
should be proportionally shorter, and since it contains less energy (volume) it
should be quieter. From a common parameter, bubble size, we will calculate
the pitch, duration, and amplitude as separate functions.

Here I've redesigned the envelope to show an efficiency. The curve obtained using `pow~` can be approximated for short sounds using only multiplies, which is
a little more efficient. A line generator rises immediately
to 1.0 and then falls to zero in a time given by a value
passed through the inlet. The complement of a quartic
curve appears on the first outlet, which will be used as
the bubble pitch envelope. By taking the square one more
time we obtain the 6th power, which falls to zero a little quicker than the pitch rises. This envelope replaces
the exponential rise and attack-decay used previously.
Results aren't quite as nice as before, but it shows how a

Figure 35.10
Two-curve envelope.

patch can be simplified where a less accurate model will do. This dual output
envelope is subpatched as `pd env4pow`.

Each bubble sound is going to be created by a number ranging from 0.0 to 1.0 that represents its size. So,
next we redesign the bubble sound to use the new envelope generator, with amplitude, base frequency, and
duration dependent on the supplied size parameter. A
float value appearing at the inlet is distributed to three
functions. The first (left branch) multiplies the size factor by 90ms to get longer sound durations for bigger
bubbles. In the centre branch we obtain the pitch value,
which is the complement of bubble size (bigger bubbles
having lower pitch). A scaling factor of 300Hz and an
offset of 100Hz are applied to a fixed base of 2kHz.
Finally we obtain an amplitude factor proportional to
the bubble size (right branch) and add a little offset so
that even small bubbles make a sound.

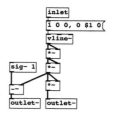

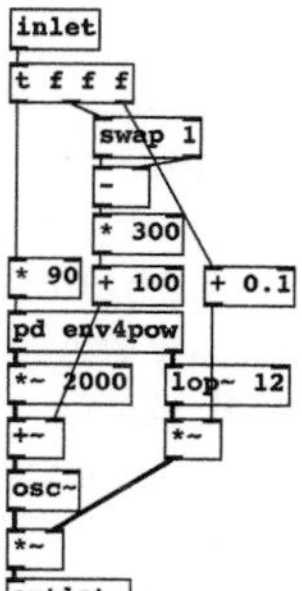

Figure 35.11
Bubble with parameters.

Finally, we combine four of these generators into a polyphonic bubbling
sound. We need a metronome to create events. As an aside, in my opinion this

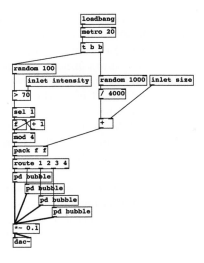

Figure 35.12
Polyphonic bubble factory.

method is lacking. It would be nice to improve it here, but we must move on. We've already looked at a time distribution based on prime numbers, but you may like to refer forwards to the Poisson time distribution examined in the chapter on raindrops. To obtain randomly distributed bubbles a uniformly distributed number between 0 and 100 is compared to an **intensity** inlet (initially 70) to see whether to generate a bang. Each bang advances a cyclic counter, the output of which becomes the first element in a list used to route the bubbles to generators. At the same time we generate a small size variation which is added to the **size** inlet. Two element lists passed to route are stripped of their first element. The remaining float is sent to one of four possible outlets, each of which activates a bubble generator. The size inlet should be between 0.0 and 1.0, and the intensity inlet should be between 70 and 99. This patch will be used in a later example for the bubbles made by poured liquids.

Conclusions

We've taken a good look at the physics of bubbles and sounds produced by the changing shape of an air cavity. Pitch is affected by the bubble size, and the rate of pitch change by the speed of the surfacing bubble. The behaviour of bubbles is determined by several factors like the density of both fluids. Bubbles from a steady source of gas behave like a relaxation oscillator.

We've seen how prime numbers can be used to produce intervals that don't sound periodic, thought about the effects of random number distributions, seen how to use the `pow~` object to create an exponential power curve, and seen how a more efficient approximation can sound almost as good.

Additionally, we have seen how to build deeper abstraction stacks where the arguments of higher ones are passed in as the arguments of deeper ones. And we have looked at polyphony, where more than one instance of the same sound happens at the same time. The problem of voice management has been explored, and we saw why round robin voice allocation is a better idea than triggering instances randomly—because the same instance may be triggered again before it has finished.

The experiments and formulas of Newton, Reynolds, Davies, Taylor, and Stokes are all important to understanding bubbles, so some are given in the references section. You are encouraged to read these, and the work of Van den Doel, to understand a more elaborate model before moving on to the next practical on flowing water.

Exercises

Exercise 1

From the Minnaert formula, how do viscosity and temperature change the sound of bubbles? What would you expect to hear from bubbling lava and boiling water?

Exercise 2

Wrap the bubble factory in a control structure so that bursts of bubbles emerge according to their size.

References

Leighton, T. G. (1994). *The Acoustic Bubble*. Academic Press London.
Leighton, T. G., and Walton, A. J. (1987). "An experimental study of the sound emitted from gas bubbles in a liquid." *Eur. J. Phys.* 8: 98–104.
Stokes, G.G. (1851). "On the effect of the internal friction of fluids on the motions of pendulums." *Cambridge Phil. Soc.* 9:8–106.
Ucke, C., and Schlichting, H. J. (1997). "Why does champagne bubble?" *Phys. Tech. Quest J.* 2: 105–108.
Walker, J. (1981). "Bubbles in a bottle of beer: Reflections on the rising." *Sci. Am.* 245: 124.

Acknowledgements

Thanks to Coll Anderson for the bubbles sample used during analysis.

36

Practical 13
Running Water

Aims

In this practical we will produce the sound of a flowing liquid such as water running in a stream. Running water is a sound we nearly synthesise quite by accident in a number of ways:

- With a randomly wobbling resonant filter applied to a complex source.
- By applying FFT-based noise reduction with a high threshold to noise.
- Subverting the MPEG audio compression algorithm.
- By granular synthesis, such as chopping speech into fragments.

None of these lends itself to efficient client-side synthesis or yields predictable results. Our aim is to reduce the process to its bare essentials and provide an efficient model for moving fluids.

Analysis

Like fire, water is an extent, emitting sound from many points. Unlike fire, it is a homogeneous production; there are many separate events but each has the same mechanism. The area of activity is the surface of the fluid, and in particular small cavities formed by turbulent flow. Water does not make a sound just because it moves; it can move silently in the right conditions. A large body of slow-moving water flowing smoothly in a stream makes practically no sound at all, as does a thin film of shallow water flowing quickly over a smooth steel plate. If we introduce irregularities or obstacles into the flow, such as placing a stick in a stream or introducing bumps and scratches to the metal plate, we hear a sound. The sound in the deep water will be much lower than that in the shallow water, and it is more intense for faster flow. The phenomenon behind the sound is turbulence, which we will look at in more detail when we consider wind, but for now let's just list the factors influencing moving fluid sounds.

- Depth.
- Speed of flow.
- Impedance. Obstacles like rocks.
- Viscosity of the fluid.

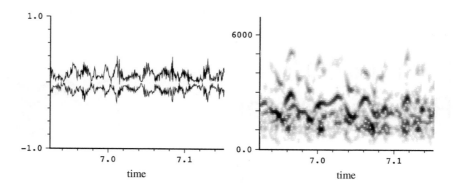

Figure 36.1
Time plot and spectrogram of running water.

In figure 36.2 we see a rock obstructing the flow of water moving left to right. At a distance from the rock the flow is regular, or *laminar*, but at the near side of the obstruction the level of the fluid is raised, causing some part of it to move outwards and downwards around the obstruction. Spinning vortices moving in opposite directions form on each side and continue downstream until they meet after a short distance on the far side of the obstruction. The front view shows the effect as these come together, creating tube-like disturbances in which air becomes trapped. Much like the bubbles we considered earlier, these change shape, narrowing and forcing the air out of the cavity to produce an oscillation. Of course, this is just one of many obstructions found on the irregular bed of a stream, and some will produce different physical movements and cavity shapes than others. Although we have not quantified "impedance" in any proper sense, it's apparent that all the other variables like speed, depth, and viscosity remain constant for any local area, so we can expect all turbulent cavities to form under nominally uniform conditions and make similar sounds.

The psychoacoustics textbook *Thinking in Sound* (McAdams and Bigand) doesn't specifically mention water in the context of auditory scene analysis, but we can use some of this perceptual psychology to understand why water is identified as such by the brain. Sounds with a common formant and similar spectra happening in a continuous timeframe are ascribed to the same source. Discrete sounds suggest a simple single source, whereas dense and complex sounds overlapping in a continuous way indicate a collection or expanse of similar sources. Uniform features of sound, like the average spectral distribution, suggest a common underlying cause, so we will tend to lump together all the little component sounds of water as one phenomenon. Flowing sounds suggest a fluid basis. But what do we mean by "flowing sounds"? A feature of running water is that each part of it seems to flow into the next. We are unable to say

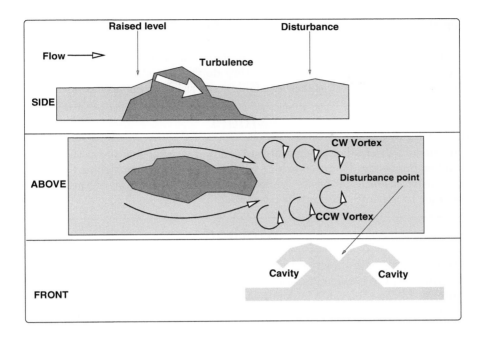

Figure 36.2
Formation of cavities by an impedance such as a rock.

where one event begins or another one ends, so we hear an unbroken stream of short events happening on top of each other as if they were one.

Let's reason by considering two limiting conditions. What is the most complex imaginable sound of water? The answer is the sea on a stormy day, or maybe the sound of a vast waterfall. What does this sound like? It sounds a lot like pure white noise, a spectrum so dense and expansive that no single event can be heard within it. On the other hand, what is the simplest sound we can associate with water? It is the bubble we created in an earlier exercise, a single event producing an almost pure sine wave. Now, this gives a clue. It would be fatuous to say that the sound of running water lies somewhere between a sine wave and noise, because all sounds do, but it isn't without merit to say that the mechanism of running water is somehow connected to the composition of thousands of droplet- or bubble-like sounds all together. These are whistles and pops of air trapped inside cavities formed under turbulence.

Looking at the features of figure 36.1 should confirm this. A spectrogram of running water looks remarkably like an artistic impression of running water. There appear to be waves. Sometimes they disappear from view or are obscured beneath other waves that cross them. Each is a narrow band of frequencies caused by trapped air singing in a cavity. Each trace in the ensemble of over-lapping lines is presumably a single resonating cavity. As with bubbles, the cavity is diminishing in time, so the spectrogram lines tend to rise as the frequency increases. But unlike bubbles they don't move cleanly in one direction; they wobble and distort, sometimes falling and rising again as they decay away.

Model

Our model will produce an ensemble of gradually rising sine waves that wobble at a low frequency. Their behaviour will be random, but constrained to behave in a distribution appropriate for water. We will need many of them layered together to generate the correct effect.

Method

The sonic properties described above lend themselves well to granular synthesis. However, the implementation we are going to build is not strictly granular synthesis in the commonly understood sense. The term "granular" applies well to the model, but not necessarily to the implementation. We won't use lookup tables or fixed envelope functions as with orthodox granular synthesis. So, when we say "running water is a granular sound," that doesn't imply that we must use a particular implementation or technique to produce it; in fact it would be rather inefficient to do so. We will design an algorithm that takes the inherent properties of properly distributed noise and applies this to the pitch and amplitude characteristics of another source. Technically we might call this a modulation method, a mixture of AM and FM using noise. As you will see, it's really a development of the bubble patch, with a few efficient tricks to make it compact. Let's develop it in a few steps to make the reasoning clearer.

DSP Implementation

Simple Moving Water

We'll begin by taking a sine wave and applying a randomly moving signal to its

frequency; this should give us a texture that at least hits on some of the properties we would expect to find in moving water. An important choice is the granularity, or the frequency of the controlling low-frequency source. We begin with control rate signals producing variations in the 1ms to 100ms range.

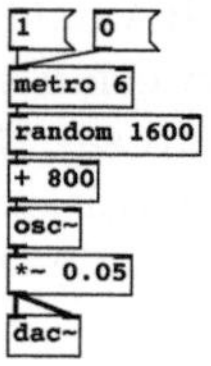

The Pure Data patch in figure 36.3 uses a metronome to trigger random numbers in the range of interest. We don't want fluctuations going all the way down to zero, so let's add a fixed offset of a few hundred Hz to get the base of the sound spectrum. Notice that the patch is attenuated quite a lot, as it's possible to make some unpleasant sounds this way. The

Figure 36.3
Message rate
random sines.

first thing wrong with this result is an occasional clicking. It may have a vague resemblance to water, but also to a kind of alien sound like a broken shortwave radio. When the random generator switches values there's no reason it won't happen right in the middle of an oscillator cycle, and if the new value is very different from the previous one we hear an unpleasant discontinuity. Another thing wrong is the balance of rising and falling frequencies. As we saw from the analysis the predominant behaviour of the sine sweeps is upwards, with the diminishing cavities, and far fewer move down except briefly. At present our patch gives an equal balance of up and down sweeps.

Slew and Differentiation

The next patch improves things with three tricks. First, an audio rate line segment is set to track the incoming random values at a fixed rate of change. This gives a *slew rate*, a minimum time the signal can take to move between any two values. Also we'll add a low pass filter in an attempt to knock down any corner transitions containing too much high frequency. Finally, we'll use differentiation with `fexpr~` and `clip~` to get changes that are positive. Modulating the sine wave by positive excursions means we get rising sine segments.

Starting with a `metro` set to 12ms, a random number between 400 and 2000 is created and packed into a list for `line~` along with a `slew` value (between 0 and 5). The oscillator is therefore wiggling around making random frequencies, but can only slide between them at the slew rate. Meanwhile we apply `fexpr~` with the expression $x1 - $x1[-1]. This expression means: return a signal that is the current signal (at the inlet) minus the last signal sample. It is a one-sample difference equation. By clipping this to a range of 0 to 1 we ignore any negative differences which happen when the signal is falling. Adding a bit of low pass at 10Hz avoids any abrupt changes, so when the oscillator is modulated with this control signal we mainly hear smoothly rising sine bursts (with occasional downward dips that slip through).

Figure 36.4
Applying slew and
differentiation.

Bilinear Exponential Distribution

There's still a few things not right, though. One is the frequency distribution. Our random source gives a range of uniformly distributed values, and that's not what we want. Our ears tend to notice a pitch centroid or mean pitch value in natural sounds. In any given situation the most likely frequency range is quite narrow, and other frequencies above and below this become increasingly unlikely.

In many natural processes this distribution is exponential, so it's very likely that a subsequent frequency will be close to a recent value, but very unlikely it

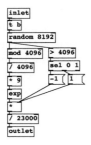

Figure 36.5
Bilinear exponential
random numbers.

will be far away. The patch shown in figure 36.5 produces bilinear exponential random noise centered around zero. It produces a pattern of numbers that are both negative and positive with a strong tendency to be close to zero. We start by picking a random integer from a fairly big range of 8192 in order to have sufficient resolution. If this number is greater than 4,096 (half the range) then we multiply the output by +1 making it positive; otherwise a multiplier of −1 gives us a negative output. With ▣mod and ▢ it's processed into to a range between 0 to 1; then multiplying by 9 before ▣exp and dividing by 23000 afterwards coerces the final range to be between −1.0 and +1.0.

Flowing Water Generator

Finally, let's insert the new random distribution into a slightly modified version of the last moving water patch.

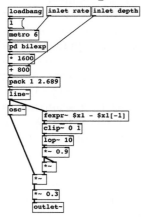

Figure 36.6
Running water with correct
distribution.

The main change you can see in figure 36.6 is the addition of a squaring function in the differentiator branch. Without it the effect sounds a little too noisy and dense, but this expands the range so we only hear the strongest changes. The addition of inlets and outlets can now be made to obtain a reusable subpatch or abstraction. These correspond to **rate** to control the metronome (which sets the density and apparent rate of flow), and **depth** to set the central frequency. A slew rate of 2.69 is hardwired into the patch. You can change this to whatever you like to create slightly different water effects. A low value makes a much "harder" sound that is more like drips or poured water, while a larger value gives a gentle, soft flow more like a stream. You may also like to change the 1,600 multiplier for frequency. A lower value will give a deeper-sounding effect, like a large slow moving stream. On its own the sound of this moving water generator is quite weak, so you should instantiate three or four and play with the input values to hear an effect with more density and variation.

Results

Source . . . . <http://mitpress.mit.edu/designingsound/water.html>

Conclusions

The sound of running water is made by many small cavities resonating. We can approximate this behaviour by modulating the frequency and amplitude of a sine wave with the first difference of low-frequency noise. The correct noise distribution is needed to make the effect realistic.

Exercises

Exercise 1

Starting with nice clean recordings of running water, analyse the spectrograms. What are the average frequency variations? Either by inspection, or using a statistical package, what relationships can you find between this average and depth or speed of flow?

References

Franz, G. J. (1959). "Splashes as sources of sound in liquids." *J. Acoust. Soc. Am.* 31: 1080–1096.

Minnaert, M. (1933). "On musical air-bubbles and the sounds of running water." *Phil. Mag.* 16: 235–248.

Mallock, A. (1919). "Sounds produced by drops falling on water." *Proc. R. Soc.* 95: 138–143.

McAdams, S., and Bigand, E. (1993). *Thinking in Sound: The Cognitive Psychology of Human Audition.* Oxford University Press.

Pumphrey, H. C., and Walton, A. J. (1988). "An experimental study of the sound emitted by water drops impacting on a water surface." *Eur. J. Phys.* 9: 225–231.

Van den Doel, K. (2004). "Physically based models for liquid sounds." *Proc. ICAD 04-Tenth Meeting of the International Conference on Auditory Display,* Sydney, Australia, July 6–9.

37

Practical 14
Pouring

Aims

Our aims here are to use a model of poured liquids in a small container to illustrate codependent parameters. We will create the sound of water pouring into a glass from a constant height at a constant rate and see how this breaks down into several parameters that are linked.

Analysis

Study the process depicted in figure 37.1 where a glass is filled from a tap. Although the glass is shown as a conical section we will assume it has straight sides and so the volume is directly proportional to the height of liquid in the vessel Dl. As time progresses, Dl, which is the integral of a constant rate of flow, increases until the glass is full. At the same time, four other variables decrease. I have shown them as linear changes on an arbitrary axis separated only for illustration. The first of these is Dc, the height of the column of water from the tap to the liquid surface in the glass. As Dl increases Dc gets smaller, so $Dc = Dco - Dl$ where Dco was the initial distance from the tap to the bottom of the empty glass. Also decreasing in an opposite relationship is De, the height (and hence volume) of the empty space above the liquid. Having fallen through a height Dc the water gains kinetic energy, so it penetrates the surface drawing down bubbles and making a sound. The depth of penetration Dp and the average size of the bubbles formed are also proportional to this energy. Since $v^2 = v_0^2 + 2gx$ and $E_k = 1/2mv^2$, for mass (m), height (x), initial velocity v_0, and gravitational acceleration (g), the net result is that most of these terms cancel out and the penetration depth and bubble size is proportional to the column height Dl. Substituting $E_k = 1/2m(v_0^2 + 2gx)$, and with $v_0 = 0$, $E_k = mgx$. For constant flow and hence mass m and constant acceleration g, we get $E_k = x$. Since $x = D_c$ (the distance from the tap) is decreasing, so is E_k, which means less water is displaced by the flow and depth Dp decreases too.

Model

We know that the sound of water depends on the rate of flow and the depth of the water, so as the liquid level increases this pitch parameter will decrease.

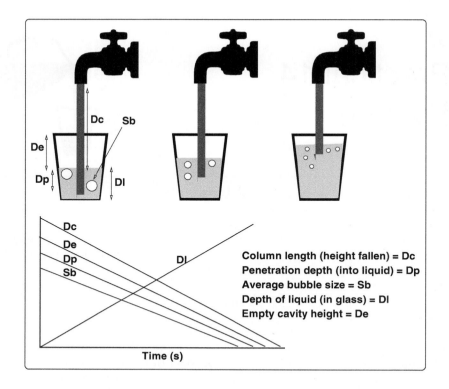

Figure 37.1
Water poured into a glass from constant height.

And we know that the size of emerging bubbles determines their frequency, so these will increase in pitch as the level rises. Finally, we know that a half-open tube will give a quarter wavelength resonance that depends on its length, so we have a resonance that increases in frequency with liquid volume. So, in summary, we have:

- A turbulent liquid flow of constant rate whose energy decreases with time.
- A volume of liquid whose depth is increasing in time.
- Production of bubbles (exponentially rising sine waves) whose diameter decreases with time.
- The above sounds contained in an open tube whose length decreases (resonant frequency increases) with time.

Method

We will take our flowing water and bubble models from previous chapters and combine them with a resonant tube model. The parameters of each will be expressed as functions of a single time parameter for how full the glass is.

DSP Implementation

We've already seen how to make a bubble factory and how to make running water. Those patches will be reused here. You will see them in the context of the final patch shortly.

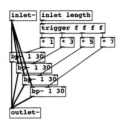

The only thing we haven't seen so far is the vessel itself, a model of a semi-closed pipe with a changeable length. Recall that a resonance in a semi-open pipe must have an antinode at one end and a node at the other, so it acts to emphasise odd harmonics. Here we have four band-pass filters set to 1, 3, 5, and 7 times the main frequency. A resonance of about 30 seems to work well for this application. Because the bubbles and running water produce fairly pure tones, this needs choosing well. Too high and peaks will blast through much too loud when they coincide with a res-

Figure 37.2
Semi-open pipe.

onance. Too low and the effect of the resonance will be hard to hear against a background of such pure tones. The effect comes to life as you move the frequency, so long as the water flow density is high enough.

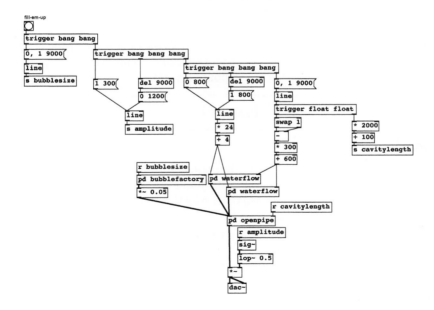

Figure 37.3
Water poured into vessel changing four codependent parameters simultaneously.

All the important parts of the implementation are shown in figure 37.3. It is basically four line generators which move all the parameters in the right range and time. The pouring gesture takes 9s in total, so each line segment scans over this time. The first line (left) raises the bubble size between the largest and smallest available. The second provides an overall amplitude to the effect, rising quickly in 300ms to full volume and then decaying in 1.2s after a 9s delay. The next line scans the rate of water flow. This is mainly constant, but to add realism for a pouring effect I've made it build from zero to full flow in 800ms and decay away in the same time once the vessel is filled. Next we have the depth of the liquid, which increases with time; however, since this is a frequency factor expressed internally as a period in the `waterflow` subpatch it's inverted in our control section. And finally, we change the cavity size, which is the length of the semi-open pipe model, sweeping from a few hundred Hertz to about 2kHz over the 9s period.

Results

◀ **Source** . . . . <**http://mitpress.mit.edu/designingsound/ pouring.html**>

Conclusions

Liquids filling a vessel change the acoustic space they occupy since the surface behaves as a reflector at the closed end of a quarter wavelength tube. Combining liquid models with a new context and thinking about the linked parameter changes gives us a way to synthesise poured water.

Exercises

Exercise 1

Write a patch for a slide whistle with a noisy flute-like excitation. Experiment with pipe resonances at inharmonic ratios and see if you can emulate a Swany whistle (often used for locomotive/train whistles in cartoons).

References

Benson, D. J. (2007). Section 3.5, "Wind instruments." In *Music: A Mathematical Offering*, pp. 107–112. Cambridge.
Cook, P. R. (2002). Appendix C, "Acoustic tubes." In *Real Sound Synthesis for Interactive Applications*, pp. 225–231. A. K. Peters.
Olson, H. F. (1952). Chapter 4, "Resonators and Radiators," section entitled "Open and closed pipes." In *Music, Physics, and Engineering*, pp. 83–100. Dover.

38

Practical 15
Rain

Aims

In this practical we will produce the effect of rain falling. We will consider the effect of short-pressure signatures as excitors for other materials and investigate another kind of statistical distribution.

Analysis

Rain is made of nearly spherical water particles approximately 1mm to 3mm in diameter. They fall at constant velocity, impacting with a variety of materials at a typical flux of $200/m^2/s$. Within any local sample all raindrops have already attained terminal velocity, so relative to one another there are no fast or slow ones. All are roughly the same size, a factor determined by their formation at precipitation under nominally uniform conditions. In different conditions the size and velocity will vary; a light mist or drizzle has much smaller drops than a heavy downpour. Because of air resistance the drop size determines their terminal velocity, which increases with larger droplets. Under normal gravity and air density 1mm drops reach about 2m/s, rising to around 10m/s for 5mm drops. Finally, raindrops are not "tear-shaped" as is commonly held. Small ones are near perfect spheres whereas bigger ones become vertically squashed (a burger shape). The factor making rain a nonuniform sound and giving it a diverse range of pitches and timbres is what it hits. Sometimes it falls on leaves, sometimes on the pavement, or on a tin roof, or into a puddle of rainwater.

Model

Impacting a Solid Surface

For a perfect droplet and surface, the model is simple. A direct geometric model yields the wave equation during collision (Miklavcic, Zita, and Arvidsson 2004). We won't reproduce this here except to say that for an unbounded, nonpenetrative impact of a fluid sphere against an immovable boundary it's possible to calculate (from Green's function and Sommerfield radiation equations) the exact air pressure signature. It looks like the curve shown in figure 38.1, which is a parabolic section. You can see how this shape arises since the pressure on the surface is proportional to the area of a slice through the sphere which is moving at constant velocity. Out of interest, I have shown the behaviour and shape of the liquid beyond the impact site on the right of the diagram. This conical "crater" shape is probably familiar from high-speed photographs of liquid impacts. It comes about because the water moves outwards faster than the surface tension and surface friction will allow it to. It has similarities to Rayleigh waves seen on the beach as ocean waves break, with the top part moving in a circular fashion over the slower underside until it falls over itself. It's also worth noting that on an irregular surface, or at high enough impact speeds, the droplet just fragments. It shatters into many other smaller ones which then give rise to secondary audible impacts. If the surface is a window pane or metal

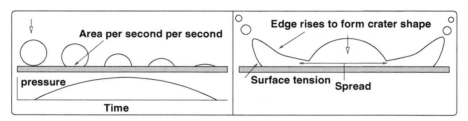

Figure 38.1
Waveform produced by impact of fluid sphere on hard surface.

roof then we can model the sound as excitation of a laminar structure by an impulse of this shape. If the surface is flexible, such as a leaf which yields to the impact, then the pressure curve is elongated. For semi-hard granular materials like soil and sand, the pressure curve creates a noisy disturbance modulated by the droplet signature. During such impacts, particles may be dislodged or suspended in small droplets and carried up to 1.5m from the impact to create further acoustic events. Think of rain on dry sand.

Impacting on a Liquid

A significant change occurs when the droplet impacts and penetrates another pool of water (see fig. 38.2). Van den Doel (2005) has made accurate synthetic models of the acoustics when a bubble is formed by the impact. As we have seen with poured water, the bubbles form when a cavity is drawn down (entrained) into the fluid which then closes (pinches off) behind the drop. A conical crater formed from the remaining energy may act as a horn amplifier for the whistle produced when the bubble collapses.

Method

Our method is a noise-based approach that uses waveshaping to turn a properly distributed noise signal into short parabolic pulses of the correct density and amplitude.

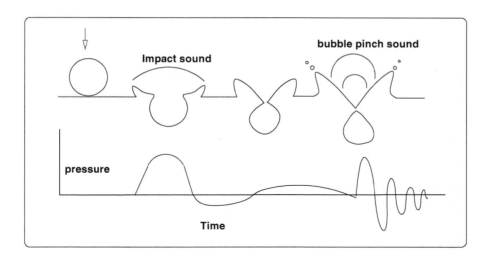

Figure 38.2
Waveform produced when raindrop hits water.

DSP Implementation

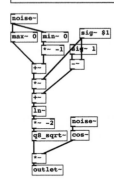

Figure 38.3
Obtaining a Gaussian noise distribution.

First let's create a source of Gaussian noise. This has a particular property sometimes called *normal distribution*. The rainfall is uniform, but for an observer in the middle of an area the average amplitude pattern of drops over time forms a bell-shaped curve when plotting the probability of all amplitudes. Note that this isn't to do with the frequencies in the noise, which will still be uniform (white noise). When we use white noise with a uniformly distributed amplitude the regularity makes the rain sound slightly wrong. Gaussian white noise can be achieved by adding up 12 or more uniform white noise sources and dividing by the total. The "central limit" theorem says that this causes the mean amplitude to form a Gaussian distribution, but using 12 sources is an expensive way to get such a subtle change. A more compact method is shown in figure 38.3 where a bell-shaped distribution is obtained from a variation of the Box–Muller transform. This transform allows us to obtain a normally distributed noise signal S_n by combining two uniform noise sources S_{u1} and S_{u2} through the equation:

$$S_n = \sqrt{-2 \ln S_{u1}} \cos(2\pi S_{u2}) \tag{38.1}$$

Notice the use of the quick square root function. We don't need good accuracy for this part so it's a perfect place to use an approximate square root instead of a more accurate and costly one. Note also that the natural base ⌈ln~⌉ is equivalent to ⌈log~⌉ with no arguments.

Rain on Ground

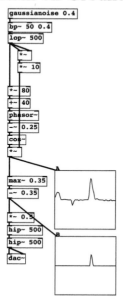

A drop generator for light rain on solid ground is shown in figure 38.4. Gaussian noise is filtered to obtain a low-frequency fluctuation which modulates the frequency of an oscillator around 40Hz to 80Hz and multiplies this by 10 times its square. This waveform is shown in graph **A**. As you can see, it has the correct features, but it also has some negative pulses and a few small ones. On its own this works well, since we can't hear that some drops are negative. Smaller ones just sound like more distant drops. However, I have included another stage to show how these can be refined to get a sparser pattern of drops that sound like light raindrops. By thresholding the signal and recentering it back to zero the result is a nicely distributed pattern of positive pulses. They may seem too bassy, but in fact, if you listen to large raindrops close to the point of hitting the earth they do sound low in frequency. From a typical observation point a few meters away the low frequencies are much weaker, so a high pass filter is needed to get the effect of rainfall on the ground nearby.

Figure 38.4
Deriving the pressure
signature of raindrops.

Raindrops on Lamina (Glass Window/Roof)

To get good rain effects we need to give each object that it might fall on a method for making sound when hit by rain. Obviously, in a real game world it would be too expensive to have every single object produce its own rain sound,

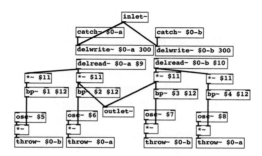

Figure 38.5
A dispersive laminar model.

so we focus on a few that are close to the observer. The remaining sound can be given by a general ambiance, which we will look at last in this chapter.

Here is a window model. Since we are dealing with rain here I will not go into this in great detail, other than to explain it generally and say that its purpose is to sound like a sheet of glass or metal when hit by small impacts. It is a kind of waveguide or reverb with two recirculating delays. The trick is that it also contains four modulators connected to an oscillator that shift the sidebands further away from the resonant frequency each time they circulate through the delays. This has a dispersive effect. The delay times give the general dimensions of the plate, so I've chosen some values that sound like a glass window, about $1m^2$. The modulation frequencies set the bands that spectral dispersion will force the sidebands to group around. These frequencies are chosen to be close to those for a square plate. It's a tricky patch to set up, because it can become unstable easily. You can also use this abstraction to make thin steel or plastic laminas.

```
raindrops 70 0.2
hip~ 9000
*~ 10
glasswindow 2007 1994 1986 1969 254 669 443 551 3.7 4.2
0.61 2.3
dac~
```

Figure 38.6
Rain on the window.

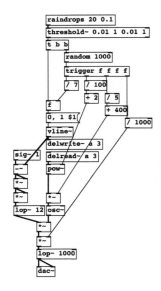

Figure 38.7
Rain on water.

Our first raindrop signature generator is abstracted, with the initial frequency of the noise filter and thresholds presented as two arguments. Combined with some high pass filtering and applied to the glass window patch we get the sound of rain on a window.

Raindrops on Water

This is a water droplet generator similar to an earlier bubble noise patch. I have used the previous drop generator in order to demonstrate a method of synchronising new audio events to existing ones. Beneath the drop generator in figure 38.7 you see a `threshold~` object. This produces a bang when the audio signal entering its first inlet rises above a certain level (given by the first argument). Each time this happens we trigger a new line envelope and generate a fresh random number. This number is used to obtain the duration, curve order, base frequency, and amplitude of each sinusoidal sweep. Using a signal delay is an interesting way of avoiding two envelopes for the amplitude and frequency. Since frequency envelope runs opposite to the amplitude, but is delayed slightly in time, we use the same line generator to derive both. A low pass on the quartic amplitude control stops the attack being too harsh if the duration is short.

Interval and Frequency

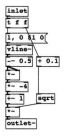

Figure 38.8
Random width pulse.

Let's think about the limitations of what we've done so far. The drop generator we just made gives a random (Gaussian) distribution of intensity, but the drop signatures have a more or less fixed width, which is tied to their interval. Because we frequency modulated a `phasor~` the faster the drops happen the shorter they are. This correlation is unnatural, but we get away with it because the generator is designed for light rain patterns and the sound produced has so far been determined by another resonant system that gets excited. If we continue adding resonators for every raindrop it's going to get expensive quickly. What would be useful is a way to get an intermediate density of rain with a controllable spectrum and distribution, without the fuss of having resonators.

Recall how Gabor gives us the key to solving this. Small pulses below 20ms in duration produce clicks whose apparent frequency is inversely proportional to their period. If we create pulses that approximate a parabolic pressure curve of a drop, but make these short, it's possible to control their perceived spectrum without any further resonators. In figure 38.8 small values at the inlet create short line segments that are shaped into a parabolic pulse. Their intensity is inversely proportional to their frequency: it's the square root of their period (plus a small offset), which compensates for the Fletcher–Munsen effect that would make the bright drops seem excessively loud. This brings the frequencies closer to a $1/f$ or pink distribution.

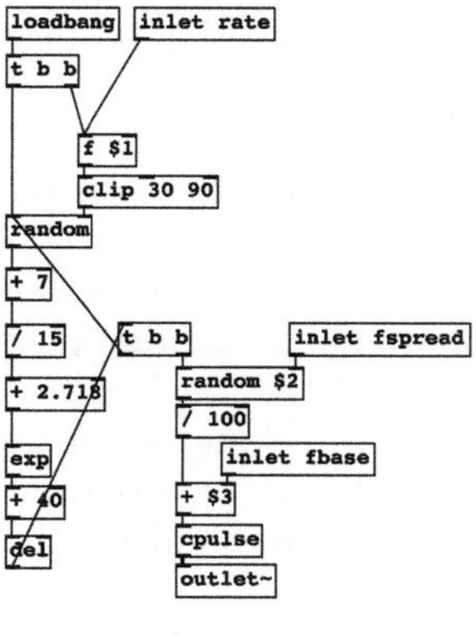

Each of these click generators will be contained in a timing patch shown in figure 38.9. You can see that this has neither a metronome nor phasor, but works in an endless loop by feeding back an initial message from `loadbang` through a `delay` and creating a random delay each time. Note here the way we use `exp` to create exponentially distributed delay periods. The rest of the operations are fudge factors to place the delay times in a sensible range so that an argument of 50 for $1 gives a reasonable rate. Generating random time periods with this distribution gives us Poisson timing, which happens to be the same as that observed for rainfall. Spread and lower (base) values for the click period are

Figure 38.9
Poisson interval.

given by parameters \$2 and \$3. The click generator itself, `cpulse`, sits next to the outlet. A spread of 12ms and lower limit of 0.1ms works well.

Figure 38.10
Poisson distributed
rain clicks.

Instantiating a few of these abstractions as shown in figure 38.10 and giving their sum a high pass above 900Hz produces the rain effect. Each is fairly inexpensive, so you might like to try about 10 or 15 of them with different frequency spreads and timings. Although we take all raindrops to be equal as they fall from the sky, rain may also drip from objects where it accumulates. Under a tree, for example, you will get larger drops falling. Since they must build up from smaller ones, the larger, heavier drops will be less frequent. This patch is most useful for the high-detail component of rain drips onto concrete and roads, as these tend to produce a high-pitched ping. The limit of this patch comes at about 10 instances, mainly because the random number generator is not great in Pure Data, and because we've quantised (given a finite lower resolution) to the delays around 1ms. That means a bunch of patches started at the same logical time will eventually have too many drops that are coincidental. Above this density we need to move to signal domain noise-based techniques, which is the subject of the next section.

General Ambient Rain Noise

Combinations of different rain sound generators should be used with varying levels of detail and crossfaded to obtain a realistic and efficient effect. Detailed generators should be supplemented with broad strokes of coloured noise. Filtered noise at about 10Hz and 300Hz can give us a thundery rumbling noise, which isn't meant to be "thunder" per se, but rather the low-frequency band of sounds we might expect from raindrops hitting bigger things like dry ground or

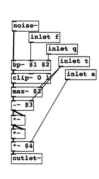

Figure 38.11
Another way of
obtaining rain-
like noise.

large human-made objects like car roofs. High-frequency noise is surprisingly quiet; it generally comes from secondary excitations. You might not think it, but a significant amount of soil or sand is eroded by heavy rain, and these tiny particles being thrown around contribute to the high-frequency components. The general spectrum of rain, sometimes called "comfort noise," is "pink" or "$1/f$ noise," and it has a calming, soothing effect. Ambient keypoints with a strong colour can be used to give an immersive spacial aspect if they are placed on objects that would sound strongly in those bands during heavy rain. To give further context you should apply running water effects to drains and gutters in a scene where it is supposed to have been raining for a while.

A patch that will be useful as a basis for rainy textures is named `drops` and given in figure 38.11. What we have here is an abstraction that provides the fourth power of thresholded, filtered noise. The output is sharp spikes with a density and colour adjustable by changing the parameters. It doesn't enjoy the Gaussian intensity distribution, in order to remain cheap, so it has a tendency to give occasional harsh spikes. It should be used sparingly as a background filler somewhere at the level of detail between the previous Poisson rain and purely noise based sources. Arguments and inlets are for frequency, resonance, threshold, and amplitude. A frequency of about 10 with a small resonance around 0.1 works okay.

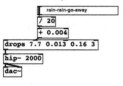

An example instance (fig. 38.12) is high passed above 2kHz with a frequency of 7.7, resonance of 0.013, threshold 0.16, and amplitude 3. The parameters are highly codependent, so you will need to set all of them carefully if you change anything, especially the threshold or resonance. Too much resonance, even by a small degree, leads to a "frying" sound.

Figure 38.12
Setting up an instance of
the filtered noise spikes.

Control Structure

Rain gives a fascinating detailed composite that provides much information about the environment. It sounds different as the rain storm progresses, often starting with large drops on dry ground which have a soft low-frequency signature. Later, as mud and puddles form, it becomes the sound of rain on water pools or wet ground. An "intensity" control should therefore fade in each of these stages, fading out the unused ones as the scene progresses. You will probably want to use `switch~` units to kill the unused DSP sections when constructing a run-time rain actor. Most interesting is where you combine wind and rain, using the ambient wind velocity to drive the density of rain drops. We will look at this later when considering wind effects.

Conclusions

Rain provides a vast range of sound effects because it's the objects the rain collides with that give so much variation. In this exercise we have looked at statistical processes and considered distributions of time, frequency, and intensity. Particular intensity and timing patterns may be obtained from Gaussian and Poisson formulas. There are some common numerical tricks for obtaining these cheaply. A realistic rain effect involves combining many sources with attention to details of timing and material structure.

Exercises

Exercise 1

Experiment with the dispersive lamina model, tight reverberations, and different sources of spikey noise to obtain the effect of rain on a tin roof or rain heard inside a car.

Exercise 2

Use a spectrum analyser to look at the frequency curves of rain recorded while moving through various locations. Can you identify the contributions of objects such as leafy trees or car roofs? How does this differ from the spectrum of rain recorded in wide-open spaces like a field or in the desert? Try synthesising these general ambiances using only cheap noise bands.

Acknowledgements

Thanks to Martin Peach and Charles Henry for helping develop the Box–Muller transform in Pure Data.

References

Lange, P. A., Van der Graaf, G., and Gade, M. (2000). "Rain-induced subsurface turbulence measured using image processing methods." *Proceed. Intern. Geosci. Remote Sens. Sympos. (IGARSS) '00*, pp. 3175–3177. IEEE.

Medwin, H., Kurgan, A., and Nystuen, J. A. (1990). "Impact and bubble sounds from raindrops at normal and oblique incidence." *J. Acoust. Soc. Am.* 88: 413–418.

Miklavcic, S. J., Zita, A., and Arvidsson P. (2004). "Computational real-time sound synthesis of rain." ITN Research Report LiTH-ITN-R-2004-3, Department of Science and Technology University of Linkoping, Sweden.

Pumphrey, H. C., Crum, L. A., and Bjorno, L. (1989). "Underwater sound produced by individual drop impacts and rainfall." *J. Acoust. Soc. Am.* 85: 1518–1526.

Van den Doel, K. (2005). "Physically-based models for liquid sounds." *ACM Trans. Appl. Percep.* 2, no. 4: 534–546.

39
Practical 16
Electricity

Aims

The sound of electricity is useful for signifying technology, danger, lightsabers, and evil genius laboratories, to name a few. Here we construct the sounds for sparking, arcing, and humming.

Analysis

Electricity is like a fluid, made of free electrons. Like wind and water, we can say the thing itself makes no sound but does so when it moves and interacts with other things. To understand these sound sources we need to understand a little about electricity itself.

Electromotive Force

Franklin, Volta, and Faraday developed the early theories of electricity as a fluid called a *charge*. Electricity moves from a place of high *potential*, where there's a lot of electronic charge, to a place of low potential, like water flowing downhill. Electrons are in everything, but where they are free as in a conductor, they can move by pushing each other along and causing a charge to flow, called a *current*. While the electrons themselves move slowly (less than a meter per day!) they behave like a continuous stiff object so the group propagation (of a change in current) is very fast, close to the speed of light. Sounds produced along an extent by electric forces can be assumed to occur instantaneously. Of course we rely on this fact when two or more loudspeakers are connected to the same circuit; each emits the same sound instantly to gives us *correlated sources*. To make a current flow, some kind of electric force is needed, called a *voltage* or *electromotive force (EMF)*, which is the difference between the highest potential and the lowest one somewhere else along a conductive path.

Alternating Current

The invention of AC as a transmission method by Tesla created the modern domestic electricity grid and gave birth to the sound we most associate with electricity. Electricity travels better as AC because there is less loss caused by heating. A low hum at 50Hz or 60Hz is the frequency at which the AC power oscillates. Even a sine wave at this frequency is suggestive of electricity to most people.

Electromagnetism

When a current travels it causes a magnetic field, and ferromagnetic materials in this field are caused to move. Ampere and Fleming showed that electricity, magnetism, and movement are all linked. This theory of electromagnetic dynamics gives us microphones, loudspeakers, electric guitars, tape recorders, motors, generators, radio—in fact just about every facet of modern life stems from it, but it also explains the sounds made by electricity. One of these is a humming sound emitted from metal objects close to an AC current. Transformers used in power supplies emit a hum because they vibrate at the frequency of the AC power.

Resistance and Heating

Ohm discovered that electricity moving through a conductor causes it to get hot. From this we get electric heaters and lightbulbs. But heat may produce sound by expansion, so the sounds of electric sparks are rapid heating of the air as it briefly conducts a current. This can range from a quiet crackling caused by static electricity, to loudly snapping sparks or huge bangs of thunder when lightning strikes. They are all the same phenomenon. Normally air is an insulator without free electrons, but its properties (dielectric) can be overcome by a large enough voltage. The force is so great that the molecules "break," rather like water bursting through a weak dam. They lose their electrons and become *ions* that conduct.

Electrochemical Action

Volta also discovered the link between chemical ions and electronic charge, inventing the battery. Conversely, an electric current can cause gas bubbles to cavitate in an ionic liquid like water, decomposing it into hydrogen and oxygen. So bubbling may be part of the sound produced when electricity meets water. In damp air sparks may hiss or squeal as charge dissipates through "corona streamers" that are not fully formed sparks, and in the presence of water high-voltage electricity can fizz and hiss quite violently.

Model

With many possible sonic manifestations of electricity, it is hard to arrive at a single sound model, but we know that a good sound will encompass some sparking, humming, and the characteristic $50 - 60$Hz AC signature. Sources of such sounds might be an arcing neon sign transformer or a pylon.

Relaxation

Remember we mentioned electricity in the context of a dripping tap or relaxation oscillator? The fluid nature of electricity makes larger-scale modulations based on accumulated potential possible. In an arcing sound source the charge builds up somewhere that has capacitance until it reaches a potential where it can jump through the air as a spark, heating the air to an ionic plasma and making an electrically conductive path. But this rapidly disperses and cools in a normal atmosphere so the conduction path is broken as cold, insulating air rushes back in. The sparking stops. Meanwhile, the source of (presumably limited) current keeps flowing towards the gap, building up the charge again. This cycle repeats, often in a periodic pattern, with charge building up and then discharging.

Phasing

We looked at the effect of phasing earlier. Recall that it happens when two or more copies of the same (or very similar) signal are delayed a short time relative to one another and mixed. Since a spark moves very fast it is effectively a simultaneous extent, radiating acoustic waves in a cylinder rather than a sphere. Parts of the sound signal arrive at some location at different times depending on the spark length and the observation point. Additionally, sparks may "dance," following paths that are similar but never exactly the same. This causes many copies of slightly different pressure patterns to arrive at the listening position over time. Phasing can also occur in AC circuits like transformers where two circuits with slightly different reactivity (AC impedance) are in close proximity. This leads to a slow shifting of the spectrum as different vibrating parts slip in and out of phase with one another.

Resonance

The phasing effect in AC transformers is a feature of circuit resonances, but resonance is also relevant to the acoustics of sparking sounds. The sound of a spark in an anechoic chamber is almost an ideal impulse (which is why spark gaps are used to do impulse captures), so the sound of the crackle is influenced greatly by the surrounding material. Detailed analysis generally shows spark sounds to contain at least one prominent echo- or reverb-like resonance.

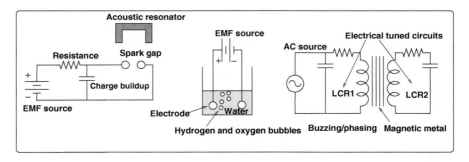

Figure 39.1
Sounds produced by electricity. (A) Crackling from spark discharge. (B) Bubbling or hissing from electrochemical reaction. (C) Buzzing and phasing from magnetic induction and electrical resonance.

In summary, then, we expect to hear a mixture of buzzing, phasing, sharp crackles, hissing, and high-frequency squeals where high-voltage and current AC electricity is present. Some of these result from expansion and stress effects of rapid heating, while others are caused by electromagnetic induction making metals vibrate. What we will model is a high-voltage AC transformer with some bad insulation that allows humming, arcing, and sparking to happen.

Method

We will introduce a new technique called a *chirp impulse*. Slowly beating/ phasing patterns will be obtained by mixing oscillators at close frequencies and then modulating a chirp impulse with this signal. Resonant effects are achieved with short time comb filters and loud sparking sounds with a combination of short impulses, noise, and a sharply tuned resonant filter bank.

DSP Implementation

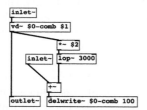

Figure 39.2
Comb unit.

Figure 39.2 shows the comb we will use to slightly shift signal copies around and act as a resonator. The top left inlet controls the delay time of a variable delay whose time is also given by the first abstraction argument in case we just want it fixed. Typically this value is very short, somewhere in the area of 10−30ms. We scale the delayed signal by a factor given as the second abstraction argument, add it to the incoming signal from the second inlet, and feed it to the delay. This means there is a feedback path and positive (reinforcement) of the input and delayed signal. This abstraction is denoted `comb` in the final patch.

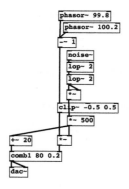

Figure 39.3
Hum source.

To make a hum sound we take two phasors with a small frequency offset between them. These frequencies are important. We hear hum as a mixture of 50−60Hz and 100−120Hz because as induction causes a vibration it's rectified giving the absolute value of the waveform. This causes an apparent doubling of frequency. A phasor is chosen instead of a sine to give a wide spectrum, but you could substitute any shaping function here to simulate different transformer or surface amplification effects. The frequency difference in figure 39.3 will give a slow beating at 0.4Hz. After summing the phasors we subtract 1.0 to centre them on zero again and clip the result harshly to add more harmonics. If you require more bass in the sound then take the cosine of one phasor and mix in some sinusoidal components. To add variation a random LFO is obtained using a noise source, second-order low-pass filter, and squaring to expand the result and make it unipolar. Since this modulator signal is weak it needs boosting. It's applied to modulate the hum amplitude and the comb delay time, increasing the phasing effect as it gets louder.

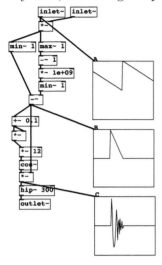

In figure 39.4 we see an abstraction for a high-frequency chirp pulse generator with diagnostic graphs attached to make the explanation clearer. Into the first inlet comes a phasor. Note that the phasor is reversed. The second inlet admits a slow randomly fluctuating signal that is greater than 1.0. The signal immediately following [*~] is therefore a magnified version whose amplitude wobbles gradually up and down. It is split into two branches and the right-hand branch is subtracted from the left. On the left we simply take a portion of the phasor that is less than 1.0, so it rises from 0.0 to 1.0 and stays there. On the right we take the remainder of each phasor cycle above 1.0, bring it back to sit on zero, then multiply it by a huge number and limit that range to 1.0 again. What we get is a square wave that can be subtracted from the left branch to leave a normalised phasor squashed in time. Because the input amplitude is being modulated the length of these will vary.

Figure 39.4
Chirp pulse.

Now, the chirp impulse rises exponentially in frequency, so increasing frequencies have proportionally fewer cycles. The overall spectrum of the chirp is governed by the frequencies on which it starts and finishes, and the time it takes to scan. By adding an offset, then taking the square of each phasor pulse we can obtain a curve starting at some value and rising with a square law. If we multiply this by a scaling factor (12 in this case), then take the cosine, we get a short sweep of a sinusoidal wave. By changing the offset and scaling value it's possible to move the peak in this spectrum to where we like. Values of 0.1 and 12 give a peak somewhere near 5kHz. But this depends on the slope of the input phasor pulse, which is changing randomly because its duration is changing randomly. What we get are different colours of short clicks as the random modulator moves. With a driving frequency of 100Hz this gives a great electric buzzing sound like sparks from a varying high voltage.

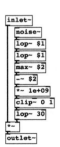

Next we would like a way to switch this on and off at random, so that bursts of sparks happen. In figure 39.5 is a random gate. Noise is low-pass filtered below the first abstraction argument. The combination of [max~] and [-~] place a lower limit on the noise signal so that only the peaks poke through, and then move the base back to zero. Multiplying by a big number and

Figure 39.5
Random gate.

clipping again gives us a square wave with a random duty cycle. To make sure it isn't too clicky when switching on or off a low-pass filter slews the transition.

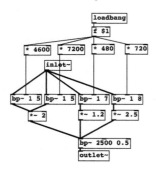

Figure 39.6
Spark formant.

Electrical buzzing we've obtained so far is only half the story. We need some big sparks to make the effect sound frightening. What we can do is fire bursts of noise or chirp impulses into the filter shown in figure 39.6 (named spark6format in the next patch). This is a four-band EQ, a filter bank designed to give some tone to a short, sharp crack. The ratio of centre frequencies is taken from a recording of a real spark in a small metal box. Even though there are only four bands this is sufficient to impart the right feel to an impulse. The frequencies may be shifted by the first argument when creating this abstraction. Notice the relative amplitudes with the peak at 720Hz. A second gentle filter in cascade centres the spectrum on 2.5kHz.

Before putting together all the components, we must finish off the loud spark generator. We need something to drive the filter bank with. Shown in figure 39.7 is an excitation source that comes in two parts, one to drive a short quartic envelope that produces a blast of noise and another to sweep a sinusoid down over the range 7kHz to 20Hz. We never actually hear much of the 20Hz side of things because the envelope (taken from the same line) decays away before we get there. When fed into the filter bank at the bottom, the result is a loud snap like a powerful electric spark. This abstraction, used in the final patch, is called snap.

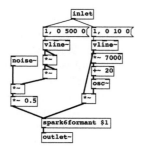

Figure 39.7
Spark snap.

Now we come to assemble whole effect as seen in figure 39.8. Two phasors are clearly visible at the top, tuned to 99.8Hz and 100.2Hz. Again, subtracting 1.0 centres them on zero (because we added two phasors of amplitude 1.0 so the total amplitude was 2.0). This signal, in the centre of the patch, is modulated by a 2Hz positive random source. It gets clipped into a small bipolar range and sent to the comb filter, but also to two other destinations, a threshold and another chain to the left. This is where we leave this signal for a moment; we will come back to it shortly. Looking to the far top left, one of the phasors drives the chirp pulse generator to make arcing noises. The tone of the arcing is set by a random modulator at 0.1Hz. Notice the offset of 3.0 here to keep the chirp pulses short. A random gate now switches the arcing on and off at around 3Hz. The threshold value, here 0.005, needs to be set for each frequency because as the filter cutoff in the random gate gets lower in frequency its amplitude output decreases.

So, we now have an arcing sound made of high-frequency chirps driven at the phasor rate of 99.8Hz and randomly modulated at about 3Hz. Before sending

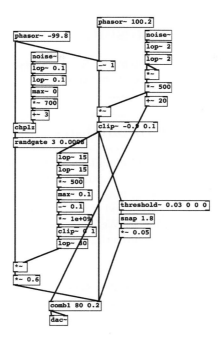

Figure 39.8
Hum and sparks.

it to the comb filter to liven it up before output, it is modulated once more by another signal coming from the code block to left of the diagram. Let's now return to the signal at the outlet of `clip~`. Low passing this at 15Hz gives us a signal that tracks the level of the buzzing amplitude. Remember that this is drifting in and out of phase with itself, beating at about 0.4Hz. What this section does is let us modulate the arcing at the same frequency as the beating. As the buzzing rises and falls in amplitude it passes the threshold set by `max~` and switches on the arcing noise. This makes sense because the arcing should occur as the intensity of the hum (and presumably voltage) rises.

Now follow the right-hand branch from `clip~`. The `threshold~` object triggers a big snapping spark every time the buzzing amplitude rises above a certain level. For `threshold~` to send out a bang the amplitude must pass its first argument. The remaining arguments set the level the input must fall to before a retriggering can occur and the minimum time between bang events. So, all three parts, buzzing, arcing, and loud sparks, are now combined at the comb input whose delay is modulated at the same rate as the buzzing. The whole system seems to undulate in phase and amplitude as if in a relaxation cycle, and occasionally, when the arcing is very high (because both random modulators are in phase), a big spark happens.

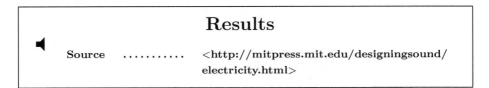

Results

Source . . . . <http://mitpress.mit.edu/designingsound/
electricity.html>

Conclusions

A broken electrical transformer can be modelled. Along the way we have learned how to produce high-frequency chirp impulses and loud snapping sparks, and how to obtain a slow beating by mixing waves with very close frequencies. A new `threshold~` object has been introduced that allows message domain events to be triggered by signal domain levels. We have also learned how to liven up an otherwise dry sound with a comb filter that can be modulated to give a feeling of movement.

Exercises

Exercise 1

Produce the weapon sound for a "lightning gun" or other fictitious game weapon. Experiment with fizzing and hissing sounds modulated by the buzz to make the sound of things frying in the electric current.

Exercise 2

Create a new arc generator that can produce small and large sparks. What is the problem if you modulate large sparks too quickly? How can you get around this using polyphony (more than one spark object)?

Exercise 3

In preparation for the next section, listen to impulse responses from halls and outdoor areas. What are the characteristics of a very loud and short impulse in a reflective space or over large distances?

References

Peek, F. W. (1929). *High Voltage Engineering*. McGraw-Hill.
Tesla, N. (1888). *A New System of Alternating Current Motors and Transformers*. American Institute of Electrical Engineers.

40
Practical 17
Thunder

Aims

The aim of this practical is to produce a stylised approximation to real thunder useful for animations and games. We will discuss some of the theory and synthesis methods needed to make natural-sounding thunder. But since this is a very detailed subject, somewhat beyond the scope of this book and rather expensive in CPU cycles, we'll opt for a compromise between two kinds of model.

Analysis

Wave During a Single Strike

When 10 billion joules of energy are released as electricity, air in the path of the spark becomes a plasma, heated to 30,000 degrees. This causes the air to expand very rapidly, and since the speed of electrical propagation is almost the speed of light it happens simultaneously along the length of the bolt, resulting in a cylindrical shockwave radiating outwards. The duration of each lightning flash is very short, so expanded air quickly cools and collapses back, causing a negative disturbance. The name of this effect is an *N-wave*, because of its time domain shape.

Tortuosity

The cylindrical wavefront moves perpendicular to the path of conduction, but a bolt of lightning is not straight; it twists and turns through the air, following ionised particles that provide a path of least resistance. On average it changes direction about every 10m, and a bolt can be 2km long, so 200 or more cylindrical waves from different sections interact as they meet. This zig zag geometry is called *tortuosity* and it has a direct effect on the sound we hear. In fact, one could say the sound of thunder and the shape of the lightning are intimately linked: thunder is the sound of the shape of lightning. This is why every thunder sound is different, because every lightning strike is different.

Multistrike Discharges

Once it has forged a path through the air it leaves a trail of ions that make the path more conductive, so the remaining electrical energy in a cloud tends to flow through the same path many times. Up to 50 strikes through the same path have been observed as little as 50ms apart. Just as a capacitor discharges through a resistor the charge in the cloud decays away. In figure 40.1 you can see that if the energy needed to overcome the insulation of air and create a spark remains fairly constant then the time between strikes tends to increase. In fact there is a mixture of both time and energy decay with the first strike being the most intense and the remainder getting less energetic and less frequent, until they reach some lower threshold point where the lightning no longer has enough energy to break down the air and strike again.

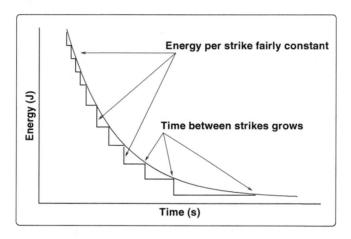

Figure 40.1
Discharge of multiple strikes.

Propagation and Superposition

An observer some distance from a strike will receive different sounds from the event at different times. If we approximate the (cloud-to-ground) bolt as a straight line perpendicular to the earth, then it forms the opposite side of a right triangle with the observer at the end of some adjacent distance, and the path of propagation is the hypotenuse to some point on the bolt at some height. Now, since we know that sound is emitted from all points on the bolt simultaneously, some must arrive at the observer later than others (and travel a greater distance). Those travelling from high up the bolt are subject to more propagation effects, since they travel further to reach us. Those from near the ground are also subject to diffraction, refraction, and reflection. We will briefly consider these next. In figure 40.2 you can see a representation of shockwaves coming from a tortuous strike. Some of the waves will reinforce, creating enormously loud bangs, while others will cancel out. The lines traced from points on the strike to the observer represent different propagation times so you can imagine how a single, simultaneous strike is stretched out in time.

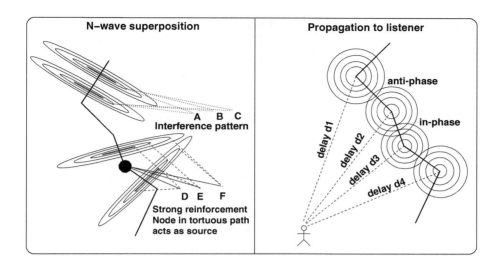

Figure 40.2
N-wave interference at the observer's position.

,

Reflection

The kind of reflections that interest us can be considered as two types. There are well-formed discrete ones from large buildings, mountains, and flat ground. These result in copies of the thunder signature which are individual echoes. The second type are scattered reflections, from trees, uneven ground, and small buildings and objects. These are reverberant and consist of thousands of tiny copies of the signature in such close time proximity that they blend into a noisy signal.

Attenuation

Recall from the chapter on acoustics that the energy of a wave is attenuated by geometric spreading and by imperfect propagation effects like dispersion and absorption. This causes the wave to lose definition, to be distorted. Generally the result is a loss of high frequencies and a deadening of the wave's sharp edges; it becomes blunt and dull. Sharp N-waves from the strike become more like pairs of rounded, parabolic pulses at great distances. The waveform in figure 40.3 shows how an initially high-energy N-wave is tamed with distance.

Diffraction

When the sound is reflected by uneven but regular structures, such as undulating hills or rows of buildings, it may be subject to *diffraction*. This is like the rainbow patterns seen on a data disc, and the effect is to send the sound in different directions according to its frequency. An observer may perceive the

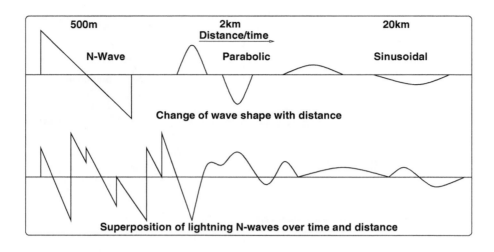

Figure 40.3
Waveform produced by N-wave superposition at a distance.

effects of diffracted sound as a filtering effect, like a swept band pass that picks out a range of frequencies in time order.

Refraction

This is a bending of the sound path by changes in air density between the strike and the observer. In a thunderstorm there are often areas of high- or low-temperature air and areas of wet or dry air in close proximity. The general effect is to curve the path of sound upwards so that in certain situations you are not able to hear the direct strike of the lightning at all, only reflections.

Net Effects

Environmental factors are summarised in figure 40.4. All these physical processes lead to a complex net effect at the observation point, so the sound of thunder depends not only on the shape and energy of the lightning, but very much on the surroundings, weather, and observer's location.

Model

Let us list some of the sonic effects of the physical processes described above.

- Impulsive strike made of N-waves arriving at observer's location.
- Decaying energy profile of multistrike flashes.
- Reverberant aftershocks from buildings, trees, mountains.
- Deep bass tail of refracted low frequencies.
- Comb filter due to constructive and destructive interference.

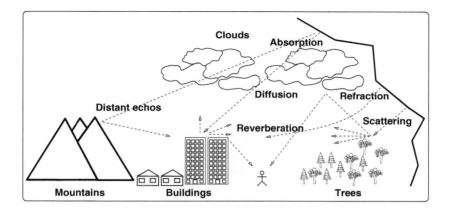

Figure 40.4
Environmental factors in thunder sound.

A general description of the effect is as follows. An initial burst of very high energy appears simultaneously along a line some distance away. Cylindrically radiated acoustic energy arrives from the closest point on this line with a loud, noisy shockwave. Radiation from other points on the line continue to arrive, and since they interfere constructively and destructively there is a time pattern of loud bangs interleaved with silences. Reflections from the initial shockwave, now travelling as planar waves, are filtered by absorption, diffusion, and refraction to arrive several seconds after the event.

Method

We shall use a mixture of noise sources, staggered delays, waveshaping, and delay-based echo/reverb. Several components will be created, each producing a particular layer of the total thunder effect, and these will be mixed together and delayed relative to one another.

DSP Implementation

Strike Pattern Generator

The patch shown in figure 40.5 generates the initial strike pattern, a sequence of values that get successively smaller and further separated in time. It begins by receiving a bang on its inlet which resets an accumulator. First the float is loaded with 0, then the accumulator is incremented by one so that the initial value is small but non-zero. The first number (1) is flushed through the accumulator to `moses` which only passes numbers less than 100. Since the first number is 1 it passes through `moses` and starts a `delay`, which 1ms later emits a bang. This bang activates `random`, producing a random number between 0 and 99.

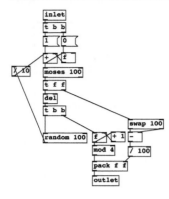

Figure 40.5
Strike pattern generator.

Now you see the feedback loop. The random number is divided by 10, giving us a value between 0 and 9.9, which is fed to the accumulator. On each iteration the delay time increases along with the value in the accumulator. To the right in the patch diagram the current delay time is tapped off and coerced into a decreasing value between 1 and 0, while a bang message cycles a constrained counter round to tag a list pair with a number between 0 and 3. These lists will be distributed by a `route` to sound generators for the thunder strike. The process stops when the delay time rises beyond 100ms and is no longer passed by `moses`. An average of 20 messages are generated on each activation.

Single Strike Sound Generator

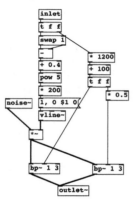

Figure 40.6
Strike sound generator.

Four copies of figure 40.6 denoted `strike-sound` are used to create a clatter of noise, so that they can overlap polyphonically. Basically, each is a pair of band pass filters, a noise source and an envelope. Values at the inlet represent the intensity of noise bursts to be produced. Larger values will produce brighter, shorter noise bursts, and smaller values will make dull, long bursts. A value at the inlet, in the range 0.0 to 1.0, is routed to two branches via the first `t f f`. The complement is taken so that smaller values will make longer envelope decays, and the decay time is computed as a fifth power, offset by 0.4. These values give short decays of about 50ms and long ones of 3s or more. On the right branch the first filter frequency can vary between 100Hz and 1300Hz, while the second filter mirrors this at half the frequency; thus we have two fairly wide bands to colour the noise.

Multistrike Sound Combo

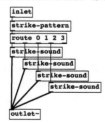

Figure 40.7
Polyphonic strike
sound generator.

Here are four instances of the above sound generator allocated round robin by `route`. When the pattern generator receives a bang, it emits the first few messages quickly. They create short bright sounds. As the delay between messages increases so does the length of each noise burst, so the effect is a fairly continuous sequence of overlapping sounds that mimic decreasing energy. Output from this patch is mixed with the following patches; it forms one of several that make up our complete thunder effect. It isn't particularly good, but this is left as is for reasons of efficiency. Thunder heard very close (less than 500m) has an incredibly loud and sharp bang to it, completely unlike the "castle thunder" we are simulating here. But further away it's unusual to hear the bang in a well-defined way, since spreading of the shockwaves has already begun. So, this part represents a cheap compromise. You may like to experiment with adding your own initial strike sounds to the effect, perhaps using techniques we will explore later on the subject of explosions.

Damped N-Wave Rumble Generator

Following the initial strike, which comes from the closest part of the lightning near the ground, come the time-delayed shockwaves propagated to make a rumble. Perhaps the most difficult part of a good thunder sound is to create this texture for the rumble properly. Using only low-passed noise produces poor results that are no good for anything but a cartoon sketch. However, following the physical model given by Few (1990, 1982) and Ribner and Roy (1982) is a computationally expensive way to go about things, and certainly not possible to use for real-time procedural game audio objects on current microprocessors. Several shortcuts have been discovered while attempting to make thunder sounds for film use, and some are capable of producing astonishingly realistic, even frightening thunder sounds, but all are a bit too complicated to describe here. What we need is something that works a lot better than filtered noise, but is simple enough to understand and create for this practical.

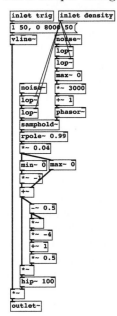

A shortcut to generating hundreds or thousands of separate N-waves and mixing them with different delays to create a thunder roll is shown in figure 40.8. This cannot create the detailed initial strike, which is why we've used a noise-based approximation, but it can give some nice detail to the main body of the thunder effect. It works by producing a randomly rising and falling ramp which is then shaped to produce parabolic pulses with a controllable density. We start with two independent noise generators (it's important that they are independent, so this operation cannot be factored out). Each is subjected to a second-order low-pass filter to get a slowly moving signal. In the right branch we rectify this signal, taking only the positive part with `max~`, and then it is scaled to drive a phasor. A multiplier of 3,000 is necessary to recover the rather small level after such strong filtering. The `phasor~` is driven at around 10Hz to 20Hz. A similar process is applied to the noise in the central branch; however, it isn't rectified, because we want a slow signal swinging positive and negative. Both are combined with `samphold~`. Falling edges from `phasor~` freeze the value on the left inlet of `samphold~` to produce a stepped waveform with random step heights and change intervals. This is integrated by `rpole~` to provide a "wandering

Figure 40.8
Rumble signature.

triangle wave" which is then corrected to be only positive by taking its absolute value. Finally, it is applied to a parabolic shaper so we get a rumbling sound made of many half-circular excursions, very much like the signal you can observe in recordings of distant thunder. An envelope (top left, left branch) gives an 8s decay to modulate the final result.

Afterimage (Environment)

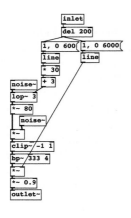

After the rumble and clatter of directly propagated waves come the first echoes. With such an energetic initial strike these seem to arrive from every direction. What characterises them is the filtering effect of reflection. Bouncing off buildings and trees reduces the top and bottom frequencies to leave more mid-range. Shortly we will look at how to make a multitap delay with individual colouring of echoes, but I've included this next patch because it's a neat trick to fake echoes for thunder (and can give some quite nice results). It can be used as a "filler" mixed into the explicit echos to make a denser and more colourful effect. In figure 40.9 two independent noise sources are used with one modulating the other. Notice the large gain of 80 on the low-passed modulator noise and the `clip~`, which work together to make a stuttering or gated effect on the modulated noise. As the low-pass cutoff is moved by a `line` the noise signal becomes quieter and less broken up.

Figure 40.9
Mid-range afterimage.

Filtering it into a band around 300Hz produces a mid-range clatter that sounds like reflections from buildings. This effect, called `afterimage` in the main patch, is delayed from the start of the sound by 200ms. You may like to make a control to set this delay manually.

Deep Noise

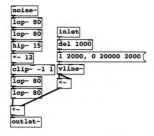

Most of the previous components deserve some measure of high-pass filtering, because they are so volatile in the low-frequency range. But a thunder sound needs some guts, especially for good sound systems where you want something to drive the subwoofer. So, it's best to derive this part separately and have control over it. The arrangement shown in figure 40.10 uses noise low-pass filtered at 80Hz. This "black noise" has a powerful, unsettling effect. To add harmonics it is overdriven and filtered again to smooth off any sharp edges. This part doesn't start until a second after the strike, and it builds up slowly to create a dramatic

Figure 40.10
Low-frequency texture.

crescendo towards the end of the sound effect.

Environmental Echos

This effect gives distance and space to the sound by creating a multitap delay, where each echo is returned by an abstraction that has its own tone. All input and output is carried over send and receive channels so there are no inlets or outlets. Using the abstraction is a matter of instantiating as many as you need. A collection is shown in figure 40.11. The addition of a `switch~` allows the DSP for this whole part to be switched off when not in use, as it can be quite CPU hungry. The abstraction that generates each echo tap is named `udly` and shown in figure 40.12. It creates a single echo with filtering and panning. Although it is really quite simple, just a `delwrite~` to write the delay buffer, a `delread~` to get the echo back and a band-pass and panner unit, there are a couple of things to note about how it works.

Figure 40.11
A box of delays.

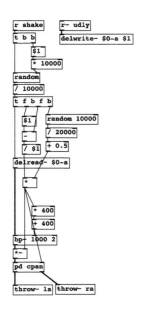

Figure 40.12
A single reflection.

The idea is to instantiate lots of them, maybe 30 or 40 if CPU power is plentiful, and allow each to assume a random value when the **shake** receiver is banged. To avoid clustering of delays around integer marks the maximum delay time D_{max} is multiplied by a large random number and divided again to place it in the original range. This is subtracted from D_{max} and divided by the same number to get the inverse, and then scaled again by a random number. This gives a value which is used to set the filter cutoff and pan position between 0.0 and 1.0. Echoes which are delayed by a short time are brighter and further to the left of the stereo image, and echoes appearing after a long time are softer, lower, and further to the right. Finally, there is a **distance** abstraction that comprises comb and low-pass filters. You may refer to the chapter on helicopters to see how this works, but since it's not absolutely essential to the sound I've omitted a description here to avoid repetition. The complete arrangement is shown in figure 40.13. The environmental effect patch is packaged into the subpatch **box of delays**. This exercise is left quite open-ended. You may like to try mixing and patching

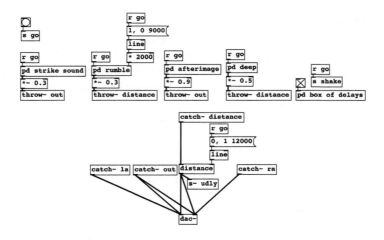

Figure 40.13
A patch to produce thunder made of several separate components.

the components in different ways. A great many thunder effects can be obtained by changing the filters and delay timings. An interesting effect is when, due to combined refraction and ground propagation, a powerful low rumble precedes the main strike. Comb filter sweeps can be put to good use to mimic the effects of superposition from many points.

Results

Source . . . . <http://mitpress.mit.edu/designingsound/thunder.html>

Conclusions

Synthetic modelling of thunder is potentially very expensive if done with finite element arrays and a detailed environmental model, so we must cheat. Breaking the sound into layers and cheaply synthesising each one provides a reasonable approximation that can be deployed in real time.

Exercises

Exercise 1

What differences might be heard for cloud-to-cloud lightning passing overhead with the observer immediately below? Research the effects of absorption by water vapour and try to create the effects of thunder high in the clouds.

Exercise 2

Using Ribner and Roys 1982, work with a computer animation artist to produce a sound accompaniment to randomly generated lightning shapes (see Glassner 2000).

Acknowledgements

Thanks go to: Joseph Thibodeau for his initial MATLAB implementation of the N-wave model; Randy Thom for suggestions, criticisms, and help with model improvements; and the guys at Lucas Arts (Skywalker sound) for use of computing time.

References

Bass, H. E. (1980). "The propagation of thunder through the atmosphere." *J. Acoust. Soc. Am.* 67: 1959–1966.

Bass, H. E., and Losey, R. E. (1975). "The effect of atmospheric absorption on the acoustic power spectrum of thunder." *J. Acoust. Soc. Am.* 57: 822–823.

Farina, A., and Maffei, L. (1995). "Sound propagation outdoors: Comparison between numerical previsions and experimental results." *Volume of Computational Acoustics and Environmental Applications*, (ed. Brebbia, C. A.), pp. 57–64. Computational Mechanics Publications.

Few, A. A. (1970). "Lightning channel reconstruction from thunder measurements." *J. Geophysics* 36: 7517–7523.

Few, A. A. (1982). "Acoustic radiations from lightning." *CRC Handbook of Atmospherics*, vol. 2, ed. Volland, H., pp. 257–290, CRC Press.

Glassner, A. S. (2000). "The digital ceraunoscope: Synthetic lightning and thunder, part 1." *IEEE Computer Graphics and Applications* 20, no. 2.

Hill, R. D. (1971). "Channel heating in return stroke lightning." *J. Geophysics* 76: 637–645.

LeVine, D. M., and Meneghini, R. (1975). "Simulation of radiation lightning return strokes: The effects of tortuosity." *Radio Sci.* 13, no. 5: 801–809.

Ribner, H. S., and Roy D. (1982). "Acoustics thunder: A quasilinear model for tortuous lightning." *J. Acoust. Soc. Am.* 72: 1911–1926.

Ribner, H. S., Wang, E., and Leung, K. J. (1971). "Air jet as an acoustic lens or waveguide." *Proc. 7th International Congress on Acoustics, Budapest*, vol. 4, pp. 461–464. Malk/Nauka.

Sachdev, P. L., and Seebass, R. (1973). "Propagation of spherical and cylindrical N-waves." *J. Fluid Mech.* 58: 197–205.

Wright, W. M., and Medendorp, N. W. (1968). "Acoustic radiation from a finite line source with N-wave excitation." *J. Acoust. Soc. Am.* 43: 966–971.

41
Practical 18
Wind

Aims

The sound of howling wind is the first thing that comes to mind for many outdoor scenes. Usually we add keypoint actors to a game level that are long loops of recorded wind, so it is one of those sounds that either occupies a lot of sample memory or is conspicuously repetitive. Normally, wind is something sound engineers go to great expense and trouble to avoid when recording. Good recordings of real wind effects are hard to come by. Unless you can find the perfect sheltered spot, the conditions necessary to get the howling and whistling, even with great wind shields, just result in a rumble. So, even for films, it is often synthesised. Here we will design a low-cost dynamic wind sound generator that produces realistic gusts and wails in a pattern that constantly changes according to a local wind speed factor. This is one of the few exercises where we will make use of stereo in order to demonstrate placement of objects within an audio scene.

Analysis

What Sound Does Wind Make?

In theory, wind makes no sound at all. Wind sounds are an *implicit production*; it is *other* things' obstructing the wind that causes a sound. But since sound is moving air, and wind is moving air, why can't we hear wind directly? Propagation of sound in a gas is by longitudinal waves, compression, and rarefactions above about 18Hz. Certainly the air is moving a lot when it's windy, but these movements are in a single direction, or backwards and forwards at a slow rate compared to sound waves. If wind can be said to make a sound, it is super low frequency, measured in millihertz (mHz), outside our hearing range. So why do we associate wind with a ghostly wailing noise? The sound it makes, like so many other phenomena, is an interaction between at least two actors. Before wind can make a noise it has to hit something. When it hits a rock, or a telephone pole, or the jagged brickwork of a building, something interesting happens: turbulence.

Model

Large Static Obstructions

Consider an irregular surface such as concrete with the wind blowing over the surface. On a microscopic scale this comprises many small cavities of varying depth, L, and diameter, W, so that we may simplify the surface to that of figure 41.1, where each cavity behaves like a small tube. To accurately syn-

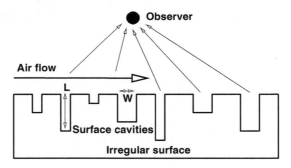

Figure 41.1
Noise produced by a rough surface.

thesise this we would need an unreasonable number (thousands or millions) of resonant filters, each corresponding to a cavity adjacent to the air flow. Statistically, though, any surface will have an average scale. Summing these will give us a distribution around a single peak, which can easily be simplified to a single filter and white noise. For any large irregular object with a rough surface we can just use an ordinary low-resonance band-pass filter. The centre frequency will be fixed and the amplitude will increase with wind speed.

Flexible and Movable Objects

Sounds may emit from objects simply because the wind excites movement within them. A clanging metal street sign pivoted horizontally moves up and down as air pressure and gravity act to cause oscillation. Energy is exchanged between angular velocity and gravitational potential energy. One of the most interesting and physically complex wind effects is a flapping flag. The exact balance of forces is still not fully understood, and some rival models exist that explain the motion in slightly different ways. Generally we can view it as an aeroelastic quasi-oscillation, for a taut fabric diaphragm with one free end, stimulated by chaotic waves in the boundary layer. If there was no turbulence the flag would be subject to three main forces shown on the left-hand side of figure 41.2. The vector sum of gravity, support from the flagpole, and the action of incident wind produces an overall effect that stretches and raises the flag. It is under tension from all sides like a square drum skin. Air moving past it on one side lowers the pressure and pulls the flag sideways. Two forces then act to

straighten it out. As it moves sideways and presents an area against the flow
it is pushed back. At the same time, because it is taut and elastic it tends to
flatten itself like any membrane. Waves then travel along the flag, accelerating
and increasing in amplitude towards the free end. At the free edge where strong
vortices are spinning, the fabric may overshoot and fold back on itself creating
a loud periodic snapping sound. Strong flapping occurs where the natural resonance of the flag as a membrane and the frequency of vortex shedding most
closely coincide.

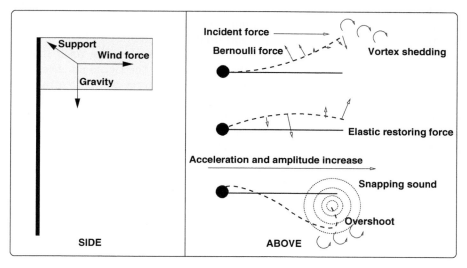

Figure 41.2
Flapping flag.

Breakup and Mode Switching

If you are a flute player you will know that blowing too hard can overdrive the
instrument and produce a sudden switch to a new harmonic or no sound at all.
Listen carefully to the wind and you will notice that some sounds only happen when the wind drops. They happen at certain wind speeds but not others.
The transition to turbulence happens over a range of Reynolds numbers, and
throughout this range resonances may occur that vanish for larger velocities.
Examples are the low moaning howl in recessed doorways and traffic under-
passes, or the noise of drain pipes. Such spaces offer a clear resonant cavity,
often in the area of a few tens or hundreds of Hertz, which only sound when the
wind hits a precise speed. So for some objects, we don't have a simple linear
relationship between air velocity and amplitude or frequency.

Whistling Wires

Immediately behind the perfectly circular object in figure 41.3 we may think of
a cone or shadow of low pressure (A) forming on the far side. Because the wire

or pole is perfectly symmetrical, the choice of whether to flow to one side or the other is finely balanced, and any small disturbance in the low-pressure areas on the sides V1 and V2, where the flow is fast and unstable, will tip this balance. Low pressure forming on one side will tend to pull the cone at A sideways to position B. Because air is compressible the difference between areas A and B now constitutes a restoring force, moving the cone of low pressure around to position C. The result is an unstable wake vortex, a "wagging tail" of airflow (called a *von Kármán vortex street*) that oscillates back and forth as vortices are shed alternately from each side of the obstruction. This *aeroelastic effect* can produce highly pitched (though not simple harmonic) aeolian noise with a sharp center frequency inversely proportional to the diameter of the wire and proportional to the wind velocity. At the same time the wire itself may be pushed forwards by incident air or pulled sideways by the Bernoulli effect. The wire is generally elastic and so an internal restoring force works to straighten it. This motion *is* simple harmonic just like any musical string, but the combination of forces, some random and some harmonic, adds up to a vector that moves the wire in a spiraling roulette. An observable example that results in periodic collisions is the rope on a flagpole or sailboat mast spinning round and banging against the pole.

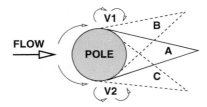

Figure 41.3
Quasi-oscillation of a whistling wire.

Windy Scene

The sounds of a windy day must take into account proper causality. Things are not just randomly excited into motion but follow a pattern appropriate for correct auditory scene construction. A feature that perceptually identifies wind to us is parallel movement. Remember from psychoacoustics that sounds linked by an common underlying feature are assumed to have a common causal property. When wind rises and falls we expect to hear a chorus of whistles all rising and falling together. However, they do not rise and fall in perfect unison. Consider the flag, tree, and wires in figure 41.4 where the wind is moving at 30m/s (approximately 100km/h). If the wind velocity increases to 40m/s in a short gust we will hear the gust propagate across the scene from left to right. Ignoring the 340m/s propagation of sound waves to the observer, there will be a time delay of one second between the flag increasing its flapping and a rise in

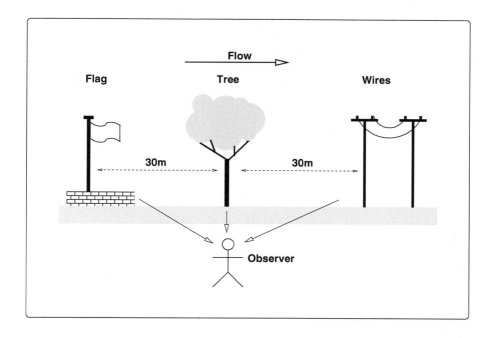

Figure 41.4
Wind propagation in a real scene.

the intensity of the rustling leaves. One more second will pass before the pitch of the whistling wires changes.

Method

We will use noise and filters to emulate chaotic signals with the appropriate spectral characteristics. Low-frequency noise will be used to obtain a varying local air velocity. Amplitude-modulated wideband noise will form our background effect, and narrow band-pass filters will provide the effects of quasi-periodic "whistling" produced by turbulence. Subtle amplitude modulation and frequency modulation effects may be employed to add realism to whistling wires. Excitations are delayed by appropriate propagation times for a realistic stereo image.

DSP Implementation

Control Layer

The left-hand side of figure 41.5 is just a test oscillator so that we can do the first job of getting our control layer working. What we want is a slowly varying normalised control signal that represents the wind speed within a local

Figure 41.5
Wind control.

frame of reference. We generate this inside the `pd windspeed` subpatch that we'll look at in a moment. Signal values will be picked up by variable delay units for each component of the wind sound, so we write them to `delwrite~ a 3000`. In this test case the control signal just generates a sine wave in the range of 200Hz to 400Hz.

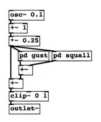

Figure 41.6
Wind speed.

We begin with a slow moving oscillator. In a video game or other installation the global wind speed value might be taken from an external variable, but here we simulate a slow rise and fall over a period of 10s. Adding 1.0 to the oscillator places the value above zero, and multiplying by 0.25 reduces its amplitude from 2.0 to 0.5. One copy goes directly to the output via a `clip~` to keep it in the range of 0.0 to 1.0. Two other subpatches are driven from the steadily moving signal to provide random variations at different scales. The subpatches `pd gust` and `pd squall` each generate a noisy signal to fill up the remaining 0.5 of the signal range. Gusts happen in the 0.5Hz range (2.0s) and squalls happen in the 3Hz (0.33s) range.Hz.

The subpatch of figure 41.7 generates the gusts. An independent white noise source is low-pass filtered (6dB) and DC blocked to obtain a slow random signal without any constant offset. Multiplication by 50 returns it to an amplitude of about 0.25. Take careful note of the scalings on the right-hand side of figure 41.7. Our input signal has an amplitude of 0.5. However, we do not want the gusts to increase linearly but in a square law. At low wind speeds the flow will be steady, but gusts will appear strongly above half speed. We add 0.5 to place the signal closer to 1.0 without changing its excursion, then square it, and then subtract 0.125 to place it back around the local zero (which is the amplitude of our oscillator). At all times the signal is within a normalised range.

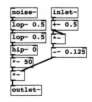

Figure 41.7
Wind gust.

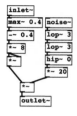

Figure 41.8
Wind squall.

A slightly different scaling approach is used in figure 41.8 where we take the control input and place a lower bound of 0.4 on it. Therefore, only the remaining 0.1 (20%) has any effect. This means squalls won't happen at all until the wind speed is close to maximum. Subtracting 0.4 returns the base to 0.0 and scaling by 8 before taking the square gives an expanded amplitude curve. Notice that both `pd gust` and `pd squall` have independent noise sources. These must be independent sources to produce the proper chaotic effect.

Stereo Panning

Before moving on to create some actual wind sound sources let's define an abstraction `fcpan` as shown in figure 41.9 to pan our sounds into a stereo image. It's similar to one shown in an earlier chapter but without a control input. The panning is power preserving (cosine tapered) with the position set by the instance argument between 0.0 (full left) and 1.0 (full right). The arrangement seen in figure 41.10 is a pattern we will be repeating several times. To save on audio signal noise sources, one global source is broadcast to any other patches that need it. Each patch outputs to a `fcpan` object, which then connects through two `throw~` units to a stereo bus.

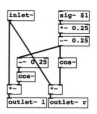

Figure 41.9
Fixed cosine panner.

Wind Noise Generator

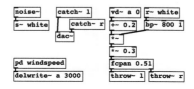

Figure 41.10
Static noise.

Wind speed is received at `vd~` with a zero delay. This patch is to make a general background ambiance, so we add 0.2 to the signal to make sure it never hits zero and becomes completely silent. A single wide band of noise centered around 800Hz is modulated by the wind speed. It gets louder when the wind is strong and quieter when the wind is light. A panning value of 0.5 places the source in the centre (note: an extra digit that makes the panning 0.51 is only there to make the patch print nicely). Scaling must be done before the panner to save having to duplicate objects per channel. The bus receivers `catch~` connect directly to the `dac~`.

The patch in figure 41.11 shows a slight modification to the one above. Now we introduce a single zero filter that sweeps against the low pass. Values between 0.2 and 0.72 sweep the notch from near the fixed filter at 800Hz up to a few kHz as the wind speed increases. Using a notch adds an interesting effect: preserving the bulk of the broadband spectrum while adding some movement. Combined with strong amplitude fluctuations around 3Hz when the wind is squally we get a good ambient effect. This patch should be mixed quietly into the final wind scene.

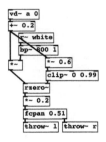

Figure 41.11
Swept noise.

Whistling

The next patch of figure 41.12 repeats the broadcast noise and stereo bus pattern of figure 41.10. Just to be clear, if you are building the wind scene by adding these patches to the same canvas there is no need to duplicate these parts. There are two separate whistling wire sources here.

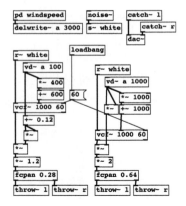

Figure 41.12
Whistling wires.

Each is a narrow-band variable filter whose centre frequency is a function of the wind speed. The first is situated between 600Hz and 1kHz, while the second is in the range 1kHz to 2kHz. Amplitude follows a square law so they are quiet when the wind speed is low. The first has a small offset of 0.12 added to the amplitude value before squaring in order to raise the threshold. This sets the speed at which the source seems to appear; in effect it sets the critical Reynolds number for the object. Panning values of 0.28 and 0.68 are fairly arbitrary and serve to place them slightly to the left and right of the scene. Pay particular attention to the values in the [vd~] units now. They are set to delay the wind-speed control by 100ms and 1000ms, causing the whistle on the right to follow behind the one on the left. In other words, the wind direction in this model is left to right with respect to the observer.

Tree Leaves

This isn't a particularly good leaves effect, but I've included it because it does show some useful techniques. Notice first of all the delay of 2s followed by a low filter. This lags the effect considerably so it follows behind the wind movement. If you notice the way leaves on a tree sound, they seem to have a kind of inertia.

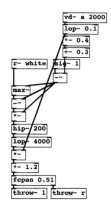

They take a while to build up their energy then take a while to quiet down once the gust stops, probably because springy branches keep them shaking for a while. Next, the control signal is reduced, then inverted, so it moves down from 0.7 to 0.4. Applying this to `max~` and `-~` creates a mask that passes only the top excursions. If there is a high value on the right inlet of `max~` (a low wind speed) then only a few spikes of the noise pass through, producing a sparse crackle. As the wind speed increases, the `max~` threshold lowers and more noise spikes come through, making a denser sound. Subtracting the threshold from the output returns the signal base to zero, and scaling it by the same threshold restores it to a normalised amplitude, so sparse crackles sound as loud as dense ones. To approximate rustling leaves a pair of filters reduces the low and high ends of the spectrum.

Figure 41.13
Tree leaves.

Howls

Now let's add some moaning and howling to the scene. This is what we expect from resonant spaces like pipes and doorways. To make this effect interesting we'll implement a critical range of Reynolds values and have each howl appear within a particular range of wind speeds. The two patches shown in figure 41.14 are almost identical. You may abstract the patch and make arguments of the band-pass frequency and oscillator values in order to create a few slightly different instances. Starting with the signal from `vd~`, each howl is set to come in at slightly different times of 100ms and 300ms. Next we use `clip~` to pick out a range of wind speeds over which the howl will occur. Subtracting the lower clip value resets the base to zero. Multiplying by 2.0 and subtracting 0.25 sets the domain for a single positive going sine cycle from `cos~`. Because this can be brief if the speed moves quickly past our threshold window, a low-pass filter slugs the movement to always take a couple of seconds. The next part is interesting. We amplitude modulate a fixed and narrow band of noise. This gives a noisy oscillator sweep with side bands that behave like a fixed formant, just as the changing vortex frequencies excite the resonant space in a forced oscillation.

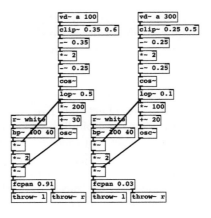

Figure 41.14
Howling wind.

Results

◀ Source . . . . <http://mitpress.mit.edu/designingsound/
                               wind.html>

Conclusions

The sounds produced by wind are interesting and varied. Moving air creates
many modes of excitation. It can blow objects along so they roll and scrape. It
can induce oscillations and swinging. It can produce whistles and howls through
turbulence and resonance. And it can produce single or periodic impacts by
banging objects together. A windy audio scene will take into account the speed
of the wind and behaviour of individual objects including their position relative
to the listener.

Exercises

Exercise 1

Modify or improve the rustling leaves patch or create your own algorithm for
leaf like textures with controllable density.

Exercise 2

Experiment with adding different models for blown, shaken, or rolling objects
into your windy scene. Maybe try the sound of a tin can (from an earlier

practical) rolling past the observer. You can use looped or processed samples in this exercise, but the key point is to try to make your objects respond to the wind speed and integrate them into the scene in a coherent way.

Exercise 3

Modify the density of a rain generator to respond to wind speed and create a scene where the wind lashes the raindrops as it gusts.

Exercise 4—Advanced

Now that you understand a little about wind and turbulence, have a go at implementing a flapping flag. Try to make your model as cheaply as possible, avoiding directly modelling the fabric as a laminar skin. Investigate the phenomenon of alternate vortex shedding and try to obtain an efficient source of similar quasi-periodic chaotic oscillations. This is not an easy exercise to do purely in the signal domain.

Practical Series Machines

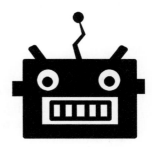

> The factory of the future will have only two employees, a man and a dog. The man will be there to feed the dog. The dog will be there to keep the man from touching the equipment.
> —Warren G. Bennis

Machines

Hyperreality and Artistic Licence

Listen to the sounds in sci-fi films like *The Matrix*, *Stargate*, *Mission Impossible*, and so on. These sounds are hyperreal, with bizarre clockwork mechanisms and pneumatic actuators. In reality, countdown timers (why do they use them?[1]) don't need to beep and click. The button that releases the escape pod bay doors isn't going to make a satisfying clunk-hiss, at least not in the cabin. So, does that mean we should abandon all physical principles and leave machine sound design purely to our imagination? No, not at all. While such sounds may be fanciful, they work because they invoke and extend psychological responses indicative of real mechanics and electronics. We have to take basic familiar physics and build on it. Before we can move into hyperreality we need to establish a solid operational base in reality; then by extrapolation, exaggeration, and morphing we can reach out into the hyperreal.

Basic Components

Starting with principles based in reality, what kinds of sounds are we going to need? A perfect machine would make no noise at all. Why? Because a noise

---

1. "The Top 100 Things I'd Do if I Ever Became an Evil Overlord" (circa 1994, Anspach, Chamness, Welles, Williams, Knepper, Vandenburg et al.). See <http://www.eviloverlord.com>.

indicates some inefficiency, either friction, collision, or some other waste of energy. Yet whenever we encounter alien races of vastly superior intelligence, it seems they have also failed to perfect mechanics, because their spaceships and machines whir, grind, click, and rattle as badly as those of the next species. No matter what part of the universe you visit, you will always find these few basic devices:

- Levers, clunks, clicks, "kerchink."
- Ratchets, series of clicks.
- Relays, chattering, buzzing.
- Motors, complex periodic waveforms.
- Pneumatics, hissing gas.
- Electronics, "bleep bleep" noises.
- Transformers and electricity, humming or whining.
- Forcefields, pulsating hum of electric/magnetic field.
- Data transfer, modem-like sounds.
- Fans, rotor/propeller noise.
- Start-up and shut-down sounds, rising and falling noises.
- Alarms, Klaxons, beeps, buzzers.
- Operational sequencing, control timings.

For now we are going to place limit on how far into unreality we go and study the real objects listed below. A later section deals with some of the above sci-fi noises. At that point we will wave goodbye to the constraints of physical reality and begin working with purely synthetic sounds judged on the merits of how cool they sound.

Control Code

The last item on the list above is special. As we progress we will meet more and more sophisticated control-level programming. Many machine sounds are themselves complex, being made of several subparts. We will frequently use the `delay` and `metro` objects to create fast sequences of messages. Sometimes, choosing the precise timing values for control is as important as the audio DSP making the actual noises.

```
                    The Practicals
```

- Switches, as a study of simple click sequences.
- Clocks, to investigate intricate periodic patterns.
- Motors, the basis of rotating machinery.
- Cars, as a study of a complex system using waveguides.
- Fans, turbulent airflow over moving objects.
- Jet engine, heuristic modelling based on spectrum.
- Helicopter, a complex machine with many parts.

42

Practical 19
Switches

Aims

We begin this section on machine sounds by creating some clicks and clonks. These might be used as stand-alone effects for buttons in software applications, or as part of a larger ensemble for a mechanical device in a film or game. They make an interesting study because the sounds are very short but require a good measure of careful design to get the details right. The principles behind making short idophonic impact sounds will be useful as we develop more complex mechanical models.

Analysis

A few common parts are found in all switches. There is the physical switch itself, the *actuator*, which might be a metal bar lever, a circular plunger, or a plastic tab. To make electrical contact a switch has one or more *poles* and *throws*. These are the metal contacts which move into position to conduct electricity. For some switches there is a locking mechanism, as found in push-on/push-off type switches. Finally there is the resonance of the switch housing or the panel on which the switch is mounted.

Model

When a switch is activated, a throw arm moves across, pushing metal contacts into place. To keep a good electrical connection, and to weather the stress of many thousands or millions of operations, the contact is usually made from a strong, springy material like phosphor-bronze, which bounces briefly against the pole. This is where the requirement for switch *debouncing* comes from in electronic circuits. Although the bounce is tiny, perhaps only a few milliseconds, the ear can pick it up as a metallic ringing sound, or short "chatter." So that switches are not accidentally activated they often hold the throw bar between springs, or against a tapered guide. This arrangement, called a *biased* switch, means a certain force must be applied to move the throw past the mid-point of the taper. Once this point is passed the energy stored in the spring pulls the throw quickly against the pole, minimising the bounce time where sparks might happen. The energy needed to close or open a typical switch is a few

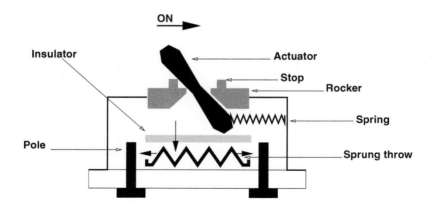

Figure 42.1
Electrical sprung-throw rocker type switch (common light switch).

millijoules, and of course this all ends up as sound or heat. In this practical we shall develop several varieties of the model with different hypothetical components. The number of switch designs and the sounds they make is enormous, so use these principles with liberal artistic license to make your own creations. Certain designs have their own characteristics, such as:

- Momentary action: Single short ping, sprung throw.
- Rocker switch: Two clicks and clunk as actuator hits stop.
- Rotary switch: Multiple clicks and rotary slide sound.
- Slide switch: Friction slide prior to contact.
- Latching push button: Double click and latch, slightly different sounds switching on than off.

Method

We will employ parallel band-pass filters to produce a metallic resonance, short recirculating delays for body waveguides, and a mixture of different complex noise-like sources. Small time offsets will be produced by delays in the message domain.

DSP Implementation

Simple Switch Clicks

Let's start with a crude but efficient implementation of a component to make clicks. A source of filtered noise modulated by a fast envelope gives us tones like a small metallic or hard plastic impact. A `vline~` in figure 42.2 rises to 1.0 in one millisecond and decays away in 20ms.

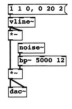

A centre frequency of 5kHz and resonance of 12 give an approximately correct spectrum. While it makes a nice single click the sound lacks complexity that might convince us it's a switch. Sequencing a few of these several milliseconds apart creates a nice clicking sound. The abstraction in figure 42.3 encapsulates a simple filtered noise click with three parameters. The first two are the attack and decay times of the envelope, and the third is the centre frequency of the noise band. If you want, replace the `noise~` with a signal inlet so that this generator can be factored out.

Figure 42.2
Switch click.

We could omit the attack time since all clicks tend to have negligible onsets, but you will find it useful to offset the attack if you create denser tones by blending clicks of different frequencies on top of one another. We name this abstraction `switchclick` and instantiate four with centres at 3kHz, 4kHz, 5kHz, and 7kHz in figure 42.4. Those at 3kHz and 4kHz correspond more to plastic tones while the others tend towards a metal texture. The delays are chosen so that the two plastic-like sounds happen first, then a metal click shifted by ten milliseconds, which roughly corresponds to the timing of a small panel switch.

On its own the switch sounds a bit too bright and neutral, so I've added some body resonance. Using a short delay with a little feedback through a low-pass filter gets us a sound

Figure 42.3
Click abstraction.

more like a switch attached to some piece of equipment. By changing the delay times, feedback values, and filter characteristics it's possible to get the switch to sound different, as if it were mounted on a metal plate. You will perceive

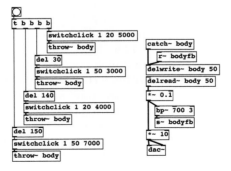

Figure 42.4
Four-click sequence with body.

some backwards-masking effects, as the clicks are very close together and it is hard to pick out their sequence order. A big difference in the total effect occurs once you have three or four clicks in close time proximity.

Slide Switch

The above switch sound lacks detail. In particular, single bands of noise provide only a rough sketch of what we want, and it's hard to find the balance between a wide bandwidth that sounds crunchy or noisy, and having them too tight which produces a nasty overresonant ring. We need more tailored signal sources for our click and slide components. Let's begin with a simple way to approximate a short metal ping.

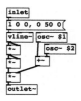

Figure 42.5
Shortping.

From the section on psychoacoustics you will remember that pitch and spectral discrimination decreases as we move into high frequencies. Not surprisingly, quite complex high-frequency vibrations like a small spring or tiny metal plate may be approximated with only two or three sinusoidal waves. In figure 42.5 we see a pair of sine oscillators, which will be tuned to frequencies near 10kHz. Once again, a short square decay envelope modulates them to produce a quick "ping" sound of 50ms duration. When added to a noise-based metal click this really boosts the presence of the sound. It produces a much more solid and focused effect. Let's call this abstraction `shortping` and use it later.

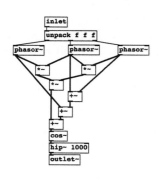

Figure 42.6
Pnoise.

White noise sources have an unfortunate property here. For very short sounds it's hard to know whether any segment taken at random will contain the frequencies we want; hence there is a random fluctuation in the level of each click produced by band-filtered white noise. What if we were able to produce a signal-like noise but with a more controlled spectrum? The abstraction in figure 42.6 shows such a method. This creates a spectrally dense signal that works like noise, but only within a certain bandwidth. Ring-modulating three phasors (and modulating the first stage sidebands from each pair) gives a very "jagged" waveform. Frequencies are chosen to produce a dense distribution around one point. Taking the cosine of this signal is equivalent to summing many sine waves centred around the base frequency so we get a similar effect to a band of filtered noise. However, unlike a true random noise source, this "additive cluster noise" is guaranteed to have the same strength of each partial at all times. Let us denote this abstraction, which takes three frequency parameters to set the noise colour, as `pnoise`.

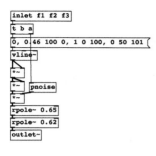

Figure 42.7
Slideclunk.

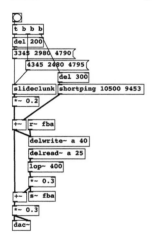

Figure 42.8
Slideswitch.

Now let's use `pnoise` in a new abstraction to produce more detailed metal clicks. We will call this `slideclunk`. Three frequencies for the noise generator are passed in as a list and separated from the bang message by a trigger. Look at the envelope message in figure 42.7 carefully. The aim here is to produce a slide switch sound. We assume that the body creating the click is the same thing the switch actuator slides over. Starting at zero we build the line segment up to 0.46 over 100ms before it suddenly jumps to 1.0, and then decays to zero in 50ms. The quartic function before the modulator sets the correct attack and decay curves to give us a "ssshh-Tunk" as though a slider has been moved over a surface and then clicked into position. A pair of `rpole~` filters in cascade gives us a peak to colour the noise.

Finally, we combine the metal ping with a `slideclunk` source in the patch in figure 42.8. A bang button begins the sequence of three events, two short clicks based on the dense modulation noise and a little metallic ping which is mixed onto the second click. Experiment with different values for the noise colour. In this example 3345, 2980, and 4790 were chosen by hand using faders. The second click, which has modified noise colour parameters, is delayed by 200ms from the first so we get a double-click effect. There is a 100ms delay between triggering a click and the peak in its output, so the ping is delayed by a time of 200 + 100 = 300ms to coincide with the peak in the second click. After scaling the clicks to mix nicely with the metal ping their sum is tapped into a single delay body waveguide, which accentuates low-frequency peaks from 40Hz, to 400Hz, so we get a solid sounding panel resonance. A direct signal is sent in parallel with the body resonance to the output.

Results

🔊   Source   ....   <http://mitpress.mit.edu/designingsound/switches.html>

Conclusions

Carefully timed excitations of a small plate or box model can produce switch and lever effects. Each click corresponds to a mechanical event. The surface on which the switch is mounted strongly influences the sound.

Exercises

Exercise 1

Why does a push-to-lock button have a different sound for switching on than switching off?

Exercise 2

Record and analyse a light switch sound from the room you are in now. Find the formant peaks by tapping the housing and do a quick calculation based on materials and size to compare with what you hear.

43
Practical 20
Clocks

Produce the sound effect for a ticking clock, paying attention to principles of its physical construction. Allow some room for modifying materials and scale so that a small wristwatch or a large grandfather clock can be made with minor adjustments.

Analysis

What Is a Mechanical Clock?

Before digital timekeeping, clocks and watches worked using "clockwork." Clockwork means an arrangement of real mechanical cogs, levers, and springs. The main mechanical component of a clock is the escapement. Instead of an electrical battery the energy to work a mechanical clock is stored in a tightly wound spring or weights on strings, but to get the potential energy stored in the source to escape evenly, at a constant rate, a pendulum was needed. Huygens and Galileo are generally considered the inventors of the mechanical clock, having worked out that a pendulum in a constant gravitational field will always swing at rate determined only by its length. An escapement couples a pendulum or other tuned system to a circular cog so that the cog advances only one tooth of rotation for each swing of the pendulum. That turns a constant reciprocating motion into a quantised rotational motion. There are many ingenious mechanical solutions to the escapement, including the Verge escapement, the anchor escapement, and the gravity escapement, each making a slightly different sound because of the way its parts collide and interact. Watches were not possible until John Harrison invented an alternative to the pendulum using counter-balanced reciprocating wheels compensated for temperature and acceleration. This exceptional piece of engineering was done to claim a £20,000 prize offered by the British government, since a highly accurate chronometer could revolutionise navigation and naval practice. For two centuries watches and clocks were based on Harrison's reciprocating wheel, the sound of which is what most people think of when they imagine a ticking watch. In case you are thinking clockwork is a dead art, think again. Precision military timers still use clockwork since it cannot be destroyed by the EMP from a nuclear discharge, and radios for use in remote regions where there is nowhere to buy batteries also use the technology. Because of portable energy shortages, and as power requirements for electronics diminish, nanoscale mechanical engineering combined with advanced pneumatics may well bring a revival of "clockwork" technology.

Model

A clock is a deterministic chain of events, each one causing another. That is where the expression "working like clockwork" comes from: it is an allusion to the regularity and certainty with which an event will cause another to occur. Each operation, we assume, causes some kind of sound, a tick or a tock, a clunk or a click. If you sample a real mechanical clock and slow it right down you will hear something interesting. Each tick is actually a fine microstructure, always the same, consisting of dozens of distinguishable events. What are these "ticks"? They are the movements of cog teeth against other cog teeth, of levers against ratchets and of the hands on the clock face moving and bouncing. A simplified energy model in figure 43.1 shows potential energy stored in a spring released through an impedance and quantising system. The armature above the sawtooth cog oscillates backwards and forwards, allowing it to move round anticlockwise one tooth at a time, at a rate of around 4 to 8 times per second. A system of gears slows down the resulting rotational motion to provide movement for the dial hands. As each cog rotates and collides some energy is lost to friction and damping. Vibrations are coupled to the clock body and hands, which resonate and amplify the sound.

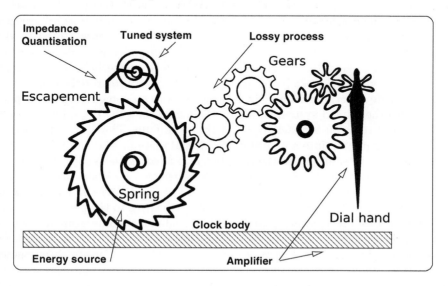

Figure 43.1
Energy flow in a clockwork system.

Method

The key to making a clock is in the control code. A good method for this is to use a delay chain or rapid counter. We will start with a regular metronome and feed each bang into a message delay chain to get a very fine-grained sequence of control events. Most importantly, this keeps everything synchronous. We don't have parts of a clock sound shifting around in phase, which sounds completely wrong; each tiny detail must appear in its correct place within each tick. Having built a switch, it's a few simple steps to building a ticking clock. If you haven't looked at the switch example I suggest you go back and complete that section now. The only significant difference between the single switch sound and something that approximates a ticking clock is the complexity of the control code, the tunings of the metal click noises, and the shape and size of the amplifying body object. Again we will build a metal click sound based upon filtered noise. We will then arrange those clicks into more complex patterns creating little clusters of metal click events, which we'll call clicks, and then arrange these into larger clusters, which we'll call ticks. Again we'll use mostly metal formants in the 4kHz to 9kHz range. Most of the parts in a clock are small, only a few millimeters or centimeters in diameter. However, we can always build in ratio-based scaling functions so that our clock can be scaled up from a small wristwatch to a mighty church clock.

DSP Implementation

Figure 43.2
Square decay
envelope.

Let the abstraction `sqdec` be a square law envelope curve as shown in figure 43.2. A bang at the trigger inlet passes a float given by the first argument to a message box, where it is substituted as the time value of the decay segment of a two-part line. The first part of the line rises to 1.0 in 1.0ms, from where it decays to zero. The square of the output of `vline~` is then sent to the signal outlet. A short 1.0ms rise time prevents very sharp clicking but is otherwise inaudible. We will use this abstraction to produce metallic clicks by modulating bands of sharply tuned noise. In figure 43.3 the new object is instantiated with a 40ms decay and tested using a graph of 1000 samples. You should hear a short click at the audio output and see the decay traced in the graph window.

Now we include `sqdec` in a higher abstraction `mclick` which produces short metallic clicks. This is shown in figure 43.4 Three instances are created along with three band-pass filters having a resonance of 30.0. The filters are connected in parallel to a source of white noise. Noise is taken from an inlet so that we may reuse the same noise source for several click generators. The output of each filter is modulated by its own decay envelope. All

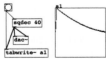

Figure 43.3
Envelope test.

decay times and filter frequencies are taken as abstraction arguments in the
order $\{f_1, d_1, f_2, d_2, f_3, d_3\}$ where f_n is a band frequency and d_n is a decay time.

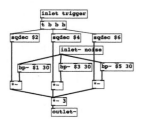

Figure 43.4
Metal click.

To recover a louder signal from the very narrow
filters we multiply the output signal by 3.0. An alternative arrangement would be to place the filters post-
modulation. When this is done the filters tend to
ring for a short time after the noise burst has finished. You can experiment with doing this if you like
and listen to the subtle difference. The reason for
patching as shown is that if we want even narrower
bands with resonances of 40.0 or higher we lose control
over the decay time by letting the filters ring. Placing the filters before the modulator allows us to have
both very narrow bands and very short decays if we
like.

An unusual, and slightly difficult to read, control element
is given in figure 43.5 and denoted `bangburst`. This produces
a series of ten numbers in quick succession for every bang
received at the inlet. In *pd-extended* external objects called
"uzi" and "kalashnikov" perform similar functions but producing bangs instead. This object allows us to create fine-
grained click sequences when used with `select` as you will see
in figure 43.6. It works rather like a normal counter except
for two differences. First, there is a `delay` in the incrementor
branch that forms a feedback path. When a bang is received it

Figure 43.5
Bang burst.

triggers the float box, which is incremented. The float is sent to the output, and
also passed back to the cold inlet of the float box. Meanwhile a bang message is
briefly delayed before triggering the float again. This would continue counting
up indefinitely were it not for the second difference, a `moses` object between the
float and increment object. For numbers greater than 10.0 a message box is
triggered that resets the float to zero.

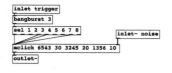

Figure 43.6
Clock tick.

Combining figures 43.5 and 43.4 we obtain
the abstraction of figure 43.6 denoted `clocktick` in
the main patch. Each bang received on the inlet
causes a fast sweep through the `bangburst` counter
to provide a pattern of bangs according to the
patching of `select`. You can play with arranging
these to get different tick-tock sounds, or creating more than one `mclick` with slightly different
characteristics. Once again, the noise source is
deferred to the outer level so we can factor all the noise to one generator.

You may patch up the `mclick` object to test it as shown in figure 43.7 by
providing a noise source and graph. Here, the graph **a1** is 2,000 samples long,
enough to capture about 20.0ms showing the three frequency bursts. Experiment with different frequencies and decay times to get a good result.

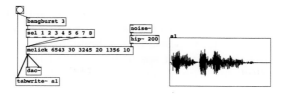

Figure 43.7
Tick test.

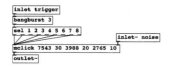

Figure 43.8
Tick 2.

Two copies of the tick are suggested. Here we have another which is identical to the first except for different frequencies and a different timing pattern. You can either make a new subpatch or create an abstraction. If you want to make a more complex and subtle clock sound you may prefer to devise a way to abstract the select timings so they can be passed as arguments.

The escapement ratchet is the fast high ticking sound we hear in a clock or watch. If you like it is the master clock of the whole device, so it operates at a multiple of the other cogs movements. Our ears aren't so good at detecting the spectrum at such a high frequency, and the escapement wheel is often only about 5mm in diameter. Most of the high ticking sound comes from the little compensator spring attached to it, which rings with a fairly pure bell-like tone at a high frequency. Instead of using filtered noise for the escapement ratchet I've used a pair of sine waves at 8.0kHz and 10.0kHz. Alternating between these frequencies provides a chattering, brush-like noise of a tiny spring.

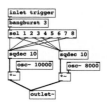

Figure 43.9
Escapement.

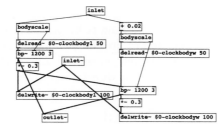

Figure 43.10
Body resonance.

The sounds from the mechanical action of the cogs and escapement sound dry and lifeless as they are. We would never hear them in isolation like this. To bring the sound to life we must add a body to the clock that mimics the housing and dial face. As you see in figure 43.10 this is done with two delays in partial feedback with band-pass filters in both signal paths. The delays are arranged and tuned to approximate a box section of length l and width w.

The object of figure 43.11 calculates the parameters for the delays and filters. Filter frequency is the reciprocal of the delay period. We use two of these to obtain slightly different length and widths, although the box simulation is nearly square. A resonance of 3.0 with a feedback factor of 0.3 provides a sound appropriate for hard plastic or well-damped thin metal sheet, while an input value of 0.1 gives a delay time of 10.0ms and a filter frequency of 1.0kHz.

Figure 43.11
Body scale.

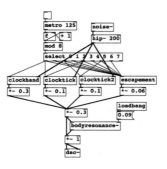

Figure 43.12
Clock, all parts.

Now we go up one more level of abstraction into the control code of the top patch as seen in figure 43.12. By adding another counter and selector, this time using a metronome, we fire off tick1 then tick2 on beats 1 and 5, and 3 and 7 respectively. The escapement ratchet fires on every beat and a clunk sound for the moving dial hand is triggered once per second. Lastly the delay-based body resonator is added in parallel with the direct sound to give it character.

Conclusions

A clock sound is nothing more than a detailed, periodic pattern of short clicks coupled though an appropriate body resonator. The body resonance is easily modified and can produce wooden or small plastic sounding clocks, though changing the scale of the body while keeping the mechanism fixed sounds interesting but strange. The abstractions can be rewritten so that the timing and apparent size of all components can scale together.

Exercises

Exercise 1

Completely rebuild the synthesis method of the clock. Keep the same model but replace noise band synthesis with Dirac pulse, FM, or another method of your choice. What advantages and disadvantages can you discover for different methods of synthesising short clicks and impact noises?

Reference

Gazeley, W. J. (1956). *Clock and Watch Escapements*. Heywood.

44
Practical 21
Motors

Aims

In this exercise we will produce the sounds of some electric motors. Motor sounds are essential for machine noises, sliding doors, drills, robots, and much more. There are many motor designs; some use AC electricity, some use DC. Some have a rotor that surrounds a stationary core, whereas others have an axle that spins within a stationary frame. Some have brush contacts, others use induction to transfer power. We will consider the common brush and commutator DC type here, but we will try to make it flexible enough for a wide range of effects.

Analysis

Let's look quickly at some operational theory. The *rotor* is the bit that spins; it's usually in the middle and connected to an axle or *shaft*. It usually has a coil wound around it and so is often the heaviest component. The *stator*, that's the outside bit that stays still, is a cylinder of permanent magnets or coils producing a stationary magnetic field. The axle is held in the middle by two plates, the *dimes*, one at each end, which usually have some kind of *bearing* to lubricate them. A typical DC motor works by having two or more brushes which conduct power to the rotor coil through a broken, slotted ring called the *commutator*. On each half-turn the flow of electric current is reversed so that motion is always in the same direction. Lastly the motor has some kind of housing or frame which will resonate. We don't need to go into details of physics and electromagnetic theory here—we know what happens, power is applied and it spins—but the mechanics are worth a few words. In a DC motor the brushes make contact with the commutator, at least twice and sometimes many more times per revolution. Each time this happens we hear a little click. The click may be due to the brush moving over different materials, first a metal conductor and then an insulator, then a conductor again. Sometimes ridges on the commutator move the brush in and out slightly as it rotates. Sparks may happen between the commutator and brush, since disconnection from the coil causes a high voltage back-EMF because of the coil's inductance. While the rotor is spinning it makes

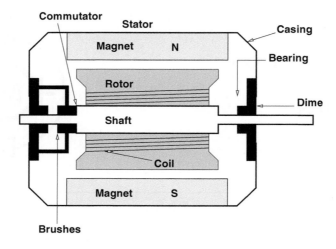

Figure 44.1
Side view of DC electric motor.

some other sounds. Even a nearly perfect motor isn't completely balanced, so some slight eccentricity of the spin will produce a vibration in the housing.

Some friction in the bearings may cause a regular squealing sound too. By far the most prominent noise is due to the way forces change as the motor revolves. A DC motor moves in pulses, at least two per cycle. Its angular motion (or more correctly, the torque) builds and then collapses as current is applied then disconnected by the commutator. This makes a different sound from a brushless AC motor, which applies a constant rotational force and so is much quieter.

Model

Speed

The speed curve of a motor is an important feature of its sound; it's a signature that helps us recognise a motor. Because the rotor is heavy it takes a while to build up angular velocity. The lighter and smaller the motor the faster this happens. A big heavy motor, or one under a lot of load, will take longer. However, in all cases we observe a certain shape. When the motor is spinning slowly a big current flows through it and its torque is high. Its angular acceleration is high at this point. After a while it reaches an optimal speed, even when not loaded, where it won't spin any faster. As it approaches this point the torque and the change in angular velocity decreases, flattening off at the motor's top speed. When the power is removed the decay in speed is more linear since only friction and load, which are constants, act against it. Motor speeds are specified in RPM. To get Hz from RPM we divide by 60, so a motor that spins at 30,000 RPM will give us a signal frequency of 500Hz.

Materials

The components of a motor significant to its sound are usually metals. Motors with plastic parts are common in low-power toys, but not in heavy-load applications like robots or electric doors. We need to remember that much of the vibrations happen because the motor is connected physically to some mounting or other material. A motor held freely in the air or mounted with a well-damped rubber grommet makes far less noise. Therefore, we need to keep the overall physical system in mind when designing the sound of complex machines, by coupling some of the sound from the motor to other parts.

Method

We will start by constructing an envelope generator that behaves correctly for speeding up and slowing down. Everything is synchronous, so a single phasor will drive the model. Brushes and sparks produce noisy clicks which will be modelled with a modulated noise source, while the pulsing movement of the housing will be obtained from a raised cosine waveform.

DSP Implementation

The speed envelope generator, figure 44.2a, is made up of two parts. It looks a lot like the logarithmic attack-decay envelopes we have made before, except for the growth and decay rates.

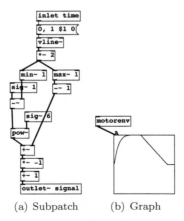

(a) Subpatch   (b) Graph

Figure 44.2
Speed control envelope.

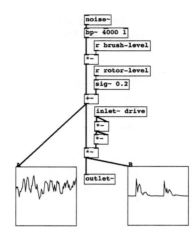

Figure 44.3
Rotor.

Beginning with the output of `vline~` which produces a single rising line segment, multiplication by 2.0 and then splitting the signal around 1.0 gives us
two branches that will be summed. To obtain the attack portion we raise the
complement to the power 6.0. This provides a fast-growing curve that levels off
approaching 1.0 when inverted. The right-hand branch provides a linear decay,
simply by inverting the line slope. Because the result is below the zero line we
add 1.0 to turn it back into a positive envelope curve. If you wish, split this
envelope generator component into two separate pieces, one for switching on
and one for switching off the motor, so that you can hold the envelope level
constant indefinitely. As it is there's no sustain portion, because we just want to
demonstrate the main features of this sound effect. The graph of this envelope
generator is seen in figure 44.2b.

In figure 44.3 is a subpatch for the rotor. A phasor on its own is much too
pitched, like the police siren sound we made in an earlier exercise. We want a
sharper, more clicking sound. To obtain this we use the usual trick of shaping
the decay of each phasor cycle by taking its square or higher power; in this
case the quartic decay (4th power) seems fine. By mixing a little constant DC
against the noise with `sig~` we can get a mixture of noisy clicking sounds for
the brushes and a more pitched sound for the rotor spinning. The first graph in
figure 44.3 shows a mix of band-pass filtered noise and DC. Passing the noise
through a 4kHz filter with a wide bandwidth tames it by removing all the high
and low components. Adding the DC gives us a noise signal raised above zero,
so that when it's modulated by the modified phasor we get unidirectional spikes
of noise, as shown in the second graph.

In figure 44.4 we see the second sound source in the motor model. Pulse-like vibrations are obtained using a cosine raised according to $y = 1/(x^2 + 1)$, which with a multiplier of 2.0 before the `wrap~` gives a pulse wave at 4 times the base frequency and $1/4$ the original width. This sounds harder and thinner than a cosine of the same frequency. The output is scaled by `stator-level` after shifting by 0.5 to recentre it. Narrower pulse widths give the motor sound a smaller and faster feel. Mixing the stator, brushes, and rotor is a matter of taste. According to our model the stator should run at a subharmonic of the rotor, which is not the case in the example because a higher stator whine seems to work better. You should find you need only a small amount of the noisy brush sound to create the right effect, but if you want a harder or less stable motor that sounds a bit old then play with the noise band pass or try adding some jitter noise to the phasor frequency inlet.

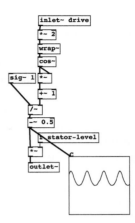

Figure 44.4
Stator.

Combining these with a master oscillator and GUI components in figure 44.5 we have a bang button to start running the motor envelope and six normalised sliders which send parameters to the model. The first sets the total time, start plus stop. This value is picked up by the `runtime` receive object just above the float box and multiplied by 20,000ms (20s). Upon receipt of a bang message the float object sends this time value to the envelope, which then rises and falls. Three more faders set the levels for different sonic components, a pulse-like wave from the stator vibration, noise bursts from the brushes, and a click-like sound from the rotor. A copy of the envelope, signal on the left branch modulates overall amplitude, since the sound intensity roughly matches the motor speed. A copy of the envelope signal on the right branch goes to `phasor~` via a scaling which determines the maximum motor speed. To make the phasor negative going `max-speed` is multiplied by a negative number. The phasor then drives two subpatches, giving the noisy rotor spikes and the pulsating stator body. They are summed explicitly before a volume envelope is applied, then finally multiplied by `volume`.

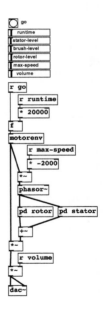

Figure 44.5
Motor.

This next trick can be tried as an experimental alternative to a delay-based resonant housing. The fixed frequency peaks (or formants) from an object body

tend to be highlighted as another moving frequency
sweeps across them. One way of thinking about the
motor housing is as a fixed tube with an excitor spinning
inside it. At certain frequencies the rotor will strongly
resonate with the housing. At others there will be almost
no resonance. There are many resonant modes where
this happens, so over a long sweep you will hear a slow
beating effect as resonances fade in and out. Instead of
a delay we can use FM as a kind of resonance by keeping the carrier fixed but moving the modulator. This is
the opposite of how FM is usually used for musical purposes. A fixed carrier represents the unchanging body
of the motor, so the signal from the rotor becomes the

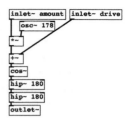

Figure 44.6
FM body resonance.

modulator. The original carrier is mostly filtered out, so we only hear the modulation sidebands coming in and out. When the carrier and modulator are at
noninteger ratios the sidebands will be weak and inharmonic, giving a noisy
metallic rattle. When the carrier and modulator align in an integer ratio, a
peak of strong sidebands in the harmonic series of the modulator will briefly
appear. Treating this signal with some distortion is great where we want to
simulate the motor rattling on its mounting.

Results

Source   ....   <http://mitpress.mit.edu/designingsound/
motors.html>

Conclusions

A motor is a case of a spinning oscillator, but with extra resonances and periodic features from the brushes or housing. Even though the decay is linear,
a heavily loaded motor may seem to stop almost instantly. We haven't taken
higher-order friction effects into account, but remember that loss is proportional
to (angular) velocity. Also, this model assumes a constant power source applied
and removed. You may find a slightly more realistic sound for robots is a proportionally controlled motor known as a *servo*. That sound has sharper start
and stop stage because power is varied to obtain the correct speed. Accurate
position control motors are carefully damped and tend not to "overspin."

Exercises

Exercise 1

If you have some sound samples of motors, examine their spectra to see how
the attack and decay stages vary with load.

References

Deitz D., and Baumgartner, H. (1996). "Analyzing electric-motor acoustics." *Mech. Eng.* 118, no. 6, 74–75.

Finley, W. R., Hodowanec, M. M., and Holter, W. G. (2000) "An analytical approach to solving motor vibration problems." *IEEE PCIC-99-XX.* Siemens Energy & Automation.

Yannikakis, S., Dimitropoulou, E., Ioannidou, F.G., and Ioannides, M.G. (2004). "Evaluation of acoustic noise emission by electric motors of bench engines." *Proc. (442) European Power and Energy Systems.* ACTA Press.

45
Practical 22
Cars

Aims

In this practical we will analyse the sound producing and shaping elements of a more elaborate acoustic system. We will begin with constructing the piston signature of an engine and then apply a new trick, warping a static waveguide to introduce FM that can cheaply model the nonlinear behaviour of a periodically overdriven tube.

Analysis

Engine

In figure 45.1 you can see a four-cylinder petrol engine that works as follows. The crank shaft rotates so that each of the pistons moves within a cylinder at a different phase from the others. On its initial intake cycle, with the fuel valve open, a mixture of fuel and air is drawn into the cylinder, while the exhaust valve remains shut. After the piston has reached the bottom of its trajectory the fuel valve closes, sealing the cylinder.

Moving upwards, the piston compresses the mixture, increasing its temperature until a spark ignites it. An explosion occurs just as the piston passes its azimuth so it is forced rapidly downwards, giving rotational energy to the drive shaft. On its next upward movement exhaust passes through the now open outlet valve and into the exhaust chamber. This cycle of four strokes, intake, compression, ignition, and exhaust continues so long as fuel and air are supplied. A battery is used to create the initial spark that starts the process, but once running electricity is taken from an alternator coupled to the drive shaft, more fuel and air are all that are required.

All the rest of the engine, turbo chargers, fan belts, and so forth, are extras that contribute to cooling and efficiency, although they obviously contribute to the sound too. The greatest differences in engine sounds come from having more or fewer cylinders, and the design of the exhaust system. An important character of the engine sound is determined by the behaviour of the exhaust valve. It is only open for half of each cylinder's rotation, on every other cycle. The upward motion of the cylinder expels hot gas under a high pressure and then the valve closes as the cylinder begins to move down. So there is no negative pressure cycle coupled to the exhaust chamber. The engine sound may therefore be

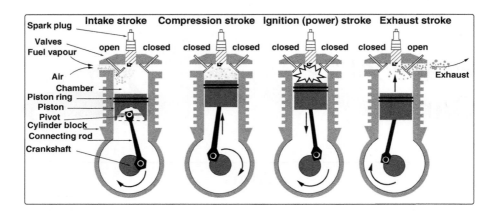

Figure 45.1
The internal combustion engine.

characterised as a rectified and truncated sinusoidal wave coupled to a resonant cavity. In a four-cylinder engine we will hear four of these on staggered phases.

Other Sources

The engine sound dominates in terms of intensity, but in addition to the other components like fans, cams, gears, and drive shafts, the second-loudest source of sound in a moving vehicle is the friction of its tyres on the ground. Rubber has strange transphase properties much studied by mechanical engineers and transport scientists; it squirms, squeals, and emits interesting patterns of noise that depend on temperature, speed, and load.

Exhaust

A two-stroke engine works a little differently, which is interesting to mention here because of how this difference affects the sound. It uses the exhaust impedance in a much more sophisticated way. Unlike a four-stroke engine that drives exhaust pulses into the pipe, a two-stroke uses the exhaust like a tuned system to blow back through the cylinder, flush out remaining exhaust gas, and induct fresh air/fuel mixture in, by taking advantage of a standing wave that is deliberately amplified. This is achieved with a trapezoid-shaped expansion cavity between the engine and the tailpipe.

The exhaust design shown in figure 45.2 makes a big difference to our engine sound. Explosion of one or two litres of compressed petrol and air certainly makes a big bang. You can hear this if an engine "backfires," if the exhaust valve remains open by accident. But since the aim is to turn this into motion in as efficiently as possible we may take the piston to be a near-perfect damper. A properly working 5kW petrol engine operating at $1800 RPM$ obtains only 5 percent to 10 percent efficiency, so a portion of the remaining energy that doesn't end up as heat must produce sound. Otherwise, exhaust gas is expelled

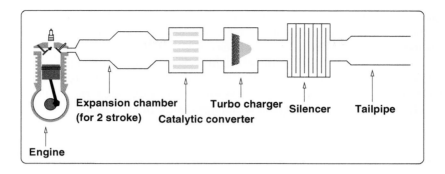

Figure 45.2
Exhaust system components (some optional).

in a controlled fashion, and we can view the exhaust system as a driven resonant oscillation. In fact, resonance is undesirable, because it would lead to increased vibration at certain speeds, so a good exhaust design minimises this as much as it can. However, any resonances that exist will radiate from the exhaust pipe body itself at various places along its length. These will all have different phases to each other as the pulse of exhaust gas travels down the tube. But what about radiation from the engine?

Engine Block and Chassis

The engine block is thick in order to contain high pressure and couple high mechanical stress, so it absorbs most of the explosive pulse. The remainder is radiated from its generally large (about $4m^2$) surface area as a dull thud. Since the engine must be soundly mounted to the vehicle chassis, the third-loudest source of sound is not from the engine block itself but radiation of these pulses from the vehicle body.

Changing Speed

The greatest difficulty in synthesising engine sounds is that it is relatively easy to obtain the sound of an engine at constant speed, but rather hard to model as it changes speed. This is because of the phase relationships between the engine's piston pulses, the exhaust signature, and vibrations from the body. An engine whose rotational speed is changing produces changing patterns, standing waves, within the exhaust and chassis. This causes an interesting change in spectra which is not necessarily related to absolute current rotational velocity, but to earlier rotational velocities. The entire vehicle is a resonating system much like complex filter with many feedback and feed-forward paths.

Sputter and Jitter

Something to avoid when designing engine sounds is to have them too perfect. Even well-made engines have small timing and amplitude irregularities.

The fuel mixture obtained on each cylinder firing might not be uniform, as the air intake and fuel supply can vary slightly. Modern vehicles have electronic ignition, but even these rely on some electromechanical feedback to decide the exact moment of discharge. A diesel engine relies on thermodynamic principles, which are inherently imprecise. A characteristic sound feature is that if some change occurs to the mixture it affects all cylinders one after the other, so the cylinders do not behave completely independently of each other.

Model

Let us summarise some sources of sound in a motor vehicle.

- Explosive pulses radiated directly from the engine block (dull thuds).
- Pulses coupled through the vehicle body (noisy vibration pulses).
- Radiation from the exhaust pipe surface.
- Pulses from the mouth of the tailpipe.
- Additional sounds, tyres, fanbelt, turbo charger, etc.

A thorough model of a car engine really needs an elaborate network of waveguides, and we will use some waveguide principles, but to do so would require a rather expensive cascade of scattering junctions and delay lines. To obtain a more computationally efficient model we need to exercise a little creativity and cunning. We shall begin, as always, at the source of energy, with the piston movement obtained from a phasor split into several subphases. We can view the engine, exhaust, and body as a series and parallel network of secondary excitations, each occurring as the explosive pulse propagates through the system. Unlike a trumpet or musically tuned pipe the exhaust exhibits plenty of nonlinearity, being overdriven to produce effects rather like distortion or waveshaping. The catalytic converter and silencer behave as absorbent low-pass filters, so the sound at the tailpipe is much reduced in high frequencies. We should also take into account two propagation paths or speeds, those of vibrations through contacting metallic components which move at around 3000m/s and acoustic pulses moving at the speed of sound. Because the exhaust is usually on only one side of the vehicle there will also be some directionality to the sound, with a different balance behind or in front of the vehicle.

Method

A mixture of phase splitting, wrapping, delays, and filters will allow us to place various excitations having different tones within each engine cycle. An interesting trick to obtain nonlinearity is to timewarp the exhaust waveguide so that it behaves like an FM modulator, thus adding higher-frequency sidebands like a waveshaper. We can use small amounts of noise to model subtle timing irregularities found in a real mechanical system and add sputter and knocking sounds at the piston.

DSP Implementation

A Toy Boat Engine

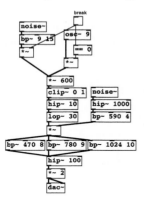

Figure 45.3
A "toy" engine.

We start with a simple example this time. We will build up through several stages of improvement. Machine and engine sound design is quite fun, but requires careful listening and creative programming to get the right sound and behaviour. In figure 45.3 you can see a cartoon engine, something you might code in a few minutes for a simple game. It has a very low level of detail and realism. Yet it contains some of the essential features we've just analysed: a piston, the ability to add jitter, and a rudimentary exhaust port. Starting with the top `noise~` and `osc~` units, fixed at 9Hz because this model behaves very poorly for any speeds outside 5Hz to 11Hz, we can switch between them to create a faltering sound like the engine is running out of fuel. Amplifying, then clipping, reduces the waveform to more or less a square wave. The following filters behave like the outlet valve terminating the exhaust system. They change the square wave to a pulse with rising and falling curves. This modulates high-passed noise centred around 600Hz into a formant filter comprising three parallel band passes with frequencies picked by ear for a fairly "clonky" sound. Picking some good filter frequencies might give you other basic machine sounds. But the problem with this design comes when you move the speed. Try it. Above 11Hz you will hear the effect lose detail and smudge into an incoherent mess. That's because we are using the trick of just letting coloured noise fill in a gap that our imagination tells us is an engine because of other features. It has no real harmonic structure at all, so the illusion breaks down as we are forced to try harder to discriminate events in time.

Inertia for a Four-Cylinder Engine

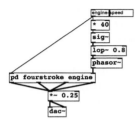

Figure 45.4
Slugging speed.

In figure 45.4 you can see an instance of a four-cylinder engine, which we will build next. Notice that it has four outlets, one for each cylinder. This implies that it's not a finished design; we're just summing the four sources to get an idea of how it works. Depending on the design we might like to route these four sources through different waveguides, which we will do later. Looking at the input, the engine is driven by an external `phasor~` whose frequency control is low-pass filtered. This gives us an important effect you should incorporate into all engine designs: inertia. Mechanical systems can seed up and slow down at a limited rate, and can sound wrong if you change speed too quickly. A top speed of 40Hz corresponds to $2400RPM$, but since there are four cylinders you will hear pulses at 160Hz for top speed.

Building the Four-Stroke Engine

The arrangement shown in figure 45.5 looks quite complicated, but it isn't really. It's just four copies of the same process in parallel but shifted in phase. Each cylinder pulse is obtained from a familiar $1/(1 + kx^2)$ shaper (along the

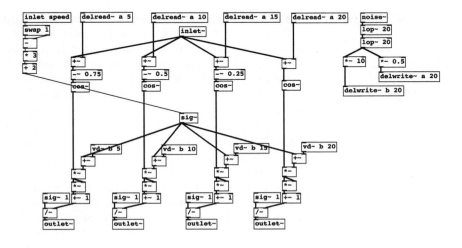

Figure 45.5
A four-cylinder engine.

bottom row), fed with a cosinusoidal wave. By subtracting 0.75, which corresponds to 3/4 of a cycle from the first, then 0.5 for a half-cycle shift from the second, and so forth, then taking the cosine of these shifted signals, we obtain four cosinusoidal phases from the same phasor. One interesting thing that makes the patch work is the addition of timing and pulse width jitter. A noise source (top right) filtered to around 20Hz is fed to two delay lines in different proportions. Delay-read operations spaced 5ms apart produce the effect of a fuel and air stream that feeds each cylinder in succession, so any jitter pattern is copied across the cylinders in a wave, giving a quite realistic result. One set of delay-read objects adds some noise to the pulse width, and another to the firing timing. These only need to be small values to create a subtle effect. Another thing to note is that we modify the pulse width as a function of speed. At low speeds the pulse width is narrower and so contains more harmonics, but as the engine seeds up the pulse width widens. This avoids the engine sounding too harsh at high speeds where aliasing might occur, and it mimics the low-pass effect of the exhaust impedance.

Exciting New Overtones

The next two parts are quite complicated, so work through them slowly and try to follow the signal path. We will combine an overtone generator with transmission delays and a waveguide into a fairly advanced engine patch in the last part. Starting with the overtone generator shown in figure 45.6, there are four

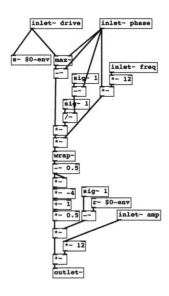

Figure 45.6
Overtone excitation.

inlets, a driving phasor d, a phase shift control p, a frequency control f, and an amplitude control. You should recognise a parabolic wave function about halfway down, $y = (-4d^2 + 1)/2$, which turns a zero-centred phasor into a circular curve. The incoming phasor (on the **drive** inlet) is split somewhere between 0.0 and 1.0 by the value on the **phase** inlet. Subtracting this value moves the driving phasor back to zero, and multiplying by $1/(1 - p)$ renormalises it. Then we multiply by $12pf$ to get a curve going much greater than 1 aligned with the current phase. Wrapping this, applying the parabolic function, and then enveloping it with the complement of the original phasor gives us short bursts of pulses that decay away. We can position the phase and frequency of the pulses independently. The upshot of all this is that it's possible to add clanking or knocking noises on every turn of the engine, and to control the relative tone, intensity, and position of these. Although a little difficult to follow, this type of *phase relative* synthesis is a very efficient way of getting good results.

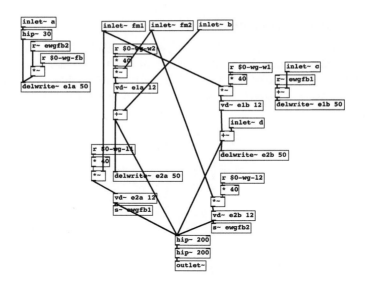

Figure 45.7
Nonlinear warping waveguide.

A Warping Circular Waveguide

This next subpatch offers a nice way of getting an exhaust waveguide that gives impressive results without using multiple bidirectional delays and scattering junctions. What we have is a circular delay chain broken into four quadrants. Delay e1a feeds into delay e2a, e2a into e1b, e1b into e2b, which feeds back into the start. At each point in the circle we can introduce a new signal via inlets a, b, c, and d. These represent points along the exhaust pipe where new excitations (given by the overtone excitors) happen. What really gives this system its character is that we can warp the waveguide to perform a kind of FM. Two anti-phase-delay offsets modulate the variable delay lines, so the total length of the pipe remains unchanged while signals moving within each of the four quadrants are time compressed or expanded.

Advanced Engine Design

In addition to having a set of overtones that can be varied relative to the driving phase, and a waveguide where we can change the length and pipe diameter, four transmission delays offset the excitations by a fixed time. This time is independent of the phase shift, so vibrations that take some time to propagate through the vehicle body are possible. This leaves us with a grand total of 23 controls to set.

- Cylinder mix—the level of the four cylinder engine model
- Parabolic mix—level for vibration of the whole engine
- Engine speed—main engine frequency

- Transmission delay 1—time delay to first overtone
- Transmission delay 2—time delay to second overtone
- Transmission delay 3—time delay to third overtone
- Parabola delay—relative shift of pistons to engine movement
- Warp delay—move the nonlinearity up and down the exhaust
- Waveguide warp—the amount of FM applied in the waveguide

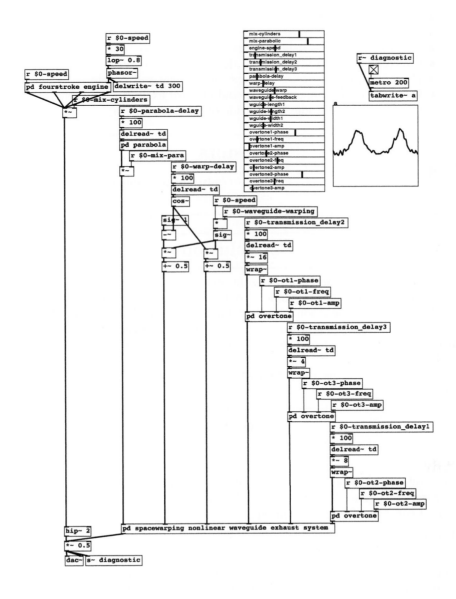

Figure 45.8
Advanced engine with multiple transmission paths and warping nonlinear waveguide.

- Waveguide feedback—liveness of the pipe resonance
- Waveguide length 1—first quadrant delay time
- Waveguide length 2—second quadrant delay time
- Waveguide width 1—third quadrant delay time
- Waveguide width 2—fourth quadrant delay time
- Overtone 1 phase—offset of excitation 1 relative to cycle
- Overtone 1 freq—maximum spread of first excitation spectrum
- Overtone 1 amplitude—amplitude of first excitation
- Overtone 2 phase—offset of excitation 2 relative to cycle
- Overtone 2 freq—maximum spread of second excitation spectrum
- Overtone 2 amplitude—amplitude of second excitation
- Overtone 3 phase—offset of excitation 3 relative to cycle
- Overtone 3 freq—maximum spread of third excitation spectrum
- Overtone 3 amplitude—amplitude of third excitation

Results

◀ Source   . . . .   <http://mitpress.mit.edu/designingsound/
                                     cars.html>

Conclusions

A wide range of car and truck engine sounds are obtainable from this patch. Modifying the number of cylinders could allow motorbikes or chainsaws to be modelled, though the resonant behaviour of a two-stroke engine needs further analysis. An engine sound can be represented as a series of excitations happening as a consequence of an explosion, starting in the engine cylinder and ending with radiation from a number of parts. A network of variable delays and feedback loops gives us a way to model the propagation and resonance of these pulses.

Exercises

Exercise 1

Research the more interesting role of the exhaust resonance in a two-stroke motorcycle engine. Why is a motorbike with a smaller capacity engine louder than a car, even if it has a silencer?

Exercise 2

Model some other elements of a large engine, such as the mechanical transmission. Pick an example to model; maybe try to make the chugging sound of a ship engine room or an eight-cylinder propeller plane engine.

46
Practical 23
Fans

Aims

Let's now consider a rotating air fan. This study of spinning object sounds will also be useful for ventilation noises, helicopters, propeller planes, and bullet ricochets, while the principles of turbulence caused by an edge cutting the air will be helpful for sword swishes.

Analysis

A typical fan or propeller consists of several equally spaced and sized blades fixed to a central node that is rotated by an angular force. Domestic ventilation fans are usually driven by an electric motor, whereas helicopters and propeller planes employ an engine. The purpose of the device is to turn mechanical rotational energy into fluid movement, which is achieved by having the blades angled so their sideways motion creates an inclined plane forcing the fluid in a direction perpendicular to it. The differences between a fan, a propeller, and a turbine are in their utility. A fan is used to move air, a propeller to move the object attached to it, and a turbine to turn fluid motion to rotational energy. Sounds produced are largely unaffected by these purposes.

Recall that spinning objects are one of the simplest physical sources of sound. As long as the object is irregular, or does not have a perfectly smooth surface, there will be perturbations of the surrounding air at the same frequency as the angular motion of the object. Yet the sound of a fan is not a sinusoid; it is much more like a noisy source, and some distance in front of a typical ventilation fan we perceive a more or less steady airstream. So, how does the sound we actually hear relate to the physics of the fan?

Model

In figure 46.1 you see a front view of an eight-bladed fan. In some respects it is a regular, rather than irregular object. If we were to add more blades, it would, in the limit, become a disc, and spinning it would make almost no sound. You will notice that fans with many blades are generally quieter. But here we have

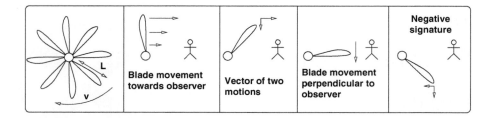

Figure 46.1
Pressure around a rotating blade.

eight gaps between the blades, and each blade is angled, so at some point in front we would expect to receive eight pulses of air per rotation, each a compression formed as a blade moves round. In this simple analysis we could model the sound in front of the fan as a series of pulses with a frequency given by the number of blades times the frequency of rotation.

Let's take a different look at the process. The other parts of figure 46.1 show another limiting condition where we have removed all the blades but one, and the observer is standing to the side (in the same plane as the rotation). We can consider the blade as a rod of length L rotating with angular velocity ω about a fixed point. Since the angular velocity is fixed, the distance moved by some point on the rod (the opposite side of a right triangle where the rod forms the adjacent and hypotenuse over some time interval) increases with distance from the centre. The tip is therefore moving much faster relative to the air than the middle, at a velocity of $2\pi L\omega$. For a 10cm blade at 2000 RPM this is about 21m/s, a speed that will be greater than the Reynolds number for a modest blade width, so we expect turbulence and consequently noisy emissions. The tip could be considered a point source of noise, and because the tip moves at constant angular velocity its spectrum remains fixed. As a more sophisticated model we could consider the noise source from the blade turbulence to be modulated by the pulsating air flow, occurring at about 33Hz for the example given. Since we have eight blades the apparent frequency will be 264Hz.

But our listener is positioned to the side of the rotation. How does this affect the sound? Since the tip is moving in a circle, it changes its location relative to the observer. At some point the blade is moving towards the listener, shown in the first frame. By Doppler we expect any waves emitted from the tip to be compressed and their frequency to increase at this point. In the next frame we see the blade at 45° and some part of the movement vector is towards the observer and some part perpendicular, until in the next frame the blade is moving sideways, past the observer, and then finally receding in the last frame. At this point we expect a second Doppler shift dilating the wave and lowering frequencies in the noise.

Method

To implement this model we will use the waveshaping technique of $1/(1+x^2)$ to obtain a narrow pulse. We will then introduce some noise and modulate this with the pulse, and to effect a Doppler shift a mildly resonant band-pass filter will be swept over each noise pulse. As we have examined, the sound from the blades depends on the listening position. This gives us an interesting parameter we can add to alter the mix of pulse, noise, and Doppler shift depending on the observer's angle to the plane of rotation. For ventilation units this is not much use, but as we will see later it is extremely effective for aircraft fly-by sounds.

Implementation

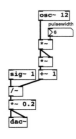

Figure 46.2
Fan pulse.

An oscillator running at 12Hz is multiplied by a scaling factor and then squared. The scaling factor sets the pulse width. The frequency of pulses is twice the oscillator frequency since squaring rectifies the sinusoid and produces unidirectional positive going pulses. The upper limit of the pulse amplitude is 1.0, which is added after squaring, because where the oscillating wave is 0.0 then $0.0+1.0=1.0$ and $1.0/1.0=1.0$. The sense of the pulses is therefore inverted by this operation. For non-zero and larger values of the sine wave $1/(1+kx^2)$ disappears towards zero, more quickly for larger scaling values of k, so the pulse narrows but remains at a constant amplitude. An oscillator value of 12Hz therefore gives pulses at 24Hz which would correspond to 180 RPM for an eight-blade fan. Play with the pulse width to see where the best effect is, I think about 5 is quite good.

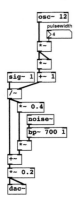

Figure 46.3
Fan noise.

Here we have added the noisy component to the fan. The exact spectrum of the noise is hard to predict and should be accomplished by experimentation. The shape of the blade influences this sound. Some fan blades are linear slopes, while others scoop the fluid with an exponential curve or one that increases toward the blade tip. Aerodynamics such as vortex shedding and standing eddies around the fan assembly can cause quite resonant behaviour for certain speeds and designs. A value of 700Hz seemed right for a fan at this speed, but the resonance is low, so the noise has really quite a wide bandwidth. This noisy part should not be too loud. It is mixed in parallel with the pulse after being modulated, then scaled by 0.4. The final mix is scaled by 0.2 to produce a sensible output amplitude.

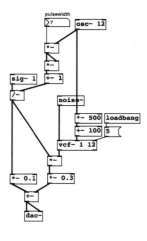

Figure 46.4
Fan Doppler.

Now we see the addition of a filter sweep to emulate a Doppler shift for fast moving blade tips. This design has some problems; it works well for slow movement but goes wrong as the speed gets too high. Moving the filter too quickly creates harsh modulation artifacts, and although `vcf~` is a robust design it is difficult to make filters that do not have problems when swept sharply. To get around this we do not sweep the filter with the narrow pulse, but use the oscillator output instead. Of course this swings positive and negative. Negative cycles are meaningless to `vcf~`, but if you are translating this design to another implementation be especially mindful of the way this is designed or you will get an unstable filter. The sweep range is between 0Hz and 600Hz with a resonance of 5. Since the modulating pulse is narrower than the sinusoid sweeping the filter we get a very interesting effect by changing the pulse width. With wide pulse widths a nice swooshing is heard, but narrow widths give us a tight purring sound. Varying the width with speed could produce some interesting startup and shutdown effects.

Next we move on to an interesting trick. Part of the reason for doing this is to get around the limitation of the filter slew in order to have better results for faster-spinning blades. But it also allows us to properly model what happens in this case. For very long blades, such as those on aircraft propellers, the velocity of the tip can reach a high value. As the speed of the blade approaches 340m/s a sonic pressure wave forms in front of it. Pulses shed from the tip change from being a smooth chopping sound to being loud snaps as accumulated energy is suddenly released. Fan and propeller blades are almost always kept slower than Mach 1.0 because they would be damaged. This is surprisingly easy to model using a variable delay. We remove the filter completely and feed a mix of noise and pulses to `delwrite~` with a 400ms buffer. These are read by a variable delay whose index is modulated by the oscillator. As the value increases the sound in the buffer is squashed into a smaller space, increasing its frequency, and as it swings through zero into the negative range the sound is stretched out and lowered. This is the usual implementation of Doppler shifting, although this example is very crude since it takes no account of the correct phase shifts for a real propeller. Experimenting with different pulse widths and the value labelled *chop* should give some

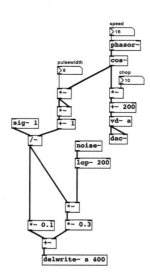

Figure 46.5
Fast blades.

good effects. This is the implementation we will use later for plane or helicopter propellers.

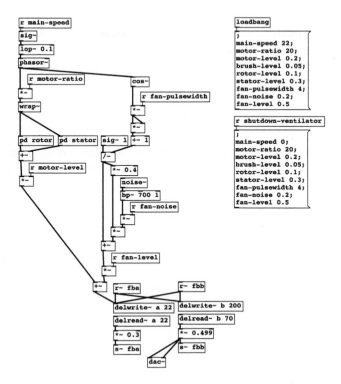

Figure 46.6
A full ventilation system with pipe simulation and shutdown effect for game.

Finally, let us combine one of our fans with an earlier motor and pipe simulation to create a complete effect. This object would be placed in an interactive game world as an ambient keypoint with additional startup and shutdown controls if required. The motor drives the fan, and both are coupled to a pipe resonator. The object might be spatialised to appear on a wall as a point source, or connected to ducting down which the player may crawl. Variations on this patch could produce other static machinery like refrigerators or heating units.

Results

Source . . . . <http://mitpress.mit.edu/designingsound/fans.html>

Conclusions

An irregular rotating object creates turbulence if it moves fast enough, and because fan blades move fast they compress and rarify the air. Depending on the listener's position a Doppler effect may be observed that modulates the turbulent sound.

Exercises

Exercise 1

Experiment with the idea that as the number of blades becomes large and the gaps between them diminish the sound tends to become smoother and quieter.

Exercise 2

By synchronous coupling, add a variation on the earlier engine to a powerful-sounding fan model to obtain a propeller plane effect. Place it into an environment such that a fly-by effect incorporates the changing observation of the propeller angle. Add some overall Doppler movement to finish off the effect.

47
Practical 24
Jet Engine

Aims

In this practical we will produce the sound of a jet plane. Specifically, we focus on production of a single engine of the turbofan type found in small commercial aircraft. Jet engines found in military fighter jets share much in common with this design, but to simplify the analysis we will concentrate only on the broad characteristics of a simple engine design. You can extrapolate from this design to add details for more specialised examples.

Analysis

Operation

A turbine is a shaft fitted with several propellers with a large number of blades. It is spun to draw air into a cavity that is tapered so that the air is compressed and moving very fast. It enters a combustion chamber where it is mixed with vapourised kerosene or propane and the mixture is ignited with a spark.

Expanding combustion products (mostly carbon dioxide and water vapour) increases the pressure further as it exits through the exhaust and provides thrust. During the exhaust stage it drives a second turbine, which is connected to a large fan at the front of the engine. This draws cool air around the outside of the turbine and mixes it into the exhaust stream. Once ignited the process is self-perpetuating and continuous so long as fuel is supplied. The combustion actually happens over the surface of a "can" which behaves like a wick and Davey lamp shield to prevent the flame going out (flameout). This means that flames don't actually come out the exhaust. Where you see planes with flaming exhausts this is fuel deliberately burned in an extra stage called *afterburn*, which gives some extra thrust. A central shaft is shown in figure 47.1, but this comprises two or more concentric shafts. In other words, the turbo fan, compression blades, and exhaust turbine are not necessarily in synchronisation. This allows careful control of the pressure at various stages, which stops engine flameout or overheating.

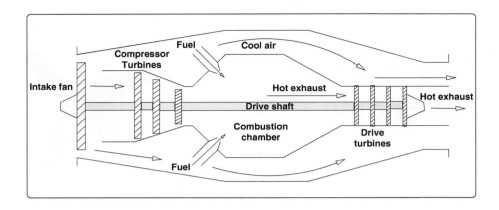

Figure 47.1
Simplified jet engine.

Gas Turbulence

Initially the flow of air through the engine is regular and mostly laminar. A quiet and steady hissing sound is heard as air blows out the back of the engine. Noise profiles built over a very long averaging time are shown in figure 47.2. The change in spectrum as engine speed increases is clear.

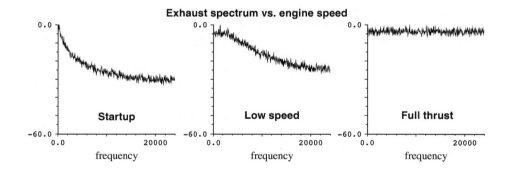

Figure 47.2
Averaged noise profile at increasing engine speeds.

Once the fuel is ignited exhaust pressure increases enormously and the air-flow is supersonic. As cool air mixes with hot exhaust it forms a quasi-periodic series of conical shockwaves that emit from the exhaust. This strongly modulates the noise into a banded spectrum. It fills up the mid-range, though there is still most activity in the 300Hz to 1.2kHz range that appears as a popping or rumbling sound from a distance, like the frictional excitation of an object being dragged over a surface. At full speed the turbulence is so intense that the spectrum approaches white noise, being virtually flat. Some turbine components are shifted upwards beyond the limits of human hearing as the energy goes above 20kHz. Eventually the exhaust sound takes on a ripping, whooshing sound of high-pass filtered noise and the turbine sound begins to dominate again.

Turbine Sounds

There are dozens or even hundreds of blades on many turbines staggered along the conical cavity. Even at low speeds of 2,000RPM the modulation of the airstream causes audible oscillations in the range of 100Hz to 1kHz so that a strong whining is heard. The partials in a turbine sound are strongly focused and result from complex beat frequencies between the blades at different stages of the airflow. What is interesting is although the dynamics are complex, the spectrum shifts almost perfectly linearly; in other words, we only need to know the spectrum of a turbine arrangement at one speed and we can shift it up and down to produce realistic results.

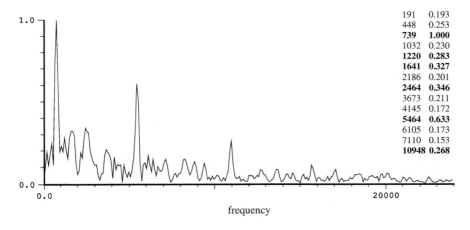

191	0.193
448	0.253
739	**1.000**
1032	0.230
1220	**0.283**
1641	**0.327**
2186	0.201
2464	**0.346**
3673	0.211
4145	0.172
5464	**0.633**
6105	0.173
7110	0.153
10948	**0.268**

Figure 47.3
Prominent components of turbine.

Housing and Resonances

The jet engine is uniquely interesting in this regard, as it is designed to minimise standing waves and resonances that might cause mechanical fatigue. Although the interior surface is smooth and reflective, the supersonic airflow means there is no back propagation upstream. Certain speeds do accentuate turbine components somewhat, but we can make a simplification for all but very low speeds by ignoring the contribution of the housing. All the important sounds are emitted to the rear through the exhaust.

Model

Two separate models are combined. The first provides a turbine sound, which is an inharmonic spectrum composed of separate sines obtained by analysis. The second is a turbulent forced flame model produced from carefully banded and overdriven noise. At low speeds the turbine sound is dominant but is quickly overwhelmed by a very loud noisy component as speed increases.

Method

A five partial additive synthesis subpatch is used for the turbine. Analysis values are multiplied by a speed scalar, keeping the same ratio. For the turbulent gas component a cascade of filters and nonlinear functions are used to produce a sound that varies with speed, moving from an even low-passed hiss at low speed to a highly distorted wideband roaring at high speed.

DSP Implementation

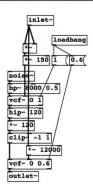

Figure 47.4
Forced flame.

A forced flame model adapted from a "flamethrower" patch is shown in figure 47.4. A normalised input controls the thrust which increases in density by a square law. The response is obtained by taking white noise through a fixed filter, constraining it to a middle-range band gently rolled off around 8kHz. A very gentle filter moves over the bottom range against a second fixed high-pass. This gives us a sweep that increases dramatically in amplitude while avoiding any very low frequencies that would cause "bursting" or audible fragmentation of the sound. After multiplication by about 100 we clip the signal harshly to create a wide band of harmonics. This signal is passed through a second variable filter that changes frequency linearly with the control input between 0 and 12kHz. At low control values, hardly any signal passes the first filter stage, so the low-frequency noise is not clipped. At medium control levels, frequencies passed by the fixed band pass are at a maximum, so the output noise is highly distorted and coloured. At high control levels, the clipping is less severe again, so we hear a brighter whooshing sound.

We implement a simplification of the turbine analysis data in figure 47.5 using only five components. By experimentation, the most important five partials are taken from an averaged analysis of the engine running at constant speed over about 60s (different from the snapshot shown in figure 47.3). This gave $3,097$Hz, $4,495$Hz, $5,588$Hz, $7,471$Hz, and $11,000$Hz as the main frequencies. To scale them, the list is unpacked and each frequency converted to a signal so that it may be smoothly modulated by the engine speed control. A separate ⬚osc~⬚ oscillator mixed in approximate ratio provides individual partials

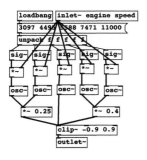

Figure 47.5
Turbine.

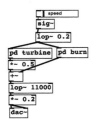

Figure 47.6
Jet engine.

so the phase of each is independent. Perhaps a better way would be to derive all in synchronous phase, and the "lobed" shape of the partials around a strong center component suggests FM or AM may be a an efficient way to approach this. However, it seems that the nonsynchronised drive of each turbine is quite important to the sound, so this is a case where separate oscillator phases are good. Before output a little clipping is applied, which introduces sidebands that fill up some of the sparse spectrum.

Combining the two sources is straightforward. The speed control is turned to a signal and slugged by a low pass to provide smooth changes. A real jet cannot exceed a certain angular acceleration without damage, so this limiter adds realism. Both the exhaust turbulence and turbine are tweaked to work with the same normalised control range, corresponding to about $1,000$ through $50,000$RPM of real angular speed. After mixing, a rolloff above 11kHz is used to tame some of the noise at high speeds. The effect works best if the engine is controlled in a realistic way, reaching an initial "warm-up" stage after ignition and then letting the speed increase very slowly.

Results

Source   ....   <http://mitpress.mit.edu/designingsound/jetengine.html>

Conclusions

Jet engines can be modelled by two separate processes, one for the turbine and one for the exhaust gasses. The spectrum of the exhaust depends on gas velocities and changes considerably with thrust.

Exercises

Exercise 1

Add four engines together to make a large passenger jet. Can you factor out or simplify any parts? What happens, in terms of beating and phasing, if the engines are at slightly different speeds?

Exercise 2

Place a simple jet aircraft in a velocity context relative to a ground observer. Produce a Doppler effect with scaled panning and amplitude curves for a fly-by.

Acknowledgements

Thanks to Paul Weir at Earcom for the jet engine recordings.

Practical 25
Helicopter

Here we experiment with helicopter sounds. This section will explore the notion of a complex composite sound that changes according to interactions between several components and the observation point.

History

Although the ancient Chinese played with flying toys that had spinning rotors and Leonardo da Vinci proposed a flying machine based on this principle, it wasn't until 1907 that the Frenchman Paul Cornu got something capable of carrying a man to briefly fly. After this milestone, which was the helicopter equivalent of the Wright brothers' famous 1903 Kittyhawk advance, a further 17 years passed before Etienne Oehmichen flew a kilometer in 1924, and another 12 before the German Focke-Wulf Fw 61 became the first practical production helicopter in 1936. The solutions to many of the problems encountered designing a practical helicopter are still with us today, and are reflected in the diversity of designs.

Operation

The sound of a helicopter is generally characterised as a "whup whup" produced by the main rotor. This is certainly an important contribution to the sound, but other parts play an equally significant role.

Engines

A helicopter consists of a powerful engine. Getting an engine powerful and light enough to lift a rotary flying machine was one of the major obstacles to producing helicopters. To give you an idea, the CH-47 "Chinook" uses two Honeywell 55-GA-714A engines of 4,733 hp. That's a combined power output of about $7,060 \mathrm{kW}$, equal to the electricity requirements of a small town. Early models used one or two internal combustion engines of 4-, 8-, or 12-cylinder designs, and many helicopters still flying today have more than one engine coupled to the same drive shaft. Most modern designs have replaced this with a gas turbine engine.

Gearboxes

In a typical design there are three gearboxes, one for the main drive to the overhead rotor, an intermediate gearbox at the rear, and a smaller one in the tail. These are necessary because the engine, main rotor, and tail rotor must all spin in an independent fashion, so various clutches and gears are needed to transmit power.

Rotors

In the classic design there are two rotors spinning in perpendicular planes. The main rotor gives lift while the tail rotor counteracts torque that would spin the fuselage around in the opposite direction to the main rotor. Each consists of independently controllable blades that can change their pitch via hydraulic servos. The combination of main rotor blades is controlled by the *collective*, which gives lift to the vehicle. As the blades rotate they cut into the air with different density and relative speed, so in order to remain stable while giving forward thrust a second control called the *cyclic* changes the blade pitch at different points in the rotation. Because there is more lift from the blade when at the back, the whole rotor assembly is able to tilt forward, keeping the stress on the blades equal. Not only does the tail rotor compensate for torque produced by the main rotor, it can be used as a rudder to rotate the craft. Another way of turning is to bank sideways using cyclic control, so the helicopter has many degrees of freedom. Each manoeuvre links several components together, so a helicopter is a complex thing to fly. From our point of view, it makes the sounds produced very interesting. For example, the tail rotor speed is linked to the angular acceleration of the main rotor.

Helicopter designs

Not all models have a tail rotor. Some use contra-rotating blades to equalise the torque. These may be placed one above the other on a coaxial drive shaft, or as tandem rotors side by side. The Chinook allows the two 18.29m, three-bladed rotors to swing inside each other's radius of rotation, so they are phase locked and can never hit one another. Other designs take the tilting drive to an extreme and have independently pitchable engine pods like the 1979 Bell Textron 301 XV-15, a tilt-rotor vehicle that uses 7.62m propellers and two 1500 hp Lycoming LTC1K-4K engines on independently flexible mountings to fly like a helicopter or a plane. Other designs are the Notar (No tail rotor) which uses turbine accelerated engine exhaust as side thrust and the vectored propeller design (such as the X49-A), both of which make the vehicle quieter.

Some more design examples include the Flettner FL 282, one of the earliest military helicopters of late 1940s design. It had one engine, a radial Bramo Sh 14A of seven cylinders and 160 hp power output, connected to a single rotor spanning 11.96m. The Sikorsky S-55/UH series (1950s) is a typical tail rotor design which employs one Wright R-1-300-3 piston engine of 800 hp with a main rotor span of 16.15m. And the Bell 204/205 H-1/UH/AH-1 Iroquois "Huey" (Mid 1950s) is the classic "Vietnam war era" medium-sized military example, the first mass-produced helicopter powered by a jet turbine. Another

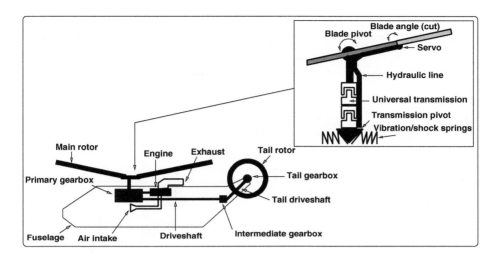

Figure 48.1
Main components of helicopter and operation of rotor blades.

example might be the UH-1B (1965) with a 960 hp T53-L-5 turbine engine with a two-blade 15m rotor.

Helicopter Sounds

Downdraft

Considering that the 7MW of power produced by a CH-47 all goes into moving air, we can expect something quite loud. Fortunately, the bulk of this creates useful thrust resulting in a subsonic downwash. Of course, this immense wind will excite many noisy responses, especially at low altitudes where the ground effect and recirculation occur to accelerate the air to high speeds and pressures. So one of the sounds is a windy rushing noise. It contains high frequencies that diminish greatly over distance, one reason why the sound is a chopping effect at distances but much more complex and noisy up close, and is heard especially loudly as the aircraft passes overhead, or rather immediately after it passes at higher altitude.

Engines and gears

Obviously the engines generate a lot of noise. Twin engines are either linked, and thus in phase, or one of them is a backup engine that is decoupled from the drive unless one fails, so we don't expect to hear engines beating in these designs. Nontandem VTOL vehicles, on the other hand, have independent engines, so both of them are apparent in the sound. Internal combustion engines coupled to an exhaust are not very different from car or truck engines in sound and may be modelled similarly, using pulse sources and waveguide apertures. Gas turbines are quieter but occupy a different spectrum, having the whining

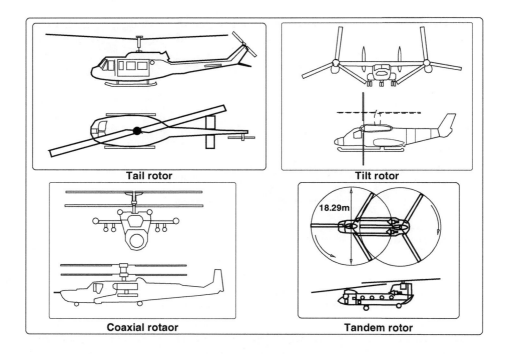

Figure 48.2
Different helicopter designs showing tail and main rotor configurations. Top left: UH-1 style classic single with tail rotor. Top right: XV-15 type tilt rotor aircraft. Bottom left: Kamov Ka series concentric coaxial rotor. Bottom right: CH-47 Chinook tandem rotors.

character we saw earlier when studying jet aircraft. As mentioned before, efficient mechanical devices should not make much noise, but the complex system of transmission and gearboxes in a helicopter contributes quite a lot to the sound. This may be a high-frequency squealing or whirring noise that is separate from the engine source.

Fuselage vibration

While vibration leads to fatigue and is undesirable, there is a lot of radiation from the body which acts an amplifier for mechanical sounds. Typical construction materials are aluminium, titanium, and glass fibre carbon composites. Sheeting is thin to reduce weight, so some hollow metallic resonance similar to a large car body contributes to the total effect.

Rotors

We have already studied fans and understand how they make a noise through turbulence and periodic compression and rarefaction. But unlike fan blades that may reach close to supersonic tip speed a helicopter blade must never do so. Mach shock waves would tear such a large area to pieces, and besides, Mach effects reduce lift. The edges rarely reach speeds in excess of 300m/s, but the effects of compression and rarefaction are still important. Period obviously varies, but in flight a typical rotation of 300RPM for a two-bladed rotor gives 10Hz. On such a large scale there is time for vortices to form in the wake of one blade which are hit by the next blade. This irregularity of density causes sound to be emitted from specific locations, and the constructive interference gives rise to directional patterns. Being smaller, the tail rotor spins faster, and as we have already considered this is an independent speed that depends on the torque created during a particular manoeuvre. Frequencies of 800RPM (14Hz) to 2000RPM (33Hz) with anything from 2 to 16 blades are found, so anything up to 500Hz is possible.

Blade noise and slap

We know the blade tips are not supersonic, so what causes the very sharp snapping that sounds like shockwaves? It seems that three separate processes contribute to rotor sound. A moving blade produces a signature not unlike the N-wave of a shock, but softened in time, with a parabolic approach and retreat and a sudden change in direction in the middle. One constant contribution to this waveform is caused by the thickness of the blade, called the *edge noise*. From this we get a turbulent broadband noise modulated at the rotation rate. Another contribution, which depends on the lift or blade pitch, is the aerodynamic signature, which is more pitched. Because of the cyclic modulation of blade pitch this changes throughout each rotation. Finally, there is *blade slap*. Vortices from the leading blade tip trail into the next advancing blade. As you probably know from air travel, a fast-moving object hitting pockets of air at a different density creates bumps, so the vortices cause sudden impulses that excite the rotor blade. They spiral inwards, usually hitting the trailing blade somewhere about 90 percent of its length. The excitation changes with speed but in certain positions they all line up, reinforcing one another and steepening the slope to make a loud bang like a shockwave. It is complicated to predict where this will happen as it depends on blade pitch, air velocity, and observer location, but we get a range of waveforms that change between a dull parabolic rise and fall to a sharp skewed sawtooth-like wave. It is not only the broadband noise from blade turbulence that is modulated by the low-frequency rotor; the engine and exhaust signals are also caught up in the same pulsating stream, so they are frequency modulated (by Doppler) at the same rate. Blade slap does not occur in all conditions or for all designs of helicopter. Some designs are very quiet and only emit regular edge noise and engine sounds. Blade slaps seem to occur once a critical threshold of pitch, area, forward velocity, and rotational velocity is passed, so it may occur during banking or sudden bursts of lift. Because of this, flight manoeuvres and sound are linked.

Directionality and location

If you listen to a recording of a helicopter approaching from a distance, passing overhead, and into the distance again, there are three distinct phases. To begin with, there is a certain chopping sound from the blade edge with not much engine sound at all. The rotor throws out waves of compressions that are strongest closer to the plane of rotation, so in the distance where the angle between the rotation plane and the observer is small it is heard loudly. Another angle 30° below the rotation plane is where the blade slap sounds loudest, so for a passing helicopter this part reaches a sudden peak. Below the plane of rotation, immediately below the aircraft, we do not hear the chopping sound but a steady downwash. The engine sound is carried by this and sounds quite loud and continuous. Behind the aircraft the tail rotor and exhaust are heard more clearly.

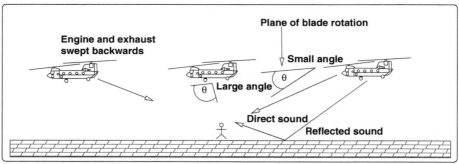

Figure 48.3
Position-dependent factors.

In addition to the change in blade angle there is a constantly changing difference between the path of the direct and reflected sounds leading to a phasing/flanging effect. You may also notice that on a calm day the volume of a distant helicopter seems to get louder and quieter as if there was a wind carrying the sound. If the vehicle passes to the side at a distance of several hundred meters the chopping can wax and wane depending on the position. This is due to directionality of compressions that radiate out like spokes of a wheel, leading to loud and quiet spots.

Model

Our initial model will include a wave signature for a simple rotor. Having studied fans and propellers, it's easy enough to construct a modulation of filtered noise that gives the right kind of effect. This first component corresponds to the edge effect, which is only half the story; so to improve on this a second signature will be added corresponding to vortex collision and aerodynamic lift signatures, which can be phase shifted relative to each other. Next we construct a tail rotor and an engine with exhaust and gearbox noise, and then use the rotor signature to modulate this too. Finally, the addition of fuselage resonance and movement effects will complete a realistic model. Values will be chosen for a generic medium-sized vehicle, leaving the option to scale components wherever possible. For the main rotor harmonics we try several predictive models and combine these with experimental data. Qualitatively speaking the blade behaves like a springy rule, but it is stressed along its length. One model is of

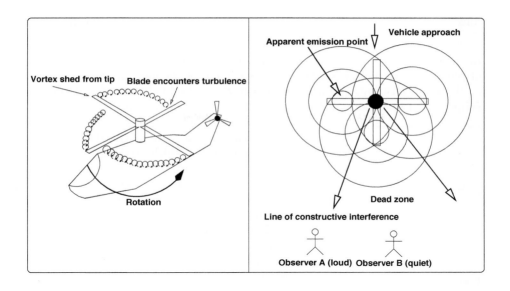

Figure 48.4
Left: Vortices from high-speed blade spiralling into next blade. Right: Interference patterns causing directional loudness and phase changes.

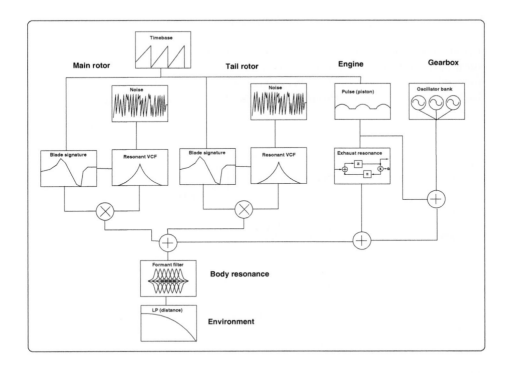

Figure 48.5
Simplified model of main components.

the blade as a string under tension from the centripetal force of rotation struck or plucked at 9/10 of its length. Another is a struck, hollow bar section excited in the same position, and another model views the blade as a cantilever bar supported at one end by a damped coupling to the drive shaft.

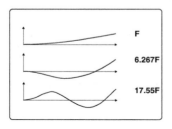

In reality the blade exhibits some properties of all these models in flight. Typical dimensions are 10m length, 0.5m width, and 0.2m thickness, with the Young's modulus and density per unit length being appropriate for aluminium with a 10mm thickness. Doing some rough estimates and aggregating the three models we arrive at a figure of 200Hz with a strong harmonics near $2f$, $2.7f$, and $6.2f$. Experimental data gives us readings between 80Hz and 300Hz with two strong harmonics that vary between $2f$ and $3f$, and $5f$ and $6f$. Analysis also reveals a variation between one well-formed impulse and several impulses in close proximity (which may be reflections in the recording echoed from the fuselage or ground).

Figure 48.6
First three vibrational modes of clamped bar.

Method

Fixed and variable delays will be quite important in this exercise. They will be useful for Doppler shifting of the angular blade velocity and whole vehicle movement as well as phasing effects and producing an engine/exhaust system. Rotor waves will be synthesised piecewise based on a skewed triangle source and waveshapers.

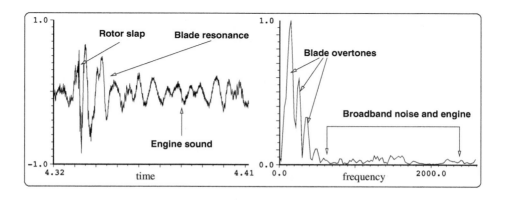

Figure 48.7
A single beat of a recorded helicopter sound, showing engine sound and blade overtones around 100Hz.

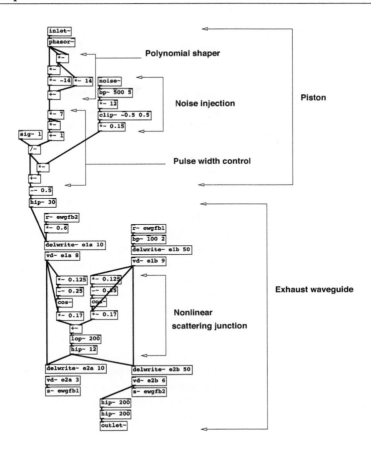

Figure 48.8
Engine, piston plus exhaust waveguide model.

DSP Implementation

To begin, let's consider the source of power for the vehicle. In this example, we will use a piston engine since we have already seen how to make one for a car. There are two main parts, the piston pulse generator and a waveguide for the exhaust pipe. The latter is a fixed filter that imparts a ringing to the pulses, but it is also a nonlinear filter that acts as a distortion or waveshaper. Starting with a `phasor~` at the top of figure 48.8, we employ a polynomial $14x^3 - 14x^2$ to provide a "shark fin" pulse (like a sawtooth but rounded on the top) and then a $1/(1 - kx^2)$ shaper to narrow the pulse. The result is a regular knocking sound with plenty of harmonics, although the spectrum is band-limited. Following this we have four delays arranged in a circle with feedback; another way of looking at it is as a bidirectional delay line. The ends of each delay pair correspond to the exit impedance of a pipe, so since they are partly open and partly closed we give a little feedback as reflection and tap off some of the signal as output. In the middle is a *scattering junction* that allows some of the back-propagated sound to mix with the forwards-propagated sound. This behaves like a hole in a flute, with the difference being that we limit the amplitude and spread the spectrum using part of a cosine cycle as a waveshaper. What we get is a pipe model that can be overdriven to give bright knocking sounds.

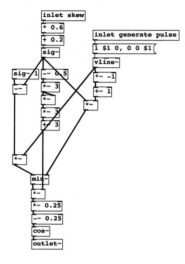

Here is the impulse generator for our main rotor. Looking at the diagram in figure 48.9 you can see it resembles a triangle wave generator followed by a cosine function. A steady cosinusoidal wave would be produced if both rising and falling parts were equal and linear. However, we introduce a variable breakpoint. Because the amplitude would change as we move the breakpoint, a crude compensation factor is applied to keep its amplitude flat. We then use the first 1/8th of the cosine cycle to turn the triangle into a pair of curves that meet at an apex. Changing the skew factor warps the pulse from a half-parabola in one direction to a half-parabola in the other, and in between we see a range of pulses where we can move the point at which the peak occurs.[1] With `vline~` and a message substitution, we may vary the duty cycle of each pulse after the timing is obtained from a metronome.

Figure 48.9
Asymmetrical triangle with variable slope.

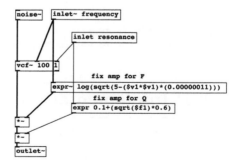

Figure 48.10
Flat amplitude noise source.

Changing the cutoff frequency and resonance of a variable band-pass filter normally alters the output amplitude. In Csound there is a filter unit called **reson** that has an interesting property of keeping constant amplitude. This

---

1. This is a form of phase distortion synthesis.

is our attempt at producing a similar filter, or rather a source of noise with a filter that maintains a constant level no matter how narrow we make the band or where it is moved in frequency. Expressions are annoying because they are not very efficient, but in this case they provide a compact way to express two compensation functions that adjust the makeup gain as we adjust frequency or resonance. It's possible to design the patch without this, but the sound is very sensitive to noise generated at this point and so it becomes fiddly to keep changing gain controls each time we move the frequency. This subpatch is named `flatnoise` in the main patch.

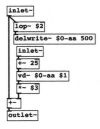

Before assembling the complete main rotor, here is an abstraction that gets used a few times (fig. 48.11). It is called

Figure 48.11
Movable delay.

`mdel` and is a movable comb delay, with a direct signal in parallel with a filtered and delayed version. Its purpose is to add blade harmonics by frequency modulation whenever its delay time is modulated by the rotor pulse source. What we have in effect is an FM synthesiser, but with precise control over the wave shape. We add harmonics by stretching

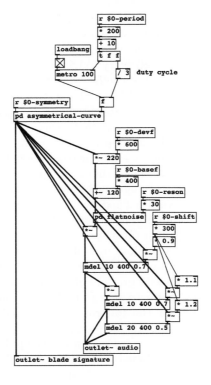

Figure 48.12
Main rotor.

or squashing copies of the pulse and mixing them onto each other. This corresponds well to the time domain waves seen in recordings of helicopter rotors and provides the blade slap sound.

A complete rotor sound simulator shown in figure 48.12 uses three movable comb delays, one set at 10 percent above, and two set 10 percent and 20 percent below the fundamental of the blade pulse (the scales affect period rather than frequency). At the top of figure 48.12 you see the metronome driving an asymmetrical pulse generator and a receiver from the period control. We have several other controls that can produce a variety of rotor sounds. Three of them modify the noise filter for broadband (edge noise) emission from the rotor; they set the frequency deviation, base frequency, and width of the noise band. A shift control varies the amount of FM applied to pulse copies and can change the sound between a soft swoosh and a harder slap. Notice the blade profile is also carried to an outlet for later use; maybe we can modulate the engine with a simulation of broken downdraft.

In figure 48.13 a graph on parent wrapper for the main rotor exposes the control sliders and abstracts the whole patch. Originally I tried two of these more sophisticated propeller models, one for the tail rotor too, but it seems like overkill since the tail rotor can be achieved with a far simpler setup. As an interesting aside, what we have here are many of the controls necessary to change the apparent position and speed of the helicopter. Changing the pulse symmetry exchanges the slap and whoosh. At its mid-point these appear simultaneously and give a good approximation to the

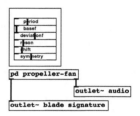

Figure 48.13
Control level of the main rotor.

sound heard directly below the helicopter if the engine level is also increased. To either side they give the impression of hearing the helicopter from the front, back, or sides where the phase of edge noise to blade slap changes.

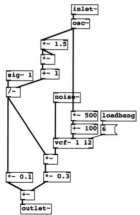

Figure 48.14
Tail rotor.

In figure 48.14 a simple tail rotor is implemented with a fixed width pulse generator and band-pass filter. This seems to spin between 3 and 5 times the main rotor speed in many recordings, which seems quite low, but if the aircraft is moving along at constant velocity and doing little work the torque would presumably be low with less need for the tail rotor to spin fast. We have an independent control for the tail rotor speed, and for a realistic effect this should probably increase when the lift of the main rotor increases. The pulse and swept noise are combined (remember that vcf~ bottoms out, giving no "negative" frequencies so the modulation apparently swinging −400 of zero is merely truncated). The noise centre is therefore about 250Hz.

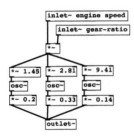

Figure 48.15
Gearbox sound.

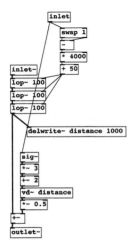

Figure 48.16
Distance filter.

A gearbox is implemented with three sine oscillators to give a high-pitched whine. It is a reduced version of the turbine sound generator. Gear sounds are linked to engine speed, but the ratio of engine speed to gear frequency needs to be adjustable. Small levels are satisfactory to create the right effect, so the gear sound must be attenuated somewhat. The numbers are fairly arbitrary; listening to some examples it seemed there were three higher-pitched components, probably corresponding to each of the three gearboxes, at 1.5 times the engine fundamental (main gearbox), twice the engine frequency and ten times the engine frequency. The last two may be the tail rotor gearing. Of course not all helicopters have this characteristic, so you should analyse and experiment with different frequency ratios for other models.

A distancing effect comprising a steep low pass to roll-off broadband noise with distance is shown in figure 48.16. In the far distance a gentle throbbing between 50Hz and 80Hz dominates the sound, with occasional bursts of rotor slap closer to 1kHz poking through. As the aircraft approaches, rotor slap and engine noise become louder. We haven't implemented a fly-by or overhead effect (this is left as an exercise), but a sudden dip in rotor noise and a peak in engine tone is characteristic of many recordings, along with the expected Doppler movement. I've implemented a delayed ground reflection that changes with distance. You can hear this very clearly in most aircraft fly-bys. On approach, a phasing effect sweeps upwards and then back down again as the aircraft recedes. The elements are all combined into a final sound object in figure 48.17.

Results

🔊 Source . . . . <http://mitpress.mit.edu/designingsound/helicopter.html>

Conclusions

A helicopter is a machine made of many parts and so is a composite sound source. Many of these parts correlate in function, so certain flight manoeuvres change several parts of the sound at once. The sound also depends on the observer's location and the helicopter's speed, rotation, and altitude. A

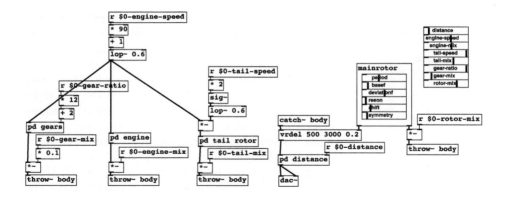

Figure 48.17
Complete helicopter sound object plus distancing filter.

composite constructed from individual parts, engine, exhaust, main and tail
rotors and gears can produce a convincing helicopter sound source.

Exercises

Exercise 1

Find a particular model to study. Working from as many recorded examples as
you can find, modify and tweak the helicopter model to simulate one particular
aircraft.

Exercise 2

Complete a fly-by effect with correct changes to engine/rotor levels as well as
Doppler. Add extra wind effects for the downwash as it passes directly over.

Exercise 3

By analysis or calculation work out the changes in tail rotor speed, engine gearing, and blade pitch for two manoeuvres like lifting off and banking sideways.

References

Froude, W. (1878). "On the elementary relation between pitch, slip, and propul-
sive efficiency." *Trans. Inst. Naval Arch.* 19: 47–57.
Froude, R. E. (1889). "On the part played in propulsion by differences of fluid
pressure." *Trans. Inst. Naval Arch.* 30: 390.
Leishmana, J. G. (1999). "Sound directivity generated by helicopter rotors
using wave tracing concepts." *J. Sound and Vibration* 221, no. 3: 415–441.

Leverton, J. W. (1983). *Helicopter Blade Noise.* Institute of Sound and Vibration Research, University of Southhampton, and Westland Helicopters, Yeovil, England.

McCluer, M. S., Baeder, J. D., and Kitaplioglu, C. (1995). *Comparison of Experimental Blade-Vortex Interaction Noise with Computational Fluid Dynamic Calculations.* American Helicopter Society Annual Forum, Fort Worth, Texas.

Olson H. F. (1952). "Resonators and radiators." In *Music, Physics, and Engineering,* chapter 4. Dover.

Polanco, F. G. (2002). *Determining Beam Bending Distribution Using Dynamic Information.* Airframes and Engines Division, Aeronautical and Maritime Research Laboratory Defence Science and Technology Organisation, Victoria, Australia.

Rankine, W. J. M. (1853). *General Law of Transformation of Energy.*

Rankine, W. J. M. (1858). *Manual of Applied Mechanics.*

Rankine, W. J. M. (1865). "On the mechanical principles of the action of propellers." *Trans. Inst. Naval Arch.* 6: 13–39.

Practical Series
Lifeforms

The ceaseless tides of selves, ever
passing away before your eyes.
—Daevid Allen

Living Things

There are two very remarkable things that distinguish sounds made by living
organisms from all other types of sound, material composition, and intelligence.

Material

The first difference is what living things are made of. Everything else in the
world is either a solid, liquid, or gas, and we have already looked at the properties of these forms in some detail. But living things fall into a kind of in-
between category. Of course they are still made of solids, liquids, and gases,
because that's what physics allows, but the *properties* of living tissue is not
really like any of these. The earliest life forms were really a sort of resilient
jelly made of long molecule chains. Archaean methanogens hanging around in
boiling mud pools 3.6 billion years ago could best be described as "a kind of
goo." It took another 3 billion years before Cambrian-era creatures had a strong
enough outer structure to squirt water, probably making the first underwater
squelches. Today we see enormous material diversity in life. The most abundant
creatures are still insects with hard exoskeletons. But most other things like
mammals, fish, and reptiles are largely a soft, flexible muscle tissue. It neither
transmits sound nor vibrates very well. In fact, all creatures have evolved to
avoid resonances except where they are useful.

Intelligence

The other difference is intelligence. Living things have intent, thoughts, purposes. Throughout this journey we have seen increasingly complex control structures. We've looked at idiophonic objects that are so lifeless they don't make
a sound unless something bumps into them or they fall under gravity. Next

we saw how forces of nature made sounds through large-scale dynamics, determined by random, indifferent processes, albeit unfathomably complex ones. With machines we have seen the possibility for elaborate periodic behaviour, but these were designed by intelligent beings. So, now we get to the top of the pile. Living things exhibit the most complex control structures of all. With intent comes communication, warnings, orientation signals, in fact most of Chion's listening strategy list (see pp. 104–107) can be turned around to form a sounding strategy list. The signals produced are incredibly subtle and varied in tone, modulation, and rhythm. They may take hundreds, even thousands of parameters to capture. And we still don't understand what most living creatures are trying to communicate or probe.

Behaviour

To help make sense of the sounds made by living things we can posit two useful categories, sounds made by movement and vocalisations.

Movement

These are the sounds creatures make by way of simply being alive. The only proviso is that they are active rather than passive sounds. So, branches blowing in the wind don't count, even though trees are alive. However, the earliest active airborne sounds might have come from vascular plants 2.5 billion years ago. Based on cellulose, they were the first lifeforms to have a hard and strong enough structure to spread seeds deliberately. Pine cones or gorse pods can be heard cracking in the summer heat as they spit out seeds. Of course, by movement what we really mean is animal behaviour, walking on legs or the flapping and buzzing of wings.

Vocalisations

Vocalisations are any deliberate sounds produced by the creature itself. Insects rub their wings together to make calls. Snakes can hiss. Frogs blow air through resonators in their throats. And eventually, through evolution, this leads to animals that can sing, squawk, bark, meow, and talk. What distinguishes vocalisations from all other sounds is that they are deliberate, they are designed; so animals are sound designers too.

The Practicals

There are four practicals in this part.

- Footsteps: an exercise in animal movement.
- Insects: a look at buzzing flies and chirping crickets.
- Birds: sounds of the avian syrinx.
- Mammals: some more complex vocalisations based on a resonant tract.

49
Practical 26
Footsteps

Aims

This first practical section on living creatures is a bit unusual. We are going to create the sound of human footsteps. There are a few surprises here. You may think footsteps to be a fairly simple sound problem, but in fact they are rather more complicated than they first seem. Although you might not think of footsteps as "animal sounds," they are one of the simplest introductions we can have to the subject of biomechanics.

We further illustrate the decoupling of control and synthesis parts. The walking mechanism is particular to the animal, while the sound is governed by the surface on which it moves. We will see in this practical, and later exercises with bird and mammal sounds, that living creatures generate complex control signals. A brain and nervous system connecting to many continuously controllable muscles is capable of producing more complex patterns of forces than any mechanical or inanimate natural sound sources we have seen so far. As well as the inanimate physics, we must consider behaviour and intention. In light of this knowledge, it will become clear why procedural audio is superior to data-driven (sampled) sound in interactive applications. Reflecting on the complexity of walking, you will understand why film artists still dig Foley pits to produce the nuance of footsteps, and why sampled audio is an inflexible choice for video game footfalls.

Analysis

What happens when we walk? It is a subject that has been researched extensively, and new insights are still emerging, but here is a simplified summary. Consider the human body standing at rest. Weight is distributed evenly on both feet, which have a relatively small surface area. There is a force, a pressure exerted on the ground, which is balanced by a reciprocal force from the ground supporting the body. We call this the *ground response force* or *GRF*. A smaller surface area means a higher GRF, so standing on tiptoe produces a higher pressure than standing with feet flat. As we move forward, weight is shifted from one foot to the other and energy is expended by muscles to propel us along. Biochemical potential energy becomes movement, as well as sound and heat.

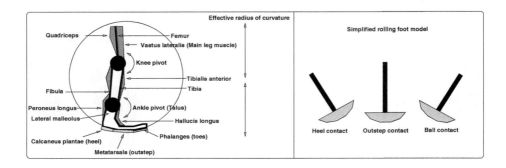

Figure 49.1
Biomechanical summary and simplification of the foot during walking.

Action of the Foot

The foot does not just plant itself squarely on the ground. There are three phases to each step. During the first phase the heel contacts the ground. This part is much harder than the rest, the bony calcaneus of the heel pivots on the ankle talus, and two muscles (peronius and hallucis longi) rotate the foot. Weight is then shifted onto outer tarsals and each foot rolls along the ground, ending on its toes, or ball of the foot. This process is simplified in the second frame of figure 49.1. It can be seen that each foot behaves as if it were an outer rim of a circle whose radius is about one-third of the total leg length. The final phase is where work is done. Force comes from a complex application of many muscles; two (vastus lateralis, tibialis anterior) work to straighten the leg and push the weight forward. Other (antagonist) muscles are used to bend the leg and balance during different phases of locomotion.

Modes of Movement

We can identify three different kinds of movement: creeping, walking, and running. Each has a different motion and a different purpose. Creeping is generally a predator's behaviour and works to minimise the pressure changes on the ground in order to reduce sound. Running maximises locomotive acceleration, whereas walking is a compromise behaviour that maximises locomotion while minimising energy expenditure. The body moves in a pendulum motion during these activities, so the weight moves up and down around the centre of gravity while the spine also twists the body at the hips. In this way energy can be converted to gravitational potential and stored to effect efficiency. In terms of sound, these factors cause different patterns of GRF pressure, which we will examine now.

GRF Pressure Signatures

Speed of movement determines the time the foot is in contact with the ground. Any GRF pattern is compressed or dilated as the actor's speed changes. Here is

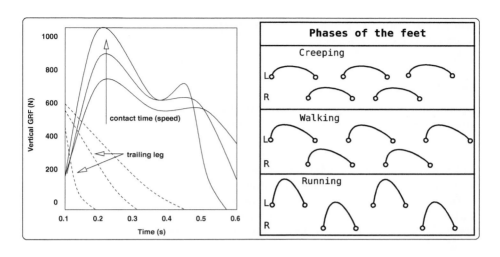

Figure 49.2
GRF curve and foot phase changes with actor speed.

one reason why sampled footsteps sound wrong. The length of each step must change with the speed while the sound from ground texture interaction must remain constant, an obvious appeal to synthesis rather than sampling.

Within each walking cycle the pressures of each step change phase, depending on running, walking, or creeping behaviour, so a different GRF curve is observed. Simplified GRF curves are shown for a small range of speeds in the left frame of figure 49.2; perhaps you can mentally extrapolate these to see where they lead as we move towards a very slow creep or fast run. The shape is also influenced by whether the actor is accelerating (doing positive work), slowing down (doing negative work), or moving at constant velocity. When accelerating to a sprint the greatest GRF occurs in the ball phase as you push off on each step. When slowing down the heel digs in to cause friction, and so the first phase is strongest. During constant velocity movement, the outstep tries to remain in contact for as long as possible, shifting the weight slowly forwards, so this has the greatest GRF and duration. Another factor influencing the GRF curve is ground incline. Walking up a hill places more emphasis on the ball phase, whereas descending a mild slope will shift GRF patterns towards the heel.

Locomotion Phases

So far we have only considered the GRF phases of one foot. What also changes is the relationship between two feet. A simplified illustration is shown in the right frame of figure 49.2. While walking there is a considerable overlap of contact. The trailing foot does not leave the ground until the leading one has moved into its second phase. Creeping along we tend to keep both feet on the ground for as long as possible. Once the pattern becomes a run there are times when neither foot touches the ground, and the actor bounces along sometimes only on the balls of the feet.

Ground Texture Acoustics

Given a force curve which we can create by knowing the actor speed, weight, approximate foot area, and some footwear material with a certain hardness, we can approximate the acoustic interaction with a range of surfaces. The impulse given to the ground is the product of force and contact time, which will give us a possible excitation pulse for filter bank or waveguide models of hard materials like wood, concrete, stone, and metal. Tempering the sharpness of this pulse allows us to introduce a measure of hardness. For highly resonant surfaces like metal panels the contact time increases damping, so we can integrate the GRF to obtain a decay time. Granular textures like gravel can be obtained by directly driving a crushing model with the GRF so that grain density and energy is directly proportional to the pressure. Unusual textures like snow deform asymmetrically, causing a squealing sound as frictional stresses cause heat, melting, rebonding, and permanently altering the structure (crushing it to ice). We may also employ thresholds on the GRF to obtain nonlinear effects like creaking wooden floorboards, or even trigger world events like ice breaking.

Model

Our model will be broken clearly into two sections, one for control and a set of synthesisers specific to the ground texture. A control system that models human walking comprises a bistable or reciprocating mechanism, two legs, and two feet. Phases for six control parts, ball, edge, and heel on each foot, are derived at two levels. The first splits the phase of a master oscillator to obtain a pair of subphases that can vary in duration and position within the main cycle. These are further split into three GRF contributions which are summed to form the resultant curve for each foot. Most importantly, of course, we need at least two sound generators that can overlap. We should be aware that there's no restriction to a single, exclusive surface texture. Synthesisers can be blended to produce mixtures of grass, soil, gravel, or any combination. This allows smooth transitions across changing terrain instead of having a discrete sound for each categorised texture that changes abruptly at a boundary. Since each texture will use the GRF curve differently a preconditioner is used to shape the curve accordingly. The model is summarised in figure 49.3.

Method

This is best implemented by a synchronous system that splits a phasor into two windows. Half-cycles of a cosine function could be used to approximate contributory pressure curves, but with similar efficiency we can get much better

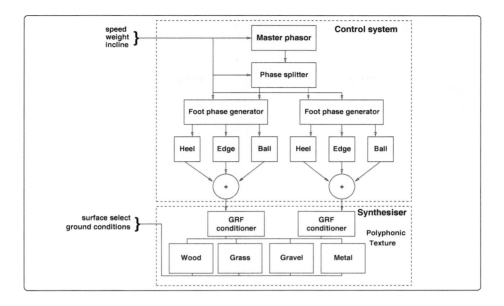

Figure 49.3
Model schematic for procedural footsteps.

results from a polynomial approximation to the curve seen in figure 49.2. To demonstrate the sound production process a granular synthesis method will be used to produce a gravel type texture; other surfaces are left as exercises for the reader.

Implementation

Let's begin with a two-phase oscillator that has variable overlap. The patch shown in figure 49.4 is a test version of what will be abstracted, with two outlets appearing in place of the oscillators below the dotted line and an inlet in place of the slider. First focus your attention on the little message domain collection on the far left. The purpose here is to shut down the output of both GRF curves (both feet) when the player stops moving, otherwise one of the texture synthesisers could be left hanging, making a continuous sound. Another function performed by this code is to reset the oscillator phase when the player starts moving again, so he always moves the right foot forward first rather than continuing from the last phase where he stopped. The remainder of this description will deal with the signal process to derive two overlapping phases. Beginning at the top with `sig~` you can see the main phasor has a range 0.0Hz to 6.0Hz and feeds two parallel process chains. Both of these are inverse functions of frequency (we first take the inverse of

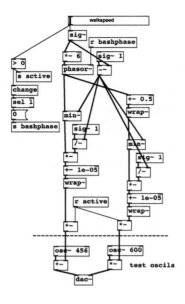

Figure 49.4
Two-phase variable overlap phasor.

walk speed). Using ⬛min~ caps the phasor at some level. We take the reciprocal of that level and multiply the capped phasor by it, thus restoring an amplitude of 1.0. This is the same for both sides except that the right side is offset by 180°, achieved by adding 0.5 and wrapping the signal. For small frequencies the duration of each phase is near 1.0, for both feet, so GRF curves will overlap. For fast frequencies (high speeds) the durations diminish towards zero. In the middle range is a critical point where the player breaks between walking and running. The final version of this abstraction is tweaked somewhat to create nice ranges for walking and running sounds; if you do not have the disk examples to play with you should experiment with adding offsets to frequency and overlap points yourself.

In order to produce each part of the GRF curve we need a better approximation than

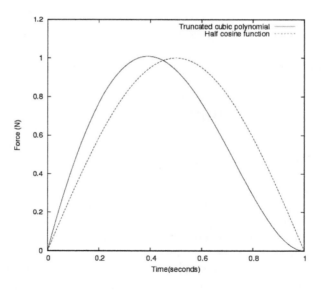

Figure 49.5
Comparison of cosine curve with polynomial pulse.

a half cosine. Notice that the polynomial curve is pushed to the left; pressure builds more quickly but decays more slowly after a second turning point on the decay side that makes the pressure approach zero more gracefully. The coefficients 1.5 and 3.3333 were found experimentally after approximately fitting the curve to real data. The implementation is a factorisation of the general cubic form that lets us use the least number of multiply operations.

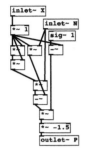

This patch implements $1.5(1 - x)(nx^3 - nx)$ where $n = 3.3333$. With x in a normalised range we find that altering n reduces the amplitude, widens the pulse, and reduces the rise time, a perfect combination that fits with experimentally observed GRF pressures. Following the flow in figure 49.6 we have, in the left column, $1 \times x^2 \times x$ giving us x^3. This is multiplied by n to obtain nx^3. In the second column we have a single multiply taking x and n, which is then subtracted from the first term to produce $nx^3 - nx$. Finally, we multiply by $1 - x$, obtained in the third column, and by 1.5 to arrive at the final factored polynomial. The initial multiplier of 1.0 is, of course, redundant. It was originally there to experiment with another coefficient of x but is left in the final patch only because it makes the diagram easier to read by acting as an anchor point for the signal connections.

Figure 49.6
Pulse generator using polynomial.

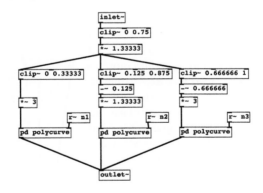

Figure 49.7
GRF curve generator.

Here is the crucial GRF curve generator. A superposition of three polynomial curves, implicitly summed at the outlet, is obtained by splitting the phase of the incoming line segment. First we modify its time, compressing it to three quarters of its original duration. Following this are three parallel flows, each of which splits off a different part of the line using clip~, subtracts the bottom offset to return its base to zero, and then scales it by a factor that returns it to a normalised range. These three subphases then each feed a polynomial pulse generator. Three receivers to set the curve shape for heel, ball, and edge roll are made available; these will be satisfied in the parent patch with some controls.

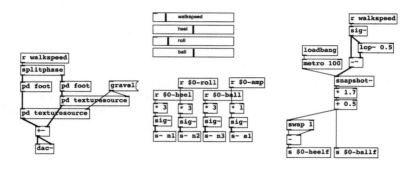

Figure 49.8
Complete footstep generator.

Before looking at the patch that actually generates some sound (which is not very important to this exercise), let's examine the final arrangement of components for producing realistic footstep patterns. At the top is the first object we made, a two-phase timebase that overlaps the left and right line segments more as the frequency decreases. Two feet are attached, one for each phase, which contain the polynomial GRF curve generators. The control signals from these now feed a texture generator that can be tailored to whatever surface we wish. Observe in the middle a set of controls for actor speed and curves of ball, heel, and edge roll.

Remember that altering these changes our perception of whether the footsteps are accelerating or slowing (doing positive or negative work), or whether the player is walking up or down a slope. On the right I have added a second-order control system as a demonstration. The filter and snapshot units form a signal-to-message domain differentiator. This gives a positive value if the player is accelerating and a negative one if he slows down. Moving the walk speed fader quickly will change the heel-to-ball ratio more.

You are encouraged to try and devise your own texture synthesisers to work with the GRF curve generator. There are a number of interesting possibilities,

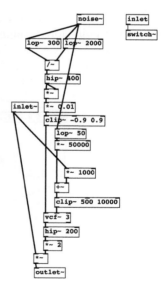

Figure 49.9
Crunchy gravel texture generator.

including using it as an index to a grain sample player that stores fragments
of sampled footsteps. Here I show a rather esoteric grain generator that makes
wet gravel-type sounds. But first, notice the DSP block control on the right.
Footstep sounds are clearly noncontinuous, so we can reduce CPU use by shutting down the audio computations when the player isn't moving. This basically
takes all the computations in this subpatch out of the loop when `switch~` is turned
off. Now let's describe the texture generator. Look at the objects above the first
`clip~`, which divide two filtered noise streams and then square a high-passed version of it. Clearly these will produce very high-signal peaks when one of the
signals approaches zero. The idea is to produce a certain distribution of spikes,
each of which would correspond to a crunch of gravel. The second part of this
patch is a modulator based on low-passed noise at 50Hz, amplified enormously
and clipped into a range of 500 to 10000, which will be the frequency of grain
spikes filtered by the `vcf~`. Values are chosen such that as the incoming GRF
curve increases the density and tone of the spikes rises.

Figure 49.10
Wrapping a source
to reduce CPU use.

Here is an accessory to the patch above. It is a wrapper,
meaning the gravel texture generator should be placed here,
inside this patch, with inlets and outlets passed in and out
of the generator to the outside. All it does is look at the
level of the GRF control signal and decide when to switch
the texture generator on or off. Because the control is in the
signal domain we cannot place this code inside the actual
generator, because once switched off all signal computation
would cease and there would be no way for the generator to
know when to switch back on again.

Results

🔊   Source   . . . .   <http://mitpress.mit.edu/designingsound/
footsteps.html>

Conclusions

Footsteps are more than simple clonks; they are complex patterns generated
by an elaborate biomechanical process involving different muscles and different
parts of the foot, and they change according to the behaviour of the actor.
We can model them using curve generators that approximate the force on the
ground and the way this force changes in different circumstances.

Exercises

Exercise 1

Design a texture generator for soft earth, dry grass, or other surfaces. Experiment with crossfading between different layers of textures so that the player

can move across dry earth, then earth with grass, then earth with small stones, and so on.

Exercise 2

Replace the human foot GRF with a single pressure pulse generator, but then modify the overlapping multiphase timebase to create the patterns for a four-legged creature like a horse. Work out how to generate trotting, cantering, and galloping patterns for the animal.

References

Adamczyk, P. G., Collins, S. H., and Kuo, A. D. (2006). "The advantages of a rolling foot in human walking." *J. Exp. Biol.* 209: 3953–3963.

Cook, P. (2002). "Walking synthesis: A complete system." In *Real Sound Synthesis for Interactive Applications*, chapter 15, pp. 191–200. A. K. Peters.

D'Aout, K. "Study of the locomotion of the bonobo (Pan paniscus): A model for the evolutionary origin of human bipedalism." <http://webh01.ua.ac.be/funmorph/Bipedalism>

D'Aoŭt, K., Vareecke, E., Schoonaert, K., Declercq, D., Van Elsacker, L., and Aertt, P. (2004). "Locomotion in bonobos (Pan paniscus): Differences and similarities between bipedal and quadrupedal terrestrial walking, and a comparison with other locomotor modes." *J. Ana.* 204(5): 353–361.

Mehta, C. (2006). "Real-time Synthesis of Footfall Sounds on Sand and Snow, and Wood." (Granular cell based approach.) Thesis.

Vereecke, E. "Comparison of the bipedal locomotion of gibbons, bonobos and humans." <http://webh01.ua.ac.be/funmorph/evie>

Willems, P. A., Cavagna, G. A., and Heglund, N. C. (1995). "External, internal, and total work in human locomotion." *J. Exp. Biol.* 198: 379–393.

50
Practical 27
Insects

Aims

Here we shall examine some sounds made by insects. Many of them are remarkably simple, others are more difficult to model. Diversity arises from the multitude of ways insects make noises. Some are pure tones, high-pitched or nearly ultrasonic whistles. Others are frictional sounds of tiny hairs or other body parts rubbing together known as *stridulation*. Beating wings create waveforms that follow the oscillatory patterns of the insect's body. In many cases the sounds are deliberate, mating calls, territorial warnings, or orientation signals, so the insects have evolved to make them as loud as possible and in a highly controlled manner. Our aim is to make this practical section as fun and informative as possible, bringing together several analysis and synthesis methods, so we will look at several examples in quick succession, picking various modelling and synthesis techniques to implement them. Finally, we will place a collection of varied insect sounds into an environment to make a virtual jungle scene.

Analysis

Each species and subspecies makes a different pattern and tone. To humans these may sound superficially similar, but insects brains are highly tuned to recognise nuances at the waveform level. There are at least three scales of detail to consider. The individual waveforms are a result of the production mechanism. At a physical level we see a basic sounding method, whether rubbing body parts, beating wings, or clicking limbs against resonant shells or other resonant body parts. The next level of organisation contains collections of cycles. The number of tiny clicks in a beetle call or cricket chirp are important, governed by the biology, size, and age of the example. Often this level of detail is deliberately controlled by the creature and can be considered *communication*. At a higher level we observe large-scale behaviour, sometimes apparent only as statistical features. The average time a fly remains in flight before settling and the length of groups of chirps separated by exact pauses in mating calls are macro features of the sounds.

Field Cricket

A most common sound effect for outdoor scenes like grasslands is the chirping cricket (Gryllus). It emits a regular burst of sound about once or twice per second for many minutes, then pauses for a while before resuming. From biological research we know it does this by rubbing tiny hairs together and employing its wings, hard resinous protein discs, or sacs of air as resonators. Let's take a look at a field recording of a familiar North American example. This sample is several seconds in duration.

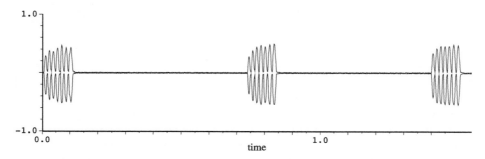

Figure 50.1
Wave of a cricket chirp.

Notice the regularity of each burst, somewhere near 0.12s duration separated by 0.7s pauses. You can see another interesting thing, that each burst consists of exactly seven smaller features. They begin at an amplitude of 0.25 and rise to about 0.5. Let's zoom in on one of these and see the waveform and spectrum.

The shape of each burst seems to have an attack like a parabolic rise, and a tail that lies between exponential and linear. This is a good indication of a driven resonator. Inside each burst is a packet of strongly periodic sound with one very strong harmonic, a little noisy irregularity, and two other harmonics that suggest a sawtooth- or relaxation-type signature. Looking at the waveform very closely (not shown here) we find this is indeed the case, something between a triangle and sawtooth, as we might expect from the stimulation of a flexible hair. The first (fundamental) harmonic is at 4.5kHz, the second much smaller one around 9.0kHz, and a very quiet one near 13.5kHz. Pulses towards the end of the chirp fall in frequency slightly; careful analysis of several examples shows this reaches 3.9kHz, a change of 600Hz, or roughly a 10 percent drop. Perhaps the creature expends less energy than at the start of the chirp, but some biolomechanical reseach suggests that certain species have varying lengths of ribs so the effect is like rubbing a comb with tapering teeth.

If we analyse many of these chirps it seems there are sometimes two peaks near the fundamental, with one a bit lower or higher than the other. In the

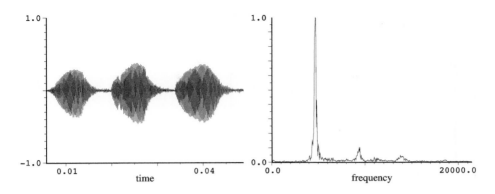

Figure 50.2
Closeup waveform and spectrum of cricket chirp.

example analysed, two are spread either side of 4.5kHz at values like 4.4kHz and 4.6kHz. This could be due to modulation with a reflected signal, but we know the recording was made in an open field. The reason is that the cricket has two wings and is rubbing them both at the same time. Is it worth replicating this dual source sound for the sake of realism? Maybe, for a high-quality effect, but for an approximation more suitable for a real-time game we can probably make the efficiency of using only one source and adding some noisy modulation to the system to help spread the frequencies a bit.

Flying Insects

The frequency of wing beating varies between 50Hz for large insects with synchronous wing muscles, and 2kHz for small flies with independent wing control. The sound is strongly influenced by the presence of two strong sources that may not necessarily be in phase or of equal frequency. The phase of both wings received by the listener will change as the insect moves about and changes orientation. Due to its small size a fly emits sound from its entire body, which moves in resonance with the wing beating. Biomechanic analysis of common flies (Phormia [Nachtigall 1966; Wood 1970] and Drosophila [Bennet-Clarke and Ewing 1968]) reveals wing movement in a figure-of-eight path, with a very fast exponential upstroke and a slower linear downstroke. The wing is rotated between these two phases so that thrust is obtained on the downstroke, but the wing angles sideways to quickly return to the top position. Pressure waveforms measured immediately behind the insect show a strong correlation to this wing pattern. Spectrally, we observe the result as close to a sawtooth with an accentuated second harmonic. This waveform at a constant frequency sounds nothing like a fly, however; the frequency of a real fly varies a lot. To us the air seems uniform, but to a fly, especially outdoors, it is filled with density and velocity variations. To navigate this invisible landscape, the fly,

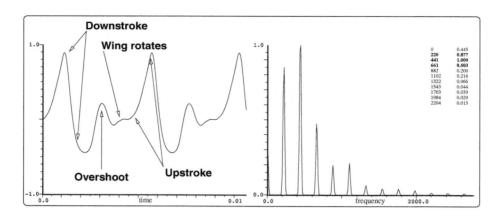

Figure 50.3
Correlation of wing action with pressure wave (from Bennet-Clark and Ewing 1968).

with a very fast nervous system, changes its wing frequency greatly in a short space of time by as much as 20 percent. This seems to produce an irregular warbling vibrato. Insects with independent wing control evolved to be much more agile than larger ones without this ability. Mosquitoes and midges, having such light bodies and high manoeuvrability from independent wing control, can almost flip around in mid-air. As they do so they emit a chorusing-like effect and a sudden spectral peak where one wing slows down while the other speeds up.

Cicada

A rapid, noisy clicking sound produced by cicadas comes from flexible ribs with a semi-circular cross section on their abdomens called *timbales*. As the abdomen muscles contract the ribs click in the same way that a plastic dome push button does, flexing inwards. The cicadas body contains hollow air sacs that act as resonators to amplify the sound. When the muscles relax the ribs pop out again making a second sound. Let's call one of these gestures a *chirp*, from which more complex sounds are built. By rapidly modulating their abdomens a more or less constant noisy rattling is produced. They alternate between several different sounds, short click-like chirps, regular and long chirps, bursts of strong noise that sound like sand dropped onto paper, and a continuous whirring sound. Each chirp is made of many tiny clicks of varied frequency surrounding two centres each of about 1kHz bandwidth at 5–6kHz and 7–8kHz. The lower group is somewhat louder than the upper one, but we can see a definite notch in the spectrum at 6.5kHz. The timing of each chirp is quite regular; with five bursts in a 0.2s period, the modulation is about 25Hz.

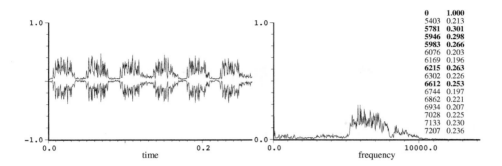

Figure 50.4
Waveform and spectrum of a common North American cicada (recording courtesy Dr. Thomas
E. Moore, University of Michigan Museum of Zoology, Insect Division).

Looking closer, it's apparent that the small-scale structure is quite noisy.
There are dozens of clicks per chirp, 20 peaks in a 0.02s period, giving a
modulation of 1kHz. But they are not of regular amplitude. In fact some
clicks are completely missing and some seem more bunched up than others.
Taking the average spectrum over this window confirms the distribution as
lying in two bands somewhere between 5kHz and 9kHz with a gap between
them.

Model

The cricket sound can work nicely as a pulse and resonator system, or by direct
spectral synthesis using FM or AM. The flying insect is best approached by
studying the pressure patterns made by the wing oscillation and using shaping
functions to approximate different segments piecewise, although it may also
be approached as a pulse resonator model. Perhaps the most difficult is the
cicada because of the spectral density of its call made by such rapid movement
of so many timbales. For this a noise-based approximation serves us efficiently,
although a more literal model with several dozen filters can produce very natural sounds, but with consequent cost.

Method

More than one method can be employed for each model. Excitor and resonator
approaches seem to be best for most cases, especially since the hard, fixed
resinous shells of many insects lend themselves to fixed filters and short, sharp
pulses for excitation. Complex calls may be accomplished well in the message

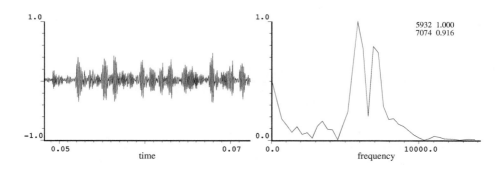

Figure 50.5
Close-up wave and averaged spectrum of a common cicada chirp.

domain, which seems appropriate since they are quite musical. Flying insects require attention to subtleties of waveform changes that occur during flight, so a method that allows fast parameterisation is desirable.

Implementation

We will now proceed to implement each of the three cases discussed above. Context is quite important since we are not used to hearing insects so close and dry, and they may seem unrecognisable outside a plausible environment. You might wish to experiment with listening using a woodland reverb or hearing ensembles of insects by instantiating many of them with slightly different parameters into a stereo listening space.

Field Cricket

A model is shown in figure 50.6. Let's demonstrate how we can make this sound using a very efficient method that uses only one phasor and some cheap arithmetic. This way we could populate a scene with scores of these creatures at very low CPU cost.

First we design the modulator signal. If the repeat time is 0.7s the required base frequency is 1.43Hz. Each burst is 0.12s, and the remaining $0.7-1.2 = 0.58$s is silent, so we must multiply the phasor range of 1.0 by 0.1714 to get the right duty cycle. Although the timing of the slow phasor is correct it now moves to 1.0 and stays there, which is not what we want. We want it to move from 0.0 to 1.0 and then return to 0.0, which `wrap~` provides. The remaining operations in the first column convert the phasor to a parabolic pulse $(-4(x-0.5)^2 + 1)$.

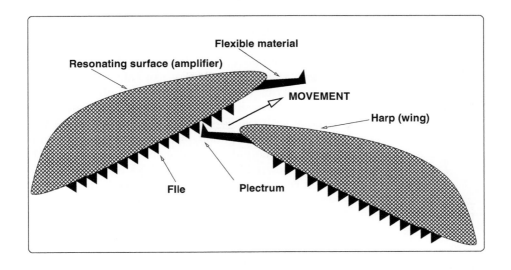

Figure 50.6
A cricket wing.

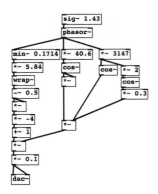

Figure 50.7
Field cricket synchronous AM
method.

Subtracting 0.5 puts the line around zero with half its original amplitude, and squaring produces two curves, one for the positive and one for the negative part, that meet at zero. Flipping the sign, recentering and adding an offset makes this a circular hump that sits on zero. Now that we have a slow modulation, we need to obtain the fast source that makes the little clicks in each chirp. If each burst is 0.12s and contains 7 segments then the frequency of modulation is 58Hz, so we can derive this from the base by multiplying by 40.6. Taking the square of the cosine of this value produces positive going pulses with which to modulate the main frequencies. On the right we derive these frequencies from the base phasor in a similar fashion, $1.43 \times 3147 = 4.5$kHz, plus a second harmonic at twice the fundamental and about one-third the amplitude. This seems good enough without a third harmonic, which is very quiet anyway.

Field Cricket 2

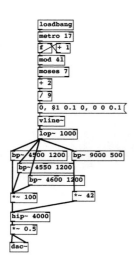

Figure 50.8
Field cricket pulse and
band-pass method.

As an alternative, let's look at a different way to
achieve a similar result. We can calculate that each
click is 17ms apart, so let's begin with a timebase
that produces clicks continually at that rate. This
is done with the `metro` object. How many pulses will
there be in one period of 0.7s? Dividing the chirp
period by the pulse period gives 700ms/17ms = 41,
so let's now add a counter and `mod` operator to constrain counting over this range. To split this number
stream into groups of 7 and 34 (the remaining silent
pulses), `moses` is used. So that the pulses grow in amplitude the number is scaled into a range 0.2 to 1.0 by
adding 2 and dividing by 9, then substituting that
value as the upper limit of a 0.2ms pulse obtained
through `vline~`. Because these pulses are a little bit too
sharp, a low-pass filter softens them before we feed
them to some high-resonance band-pass filters which
produce the correct tone. Unfortunately this leaves a
residual low frequency at the pulse rate, so a further
high pass removes this. The result sounds much too
mechanical and unnatural with only two bands, so I've
added an extra two peaks very close to the fundamen-
tal to provide the effect of two wings at close frequencies. Notice the high gain
needed to recover the ringing signal from the filters when excited by such a
short pulse. This leads to a potentially troublesome patch that can make loud
clicks on startup if the filters are not initialised carefully. It works nicely in
Pure Data, but beware if you are translating this patch, and be sure to zero
any signal prior to the filters and trap any initial DC components.

Cicada

An approach is summarised in figure 50.9. We start with some harsh preconditioning of the noise source to keep it well inside the 5,000Hz to 8,000Hz band.
Extraneous frequencies in the lower region seem to badly affect the sound by
bleeding though as modulation artifacts, so we kill everything we don't want
in the spectrum first.

Two narrow peaks are split off at 5.5kHz and 7.5kHz and subjected to
a modulation at 500Hz, which widens up the sidebands and gives us a time
domain texture like that observed in the analysis. A pulse wave is derived from
a cosine oscillator using the $1/(1 + x^2)$ method to modulate the noise bands.
The width and frequency of this are controllable to set the singing call. Three
examples heard from the analysis recordings are switched between at random.
Modulating the noise after such high-resonance filters works to keep the sound

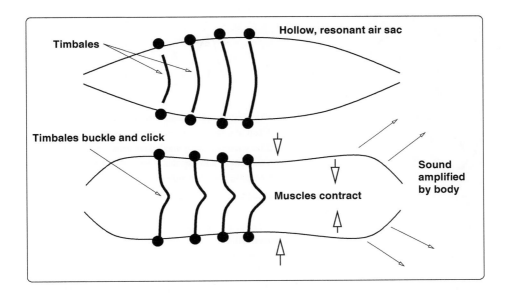

Figure 50.9
Timbales of a cicada.

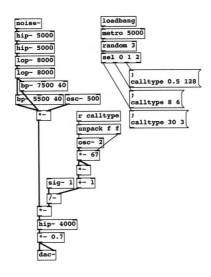

Figure 50.10
Cicada with three call types.

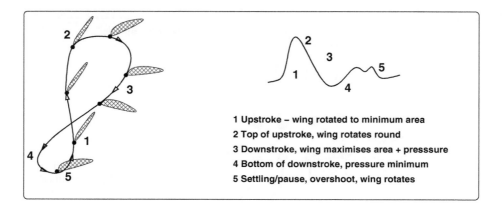

Figure 50.11
Housefly wing movement.

tight and dry. An alternative arrangement that works well for single chirps is to put the filters post modulator, so they continue to ring slightly after each chirp; this is probably much more like the natural model, but for fast modulations (the whirring part of the call) it makes a mess as new components in the noise interact with what is left recirculating in the filter.

Housefly

Although Bennet-Clark and Ewing (1968) give us analysis of a fruitfly, it will serve as a good enough model for a housefly, with the big difference being the frequency of wing beating which is about 340Hz in a typical example. A depiction of the wing movement appears in figure 50.11 and a model summary is shown in figure 50.12. Our method will be direct waveform approximation in the time domain. There are several possible solutions, such as using a table oscillator or polynomial curve fitting, but here we use a piecewise approximation.

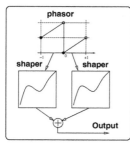

We also take advantage of the fact that time-reversed signals have the same spectrum as forward ones, because to do this with a single phasor instead of a triangle it would be much more tricky. However, the anomaly you will see on the down cycle of the wing time domain plot looks wrong, but sounds okay; it is merely a bit of the waveform that has been shifted to the wrong place in time. Starting with a phasor an asymmetrical triangle wave is obtained. The rise time is about twice as fast as the fall time, as shown in graph A.

Figure 50.12
Summary of fly method.

The arrangement of [min~] objects is similar to a triangle shaping patch seen earlier in the helicopter rotor. If the left branch multiplier was 0.5 the waveform would be symmetrical; however, we reduce this to 0.2, which tilts the triangle to the right. This also reduces its amplitude, so an additional scaling factor of 6.0 brings it back to the range 0.0 to 1.0.

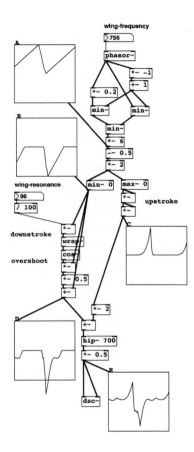

Figure 50.13
Direct signal implementation of housefly wing.

Next we split the triangle into two half-phases. Let's follow the nearest one on the right side first, which gives the wing upstroke. A quartic function is taken to give it a fast-rise curve as shown in graph C, and it is then scaled by 2.0 and added to the output. Meanwhile, the negative half-cycle shown in graph B forms the downstroke of the wing. Remember this gives the greatest pressure pulse as the wing is rotated to lift the fly. It also ends in an underdamped wobble. We obtain this behaviour by taking the cosine of a scaled and wrapped version of the segment so we get a little burst of sinusoidal wave. This is enveloped and added to the original downstroke half-cycle and can be seen in graph D.

Finally, we add these two parts together, upstroke and downstroke, which is shown (after a high-pass filter) in graph E. Note that a frequency of about 750Hz is chosen to make the graphs look nice. On the left side you can see an adjustable parameter for the prewrapping scale. This sets the frequency of the wing resonance and can be tweaked to get the right underdamping response. Next we will abstract this patch to make a single wing object with frequency and resonance controls before assembling two of them into a full fly effect.

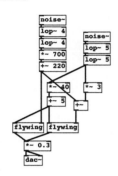

Figure 50.14
Buzzing housefly.

Two noise generators are needed to give variation to the basic wing movement waveforms. The first works around 4Hz to modify the beating frequency of both wings. Modulating each wing separately sounds completely wrong, so even though we want some slight variation in wing speed both must be derived from a common source. Even though the average housefly frequency is 340Hz, for some reason 220Hz sounds about right for this creature, so it's turned out to be quite a big fly. Making changes to the wing model, perhaps by high-passing at a higher frequency or modifying the slopes, should yield examples that work well at other frequencies for mosquitoes and so forth; but there tends to be a "sweet spot" for any model where things seem to work best. A second noise source is used to modulate the resonance and a slight offset to the second wing. This creates a natural extra buzz as the fly seems to move around. Try panning the example back and forth and using the rate of change of position to modulate this wing resonance too.

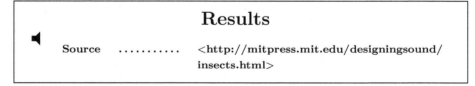

Results

◀ **Source** .... <http://mitpress.mit.edu/designingsound/ insects.html>

Conclusions

A wide range of analytical techniques can be used to understand intricate animal sounds. We can use high-speed video and slow-motion replay to follow beating wing patterns, microscopy to look at their anatomy, as well as the usual spectral and time analysis of waveforms. Each has a unique and special way of making its call.

Exercises

Exercise 1

Imagine you have been given the task of designing an outdoor scene for a particular location and time. Research the creatures you would expect to find in that setting. Locate recordings or studies of the insect calls and implement some of them as closely as you can.

Exercise 2

Emulate the katydid (Pterophylla), common in the Americas and Canada. How do you think it makes the changes in resonance that give a chattering sound?

Exercise 3

Insects' calls have meaning. They are like radio transmitters and receivers, highly tuned to one another's sounds. Make a pair of insects that communicate. When one calls, the other responds. Place them in a stereo field so that you hear them calling across to each other.

Acknowledgements

Analysis recordings courtesy of Coll Anderson, David L. Martin, and Dr. Thomas E. Moore.

References

Aidley, D. J. (1969). "Sound production in a Brazilian cicada." *J. Exp. Biol.* 51: 325–337.

Alexander, R. D., and Moore, T. E. (1958). "Studies on the acoustical behaviour of seventeen year cicadas." *Ohio J. Sci.* 38, no. 2: 107–127.

Bennet-Clark, H. C. (1970). "The mechanism and efficiency of sound production in mole crickets." *J. Exp. Biol.* 52: 619–652.

Bennet-Clark, H. C. (1998). "Size and scale effects as constraints in insect sound communication." *Phil. Trans. R. Soc. Lond. B* 353: 407–419.

Bennet-Clark, H. C. (1999). "Resonators in insect sound production: How insects produce loud pure-tone songs." *J. Exp. Biol.* 202: 3347–3357.

Bennet-Clark, H. C., and Ewing, A. W. (1968). "The wing mechanism involved in the courtship of Drosophila." *J. Exp. Biol.* 49: 117–128.

Chapman, R. F. (1982). *The Insects: Structure and Function.* Harvard University Press.

Davis, W. T. (1943). "Two ways of song communication among our North American cicadas." *J. NY Ent. Soc.* 51: 185–190.

Josephson, R. K., and Halverson, R. C. (1971). "High frequency muscles used in sound production by a katydid. I. Organisation of the motor systems." *Biol. Bull.*, Marine Biological Laboratory.

Koch, U. T., Elliott, C. J. H., Schaffner, K. H., and Kliendienst, H. U. (1988). "The mechanics of stridulation in the cricket Gryllus campestris." *J. Comp. Physiol. A* 162: 213–223.

Nachtigall, W. (1966). "Die Kinematick der Schlagflugelbewungen von Dipteren: Methodische und analytisch Grundlagen zur Biophysik des Insectenflugs." *Z. Vergl. Physiol.* 52: 155–211.

Wigglesworth, V. B. (1972). *The Principles of Insect Physiology.* Halsted.

Wood, J. (1970). "A study of the instantaneous air velocities in a plane behind the wings of certain diptera flying in a wind tunnel." *J. Exp. Biol.* 52: 17–25.

Young, D. (1990). "Do cicadas radiate sound through their ear drums?" *J. Exp. Biol.* 151: 41–56.

51
Practical 28
Birds

Aims

To understand and synthesise the calls of birds.

Analysis

Birds make sound using an organ called the syrinx, which is their equivalent of our voice box (larynx). Unlike the mammalian larynx which is high in the trachea the syrinx lies deep down at the base where the bronchi split off. It is surrounded by an air sac which acts as a resonator or coupling (via the external tympanic membrane) to the lower breast; so not only do birds sing through their beaks, they resonate their whole breast and throat area.

The syrinx is highly developed in songbirds (oscines) and serves many functions, communicating territorial and sexual information, predator warnings, and information about food. Elaborate song is presumed to be a demonstration of fitness and intelligence for mating calls, but some birds seem to sing because they like to, or they mimic other sounds as if tying to make sense of their world. Birds are unique in being animals that can control both lungs separately for vocalisation (Suthers 1990). A complex system of muscles around the syrinx, bronchi, and trachea modulates air pressure while inhaling and exhaling. This allows some birds to sing continuously (the nightjar can sing for nearly 20 minutes without pause). Control of the syringial muscles gives birds control over the amplitude and frequency of call. The neurology (Max Michael 2005) and physiology of this has been studied in depth, and it is a fascinating process.

In the centre of figure 51.1 you can see a small, triangular-shaped component called the pessulus that sits on the surface of a sac made of flexible tissue. It is a hard bony material, so it has some mass and can swing from side to side within the syrinx cavity. This sac has tight skin on its side called the semilunar tympanic membrane that amplifies movement to produce sound. Directly opposite it, on the outside of the syrinx, is a corresponding membrane that seems to transmit sound out of the syrinx and into the thoracic cavity, to the breast. On each side of the interbronchial sac are two lips (labia) that admit air

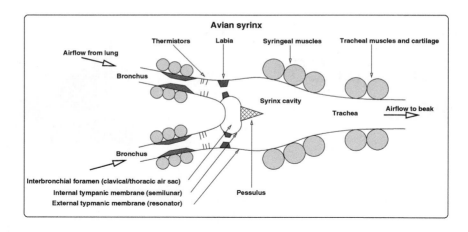

Figure 51.1
Anatomy of avian syrinx.

from each bronchus. The flow of air within the bronchi is controlled by muscles
and cartilage that dilate or constrict to control the pressure.

Pressure pulses are developed by the bronchial muscles acting with labia
at the entrance to the syrinx. The whole syrinx is surrounded by muscles, but
further up towards the trachea there is another set; thus the pressure into and
out of the syrinx is controllable. Sound production is not perfectly understood
but is certainly a combination of resonances from the membranes and interactions of the labia, cartilage, and trachea entrance as the creature carefully
changes these impedances to create song (Fagerlund 2004). It seems the bird
can feel the airflow using tiny hairs, called thermistors, in each bronchus, so
this almost certainly plays a part in some feedback mechanism. One attempt
at understanding the sound of the syrinx focuses on the FM/AM nature. If
we assume the output impedance is high and each side of the cavity to be a
Helmholtz resonator, then the frequency of it is dependent on the volume, but
the effective volume varies in inverse proportion to the pressure on the opposite
side of the syrinx.

As the pessulus moves across to the left side, pivoting on the clavical sac,
it simultaneously reduces the volume and increases the pressure on that side.
At the same time the labia move together, constricting air flow through this
side. The speed of the air moving past the opposite side is now fast and the
pressure lower, so the pessulus moves back to the right side, opening the left
labia and letting out a pulse of air that has built up. These pulses of air enter
the resonant cavity and produce a burst of frequency. By varying the syrinx
muscles the bird can control the frequency of these bursts, and by varying the
tracheal muscles it can control the impedance of the outlet port to perform
amplitude modulation.

Model

Smyth and Smith (2002a,b) and Fletcher (1993, 2000) have made detailed models of the pressure, volumes, and impedances in the syrinx. We could build a waveguide model from this basis, but it would be expensive for a real-time procedural audio design. Fortunately there is an enormous body of work on the spectral characteristics by Beckers, Suthers, and Cate (2003a,b) and other researchers that allows us to take a different approach. Kahrs (2001) and others have noted that an AM/FM approach yields excellent results when constructed carefully.

Some non-oscine species have rough and chaotic calls, like the seagull, jackdaw, and crow. Fletcher (1993) points to a the syrinx behaving in a chaotic fashion when the muscles are loose and the airflow strong; so in fact a waveguide model may not be appropriate at all. For this case we could look to FM with feedback or another quasi-periodic astable system. What we shall do is take a hybrid approach by treating the bronchial passages as two separate pulse generators, but give them natural parameters. Combining these with AM/FM and a resonant filter will achieve the syrinx and trachea approximations we need. The heart of the synthesis model is extremely simple, but as we shall see, the parameters needed to control this in a useful way become unwieldy.

Method

Both pulse waves are derived by the now familiar $1/(1+x^2)$ shaping of a cosine. Ring modulation combines the sum and difference of sidebands that we can mix individually to form the carrier of an FM stage. Two parallel band-pass filters with variable resonance provide a crude tracheal passage, and a final-stage attenuator and high pass perform the work of the horn-like beak. Each of the components will now be examined separately before assembling them into a complete birdcall synthesiser.

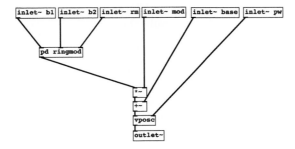

Figure 51.2
Syrinx model.

DSP Implementation

Here is the core of our birdcall synthesiser (fig. 51.2). Starting on the left, there are two inlets from the bronchi that will carry pulses into the ring modulator. A third inlet is the ring modulator balance that varies between the sum and difference of the incoming waves. Output from the ring modulator is scaled by the signal value on the fourth inlet and added to an offset (fifth inlet), giving us the base frequency of the bottom pulse oscillator. We can vary the pulse width of this from the last inlet.

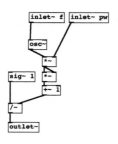

Figure 51.3
Pulse wave oscillator.

Three pulse oscillators, seen as `vposc` in the parent patches and shown in figure 51.3 opposite, are used. One is used for each bronchus/labia port and one for the syrinx simulation. Frequency is set by the first inlet and pulse width by the second. We tend to use small deviations from a raised cosine here, with values on the pulse width inlet ranging between 1.0 (raised cosine) and 3.0 (slightly narrowed pulse). The result of course is not centred on zero, so both inputs to the ring modulator have a DC offset that propagates through the patch. To simplify matters we have not recentred the pulses; the DC component is dealt with by filters later in the chain.

For convenience the ring modulator is given here again (fig. 51.4). Recall from the chapter on shaping that multiplying two signals moves the harmonics by their difference and adding them performs simple superposition that leaves them unaltered but combined. For two harmonics at the inlets we can expect a mixture of potentially four harmonics at the output, depending on the value of the crossfader. A value of 0.0 at the right-hand crossfader inlet produces only difference components, while a value of 1.0 gives only the sum. At 0.5 we get an equal mixture of both.

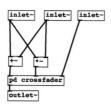

Figure 51.4
Ring modulator.

Finally, here are two filters in parallel for the trachea (fig. 51.5). These focus the driving oscillation of the AM/FM syrinx into a narrower band. We can expect some undesirable modulation sidebands, especially at low frequencies where they may be reflected around zero. Fortunately the deviations needed are mild so there won't be any problems with sidebands getting above the Nyquist and folding over at the top. A waveguide model for the trachea would be nice, but most of the character we are interested in comes from the syrinx, and so any realism advantage gained by a more sophisticated output tract might be too subtle to warrant the extra cost. Resonance of this component remains fixed during each call and should be between 2.0 and 5.0.

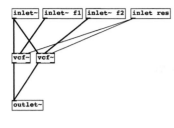

Figure 51.5
Two-filter trachea approximation.

Now we want to connect all these parts together to make the complete bird, so this is where things get interesting. There are 11 parameters in total, summarised in figure 51.6. Although we've captured the essentials of the sound, the spectrum of birdcall, real birdcalls are complex—not because the production mechanism is complex but because of the huge amount of control data needed to run it.

Going back to our earlier observations on living things, they make sounds that have semantics and even simple living things will make astonishingly complex neural patterns to control movement and voicing. Let's suppose we could simplify birdcall to one envelope per parameter and make each sound a short phrase lasting less than one second. Then we could connect together these phrases into more elaborate calling. If we control each with an envelope that has an attack time, decay time, initial level, and final level we will have 44 parameters to play with, a lot for what will be unsophisticated behaviour.

Parameter	Value range
bp1 Left bronchus pressure (pulse frequency)	0Hz to 10Hz
bp2 Right bronchus pressure (pulse frequency)	0Hz to 10Hz
bw1 Left bronchus impedance (pulse width) (scalar)	1 to 4
bw2 Right bronchus impedance (pulse width) (scalar)	1 to 4
rm Ring modulation mix (scalar)	0.0 to 1.0
mod FM modulation index (frequency)	0Hz to 200Hz
bf Syrinx base frequency (frequency)	80Hz to 1kHz
pw Syrinx pulse width (scalar)	0 to 4
tf1 First trachea formant (frequency)	50Hz to 3kHz
tf2 Second trachea formant (frequency)	50Hz to 3kHz
amp Attenuation (absolute fsd)	0.0 to 1.0

Figure 51.6
Birdcall synthesiser parameters.

Remember that for real-time synthesis we always try to avoid memory access, because if everything can be done in registers it's much faster, and memory access hinders parallelism for the DSP tree. However, in this case we will choose an easy way out, partly because it demonstrates the joys of using arrays as control envelopes. To translate this patch for proper procedural use you should create breakpoint parameter lists. Here I am going to create a table of $1,024$ points for each parameter and read them back using the `tabread4~` object. Included in the supplemental online material are some other birdcall

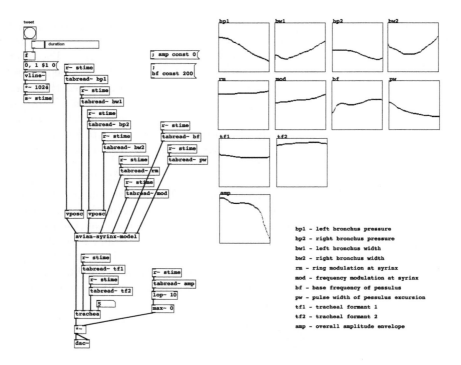

Figure 51.7
Bird with table-based parameter control.

synths based loosely on this one and Hans Mikelson's Csound implementation. One of these includes an "autotweeter" that randomly generates birdcall-like gestures. This would be ideal for virtual world creatures where we just want to spawn some that will twitter away forever, making interesting noises without further intervention. This example is more useful for making single sound instances that you can record to use as samples.

Results

Source . . . .   <http://mitpress.mit.edu/designingsound/
birds.html>

Conclusions

Birds produce sound using a resonant cavity that works like a modulator. The avian syrinx is a complex organ of muscles, membranes, and cartilage. Even though we can mimic its spectral behaviour, making complex calls requires intricate parameterisation of the synthetic model. Birdcall is a fascinating subject that has been studied for a long time and from many angles. We could go much deeper into studying the calls of various song birds and the strange sounds made by other species, but this is left to the reader's imagination, further research, and experimentation.

Exercises

Exercise 1

What effect do these sounds have on cats and other birds? Try extending the bandwidth right up to the limits of the reproduction system, using a 96kHz sample rate. Does this change the way other animals react to it? What does this say about the human hearing range and the information carried in the sound of real birdcall?

Exercise 2

There are thousands of birds recorded and documented. Pick one to study and find out as much as you can about its habitat, calls, and behaviour. Model the sound as closely as you can.

Exercise 3

How does the AM/FM syrinx model fail for non-oscine species? Can you obtain a crow or duck quack? What more elaborate alternatives might be used for synthesising these species? Use a noisy excitor or chaotic oscillator and a three-port waveguide to create a seagull or duck call.

Exercise 4

How could you analyse, represent, and sequence real birdcalls? Try using a pitch follower and FFT to translate some real calls into parameter lists for a bird synthesiser in order to mimic real species.

Exercise 5

Listen to the exchanges between wood pigeons or owls. Create a pair of birds that can call back and forth, making appropriate responses.

References

Beckers, G. J. L., Suthers, R. A., and Cate, C. (2003a). "Mechanisms of frequency and amplitude modulation in ring dove song." *J. Exp. Biol.* 206: 1833–1843.

Beckers, G. J. L., Suthers, R. A., and Cate, C. (2003b). "Pure-tone birdsong by resonant filtering of harmonic overtones." *Proc. Natl. Acad. Sci. USA* 100: 7372–7376.

Brackenbury, J. H. (1989). "Functions of the syrinx and the control of sound production." In *Form and Function in Birds*, ed. A. S. King, and J. McLelland (pp. 193–220). Academic Press.

Casey, R. M., and Gaunt, A. S. (1985). "Theoretical models of the avian syrinx." *J. Theor. Biol.* 116: 45–64.

Fagerlund, S. (2004). "Acoustics and physical models of bird sounds." HUT, Laboratory of Acoustics and Audio Signal Processing, Finland.

Fletcher, N. H. (1993). "Autonomous vibration of simple pressure-controlled valves in gas flows." *J. Acoust. Soc. Am.* 93: 2172–2180.

Fletcher, N. H. (2000). "A class of chaotic bird calls." *J. Acoust. Soc. Am.* 108: 821–826.

Goller, F., and Larsen, O. N. (2002). "New perspectives on mechanism of sound generation in songbirds." *J. Comp. Physiol. A* 188: 841–850.

Kahrs, M., and Avanzini, F. (2001). "Computer synthesis of bird songs and calls." In *Proc. of the COST G-6 Conf. on Digial Audio Effects (DAFX-01)*. Limerick, Ireland, Dec. 6–8. DAFX.

Lavenex, P. B. (1999). "Vocal production mechanisms in the budgerigar (Melopsittacus undulatus): The presence and implications of amplitude modulation." *J. Acoust. Soc. Am.* 106: 491–505.

Max Michael, D. (2005). "Evolved neural dynamics for synthetic birdsong." Thesis Msc., Evolutionary and Adaptive Systems, Univ. Sussex, Brighton, UK.

Smyth, T., and Smith, J. O. (2002a). "The sounds of the avian syrinx: Are they really flute-like?" In *Proc. of the 5th Int. Conf. on Digital Audio Effects (DAFX-02)*, Hamburg, Germany, Sept. 26–28. DAFX.

Smyth, T., and Smith, J. O. (2002b). "The syrinx: Nature's hybrid wind instrument." First Pan American/Iberian Meeting on Acoustics, Cancun, Mexico, Dec. 2–7.

Suthers, R. A. (1990). "Contributions to birdsong from the left and right sides of the intact syrinx." *Nature* 347: 473–477.

52

Practical 29
Mammals

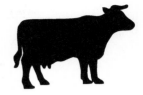

Aims

This chapter concerns producing animal sounds, specifically mammals. Modern acoustic and computational research focuses on natural speech synthesis. There are many books and papers on this subject. But here we will think about the general principles as they might apply to all animal sounds, from mice to lions. We will create a simple glottal pulse source and vocal tract model in order to experiment with roaring lions and mooing cows, before investigating a model of human vowel production that you may build on to make singing or speaking synthesisers.

Analysis

Mammals generate sound by expelling air from their lungs through the trachea and around the glottis which vibrates. This vibration is tuned by muscles which control tension, then amplified and filtered by the remainder of the tract up to and including the mouth, lips, and nasal cavities. Vocalisations are for communication. They may be an attempt to attract a mate, or demonstrate fitness, strength, and lung capacity. They may be a warnings or indicators of food, so must carry a distance. And they can be a form of localisation to signal others when hunting.

Films and cartoons always require new and interesting creature noises, meaningful vocalisations, or even talking animals. Cross synthesis, resonant imprinting with LPC and vocoders, or warping real animal recordings are all useful techniques. Studying the nature of animals and their vocalisations can help greatly with this task. Another motivation for researchers creating animal sounds by synthesis is to try to communicate with animals. Synthetic calls for dolphins, seals, bats, and other mammals have provided fascinating insights into behaviour and helped us understand animals.

Many animals recognise individuality, emotion, and intention in others. A female seal can find her pups in a crowd of thousands of others by their calls. It is as if all living things have some common understanding of sound communication at a fundamental level. Most are frightened by a lion's roar, because it indicates great size and strength. Because this is an active research area in biology and acoustics, there are many recordings of animals available as scientific

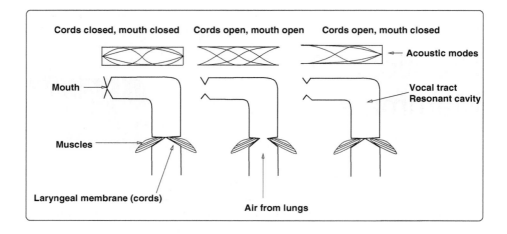

Figure 52.1
Opening and closing of the cords to produce pressure pulses and modes of resonance in the tract.

data to study, so it's a rich area for analysis. Let's begin by reviewing the standard wisdom on the vocal tract due to Morse (1936), Fant (1960), and others.

The Vocal Cords

The cords or laryngeal membranes are a loose area within the respiratory tract surrounded by muscles that can contract and tense the tissue. This produces oscillatory motion as air is expired, like the neck of a balloon. Air pressure forces the constricted section open, leading to a pulse of air. The elastic action of tissue, combined with the Bernoulli effect as air moves over the cord surfaces, pulls them back together, stopping the air flow again.

The natural frequency of this apparatus, which we denote F_0, is determined by the size of the cords, the muscular force used to constrict them, and the pressure developed by the lungs. It varies greatly depending on the size, species, and age of the animal. Our voices have a frequency around 100Hz to 200Hz in adult male humans, 200Hz to 300Hz in adult female humans, and up to 350Hz in children. For cats this rises to 500Hz, and for buffalo, walrus, and lions it can be as low as 30Hz.

How can we know what the vocal cords themselves sound like without the rest of the vocal tract? Miller and Mathews (1963) and Rothenberg (1968) found ways of inverse filtering and using air velocity measurements to determine that the waveform is a slightly asymmetrical pulse, much like a narrowed raised cosine, which rides on top of the main flow from the lungs. Tightening of the cords can narrow this pulse slightly without changing the fundamental frequency.

Of course, not all animals have cords like humans. Monkeys and even sea lions have similar biology, but lack the sophisticated resonance control that makes human-type speech possible. Cats and dogs, on the other hand, have a different mechanism that produces a rippling effect of several pulses in combination. As air moves over soft, loose tissue it causes wave-like motions, flapping much like a flag. The intensity and density of the pulses therefore depends on the air velocity over the membrane. Lion roars start soft and low with distinct glottal pulses, building to a dense roar. Frequency also moves up and down, starting as low as 30Hz, building to around 240Hz, and then dropping to around 120Hz.

The Vocal Tract

With the mouth and vocal cords open, the tract behaves like a semi-open pipe. With either end closed the resonant mode changes. During normal speech and singing the human cords stay mostly closed, so the behaviour is of a half-open pipe. But when screaming or voicing a stopped consonant or pre-plosive, the tract is respectively wide open or mostly closed at both ends. The natural resonance of the voiced modes in a human vocal tract are given by its length, about 17cm, for which we get a quarter-wavelength mode. Setting $l = 0.17$, then $F = c/\lambda = c/4l = 340/0.68$. This gives us frequencies of 500Hz, $1,000$Hz, $1,500$Hz ... Knowing the length of an animal's vocal tract we can work out the characteristic resonances.

Articulation

The length calculation above gives a general resonant behaviour, but most animals can either shorten or lengthen the tract, or apply other muscle structures to constrict it in certain locations. Furthermore, the shape of the mouth, lips, and tongue can change and a flap called the velum can open and close to admit more or less air into the nasal cavity.

Adapted from Fant (1960), the illustration in figure 52.6 shows cross sections through the human vocal tract at various places along its length. The shape obviously has some impact on the resonance, but as a simplification we only need consider the total area of any cross section. In some places it is much wider or narrower than others. The difference between humans and other mammals is that we have a fixed larynx, which is much lower. This allows us to use the full range of the vocal tract for communication. Other animals that vocalise only occasionally, like ruminants, must move their larynx out of position near the top of the respiratory tract and down into a position where it can effectively resonate.

For dogs and cats this movement is large. For sounds like whining and snorts, most species do not move their larynx and the velum remains open, so a nasal formant is always present. For loud sounds many species close the velum so air doesn't pass through the nasal cavity. This all varies greatly between species, but the general principle is the same; we can reduce the tract to a cascade of short pipe models separated by impedances that create some back propagation and resonate like a partially closed pipe.

Model

The resulting model is a set of filters, each of which corresponds to a section of the tract and its resonance. The collective result of these is a formant with several poles and zeros. Peaks are denoted F_1, F_2, and so forth. For speech synthesis the filters can be dynamically changed in frequency and resonance to mimic the changing articulation of the vocal tract. Speech synthesis was first done this way using electrical LCR filters (Klatt model) and later turned to digital methods.

Method

We can use cascades and parallel forms of resonant bandpass filters. Vocal cord sources will be variations on pulse generators to provide control over width and clustering. All vocal and creature sounds obviously require extensive use of dynamic filters. In speech synthesis the problem is how to control these filters to model elaborate tract articulations, but for animal sounds we can use cruder control gestures.

DSP Implementation

Two short examples follow, one to make animal sounds and one to make human vowels.

Animal Sounds

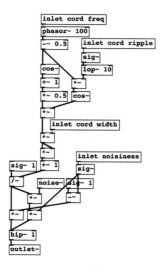

Figure 52.2
"Flapping" waveshaper.

An elaborate pulse source shown in figure 52.2 looks a bit like a regular $1/(1 + kx^2)$ waveshaper with the cord width inlet controlling the pulse width. However, notice the additional cosine function running in parallel at the top. This is performing a modulation with the other cosine to produce a packet of cycles shaped nicely at each lobe. The first cosine is raised above 0 and behaves like a windowing function on the second one. Because the line (scaled by cord ripple) produces a higher frequency containing more cycles it increases the number of pulses per glottal click and changes the spectrum. After shaping to obtain unipolar pulses of controllable width, some noise is modulated by the signal and then mixed in to provide a noisy component. The noisiness inlet crossfades between pulses and modulated noise. Narrow pulses with lots of ripple and some noise give a harsh, gritty, snarling excitation, whereas wide pulses with little or no ripple and noise give a smooth, humming source.

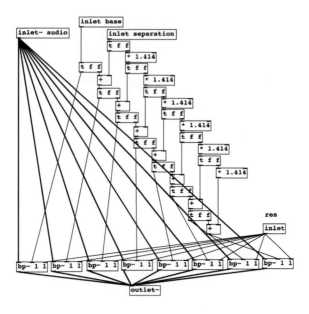

Figure 52.3
Parallel band-pass comb filter.

In figure 52.3 we see how to model the vocal tract. Unlike a human tract where we want individual formant control, this one contains a bunch of filters that behave like a comb filter. The spacing between them, the total frequency range covered, and the overall resonance are all controllable via inlets. This seems to work well even though `bp~` objects don't change their centre frequency nicely when using message domain control. A few clicks are heard, but rarely. If you aren't satisfied with this then experiment with changing them to `vcf~` units and adding some more smoothing on the frequency controls, or try a variable delay-based comb filter instead.

Some way of providing articulation is needed, so figure 52.4 is an envelope that gives a warped half-cosine cycle where you can adjust the rise and fall sides separately. The line scans a quarter of the cosine function, so we need a $\pi/2$ multiplier, then turns around and reverses back to zero. Rise and fall times are stored in the `float` objects and the balance between rise and fall time is used to scale them. We don't want the output to sit on zero, so rather than give offsets to every parameter we add 0.25 here before output.

Combining the cords' pulse source, tract comb resonator, and articulation envelope with some controls we arrive at figure 52.5. Controls are given to set pulse width, ripple, pulse frequency base and excursion, pulse noise, tract resonance, length characteristics, duration, and rise/fall for the articulator. It can produce some interesting sounds from cute kittens to nasty monsters.

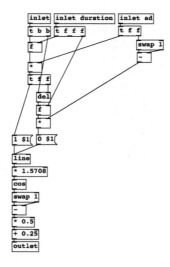

Figure 52.4
Soft rise and fall curve.

Human Vowels

The vowels are most strongly characterised by the relationship between the first two formants F_1 and F_2, so can be arranged in a 2D plot giving a "vowel space." Diphthongs are double vowels, such as aʊ in the word ab**ou**t. Unsurprisingly the common ones are close neighbors in the vowel space. To move between them and make natural speech one needs an interpolation method to smoothly morph the filter parameters. Although animal sounds do not have complex speech-like characteristics, they do obey the same rules of geometry and resonance that describe a possible space of modes, so adding interpolation might help with those too.

The human vocal tract shown in figure 52.6 is only three band-pass filters, one for each formant. The frequencies are stored in messages as three element lists and unpacked to each filter. Be careful of nasty pops when the patch is initialised and the filters are flushed out.

Results

Source .... <http://mitpress.mit.edu/designingsound/mammals.html>

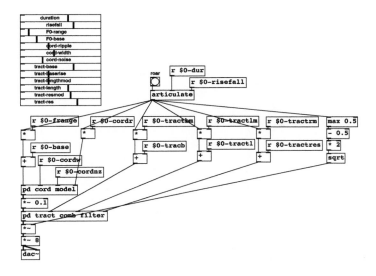

Figure 52.5
Animal sound generator.

Conclusions

A vocal tract model is essentially a set of band-pass filters arranged to mimic the changing diameter of a long passage. Feeding noisy or click-like pulse excitations into a vocal tract model can produce animal sounds. Human vowel sounds can be produced by selecting the appropriate formant frequencies for a vocal tract model.

If you are going to experiment further with speech you will almost certainly need textfile or database input in order to handle the complexities of control data. You might also like to learn IPA phonetic notation and study some of the references given on linguistics and phonetics before attempting anything like a text-to-speech system. For detailed animal sounds you may find it useful to use Praat (see below) or another good spectral analysis system in order to reveal what is going on.

Other Tools

An excellent analytical and synthesis environment is the Praat software by Paul Boersma and David Weenink of Institute of Phonetic Sciences, University of Amsterdam. It is freely available for all platforms (but not open source as of 2008) on the Internet. Download and experiment with this if you want good spectrographs and vowel analysis tools.

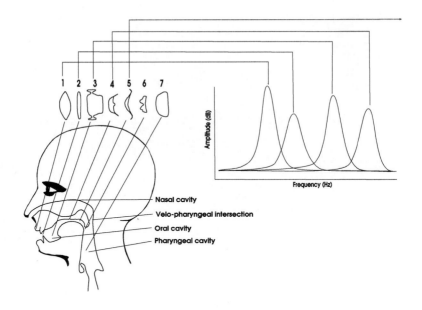

Figure 52.6
Human vocal tract and its model as a set of filters.

Phonetic	Example	F1	F2	F3
i:	M<u>ee</u>t	280Hz	2250Hz	2900Hz
ɪ	Sh<u>i</u>p	400Hz	1900Hz	2550Hz
ε	P<u>e</u>t	550Hz	1770Hz	2490Hz
æ	C<u>a</u>t	690Hz	1660Hz	2490Hz
ʌ	L<u>o</u>ve	640Hz	1190Hz	2390Hz
u	R<u>oo</u>t	310Hz	870Hz	2250Hz
ʊ	H<u>oo</u>k	450Hz	1030Hz	2380Hz
ə	<u>A</u>bout	500Hz	1500Hz	2500Hz
ɑ	F<u>a</u>ther	710Hz	1100Hz	2640Hz

Figure 52.7
List of human vowel formants (compiled by Tim Carmell, spectral database at Center for Spoken Language Understanding, Oregon University).

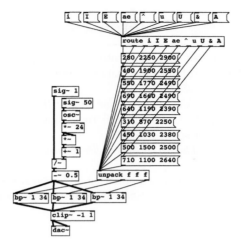

Figure 52.8
"Schwa box": human vocal tract resonances for vowels.

Exercises

Exercise 1

Pick an animal to study. Find something for which you can source lots of good recordings and spend time listening to it. Use analysis tools to plot F_0 frequencies in different calls and try to map the tract formants. Make biological estimates of its vocal apparatus, lung capacity, and vocalisation habits, and then see if you can synthesise this one animal as well as possible.

Exercise 2 (Advanced)

Try making animals talk. This is a sound design skill often needed for games, fairy tales, and children's media. A "Dr Doolittle" patch will probably be a kind of cross synthesis where you isolate the excitations and resonances, then impose human-like tract formant gestures upon them. Experiment with sub-band vocoders, LPC, Fourier analysis, or any other transform you like to analyse the data and separate the components. You will find that separating the voiced (pitched vowel) and unvoiced (fricatives, plosive consonants, etc.) from each other helps a lot. Mixing in the original human actor's voice to some degree is essential if the hybrid sound is to be intelligible.

References

Charrier, I., Mathevon, N., and Jouventin, P. (2002). "How does a fur seal mother recognize the voice of her pup? An experimental study of Arctocephalus tropicalis." *J. Exp. Biol.* 205: 603–612.

Erkut, C. (1998). *Bioacoustic Modeling for Sound Synthesis: A Case Study of Odontoceti Clicks.* Helsinki University of Technology, Lab. of Acoustics and Audio Signal Processing, Espoo, Finland.

Fant, G. (1960). *Acoustic Theory of Speech Production.* Mouton. (Second printing, 1970.)

Fant, G. (2000). "Half a century in phonetics and speech research." FONETIK 2000, Swedish phonetics meeting, Skövde, May 24–26. Dept. Speech, Music, and History, KTH, Stockholm.

Farley, G. R., Barlow, S. M., Netsell, R., and Chmelka, J. V. (1991). *Vocalizations in the Cat: Behavioral Methodology and Spectrographic Analysis.* Research Division, Boys' Town National Research Hospital, Omaha.

Fitch, W. T. (2000). "Vocal production in nonhuman mammals: Implications for the evolution of speech." *The Evolution of Language: Proceedings of the 3rd International Conference*, pp. 102–103.

Fitch, W. T. (2006). "Production of vocalizations in mammals." In *Encyclopedia of Language and Linguistics*, edited by K. Brown, pp. 115–121. Elsevier.

Fitch, W. T., and Kelley, J. P. (2000). "Perception of vocal tract resonances by whooping cranes, Grus Americana." *Ethol.* 106, no. 6: 559–574.

Hillenbrand, J., Getty, L. A., Clark, M. J., and Wheeler, K. (1995). "Acoustic characteristics of American English vowels." *J. Acoust. Soc. Am.* 97: 3099–3111.

Mergell, P., Fitch, W. T., and Herzel, H. (1999). "Modeling the role of nonhuman vocal membranes in phonation." *J. Acoust. Soc. Am.* 105, no. 3: 2020–2028.

Miller, J. E., and Mathews, M. V. (1963). "Investigation of the glottal waveshape by automatic inverse filtering." *J. Acoust. Soc. Am.* 35: 1876(A).

Miller, R. L. (1959). "Nature of the vocal cord wave." *J. Acoust. Soc. Am.* 31: 667–679.

Morse, P. M. (1936). *Vibration and Sound.* McGraw-Hill.

Ohala, J. J. (1994). "The frequency codes underlies the sound symbolic use of voice pitch." In *Sound Symbolism*, L. Hinton, J. Nichols, and J. J. Ohala (eds.), Cambridge University Press. 325–347.

Peterson, G. E., and Barney, H. L. (1952). "Control methods used in a study of the vowels." *J. Acoust. Soc. Am.* 24: 175–184.

Riede, T., and Fitch, W. T. (1999). "Vocal tract length and acoustics of vocalization in the domestic dog Canis familiaris." *J. Exp. Biol.* 202: 2859–2867.

Rothenberg, M. (1968). "The breath-stream dynamics of simple-released-plosive production." In *Bibliotheca Phonetica VI.* Karger.

Stevens, K. (1998). *Acoustic Phonetics.* MIT Press.

Sundberg, J. (1991). "Synthesising singing." In *Representations of Music Signals*, chapter 9, ed. G. De Poli, A. Piccialli, and C. Roads. MIT Press.

Weissengruber, G. E., Forstenpointner, G., Peters, G., Kubber-Heiss, A., and Fitch, W. T. (2002). "Hyoid apparatus and pharynx in the lion (Panthera leo), jaguar (Panthera onca), tiger (Panthera tigris), cheetah (Acinonyx jubatus), and domestic cat (Felis silvestris f. catus)." *J. Anat. (London)* 201: 195–209.

Practical Series Mayhem

Boom, Boom, Boom, Boom,
Boom, Boom, Boom,
Boom, Boom, Boom, Boom,
Boom, Boom, Boom.
—"The German Guns," Pvt. S. Baldrick (1917)

Killing Things

We now move, inevitably, from life to death. It's time for—blowing things up and killing each other. What is interesting about this subject is that many of the acoustic rules we have become accustomed to break down. The only comparable example we have seen is with thunder, but we did not explore the more difficult details of shockwaves at that point. With explosions and supersonic events sound starts to behave in some strange ways, which is what gives these sounds their character and makes them fun.

The Practicals

There are three practicals in this part.

- Guns: supersonic bullets, automatic fire, and reload sounds.
- Explosions: the strange behaviour of shockwaves and highly dynamic gases.
- Rocket launcher: a complete look at a complex game weapon.

Acknowledgements

I would like to thank Charles Maynes for his help researching the firearms chapter.

53
Practical 30
Guns

Aims

The purpose of this practical is to study and make gunshot sounds, which are essential to fighting games and action films. In addition, we'll see how adding reload sounds that reuse parts of the model leads to a coherent, modular object.

Analysis

Listen to the gunshots in a spaghetti Western: they go on forever with vast reverb effects and almost comical ricochet sounds, even when they hit somebody. A huge part of any gunshot recorded in an open environment is the reverb. These dramatic effects are something you may embellish your work with later, but for now we will focus on the pure, dry sound of a gunshot without any reverb. So, step one is isolating the actual gunshot from environmental effects. A real gunshot recorded in an anechoic chamber is remarkably short. It's more than just a burst of noise, having a well-defined structure emerging from its physical process. First let's consider that most guns are made of several parts. For a rifle the stock is a large, often heavy part to stabilise the weapon. Military combat weapons tend to be constructed for lightness, so there is a design compromise made here. A massive stock absorbs more impulse on firing but is obviously heavier to carry around, so many military rifle designs use a spring-loaded mechanism to provide some relief from the recoil impulse. The primary purpose of the stock, therefore, is to couple the weapon to the body at the shoulder. There are three other parts that have significance to the sound. The barrel is a strong circular tube with a small diameter that fits the calibre of the ammunition used. Its length has some bearing on the sound produced. Shorter barrels produce a louder sound for the same calibre. Connecting the barrel to the stock is a housing that contains some light components, usually made of steel: a spring, trigger mechanism, and chamber for the round to sit in. Other wood or metal parts around this mid-section are sometimes called the *furniture*. For single-shot rifles this is all we have, but for automatic assault rifles and some handguns there is a detachable magazine that sits beneath the base containing further rounds and a spring to feed these into the chamber.

Detonation

Some initial energy is stored in a compressed spring. When you pull the trigger the spring actuates a firing pin, which impacts with the base of a tiny brass shell. In the bottom of each round is a primer charge, held in a thin brass bubble. This explosive, sometimes an unstable metal fulminate, detonates on impact. It's only a tiny charge, no bigger than a toy cap gun. It sets off the main charge of cordite (nitro-cellulose and nitro-toluene) in the main body of the shell. Because it's a high explosive the detonation happens almost instantly, unlike a cannon or firework using black powder that "deflagrates" (burns normally). The actual period of detonation is very quick.[1] The explosive disintegrates at between 5,000m/s and 8,000m/s, so a 10mm shell has used all its fuel in about 2µs. During this time a large amount of energy is released. To get a feel for the numbers, consider that a rifle round travelling at 800m/s contains the same kinetic energy as a 500kg motorcycle travelling at 80km/h, the reason being a high velocity due to the quick detonation time and the formula for kinetic energy being $E = 1/2MV^2$, for mass M and velocity V. Ranges of kinetic energy are from 11kJ/kg for a handgun to 500kJ/kg for a sniper rifle bullet. Since a large amount of energy is released in a short period the power is extremely high, up to 500GW for a rifle bullet. So, the sound of a shell exploding is like a single extremely loud click, for which we have a name: an impulse.

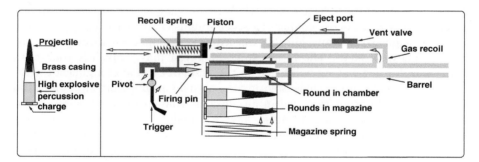

Figure 53.1
Schematic operation of automatic rifle.

Excitation

When the shell detonates it sets everything else in vibration. A shockwave moves outwards through the other components as if the gun had been struck hard at the point of the chamber. In one analysis, the sound of the gun firing is the convolution of the weapon body response with the impulse of the shell detonation. This excitation wave is primarily longitudinal and its speed in the (usually steel) barrel is well matched to detonation speed at about 5,000m/s.

---

1. Detonation is damped to avoid excessive brisance from shattering the barrel.

About 10 percent of explosive energy is lost to mechanical vibration of the weapon, which, considering the large starting value, is still significant. Magazine, stock, and housing then act to amplify and radiate this energy. Without internal recoil damping it is as if you hit the stock and housing hard with a hammer. Consequently, this part of the sound depends greatly on the weapon construction.

Expulsion and Gassing

Hot expanding gas drives the bullet down the barrel, which has rifling that spins it for stability in flight, so the bullet is slowed down by this process. Friction imparts a second force on the barrel in the same direction as the bullet. A wave of high pressure causes the barrel to radiate, but this sound is insignificant compared to the enormous volume of gas released as the round exits the barrel. Behind it comes about 100 litres of hot nitrogen, chlorine, and hydrogen, which explode in the air causing a flash. This sound, called the *muzzle signature*, is much lower in frequency than that produced by the shockwave excitation, more like a bursting balloon and several milliseconds in duration. It accounts for 20 percent of the cartridge energy. Some designs include barrel porting or muzzle brakes to reduce recoil, which lengthens the outgassing time and directs more low-frequency sound energy to the side of the weapon.

Recoil and Automatic Weapons

In an automatic weapon some of the expanding exhaust is tapped off to drive a *recoil* system. This recompresses the firing spring and drives a mechanical assembly that ejects the spent shell, chambers another from the magazine, and opens a valve to release the recoil gas. The receiver, a housing which contains the magazine fastener, is separate from the bolt and locking lugs. When these parts move to facilitate reloading for automatic and semi-automatic handguns and rifles, their action produces the mechanical sounds that help identify the weapon.

Some weapons, such as the M16, do not use a gas recoil piston but instead employ a *gas impingment system*, where exhaust gas directly cycles the weapon. In the Sear system, used for machine guns, if the trigger is not in position to catch the firing plunger another shot is fired, and the process continues in an oscillation that takes energy from each exploding round and repeats at a frequency set by the resonance of the spring and recoil chamber. Spring stiffness and gas pressure set this rate, so when a gas stem gets dirty (in gas impingment systems) the repeating rate may slow as the gas channel is fouled by powder residue. In semi-automatic weapons only one round per trigger pull is expelled and the mechanism cycles and resets itself, ready for the next triggering. A technique known as "bump firing" allows the simulation of fully automatic fire.

Heat and recycled mechanical energy accounts for up to 40 percent of the cartridge energy, so some cooling is needed to stop automatic weapons overheating and jamming. This presents an awkward design compromise since a large area must be given over to this. In the AK-47 design the gas recoil piping is left exposed over the barrel to cool in the air, while other designs couple to the housing to act as a radiator. Of course this also acts as a good sound radiator too.

Bullet Sound

After barrel friction, the remaining 30 percent of the explosive energy goes into the bullet as kinetic energy. Air that was in the barrel moves ahead of it, faster than the speed of sound. Therefore the bullet carries a supersonic shockwave at its tip as it exits. This disturbace sounds like a loud bang as the bullet moves past any observer downstream in the line of fire. Since it moves faster than the muzzle signature from the fired weapon, it is heard first. If you hear a bullet you're okay, it missed you—then you hear the shot, often some seconds afterwards.

Relative Intensity and Position

For the shooter, especially with a suppressed weapon, the sound is dominated by the excitation pulse and any echo from the outgassing. At this position the muzzle signature is affected by phase cancellation reducing the perceived intensity due to the air displacement away from the firearm. But downrange, in the cone of 45° to the line of fire, the sound is different. At less than 1m the intensity of the muzzle signature is between 140dBSPL and 160dBSPL, falling to 130dBSPL at 10m. In contrast, the housing and stock excitation may be as low as 100dBSPL. In any recording made downrange the latter is barely significant.

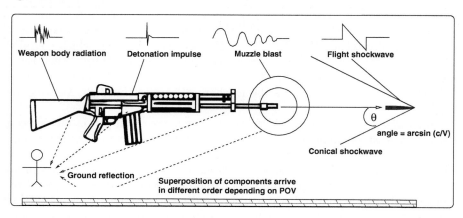

Figure 53.2
Contributory waveforms to gunshot sound.

As the bullet moves it generates a shockwave that spreads in a cone behind it. The shape of the shockwave is an N-wave with a fast rise, linear transition, and fast return. This is barely audible from the shooter's position compared to the muzzle blast, but in front of the shooter this is the louder component. The angle of shockwave spread depends on $sin^{-1}c/V$, where V is the bullet velocity and c is the speed of sound. Typical bullet velocities and their shock-wave angles are 680m/s (giving a cone angle of 30°) up to about 850m/s (giving a shockwave angle of 25°. When the bullet moves at exactly the speed of sound $c = V = 340$m/s the shockwave is at 90° and so moves in the same direction as the bullet. To the side of the weapon there is a mixture of sounds, with their relative times depending on angle and distance.

Even in an open field one echo is always found: the ground reflection of the muzzle signature and bullet flight sound. We also expect to hear ambient reflections from nearby buildings, trees, and then late echos from distant objects. Large mounted guns coupled to the ground can send shockwaves through the earth at up to five times the speed of sound in air, so these may arrive ahead of the projectile on dense (granite) terrain, giving artillery targets a brief warning. Let's summarise the contributory sounds and factors shaping the sound:

- Detonation impulse (munition signature)
- Gassing (muzzle signature)
- Body ring (weapon furniture signature)
- Automatic recycling (mechanical signature)
- Bullet flight (supersonic crack, Mach signature)
- Early reflections (bullet flight and muzzle ground reflection)
- Ambiance (trees, buildings)
- Observer position (shooter, downrange or side)
- Subterranean propagation, from heavy weapons

Model

Our model will comprise several separate components, each producing a short sound that can be mixed to provide a superposition appropriate to an observation point. Each component has a delay to offset it against the others. A filter bank creates the modal character of the weapon body. This can also be used for handling noises such as reload, chambering bolt and magazine slides when excited by a suitable friction pattern.

Method

The detonation is provided by a chirp impulse. We are not able to produce a suitably energetic impulse in the short time of a few microseconds using digital synthesis since only a few samples would be available. A critically short (about 10ms) sine sweep produces the correct effect. Muzzle blast is a much lower frequency, but again we will use a short sweep around 100Hz to obtain the required density. The weapon body is simulated with a set of series band-pass filters and excitation of the weapon will be a short noise burst. The N-wave shock signature is produced directly by a `vline-` object with a delayed and low-pass filtered version accounting for ground reflection. Some distortion using a `tanh-` or table transfer gives more high-frequency energy to the sound in order to brighten it up.

DSP Implementation

Figure 53.3
Shell chirp.

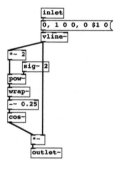

Figure 53.4
Barrel wave.

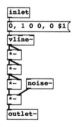

Figure 53.5
Excitation noise.

An efficient chirp impulse generator is shown in figure 53.3. This is used for the shell detonation. It can be scaled in time and frequency from shorter high impulses to longer lower ones by passing a different number to the inlet. Typically 30ms to 60ms is appropriate. Substituting this value in the decay time of a short line produces a burst of constant amplitude decaying in frequency. The values of 64 and 1.05 in the power function create a sweep over 10kHz, down to a few hundred Hz in about 50ms. An offset of -0.25 to the cosine function gives us a sinewave burst starting and ending on zero.

For the muzzle bang emitted at the end of the barrel a similar arrangement is used. This time we want a burst at about 150Hz with a smaller decay in frequency. You will notice in figure 53.4 that we also envelope the burst with the decaying line so it fades away unlike the detonation pulse which has constant amplitude. From the coefficients given there will be $2^2 = 4$ cycles of waveform. A typical duration is 20ms to 40ms, so in this period we will obtain a burst between 100Hz and 200Hz maximum frequency. Again, starting at -0.25 produces a sine wave beginning on zero, so we can mix this into the previous burst without clicking. In fact there is a short delay of perhaps 1ms or 2ms between detonation and muzzle signature in some examples analysed. This is the time it takes for the bullet to travel down a 1m barrel at a velocity of about 700m/s.

To excite a filterbank representing the weapon body and bullet sound we need to produce a short burst of noise. The decay time of this is rapid, so we use a decay made up of three cascaded squaring operations. The decay time, substituted from the inlet into the last message value for the line, will be about 200ms. At 100ms it will be virtually inaudible at 0.003906 of its initial amplitude. White noise is used because the filter will represent the combined resonance of the gun housing, barrel, and bullet crack, and we will need a broad range of bands. A set of parallel bandpass filters shown in figure 53.6 makes up the weapon body resonance. This is patched as an abstraction so we can fix the resonance as the first argument, although a value at the third inlet can be used to override any creation argument. A list of eight centre frequencies is given at the second

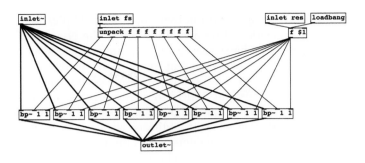

Figure 53.6
Body resonance.

inlet and unpacked to each filter. These frequencies remain fixed throughout the sound.

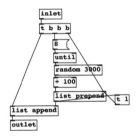

Figure 53.7
Randomiser.

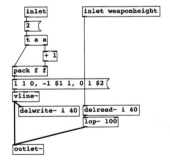

Figure 53.8
N-wave shock profile.

Setting up each frequency for the resonance can be time-consuming, so a randomiser patch helps us find good values. We usually find that a group of four between 200Hz and 800Hz make a good formant for the body resonance and another cluster around 2.5kHz work well for the barrel radiation. When you find a set of values that work well, store it as a message box list for a preset weapon character. Using an `until` object, eight random values in the range 100 to 3,100 are successively appended to a list, which is sent to the filter bank. You might like to experiment with two groups of four filters instead. Using two filters, one delayed for the muzzle shot and housing, plus an earlier one for the bullet sound, you can realistically range the weapon from an observation point downrange. In other words, if the point of view shifts from the shooter to the target the relationship between the components changes. In fact this technique is used in real life analytically (in reverse) to range enemy snipers.

To create a shockwave we need a short N-wave and a damped ground reflection a few milliseconds later. A bang at the inlet of figure 53.8 creates a float message of 2.0.

It's packed into a list along with another copy of itself plus 1.0. These two numbers represent transition time and duration of the N-wave. Substituting into a message for `vline~` we have: rise to 1.0 in 1.0ms after a delay of 0.0, move to −1.0 in $1ms after a 1.0ms delay, and finally move to 0.0 in 1.0ms after a delay of $2ms (where $2 = $1 + 1.0). A copy of this symmetrical N-wave pulse is delayed and slugged by `lop~` at 100Hz to create a reflected image that can be adjusted to modify the apparent height of the passing round. The complete gunshot synthesiser with a number of additions is shown in figure 53.9. Number boxes are provided to tweak the detonation impulse, barrel characteristics, and noise decay time, as well as the delays between the onset of each part. All parts of the combined signal pass through the filter bank whose resonance and centre frequencies are settable in the middle of the patch. Some distortion can be applied using the `tanh~` function (substitute a table lookup if `tanh~` is not available). This helps create the impression of recorded gunfire, which is invariably over level. It also to adds natural compression applied by saturation in the barrel and in the observer's ears. Part of the final signal is delayed and given to a `rev3~` reverb unit. Remember that as game sound developers it is not usually our place to add reverb to sounds. This should be taken from level geometry

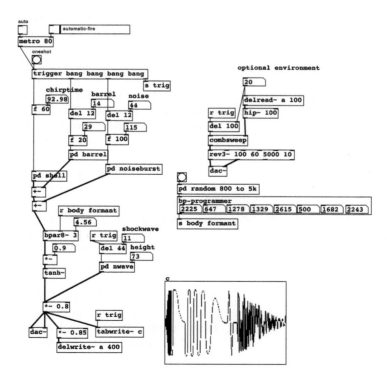

Figure 53.9
Complete gunshot simulation.

appropriate to the context, or the sound would be completely wrong when moved from a reverberant urban street to a furnished room indoors. However, while designing gunshots this "sweetener" reverb can be a useful aid to hearing what we are doing with such short sounds. It should be taken out of the code before embedding the procedural gunshot generator in a weapon model, so the reverb is left to subsequent design determined by the real-time context.

Weapon Sound Variations

Contrary to widely held belief, it isn't possible to tell the difference between types of firearm at any significant distance. This is because the body excitations unique to an example are lost at anything over 100m. It is, however, easy to distinguish calibres, so a rifle at 100m will sound different from a handgun due to the cartridge size. Over large distances such a short impulse spreads due to atmospheric effects, so the environmental factors including reflections dominate the sound. Weapon variation is therefore a sonic attribute particular to the shooter, an observation point directly behind the weapon where the muzzle signature is much quieter and the body excitation can be heard clearly. While the total discharge time (detonation and muzzle blast) may be as low as 2ms, the weapon body may continue to ring for much longer, maybe several hundred milliseconds. Other attributes that can identify the weapon are automatic rate of fire and the number of rounds discharged in successive groupings per magazine.

Assault Rifle—AK47

Original wooden stock Russian 47 (not the Chinese plastic or open stock) has good separation of crack and furniture signature at the shooter's position. There is a prominent wooden knocking sound coming in about 90ms after the impulse.

Assault Rifle—M16

The M16 is a light weapon compared to the AK47, about 7 to 9 pounds in weight when loaded. Box section steel housing gives the body resonance a hollow and light metallic "donk."

Sniper Rifles—Short, Sharp Crack

This has a high-velocity muzzle exit. Many assume a sniper is a "big gun" in games; in fact many sniper rifles are .22 calibre. The sound is shorter and harder. Larger Barrett and L96 have a high-calibre round (.50 BMG) and the Barrett is side vented to remove some flash and dampen the output intensity, from where it gets a peculiar "whizz." A 5.56 round is high velocity at 930m/s, whereas a .50 BMG round will have a muzzle velocity of approx 988m/s. The shockwave from the .50 will be much louder and broader in frequency, which will provide greater excitation to the surrounding enviornment.

Suppression

Allowing the gas to bleed into a larger volume before it exits the muzzle reduces the sound. Rifle suppressors (available up to 20mm) will reshape the report, giving a different sound. This also affects the projectile velocity, slowing it down.

Semi-Automatic Machine Pistol

These produce a tight, gassy, smaller body sound. The Uzi, H&K Mp5, and similar 9mm weapons all share a similar ringing; they are noticeably less brash than a rifle and sound more like a rapidly fired pistol.

Musket, Large-Calibre Handgun .357 Magnum

These project a subsonic ball or jacketed round, which does not cause a Mach shockwave. The discharge time of black powder is longer than a high-velocity rifle round, maybe 30ms to 80ms. Heavily suppressed rounds may also travel slower than sound.

Reload

Let's extend the weapon to include a reload sound. This is the operation of sliding a bolt to tension the firing spring. Since we have created a body resonance filter for the weapon, why not reuse that? This shows how modular construction of procedural sound not only gives nice efficiency, it leads to an automatically cohesive effect. If the body of the weapon changes, then the shots and the reload sound are automatically aligned.

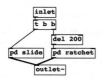

Figure 53.10
Combined reload source.

Here we see the top level of an additional subpatch called `pd reload`, which contains two other subpatches separated in time by a 200ms delay. When banged it first produces a friction sliding effect and then a locking catch sound made up of several clicks. The idea is that we do not give these sounds their complete character; we simply produce the sounds as if they were in isolation from the weapon body. When they are fed into the body filter we should get the correct effect that matches the sounds of the shots, making the ensemble sound like a coherent object.

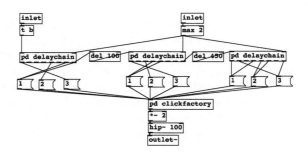

Figure 53.11
Locking mechanism click sequence.

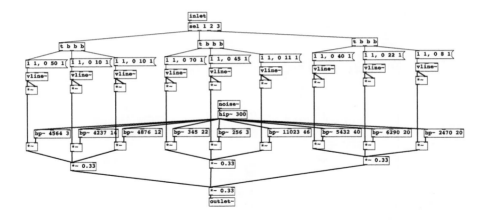

Figure 53.12
Click factory: metallic clicks for reload sound.

To sequence the clicks for our locking mechanism, a pair of cascade delay chains are used. These have inlets that propagate a bang from left to right, so each successive delay chain is connected to the end of the last. It provides a rudimentary sequencer. Notice this is exactly the same technique we used to make clockwork sounds. There are three separate clusters of clicks addressed by sending a message containing a float 1, 2, or 3 to the subpatch called pd clickfactory, shown in figure 53.12. A second inlet for each delay chain scales the total time, so we can speed up the reload action time without affecting the tone or spacing of the smaller micro-events from which it is built.

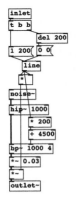

Figure 53.13
Slide friction source.

Here is how we make the actual click clusters. The diagram in figure 53.12 should seem familiar. It is the same brute force implementation we used in the clock object. Several sources of narrowly filtered noise are derived to simulate the short impact of mechanical parts; each noise band has its own brief envelope. They are clustered together in threes and tuned to sound like a small catch falling into place, a ratchet, and the clunk of an end stop.

Preceding the locking sound is a slide noise. This represents a bolt being drawn back and rubbing against the sides of a slot that guides it. Metal on metal gives rise to noise with a character that has a peak sitting somewhere between 1kHz and 5kHz. It depends on the surface finish of the metal, how rough or smooth it is. The peak depends on the speed at which the two parts are rubbed together. As the bolt moves in, a smaller amount of it is free to vibrate, so one component of the sound rises slightly as the bolt is

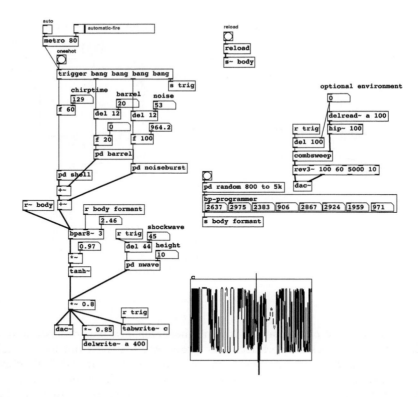

Figure 53.14
Addition of reload sounds to weapon body.

drawn further. A 200ms line is turned to a square law curve that sweeps a band-pass filter between 200Hz and 4.7kHz in cascade with a highpass above 1kHz. The final diagram of figure 53.14 is the same as figure 53.9 but showing how we add the reload sound to the weapon body. We add it into the signal chain before the filter bank since the reload bolt is coupled to the body, like the chamber and barrel. It should probably be attenuated much more for a realistic balance.

Results

Source   . . . .   <http://mitpress.mit.edu/designingsound/guns.html>

Conclusions

In summary, gunshot sounds are composed of several parts and their exact combination depends on where the observer stands. We can simulate gunfire by combining these components at a small scale of just a few milliseconds. For the shooter, different material compositions and structure of the gun has an effect on the sound, but downrange most guns sound the same. Muzzle signature is directional, and the bullet also produces a sound that can't be heard behind the weapon but is loud to an observer at the side as it passes. We can combine body resonances used to colour the shot with friction patterns to obtain handling noises.

Exercises

Exercise 1

Create the correct localisation heard 500m from the firing position where rounds at a velocity of 680m/s are missing you by 50m.

Exercise 2

Research exterior and flight ballistics, spin, tumble, and coning. Try to create the sounds for subsonic bullets passing or ricochet effects.

References

Maher, R. C. (2006). "Modeling and signal processing of acoustic gunshot recordings." In *Proc. IEEE Signal Processing Society 12th DSP Workshop*, pp. 257–261, Jackson Lake, WY, September 2006. IEEE.

Maher, R. C. (2007). "Acoustical characterization of gunshots." In *Proc. IEEE SAFE 2007: Workshop on Signal Processing Applications for Public Security and Forensics*, pp. 109–113. Washington, D.C., April 2007.

Pääkkönen, R., and Kyttala, I. (1992). *.308 suppression*. Finish Ministy of Labour.

Stoughton, R. (1997). "Measurements of small-caliber ballistic shock waves in air." *J. Acoust. Soc. Am.* 102, no. 2: 781–787.

54
Practical 31
Explosions

We investigate the different types and sounds of explosions. Many explosion sound effects used in films and games are generic stock recordings with little relation to the image they accompany. Often they are library elements rehashed with new effects. Because the physics of explosion sounds is rather detailed we can't possibly cover all of it. Hopefully what can be achieved in this section is to provide food for thought about the realism or feelings conveyed by an explosion sound effect, including power, distance, duration, environment, and secondary effects.

Analysis

An explosion is a sudden release of energy, usually but not always resulting in a rapid change of air pressure and formation of a shock wave that travels faster than the speed of sound. A wave of increased pressure called *overpressure* moves away from the source of explosion. This may be followed by a negative inrush of air in reaction to the initial blast, sometimes with more damaging results. A fast shockwave gives an explosion a shattering effect or *brisance*, whereas slower explosions are *propellants* that gradually push things out of the way.

A typical overpressure curve is shown in figure 54.1. In the first phase the air pressure builds very rapidly. With a supersonic shockwave this line is almost vertical. Next it decays at a slower rate, then overshoots to becomes negative, creating a "blast wind" that can pull out windows or demolish structures weakened by the first shockwave. Further pressure changes may occur as the air stabilises back to atmospheric pressure again.

Rupture

Not all explosions require explosives. Any compressible fluid under high pressure can cause an explosion if its container fails. Boiler explosions or failure of compressed gas cylinders can have devastating effects. This usually starts with a small leak around a point of weakness, which leads to a chain reaction known as the "fluid hammer effect" that fractures the container. It's worth noting that not all explosions release heat. Rapidly sublimating carbon dioxide can be used as a safety explosive in mining; the net effect of the explosion is to

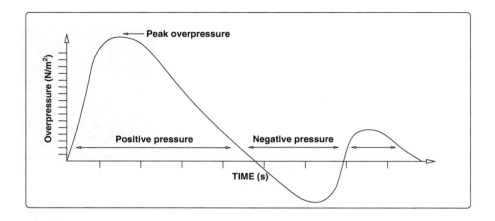

Figure 54.1
Overpressure at some point distant from explosion.

cool down the surrounding material. Volcanoes, geysers, and earthquakes are natural occurrences that can have explosive effects due to a sudden release of accumulated fluid pressure or material stress.

Deflagration

A burning mixture of fuel and oxygen releases hot exhaust gases that have a larger volume than the precursors. If it is contained by a sealed vessel then pressure builds until the container ruptures. Furthermore, the reaction speed often increases with pressure, so gunpowder that merely fizzles on its own will explode if confined. This use of propellants in early firearms like cannon is denoted "low explosive" action.

Conflagration

Even without any container, a mixture of the right proportions can burn violently. A conflagration of explosive air vapour mixture is the familiar film explosion. Most Hollywood explosions are achieved with kerosene, which is safe to handle until deliberately vapourised. It creates a wonderful show of light and smoke, but no brisance. Overdubbing with big explosion sounds is required because the overpressure wave is very mild. Of course this doesn't mean vapour conflagrations are not dangerous; fuel-air bombs cause enormous destruction by the negative overpressure they create when consuming atmospheric oxygen, and can destroy buildings.

Detonation

High explosives undergo a chemical chain reaction that moves with enormous speed through the whole mass. A shockwave, initiated by a smaller primary charge, propagates through the material disturbing chemical bonds. These disintegrate and release more energy, which pushes the shockwave forward further. Behind the detonation wave the explosive expands, usually to a mixture of gases that may then further deflagrate. Technically speaking, any shockwave moving faster than the speed of sound is a high explosive. Detonation speeds range from 340m/s up to almost 10,000m/s.

High Explosive Weapons

Game and film sound effects you may be trying to create are various bombs, grenades, and so forth. Not only do these contain high explosives that detonate, they are often surrounded by a strong container designed to fragment. This means the pressure is extremely high when they burst, and because it is sustained by containment some of these are the loudest explosions. Shrapnel fragments ejected from the explosion move supersonically, initially up to the speed of detonation, so they behave like bullets we looked at earlier, trailing a detached Mach shockwave and making a snapping sound as they pass by.

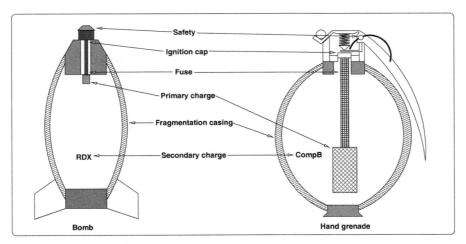

Figure 54.2
Explosive devices.

Explosion Sounds

The sound produced is no indicator of destructive force. Civilian demolition makes use of very high-brisance explosives, which create unusually short sounds. These short, loud cracks are in the order of a few milliseconds and are particularly hard to capture or synthesise but will pulverise any material in the shockwave path. Only small amounts are needed; the gaseous products may be small, and there are few flying fragments. The explosive just weakens critical structures, causing the target to collapse under gravity. Much like the gun sounds we looked at, these sounds depend greatly on the material coupled to the blast. For example, lock cracking charges sound like a door being hit extremely hard. Sounds of high explosives in a complex environment are particularly interesting. Shockwave superposition plays an important role as shockwaves are reflected from the ground or buildings. Bombs may be carefully detonated above ground to focus shockwaves in a particular destructive pattern where the direct blast wave meets the reflected ones. Gunfire or grenades heard in an urban environment may produce strange whines, flutter noises, and other secondary effects as shockwaves are focused into corners.

Movement of the Explosion

Common to many explosions, but most familiar from atomic bomb blasts, is the mushroom cloud, which has a toroidal circulation of hot gas (figure 54.3). This moves upwards due to convection above the seat of the explosion and downwinds of cooler air falling at the outside. To an observer some distance from the fireball an interesting effect is heard. The subsonic roaring sound of burning gas follows two paths, one direct and one reflected. Since the ball of gas is moving upwards an interference occurs at the observation point that sounds like a comb filter swept down in frequency. This arrives much later than the initial shockwave boom.

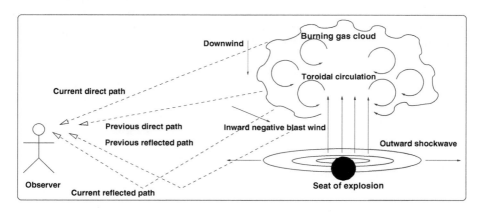

Figure 54.3
Comb and phasing effects produced by a moving source of sound.

Interactive Effects

As we have already noted, some of the sound comes from structures excited by the explosive force. Doors and shelves may rattle, objects are overturned, and pieces of shrapnel hit stationary obstacles. Other sounds may be fragmentary, like shattering glass, crumbling concrete, and so forth. These all produce secondary sources in the vicinity of the explosion. Additionally, early subterranean waves arriving before the airborne shock might set objects close to the observer moving.

Medium Effects

Sounds carried from the seat of the explosion and its immediate vicinity are propagated on top of the overpressure signature. This has an effect as if the explosion were moving rapidly forwards then backwards from the observer, changing the pitch of received waves like Doppler effects from a moving source. The supersonic shock is really sounds from the initial blast compressed into a single wavefront. At great distances this slows down to transonic speeds and dilates, where it releases the compressed sound waves in a single dull thud. Sounds following this point may have the impression of slowing down or receding. Although the blast may contain high frequencies, those arriving at a distant observation point in the later stages of negative overpressure can be slowed down to become a wall of bass. This gives the impression that the explosion persists for longer than it actually does.

Model

A detailed physical model of an explosive event is impossible, so any model must be spectral and approximate. We must try to incorporate the following features.

- Early ground waves (prerumble or dull thud)
- Initial shock front (dilated N-wave)
- Burning gasses from a moving fireball (phasing/roaring)
- Collisions and fragmentation (noisy textures)
- Relativistic shifts in frequency (time dilation and compression)
- Discrete environmental reflections (echo and reverb)

Method

This patch is somewhat similar to the thunder example from an earlier chapter, another kind of explosion. Again the approach is to build up the sound in layers, giving attention to each of the features discussed above. A short chirp impulse will form the attack, followed by shaped noise to create the loud blast, then a rumbling fireball made from low-passed noise. Except for the initial impulse, both components are delayed slightly relative to the start and both can feed into two effects. The first effect is a moving variable delay which creates a Doppler type effect made by the distortion of the medium around the explosion. The second is a slow-moving comb filter to give the effect of the rising fireball.

DSP Implementation

Shockwave Impulse

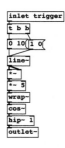

This subpatch uses a wrapped line method to obtain a chirp. A bang arriving at the `trigger` inlet fires a message to `line~` setting it to 1.0, then immediately follows up with another message telling it to move to 0.0 in 10ms. The direction is from high to low since we want a sound that is weighted towards low frequencies, and squaring the signal ensures that the initial click of high frequency is short while the lower body and tail of the chirp are longer. There are five cycles in the chirp, with the sweep moving between $1/10\text{ms} \times 5 = 500\text{Hz}$ down to 0Hz. Stopping on 0Hz means there will be a DC offset, so a `hip~` acts as a DC trap to pull the signal back to zero. This creates a nice dull thump, which is exactly what we want.

Figure 54.4
Chirp of initial shockwave.

Blast Noise

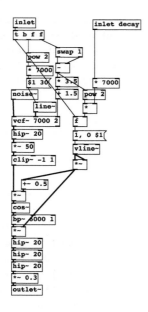

Although figure 54.5 seems quite elaborate it is only filtered noise and a waveshaper with a few extras to set up the correct behaviour. A float at the left inlet triggers a descending line which sweeps the frequency of `vcf~` depending on its value, from a maximum of 7kHz. The `pow` is used to make a curve so that small differences result in larger sweeps. Notice that the blasts are quite short at 30ms. We trigger a few of these in quick succession with decreasing brightness. Filter resonance is inversely proportional to cutoff frequency, so bright blasts, $Q = 1.5$, have a wide bandwidth, while lower ones, $Q = 5$, are more resonant. Noise is passed through this filter, then amplified and clipped. The overdrive gives us a noise source like a random square wave, digital noise that is either on or off. Now comes the interesting bit. We use this signal (which is sweeping downwards in frequency) and add it to a fast-moving line which is then applied to a cosine function. We get "sinusoidal noise," which is moving about in frequency a lot but bounded in amplitude between -1.0 and

Figure 54.5
Noisy blast generator.

1.0. This allows us to make very brutal frequency sweeps keeping a constant amplitude, which would be hard to do with filters alone. This noise is focused with a gentle band pass at 6kHz and modulated by the line making the sinusoidal sweep. The technique can be used for making fragmentation- and smashing-type effects; we get very loud, harsh, and short noise sweeps that can be controlled in tone.

Blast Control

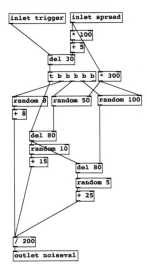

A sequence of short blasts is created by the patch in figure 54.6. Everything is done in the message domain. When a bang arrives it passes through a sequence of delays that trigger random numbers to create further delays or output values. Starting top left, the initial bang is delayed by 30ms, or whatever the **spread** inlet provides, down to a minimum of 5ms. Three further random numbers are generated, two of which set delay times. The third number is given an offset (8) and output after scaling by 1/200. Two more numbers arrive sometime later, delayed en route by random amounts. Increasing **spread** lengthens the gap between each event, but leaves the possibility that the second and third blast may be very close together. In practice this seems to work well, as many explosion recordings have a double "bam-bam" immediately following the shock, possibly due to ground reflection. So, we get a sequence of three increasing random numbers with adjustable separation. This subpatch feeds the above blast noise generator to

Figure 54.6
Blast control.

provide a quick succession of three harsh noise blasts.

Fireball

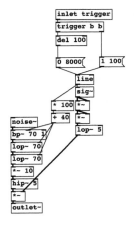

Here's the final sound layer, which gives the guts of the explosion, a long rumbling boom. It is fixed at 8s duration, though you may like to add a control for this. The rise time is not instantaneous, a value of about 100ms seems to work better and I've used a message domain **line** so that the filter cutoff and amplitude can be controlled from the same line segment. Low-passed noise is swept upwards and downwards a small amount, from 40Hz up to 140Hz and then slowly back down again. Modulating amplitude with a quartic curve makes a nice reverb-like tail while giving a full body for the first 2 seconds. Notice a fairly high gain factor of 10 right before the DC killer, making the output of this subpatch quite hot. This is done so that you can apply a volume control to the fireball boom and still be able to overdrive it into a subsequent **clip~** unit for an extra meaty effect.

Figure 54.7
Fireball rumble.

Environmental Effects

Two environmental effects that greatly enhance our explosion are shown in figure 54.8. The first is a "pressure wave effect." Starting with the left inlet, the signal is fed through to the outlet almost unaffected, except by a low pass. Some of the signal is tapped off and fed into a delay buffer. It appears on the outlet of vd~ 500ms later, and some of it is fed back into the delay to recirculate. The net effect will be an ordinary echo, until a bang arrives at the `trigger` inlet. After a bang arrives, and a short time delay has passed, a long, slow line segment is started which begins to shorten the delay. This raises the pitch of any signal still recirculating in the buffer. It is similar to a tape delay effect often used in music, but in the context of an explosion it mimics the effect of a pressure wave following behind the shockwave which time-compresses the echoing sound.

The second effect is a comb filter and appears on the right in figure 54.8. In this case the input signal goes straight into the delay buffer, which has three taps spaced at 10ms, $10 + $ `width` ms and $10 + 2 \times$ `width` ms. Combining them

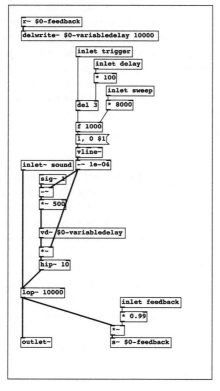
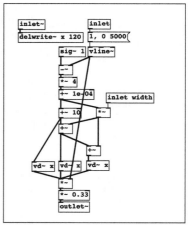

Above: Swept comb filter

Left: vari–delay pressure wave effect

Figure 54.8
Pressure wave effect and comb filter effects.

creates a phaser/flanger with notches that colour the sound. When this is swept downwards it gives the effect of a rising fireball, where the direct and ground reflected signals move relative to one another.

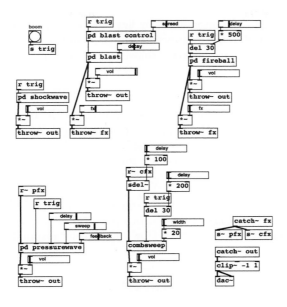

Figure 54.9
Complete explosion effect.

Putting all the parts together results in the patch of figure 54.9, consisting of three parts: impulse, blast noise, and fireball rumble. These can be mixed and routed to effects to create the right blend. Controls are provided for the delay offsets, relative volumes, effect depth, and sweep times.

Results

Source . . . . <http://mitpress.mit.edu/designingsound/explosions.html>

Conclusions

Explosions create a high-pressure wave that excites the environment. High explosives make a supersonic shockwave with slower waves following behind. We can model the sound of explosions using layers to create each physical effect.

Exercises

Exercise 1

How do urban gunfire detectors used by law enforcement work? How can these detectors tell the difference between a gunshot and a firework? Study good quality recordings of high and low explosives and determine differences in the initial attack portion.

Exercise 2

Create the short, hard sound for a high-explosive grenade to be used in a combat game. How can you work with the game world reverb to localise and colour this explosion? How is it different from a flashbang (stun) grenade? What role does occlusion play, and how is this different for supersonic and sub-Mach waves?

Exercise 3

You need to create the effect for a very large but distant explosion. Think about the colouration and timings of the various parts. As with an earthquake, consider the objects near the observer. How might they respond to powerful low frequencies?

References

Brode, H. L. (1956). *The Blast Wave in Air Resulting from a High Temperature, High Pressure Sphere of Air.* Res. Mem. RM-1825-AEC, Rand Corporation, Santa Monica, CA.

Olsen, M. E., Lawrence, S. W., Klopfer, G. H., Mathias, D., and Onufer, J. T. (1980). *Simulation of Blast Waves with Headwind.* NASA Ames Research Center Moffett Field, CA 94035.

Yngve, G. D., O'Brien, J. F., and Hodgins, J. K. (2000). "Animating explosions." In *SIGGRAPH 2000*, New Orleans, LA. ACM.

55

Practical 32
Rocket Launcher

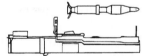

Aims

No game weapon gives quite as much satisfaction as the rocket launcher (except maybe the chainsaw in CQB). As well as showing how to make the sound of a rocket launcher, this final part of the weapons chapter aims to gently introduce some more concepts for designing sound objects as used in games. We will approach the implementation in a slightly different way, thinking about states and how components of a sound object interact. As we saw with the gun example, where reload sounds were added to an existing weapon body, a powerful principle to use in procedural audio is reusability. This is the most complex example that can be presented in this book because of space limitations; however, it will give you an idea about the kind of programming tactics needed for procedural sound objects.

Analysis

Let's briefly review some technical data. For realism we must distinguish between superficially similar weapons that are in fact rather different. Technically a rocket launcher is either a man-portable anti-air weapon like the stinger, or a rocket-propelled grenade such as an RPG7. The former is completely recoilless, having an open back, while the latter, partially open, is designed to produce a back pressure and can give quite some kick. This affects the sound of launch. Neither should be confused with recoilless rifles or guns such as the Carl Gustav or M67 which burn up all their propellant in the tube but use a countermass or recoil back vent. We will take the M72A2/A3 LAW as our target model for this exercise. The 1kg rocket is 51cm × 66mm and has six spring-loaded fins that pop out to stabilise it as it flies at a velocity of 145m/s. The composite alloy tube is 93cm long and is a disposable housing designed to fire one rocket with an effective range of 200m and a total bombardment range of 1km. Like many HEAT or RPG weapons the warhead will explode after a timeout or on hitting something solid enough. Many game weapons, like the rocket launcher in Half-Life, have exaggerated burn times. A typical shoulder launched rocket uses all its propellant in less than 2s and its momentum completes the remainder of its range. For artistic license we will use the specs of the M72 as a guide, but will make our launcher reloadable and have rockets that burn a bit longer.

Model

Acoustically the unloaded empty tube, open at both ends, behaves as a full wavelength resonator with $\lambda = l = 0.93$ giving $f = c\lambda = 366\text{Hz}$ and all harmonics. With a projectile inside we have a closed-tube quarter-wavelength resonator such that $\lambda/4 = 0.93 - 0.51$, giving $f = 571\text{Hz}$ with odd harmonics. What about vibrational modes? The first circular mode (for a thin-walled tube $f = \sqrt{E/\mu}/\pi d$, where μ is mass density and E is Young's modulus of elasticity and d is the diameter of the tube) for a 66mm × 1m aluminium tube gives about 40kHz, way too high to be relevant to our synthesis. The first and second bending modes, on the other hand, come out at about 300Hz and 826Hz and longitudinal vibration (up and down the tube) at about 3200Hz. This gives us some idea of the sounds we might expect handling the tube loaded and empty, dropping it, or reloading it with a fresh rocket.

Method

Most of the work will be done by narrow band filters to build the tube model. This allows us to easily change the apparent capacity from loaded to empty. Handling noises are produced with a simple additive method. The rocket itself will use comb-filtered noise and its own resonant tube model, again produced by narrow filter methods.

DSP Implementation

We need to start with an overview of the whole system in order for this exercise to make any sense.

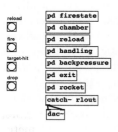

Figure 55.1
Top-level patch.

The top-level patch is shown in figure 55.1. There are no connections, just a bunch of subpatches and some action buttons along the left side that communicate to destinations within the subpatches. The first subpatch maintains the system state. The second is a chamber, a wrapper around the tube model to control how full or empty it is. Next are two subpatches dealing with the reload, handling, and trigger click sounds. Finally, there are three subpatches dealing with actually firing the rocket, a tube backpressure model, the chamber exit effect, and the actual rocket, which itself consists of a tube model. In figure 55.2 is an action-state diagram that helps explain the components and their relationships. You can see there are really two objects, the launch tube and the projectile, that exist within the environment. Before firing they will be coupled, with the rocket inside the tube. After firing they are separate, and the projectile accelerates away. The listening location will be close to the launch tube, since this sound is to be rendered from the player's point of view. The launch tube comprises an

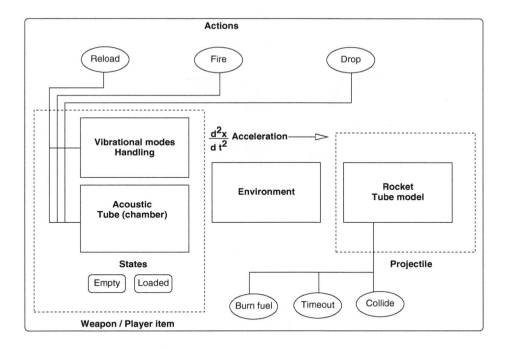

Figure 55.2
Actions and states of the sound object.

acoustic tube model and a set of vibrational modes for handling and dropping sounds. Six actions are attached to the system: reloading, firing, and dropping the launch tube, plus burning, target collision, and timeouts for the rocket.

Launch Tube

For the launch tube chamber a patch is shown in figure 55.3 made from four band-pass filters. The signal to be placed inside the tube as an exciter arrives via the `catch-` destination. A little of it is fed directly to the main output bus while the rest goes through the filters in parallel. The effective length of the tube is set by the `chamberf` parameter. It is multiplied by a series of factors, being either odd (1, 3, 5, 7) or odd and even (2, 3, 4, 5). An internal parameter destination `chamberclosed` sets whether the tube model is half open (with the rocket in) or fully open (with the rocket launched), while the resonance of the tube is picked up by `chamberres`.

Fire State

Look now at figure 55.4, the patch for controlling the fire state. When the fire button is pressed a bang picked up on `firebutton` triggers the value stored in a float box. The value is either 1 if the chamber is empty, or 0 if it is loaded with a rocket. If it's 1 then the bang message passes to the right of `moses` and activates

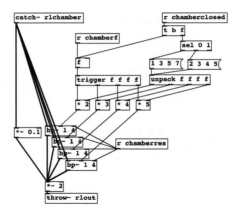

Figure 55.3
Launch tube.

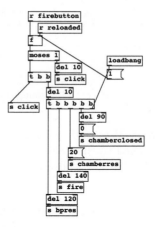

Figure 55.4
System state.

the firing click after a 10ms delay, but nothing else. If the tube is loaded then the message passes to the left of moses triggering a sequence of events. First a message is sent to the cold inlet of the float box to say that the tube is now empty. So here the tube maintains its own status, full or empty. Meanwhile two other messages are scheduled through delays, to set the chamber harmonics and resonance for launch. A bang is also sent to another subpatch that will produce a loud backpressure sound, a kind of dull thump.

To understand how the sequence of operations creates the launch sound refer to figure 55.5, showing the rocket exiting the tube. While it is in the tube a short half-open pipe is formed. As it's launched the pipe length grows rapidly and suddenly becomes a fully open pipe as the rocket leaves.

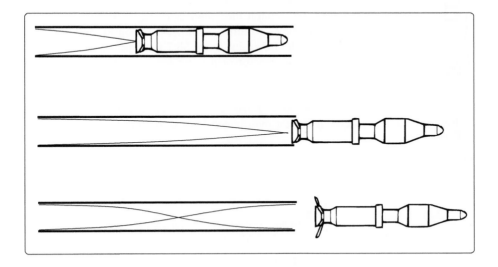

Figure 55.5
Acoustic behaviour of the tube loaded and unloaded (at firing).

Launch

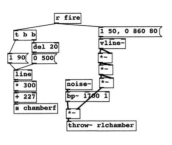

Figure 55.6
Exit sound.

As the rocket leaves the tube (fig. 55.6) a `line` object sweeps across the chamber frequency to give the effect of the rocket moving out. When loaded, the rocket occupies a bit more than half the tube, so the sweep is between about 230Hz and 530Hz (to hit the resonances). At the same time a band-filtered noise burst around 1700Hz is given a sharply curved envelope and fed into the chamber cavity. Coinciding with the moment the rocket leaves the tube a message is received to switch the modes of the launch tube, giving a nice empty-sounding ring. The noise blast continues for about 500ms after the rocket has left to allow the tube some ring time and blend into the next component.

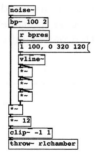

Figure 55.7
Backpressure.

Accelerating so fast, the gas from the rocket cannot escape the tube quickly enough. Even before the projectile fully exits a considerable pressure builds up in the tube. Once the rocket leaves and both ends are open this excess pressure is released faster. The effect is a tamer version of the barrel gas expansion modelled in the gunshot exercise. It is a low-frequency "whump" somewhere around 100Hz.

The patch shown in figure 55.7 is responsible for this. It is activated on receipt of a bang via the **bpres** destination, which triggers a `vline~` object. Another steep power curve envelope is used, this time rising in 100ms and decaying in 320ms. The noise, post-modulation, is quite severely clipped, to give a strong overdriven knocking sound.

Rocket

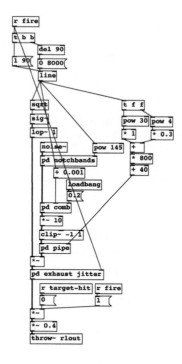

Figure 55.8
Rocket.

The rocket itself would be a separate object, although in this exercise it is included within the same patch example. Ideally the rocket would emit an accurate representation of a real rocket sound. It would actually get louder and more energetic sounding during the short time the fuel burns away. Environmental modelling for movement would then be applied to it so that distance produces a decaying, dulling effect from the shooter's point of view.

With a proper two-object implementation the sound would immediately work when passing an observer, or approaching the target, without having to make separate sounds for all cases. However, in this example we fake some of that, just to show some of the principles that should be employed in the environmental model for the rocket. In figure 55.8 we see the rocket patch. In many ways it is similar to the launch tube model, since a rocket is no more than a propellant burning in a half-open tube.

Again, a line envelope controls the burn time, although this time we use a square-root-shaped curve for the main modulator. The effect of the fuel burning is interesting. With time, an increasing surface area burns, and greater pressure is produced. But at the same time the size of the cavity increases, lowering the tone. These dynamics don't cancel each other out, but they produce an interesting set of changing resonances that characterise a rocket sound. The fuel effect is obtained by the `notchbands` filter which sweeps upward in a power curve, while at the same time a `comb` filter sweeps over the noise before it is placed in the `pipe` model whose size is slowly increased.

For a man-portable SAM like the stinger, the rocket accelerates at an extremely high rate, reaching Mach 4 in about the time it takes to burn all its fuel. This means there is an extreme downward Doppler shift, and at some point not long after launch the sound stops being heard at the shooter's position. Here we have a compromise between a realistic and artistic effect. Giving the rocket sound some `exhaust jitter` fakes the environmental effects of wind shear and strong ground effects. Finally, we need some way to turn off the rocket sound when it hits a target. You'll probably want to download the code rather than build this, but so you can implement the rocket just from this book I've included the internal components of the rocket in figure 55.9, which we will not discuss further.

Reload

To reload the weapon a new rocket slides into the tube. When fully home it interlocks with the arming and firing mechanism. The first part of this sound is a frictional noise during which the tube length, in half-open mode, is swept the opposite way than for launching, so it gets shorter. The locking sound is a couple of clicks applied to the chamber in its loaded configuration. All the components needed are shown in figure 55.10. On receipt of a bang at `reloadbutton` some handling noise is triggered, the chamber is switched to closed mode, and its resonance configured before a slow line sweeps over the chamber frequency. The friction is produced by some unipolar high-pass-filtered narrow band noise around 6kHz. Clicks for the locking mechanism are produced by 20ms bursts of noise around 5kHz with a square law envelope. This subpatch also includes some initialisation for the launch tube using `loadbang`.

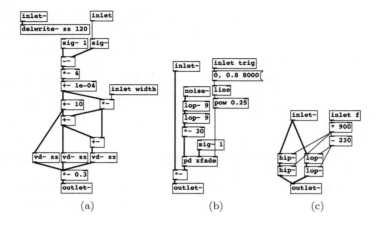

Figure 55.9
Left to right: (a) Comb filter. (b) Exhaust jitter. (c) Notch filter.

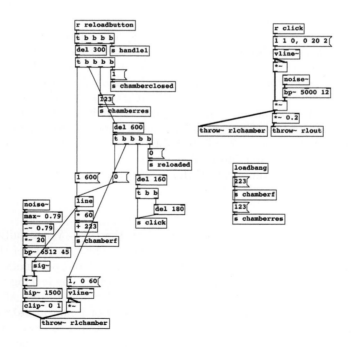

Figure 55.10
Reload sounds for the launch tube.

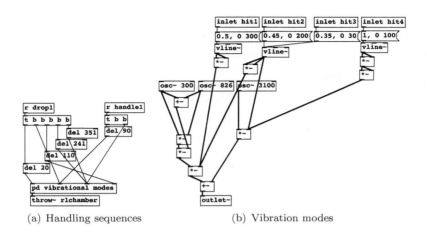

(a) Handling sequences   (b) Vibration modes

Figure 55.11
Handling noise sequences and vibrational modes of the launch tube.

Handling Noise

Two bending and one longitudinal mode are produced by sinewave oscillators. Mixing together ring-modulated and direct combinations of these gives us the right properties for side and edge collisions with the tube. These short sounds are also fed into the acoustic tube model as well as having a direct (outer surface radiated) signal. When the tube is dropped four noises are activated in a short sequence using `delay` objects. This simulates an end collision and brief bouncing back and forth to excite some side collisions. The handling sound triggered for reloading is a shorter version that just excites a quieter end collision, for the rocket knocking against the launch tube. In a proper game context these could all be parameterised by real-time data from the animation, particularly the drop collisions that should be derived from the physics engine. Of course, because of the tube state, different sounds are heard if you drop the tube when empty or loaded.

Results

Source   ··········   <**http://mitpress.mit.edu/designingsound/rockets.html**>

Conclusions

Rockets, grenade launchers, mortar tubes, and so forth can be modelled with acoustic tubes. There is not much new here as far as synthesis or techniques go, but we have seen how many components can be combined to build a more complete sound object with statefulness. Strictly, for game objects, state should rarely be built into sounds themselves. The main object code should maintain an authoritative version of all states. However, we have seen how states can be applied to things like whether a weapon is loaded or not.

Exercises

Exercise 1

Produce the sound effect for a fixed mortar tube. Use a detailed tube model with at least five acoustic and three vibrational modes to get the correct sound of the grenade falling down the tube.

Exercise 2

Experiment with adding Doppler shifts and better environmental effects to the rocket model. Place a listening position so that you can hear it approach fly-by.

Practical Series Science Fiction

Space: the final frontier.
—Gene Roddenberry

Sci-Fi, Fantasy, and the Unreal

Introducing machines we talked about "hyperrealism," the way that synthetic and analytical sound design allows us to reach out from an established base in reality and go beyond. It became apparent that we could use mechanical and physics knowledge to create arbitrary devices from imagination alone. Now we are going one step further, to enter the realm of the unreal. However, you will not want to completely abandon established techniques. As they are sublimated by experience you will simply no longer be aware of needing them for support. This is a point of liberation. In a way it is why we worked so hard, to learn so many rules, only to let go of them. A pianist practices scales, but for entertainment plays music. That's not the same as letting go of our common sense and only improvising wildly. On the contrary, it's time to take a look at a different side of sound design that requires as much thought and skilful application. Hereafter we need to be more sensitive to the meaning in sounds. Fantastic devices like hovercars, lightsabers, teleport transporters, and spaceship engines are as difficult to create as real sounds, maybe more so because there is no blueprint given by nature. It is time to stretch the muscles of metaphor, simile, onomatopoeia, and juxtaposition. If what we have been engaged in so far is technical writing then this is the "poetry" of sound design.

Synthesisers and Sci-Fi Sound Design

Synthesisers and science fiction share a strong common history. Throughout the 1950s, 1960s, and 1970s a constant quest sought new and interesting sounds to enthuse the listener with a sense of magic and wonder. This was driven by a perception of synthesisers having unlimited possibilities, as humankind seemed to have unlimited possibilities when we ventured to the Moon in 1969. Culturally, the postwar and "cold war" period was an optimistic time. Although we live in darker times now, where technology is often seen as a dystopian enemy, we should not forget the optimistic roots of synthetic sci-fi sounds that carried magical, engaging, wonderful connotations.

Some notable early practitioners were the Barons, a husband-and-wife team who worked on *The Forbidden Planet* in 1956. The sounds for the Krell and their monsters from the id were created using self-destructing electronic circuits, a profound work of art if not the most practical way to synthesise sound. Their work remains unique to this day. Later in the UK, Briscoe and Mills of the BBC set up the Radiophonic Workshop, a hothouse for new technological sound design where talented pioneers (Hodgson, Baker, Derbyshire, Oram, Clarke, Kingsland, Limb, Howell, and Parker) experimented with new methods of sound creation.

The idea, to discover new sound production processes, was apparently an enormous success evidenced by prolific output in the heyday of the Radiophonic Workshop. Sound for television series like *Dr Who* and *Quatermass* relied on strange and unique noises from custom modular synthesisers, optical Fourier transforms, and hybrid electromechanical signal generators. Then, as with all revolutions, it overreached, precipitating a countermovement. As the popularity of sci-fi waned, a backlash against synthetic and unreal sound reigned, until in the late 1970s George Lucas and Ben Burtt took up the torch again. Founding Skywalker Sound off the back of the immensely successful *Star Wars* franchise, they continued the tradition of using synthesis creatively for fantasy-world stories. Today the tradition is as strong as ever, with long-running institutions like *Star Trek* keeping synthesis at the heart of sound design.

Of course not all sci-fi sounds are synthesised, and you should not see digital synthesis as a panacea for sound design in any genre. As you will see, two of the sounds we are going to look at are digital simulations of sounds created from real-world sources. Sound design has matured as an art, and pure synthesis has found its place alongside traditional recording. Modern fantasy sound design for film and games relies on hybridisation, cross-synthesis, and blending the synthetic with the real. As a contemporary master of the art, David Randall Thom says that "creating unreal sounds (with synthesisers) is very easy." What I think he means by this is that the space of interesting synthetic sound is so extensive it's easy to get lost and seize upon a sound that has no semantics. So, using synthesis for this task doesn't require the same attention to sonic meaning as working with recorded material; it requires much more. That is why I left this section, which many people would consider the "fun stuff," to the end: using synthesis to work only from your imagination will take all the knowledge you have accumulated so far to get good results.

The Practicals

- Transporters: create the effect of beaming down.
- Computer babble: R2D2 and other computer chatter.
- Red alert: starship sirens (advanced analysis).

56
Practical 33
Transporter

Create a *Star Trek* transporter sound.

Background

A transporter scans the complete quantum state of any object, employing a Heisenberg compensator to remove measurement uncertainty, then transfers this mass-energy information to a remote location within 40×10^3km. Invented in the early twenty-second century by Dr. Emory Erickson the device can transport objects in real time with scanning, projection, and reassembly taking between 2 and 2.5 seconds. Anybody standing in the beam simply disappears and reappears elsewhere. This obviously involves considerable energy since all the mass must be converted to energy and back again.

The Sound of a Transporter

What are we to make of this? Imagine you have been given the task of designing the transporter sound in the 1960s. Transportation is a process, something progressive and moving, so it has a beginning, buildup, and conclusion. It is clearly an intricate and complex affair and the sound reflects this. The use of a strange and mysterious energy process implies something magical in the sound. Neither Roddenberry, *The Next Generation*[1] creators, or Starfleet manuals fully explain the process. Anyway, it seems the sound in the original series (TOS) is based on a cymbal or æolian harp, possibly in combination with an early vocoder. A vocoder is a real-time effect that operates on two signals to produce a third, new one. The output amplitudes of a bank of narrow filters with fixed separation are controlled by those from another filter bank used to analyse a sound. The spectrum of the analysed sound is thus imparted to whatever passes through the first filter bank. In TNG[2] the sound is developed slightly but keeps much of the original character. Both examples share important features. One of these is

---

1. The original series ran from 1966 to 1969.
2. *The Next Generation* (TNG) ran from 1987 to 1994, incorporating much of the original sound design.

a musical scale. The narrow noise bands are in a whole-tone scale starting on C above A 440 and extending several octaves upwards. The second characteristic is an undulating or shimmering modulation of the bands combined with a soft sweep that scans slowly upwards.

Model

We will synthesise a complex metallic spectrum like that of a cymbal and pass it through a bank of narrow filters spaced in a whole-tone musical scale.

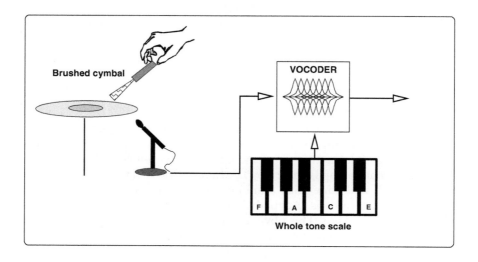

Figure 56.1
A possible production mechanism for the transporter sound.

Method

We will directly fix the band frequencies, repeatedly multiplying a base frequency by a whole tone ratio of 1.12247. Using 12 bands should be enough to get the general effect and allow the complete patch diagram to be shown here, but you can add more if you wish to get a better sound. A crude cymbal approximation is obtained by frequency modulating triangle waves and then sweeping a flanger over this signal. The addition of a simple reverb gives the effect more smoothness.

DSP Implementation

Most of the patch is exposed in figure 56.2. At the top left is the signal source for the cymbal texture. It consists of a two-stage FM process using triangle waves. The centre frequency of the spectrum is a little above C 466. The sideband spacing and modulation amount is chosen to give a dense spectrum. This is fed to a delay buffer x with 120ms of memory allocated.

In the middle is a flanger effect built around three `vd~` variable delays spaced 12ms apart and a feedback path back into `delwrite~`. Once a start message is received from the button via the **beam_me_up** destination a 12-second sweep is commenced. The line envelope also controls the amplitude of the flanged noise signal before it is fed into the filter bank.

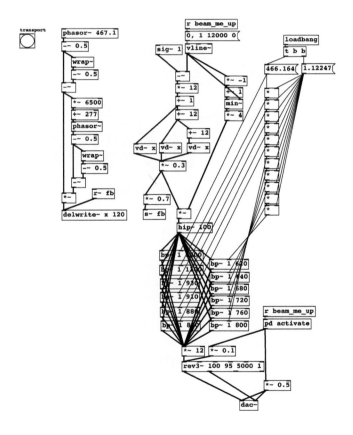

Figure 56.2
A sound similar to the *Star Trek* transporter.

Ten parallel band-pass filters make the filter bank at the bottom of figure 56.2 (they are cluttered in the diagram, but you should be able to understand since they are connected in parallel). Their resonances range between 1,200 for the lowest frequency to 800 for the highest. This means their output is virtually a sinusoidal waveform. The frequency spacing is derived from the multiplier chain on the right of the patch. This has a base frequency of 466Hz and an interval of 1.2247. The sum of all filters is fed to a reverb unit.

To complete the effect, a transporter activation sound is shown in figure 56.3. This is also an FM process. It appears in the main patch near the bottom, also receiving a message to start it when the `beam_me_up` button is pressed.

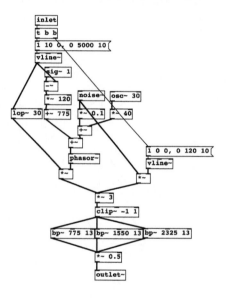

Figure 56.3
Transporter activate.

Conclusions

Dense metallic spectra can be obtained cheaply with FM. Movement can be added using chorusing. Musical scales can be obtained from a base frequency and interval multiplier. Most importantly, we can produce sound effects that are suggestive of some imaginary physical process.

Exercises

Exercise 1

What might be the significance of a whole-tone scale in this effect?

Exercise 2

Study the TNG transporter effect and try to emulate it with a higher-quality vocoder. There is some sparking effect that might be a bell tree. How could you synthesise that?

References

Joseph, F., et al. (1975). *Star Fleet Technical Manual*. Ballantine Books.

57

Practical 34
R2D2

Aims

The aim here is to make "computer babble." This is frequently heard on the bridge of starships, computer rooms, and for robots. I'll show you an implementation that mimics the *Star Wars* R2D2 robot as inspiration for creating other similar patches for your science fiction needs.

Analysis

Plenty has been written about *Star Wars* sounds, and it's not my intention to exactly replicate the sound of R2D2 here, but these patches show a relatively simple way to get a similar effect. From observation, R2D2 in the *Star Wars* films sounds like a few familiar things. He has something in common with birdcall. A blackbird exhibits quite a few spectral and amplitude gestures like the lovable tin can: there are modulation sweeps, pitch and modulation sweeps, only pitch sweeps, constant pitches, and breaks of continuous or very broken calling. For a while I wondered whether some of the R2D2 sounds were treated birdcall, possibly with ring modulation. Another sound that comes to mind is the 303 acid sound, especially regarding the pitch slides, so there is a suggestion that a sawtooth waveform and resonant filter near self-oscillation plays a part. In fact many of R2D2s sounds were realised on an ARP2600 by sound designer Ben Burtt, but not all the sounds are synthesised. About half are generated electronically: "the rest are combinations of water pipes, whistles, and vocalizations by Ben Burtt."[1] The Pure Data diagram at the end of this section looks rather complex. It is not. It looks frightening because of the large number of units needed to make it, but both the operational theory and the synthesis method at the heart of it are very easy indeed. If you've come this far through the practicals you are going to laugh once you realise how simple it really is.

---

1. <http://filmsound.org/starwars/burtt-interview.htm>.

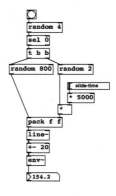

Figure 57.1
A "random random number generator."

Model

To make the babbling computer noises we are going to completely randomise the parameter space of a simple synthesiser. The timing and distributions of the random variables will be chosen to give a certain character to the sound, but other than that we won't really constrain the values except to keep them within sensible limits.

Method

FM synthesis is used for this patch. Strictly, it is in fact PM (phase modulation), but this produces very similar results.

DSP Implementation

Random Line Slides

Here is one of the most frequently used patterns in the patch. It's a random value generator. When it receives a bang message it doesn't always generate a new random number. You could say it's a "random random number generator." It first generates one random number to decide whether to generate the next. There are a few variations you will see which either output a random number, stepping from one value to another instantly, or output a line segment that slides between the previous and new value. The slide time is always derived from the metronome period. Tempo is obtained via the destination `r period` on each randomiser, which makes the slide shorter or longer as the

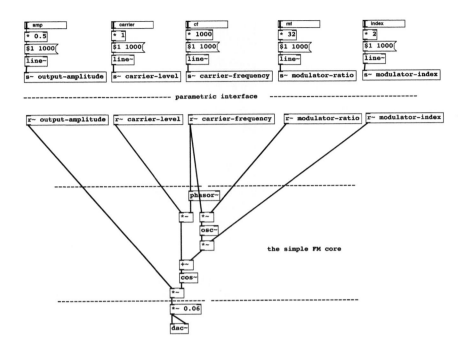

Figure 57.2
FM synthesiser for computer noises.

tempo changes. The trick is that it doesn't always slide or step; it randomly selects which one to do each time, including the chance that it will do nothing.

FM Synthesiser

Here's the synthesis block at the heart of the patch that uses FM. It is shown in figure 57.2 disconnected from some controls so that you can see the simplicity of the actual synthesiser part. Playing with the controls in this example will give you some idea of the range of sounds possible. The only things worth noting are that we are going to drive the modulation and index values well outside the normal range to deliberately introduce foldover aliasing. Why? Because it sounds cooler and more technological, that's all. If you look in the final patch there is a cascade of `lop~` and `hip~` units to kill the really low and high frequencies, but apart from that we make no attempt to control the spectrum or limit signals the way we would for a musical instrument; we actually want it to sound a bit messed up.

Complete Patch

All that I've done in the final patch is connect random value generators to the carrier frequency, modulation frequency, modulation index, and the patch

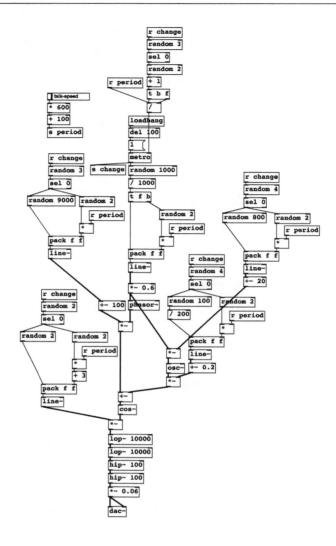

Figure 57.3
Babbling R2D2 computer noises.

output amplitude. There are a few constants to offset some values and make sure they aren't too high or low, but that's about it. Some of the constants are picked to keep him sounding quite cute and nonthreatening. If you want to extend the ranges and get different effects, try changing the carrier scaling from 0.6 to a bigger value. The patch operation is completely automatic and random. Switch it on and you don't know what might happen; it might not even make any good noises for a while, but sometimes it makes great computer babble sounds.

Results

◀ Source   . . . .   <http://mitpress.mit.edu/designingsound/
                                 r2d2.html>

Conclusions

Fanciful computer sounds can be made from bleeps and whistles sequenced by a random generator. Applying random values to the parameter space of a simple synthesiser can produce vast amounts of material for off-line (not real-time) sound design.

Exercises

Exercise 1

Listen to the bridge and computer room ambiance in *Star Trek* or other films. Try to recreate the textures you hear.

Exercise 2

Investigate state machines, fractal attractors, closed geometric sequences, and chaotic equations as other possible means of creating complex and pseudo-random controls.

58

Practical 35
Red Alert

Create the original *Star Trek* series' "red alert!" siren and learn a few more analysis tricks.

Analysis Spock?

Used in both TOS and TNG series, the classic "red alert" siren has become an iconic reference point in sci-fi. It has been used as recently as 2008 in Ben Burtt's *WALL-E* robot animation. We will use the freely available Praat analysis software for this task. Download the original red alert siren from one of the many *Star Trek*–related websites. Save the file as a mono .wav file. Open Praat and choose Read→Read from file to load the sound effect. You will now see the file in the objects list. Select it and perform Analyse→Periodicity→To pitch choosing 1000Hz as the pitch ceiling. Click OK and when it's finished analysing you should see a new object in the list. Now select a new area in the picture window by dragging a box. Select the newly created pitch object from the object list and do Draw→Draw from the action menu, choosing 200Hz to 1,000Hz as the frequency range. The plot shown in figure 58.1, which describes the movement of the fundamental frequency, gives us some valuable information immediately. Notice the curve of the pitch sweep is neither linear nor rising in a power law but circular (parabolic). It rises more slowly towards the end.

The graph doesn't tell us exactly what the frequencies of the sweep are, and you'll probably notice that it's a bit irregular. Don't worry about that, because the apparent jitter is due to the accurate pitch plotting algorithm. What we want to know is the start and end frequencies, to fit a function between them. To find the start and end frequencies select the pitch object again (if it isn't already selected) and do Query→Get minimum from the action menu. My machine tells me confidently that the start pitch is 367.3953670140852Hz; let's call that 367Hz, although I expect your example may vary. Repeat the operation using Query→Get maximum to discover that the final pitch is about 854Hz.

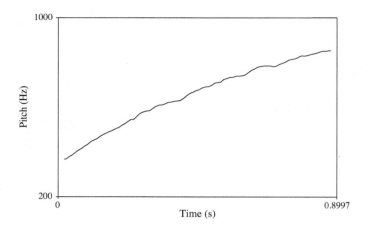

Figure 58.1
Fundamental frequency plot of TOS red alert siren.

General Spectrum and Formants

Let's take a look at where the energy is concentrated in this sound. Instead of the usual short window spectrum analysis we'll take a plot averaging all the frequency bins over the full duration of the sound. With the `sound` object selected `Analyse→Spectrum→To LTAS (pitch corrected)` gives us the bar chart shown in figure 58.2. You can see immediately there are two prominent

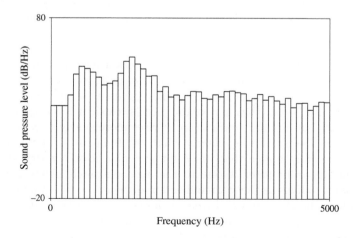

Figure 58.2
Spectral bin analysis of the whole sound.

peaks near the bottom. Let's see what frequency the largest of these has using Query→Get frequency of maximum while the LTAS object is selected. A value of about 1450Hz should be returned. Looking at a detailed spectrum of the whole file as shown in figure 58.3 you can see two clumps of energy clearly and a bunch of overtones excited around them. The first is approximately 700Hz to 800Hz and the second denser and louder group is around 1,500Hz, with two peaks.

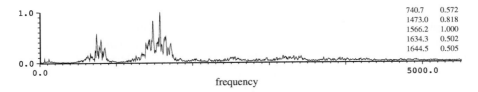

Figure 58.3
General spectrum of whole file.

Autocorrelations

Looking at the autocorrelation gives us another way to identify periodic components. It gives us a way to see how each successive wavecycle compares to the next or previous. What we are looking for this time is resonances.

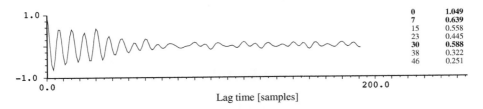

Figure 58.4
Autocorrelation snapshot from start of file.

A single snapshot from the start of the file is shown in figure 58.4, but a single graph can't show you how to use this analysis technique to its full potential. What we do is scan through the file looking for invariants, lag-time correlations that don't appear to be part of the wave harmonics. The scale makes this harder to do because the autocorrelation coefficients are in samples. Since the sample rate is that of the file (11025Hz), turning a number to a frequency requires $f = 11025/t_l$ for a lag time t_l. The fundamental appears at about 30 samples, $11025/30 = 367.5$Hz.

As we scan the file it changes in accordance with the waveform period. But there are also some values that seem fixed wherever they pop up. These are reverberations or resonances. They reveal the fixed acoustic structure of the sound. Some strong ones appear at 163, 247, and 269 samples, corresponding to 67Hz or 14.7ms, 44.6Hz or 22.4ms, and 41Hz or 24.3ms. Others not listed here but added to the implementation came out as 35ms, 11ms, and 61ms.

Waveform, Harmonic Structure

Although it changes a great deal throughout the file, the snapshot of figure 58.5 is typical of the wave, with the general harmonic shape of a sawtooth wave having equally spaced odd and even harmonics. There are two things to note. First, the second harmonic is greatly magnified. This tells us that the wave, if we assume it started as a relaxation-type sawtooth oscillator, has encountered some harmonic distortion to amplify the second harmonic. Second, some harmonics disappear momentarily as the fundamental sweeps up. This tells us there are anti-resonances or zeros in the fixed acoustic structure.

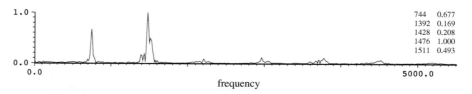

Figure 58.5
Short window spectrum of typical waveform.

Model

We now have a spectral model obtained by analysis. Without knowing exactly what the *Star Trek* red alert siren *is* we can only guess about its physical makeup. The closest sound I was able to match was that of a naval frigate. It is similar to an air-driven diphone rather than a Klaxon or cylinder siren. The rapid frequency rise time seems to add weight to this hypothesis. A fast-rising and quickly settling frequency curve with a sawtooth-like wave suggests some kind of acoustic relaxation oscillator at the heart of the sound, maybe a type of diaphragm driven by an air blast.

Method

To get a sawtooth with second harmonic distortion we could use Chebyshev polynomials; however, the rest of the harmonic profile seems like a sawtooth except for strong spreading of the bands due to some hard nonlinearity, so we take a shortcut and add just a bit more second harmonic to the waveform. A frequency sweep over the analysed range will be modulated by a fast-rising and falling amplitude envelope and the remainder of the sound's character will be given by fixed delay-based resonators and sharp filters.

DSP Implementation

Let's commence by looking at the main oscillator (seen in fig. 58.7). Its frequency starts at 360Hz (a little bit below the value we analysed) and rises to 847Hz in 900ms. To get a circular curve we take the square root of this line segment. A `phasor~` driven by this frequency sweep is recentred on zero to avoid upsetting the filters and resonators. It is mixed with some extra second harmonic (0.3) before encountering a DC trap that removes any offset when the phasor frequency is briefly zero. Amplitude control happens *before* the resonators, because we want them to behave like a system excited by the oscillator and continue to ring a little bit.

In figure 58.6 you see a fairly standard arrangement made into an abstraction that takes a delay time in milliseconds as its first and only argument. This delay feedback element will be used to make the resonators. The feedback level is fixed at 0.6. This is only to be used for short delays, so just 100ms is allocated. You can see several instances of them about halfway down figure 58.7 set to the times of fixed modes indicated by the autocorrelation analysis. In addition to five parallel resonances a loop around all of them at 61ms is added to give a bit more liveness. This value was chosen by ear to avoid interfering with the other resonances by colouring the sound too much in the wrong places. All the resonators are summed before a `hip~` removes any low-frequency circulations that might have accumulated in the delay loop; then we clip the signal hard to spread the bands out and make it much brighter and harsher. Before output a set of parallel `bp~ 1` units impart strong formants at 740Hz, 1.4kHz, 1.5kHz, and 1.6kHz.

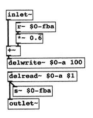

Figure 58.6
Delay feedback element.

Results

Source   . . . .   <http://mitpress.mit.edu/designingsound/redalert.html>

Conclusions

Even when we don't have a clue what a sound really is we can attack it by analysis and usually get close by looking for understandable features. This works better if we can hypothesise a physical model and take a guess at how the

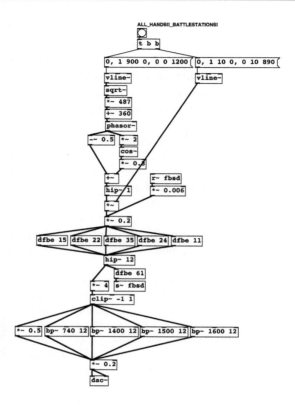

Figure 58.7
Complete patch, saw + second harmonic, resonators, distortion, and post filters to create
fixed resonance.

sound might have been made. Powerful and free tools, mainly designed for the
analysis of speech, are available for us to deconstruct existing sounds.

Exercises

Exercise 1

What are the essential differences between a siren, Klaxon, and air horn? Try
synthesising a train- or ship-type of horn.

Cover Image Sources

Fireworks: Large fireworks display. Courtesy Jon Sullivan, PDPhoto.org.

Bee: Honey bee on a flower. Courtesy Jon Sullivan, PDPhoto.org.

Bullet: High-speed photography of round fired from a .22 rifle.
Copyright Professor Andrew Davidhazy, with permission.
Rochester Institute of Technology, Department of Imaging and Photographic Technology.

Helicopter: MH-60S Knighthawk.
Public domain photo (modified). Image ID: 080205-N-5248R-005.
U.S. Navy photo by Mass Communication Specialist 3rd Class Sheldon Rowley, Feb. 5, 2008.

Bird: Humming bird in flight. Courtesy US Fish and Wildlife Services.

Twister: Storm over Cordell, Oklahoma, May 22, 1981 (modified).
Public domain photo, Image ID: nssl0054.
NOAA National Severe Storms Laboratory Photo Library.
Photographer unknown.

Lightning: Multiple cloud-to-ground lightning strokes at night.
Public domain photo. Image ID: nssl0010.
NOAA's National Severe Storms Laboratory.
Photographer: C. Clark.

Water splash: Water drop forming a "crown."
Copyright Professor Andrew Davidhazy, with permission.
Rochester Institute of Technology, Department of Imaging and Photographic Technology.

Fire: Gas flames. Courtesy Steven Kreuzer via burningwell.org.

Index

Aberration, 67
Absence, 97
Absorption, 16, 61
Abstraction, 196
    edit, 197
    instance, 196
    parameters, 197
    scope and $0, 196
Acceleration
    of human running, 549
    of vehicle, 509
Accleration
    angular, limit, 527
Accumulator, message, 179
Acousmatic (audio-visual), 97
Acoustic, 55
    exterior, 69
    intensity, 59
    room, 67
Actuator, 485
Adiabatic index, 55
Alarm sound, 347
Allocation
    random, 426
    round robin, 426
Ambient keypoint, 521
Amplitude, 20
    constant, compensator, 539
Amusia, 93
Analog, 32
    mobility, 32
    network, 32
Analysis
    autocorrelation, 643
    component, 106
    formant, 642
    Fourier, 268
    requirements, 247
Anechoic chamber, 593
Anti-node, 71

Aperiodic, 39
Archimedes' Principle, 420
Arcing, electric, 457
Array
    Pure Data, 161
Articulation, speech, 581
Asynchrony (audio-visual), 96
Attack (envelope), 89
Attention, 96
Attenuation, 58
    geometric, 60
    inverse square, 60
    thermoviscous, 61
Audio
    effect, *see* Effect
Audio-visual contract, 97
Auditory scene analysis, 99
Auditory scene, wind composite, 474
Axle, 499

Backfire, 508
Ball, foot, 549
Balloon, 41
Bandpass, 215
Bandwidth, 52
Bark scale, 83
Bearing, 499
Beeps, 333
Behaviour
    animal, 547
Bell, material, 368
Bell, shape, 368
Bell, size, 368
Bennet-Clarke, insects, 559
Bernoulli principle, 41
Bias
    encoding period, 103
    framing, 104
    positional, 103
    switch, 485

Bilinear exponential distribution, 433
Binaural
    beat entrainment, 109
Binaural pitch, 86
Biomechanics, 547
Birds, 571
Bistable
    walking model, 550
Blade slap, helicopter, 533
Blade, number (fan), 518
Blast wind, 607
Block, 128
    engine, 509
    Pure Data, 185
Boiling, 409
Bouncing, 383
Boundary, 25
    discontinuity, 28
    layer, 67, 70, 472
    loss, 66
    modulus, 25
    occlusion, 28
    phase, 26
    reflection, 26
    refraction, 28
    solid, 26
Breakpoint
    variable triangle, 538
Brightness, 88
Bronchial passage, modulation, 573
Brush
    cymbal, 629
    motor, 499
Bubbles, 419
Buffer, 128
Bulk modulus, 13
Bumping, 392
Burtt, Ben, 635
Buzzer, electromagnetic, 367

Call
    mating, 557
    warning, 557
Canvas, 152
    create, 155
Capacitance, 34

Carrier, 291, 296
Cars, 507
Cavitation, 421, 452
Cavity
    syringial, avian, 572
    water sound, 431
Channel strip, 219
Chaos, 70
Chassis, vehicle, 509
Chatter, switch, 485
Chebyshev, Pafnuty Lvovich
        (polynomials), 285
Chirp, insect, 560
Cicada, 560
Classification, 95
Clavical sac, 572
Click
    clock tick, 493
    plastic, 489
    sequence, 489
    switch, 488
Clock, 491
    clockwork, 491
Closed form, 271
Coefficient
    acoustic absorption, 69
Coherence, 58
    perceptual, 102
Cold inlet, 165
Collective, control helicopter, 530
Collision
    rigid body, 383
Combustion, 409
Combustion chamber, 523
Communication
    animal, 557
Communication, mammals, 579
Commutator, 499
Complex harmonic oscillator, 48
Composite, 409
Compressibility, 13
    water, 419
Conflagration, 608
Connection
    audio fanning, 186
    merging message, 167

Connection, programming, 152
Consonance, 86
    local, 87
Continuity, 101
    homophonic, 101
Control data, arrays, 575
Control signal, 547
Control, of lungs in birds, 571
Convection, 410
Conversion
    analog to digital, 122
    digital to analog, 121
Cook, Perry, 440
    footstep model, 556
Cords, vocal, 580
Correlation, 58
Correspondence (audio-visual), 96
Cosine
    raised, 501
Counter, 168
    constrained, 179
Coupling, 28
CPU efficiency, 185
Crackles
    electric, 453
Crackles, fire, 414
Creaking, 395
Creeping, 548
Cricket sound, plectrum, 558
Critical band, 83
Crossfader, 224
Cubic difference tones, 78
Current, 451
    alternating, 451
Curve
    GRF (ground response force), 549
    overpressure, 607
Cyclic, control helicopter, 530
Cylinder, engine, 507

Damping, of bell, 369
Data reduction, 363
Dataflow, programming, 152
Dead zone, 56
Debounce, switch, 485
Decay (envelope), 90

Decibel, 58
Decoupling, 259, 547
Deflagration, 608
Delay cascade, 182
Demultiplexer, 224
Density, 15
    air, 419
Depth first, 153
Depth, of liquid, 430
Detonation, 608
Dielectric, 452
Differential threshold (hearing), 83
Differentiation
    in fluid sounds, 433
Diffraction, 64
    Fraunhofer, 64
    Huygen, 64
    thunder, 461
Diffusion, 65
Digital
    signal processing, 123
Dime, 499
Dipole, 56
Discrimination, 93
Disintegration, 410
Dispersion, 63
    thunder, 460
Displacement
    graph, 120
Dissonance, 86
Distribution
    Gaussian, 475
    normal, 443
    Poisson, 446
Doom tone, 87
Doppler, 67
    fan blade, 518
Downdraft, 531
DTMF tones, 337, 343
Duifhuis effect, 97
Duty cycle, 333
Dynamic range, 121

Ear
    basilar membrane,
        77

cochlea, 77
human, 77
Echo
flutter, 67
slapback, 67
Eddy, 70
Edge effect, 86
Edge noise, helicopter, 533
Edge roll, foot, 554
Editor, audio, 148
Effect
Bernoulli, 580
chorus, 232
Fletcher Munsen, 446
fluid hammer, 607
ground, helicopter, 531
reverberation, 233
secondary (explosion), 610
Efficiency
petrol engine, 508
Elasticity, 13
Electricity, 451
corona streamers, 452
Electromagnet
motor, 499
Electromagnetism, 452
Encapsulation, 259
End correction, 73
Energetic maintenance, 90
Energy, 9
decay, 31
decay, bouncing, 384
degree of freedom, 10
entropy, heat, 31
equipartition, 18
flow, 10
Joule, 9
kinetic, 9
kinetic, of bullet, 594
potential, 9
sources, 10
thermodynamics, 10
Engine
four stroke, 512
internal combustion, 507
jet, 523

model, 510
parts, 508
two stroke, 508
Entrainment, in liquids, 442
Envelope, 89, 139
breakpoint, 268
curve, 210
quartic, 456
vline object, 189
Escapement
clock, 491
Harrison, 491
Verge, 491
Event, driven system, 152
Excitation, 12
bubble, 421
exciter-resonator, 12
firearm body, 594
Exothermic, 409
Expansion
air, 459
Explosion, 410, 607
boiler, 607
brissance, 607
duration, 607
overpressure, 607
propellant, 607
shockwave, 611
Expression, 213, 433
Extent, 409
homogenous, 429
External, Pure Data, 152

Factoring
causality, 416
Fader
log law, 220
MIDI, 220
smooth, 221
Fan, 517
Fant, vocal tract, 581
Fast square root, 443
Few, thunder, 465
Field cricket, 558
File
audio, loop, 227

audio, reader/writer, 226
    textfile, 231
Filter
    comb, 454, 468
    formant bank, 454
Fire, 409
    sound features, 412
Firearm
    AK47, 601
    Automatic, 602
    barrel, 598
    calibre, 593
    construction, 593
    cordite, 594
    deflagration, 594
    identification (from sound), 601
    M16, 601
    magazine, 593
    Muzzle brake, 601
    primer, 594
    reload sounds, 602
    rifle, 593
    shell, detonation, 594
    shockwave, 595
    signature list, 597
    stock, 593
    Suppression, 601
Fitch, mammalian vocal tract, 588
Fizz
    electric, 453
Flag
    flapping, 473
Flame, 410
    forced, 526
    oscillation, 410
Flameout, 523
Fletcher, bird synthesis, 573
Flow, 33
    air laminar, 70
    laminar, 430
Fluid
    electricity as, 451
Flux density
    rainfall, 441
FM
    bandwidth, Carson's rule, 301

Foldover, 303
Foley, 547
Footsteps, 547
Force, 9, 11
    buildup of, 399
    dynamic equilibrium, 18
    equilibrium, 9
    exchange, 18
    ground response, 547
    Newton, 11
Formant
    hearing, 88
Fragmentation, 612
Freedom, degrees of, 12
Frequency, 23
    angular, 40
    equation, 23
    hum, electricity, 452
    negative, 301
    of bubble, 422
    perception, 83
    resolution (hearing), 85
    response, 53
    rotor, helicopter, 532
    spinning object, 39
    voice, human male/female, 580
Friction, 366, 387
    creaking, 395
    kinetic, 396
    loss, 504
    magazine slide, 603
    static, 396
    stick, 395
    stick-slip model, 395
Friction, slip, 387
Full scale deflection, 121
Function
    Bessel, 300
    Bessel, sphere, 384
    non-linear, transfer, 283
    sinesum, 279
Fuselage, aircraft, 532
Fuselage, resonances, 534

Gabor, 292, 305
Gabor limit, 91, 415, 446

Galileo, clock, 491
Game
 acoustic environment, 320
 actor, 317
 audio engine, 319
 audio, bus, 319
 audio, controller, 319
 audio, localisation, 320
 audio, sampled, 318
 blending, 319
 event randomisation, 319
 events, 318
 keypoint actors, 320
 logic, 317
 movers, platforms, 317
 network replication, 320
 relevance, 317
 stage, level, 317
 switching, scope, 319
 VO, dialogue, 320
 VO, menu sound, 320
 world, 316
Gas
 burning ball, explosion, 610
 impingement, cycling, 595
 molar constant, 55
Gearbox, 530
GEM, 149
Gestalt
 phi phenomenon, 93
Glitch, dropout, 185
Glottis, 579
 cat, 580
 dog, 580
Granularity, 89
Graph
 traversal, DSP, 153
Graph On Parent, 199
Gravel, crunch texture, 554
Greens function, 441
Gridflow, 149
Grommet, damping, 501
Ground effect, 66
GUI
 graph, 161
 interface design, 259

 message box, 160
 number, 159
 send symbol, 344
 slider, 159
 symbol, 161
 toggle, 159
Guns, *see* Firearm

Handling noise, 618
Hardness, 17
Harmonic
 group, 371
 series of common waveforms, 274
Harmonicity, 100
Harmony, 87
Head response transfer function, 80
Hearing
 Distance perception, 80
 fatigue, 83
 frequency range, 78
 localisation, 79
 loudness, 81
 non-linearity, 78
 Source identification, 81
 threshold, 78
Heating
 of air, expansion, 452
Heel, foot, 549
Helicopter, 529
 Chinook, 529
 Cornu, 529
 Focke-Wulf, 529
 Froude, 542
 Oehmichen, 529
 Rankine, 542
Helicopter, historical development, 529
Helmholtz oscillator, 73
Helmholtz resonator, 423
Hertz, 39
Highpass, 215
Hirsh limit, 91
Hissing, 524
Hissing, fire, 413
Horn, siren, 358
Hot inlet, 165
House fly, 559

Housing
    jet engine, 525
    rifle receiver, 599
Howling
    wind, 471
Howling, wind, 479
Huygens, clock, 491

Identification, 95
Idiophonics, 365
Impact
    raindrop, 441
Impedance, 33
    physical obstruction, 429
    wind, 472
Implicit production, 471
Impulse
    chirp, 454, 598
    firearm signature, 594
    frequency, 139
    Kronecker delta, 137
    step, 131
    test excitation, 252
Inertance, 33
Inertia
    rotational (engine), 511
Information, 119
Insects, 557
Intensity, 58
Intention, 547
Inter-activity, 107
Inter-aural intensity difference, 79
Inter-aural time difference, 79
Interference, 24
    uncorrelated waves, 58
Ionisation
    of air, electricity, 452
IPA, phonetic notation, 585

Jitter, sputter (engine), 509
Just noticable difference, 79

Kerosene, 523
Kerosene explosion, 608
Keyboard shortcuts, 150, 157
Klatt, tract model, 582

Knowledge
    categorical, 113
    declarative, 112
    imperative, 113
    poetic, 113
    procedural, 112

Labia, avian, 572
Language
    common list music, 142
    Csound, 141
    programming abstraction, 141
Laplacian
    of sphere, 421
Larynx, mammalian, 580
LAW launcher, 617
LC network
    frequency of, 47
Learning (perception), 100
Least significant bit, 122
Leaves, wind, 479
Line, 139
    object, audio, 189
List
    parameters, 200
    unpacking, 200
Listening
    analytic, 106
    causal, 105
    connotative, 105
    critical, 106
    empathetic, 105
    engaged, 107
    functional, 105
    hierarchy (Chion), 104
    hierarchy (Huron), 104
    hierarchy (Schaeffer), 104
    reduced, 106
    reflexive, 104
    semantic, 106
    signal, 107
Localisation, 336
Loop, until, 180
Loss
    energy, bouncing, 386
Loss, Damping, 31

Loudness
    duration effects, 82
    Phon scale, 81
    scale weighting, 81
    Sone scale, 81
Lowpass, 215

Mach
    cone, 596
Maher, R.C, firearm acoustics, 605
Mammals, 579
Marranzano, 406
Masking
    concurrent, 98
    critical band, 98
    in-band, 98
    intensity, 83
    inter-band, 98
    simultaneous, 98
    temporal proximity, 98
Mass, Spring
    frequency, 44
Matching, 95
Mathews, Max, 267
Mathews, speech analysis, 580
Matter, 11
    bonds, 11
    mass, 11
    molecules, 11
    state, 12
Max/MSP, 149
Medium, 17
    dispersive, 23
Memory
    auditory pipeline, 103
    echoic store, 103
    episodic, 103
    pre-categorical, 103
    short term, 103
    verbal, 103
    visually augmented, 104
Message
    bang, 158
    broadcast, 171
    delay object, 168
    float, 158

input/output, 174
list, 161, 172
list distribution, 173
list pack, 172
list unpack, 172
persistence, 173
pointer, 161
selector, 158
sequence, 171
substitution, 173
symbol, 160
translation table, 344
trigger, 166
Message, Pure Data, 157
Method, 255
    additive, 256
    choice of, efficiency, 374
    choice of, flexibility, 375
    composite, 256
    granular, 257
    non-linear, 257
    piecewise, 256
    piecewise, critique, 362
    subtractive, 257
    waveguide, 258
    wavetables, 256
Metronome, 167
MIDI
    controller, 176
    note in, 175
    note out, 175
    note to frequency, 176
    object summary, 176
    sysex, 176
Miklavcic, rain, 449
Miller, speech analysis, 580
Minnaert, water flow, 435
Mixing, 134
Mode, 28
    bending, 56
    breathing, 56
    free vs clamped bar, 403
    number, 29
    of bell, 369
    switching, 473
    umbrella, 56

Model
    small housing, 376
    finite element, 468
    parametric, 106
Modulation, 141
    amplitude, 291
    bi-axial spinning, 39
    FM index, 297
    Frequency, 296
    phase, 303
    ring, 293
    single sideband, 295
Modulator, 291, 296
Monopole, 56
Mortar tube, 625
Motion
    acceleration, 11
    periodic, 39
    simple harmonic, 11
    velocity, 11
Motor, 499
Mounting
    jet engine, 525
Mushroom cloud, 610
Mute button, 221

Node, 71
Noise
    black, 466
    cluster, 488
    Gaussian, 443
    Perlin, 65
    pink, 447
    white, 136, 524
Non-linear
    discontinuity, 401
Normalisation, 123
    parameter, 201
Number
    comparison, 178
    complement, 181
    last, 182
    LFO, 229
    logical, 178
    prime sequence, 423
    random, 178

    reciprocal, 181
    Reynolds, 473, 518
    rounding, 180
    running maximum, 183
    scaling, 180
    stream lowpass, 183
Number box, 156
Nyquist, 303
Nyquist frequency, 124

Object, 152
    arithmetic summary, 177
    audio, 185
    behaviour, 316
    Boolean, 178
    change, 170
    create, 155
    duplicate, 157
    float, 166
    inlets, 165
    int, 167
    list, 167
    method, 158
    methods, 315
    MIDI, 175
    modify, 156
    moses, 170
    numerical, 177
    pipe, 168
    principles, 165
    print, 175
    route, 169
    select, 169
    send/receive, 171
    spigot, 170
    swap, 170
    timer, 168
    trigger, 166
    trigonometric summary, 178
    until, 180
    uzi, kalashnikov, 494
    views, 315
Observation point, 338
Occlusion, 62
Optimisation, 414

Oscillation
    acoustic, 70
    aeroelastic, 472
Oscillator, 39
    astable, flip-flop, 357
    bank, 269
    chaotic, friction, stick-slip, 396
    clamped rod, 49
    differential equation, 44
    driven (and resonance), 51
    free rod, 49
    frequency, 39
    geometric, 40
    initial condition, 51
    instability, 45
    lamina, 50
    LC network, 46
    multi-phase, 350
    non-linear, 401
    object, Pure Data, 187
    object, wavetable, 187
    pendulum, 46
    phasor, 41
    phone bell, 376
    relaxation, 41
    simple harmonic, 43
    string, 48
Oscine, song bird, 571
Outdoor reverberation, 359
Outgassing, 409
Oxidation, 409

Panning, 221
    law, cosine, 222
    law, linear, 221
    law, root, 222
    law, taper, 221
Parallelism, auditory scene, 474
Parameter
    abstraction, 197
    collapsing, factoring, 261
    default, 198
    efficiency, 260
    randomisation, 636
    routing, 203
    space, 260

Parameters
    co-dependent, 437
    initial, 156
Partial, 269
Patch, 152
    edit, 156
    file, 157
Patching, 155
Peaks list, 334
Pedestrian crossing, 333
Pendulum
    clock, 491
    frequency of, 46
    walking, motion, 548
Period, 23
Pessulus, 572
Phantom fundamental, 86
Phase, 24
    anti-phase, inverted, 24
    in phase, 24
    walking, feet, 548
Phase shift
    by location (helicopter), 534
Phase splitting, 349
Phasing
    arcing, 453
Phasor
    code, 131
Phosphor-bronze, 485
Physioacoustics, 77
Pinching, 419
Pipe, 71
    half-open, 439
Piston, 507
Pitch, 83
Plane
    inclined, 517
Plasticity, 16, 61
Player, game, 316
Plunger, 485
Poisson
    distribution, 426
Poisson ratio, 15
Pole
    switch, 485
Police siren, 355

Polynomial, Chebyshev, 645
Polyphony, 425
Potential, 32, 451
Poured liquids, 437
Power, 10
    explosive, 607
    Watt, 10
Praat, analysis suite, 641
Pre-computation, 273
Precedence, 91
    Haas effect, 91
Presence (perception), 84
Pressure, 9, 58
Principle
    Bernoulli, 473
Procedural Audio
    deferred form, 321
    audio engine, embedding, 324
    code translation, 324
    cost metrics, 325
    default form, 321
    denormal issues, 323
    development, 323
    DSP graph, 323
    level of detail, 322
    Pure Data, as plugin, 324
    real-time architectures, 325
    variable cost, 322
    variety, 321
Product, cosine, 292
Programming
    dataflow, 149
    parameters via list, 351
    visual, 149
Propagation, 19
Propeller, 517
PSOLA, 307
Psophometric weighting, 82
Psychoacoustic
    adjective (language), 111
    adjunctive (language), 111
    Gerund verb (language), 111
    imagination, 110
    nouns (language), 111
    onomatopoeia (language), 112
    reference points, 112

    sensation, 77
    verbalising, 111
Pulse
    asymmetrical, 539
    Dirac, 497
    fan blade, 517
    formant aligned, 582
    parabolic, 466
    polynomial curve, 552
    shark fin/dog tooth, 537
Pulse dialling, 339
Pure Data
    GUI, 153
    installer, 150
    support, 162
    test, 150
    watchdog, 153

Quadrupole, 56
Quantisation, 43
    bubble, 419
    digital, 121
    distortion, 121

R2D2, 635
Radiation, 56
    cylindrical, 463
    far field, 57
    fire, 411
    from surface, 400
    near field, 57
    pattern, 56
    pipe/horn end, 73
Rain, 441
    ambiance, 447
    on ground, 444
    on water, 445
    on window, 444
Random
    walk, 309
Reaction
    electrochemical, 452
Recognition, 95
Recoil, 595
Recording
    analytical, 251

Reflection, 62
   parallel walls, 67
   thunder, 461
Refraction, 63
   thunder, 462
Relaxation
   molecular, 61
   sparking, 452
Release (envelope), 91
Resistance, 33
Resolving power, 83
Resonance, 28, 52
   acoustic, 71
   body, clock, 496
   body, switch, 489
   of electric spark, 453
Resonator
   Helmholtz, 572
   rectangular membrane, 398
Response
   frisson, 108
   physiological, 108
   scstatic response, 108
   srientation response, 108
   stapedius reflex, 108
   startle response, 108
   stress responses, 109
Rest point, 12
Restoring force, 13
Reverb
   random incidence, 68
   time, 68
Revolutions per minute, 500
Reynolds number, 71
Ribner and Roy, thunder, 465
Rigid body collisions, 365
Rise time (envelope), 90
Risset, Jean-Claude, 267
Roaring, fire, 416
Rocket fuel, 622
Rocket launcher, 617
Roddenberry, Gene, 629
Rolling, 387
   collision pattern, 389
   Raths' model, 388
Rotation, 387

Rothenberg, speech analysis,
   580
Rotor, 499
   helicopter, 530
   helicopter, coaxial, 530
   helicopter, tail, 530
   helicopter, tilt, 530
Roughness, 87
RPG7, 617
Rubber, 508
   squirm, 508
Running, 548
Rupture, 607

Sabine formula, 68
Safety explosive, 607
Sample, 121
Sampler, simple audio, 225
Sampling, 121
   rate, 121
Scale
   and Reynolds number, turbulence,
   472
   perceptual, 88
   whole tone, 629
Scaling, 94
Scattering, 62
Schema activation (perception), 100
Segregation, 99
Select
   random, 182
   weighted, 182
Semantic, 119
Sensible bands, 84
Sequencer
   division, 229
   list, 230
   textfile, 231
   time, 227
   using select, 228
Shape
   and modes, 30
   raindrop, 441
Shaping
   by cosine fuction, 349
Sharpness (hearing), 88

Shifting
    pitch, 307
Shockwave
    cylindrical, 459
Shockwave (explosive), 607
Sidebands, 293
    FM, 298
Signal, 119
    arithmetic, 191, 205
    audio, Pure Data, 185
    cosine, 211
    delay, 191, 214
    filters, 190, 215
    flow, 119
    graphs, 125
    input/output, 189
    math, 191
    periodic, 211
    pseudo-random, 136
    random, 136
    representation, 120
    send/receive, 187
    shaping, differentiate, 217
    shaping, expression, 213
    shaping, integrate, 215
    shaping, invert, 206
    shaping, limit, 207
    shaping, line envelope, 210
    shaping, phase, 214
    shaping, polynomial, 212
    shaping, root, 209
    shaping, scale, 206
    shaping, shift, 206
    shaping, square, 209
    shaping, wrap, 207
    to message, 187
    vector, 185
Signature
    bubbles, 423
    bullet flight, 596
    wing, fly, 559
Similarity, 94
Simple harmonic motion, 20
Size
    bubble, 421
    raindrop, 441

Slew, 433
Smouldering, 411
Smyth, T, bird synthesis, 573
Sound
    grains, 305
    visualisation, 30
Sound design
    analysis, 254
    analysis, operational, 254
    analysis, physical, 254
    analysis, spectrum, 254
    analysis, waveform, 254
    as sofware engineering, 245
    critical judgement, 245
    deconstruction, 252
    design cycle, 261
    expediency, 262
    flow, 262
    integration, 247
    maintenance, 247
    methods, 243, 247
    model, 246, 252
    model, entity-action, 249
    objectification, 262
    parameterisation, 254
    placeholders, 249
    production plan, 249
    requirement analysis, 246
    research, 246, 250
    reuse, 244
    studio, 244
    support, 148
    target platform, 250
    test, 247
    tools, 147
    working from script, 337
    working from specification, 333
Sound therapy
    Beth-Abraham, 109
Spark
    ignition, 507
Sparks, electric, 452
Spectrogram, 126
Spectrum, 125
    of bell, 370
    centroid (perception), 88

equivalence, 363
jet engine, 524
Spin
  eccentric, 499
  irregular object, 517
  torque, 499
Spokeydokey, 41
Spreading function (masking), 98
Spring
  compensator, 495
Standing wave, 28
Star Trek, 629
  Red alert siren, 641
  transporter, 629
Star Wars, 635
Stator, 499
Stiffness, 14
Strain, 14
Strategy
  "old plus new," 102
  listening, 102
Stream
  of sound, 430
Streaming
  fission, 92
  fusion, 92
  pitch, 92
  temporal coherence boundary,
    92
  Van Noorden, 92
Strength, 17
Stress, 14, 410
Stridulation, 557
Strike, lightning, 459
String
  harmonics, 48
  modes, 48
Struck cantilever bar, 536
Structure, 17
  hetrogenous, 17
  temporal (perception), 88
Subpatch, 193
  abstraction, *see* Abstraction
  copy, 194
  inlet,outlet, 193
  scope, 194

Summation chains, 202
Superposition, 24
  N-Wave, lightning, 460
Surface tension, 423
Sustain (envelope), 90
Suthers, bird calls, 573
Switch, 485
  latch, 486
  momentary, 486
  rocker, 486
  rotary, 486
  slide, 486
Switch wrapper, DSP control, 555
Synchronous seqeuence, clock, 493
Synthesis
  additive, 267
  AM, 291, 561
  ARP2600, 635
  asynchonous additive, 527
  cross, hybridisation, 309
  discrete summation, 270
  FM, 432, 503, 540, 572, 632
  frequency modulation, 296
  grain cloud, 307
  granular, 305, 432, 550
  granular, asynchronous, 308
  modal, 35
  phase modulation, 303
  phase relative, 513
  piecewise, 362
  PM, 636
  ring modulation, 573
  speech, 579
  subtractive, 412
  vector, 279
  wave scanning, 280
  waveshaping, 283
  waveshaping (distortion), 597
  wavetable, 277
Synthesiser
  simple MIDI example, 189
Syrinx, 571
System
  acoustic, 55
  driven, as filter, 52
  entity-action, 36

heterogeneous, 51
modes, 53
response, 52
Seer, 595
state, 618

Table
transfer function, 283
Telephone bell, old type, 367
Temperature
air, 55
Temporal correlation, 102
Temporal integration, 82
Tesla, electricity, 451
Texture
ground, 549
Theorem
central limit, 443
Thermodynamics
ignition, 509
Thermosetting, 16
Throw, 485
Thunder, 459
castle, 465
environment effects, 462
rumble, 466
Timbales (insect), 560
Timbre, 86
Timbre space, 92
Time
division, 229
perception, 89
Timer
military, 492
Timestretching, 279, 307
Tone sequences, 349
Tortuosity, 459
Trachea, mammalian, 579
Trajectories (perception), 99
Transducer, 119
Transform
Box-Muller, 443
Hilbert, 296
Transient (envelope), 90
Transmission, 61
mechanical (engine), 514

over noisy channel, 343
telephone line, 339
tremolo, 291
Tube
partially open, 390
semi-open, 618
Turbine, 517, 523
Turbine, gas (engine), 531
Turbulence, 70, 410, 523
sounds, 71
underwater, 438
wind, 471
Two tone alarm, 348
Two tone suppression, 78
Tympanic membrane, avian,
571

Upthrust, 420

Valve
exhaust, 507
fuel inlet, 507
Van den Doel, bubbles, 427
Van den Doel, water flow, 435
Van Noorden
hysteresis, 92
streaming ambiguity, 92
Vari-delay
Doppler, 521
Velocity
angular, 387
angular, motor, 500
calculation, in steel, 21
equation, 23
group, 22
of bullet, 594
of lightning, 459
particle, 22
phase, 22
terminal, bubble, 420
terminal, raindrop, 441
wind, 473
Velum, nasal cavity port, 581
Vibration, 17
acoustic, 55
bar, 401

forced, 52
    motor, 505
Vibrato, 297
Viscoelasticity, 61
Viscosity, 61, 430
Vocal tract, human, 581
Vocoder, 629
Voltage, 451
Volume control, 219
von Kármán vortex street, 473
Vortex, 70
    chain, 70
    shedding, 519
Vowel
    Diphthong, 584
    formant list, 585
    human speech, 584
    space, 584

Walking, 547
Warm up, jet engine, 527
Warp
    space (waveguide), 510
Water, 429
    sound features, 429
Waterfall plot, 127
Wave, 17
    acoustic, 20
    compression, 19
    cycle, 23
    cylinderical, 57
    discrete points, 17
    longitudinal, 19
    model, 17
    N-Wave, 465, 596
    packet, 305
    plane, 57

rarefaction, 19
Rayleigh, 441
sawtooth, 131
sinusoidal, 132
spherical, 57
Tollmien-Schlichting, 70
tortional, 20
tracing, 67
transverse, 19
triangle, 207
Waveguide
    engine exhaust, 510
    port, 538
    scattering junction, 538
    two port, 514
Wavelength, 23
    equation, 23
Weighting filters, 82
Whine, gearbox (helicopter), 541
Whistling wires, 473
Whooshing
    jet engine, 526
Wind, 471
Wind shear, 67
Window
    Gaussian, 306
    Hanning, 312
Window pane, 442
Wings, insect, 557
Work, 10

Yield, 16
Youngs Modulus
    elasticity, 14
    materials, 13

Zipper noise, 220